Durkheim's sociology of religion: themes and theories

By the same author:
Durkheim on Religion
Durkheim on Morals and Education

DURKHEIM'S
Sociology of Religion

THEMES AND THEORIES

W. S. F. Pickering
Department of Social Studies
University of Newcastle upon Tyne

Routledge & Kegan Paul
London, Boston, Melbourne and Henley

First published in 1984
by Routledge & Kegan Paul plc
39 Store Street, London WC1E 7DD,
9 Park Street, Boston, Mass. 02108, USA,
464 St Kilda Road, Melbourne
Victoria 3004, Australia, and
Broadway House, Newtown Road,
Henley-on-Thames, Oxon RG9 1EN

Set in Times by
Input Typesetting Ltd, London SW19 8DR
and printed in Great Britain by
The Thetford Press Ltd
Thetford, Norfolk

Library of Congress Cataloging in Publication Data

Pickering, W. S. F.
Durkheim's sociology of religion.

Bibliography: p.
Includes indexes.
1. Religion and sociology—History—20th century.
2. Durkheim, Émile, 1858–1917.   I. Title.
BL60.P53 1984   306'.6'0924   83–19226

British Library CIP available.

ISBN 0–7100–9298–9

To the memory of my father, Frederick Charles Pickering (1895–1967), who unwittingly introduced me to Durkheim's last and greatest work.

Contents

Part II Taking up Positions

Part III Beliefs and Ideas

Part IV Ritual and Effervescent Assembly

Acknowledgments

This book has been in the making for several years. It is hardly surprising, therefore, that a number of people have been consulted at various times. To mention them all by name would be impossible: they are sincerely thanked as a group, which is surely something Durkheim would have approved of! One person of the group, however, should be mentioned by name and that is Steven Lukes, who more than anyone else was most encouraging and helpful when the plans for the book were first drawn up.

And with groups in mind, I certainly want to acknowledge the patience and understanding of members of the graduate seminar in the sociology of religion in the University of Newcastle upon Tyne who, over the years, have been forced to come face to face with much of the contents of this book. Their reassurance and above all, their never-failing criticisms have, I know, helped to produce a better book than otherwise would have been the case. To those who have read the entire manuscript or parts of it, I wish to extend my deep appreciation, especially to Séan Carey, but also to James Beckford, Mary Hesse, Robert A. Jones and Malcolm Ruel. They have eliminated some of the mistakes and weaknesses, and the many which remain can in no way be attributed to them.

In order to complete the manuscript I was awarded in 1980 a Personal Research grant by the Social Science Research Council. As well as being grateful for that, I also wish to extend my sincere appreciation to the President and Fellows of Wolfson College, Cambridge, for electing me to a Visiting Fellowship for that year and providing a most congenial milieu in which to work.

As on previous occasions in writing on Durkheim, I must thank Mrs A. Rule for her indomitable efforts as a typist. And now I must also thank my wife, who has given unstinting encouragement and assistance, and at the same time has suffered the fate of so many wives of people such as myself, in having to put up with her husband's long hours of work and extended absences from home. They are of far more help than perhaps they realize.

W.S.F.P.

References, notation, translations

The key to the references in the text is the author's name and the date of publication of the item mentioned. The number refers to the page number. Details of the item can be found in the bibliographies at the end of the book, under author and date. In the case of works by Durkheim, the author's name is not given in the reference and has to be assumed by the reader. If the author's name is mentioned in the sentence, it is not given in the reference.

The writings and English translations of Durkheim have been given the dating enumeration of Steven Lukes (1972:561ff.) and subsequently brought up to date by myself (Pickering 1978). One of the bibliographies is devoted solely to Durkheim's works which deal with religion and which is a slightly revised edition of a similar, earlier bibliography (Pickering 1975:305–10).

Because of the frequent references to *Les Formes élémentaires de la vie religieuse* (1912a), all references not marked by an author's name and without a date and without the word ibid., refer to this book. A given figure for the French text is nearly always followed by another, corresponding to Swain's translation (t.1915d), for example (603/422) means page 603 in *Les Formes élémentaires* and page 422 in *The Elementary Forms*. Where possible an additional number is included which refers to the translation by Redding and Pickering (t.1975a) of parts of *Les Formes élémentaires*, for example (603/422/151) means the references just cited, plus page 151 of *Durkheim on Religion*.

Where quotations are from French texts which have not been translated into English before, I have translated the passages myself. Again, although generally recognized translations of Durkheim's works have been used, in several instances changes have been made where improvements in translations were thought desirable. The prefix t. in front of a date has been inserted to show the reference is to the translation. For problems over translating certain French words such as *conscience*, *représentation*, and so on, the reader is asked to consult earlier books on Durkheim edited by the author (Pickering 1975:ix–x; 1979a:viii).

The prefix r. before a date denotes that a previous item is reproduced in a book, the date of which follows the prefix. In some of Durkheim's works a second edition is commonly used, as in *La Division du travail social* (1893b, 2nd edn. 1902b). Also, certain articles are generally referred to reprinted in a book entitled *Sociologie et philosophie* (1924a). In both these examples and in cases of a further, unchanged edition of a work by Durkheim but using different page numbers, the r. has been dropped as in (1893b/1902b:22) and (1911b/1924a:20). The relevant page for the original or early edition, as indicated, is not given. The original dates of publication are retained in order to show, amongst other things, the date when the item was available to the public.

The letters Ch. refer to a chapter in Durkheim's *The Elementary Forms of the Religious Life*, and the letters ch. to a chapter in this book or to another book to which reference is made.

Abbreviations

AJS	*American Journal of Sociology*
AS	*L'Année sociologique*
ASR	*American Sociological Review*
ASRel	*Archives de sociologie des religions*
BJS	*British Journal of Sociology*
BSFP	*Bulletin de la Société française de philosophie*
EJS	*European Journal of Sociology (Archives européennes de sociologie)*
JSSR	*Journal for the Scientific Study of Religion*
MF	*Mercure de France*
PR	*Philosophical Review*
RB	*Revue bleue*
RFS	*Revue française de sociologie*
RHPR	*Revue d'histoire et de philosophie religieuses*
RIS	*Revue internationale de sociologie*
RMM	*Revue de métaphysique et de morale*
RNS	*Revue néo-scolastique*
RP	*Revue philosophique de la France et de l'étranger*
SR	*Sociological Review*

Introductory remarks

Sociology is commonly held to be a discipline which was crystallized in the nineteenth century against the background of an accelerating industrial revolution. It can also be described as a secular or even atheistic discipline. Yet Émile Durkheim (1858–1917), one of its pre-eminent founding fathers, standing alongside Max Weber (1864–1920) and Karl Marx (1818–83), gave to the study of religion a place of overriding importance in his attempt to explore social phenomena scientifically. Although he was not an orthodox believer, he had an innate reverence for religion. Any doubts about the primacy of religion within his scheme of thought are quickly dispelled in reading his book *The Elementary Forms of the Religious Life* (1912a). It now stands as one of the classics, not only in the sociology of religion but in sociology itself. As Steven Lukes, who has done so much to revive Durkheimian studies, said in a debate: 'I went and read *The Elementary Forms of the Religious Life* and had my mind blown, and as a result I just became totally immersed in Durkheim' (in Clark 1979:131). In many respects it remains *the* classic in the sociology of religion, for no other book has supplanted it. The contributions of Max Weber are considerable, but he never produced a book on religion which dealt with the subject in the broad sweep, or raised as many issues as Durkheim did, in what, as events turned out, was his last book. But besides being a classic in the sense that it is the corner-stone of a discipline, *The Elementary Forms* is also a classic in that it is constantly read and reread. It is published and republished. It is a fountain from which one continually gains academic refreshment and insight. It is a book that goes on living.

Although *The Elementary Forms* contains Durkheim's most developed ideas on religion, to concentrate only on that book and to disregard all else he wrote on the subject, as many who concern themselves with Durkheim do, is an inadequate procedure in trying to come to grips with his analysis of religion, which is the purpose of this book. In the many articles and reviews that

Durkheim wrote and in virtually every book, there were allusions to religion (see Pickering 1975:323ff.). One can therefore only begin to understand the complexities of his thought and its paradoxes, if one is prepared to examine and evaluate the entire corpus of his writings which deal with religion and allied subjects. For Durkheim, religion is not only one social institution amongst other social institutions, it is of such significance that it explains other phenomena rather than being explained by them. It is thus scarcely surprising that it weaves its way into so many facets of social life in which he was interested. To be comprehensive, it is also necessary to give careful attention to Durkheim's many followers and critics at the time he was writing as well as subsequently. On the whole the views of his contemporaries, both friendly and hostile, especially those in France, have not up to now been given much attention (see, for example, Pickering 1975: 205–8 and 228–76).

To approach a classic which has stood the test of time and triumphed over the attacks of critics, or to come to the work of a classical writer whose mind has been shown to be outstandingly great, means that the primary task must be to expound what the man has written. This is necessary for three reasons. The first is that, as with all classical works, the ideas involved and their ramifications are numerous and complex. Often in the course of time some become forgotten and need to be revived. So, for example, there has been a notable lack of attention given to Durkheim's theory of ritual and collective effervescence. The second is that largely because of its alleged atheistic, positivist and reductionist assumptions, Durkheim's work in the sociology of religion has been subject to stringent criticism. Continued attacks, however, often bring with them distortion of what the author originally meant. By concentrating on the weaker points his thought tends to be misinterpreted and not seen as a whole. The third reason is that to focus solely on the weaknesses of Durkheim's thought is to be small-minded. He made a similar point himself in connection with Montesquieu's theory and quoted with approval Paul Janet who complained that most commentators had been interested in showing only Montesquieu's errors (1892a/ t.1937b and 1953a/t.1960b:61). It would have been better, argued Janet, to have given 'a detailed idea of the vastness and obscurity of the subject he chose and of the intellectual power with which he mastered it' (ibid.). The primary task must therefore be to try to expound Durkheim's thought. And while the present writer does not pretend to have the intellectual prowess of Durkheim, his intention is to try to follow Durkheim's own advice in the quotation from Janet and to apply it to the grand master of sociology himself.

Immediately questions are raised. How is a commentator to proceed with his work? What principles are to guide him? What are his presuppositions? Such issues raise acute hermeneutical and historical problems, some of which have been broached by R. A. Jones in his article 'On understanding a sociological classic' (1977), where he actually considered *The Elementary Forms*. There is no intention to enter into the debate of how far interpretation should be purely historical or how far sociological; nor indeed to consider in detail the issue of whether, if at all, one can approach the task free from personal and ideological bias. Or, again, to raise what principles are involved in studying historically the work of the founding fathers of sociology, for example, principles recently raised by Quentin Skinner, who in approaching the history of political theory, would emphasize the intention of the author in what he was writing. All that is intended in these remarks is to state very briefly the principles which we hope and believe have been used and by which the work should be judged. The overall task is to come to terms with Durkheimian thought about religion, not to argue about how one comes to terms with any classic or classical thought in general. Clearly such a wide issue has an important place in the academic world, but that place is not here.

For our purposes the starting-point must always be the texts themselves, the careful appraisal of what they mean and at the same time the avoidance of reading into them what the commentator would like to see. It means continually going back to the French original and trying to wrestle with it, especially where it is obscure. Careful attention must be given to key words and phrases. Indeed this book must be judged on whether or not it is a faithful account of some of the work of Durkheim. The truth of the matter is that one cannot escape from the written word, from the texts themselves.

The task is therefore to try to ascertain what Durkheim said. What he did not say, what he did not attempt to do is of little consequence. One can only judge him by what he did and by what he set out to do. Any other sort of judgment calls for a completely different set of criteria.

In letting Durkheim's ideas speak for themselves, no attempt is made to try to compare the work of Durkheim with, say, that of Max Weber, far less to try to combine them. Durkheim's sociological thought stands on its own. It is a complete system, almost like a sociological Thomism. And let it be noted that Durkheim was very much attracted to medieval philosophy (see 1938a). His work therefore stands or falls by the completeness of the system. And with whom does one conflate St Thomas? To compare Durkheim in detail with other sociologists, especially in the matter of religion, is a futile exercise, only excusable as an examination question for undergraduates.

To help elucidate the text and to understand Durkheim's aims and ideas, both his work and indeed his life have to be placed in a historical perspective. Durkheim, an enthusiastic liberal, humanist and agnostic, was very much a man of his time. This may sound a truism, but to take into account historical factors in evaluating his work, scientific and ahistorical as he claimed his conclusions to be, is imperative. His ideals cannot be understood apart from the fact that he was an ardent supporter, indeed an academic spokesman of and for France's Third Republic. Steven Lukes's intellectual biography of Durkheim, published in the early 1970s, has proved to be a model in providing a historical setting for the development of Durkheim's work. But in a study such as this, which focuses on religion, attention will have to be given to some of the religious issues of his day and at the same time to his own religious background, upbringing and ideals. On internal evidence, it has often been argued that Durkheim's thought underwent changes during his lifetime and such a possibility within the area of his analysis of religion will have to be examined.

Although one must approach all classics with a degree of reverence and a readiness to follow their logic, complexity and imagination, this does not preclude criticism and assessment. The danger is to be critical before exposition, to be devastatingly negative before the picture has been unfolded. Here is a particular weakness of sociologists, not least at the present time, when criticism seems to be their main craft. Nor must it be forgotten that Durkheim was a severe critic himself, although he was never sarcastic and vitriolic, even in his controversy with Tarde. It was his opponents who tended to be the more aggressive (see Pickering 1975:347, 356). As we have had occasion to note, Durkheim's work, particularly that on religion, has been subject to much criticism, but such criticism needs to be sifted and evaluated. In the last analysis, exposition must give rise to assessment and criticism of some kind or another.

The book has deliberately been given the subtitle 'Themes and theories'. The reason is simple enough. Durkheim's study of religion covers a vast number of topics. To write about them all and in detail would mean producing a book of inordinate length. Further, some of the topics are only tangential to Durkheim's main argument. Others cover issues now dead and buried. Some have had to be omitted because the space is required for more pressing issues. However, the main subjects that Durkheim dealt with can be readily grouped. The corpus of Durkheim's work on religion, highlighted as it is in *The Elementary Forms*, is to be divided as follows:

1 the methodology of the sociology of religion;
2 a theory of religion based on social origins;
3 the interpretation of the religion of certain Australian and other tribes;
4 ritual and collective effervescence;
5 modern religion, the decline of traditional religions, and the rise of 'secular' religions.

The first contribution mentioned, that of methodology, is still of considerable importance to the current standing and understanding of the sociology of religion and must of necessity be treated in detail. His theory of religion based on social concepts is rejected today by most scholars, but it still has a number of interesting insights which should be considered on their own merits. Durkheim's contributions to the study of totemism and the religion of the Arunta and other tribes is still open to debate, although most scholars think that at the time he wrote his contributions were outstanding. But the interest here is only for the technically competent in anthropology and will only be incidentally alluded to in what follows. Durkheim's analysis of ritual, admittedly set within the context of primitive societies, has been little explored and, it is suggested, has still a great deal to offer. But even more important is Durkheim's notion of collective effervescence, since it provides some understanding of religious change and at the same time has particular relevance in the modern context – something confirmed by the observation of Eliade (1973:21). In turn, this has bearing on Durkheim's analysis of the modern religious situation which has so frequently been overlooked. What might be called his theories of secularization will be considered, particularly in connection with the rise of what might be called the cult of man. The reader is therefore warned in advance in the light of these emphases, that the following topics have not been dealt with in detail or as subjects in their own right: animism, naturism, magic, Australian totemism, the notion of the soul, and sacrifice.

Yet there is another, altogether more controversial area. It is the sociology of knowledge which was so bound up with religion in *The Elementary Forms* and in which Durkheim was greatly interested. An earlier article which was incorporated in his book had the title 'Sociologie religieuse et théorie de la connaissance' (1909d). This branch of sociology is scarcely considered here. The criticism about such an omission is parried by the argument that to deal with the sociology of knowledge in Durkheim is to open up a vast territory which itself could be the subject of a book. It is stated unashamedly that the subject considered here – the substantive area – is religion. It is not society, social behaviour, social institutions or even epistemology. If we have concentrated on religion and drawn sharp lines of demarcation and are criticized for it, so be it. Relations with other social areas will inevitably be considered, but always one comes back to religion and so to the base of operations. We are therefore not offering a complete exposition of *The Elementary Forms*, but only those of parts that are relevant to our quest.

No attention has been given to the question of how far Durkheim's Jewish background, particularly Jewish beliefs, affected his sociology. The question is a large one, full of methodological problems, and a consideration of Durkheim's sociology *in toto* which would be necessary, is beyond the confines of this book (see Filloux 1977:36ff.).

In order not to create false expectations it must be said that in what follows there is no attempt to support an overall thesis about Durkheim's analysis of religion. Nor is there any conclusion which would allow Durkheim to be categorized as a positivist, a social realist, an idealist, and so on. Is this how one is to judge a classic or a classical writer? Is this the way to deal with the writings of Plato, St Thomas Aquinas, or Karl Marx? Is their work to be summed up by one phrase, by one characteristic, by one thesis? As if this is all that is to be said! If this is so, the notion of a classic is meaningless. Rather, there is the attempt to look at some of the many aspects of Durkheim's work on religion, each on their own merits, and to appraise them accordingly. Every effort has been made to eschew a particular ideological approach in such a task. This is the intention at the outset: how far it has been realized is another matter.

In brief, there are two purposes of the study. One is to set forth the truth about Durkheim by delineating his thought on the matter of religion. The other is to try to bring out the 'truth' of the truth of Durkheim, that is, the 'truth' of the analysis he so imaginatively put forward.

And imagination he certainly had. That will become apparent in the various propositions and assertions that he made in his analysis of religion. What is more difficult to convey is his style of writing and great knowledge. To see this it is necessary to read the author himself. As Parodi said, Durkheim wrote 'avec une érudition imposante et une force dialectique incomparable' (1919: 136).

The greatness of Durkheim is no better attested than by an Australian anthropologist, W. E. H. Stanner, an authority on Australian aboriginal religion, which forms the empirical core of Durkheim's great book on religion. Stanner wrote:

> for some at least, [there is] an impulse to turn back and to study again and again this inexhaustibly interesting scholar. There is a widespread view that everything of value which he wrote has long since been incorporated into the theory and practice of social anthropology. This does not seem to me true. (1967/r.1975:290)

It is hoped that this book in some small way responds to such a call.

Part I
Historical Perspectives

1 Durkheim's religious quest

I Adolescent changes, family life and personal beliefs

1 Introduction

If the subject of this book is Durkheim's study of religion, why should an attempt be made to consider at the outset Durkheim's personal and academic life? His aim, after all, was to undertake an objective and scientific analysis of religion according to those canons of sociology which he himself had laid down. If that is the case, if the discoveries he made are to be judged by scientific criteria, his own life, beliefs and professional achievements can hardly have any bearing on such judgment. For example, one does not need to be acquainted with the life of Faraday in order to understand and make use of his discoveries in electricity. A different kind of challenge to even a brief inquiry into the life of the man, who was to dominate French sociology and to give it new life in the two decades before the First World War, might come from the fact that much has been recently written about Durkheim's life, particularly with the publication of a definitive intellectual biography by Steven Lukes (1972). To write anything new is virtually impossible: all the facts and sources have been well worked over.

Both these questions need to be answered. The study of religion, like religion itself, is, when taken seriously, emotionally charged and ideologically evaluated. A student may set out with the strong conviction that he will be objective and fair, but few are those who in the long run achieve such objectivity. More than likely, the more radical the conclusions, the less neutral the outlook of the student. The liberal quest of many nineteenth-century academics to analyse religion without bias has in the last

3

analysis proved to be very difficult. It may well be that some writers have shown themselves to be fairer than others: the outcome is relative, not absolute. Since religion itself is based on a system or a group of values and ideas related to this world and, usually, to a world that is held to exist beyond it, it is inevitable that strong convictions enter into the study of religion, for such beliefs cut deep into matters of life and death, of what ultimately matters. Neutrality about religion, even as a subject for study, is rarely, if ever, achieved. The nature of modern disciplines associated with religion, no matter how much their aim is to be scientific – and it was certainly Durkheim's aim – are not free from the personal outlook of the scholars who work in them. In this respect personal involvement in the study of religion is markedly different from personal involvement likely in the work of natural scientists. In a study of morals, politics and religion one cannot completely filter out such values. There is obvious merit, therefore, that in coming to grips with the conclusions of a great scholar in the field of religion, one should also be aware of his personal life and the way he relates it to his academic thought and action. Such a procedure affords assistance in trying to know the way he reaches his conclusions, and more importantly, the axioms he assumes at the outset.

In a book such as this, it would be remiss not to give some attention in the beginning to Durkheim's life, and in particular to those aspects of it directly associated with religion. And while, as we have said much has been written about his life, nevertheless we dare to dig over old ground in order to bring out more pointedly his religious attitudes and outlook. Here, the beginning links up with the end, for in the last part, before the conclusion of the book, we treat in some detail Durkheim's evaluation of western religions based on evidence from his own writings and we also attempt to assess what was his religious quest, apparent in his early life and expressed in his professional achievements. Further, those who might come to Durkheim for the first time through a study of his sociological analysis of religion, because their primary interest is in religion rather than in sociology, and who may not want to read a more general account of his life in another book, would benefit from some knowledge of his life and the part he played in the French academic world of his day.

2 Boyhood, youth and the rejection of Judaism

Émile Durkheim's background and upbringing were strongly religious. He was born on 15 April 1858, in the town of Épinal in Alsace-Lorraine, into a rabbinic family. His father Moïse Durkheim (1805–96), himself the son of a rabbi, who in turn was also a rabbi's son, had come from Hagenau in Alsace in the 1830s. (For details about the childhood of Durkheim, see Lukes 1972:39ff.; Greenberg 1976.) Moïse Durkheim had wanted to complete philosophical and scientific studies in Paris before he settled down as a rabbi, but financial difficulties prevented him (Greenberg 1976:625). As events turned out, he became the Chief Rabbi of the Vosges and Haute-Marne. Of the four children of the family, two were sons, neither of whom was destined to be a rabbi. Félix, who entered commerce, died relatively young, and Émile, the youngest child, born when his father was 53 years of age, also rejected the rabbinate and opted for an academic career. Émile went, as might be expected, to the rabbinical school at Épinal and was taught Hebrew, the Old Testament, the Talmud and Jewish doctrines, and this he did whilst attending the local state school. Alpert maintains that he did not study Hebrew systematically (1939:15).

Through a personal communication made to Lukes from a distant relative of Durkheim, all seemed set for him to become a rabbi (1972:39 n.2). One assumes it was very much the wish of the family that the young boy should continue in its tradition and perhaps the local orthodox Jewish community felt the same. That he eventually said no to such a possibility must have been a disappointment to the family, especially to his father. And it was in all probability a rather emotionally wrought decision on Émile's part, for he would have realized the possibility of his family's hostility to or strong dislike of his decision. There is some evidence to suggest that Durkheim was never strongly attracted to the rabbinate. Lenoir, writing in the 1930s, made the point that he only toyed with rabbinic studies ('Les études rabbiniques ne furent qu'une velléité': Lenoir 1930:293). At what age Durkheim made up his mind not to proceed with the rabbinate, and when he told his parents, is not known. He did not talk about the event publicly nor did he mention it in his writings. It could have occurred at any time from the age of perhaps 12 or 13 until he went to the École Normale Supérieure in 1879 when he was 21, having attended the Lycée Louis-le-Grand in Paris a few years before and having failed the entrance examination to the École twice. Although details of the event are lacking, it must have been important in the life of the young Durkheim. It clearly shows that he was thought to be interested enough and clever enough to be a rabbi, and further, that he was prepared to accept the consequences of his action within the family.

The second stage in Durkheim's early religious odyssey would seem to be an episode that has now become well-known, through the account of it by Durkheim's student and close friend, Georges Davy (1883–1976) (1919:183). The setting was the state school he attended in Épinal, where he showed himself to be an able pupil. When the event occurred is also not clear: perhaps it was shortly after his bar mitzvah at the age of 13. The story is that he was considerably influenced by an elderly female teacher who was a Catholic. As a result he underwent some form of spiritual crisis by which it is said he was attracted to mysticism and in the long run to the Catholic Church. He did not take the final step of crossing the religious divide: had he done so, he would have unquestionably precipitated further turmoil in the Durkheim household, if by this time he had already communicated his intention of not becoming a rabbi. Davy does not hesitate to remark that Durkheim did not take long to free himself from the crisis; and Davy seems to want to redeem what might be thought a weakness on the part of the grand master of sociology, for it might be seen to be a failure of judgment to become entangled in an undesirable religious flirtation. Apart from the remarks of Davy, we know nothing of what happened. But it seems legitimate to ask whether it was the institutions and liturgy of Catholicism which attracted Durkheim, as Auguste Comte had been attracted by them some fifty years earlier, and when he later incorporated them into his religion of humanity. Or was it, as Davy suggests, the search for some kind of mysticism, say, in the soul seeking union with God or in a striving after saintliness? Gaston Richard (1860–1945), once a collaborator and then an opponent of Durkheim, held that there were elements in Durkheim's nature which were strongly opposed to mysticism (see chs 23.4 and 9.5). Whether Davy and Richard meant the same thing by mysticism is difficult to say. Richard seemed to imply personal attitudes towards a divine source which involved an act of worship. Davy refers to the interlude as 'feminine' or 'womanish' (1919:182). What does this mean? Does it refer to the agent of the crisis? That he had a crush on the *institutrice*? Or, again, is it Davy's biased way of describing mysticism?

A general observation might be made about Durkheim's flirtation with these forms of religion. It relates to the historical background of conversions from Judaism in nineteenth-century Europe. One might note that during the early part of the century, as Jews gradually gained their civil freedom in the face of a complicated political situation, the walls of their ghettos were broken down, if not literally, then certainly intellectually and socially. A consequence was that many of the Jews, who entered the professions which were now open to them but which before had remained closed, abandoned Judaism as a religion and were often converted to Catholicism or Protestantism, or more frequently became rationalists and agnostics. In the field of the social sciences one recalls Georg Simmel (1858–1918), an almost exact contemporary of Durkheim, a man of letters who was much interested in sociology and social psychology, and who became a Protestant. Generally, however, those who were pioneers in the human or social sciences rejected all established forms of religion. One can think of no great scholar in the nineteenth century in the social sciences who continued to practise as an orthodox Jew. Such sciences tend to be by nature agnostic or atheistic, and the personal lives of those who are devoted to them reflect a similar outlook. Two prominent examples come readily to mind: Marx with his unusual religious background – his father became a Protestant when he was 6 years old; and Sigmund Freud, who retained an academic interest in religion, but who felt that it was little more than a neurosis. Another point is that if Davy's description of the episode is accepted and the word mysticism is applicable, there are interesting though perhaps remote links with some of the facets of Durkheim's sociological thought which have escaped the attention of commentators. As we shall see, Durkheim's sociology, on account of the reverence he had for society, was thought by some to be 'spiritual' or even 'mystical' (see ch. 13.3). Such a charge is clearly quite contrary to the rationalist and scientific analysis of social behaviour which Durkheim was attempting to establish (see *The Rules of Sociological Method* 1895a/t.1938b). Patently what mysticism there is here is not that imputed to his adolescence; rather, it is associated with his so-called sociologism in which social factors are held to be of overriding importance compared with individual factors in explaining social behaviour. The alleged mysticism which was said to have engulfed his concept of society and his approach to collective *représentations* had associated with them mysterious qualities which were not far removed from the divine. Society seemed to be above scientific analysis, despite Durkheim's claim to be scientific: it had a soul (*l'âme collective*). Writing in the late 1950s, Davy went so far as to state that Durkheim's rationalism was permeated with mysticism (1960:6). Clearly one does not want to make too strong a link between the adolescent episode in the school at Épinal and Durkheim's exaltation of the concept of society; nevertheless, the parallel is not without interest.

The third step that Durkheim took in the religious journey of his younger days was the final rejection of the faith of his fathers and, with it, the rejection of all traditional forms of Judaeo-Christian religion. Once again, little by way of biographical detail is known. Perhaps this stage could be divided into two parts – intellectual and ritual – a rejection of the traditional monotheism which is at the heart of Judaism and Christianity, and the refusal to take part in synagogue worship and to follow Jewish laws and ritual requirements. His severance from Judaistic practice was probably not as decisive and as dramatic as one might suppose and there was probably no clear-cut date or event to mark it, although here once again this is speculation. A reported comment from Étienne Halphen suggests that the final break with Judaism came while Durkheim was at the École Normale Supérieure, perhaps shortly after he arrived in 1879 (Lukes 1972:44 n.2). However, he may have rejected the theological claims of Judaism at some earlier time. Filloux has suggested that he abandoned his beliefs 'very quickly' (*très tôt*) (1970:31), but the reference is vague. Did Durkheim begin to have serious doubts about the claims of Jewish belief before his short-lived flirtation with Catholicism? It does seem likely that, for some years until he took what was for him the irrevocable step of totally abandoning orthodox Judaism, he entertained considerable doubts about the truth of religion. Lukes suggests that it was his friendship with two fellow-

8

students slightly senior to himself – Henri Bergson, a Jew who also rejected his faith, and Jean Jaurès, who later became a socialist leader – which was instrumental in his eventual severance with Judaism.

The question of time apart, what were the reasons for Durkheim's rejection of Jewish and, we might add, Christian belief? In the absence of personal testimony on the part of Durkheim, one can only infer them from his academic writings, from various references and asides.

It would seem that at the very heart of his eventual disbelief was an uncertainty about the existence of God and the refusal to accept the traditional doctrines of the deity. As commonly understood, the truth of western religion turns on the fact that there is a God and that he has certain attributes or qualities – he is creator, almighty, totally good, and so on. It seems clear that certainly by the time he left the École Normale, Durkheim could not accept the claims about God made by traditional religion. For him no God, defined as a spiritual being and existing beyond the universe, exists. Similarly, there are no spiritual beings and the soul, as traditionally defined, does not exist. Durkheim believed that these doctrines, as proclaimed within the Hebraic-Christian tradition, were totally unacceptable to anyone of an honest intellectual outlook. Nothing that can be called real exists outside the world as defined by the scientific mind or by everyday experience (see ch. 15.2). All that is in the world is the result of natural processes, including of course the work of man. Such a position epitomizes the outlook of any rationalist and agnostic.

The claims of monotheism were rejected by Durkheim, it is suggested, because they did not match the findings of modern knowledge. The universality claimed by monotheism, that God is the God of the world, was contradictory to the growing awareness that in different societies around the world men had different gods. Each society had its own conception of the deity, or in wider terms, what was ultimately true. In the face of such relativism it was impossible to believe that any one form was true and, by implication, others false. As Durkheim observed in his own writings, man makes his gods, or more accurately society makes gods for men. If there were one God, supreme and universal, all men would be aware of him and worship him. Comparative knowledge about religious systems other than those of the western world, brought about by missionaries, explorers and anthropologists, weakens the authority of any one system in which the claim is made that it possesses ultimate truth and rightness in religious matters. The same kind of inherent weakness also undermines any moral system, which is held to be true beyond the particular societies in which it is found.

The clue which supports the hypothesis that this kind of thinking lay behind Durkheim's youthful rejection of religion and the opting for a relativist position, which after all was common in his day, is to be found in an essay he published in 1911, 'Jugements de valeur et jugements de réalité'. The problem which Durkheim was discussing centred on the fact that men love and aspire to the ideals of goodness, beauty and truth. Yet such ideals are never realized, although men make such a world their sanctuary. Why should this be so? Durkheim responds:

> To this question, the theological hypothesis carries some semblance of a response. The world of ideas is taken as real and has objective existence, but an existence which is supra-experimental, and the empirical reality of which we are part comes from it and depends on it. We are then attached to the ideal as to the very source of our being. But despite the known difficulties that this conception raises when one so hypostasizes the ideal, it is at the same time immobilized, and every means of explaining its infinite variability is lost. We know today not only that the ideal varies according to human groups but that it ought to vary: the ideal for the Romans is not ours, nor should it be ours, and the scale of values changes similarly. These variations are not the product of human blindness, they are based on the nature of things. How can one explain them if the ideal expresses one unassailable reality? *One is forced to admit then that God himself varies with space and time; but to what could this surprising diversity be attributed? The divine process will only be intelligible if God himself had the task of realizing the ideal which is beyond him; however, the problem would then be shifted.* (1911b/1924a:129–30/t.1953b:88–9; our italics)

Although this was written about thirty years after his rejection of orthodox Judaism, it speaks of his awareness that theological relativism militates against, indeed denies a belief in the existence of an omnipotent, absolute God, as found in the Old Testament and implied in the New Testament.

But the denial of ethnocentricism, be it religious or moral, brings with it its own problems, one of which is the denial of absolutes, and for the individual within a society making legitimate his own religious and moral beliefs. If the absolute goes, how is one to justify the rightness of one's own belief and action? Durkheim realized this and it was of constant concern to him in the development of his sociology. A society cannot be a healthy one where men live only according to half-committed beliefs and ideals. He was honest enough to face the problem in his studies on morality, education and religion (see, for example, 1909a(2)). The dilemma that he saw was that in rejecting the truth-claims of a religion or moral system, the sense of authority is very seriously weakened and so the system becomes vitiated. Some kind of surrogate authority must be found and this, Durkheim felt, was in society itself. He was one of the few thinkers of his day who saw the social weaknesses of religious and moral relativism.

It is one thing to abandon intellectually one's belief in God: it is another to cut oneself off irrevocably from a religious body in which one is deeply rooted. As an individual one can harbour doubts about religious tenets, one can even secretly deny them, for one's thoughts are hidden from the public gaze. Not so attendance at church, at the synagogue, not so the upholding of dietary laws, of abstinence and fasting. These are public acts which cannot be hidden: to absent oneself from them is to evoke query and judgment. To leave a closely knit religious group, such as that to which Durkheim was attached, may well bring upon the individual a reaction of social ostracism. Mixed marriages are also strongly disliked because of the threat they pose to the religious group and frequent in such marriages is the charge of infidelity to the group.

As we have noted, Durkheim's refusal to proceed to the rabbinate most likely brought about a degree of family unhappiness, if not a certain amount of dishonour. It seems quite likely that Émile Durkheim's discarding of the customs and beliefs of the religion in which he was brought up and his adoption of Gentile habits probably bordered on the traumatic. This is Coser's opinion also, especially as Durkheim was an Ashkenazi Jew (1971:162; see following section and the footnote). Some of the emotional turmoil and feelings of guilt may be caught in an early review that he wrote of Guyau's *L'Irréligion de l'avenir*:

> The Christian who for the first time eats a normal meal on Good Friday, and the Jew who for the first time eats pork, experience a remorse which it is impossible to distinguish from moral remorse. (1887b:308/t.1975a:35).

It is possible that he may have exaggerated the feelings of Christians in the case he cited. Apart from the fact that Protestants do not follow such a precept, the rule did not have the same status amongst Catholics (for whom it was subject to local custom) as had the taboo on the eating of pork amongst Jews. And writing a few years later in his doctoral thesis, *The Division of Labour in Society*, he again refers to the horror felt in eating a particular meat forbidden by society. Interestingly enough he observed in a footnote that a penal rule (which would include a taboo) should be conserved only if it is supported by a 'living and energetic' collective sentiment (1893b/1902b:76/t.1933b:107 n.45).

Durkheim may have thrown off his orthodox beliefs and practices, but like others before and since, no matter what their religious affiliation, he tended to conform when he visited the parental home. Perhaps not to give offence, he attended synagogue worship with his mother. One incident which Durkheim found embarrassing is recalled by Filloux (1970:301). When as professor at the Sorbonne, Durkheim, under pressure from his mother, found himself attending the synagogue in Épinal on a holy day. The rabbi, seeing the son of his predecessor in the congregation, referred to the presence of an eminent person in their midst, which he said indicated that Judaism was still a flourishing religion.

It might be noted that for reasons of conformity or otherwise, Durkheim married someone who was undoubtedly a Jewess, Louise Dreyfus. Her family home was in Alsace, where her father was in business in the iron trade. After Durkheim graduated from the École Normale Supérieure with very poor marks, perhaps due to a serious illness, he taught philosophy in various lycées until he was given a government grant to visit several German universities in the academic year 1885–6. Then in 1887 he was appointed *chargé de cours* of social science and pedagogy in the University of Bordeaux. His marriage occurred just before he went there, but nothing is known of the religious outlook of Louise Durkheim: one imagines that she tended to adopt the views of her husband and we have no knowledge as to whether their children, André and Marie, were brought up as orthodox Jews. It seems most unlikely.

3 Psychoanalytic factors

Greenberg's psycho-historical treatment of Durkheim's early years is interesting but not convincing. He argues, in using a parallel case, that of Henri Bergson, that the fathers of these two great contemporary nineteenth-century figures had in various ways failed, that the schools they had attended offered them models of success, that they both rejected their fathers in school years, and that in higher education they found a response to their needs and to their goal of assimilation into French society (1976:630). Once again the argument turns on a basic proposition of a psychological kind which uses the attitudes of sons towards their fathers to explain later attitudes and successes. These factors are also said to engender hard work and determination, not least in school and university (ibid.:633). How far one can accept Greenberg's position is in part determined by the degree to which the psychoanalytic theory of causation can be admitted; and in the case of Durkheim, whether there is in fact sufficient biographical material to substantiate the argument, even if the form be accepted. Durkheim's relations to his father are not well documented. One point that seems most doubtful, and which is of great interest to the present study, is the considerable enthusiasm that Durkheim showed for religious thought in the mid-1890s when he read Robertson Smith for the first time. Greenberg suggests that this was directly due to the death of his father, Moïse Durkheim, in 1896 (ibid.:616 n.22) (see ch. 4.2 for a discussion of the reference to Robertson Smith). It should be noted, however, that Durkheim's interest in religion always seems to have been a strong one. It is difficult to know exactly in what ways Robertson Smith inspired Durkheim, but one thing seems certain, apart from substantive issues – he offered Durkheim a new way of approaching religion. Does the discovery of a method supply the right kind of evidence in dealing with personal problems? But further, there is the problem of the dates. Moïse Durkheim died in February 1896. Durkheim in the famous reference to Robertson Smith indicates that it was in 1895 that the traumatic change occurred in his religious thinking (1970b/ r.Deploige 1911:402–3). The problem of Durkheim's relation to his father and the influence of the death of his father has subsequently been raised by Lacroix (1981), who has adopted the same position as Greenberg although he does not refer to him. The Robertson Smith episode of 1895, references to nervous complaints attributed to Durkheim, and even Durkheim's lack of political commitment as being due to a fear of castration, are all used by Lacroix to substantiate his position. But as Besnard rightly points out, as we have just observed, this does not constitute enough material on which to base a psychoanalytical argument and the material is far less than that for Max Weber in relation to his mental breakdown (1981:3). Further, the facts themselves are very dubious and the dates which are crucial to the argument are often wrong (ibid.). A psychoanalytical approach in trying to understand Durkheim's thought and action, especially that relating to religion, is a fruitless task because of the lack of adequate and firm evidence.

4 The significance of Jewishness

Further attention must be given to Durkheim's Jewish background. The place of Jews in France, particularly in the nineteenth and early twentieth centuries, is a subject that has recently received considerable attention (see, for example, Aubery 1962; Bourdel 1974). Only limited aspects of a very wide subject are touched on here.

The medium-sized town in which Durkheim was born is in the Vosges, near Strasbourg and Nancy. It is situated in a part of France where in times past Jewish refugees from the east usually arrived. They were generally of Ashkenazi descent and it is not surprising that eastern France as a whole, particularly Alsace, had in Durkheim's day proportionally more Jews than any other region of the country.[1] Épinal itself contained a large Jewish community with three synagogues. To the north, and on the same river as that on which Épinal stands, the Moselle, is Trèves (Trier) where Karl Marx, also a Jew, was born some forty years before Émile Durkheim.

The French Revolution had been one of the most important instruments in allowing Jews to leave their ghettos and in helping them to assimilate into Gentile life. However, the process of integration in Europe was not a smooth one and was continually subject to ups and downs. It received a serious setback in the 1880s, when socialists in their attack on capitalism switched their attention to Jews and accused them of being the worst offenders – accusations which Marx himself had once made, and in so doing pointed to the alleged evils of his own race. In France the crisis came with the Dreyfus affair in 1894, which dragged on for twelve long, tense years, and which has been so extensively documented. Over and above the question of the innocence or guilt of an army officer of Jewish birth, or even the question of anti-Semitism there quickly emerged issues of larger consequence – the rights of the individual, the concept of patriotism, the well-being of *La Patrie, La Nation*, France herself. Like the events of May 1968, but more decisively, the affair divided the country right down the middle. The old traditional divisions appeared: right versus left, Catholic versus Protestant; moreover, socialists themselves were divided, so were Catholics, so also were families. In the early days, mob action bordered on persecution as crowds shouted 'Death to the Jews'. The army and government administrative bodies attempted to remove from their ranks not only Jews but Protestants, republicans and Freemasons. Hostile action was attempted against any groups or individuals who were thought to be failing in a sense of patriotism. Durkheim, like many Jews at the time, suffered from verbal hostility (Peyre 1960a:14). As expected, he had no hesitation in standing on the side of the Dreyfusards not only in demanding justice for the wronged officer, but also in his support of liberal ideals which he and many others held were the foundation of the Third Republic, and which came under sustained attack during the crisis. Not only was Durkheim very quick to join the ranks of the Dreyfusards, but he also became a member of the supporting movement, the Ligue pour la Défence des Droits de l'Homme, which was formed partly on his suggestion. He became secretary for the Ligue in the Bordeaux region (for Durkheim's involvement in the Dreyfus affair, see Lukes 1972:ch. 17; also Lalande 1906:253; LaCapra 1972:76; Besse 1913:238; Clark 1973: 172–4). In 1898 he published an important article called 'L'Individualisme et les intellectuels' (1898c). In it he answered some of the charges levelled against the Dreyfusards, notably their lack of patriotism, and at the same time he helped to clarify the moral and social issues. Although the essay was of political importance, it was also significant for another reason, namely, that it was written while Durkheim was at Bordeaux and when he was beginning to formulate systematically his sociology of religion (*sociologie religieuse*) (see ch. 27). Certainly one result of the affair was increased anti-clericalism, and with this a heightened religious fervour amongst many believers. But beyond that, national division and internal hostility which had been engendered by the affair, strengthened what Durkheim had so clearly seen after the 1870 Franco-Prussian war: the need for France to realize its unity and to seek a morality based on an unambiguous, scientific foundation. For him, what happened to France during those years was an occasion of moral and political stirring: it was an example of his notion of effervescence (see chs. 21 and 22). The outcome was all to the good, for it was a great awakening which carried with it seeds of change and invigoration. Indeed, Durkheim greatly welcomed the intellectual and political activity which was fermented during the affair.

But was Durkheim drawn to the ranks of the Dreyfusards to become their stalwart supporter on account of his loyalty to Judaism, or by a conviction about republican and liberal principles? Commentators such as Filloux and Lukes feel that Judaism *per se* was not a primary consideration (Filloux 1970:257; Lukes 1972:33 n.49). Strong moral considerations about freedom and human rights were of far greater importance to Durkheim than Jewish loyalties. But could it not be argued that the situation was probably more complex and that both issues were important to Durkheim? That he so quickly rallied to the Dreyfus cause, which was initially concerned with the problem of Jewishness, might suggest that he was quite ready to assist the movement on such grounds. It should be remembered that Durkheim supported certain Jewish organizations throughout his life, provided religious orthodoxy was not the criterion of membership. During the First World War he was a member of a large number of national committees, including the Comité Française d'Information et de l'Action auprès des Juifs des Pays Neutres (Davy 1919:193). Again, the origins of justice and of the rights of the individual can be traced back in part to the eighth-century Jewish prophets about whom Durkheim had learned as a boy. He was very much aware of the persecutions that the Jews in Europe had suffered through the centuries at the hands of Christians. One wonders therefore whether Jewish loyalty was of such secondary consideration as some have maintained. But there is further evidence that the Jewish question was always with him.

During the 1914–18 war, anti-Semitism strangely enough was an ever-present threat to national unity. Durkheim was a sufficiently important figure in the public eye to suffer unpleasant attacks on account of his Jewishness, and that despite his patriotic pamphleteering (see, for example, 1915c). At one point he was castigated in the *Libre Parole* as 'a *Boche* with a false nose, representing the *Kriegsministerium* whose agents are swarming throughout France' (cited in a letter to Léon, 26 January 1916, quoted in Lukes 1972:557). He was also attacked by a senator, M. Gaudin de Vilaine, who requested an examination of residence permits to foreigners, including 'Frenchmen of foreign descent, such as M. Durkheim, a Professor at our Sorbonne' (ibid.). The scurrilous suggestion of the senator was vigorously denounced by a government official who gave high praise to Durkheim and forced de Vilaine to withdraw his remarks.

During the latter part of the nineteenth century and the beginning of the twentieth century, there was a widespread movement in France towards national unity and away from loyalty to regions. It enabled France to reach a new level of self-consciousness. The movement was without reference to religion or to political party, and it was found as much amongst Catholics as amongst anti-clericals. In the Catholic Church no better example of this is to be seen than in the Sacré Coeur de Montmartre, dedicated as it was to national repentance and unity. It was thought of as the Basilique du Voeu National. Durkheim's patriotism was of this genre. It was not to a region of France, say to Alsace, where he was born, but to the nation as a whole. It was the inevitable outcome of his early wish that France should be firmly united and as such he saw regional loyalty to be divisive.

It is the case that in later life Durkheim does not seem to

have been troubled about his Jewish origins, as for example was Sigmund Freud and perhaps Karl Marx. Quite naturally he opposed anti-Semitism, though not in a spirit of hatred: he certainly opposed Jewish extremism (1899d). He presented himself not so much as a Jew, who had guiltily rejected the faith and practice of his forebears, but as an enlightened, intellectual European liberal. There would appear to have been something in him that wanted to play down or quietly cover up his Jewishness. Was it, for example, an accident that he always referred to himself as Émile Durkheim, and not as David Durkheim? He had been given both names, David Émile. He wanted to be accepted for what he was – an intellectual, and a devoted son of France, and in particular an ardent supporter of the Third Republic (see the following chapter). And it was to the country as a whole and not to a particular region of it that he showed his loyalty. He appears to have adopted without much difficulty a 'rational', common-sense attitude towards his Jewishness and here one might recall the example of Disraeli. His background neither obtruded so as to suggest it was the basis of some emotional or intellectual imbalance: nor was it repressed or totally denied. It was quietly laid on one side. To this degree Durkheim seems to have been happily integrated into Gentile society, whilst at the same time remaining in many respects loyal to Judaism. He was *déraciné* yet felt himself embedded in a country which he virtually adored.

5 Asceticism and family life

Although Durkheim became a non-believer at a relatively early period of his life, he firmly retained some of the moral precepts and ideals projected by western religion. One of these was asceticism; not the asceticism practised by hermits and monks, not one based on extreme physical deprivation, but an asceticism tempered by moderation and manifested in the form of self-control and total dedication towards work. From his early days when he entered the École Normale Supérieure, Durkheim exhibited a firm belief in the importance of duty and moral integrity. Georges Davy, to whom we owe much of our knowledge of Durkheim's personal life, used the words '*la croyance au devoir*' as being an outstanding quality of the young Durkheim (1919:182). Let it not be forgotten that Durkheim was no Protestant who might have been influenced by the so-called work ethic: indeed he seemed to have had but little understanding of Protestantism (see ch. 23.4). He was considerably influenced by Kant and neo-Kantianism, which can be seen in his concern for morality and for a high sense of duty which he held everyone in society should have. According to Filloux, the family from which he came was austere and showed great respect for the law (1970:8). Many of Émile's friends pointed to his cold, stoical and ascetic appearance (Davy 1919:194). Work, duty and justice seem to have been the foundation of his morality and happiness, even in the days of his youth (Davy 1960:6–7, 17). He also stood aloof from the arts and from games (see ch. 19.2). Hubert Bourgin, who came to know Durkheim at the turn of the century, wrote perhaps somewhat flamboyantly about the aura of authority and seriousness that surrounded this '*maître impérieux*' (1938:224). 'One felt oneself to be under the judgment and already under the authority of a man who had devoted himself to his task, his mission, and who in admitting you to his presence and within his circle, delegated to you a place within the responsibilities he had assumed' (ibid.:217). His main joy seems to have come in talking about ideas – a Spinoza type of joy, as one writer described it. His warmth was most apparent in conversation (Davy 1919:194).

There can be no doubt that Durkheim worked prodigiously hard, and within the family he was helped a great deal by his wife in proof-reading and similar tasks (see *AS*, n.s., II:8–9; also Lukes 1972:99 n.4). His own home was described as austere, in which the overriding ideals were work and duty (Davy 1960:17). (I have seen where he lived in Bordeaux – a conventional, middle-class terraced house.) Nevertheless, Durkheim's family seems to have been an extremely happy one in which there was warmth and tenderness (Greenberg 1976:627). Certainly Durkheim was very much a family man, devoted to his wife and children. In Louise Dreyfus he was said to have married just 'the right person'. (She had no family connection with the person involved in the later political scandal.) Durkheim was devoted to his two children, although it is reported that he refused to allow his gifted daughter to pursue her education (ibid.:627 n.28). In one sense Durkheim was well prepared to take on family duties, for at the death of his father, when he was young, he became the head of the family (LaCapra 1972:28). Thus, behind Durkheim's austere moral disposition there lurked a warm personality, which made him liked amongst his collaborators, although it must also be admitted that his relations with the members of the Année Sociologie group were, at least in part, dominated by empire-building motives (see ch. 2.2). He seems to have needed collaborators more than they needed him and in many cases his relations with them were warmer than theirs with him.

One wonders how right Greenberg is in suggesting that Durkheim was ambivalent towards the family as an institution, implying an ambivalence towards his own family. Greenberg's argument rests on the fact that discipline, if not asceticism, dominated the Durkheim family. Such a characteristic of Durkheim's own family seems beyond doubt. Greenberg's position about Durkheim's ambivalence rests on the doubtful assumption that family life and discipline verging on asceticism are totally incompatible, and that there cannot be a happy home life where there is such discipline. This is a very doubtful proposition, not only in general terms, but is virtually contrary to Durkheim's own thinking. Durkheim always considered that his most treasured lecture notes, which alas have been lost and which he took with him wherever he went, were those on the subject of the family (Lukes 1972:179). This might be a pointer that family life, both intellectually and emotionally, was of enormous importance to Durkheim himself, and he believed to society at large.

6 His religious quest

We noted earlier that Durkheim firmly rejected traditional religion during his early manhood. The result was, as Filloux has said, that Durkheim 'called himself agnostic, rationalist and atheist' (1970:301). There is no reason whatever to deny the broad truth of the statement. But what is to be challenged is whether such a description, in some such form frequently repeated not only by Durkheim himself but also by his colleagues, is as straightforward an assertion as it seems to be. True, he was a rationalist in the broad sense of the word and was a devoted supporter of France's

Third Republic which was to become avowedly secular. Yet, his attitudes towards religion were not as conventionally hostile or even negative as might be imagined from one's general knowledge of rationalism in France at the time. Despite his claims to follow the dictates of reason and science, he was not the thoroughgoing debunker of religion one imagines he might have been. Indeed, to declare one conclusion of our study at the beginning, there was much about Durkheim that could be called 'religious'. What marked him off from so many of his rationalist, anti-clerical contemporaries was that, as it will become apparent, he had a great reverence for religion. One could say that he was 'religious' about religion. Evans-Pritchard, who was critical of much of Durkheim's thought, but who was largely responsible for the translation of several of Durkheim's writings into English after the Second World War, supports this view in speaking of Durkheim's extraordinary interest in religion (1960:16 n.1). When Durkheim addressed a conference of Free Thinkers and Free Believers in Paris in 1914, he declared vehemently that he was as much opposed to those who were strongly anti-religious as he was to those who were dogmatic believers (1919b). Unlike so many rationalists of his time, and indeed before his day, he never mocked or derided religion, although he was often critical about the contemporary institutional brands of it (see ch. 23).

The truth of the matter is that he saw a *via media* between traditional believers and anti-clericals, and pointed to both the desirability of new forms of religion and the fact that they were emerging anyway. He believed that the moral and social uncertainty of the times was in part due to the failure of traditional religions – Catholicism, Protestantism and Judaism – to offer a satisfying system of beliefs and rituals, which could even approximate to the intellectual demands of the day – demands based on reason and science (chs 24 and 25). The new patterns of religion which were in fact emerging were of the kind to which scientifically minded people such as himself could readily subscribe (ch. 26).

Like many French intellectuals before him, Durkheim looked for a religion without God, but which at the same time contained what might loosely be called 'a spiritual element'. From the time of the Revolution, and indeed before it, France proved itself to be a veritable seed-bed of humanistic religions and sects. As such it was an earlier and secular challenge to the religious fertility of the United States. The French Revolution did not take the logical step of abolishing religion root and branch, but attempted to create forms which were in keeping with some of its basic ideals. Such forms centred on the code of reason and the institution of ritual and festivals associated with human and moral virtues. Later there was the Nouveau Christianisme of Saint-Simon, followed by the religion of humanity of Auguste Comte, who was for a time Saint-Simon's secretary. During this turbulent period, France might show itself to be anti-clerical and anti-Catholic, and even anti-Christian, but there were always those who searched for what might be called surrogate, humanistic religions, often highly ritualized as in the case of Comte's church. The theology, however, of such religions was always based on man and on human values. The goal was to create a Christian-like morality devoid of the 'false' premises of Christian belief and free from the inimical control of the Catholic clergy. Such an end is exemplified in the title of one group, Société de Morale Chrétienne, which existed in the 1820s.

Durkheim categorically disassociated himself from these distinctive movements, which were carefully contrived inventions to bring about an institutional religion with man as its centre, accompanied by rituals in praise of him. For him new religious forms were not something which had to be deliberately engineered or promulgated: they emerged in history. Within society as a whole the new form of religion which he held was growing was one which took the shape of individualism. It was based on a deep respect for man in relation to other men and set within his social order. There existed in society a morality based on the dignity of the human personality, but which was mediated by society itself. His nephew, Marcel Mauss, said that 'morality was really the goal of his existence . . . the foundation of his mind' (1925:9). And Davy somewhere made a similar point, that anyone is destined to fail to understand Durkheim's work unless it is realized 'that morality is at the centre of it . . . its end'. Some more recent commentators have gone so far as to suggest that Durkheim was more a moral philosopher than a sociologist. Bellah wrote in 1973 that Durkheim was 'a philosopher and moralist in the great French tradition of moral thought' (1973:x) and Wallwork's book, *Durkheim: Morality and Milieu* (1972), was the substantiation of the thesis that Durkheim 'stood in the classical tradition of moral philosophy that stemmed from Plato and Aristotle' (1972:vii). Such arguments as these receive support from the fact that after the publication of *Les Formes élémentaires de la vie religieuse*, Durkheim set about writing what he hoped would be an even more important book, this time on moral philosophy. The war years interrupted his efforts and when he died he had only written the introduction (1920a; see Pickering 1979a:4).

As we have hinted, there were, however, political reasons for upholding this emerging form of humanism which appeared to sway Durkheim more than purely theological reasons. It is true, as Richter says, that all Durkheim's endeavours were affected by his search for a religion minus a transcendental god (1960:203). The reasons for such a lifelong search were doubtless deep in his psyche, but from his writings and all other evidence the urge was to discover some quasi-transcendental base on which to build political stability and strength.

It was an attempt to give a rational understanding of the sacred base for an emerging morality which could thus be strengthened and made more effective. Hence there was the prior need to understand religious life, because of its very close relation to morality and because in it is located, as nowhere else, the sacred. A deep concern for matters religious is thus at the heart of Durkheim's thought.

7 Patriotism, politics and war

Épinal is situated in an area of France renowned in the nineteenth century for its sense of identity and for its patriotism. When he was only twelve years of age, Durkheim witnessed the 1870 Franco-Prussian war fought, as it were, on his very door step. After the French suffered their unexpected and humiliating defeat – the war lasted a bare three months – it was followed by the collapse of the Second Empire, the rise of the Third Republic and the Commune of 1871 with its chaos and bloodshed. Internal wrangling between the Orléanists, Legitimists and Bonapartists gave rise to continued instability, until eventually the republicans gained a moderately firm control in 1877. They were initially a somewhat divided group, since support came from many quarters, from thoroughgoing atheists, from Freemasons, anti-clericals, liberal Jews and Protestants. They formed an alliance against extremists who threatened them from the left and from the right. The right was, on the whole, a stronger group with an alliance between royalist factions, 'nationalists' and the supporters of the Catholic Church.

One result of the war and the annexation of Alsace-Lorraine to the Germans was to engender in the young Durkheim a deep sense of patriotism and nationalism. He was struck by the uncertainty of the times, the humiliation of defeat, the multiplicity of political parties each striving for different goals, the pluralism of institutional religion. As Essertier said, he was living at the end of a century which was marked by every kind of confusion. In literature there was a vague sadness which may have exaggerated its importance, but traditional beliefs, a sense of duty, the love of one's country seemed to be at the point of sacrifice. What one held most deeply could be the subject of blasphemy and laughter (Essertier 1930:34). Durkheim was utterly convinced that a moral and intellectual crisis was afoot. Duties were no longer related to the realities of life and what was needed was a new discipline which could demonstrate the nature of the crisis and point to the need for moral integrity, national regeneration and re-organization.

The moral fibre of France was to be tried again forty-five years later with the outbreak of the First World War. Once more the French and the Germans were at each other's throats, this time with the French seeking revenge for what had happened in 1870. And once more Durkheim, like so many other Frenchmen, was emotionally stirred, and now he was a man at the height of his powers. He had no hesitation in lending what intellectual weight he could to the cause of his country. As someone who was 'passionately devoted to science, justice, his native land' (Worms 1917:567), he found that everything he stood for was threatened by the war. Even when the clouds were beginning to gather at the turn of the century, he had no hesitation in making contributions to such subjects as militarism (1899b) and later patriotism and pacifism (1908a) (Lukes 1972:350). When the storm eventually broke, Durkheim showed a burning desire to see what he called a 'moral revival', which was necessary if France were to survive (Davy 1960:6). With the memories of 1870 rekindled, he held more strongly than ever that only through a sense of unity and moral fervour, coupled with justice within society, could France gather sufficient moral and social strength so as to be victorious in the war. As a public figure, he helped by writing a series of tracts, sometimes with the help of others, with such titles as:

Qui a voulu la guerre? Les origines de la guerre d'après les documents diplomatiques (1915b);
L'Allemagne au-dessus de tout: la mentalité allemande et la guerre (1915c);
Lettres à tous les Français (1916a).

These essays or tracts formed sections of a general volume, *La Science française*, which was sponsored by the French Ministry of Education; they were in response to German manifestos justifying the war. Durkheim's essays were amongst the last he wrote, for, as we have said, he died in 1917. Davy, writing just after Durkheim's death, made a great deal of his ardent patriotism and observed that his master had launched a strong appeal to his countrymen to have 'patience', 'confidence' and 'make a maximum effort for victory' (1919:190ff.). Recently there has come to light an open letter that Durkheim wrote during the war in an educational journal (1916c). In it he pays tribute to the heroism of the French troops and to the moral greatness of France; Ferdinand Buisson, whom he followed at the Sorbonne, wrote in a similar vein at much the same time (1916). Durkheim speaks of the soundness of moral education in France, meaning secular moral education, which he himself played a large part in fostering. He calls attention, however, to the weaknesses of the French in their individualism and nonchalant attitude towards national action. The schools in the future will have to have a greater respect for authority and a high sense of discipline, though not that 'mechanical, punctilious discipline' that was once practised. Once again, he employs religious terminology in asking that school discipline 'must appear to children as something good and sacred – the condition of their happiness and moral well-being'.

The truth of the matter is that Durkheim was an ardent nationalist from his earliest days to his last. Davy recalled that in 1880, after he had been at the École Normale for a year, he rejoiced greatly during the festivities of 14 July and spent the whole day on the streets, caught up in the enthusiasm of the occasion (Davy 1919:188).

The morality which Durkheim saw emerging, and to which he committed himself, had in his eyes a sacred base in an unquestioning respect for the human personality. But it was not the human personality *per se*, in isolation, which was sacred, but rather, in its relation to society, to other people, who formed society. There were thus two principles – two 'deities' – and in this dyad Durkheim never saw any real or lasting conflict. Under normal conditions they were in complete harmony – the individual and society.

Durkheim's basically 'religious' outlook was thus in part confirmed by the fact that he was always ready to see that the most cherished ideals and ideas within a society could be described as sacred (see chs 7 and 8). The sacred was at the very heart of religion; it was also at the heart of society. Hence what is basically a religious concept is the most satisfactory and indeed scientific way of analysing a society, even a society which at first sight is thoroughly secular.

France's Third Republic, which had begun in 1870, had declared itself to be agnostic and had pursued such a policy at a time of moral and religious uncertainty. What Durkheim saw as his 'religious' task was to point very clearly to the emerging morality that was non-religious yet sacred, nationalistic yet universal in application, scientifically enlightened and yet authoritarian. Of course he wanted not only to point to the existence of such a morality, but in some way to strengthen it. Both these points are important. Obviously he was not alone in hoping to see this kind of morality firmly established in France – an essentially lay (*laïque*) morality, the authority of which was firmly established in the state. His thinking was very close to that of Louis Liard, who was his patron and Directeur de l'Enseignement Supérieur. Durkheim's unique contribution was in attempting to show the part that the new discipline of sociology could play in the moral strengthening of France along the lines proclaimed by the Third Republic.

In an anonymous obituary, Durkheim's goal in helping to bring about the stability and spiritual invigoration of France is clearly set out:

Already, during the days of his youth, following the Treaty of

Frankfurt, he abandoned the idea of psychological research on quality and quantity in order to concentrate on work of an almost new kind in France. This was in finding in the science of societies the objective base for a re-organization of national life. (Anon. 1917:750–1)

The writer makes plain the fact that Durkheim at an early age turned to sociology for what might be called political, pragmatic or ideological reasons. From the time Durkheim entered the École Normale he was attracted by the problem of social justice (Essertier 1930:34). In this he was influenced by Jaurès, who later became a prominent socialist thinker. Jaurès was one year his senior as a student at the École and through him he turned away from a formalist and intellectual approach to politics and radical philosophy. The search for moral justice received a more practical interest, although Durkheim never became a member of a socialist party. Hubert Bourgin suggests that in the last analysis Durkheim was more concerned with moral issues than he was with the development of sociology as a social science. He wrote:

the founder and principal contributor to the French school of sociology was a sociologist more on moral grounds than on scientific grounds. Sociology was for him the only and certain means of reconstructing morality, which had been shattered by the very conditions of life in our society, which was too vast and overstretched. (1938:218)

The task of sociology, as Durkheim saw it, was to construct the intellectual foundations of an imperative morality for the whole of society – a morality which was already in existence (ibid.:219). Thus, sociology had to give a 'theological' basis, which was essentially naturalistic and pragmatic, to the new quasi-religious morality that was emerging in France, and which was thought necessary for the well-being of the nation.

8 The epilogue

When Durkheim died in 1917, the medical diagnosis of his death was a stroke, but it was commonly said that he died through a broken heart (Davy 1919:181; Lukes 1972:559). Although it was held that he always had delicate health, he was irrevocably saddened when he learnt in January 1916, that his only son, André, had died in a Bulgarian hospital from wounds he had received whilst commanding a rearguard action on a retreat at the Serbian front (Anon. 1918). André had been wounded before on the western front and his health had always been somewhat uncertain (Worms 1917:568). He had been taught by his father, who realized that in his son there was a promising linguist. The series of lectures on pragmatism (1955a) were specially intended for André, and in them were Durkheim's last academic references to religion. But the loss of his son was yet one more sorrow heaped on others for, as we shall see in the next chapter, Durkheim was already weighed down by the death of many of his most promising students and collaborators, members of his *équipe*, who had also been killed during the war. Obviously the saddest blow of all was the loss of his son. At such a time of misery and desolation, Durkheim yearned, it is said, for the consolation of religion. He had written objectively about the functions of religion and the help that it gave at such occasions as he was experiencing. Now he only encountered utter misery in the form of a personal vacuum. He could scarcely talk about the death of André (Davy 1919:181–2). In the darkness which surrounded him he categorically admitted that religion offered him no hope or comfort. He wrote to Xavier Léon:

> Of course I know that the religions are there, and that their practices are rich in experience that is unconscious and full of accumulated wisdom. But their wisdom is crude and empirical; nothing resembling ritual practices has been of use to me or seems effective to me. (Letter dated 20 April 1916; quoted in Lukes 1972:556)

It is remarkable that having rejected the truth-value of all religions he should have momentarily turned to them in seeking consolation at the hour of crisis. Was the backward glance another pointer to Durkheim's religious nature? Clearly the edifice of the cult of man on which he had consciously based his beliefs had crumbled. The brittle foundations had given way in the face of the holocaust of the war. The hatred between civilized nations had rendered liberal humanism virtually untenable. Was it also such embittered suffering that caused him to forbid all ceremonial and speeches at his own funeral (Worms 1917:568)?

Society, which he seemed to worship as a quasi-deity, offered not comfort but betrayal.

2 Durkheim's religious quest

II In professional achievement

1 To greater things

As we have noted, Durkheim was chosen to be a university lecturer in Bordeaux in 1887. The initiative for the appointment seems to have come from Alfred Espinas (1844–1932), who helped to make Bordeaux in his day the foremost university in France not only for the social sciences, but for pedagogy. In 1882 Espinas, famous for his doctorate of 1877, *Les Sociétés animales*, began giving a course of lectures on education under the auspices of the Municipality of Bordeaux. The purpose was to instil into future schoolteachers a sense of the social, which according to Espinas, was the means of revitalizing the soul of France. It was a successful course and when Espinas became dean of the faculty, the government did not hesitate to create a new chair in Pedagogie et Science Sociale. Durkheim was earmarked for this when he was made *chargé d'un cours*. He eventually received the chair in 1895. Outstandingly able though he was, he had to wait a further seven years before he was appointed to the centre of academic life in France, Paris and the Sorbonne. Thus, it took him fifteen years of university life to reach the summit, but the period was the most arduous and fruitful part of his life (Lacroze 1966:169). It was said that while he was in Bordeaux he felt lonely and had a sense of powerlessness (Mauss 1979:210). The move to Paris meant that once again he followed in the footsteps of a prominent person, this time Ferdinand Buisson (1841–1932), a famous educationalist, who was made a member of the Chamber of Deputies in 1902. In 1906, after being *chargé d'un cours*, Durkheim again became professor. He never moved from the Sorbonne. In pursuing a professional life, unmarked by dramatic events, he was

30

able to establish himself as the doyen of sociology in France and in this was supported by a band of young and ardent disciples. Thus, during his lifetime he managed to lay the foundations of a kind of sociology which has now become generally accepted in and beyond the realms of his native France.

2 Disciples and the journal

Durkheim firmly believed that the new science of sociology – his particular brand of sociology, as distinct from that of Comte or of German scholars – needed to be communicated to society at large. It was not a light to be hid under a bushel. It was not remote scholarship which was intended for a few obscure academics, concerned with minor points of past history. It was intended for public acceptance and assimilation. It had an important role to play in revitalizing society. This meant that not only should its conclusions be widely accepted by educated people as a whole, but that its findings should so captivate the minds of other scholars that they would feel themselves impelled to join the ranks of those who had given their lives to working professionally within the discipline. The great merit of Durkheim's sociology was that it did indeed penetrate other disciplines and that the ideas which emanated from him found their way into history, philosophy, psychology, political science, and so on. Durkheim was thus very concerned that what he had to say should be widely received and that the science should go from strength to strength. It was very far from his mind that the kind of knowledge with which he was associated should, as it were, find its own level by haphazard channels of communication. The knowledge had to be promulgated. He was a man with a mission – a gospel to proclaim – and like all preachers and prophets he felt impelled to declare his message to all, whether they would listen or not. But as a preacher taking the initiative, he was careful, and indeed in some cases fortunate, to find places and occasions when he could most effectively proclaim his ideas. There can be no doubt that although he was never committed to a political party, he was nevertheless a skilled politician, as well as being a fine 'preacher'.

As is well known, Durkheim created around him, from relatively early on in his academic career, a band of disciples who became known as the Année Sociologique school – Durkheim's *équipe*. Many of the individual members of the group became renowned by reason of their writing and because they received academic posts in France both during Durkheim's lifetime and afterwards. We should mention the names of Marcel Mauss, Celestin Bouglé, Georges Davy, Paul Fauconnet, Paul Lapie, Henri Hubert, and so on. (Articles on the formation of Durkheim's *équipe* and some of its members constituted a special issue of the *Revue française de sociologie*: *RFS*, XX (1), 1979, see in particular the article by P. Besnard.)

We can only deal summarily with Durkheim's extraordinarily successful endeavours to develop his sociology through this working group. Perhaps the best-known description of the group itself comes from the pen of someone who was a prominent member of what might be called the second generation, Georges Davy:

> There were some in fact around him who formed as it were a spiritual family, united by the tie of a common method and a common admiration for their master. They constituted, to coin a word which was clear to him, a little society *sui generis*, the clan of the *Année Sociologique*. Durkheim created and maintained the spirit and the unity of this little society, without any tyranny by allowing full freedom to each member. He acted only through the extraordinary influence of his mind and his method. Everyone liked to go and see him, and at the same time receive his advice, and to be certain of the affectionate interest he had for them all. (1919:194–5)

It is not surprising that amongst those who criticized Durkheim were some who looked upon the *équipe* as 'Jesuits' propagating the ideas of their master (the 'pope'?) in trying to establish a secular society. This accusation, if nothing else, points to the efficiency and effectiveness of the group of followers whom Durkheim had gathered around him.

Correspondence has recently emerged, written by members of the group, such as Lapie and Bouglé, which testifies to the close and warm relations Durkheim had with his disciples (see *Études durkheimiennes. Bulletin d'information*, Paris, 1977, no. 1, *et seqq.*). Perhaps it is not too cynical to say that Durkheim, because he was fired by his sense of mission and a desire to exert his influence, had a greater need to gain the help and co-operation of a group of followers, than perhaps the followers had of that which he had to offer them. Nevertheless, Durkheim's achievement was remarkable and his ability to hold together a group of disparate young scholars, working in various fields of learning but all interested in the application of sociology to their disciplines, has often been overlooked. No other sociologist had heretofore ventured along these lines and nearly all sociologists of his day were working very much on their own – for example, Simmel, Herbert Spencer, Max Weber, Ferdinand Toennies. Nor has any sociologist subsequently been able to weld together a group comparable to that which Durkheim created and nurtured. Perhaps the only exception is the Frankfurt school in the 1930s and durings its revival after the Second World War, although no one person dominated it. Durkheim held that the very nature of the subject of sociology required a collective response. Sociology is about groups, societies, institutions, and therefore it could only be developed by such means. Of course, some might want to argue that a need for security in Durkheim's personality, perhaps due to his Jewish origins, caused him to work for a collective response – he felt it necessary to be supported by devotees (cf. the importance of 'we' in 1925a:274/t.1961a:240). There can be no doubt, as Davy stresses, that the group was very much centred on the master himself. After he died, it lost its way and eventually fell into obscurity (see chs 27 and 28).

It was not only the charismatic figure of Durkheim himself, who was the focal point of the academic zeal of the group; it was also the journal, *L'Année sociologique*, which expressed their views and which was a labour of love. Such a journal had been suggested by Xavier Léon in the 1870s, many years before the first issue appeared in 1898. Léon was to become a close friend of Durkheim and the friendship lasted until Durkheim's death. Léon was a wealthy Jew who was the editor of the *Revue de métaphysique et de morale*, which he financially supported himself. The *Année sociologique* was printed by Alcan in Paris – a firm which published all Durkheim's works as well as those of many of his group. Altogether twelve volumes containing articles and reviews were published, the last was in 1913. The publication of the journal made great demands on the editor. The attempt was to produce one volume each year and this entailed '*un labeur gigantesque*', as Davy called it (1919:195). In Durkheim's day the journal was read in France as well as abroad, and not only by sociologists but by those in allied disciplines such as psychology, history, law and philosophy. Partly in imitation of German journals, much of the space was given to a systematic reviewing of books and articles. Some volumes were given over solely to this, as was vol. XI (1910) which extended to over 800 pages. The quality of the writing was remarkably high. Only one other sociological journal in France could be said to approximate to it, and that was the *Revue internationale de sociologie*, which was started earlier than the *Année*, in 1893, with Renée Worms as its editor and which continued to be published until 1939. Its sociological outlook was eclectic, less rigorous than that of the *Année sociologique*, but it drew on scholars outside France far more than did Durkheim's journal.

The reasons which prompted Durkheim to seize the opportunity of editing the *Année* were probably many and complex: a desire to see the discipline of sociology extended as far as possible, to acquaint the public with the findings of sociologists, to have a means of allowing his own colleagues to publish their findings (Alpert 1939:47–8). It is difficult to be precise about it. No one suggested that the editorship was undertaken in order to promulgate certain ideas about religion, but religion always received a prominent place in the journal through the large numbers of articles and reviews that were published in it year by year (see ch. 27.2). It was said of the members who contributed to the *Année sociologique* that they had 'a sympathy and even admiration for religious idealism, and in particular for Christian and Jewish faith and teachings' (source unknown). Was this an idle and fanciful characterization? One thing is certain; it was true enough of Durkheim himself.

3 Influence in the realm of education

In one of his lectures on moral education, Durkheim said:

> The last twenty-five years in France have seen a great
> educational revolution, which was latent and half realized

before then. We decided to give our children in our state-supported schools a purely secular moral education. (1925a:3/ t.1961a:3)

In entering the arena of education, Durkheim did not find himself having to cut a special path, or to fight single-handed an overwhelming opposition. His aims were completely in keeping with what many others wanted, and changes of which he thoroughly approved were taking place in education. They were the reforms which in many ways made the Third Republic famous. Durkheim was certainly not alone in seeing that in the avowed policy of the Third Republic in the change to a secular education in the lycées and primary schools, there existed a means of propagating throughout France an ideology which was essentially rationalist and which it was hoped would bring about moral regeneration and social development. On this nearly all the supporters of the government were agreed. As we have said, Durkheim was unique in hoping that sociology would help to undergird the secular morality on which the hopes of so many were pinned. But Durkheim was not just a thinker; he was a man of action. For him the ultimate was praxis, defined in broad terms as a confluence of thought and action.

People cannot convincingly teach what they do not believe. If a secular education is to be successfully promulgated, teachers of traditional religious convictions, or teachers employed by the Church, are not to be entrusted with it. If the content of education is to be radically changed, so must the outlook of the teachers. From the early 1880s, under the anti-clerical leadership of Jules Ferry, an agnostic who married a wealthy Protestant, moves were made by the French government to laicize or secularize all schools. This controversial legislation, which has been extensively documented, took considerable time to carry out (see Duveau 1957; Weill 1925). The Catholic system of education, which had dominated the scene for so long, had to be dismantled. By 1906 the process was wellnigh complete and the teaching orders of the Church were no longer allowed to function as such. From then onwards free compulsory education in primary schools was put into practice. Further, in 1905, the Concordat of 1801 was finally broken and the Church was completely separated from the State: in some respects this was to the advantage of the Church, since it was allowed to manage its own affairs. From the 1890s onwards, as the religious were being excluded from teaching, a vacuum was created which had to be filled by lay teachers. It was estimated that 10,000 men and 40,000 women in religious orders had to be replaced (Bryant 1976:111). The task was gigantic and consequently members of the religious orders could still be found teaching in state schools up to the time of the First World War. The process required more legislation than that of Ferry and it came from the more vigorous anti-clericalism of the government of Waldeck-Rousseau and Combes, who capitalized on the right-wing extremism which was allied to the Church and which emerged during the Dreyfus affair.

One of the problems that faced the government was to train a sufficient number of new teachers and to ensure that they were adequately prepared to carry out new tasks that were laid upon them. In place of the religious instruction that had formerly been given, the schools were now required to provide moral and civic teaching in accordance with the ideals of the Third Republic. The teacher was thus called upon to take a full part in trying to bring about moral and social progress in society. He had to teach an adapted Christian ethic, based not on a religious foundation, but on a secular one, in many respects middle-class in orientation. The *instituteur* (the schoolmaster) – or more often the *institutrice* – was called upon to exercise an extraordinarily important role in moulding the beliefs and morals of the young, in the way the priest did formerly. Thus the curé was to be replaced by the lay teacher – the 'Black Hussar' of the Republic, in the words of Péguy, the Catholic republicanist (see LaCapra 1972:59). As the change began to take place, the two dominant figures of the parish – the *instituteur* and the curé – became rivals for the loyalty of the parish or village. Mehl, in commenting that the influence of the Protestant minister was similar to that of the Catholic priest, described the situation as follows:

> In France, the Third Republic was so conscious of this *de facto* power exercised over the parish by the parish priest, who was usually unsympathetic to the regime and hostile to the secularization of the state and of the school, that it could not assure its own stability without installing a rival authority into the parish. This rival authority was the teacher. In the same

paternalistic fashion, he became the counsellor of the
inhabitants, the organizer of their spare-time activities, and
the electoral agent of the Republic. (1965/t.1970:304)

Thus unashamedly the schoolmaster assumed the role of a teacher
of ideology, as well as imparting the three 'Rs' and other factual
knowledge. Far from unity being brought to a parish, the presence
of the rivals often meant that it was divided into two factions
which were hostile to each other.

The fact that the work of the lay teacher in many ways
supplanted that of the priest in the local community was something
which Durkheim strongly supported. Education at every level was
of vital significance for a society. For France it was particularly
the case. The teacher at the lycée, and especially in the primary
school, had a part to play in building up the nation. Perhaps his
own experience of being influenced by his Catholic *institutrice*
convinced him of the power that schoolteachers could wield over
their pupils (see ch. 1.2). In the task that faced the country in
training teachers for a new kind of work, there existed a situation
which was ideal for Durkheim's purposes, although he may not
have been conscious of this at the beginning. From the time he
began to teach in the university, he found himself having to lecture
to students who were to be future teachers and this afforded
him a great opportunity of spreading his ideas not only on the
subject of sociology but, more dear to him, on the subject of
morality too. In this way he was able to make a unique contribution to the problems of education in France and at the same
time have a vehicle for propagating his doctrine (see 1916c;
1925a).

Of the many academic achievements attributed to Durkheim,
probably the description of him as the father of the sociology of
education is the most accurate (see Pickering 1979a:99–125).
There was no sociologist before his time, and no sociologist
contemporary with him, who had given it any consideration
worthy of the name, with the possible exception, of Herbert
Spencer. Durkheim alone devoted much energy to the subject.
Between one-third and two-thirds of his teaching time in Paris
was said to have been given to educational subjects (according
to Fauconnet in Durkheim 1922a:1/t.1956a:27). Did he wittingly
choose to expend himself in this way? It is a difficult question to

answer. His primary concerns were with the science of sociology and a secular morality, but as is well known, his first academic appointment in Bordeaux was chargé d'un cours de science sociale et de pédagogie. Eight years later, in 1895, he was appointed professeur-adjoint, then professeur, and then had a chaire magistrale in science sociale (Worms 1917:564). When he was transferred to Paris in 1902 to follow Ferdinand Buisson, who was professor of education and who had been elected to the Chamber of Deputies, Durkheim was appointed as chargé d'un cours de science de l'éducation and in 1906 professor of the science of education; it was only later, in 1913, at his request that the title was changed to professor of the science of education and sociology. Durkheim's entry into university life meant that he was provided with a niche, which was accompanied by security and status, in which he could develop his primary vocation, the study of sociology. It is probably not too much to say that when he took up his duties he looked upon lecturing to would-be teachers in various institutions as an academic chore. Although he saw the importance of such lectures to those who had such an important part to play in the future of France and even in the propagation of his ideas, he never seems to have relished this particular part of his work. Even the superb set of lectures which he gave in Paris, *L'Évolution pédagogique en France* (1938a), which was intended to make future teachers fully aware of their tasks, was said to have been given as a result of the demands of the university authorities and against his own will (Lukes 1972:379). Nevertheless, whether or not he felt that his time could be better used than in giving lectures to teachers, the fact remains that his influence in this area was very great.

Durkheim has left to posterity several series of lectures on education as well as articles (see Lukes 1972:ch. 6 and pp. 617–20; Pickering 1979a:202–3). This is no occasion to try to expound his sociology of education as it is contained in these works or to assess his contribution to the discipline. The subject is vast. Our concern is much less ambitious and more practical. It is to show ways in which Durkheim attempted to ensure that his sociology and philosophy of education were universally accepted. To say that Durkheim had his own 'priests' in every town and village of the land is to make too bold a claim. On paper it seemed a possibility, but if the ideal was not realized at least it could be said that

Durkheim made a very substantial contribution to education in the France of his day and in the decades that followed.

This is in part borne out by the influence that Durkheim exerted in another area. In this case it was the government department responsible for higher education. Durkheim's political outlook has been the subject of much debate and speculation (Lukes 1972:ch. 12; LaCapra 1972:64ff.; Bryant 1976:114ff.; Filloux 1977). He never publicly allied himself to a particular political group, although he was socialist in outlook. Above all, as has been repeatedly said, he was an unwavering supporter of the Third Republic and indeed could be called one of its intellectual leaders (see 1904e; Bellah 1973:xxxvii). His political thinking was almost identical to that of the leaders of the Republic. When Durkheim went to Paris in 1902 his links with government officials became close. His advice was sought frequently. Clark has called him 'one of the most powerful university politicians in France' (1969:10). His association with influential figures in the department of education has suggested some kind of 'conspiratorial favoritism' (LaCapra 1972:33). LaCapra holds, however, that links between Durkheim and the government were not strictly of this kind but were due to a coincidence of ideas and connections with the government, and a common deep concern about the future of education in France (ibid.). Not everyone would agree with LaCapra's judgment. As Durkheim himself had received his early appointments through the government official Louis Liard, who as Directeur de l'Enseignement Supérieur appears to have paved the way for his visit to Germany in 1885 to study the teaching of social science and his appointment to the University of Bordeaux two years afterwards, so Durkheim later sought to influence university appointments through his contacts in the department of education. Or so it seems. Little evidence has yet been found. But one can point to many of those who were members of the Année Sociologique school who received teaching posts to the exclusion of other candidates not taught by or influenced by Durkheim (Clark 1968:68). One might point to Gaston Richard, who followed Durkheim at Bordeaux (see Pickering 1975:344; 1979b). The chairs in question were usually established chairs in philosophy. What Durkheim seems to have been able to do was to have them filled by sociologists of his school, or to have the titles of the chairs changed to that of sociology and then filled them with his nominees. One example is that of Bouglé, who was appointed to a chair in philosophy in Toulouse in 1902. While Durkheim was alive, no appointment in sociology to a university chair seems to have gone to a non-Durkheimian, and van Gennep, the well-known anthropologist, never received an academic appointment, nor did any member of the group associated with the Institut International de Sociologie, associated with the *Revue internationale de sociologie* (see ch. 27.3). Further, this policy seems to have persisted well after his death into the 1920s and 1930s. Such was the persistence of his influence.

4 'More a priest than a scholar'?

Durkheim's dedication to a rational-empirical sociology, but above all his sense of mission that sociology had a leading role in strengthening the moral fibre of France, was accompanied by a firm determination to propagate the ideas of the new science. This vigour on the part of Durkheim created, nevertheless, hostility and was destined to draw forth even further hostility after his death (see ch. 27.3). One frequent charge was that his attitudes, policies and actions smacked of dogmatism. Such a charge clearly carries with it religious overtones – a dogmatism associated in particular with that of the Roman Catholic Church, and never more apparent than in its ultramontanist phase in the nineteenth century. The charge of dogmatism ill becomes a rationalist, a believer in democracy, someone who stands at the edge of the camp of anti-clericals. That such a charge can be made supports the motif drawn out here, namely, that in much of what Durkheim thought and did in his personal life and in his involvement in the academic world, there is the thread of what is little short of a religious quest.

Can the charge be seriously sustained? To answer this one must look more precisely at the ways in which Durkheim was seen to be a dogmatist. One possibility can be eliminated immediately. In his personal relations and in his family life, what evidence there is all points to the fact that he was warm and generous, though ascetically inclined. Much the same might be said of his relations with the members of the inner circle of the Année Sociologique group. Within certain parameters he seems to have allowed his collaborators considerable freedom of manoeuvre (Fauconnet 1927:18). The members of the *équipe* often disagreed with their master, although not on the basic methods and aims of the discipline which Durkheim had established (Branford 1918). There were disagreements, often in the area of religion; for example, Durkheim had different views about sacrifice compared with those of Hubert and Mauss. As Mauss himself said: 'We were not just a school of blind disciples centred on a master, a *philosophe*' (1979:210). These differences remained little more than internal squabbles and were never sufficient to cause any serious severance or disruption; the only exception was that centred on Gaston Richard (see ch. 23.4). Although the group has been described as a family, it was also a band of disciples who went out into the world to promulgate the ideas of their founder. At a more personal level, he wanted the co-operation and friendship of the group and deliberately created around him a contented, devoted community of scholars.

Durkheim, ambitious for the discipline he championed, was without great personal ambition. It is true that in 1897 he applied for the chair of social philosophy at the Collège de France (*RFS*, XX, 1979:114–15). Nevertheless, he never seems to have manipulated situations so as to bring about his own professional advancement. To the contrary, there is an example, quoted by Lukes, that in 1908 at the age of 50 he turned down the possibility of the academic honour of having his name proposed for membership of the Institut. He felt that a philosopher called Evellin, of greater age than himself and at the end of his career, was a more worthy nomination (1972:377–8). Durkheim in fact never became a member, although he received the Légion d'Honneur in 1907.

If the charge of dogmatism is to stand, it must be located in a wider, academic world. Here the charge could be one of political manipulation on behalf of other people, namely, that Durkheim used his authority and influence with the government to control appointments so that his own students and colleagues received chairs and lectureships. By this means his particular kind of sociology could be taught in as many universities as possible. There is considerable truth in this. Letters have now come to light in which he proposed the nomination of Paul Fauconnet to follow Célestin Bouglé at the University of Toulouse, and nominated

Maurice Halbwachs to a vacant position in the University of Lille (*RFS*, XX, 1979:115–17). He also supported Paul Huvelin, a professor of Roman law at Lyons, for a chair in Paris (ibid.). Of course not all Durkheimians were successful, notably Marcel Mauss, his nephew, the most learned of all the Durkheimians who never realized his potential (for a résumé of the academic careers of Durkheimians, see Besnard 1979:28–30).

When Durkheim came to Paris in 1902 it soon became apparent that he was assuming a position of great importance in the academic hierarchy. For various reasons, not least because of the subject he taught, this was resented. In 1911 a group of writers using the pseudonym Agathon launched a bitter attack. Taking a somewhat traditionalist stance, they accused Louis Liard, Directeur de l'Enseignement Supérieur – Durkheim's patron indeed – of making him 'the regent of the Sorbonne, the all-powerful master' (quoted in Clark 1969:11). They argued that it was Durkheim who had won the victory for the new spirit in the Sorbonne (see also Dansette 1948, II:47). Within the paramount university of France, he had gained a place on the most important committees, including the Council. He ensured that his sociology replaced the traditional philosophy and was the official doctrine of the university. Goblet d'Alviella said that the neo-sociology was the theology of the New Sorbonne (1913:219). For students taking degrees as teachers in philosophy, languages, literature and history, their only compulsory lectures were those Durkheim gave on education (Lukes 1972:372). Thus critics were not slow in attacking what they saw as Durkheim's powerful influence – his authoritarianism – and such attacks came from both left and right. Only Republicans appeared to support him. An opponent of Marxist persuasion, P. Nizan, accused Durkheim of being 'the watchdog' of the Third Republic in guarding its official morality (quoted in LaCapra 1972:62). Hostility also came not surprisingly from Catholic quarters, not least from Dom Besse who, in his book *Les Religions laïques: Un romantisme religieux* (1913), showed himself to be not only anti-Durkheim but also anti-Jewish, anti-socialist and anti-Protestant. His chapter, 'M. Durkheim en Sorbonne', was vitriolic in its attack not only on Durkheim's 'doctrine' but on 'the president of social science', who is the 'high priest of Humanity' and 'the great pontiff of lay religion'. Such phrases as these, coupled with one that reads 'ruling over the local

priests as the cardinal', are to English ears hardly the language of
sober judgment, yet they and others like them were commonly
levelled against Durkheim and his alleged machinations, and were
even used at times by his friends (for further details, see Lukes
1972:ch. 18). There were those who went so far as to suggest that
at heart Durkheim was a cleric, not an academic. Bourgin, a
member of the *équipe*, has written:

> He was a priest more than a scholar. He was a hierarchical
> figure. His mission was religious. As a revolutionary in
> religion and morality, this scholar wished to provide the
> grounds and support for morality for his contemporaries. He
> was no preacher: he was the priest of rules, to which it was
> necessary to adhere. (1938:218)

But if priestly terms could be so readily applied by Frenchmen
to Durkheim within the setting of the university, so equally applicable were those of the prophet. We have already shown that
there was something about Durkheim which encouraged people
to see him as a charismatic leader. As Davy said, he seemed like
the prophet of some new religion (1919:194). And Durkheim
never seems to have repudiated this kind of role, although as we
shall see he deliberately rejected the religious ideology of Comte.
Witness the well-known account of Bouglé when he was walking
past the cathedral of Notre Dame with Durkheim, who turned to
him and said: 'It is from that chair that I should be speaking'.
Was this the pang of regret from a possible rabbi *manqué*, or the
wish to be acknowledged as the ultimate spokesman of the emerging sociology with its moral and religious dimensions, or again,
the yearning for a larger audience than that of the Sorbonne?
Only speculation about these questions is possible. One thing,
however, is true and that is that Durkheim had about him certain
characteristics – his asceticism and sense of mission – that
bestowed upon him the aura of an eighth-century prophet of
Israel. Contemporary society stands under judgment! It has lost
its moral fibre! It is poised on the brink of anomy and chaos!
People need to repent, to be disciplined, to be obedient to the
law, to the voice of society! Only by a change of heart will man
be happy, free and escape from disaster! Preaching in season and
out of season, Durkheim felt that he was a man for the times, a
man needed by France, by the nation, if only it would listen to

him. After his death, Pécaut wrote that Durkheim's 'faith was that society needed his ideas' (1918:2). The message of the prophet was validated by the charismatic power of the prophet. His presence was able to excite in certain people a deep moral faith (ibid.:1). He achieved a consistently high reputation for his ability as a teacher and, in particular, for his superb lecturing. He was an outstanding example in this of the ideal nineteenth-century liberal academic – precise, objective, fair, but with the fire of enthusiasm and the conviction that what he had to say was of great import- ance; that he was proclaiming some new scientific truth that had direct bearing on the well-being of society. His power over students in the lecture hall seems to have been electrifying (Bouglé 1930:281–2). Maublanc describes it in detail:

> Those who wanted to get away from his influence had to escape from his course of lectures: on those who attended them, he willy-nilly imposed the power of his mind. How could one combat the authority of his serious, muffled voice, his laboured delivery, his powerful oratory, his cutting phrases, his deliberate movement of the hands, and his eyes which, under puckered brows and behind a pince-nez, flashed, like lightning, his ascetic illumined face? He was tall, thin, upright, dressed in black, with a pale head, his nose curved like that of a Jew, his beard with patches of grey amidst dark areas – he had the air of a rabbi who was also a mystic. (1930:297)

Durkheim was in fact both prophet and priest – an ideal combin- ation of roles according to many Christian theologians. He medi- ated between God (Society) and people (Filloux 1975:42). But he did so not only by fervently proclaiming a message but by skilfully employing institutional means, bureaucratic procedures, and exerted his influence in high places so as to ensure the acceptance of his message and the enactment of its implications. But there are no prophets without an authoritarian message, and no priests without a dogmatic creed.

Like so many dogmatists, Durkheim disliked any dogmatism that threatened his own! He spoke about orthodox Christians and Jews in these terms:

> if he [a believer] values a denominational formula in an

exclusive and uncompromising way, if he believes that he holds the truth about religion in its definitive form, then agreement is impossible. (1919b:101/t.1975a:184)

But science and free thought to which Durkheim subscribed, have often contained within them that dogmatism which they have attacked. Durkheim was very intolerant of those who challenged some of the basic assumptions of science or who ideologically challenged the liberalism he so strongly upheld. Richard maintained that Durkheim's dogmatism was a denial of true freedom (1928:307). To others Durkheim's dogmatism was in his particular assumption about the priority of society, his sociologism (Maunier 1913:276; Cuvillier 1953:39; see chs 13 and 14). From his early days Durkheim strove to make sociology an incontestably scientific discipline and he hoped that the method which he adopted would be such that sociology could be placed alongside the natural sciences. Perhaps a change occurred when his hopes were not realized and he encountered far more opposition than he had anticipated. Here may be a clue to the alleged and perhaps exaggerated dogmatism of Durkheim. The charge comes from his opponents and it is often forgotten that between the 1890s and 1914 the Sorbonne was the bastion of scientific, rationalist and democratic principles. Much in the intellectual world of France at that time would seem to be challenging such ideas, for example, the thought of Bergson, Sorel, Maurice Barrès, Verlaine and Mallarmé (Coser 1971:161). When these issues were at stake Durkheim never compromised himself, and in this sense he might be said to have been dogmatic.

Thus, Durkheim may well have realized that the possession of qualities associated with the work of prophet and priest were necessary in order to achieve the end he had set himself. Only a thoroughly dedicated man could have done what he did. As Peyre has observed: 'he felt intensely and thought fervently, systematically, with his heart as well as with his brain' (1960b:xvi). An anonymous writer has said that Durkheim was not one of those who allowed themselves to be complacent, who compromised with their principles, and with their consciences (Anon. 1917:749). Peyre argues that Durkheim was forced to wage an incessant war against the forces of prejudice and conservatism. Traditional religion, idealist philosophy, and old fashioned psychology were serious threats to his social science. Confronted with this 'irrational' opposition, Durkheim and his disciples could only respond with a 'dogmatic' fervour. The rational is often impotent to overcome the irrational. One might say that sociologically the 'political' situation called for a dogmatic approach, seen most clearly in some form of control of education at various levels. René Worms admitted that such determination had the effect of benefiting the movement which Durkheim led (1917:567). More recently, Terry Clark has accounted for Durkheim's success by the political power that he was able to exert over the government of his day, by the creation of a team of followers and by an uncompromising attitude about the nature of sociology (1973:ch. 6; see also Weisz 1979:83–112).

Yet Durkheim's dogmatism was the dogmatism of the middle ground; in the matter of religion he upheld a rational approach that avoided the extremes of anti-clericalism, on the one hand, and orthodox dogmatism, on the other, and so he was able to pursue a *via media* in looking objectively at religion and avoiding the emotional overtones which were at the heart of the polar extremities. The question arises whether Durkheim's 'sensible' approach, coupled with professional determination, itself bordering on the religious, is intellectually tenable. It is this which the pages ahead attempt to answer.

3 The development of Durkheim's thought on religion

I The early period

1 The search for lines of demarcation

Gaston Richard observed that from 1895 to 1912 Durkheim was dedicated to the study of religion (1923:233/t.1975:244). He did not offer specific reasons for the choice of dates. Perhaps 1895 refers to the first course of lectures given by Durkheim on religion, although it was started in 1894. The contents of these lectures have been lost to posterity, but Marcel Mauss, his nephew, who was working under him in Bordeaux, helped to produce the material for the lectures (Mauss 1979:214). On the other hand, Richard might have chosen 1895 as the year when Durkheim received his sudden 'revelation', which came to him whilst reading Robertson Smith. The date 1912 obviously relates to the publication of *Les Formes élémentaires de la vie religieuse: le système totémique en Australie*, which stands at the culminating point of his thought on religion. Durkheim's great interest in religion, what we have called his religious quest, is apparent in every major work he published, in which some reference to religion is made, often but not always on a substantial scale. Much the same can be said for the articles he wrote. And many of the reviews he published in the *Année sociologique* were on books dealing with religion, although the section of religion had several able contributors whom we have already mentioned (see the bibliographies at the end of this book; in Pickering 1975; see also ch. 5.1 and Table 3.1).

Durkheim's academic interest in religion, however, goes further back than Richard's initial date, to the time he went to the École Normale Supérieure in 1879 and began to study under Fustel de Coulanges. It extended until the time he died in 1917.

In so far as sociology was itself a new discipline, which was being shaped in the hands of Durkheim, it is not surprising that Durkheim's approach to it underwent some change. And if, in general, his sociology shifted course, as many people believed it did, it is only logical to surmise that for this and other reasons Durkheim's sociological approach to religion also underwent change. Even before Durkheim's death, observations were made about the alleged change in direction his thought was taking in a search for sociological explanation. Somewhere about the middle of the period between 1900 and 1910, Durkheim, it is argued, began to turn away from morphological factors, such as demographical and institutional influences, and to search behind these – what might be called 'physical' or structural factors – to those directly related to ideas, to *représentations*, that is, to idealistic or 'spiritual' influences. Ever since Davy drew attention to the change in 1911, a controversy has raged which has shown no signs of being resolved. Durkheim himself did not directly enter into it. (For a discussion on this, see chs 15.4 and 20.3.) Georges Davy also stated that Durkheim turned to the study of religious phenomena after completing his doctoral thesis, *The Division of Labour* in 1893 and writing *The Rules of Sociological Method* in 1895. His great concern with religion caused him, according to Davy, to realize the importance of 'spiritual' factors in his general approach to the study of society some twelve years later, around 1907 (1911:44). Whether in fact one can make such a causal connection as this is doubtful, for it is difficult to prove in the light of incomplete evidence, and further, it was never admitted by Durkheim himself. But at least Davy's statements about the changes in direction of Durkheim's thought raised the question of changes in his religious thought, and whether there are any close parallels between the two.

Davy takes the straightforward position of dividing Durkheim's sociological thought into two stages: a 'non-idealist' stage, followed by an 'idealist' one. And it is to be assumed that he would divide Durkheim's religious thought accordingly by emphasizing the role of religious *représentations* in the second period. Other commentators have also seen the development of his religious thought to be of two stages. For most the turning-point is 1895, and rests largely on Durkheim's own confession of the influence that Robertson Smith's thought had over him. What actually happened emerged, strangely enough, twelve years later, in 1907 in a letter he wrote in the Belgian journal, *Revue néo-scolastique* (1907b). Alpert (1939:215), Parsons (1937:409n.), Stanner (1967:220ff.) and more recently Lukes (1972:237ff.) accept this confession as denoting the only significant change in his religious thought. Lukes characterizes the two stages in this way. Before 1895, Durkheim's work is seen as 'pre-ethnographic' and is contrasted with the later period when Durkheim became saturated with Australian Aboriginal studies, which were the key to his final work (ibid.:240). The early period is 'largely formal', 'rather simpliste' and containing uncertain hypotheses. His later work is 'considerably more nuanced and complex'; he 'tested, modified and extended his hypotheses'.

Another writer who appears to settle for a two-stage development of Durkheim's religious thought is Stanner. In his admirable essay, 'Reflections on Durkheim and Aboriginal religion', he suggests that Durkheim passed through a creative period between 1898 and 1907, during which time his ideas were crystallized and received confirmation in detailed ethnographic studies (1967:220,227). Is one to assume from this that little of significance occurred after 1907, or that the period before 1898 was of no importance?

If *The Elementary Forms* represents the peak of Durkheim's creativity, it should not be forgotten that it did not suddenly burst in upon the academic world unheralded or unanticipated. Much of it was communicated to university students and indeed others in a public course of lecturers Durkheim delivered in the Sorbonne between 1906 and 1907, and which constituted an early working of the book. The lectures were quickly published in summary form in an academic journal through the efforts of a listener, P. Fontana (Durkheim 1907f). Two years later Durkheim himself published two articles, 'Sociologie religieuse et théorie de la connaissance' (1909d), and 'Examen critique des systèmes classiques sur les origines de la pensée religieuse' (1909c) in the *Revue de métaphysique et de morale* and the *Revue philosophique* respectively. With minor changes, they appeared as chapters in *The Elementary Forms* (from 1909d, pp. 754–8 were omitted). These facts clearly demonstrate that Durkheim's great book did not suddenly emerge as the result of a revelation or a hastily conducted piece of research. Not only did it take a considerable time to prepare for publication – at least six years – it included a vast amount of ethnographic material which represented the fruit of many years' study and reflection. But disregarding the question of aboriginal material, the book represents the final outcome of long and continual thought which went through fairly well-marked stages.

For reasons that will be advanced, we shall divide the development of Durkheim's religious thought into three periods. Isambert has recently come to a similar conclusion (1976:37). They are:

I *The early period* (1880–95): from the time he entered the École Normale Supérieure to just before he began to read Robertson Smith;

II *The middle period* (1895–1906): from the time of his acceptance of Robertson Smith's ideas to about 1906;

III *The final formulation* (1906–17): from the time he delivered the course of lectures in the Sorbonne on the origin of religion to his death.

The dates are only approximate ones. When can ideas be said to begin? When do they change? So often it is impossible to attach any precise date, even if the individual concerned is asked to give it. As a rule ideas emerge gradually, and only after a period of gestation do they become crystallized. But the fixing of dates is even more difficult when the individual concerned is dead and has left few personal details. And in the case of Durkheim, the one sure date of 1895 is somewhat blurred. Did the event mentioned in 1895 extend over a longish period or was it immediate? And in using the only evidence we have, the dates of articles and books, there are added difficulties of knowing whether the published material was written well before the date of publication. That is particularly acute for items published around the dividing dates between the stages. It is ridiculous to suggest that the dates which we have given to the three stages of Durkheim's thought are in any way precise. Obviously we have tried to be as accurate as possible, but it might be said that the dates do little more than to indicate 'about the time of'.

Clearly there were shifts in Durkheim's thought, but they were in no way dramatic (see ch. 20.3; Bellah 1973:xlvi). One thing is quite certain; Durkheim never underwent a volte-face in the matter of religion. Most of his ideas evident at the end of his life were latent, if not abundantly clear, in his earlier writings. What one witnesses is a development and interlinking of ideas through the stages into a coherent system of great ingenuity, but as we shall show, elements of them Durkheim possessed from an early age. It should be emphasized that in relating Durkheim's thought on religion to certain periods of his life, we are not suggesting that they are marked by radical changes in his ideas, but that they relate to phases in his academic productivity in the subject which are accompanied by one or two changes and by certain shifts of emphasis.

2 Publications and substantive issues

The importance of the first period in the development of Durkheim's thought on religion lies in the fact that in it three books of his were written, two of which had largish and important sections devoted to religion. The first book was his doctoral thesis, *De la Division du travail social* (1893b); the second did not contain a great deal on religion, it was his manifesto for sociology, *Les Règles de la méthode sociologique* (1895a); the third was *Le Suicide: étude de sociologie*. The last was published in 1897, admittedly outside the period, but on the evidence of Gaston Richard, who was in charge of reviewing books in the section on criminality in *L'Année sociologique*, the book was written a good time before it went to the publishers (1923:230/t.1975:242). For this reason the book has been placed in what we have called the first period of the development of Durkheim's thought.

The young Durkheim wrote only a handful of reviews or review-articles which were associated with religion. Amongst them was a review of Guyau's *L'Irréligion de l'avenir* (1887b) and an account of Wundt's analysis of religion (1887c). Interestingly enough there were no reviews on totemism. (The details of the various items relating to religion in the three periods of the development of Durkheim's thought are given in Table 3.1, which shows the method that was employed in compiling the table. For items on totemism, see Pickering 1975:311–13).

Durkheim's earliest attitudes towards religion emerge most clearly in his review of the *Ecclesiastical Institutions* – itself a sociological study (see 1886a:65–9/t.1975a:18–23). Here he states

TABLE 3.1 *The development of Durkheim's sociological analysis of religion according to lectures, books, articles and reviews*

	I Early period (1880–95)	II Middle period (1895–1906)	III Final formulation (1906–17)
Lecture courses (Unpublished)	1894-5 La Religion	1900–1 Les Formes élémentaires de la religion	1906–7 La Religion: les origines
Published posthumously (English titles)	1928a Socialism and Saint-Simon	1950a Professional Ethics and Civil Morals 1925a Moral Education 1938a The Evolution of Educational Thought 1918b Montesquieu and Rousseau	1955a Pragmatisme et sociologie
Books published (English titles)	1893b Division of Labour in Society 1895a The Rules of Sociological Method 1897a Suicide: A Study in Sociology (see text)		1912a The Elementary Forms of the Religious Life

TABLE 3.1—*Continued*

	I *Early period* (1880–95)	II *Middle period* (1895–1906)		III *Final formulation* (1906–17)		
Articles and reviews	1886a	1897e	1901a(i)	1907a(17)	1911b	1913b
	1887b	1898a(ii)	1901h	1907b	1911c(1)	1914a
	1887c	1898a(iii)(13)	1903a(i)	1907c	1911c(3)	1915c
	1890a	1898b	1903a(ii)(57)	1907f[1]	1913a(i)(2)	1917b
		1898c	1903c	1909a(i)	1913a(ii)(6) &	1918b & 1919b[2]
		1899a(i)	1905a(ii)(2)	1909a(ii)	(7)	1968c
		1899a(ii)	1905e	1909c	1913a(ii)(9)	
		1899d	1906a(6)	1909d	1913a(ii)(10)	
		1900a(45)	1906b	1910a(ii)(2)	1913a(ii)(11) &	
		1900a(47)	1906e		(12)	
		1900c			1913a(ii)(15)	
Number of articles and reviews from above	4	21		25		

Sources: Lukes 1972: 617–20, 561–90; and the Bibliography at the end of this book. The titles of the articles and reviews are omitted, but they can be determined from the dating-enumeration given in the Bibliography.
1 Summary of lecture course, 1906–7.
2 Extempore lecture.

that sociology is not concerned with metaphysical speculation such as is normally associated with religion. By contrast, the sociologist is to examine the practical effects of what is in fact a complex phenomenon. Religion dictates to people actions, ideas and sentiments, and it also possesses its own authority. Therefore, like law and morality, it has a regulating function in society and creates social equilibrium. This means that law, morality and religion can all be legitimately studied by sociology. Belief has a priority over religious action because common beliefs are necessary for society to exist. This is historically the case. What the future of such beliefs, religious and social, will be in the West cannot be foreseen. But based on these sociological observations, religion in some form or the other can be said to go on for ever, for it is essential to the existence of society. Durkheim postulated what he thought were secondary characteristics of religion, namely, the notion of God, belief in life after death, a sense of the mysterious, a collection of individual beliefs. The important question is to find what God symbolizes 'hides and expresses'. He urged the distinction between the sociology of religions and the history of religions. Ideas change and their documentation devolves on the historian. The sociologist sees that when these changes occur the ideas no longer fulfil their functions, as they fail to ensure the adaptation of individuals to external circumstances.

In *The Division of Labour*, Durkheim emphasized the positive relation between penal law and religion in societies marked by mechanical solidarity (primitive societies). Religion always acts as a coercive or constraining force over individuals, forcing them to believe or behave in particular ways, as he says in the review we have just mentioned. Religion demands personal sacrifice from those who adhere to it. Sacrilege, which indicates the presence of religion, is severely punished in primitive societies, not least for ritual offences. With the advance of history, 'religion tends to embrace a smaller and smaller portion of social life'. Formerly religion was coterminous with the political. Today, in western societies marked by organic life, the individual is freed from the demands of belief and practice made by traditional religions. The new form of religion is without a transcendental concept of God and is focused on man himself – on the individual. The change has been brought about not least through Christianity, which itself has placed less emphasis on cult and punishment and more on morals and ideals. Free thought began to emerge through medieval scholasticism, which gave primary place to reason. Traditional religions are opposed to science, since science studies man as part of nature, and part of the universe. Philosophy became prominent as theology receded into the background, because religion lost its hold over society. Reflective thought and science undermine a belief in God, who is no longer seen to be omnipotent and omnipresent. There has yet to be a scientific definition of religion, but any such definition would not make God an essential element since Buddhism is without gods and many religious laws make no reference to gods. Religion is basically a social phenomenon.

In many respects Durkheim's *Suicide* shows a much more convincing approach to religion than *The Division of Labour*. In part this is helped by the fact that Durkheim is in the main only concerned with that aspect of religion which has direct bearing on the phenomenon of suicide. He shows how doctrinally the traditional churches in the West have opposed suicide in considering it an immoral act. Nevertheless in European countries there are different rates of suicide and Durkheim attempted to show how the social and theological characteristics of Catholicism and Protestantism in some way account for the different levels of suicide. He holds that the Church of today, because of its weak control over society, is powerless to prevent suicidal tendencies. Within a wider context, religion is a system of symbols by which society becomes conscious of itself. In the last analysis, man worships society which is seen as the gods hypostasized. Once again, Durkheim argues that the new religion in the West is centred on man worshipping himself.

3 The beginnings and early influences

It would seem that after he left the École Normale Supérieure Durkheim's interest in religion received a considerable boost from Lucien Herr, the librarian at the École, whose acquaintance was renewed when Durkheim taught at the Lycée de St Quentin in Paris in 1885–6. It was while he was at the Lycée that Durkheim was given six months' leave to tour German universities, including

Berlin, Marburg and Leipzig. About this time Herr drew his attention to Frazer's article on totemism in the *Encyclopaedia Britannica* (Mauss 1927:9; Lukes 1972:183 n.13). But first the interest was mainly in the connection which Frazer made between totemism and exogamy. Durkheim supported the idea, although Frazer later rejected it. His introduction to Frazer's article at least made him aware of the growing science of religions, which was largely stimulated by the work of such English scholars as Frazer, Spencer, Tylor and others. His acquaintance with these writers was also encouraged by his nephew, Marcel Mauss, who quickly joined Durkheim as a student at Bordeaux when Durkheim went there in 1887. As we shall see, Durkheim openly admitted that the science of religion was in the first instance an English and American discipline (see ch. 4).

There can be no doubt that in his formative years, Durkheim was far more influenced by Fustel de Coulanges in the matter of religious analysis than by Saint-Simon or Comte (Evans-Pritchard 1960:11,12n.). This can be said despite the fact that Durkheim for the greater part of his life held that the religion of the present and that of the future was one centred on man himself, a position that was held by Saint-Simon and Comte as well as by other French thinkers. The influence of Fustel over Durkheim was quite simply that Durkheim followed the academic historical analysis of the professor of classics rather than the speculations of political and social philosophers.

Numa Denis Fustel de Coulanges (1830–89) was professor at the Sorbonne and then director of the École Normale Supérieure, who before had been professor at Strasbourg and who was forced to leave after the 1870 war. Himself a *normalien* he taught Durkheim while he was at the École between 1879 and 1882.[1] Fustel's influence over those with a sociological bent stemmed from his well-known book, *La Cité antique: étude sur le culte, le droit, les institutions de la Grèce et de Rome*, published in 1864 shortly after he had gone to Strasbourg and translated into English in 1873 as *The Ancient City*. Fustel de Coulanges's argument was based on the assumption that in the matter of social institutions the Greeks and the Romans had a great deal in common. A comparison of their beliefs and laws demonstrated that their religion was at the heart of their family life. It established marriage and paternal authority, fixed the order of relationships, and governed the right of property and the right of inheritance. Extending itself beyond the family, religion formed a still larger association in connection with the city and controlled it, as it controlled the family. From their religion came every institution of the Greeks and Romans, including private law. The city based all its principles, its rules, its customs, its magistracies on it. As time proceeded, the ancient religion was modified and private law and political institutions were changed with it. Thus, Fustel argued, religion is of prime importance and is the oldest of the institutions of these ancient peoples. Of course, it had at its centre an ancestor cult in which the head of the family acted as the priest. To each family the dead are seen to be the deities and in this way deities are established for the city. Fustel held that the oldest type of religion was the cult of the dead, which he thought was the earliest element of the religion of Greeks and Romans, and according to the Laws of Manu, the most ancient form of worship among Hindus.

Keeping in mind ideas which Durkheim was to be identified with in later years, particularly during the second period (see ch. 6), it should be noted that Fustel held that religion was the absolute master, for everything had come from religion, that is to say, from beliefs which men held about the divinity. Religion, law and government were compounded and were but three different aspects of the same thing. What is more important for sociologists as a whole is that Fustel holds that ideas bring about social changes, that worship symbolized by the sacred fire is at the centre of family life in the classical world and that religion is at the centre of social life itself.

Needless to say, Fustel de Coulanges has not been without his critics; for example, he is said to have misunderstood *gens* in seeing it as only a vast agnatic family (Lowie 1937:197ff.). During his early period, Durkheim himself was critical of his teacher for deducing social arguments from religious ones (1893b/1902b:154/t.1933b:178–9). For Durkheim, religion is a reflection of some aspect of social reality (Jones 1974): but Durkheim's criticism at this point turns out to be an ambivalent one, because he reflects Fustel's thought after his 'conversion' in the second period. Durkheim, however, disagreed with Fustel over the question of the cult of the dead, which Durkheim maintained was not central in the evolution of religious ideas.

Overall, it is not surprising that Camille Jullian, an admirer and expositor of the work of Fustel, held that there were close parallels between *La Cité antique* and *Les Formes élémentaires* (see Lukes 1972:60–3). Both books showed that religion held a central place in society and that the tribe or city, which was held to be sacred, is a social whole and constitutes as well an ecclesiastical body. Also, forces are at work in society which are contrary, yet superior, to physical forces.

4 Characteristics of the period

Stanner, pointing to an earlier period, but using dates different to our own, asserted that Durkheim failed to provide in it a systematic answer to three questions: 'the intimate but elusive relations between religion and social order; the place of religion in a sociological schema; and the status of religion as determined or determining' (1967/r.1975:282). We suggest that Durkheim attempted to deal with these issues in a later period, but whether he ever solved them satisfactorily is open to dispute. Behind Stanner's observation, however, lies a more general and acceptable notion, namely, that Durkheim's approach in the first period is relatively disjointed and contains a number of important but none the less unrelated hypotheses and propositions. Compared with the full blossoming of his ideas later on, this period is marked by a crudeness and lack of subtlety in his analysis of religion (see Jones 1981). Parsons has held that in the earliest period Durkheim saw the relation between society and religion, but that he saw the importance of religion only after he had developed the notion of social control (1937:409). However, in the light of Durkheim's review of Spencer's *Ecclesiastical Institutions*, Parsons's conclusion must be challenged, for in that review, written as early as 1886, Durkheim states categorically that religion along with law and morality are control mechanisms of society (1886a:69/t.1975a:23). What is significant is that in the early period Durkheim advanced propositions which he never rejected, but which in the course of time he refined and related one to the other, in some cases introducing additional elements. As Richard said, Durkheim never really changed his basic attitude toward religion as he proceeded in his academic career (1928:299). Fundamental ideas which appeared in *The Division of Labour* and *Suicide* can also be seen in *The Elementary Forms*. Over and above the themes which interested Durkheim in this period, and which we have very briefly noted, one was of overriding concern; this was the search for the origin of religion. Like all those who were interested in the science of religion in his day, he was one with them in pursuing such a quest. In this early period he openly rejects theories of Spencer, Réville, Müller and Hartmann, and even the sociological theory of Guyau was also criticized. Durkheim did not always openly raise the question of the origin of religion, but it is clear to see that it was of enormous importance to him and that he sought an answer to it not in trying to find a unique historical event or events which were impossible to verify, but rather to find the origin of religion in the very structure of the phenomenon itself. To this end he devoted his labours.

4 The development of Durkheim's thought on religion

II The middle period

1 The 'revelation'

The period from about 1895 to 1906 constituted what were the most eventful years of Durkheim's life, not only intellectually but professionally. In their midst, in 1902, he was invited to take up the lectureship at the University of Paris. To be sure, this creative period was fruitful in the development of his sociology in general, but in particular it was characterized by a turning-point at its beginning in his sociological approach to religion. It heralded what we have called the middle period.

We might have known nothing about the event, but for an accident which prompted Durkheim to write about it publicly. It emerged in the correspondence he entered into in a Catholic philosophical journal, *Revue néo-scolastique*, in 1907. Simon Deploige, then or subsequently a priest, published a series of articles vigorously attacking Durkheim, and in particular his concept of the science of morals and his social realism. In this he was accused of bestowing metaphysical status on society and giving it a place superior to that of the individual. The articles were subsequently published in 1911 in book form as *Le Conflit de la morale et la sociologie* and it was later translated into English (1938). Not surprisingly, the articles were strongly negative in their condemnation of sociology, and in a brief, positive fashion Deploige advocated a return to the teachings of St Thomas Aquinas. Durkheim responded by reviewing the book negatively in the *Année sociologique* (1913a(ii)(15)). What propelled Durkheim to write a letter to the editor of the *Revue néo-scolastique* in the first place, however, was not so much an attack on his sociology as the charge made by Deploige that his articles had been borrowed from German authors and that he had carefully disguised the fact (1907b:606). In particular. the case against him was that he had 'simply taken over Wundt's theory of moral ends' and used it without acknowledging his debt. Durkheim defended himself by retorting that it was he who had introduced to the French public the work of Wundt and other German writers of the same school in articles he published in 1887 (see 1887c). In a second letter dated 8 November 1907, Durkheim returned once more to the charges Deploige had made against him. It was in the course of this letter that, out of the blue as it were, he acknowledged the enormous influence of Robertson Smith on his thought. Durkheim wrote:

> On page 343 note 1, it is affirmed that I found in Wundt the idea that religion is the matrix of moral and juridical ideas etc. I read Wundt in 1887 and yet it was only in 1895 that I had a clear understanding of the important role played by religion in social life. It was in that year that I found the method of approaching the study of religion sociologically for the first time. It was a revelation to me. During 1895 a line of demarcation was drawn in the development of my thought, so much so that all my earlier research had to be looked at afresh and made to harmonize with these new views. Wundt's *Ethik* read eight years previously had nothing to do with this change in direction. It was entirely the result of the studies of religious history which I had just undertaken and notably the reading of the work of Robertson Smith and his school. (1907b:613)

Durkheim again repeated the refutation of the charge when he later reviewed Deploige's book and stated that the science of religion was essentially an English and American discipline, not a German one, and that he owed a great deal to authors of those schools (1913a(ii)(15)). The confession in the second letter of 1907, describing his intellectual conversion in his approach to the sociological study of religion, has become a 'proof-text' and no analysis of Durkheim's approach to religion can fail to include it. How far the letter was well known at the time is difficult to ascertain. Very few writers seem to have referred to it, but Gaston Richard was acquainted with it, saw its importance and quoted it in his article of 1923 (1923:229–30/t.1975:241). One wonders who introduced Durkheim to Robertson Smith. Isambert suggests that it may have been two of his disciples, Hubert and Mauss, for they developed Smith's idea of the sacred and sacrifice (1976). British writers on religion, with the exception of Smith and Spencer, were not interested in sociology, although they attempted to treat religion 'scientifically'.

2 Durkheim's reading of Robertson Smith

In what ways, then, was Durkheim's thought so radically changed as a result of reading Robertson Smith? It is vexatious that despite Durkheim's reference to the event as a revelation (*révélation*), he never disclosed its nature in detail, and indeed, as we have just noted, were it not for a controversial correspondence on an allied matter, the secret in all probability would have gone with him to the grave. In the course of subsequent events, Durkheim made only a few references to Robertson Smith and they were in his essay on totemism (1902a(i)), in the 1906 lectures (1907b) and in *The Elementary Forms*. Strange to relate, there was no mention of him in the important article on defining religion (1899a(ii)). That this 'conversion experience' is so poorly documented has meant that scholars are left guessing about its content. No one knows for sure what elements of Robertson Smith were of such revelatory importance to Durkheim. Evans-Pritchard has suggested that there were four ideas which Durkheim derived from Robertson Smith (1965:56). They were: primitive religion is basically a clan cult; the cult is totemic; the god of the clan is the clan divinized; totemism is the most elementary form of religion known to man. Such a position as that of Evans-Pritchard would suggest that almost exclusive of any other hypothesis, Durkheim only adopted those hypotheses associated with totemism and the clan in their relation to religion. It was these that were of overriding importance to him. There can be no doubt that totemism seen as a primitive religion was crucial to Durkheim in his arguments in *The Elementary Forms*. But to concentrate exclusively on totemism is far too narrow an approach, and we would suggest that there are other influences at work of equal importance. To substantiate this it is necessary to take a brief look at Robertson Smith's work.

Although a theologian and Old Testament scholar, William Robertson Smith (1846–94) was interested in anthropological issues and in applying them to the Old Testament. Much of the controversy which surrounded him related to his higher criticism, which in part he learned from his studies in Germany. As a professor in Aberdeen, he was forced to vacate his chair owing to hostility from the Church of Scotland. He then went to Cambridge and, with a fellowship at Christ's College and a reader-ship in Arabic, he remained there for the rest of his life. His last book, the one which so much influenced Durkheim, *The Religion of the Semites*, showed that his interests extended beyond the Jews in considering the peoples in the area as a whole. The book was first published in 1889: the second edition of 1894, published posthumously, contained certain changes that were made in a somewhat mysterious manner. It was probably this 1894 edition that Durkheim first read.

Robertson Smith held that the religion of the Hebrews had to be considered not as an isolated religion but as one amongst, and indeed influenced by, the religions of surrounding peoples. Christianity and Islam were also examples of religions growing out of other religions, for no religion grows out of nothing (1889/1894:1–2). Thus Smith, as an Old Testament scholar, firmly stood in the camp of those who might be called advocates of comparative religion, whose origin can be traced back to John Spencer (1630–93) of Corpus Christi College, Cambridge, who is often referred to as the father of comparative religion (ibid.:vi). Another assumption that Smith made was that all religions contained two dominant components, belief and ritual. Due to the influence of Christianity, and its rejection of all that might be called superstitious, scholars in their approach to religions, including Christianity itself, began by examining the component of belief, that is, the creeds of the religion (ibid.:16; see ch. 17.1 in this volume). For Smith this method was incorrect, as many ancient religions had no creeds. It was better to examine first their ritual, which could be carried out with accuracy, since ritual was obligatory and not subject to variation which is to be found in the component of belief (ibid.:18). In early societies myths were open to change and it was obvious that people's beliefs were by no means uniform. Myths later gave place to creeds, as in Christianity. Another assumption – one that Durkheim had already accepted and which Robertson Smith stressed – was that in early societies the religious realm and the political realm were coextensive, and consequently an offence committed against a religious ordinance was in fact also an offence against the state. To study religious institutions in such societies meant also studying their political institutions. Thus, religion was not to be viewed through spiritual concepts, for it was not a means of saving souls but a vehicle of assuring the welfare of society, and as such, meant its material well-being (ibid.:29).

It is clearly evident that Robertson Smith encouraged Durkheim to make the distinction between religion and magic. In his early essay published in 1899 on defining religious phenomena, and written shortly after the 'Smith revelation', he declared that religion and magic had to be separated although the two are not always distinguishable (1899a(ii):21n.2/t.1975a:99n.24). Durkheim does not develop the point and one detects a certain amount of hesitancy on his part, perhaps due to the fact that he was attempting to define religion in terms of obligatory beliefs and actions (see ch. 9.3). However, by the time he gave the lectures on religion in 1906–7, which were the basis of his later book, he was clear in his own mind about the opposition between magic and religion, and in *The Elementary Forms* his arguments are well enunciated (58ff./42ff./119ff.). The contrast is made on the basis of his definition of religion. 'In magic there is no church', but there is in religion (see ch. 9.5). The magician creates a clientele, not a band of devoted followers who constantly consult him and who create relationships one with another by reason of common beliefs and practices. Magic is diffuse and individualistic: religion is social. Smith stressed the fact that in the eyes of religious leaders, magical practices are illicit (1889/1894:264). They therefore stood outside the realm of religion. In religion, man 'was bound always to think and act with and for the community'. To enter into private relations with supernatural powers, for that is what magic means, is to be castigated as being anti-social. Durkheim openly admits in a footnote in *The Elementary Forms* that Robertson Smith had already made the contrast between magic and religion, and we might add, in a similar way as Durkheim made it (63 n.1/45 n.2/ 162 n.28).

One of Robertson Smith's many contributions to the anthropological study of religion was, as we have just noted, in the considerable place that he gave to ritual as a basis for analysis. Durkheim also followed Smith in this respect, but whereas Smith gave prominence to ritual over belief, Durkheim was ambivalent about it (see ch. 20). His interest in ideas and *représentations*, absent at a theoretical level in the work of Smith, probably meant that in the last analysis Durkheim holds that beliefs have primacy over ritual, although in many places he appears to give ritual and belief equal importance. Certainly one undergirds the other. Smith never shared Durkheim's interest in epistemological or even metaphysical problems – problems that Durkheim held arose out of the sociology of religion.

The need to study primitive societies in order to reach an understanding of religious phenomena Durkheim did not derive from Robertson Smith; nevertheless, one feels that his position in this respect was strengthened by what he read of Smith. The clan system was held to be the earliest and therefore the most important form of social organization known to man and is associated with totemism (Smith 1889/1894:277ff.). Durkheim praised Smith for extending McLennan's ideas on totemism by showing that totemism is not just a cult of animals or plants, for it presupposes a 'likeness in nature, either natural or acquired, of men and animals (or plants)' (127/90). Smith held that the matrilineal clan, which was not to be identified with the larger household, was to be seen as the basis of Semitic society, and each clan had a sacred relation to a species animal. Smith, however, was honest enough to hold, and others have subsequently agreed, that there was not in fact much evidence for clan structure amongst the Semites. But at that stage of anthropological knowledge, it seemed likely to many that totemism was the most primitive form of social organization and that every society had sprung from it. It was logical, therefore, to deduce that the Semites had once passed through a totemic stage (see ch. 6.3).

Robertson Smith's theory of sacrifice, Durkheim agreed, was revolutionary (480–500/336–50; 1970f:635–6; see Jones 1981). Totemic sacrifice, according to Robertson Smith, was not just a family occasion, nor was it a propitiary act towards the divinity, but was an act of communion with the gods. Primarily it was a periodical public feast of clansmen and such an occasion brought the clans together. What was sacred was that which belonged to the clan. The private slaughter of animals for a man's personal sacrifice did not possess the character of the sacred which was attached to public offerings. 'No life and no obligation was sacred unless it was brought within the charmed circle of kindred blood' (Smith 1889/1894:287). Primitive men drew no sharp distinction between the existence of gods, men and beasts. There was a close relation between families of men and animals. Thus a sociological identification was possible between the god and the clan which met in the representation of the individual totemic animal. This was most obvious on occasions of clan sacrifice, when the totemic animal was slaughtered and eaten. Therefore, by this act, the clansmen ate and killed their 'god', and so entered into communion with it. Clan sacrifice, therefore, was a sacramental meal from which, as a result of 'consuming their god', men would feel strengthened and united. It was on such occasions that the totemic beast could be killed, but later this sacrificial rule was relaxed (ibid.:290). Smith also connected Semitic forms of sacrifice, which he held were totemic in origin, with those of the Romans, Syrians and Assyrians. In his theory of sacrifice, Robertson Smith's arguments were based in part on Semitic evidence, but much was also based on generalized notions of totemism which were derived from other pre-literate societies, and these assumptions were later found to be unwarrantable.

There were at least two propositions put forward by Robertson Smith which Durkheim accepted, but which misled him. First, that sacrifice began with totemism: there is no evidence to support it and many tribes do not have sacrificial rituals (see Evans-Pritchard 1965:52). Second, that totemism is universal: however, certain data run counter to the claim, since not every society has passed through such a stage, and also that in all totemic societies where an animal is held to be sacred, it is never killed – the only exception is amongst the Australian Aboriginals which Durkheim selected for his ethnographic evidence in *The Elementary Forms*. Amongst these tribes there is a complex pattern of totemism (see ch. 6.3). Generally speaking, both anthropologists and Old Testament theologians have found Robertson Smith's views on totemism and totemic sacrifice exaggerated.

Durkheim was not uncritical, however, of Smith's theory of sacrifice (see 1907f:637–8). He admitted that 'it is to the totem that humanity owes the principle of the common meal' (127/90) (and might we add, also, to Robertson Smith?) and continued:

> It is true that the theory of Smith can now be shown one-sided; it is no longer adequate for the facts actually known; but for all that, it contains an ingenious theory and has exercised a most fertile influence upon the science of religions.

In the end Durkheim rejects Smith's theory of sacrifice as he does that of his collaborators, Hubert and Mauss, in their essay on sacrifice (1899).

In another way, however, Durkheim was also critical of Smith's approach to sacrifice. The Scot classified types of sacrifice according to the method of sacrifice and the nature of the animals and food offered. Durkheim rejected this somewhat naive approach. Nor did he follow him in holding that sacred places, regions and things could be seen to be sacred on utilitarian grounds, that is, on account of their inherently obvious or useful qualities – qualities that would have been apparent to the worshippers.

Durkheim lauded Robertson Smith for pointing out the ambiguity that is to be found within the concept of sacredness and showing that it contained beneficent and antagonistic forces (584–6/ 409–10; see ch. 7.3). He also spoke appreciatively of Smith's notion of the contagiousness of the sacred (457/319–20). He noted his observation that ancient Arabs tattooed themselves with pictures of animals (164 n.8/117 n.7). But Durkheim, as we have seen, was not uncritical of Smith. Another example of this was his rejection of Smith's notion, held in common with other scholars, that the cult of nature is an extension of the cult of the dead (91/65).

The question remains: what was the flash of insight that Durkheim received from reading Robertson Smith? Durkheim refers to method – to a new way of looking at religion – to discovering, in fact, the sociological method of examining religion. And this comes not only from reading Robertson Smith, although chiefly so, but from studies of religious history. Sumpf has suggested that, in Smith's work, Durkheim grasped the notion of germinal principle. Since religion cannot be analysed as a *sui generis* entity as society could, there had to be some sense of continuity (1965:67–8; see ch. 9.2). In Smith there is to be found the notion of a germinal principle – some substructure – which accounts for distance and prevents complete disparity and fracture. This solution by Sumpf is imaginative, but one wonders whether there is sufficient evidence for such an assertion. Concepts such as continuity, germinal principle, or their equivalents, are not extensively to be found in Durkheim (but see 1899a(i)/t.1960c:350). Even more serious is the fact that, in his review of Spencer's *Ecclesiastical Institutions* in 1886 (that is, in the first period, not the second), Durkheim refers to the notion of germ (1886a:64–5/ t.1975a:16–17).

It could well be argued that in referring to method, Durkheim meant the study of totemism and nothing more, because he came to believe that *the* elementary form of religious life would reveal the nature of more complex phenomena in the realm of religion. This is Evans-Pritchard's position, as we have noted, as well as Stanner's (1967/r.1975:281). Admittedly, Durkheim did not write about the subject before 1894, although he had read books on it (for example, Frazer's early studies on totemism). But does 'methodology' refer only to totemism? Surely it is something more (Giddens (1978:83) would appear to agree also). The Scottish theologian concentrated his attention on one particular group, the Semites. He attempted to show the influence of social factors upon their religion and the influence of religion on their social life. His studies gave rise to generalizations about religion and social organization. The method was in contradiction to that particular comparative method, then so much in vogue in the hands of Frazer and others, which abstracted examples of customs, ideas and rituals from societies around the world and then from such an array of items attempted to make generalizations. We suggest that it was this concentration on one society that was so methodologically important to Durkheim. As Smith focused on the Semites, so Durkheim was to concentrate his attention on the Arunta of central Australia, and to a far lesser degree, on other totemic tribes. Using the field studies of Spencer and Gillen, and others, he made 'one well-conducted experiment' and this detailed case-study he held was adequate in the production of scientific knowledge (593/415/144). Indeed, one might be tempted to say that in the matter of method Durkheim in *Les Formes élémentaires* achieved with the Arunta what Robertson Smith achieved with the Semites. In recent years Tiryakian has supported this view.

His argument, however, goes further, and reaching beyond overt evidence, he holds that despite its intellectual appeal, the *Religion of the Semites* was a 'revelation' to Durkheim in discovering his roots as a Jew, or at least some of them (1979a:111). The position is dangerous. For one thing it is far-fetched because there is no evidence to suggest that Durkheim ever forgot his Jewish roots or needed to have them dramatically illuminated. And for another, to suggest that Durkheim's involvement in studies of the Arunta was a religious fulfilment – a discovery of what Judaism was like in some basic way – might well be offensive to Jews in so far as Arunta life is equated with Jewish life, or at least is of the same order. It would have been a different matter if Durkheim himself had made such a confession.

Another evaluation comes from Giddens who suggests that Durkheim found British and American anthropologists, including, we would add, Robertson Smith in his anthropological approach to the Old Testament, thought-provoking because in them he encountered detailed studies such as were not to be found elsewhere (1978:83). Frazer and Tylor might have employed a faulty method, but their work contained a wealth of material absent in German ethnologists on whom Durkheim had leant when he wrote his earlier work, *The Division of Labour* in 1893 (ibid.).

This kind of approach is too vague. The intellectual change of direction – one could almost call it an intellectual crisis – which undoubtedly occurred in the mid-1890s has to be located in the work of Robertson Smith. No one can be sure what in the work influenced Durkheim. Detailed issues about religion and ritual? Concentration on the social inter-relations contained in one society? The need to study in detail a primitive society? Totemism? Philippe Besnard has recently indicated that it is the third possibility that contains the nature of the change (1981:4). Between 1894 and 1895 Durkheim suddenly seems to change from a near indifference to primitive societies to a considerable concern for them, as in the 1894–5 lectures in Bordeaux on religion in which he declared in a letter to Hamelin that a large part of them were devoted to 'les formes élémentaires de la religion'. This set of lectures might be seen to cover the dividing line of before and after the 'Smith event'. They are thus difficult to place in one stage or the other. What, however, gives weight to this sensible general solution to the problem is that the lectures on religion given in Paris six years later (1901–2) were in fact called 'Les Formes élémentaires de la religion'! But the enigma remains. Do 'les formes élémentaires de la religion' refer to totemism or to something more general, say to the social components of a preliterate society without regard to its type? Any solution to the problem will have to take into consideration Durkheim's overwhelming concern with totemism, which dominated the lectures he gave in 1906 and 1907 and which was methodologically central in his book – a book which bore a title very similar to the phrase just mentioned (see following chapter, especially section 2).

3 Feverish activity

Although the middle period was a highly creative one, it was also one in which Durkheim did not publish a single book. Roughly in the middle of it he moved from the University of Bordeaux to the prestigious Sorbonne. This meant, as we have seen, that in addition to his strictly academic work, he found himself immersed in a great deal of administrative and political activity (see ch. 2.2). Further, he was forced to continue to deliver a considerable number of courses of lectures, some of which he did not appear to relish and would probably have preferred lecturing on more strictly sociological topics (Lukes 1972:619–20). These were in education (see ch. 2.3). Some he had already given in Bordeaux, others he had to prepare *de novo*. That he published no books meant that his more sustained thought reached only a student audience. For various reasons the lectures could not be published and it was only after his death that they gradually appeared, as certain disciples gained access to the texts and were prepared to edit them.

His lectures entitled 'L'Éducation morale', which he began to deliver in Bordeaux in 1898 and subsequently in Paris, appeared in book form in 1925. Nowhere, perhaps, did he more clearly enunciate his plea for a secular morality which would replace a theologically based morality than in this book. Lectures entitled 'L'Histoire de l'enseignement secondaire en France' were started in 1904 and were expanded and repeated in an almost statutory fashion at the École Normale Supérieure for the whole time that he was professor at the Sorbonne. They were published in 1938 and did not become well-known until recently either in or outside France. In the matter of religion, Durkheim outlines the role of the Church in education from its very early days to modern times. Particularly interesting are his observations about the Jesuits. The lectures point to Durkheim's great ability as a historian (see ch. 23.3).

Mention also ought to be made of lectures concerned with Rousseau which Durkheim delivered in 1901–2 and which were posthumously published in 1918 (1918b). In them there appears Durkheim's own closeness to some of Rousseau's views in the matter of religion: that law is religious in nature, that religion is the basis of social order and that a religious foundation is required for morality.

In 1896 he gave a course of lectures with the title, 'Cours de sociologie: Physique générale des moeurs et du droit'. These were extended year by year, but a definitive draft was made between 1898 and 1900 (Lukes 1972:255). They were published after the Second World War through the efforts of a Turkish professor of law, H. N. Kubali, who had been introduced to the manuscripts of the lectures by Marcel Mauss. They were published in 1950 and translated as *Professional Ethics and Civic Morals* in 1957. In these lectures Durkheim attempted to deal with basic moral and legal problems and to show that in the past religion lay close to the foundation of both of them. The importance of this book in understanding the development of Durkheim's religious thought is frequently overlooked. In it are contained in summary form nearly all his major hypotheses on religion: the notion of the sacred, religion as a non-illusory reality, the divinity as a symbolic form of society, the modern cult of the individual and so on.

In 1900–1, just before he left Bordeaux, he gave the course of lectures with the title 'Les Formes élémentaires de la religion', to which reference has just been made. Their contents are totally unknown. Clearly, from the title, they are a forerunner of his great book, and it is interesting to note that for this Durkheim changed 'religion' to 'religious life'.

That Durkheim did not have the satisfaction of seeing a book published in his name during this otherwise very fruitful period can be largely attributed to the time he spent in other activities. In addition to his lecturing and duties of administration there appeared in 1898 the first issue of *L'Année sociologique*. The importance of this journal, both for sociology and the Durkheimian enterprise, has already been noted (see ch. 2.2). The amount of effort that Durkheim put into the production of the journal was enormous. This was not only to be seen in editing and producing it, but also in writing articles and in the numerous reviews which he contributed to it. In reviewing he tended to concentrate on examining books on the family and on totemism, but he also reviewed books which were specifically about religion or which raised religious subjects. According to our reckoning, there were published during this period 21 such articles and reviews, and a good number of items relating to totemism, which he saw as being so important to his analysis of religion (see Table 3.1; Pickering 1975:311–12). Amongst the more important articles which raised religious issues the following should be noted:

'Représentations individuelles et représentations collectives' (1898b),
'L'Individualisme et les intellectuels' (1898c),
'De la Définition des phénomènes religieux' (1899a(ii)),
(with Mauss) 'De Quelques formes primitives de classification' (1903a(i)),
'La Détermination du fait moral' (1906b).

Durkheim covered many topics of a religious kind other than those just mentioned. They are too numerous to be covered separately and only the more important ones will be raised here and in the chapters ahead. From all the evidence available it would seem that he began for the first time to work on the problem of the definition of religion. This he did in one of the articles above, which appeared in the second volume of the *Année sociologique* with the title 'De la Définition des phénomènes religieux' (1899a(ii)). Whether this article was based on one or several of the lectures Durkheim gave on religion in the series of 1894–5 is difficult to know. It might be argued that it was written as a result of the new insights that he had gained from reading Robertson Smith. As we shall show, the judgment of Lukes that the essay is of little consequence is a hasty one (Lukes 1972:240; see ch. 9). In the essay he convincingly demonstrated the controlling or coercive force that religious beliefs and rituals exercise over individuals (see also 1900c). This encouraged him to attempt to define religion in terms of a coercive force in a way that fitted in with his definition of a social fact that he had established in *The Rules of Sociological Method* (1895a). He contrasted religious phenomena which emerged from society and which exerted a 'real' force over individuals with those which were associated with individual religious phenomena and which exerted a more feeble force over the one or the few. The notion of the sacred is raised, but it does not have the dominant place in his system that it was later to assume.

He proclaimed religion as the most primitive of all social institutions – the fountain from which all others have emerged (1897e). This was to be reiterated on many occasions as he postulated that religion is the basis of all social institutions (ibid.; 1899a(i)). The proposition that religion is based on the notion of constraint rests not least in the fact that its *représentations* have the form of dogmas and myths which demand acceptance (see ch. 15). By contrast, science is not based on such constraint and rests on reason and experiment; it is therefore open to intellectual challenge and to modification (1901h). Traditional religious *représentations* which claim to be true cannot in fact be accepted by intellectuals today. Science by its unfailing method has undermined religious belief in terms of knowledge about phenomena (1925a; 1905a(ii)(2)). The rationalist contention that religion will automatically die, however, is not true. In the place of traditional religious beliefs there has emerged a common belief in man himself and so man has become a god for men (1898c). Durkheim's theoretical argument rests on the proposition that at the heart of every society there are collective *représentations* which are necessary for its existence. Whether they are to be found within religion as traditionally thought of, or outside it, is beside the point (1899a(ii); 1925a; 1950a). The contemporary cult of man fits the bill admirably (1906e). Crucial to the notion of morality is the authority that supports it: in traditional societies this authority is based on God or some equivalent concept. In modern society, which rejects this particular authority, some other authority has to be found – indeed it already exists. It is in society itself. This in fact has been so all down history (1906e; 1925a). This very close relationship between society and morality, between society and religion, encourages Durkheim once again to state that God is society hypostasized (see ch. 12.2).

4 Characteristics

There can be no doubt that the ten years or so which correspond to the middle period were marked by intense intellectual activity. Durkheim had reached the high plateau of his academic life. Much of the activity was focused on religion. As has already been observed, the first period was one in which religion had full recognition within the sociological framework. The 'revelation' of 1895 acted as a spur in intensifying Durkheim's search for religion in heretofore unrecognized places. It seemed as if he had discovered that religion was the missing key to open most, if not all, sociological doors. Through the 'revelation' he had unearthed what so many had overlooked. His discovery could be said to give rise to the technical name *sociologie religieuse* and this was inevitably linked with his own name (see ch. 27). It was not that religion was explained through a study of religion, but society now had its mysteries revealed by the mystery of religion and religion itself was to be understood by its relation to society. We have already had occasion to note how during this period, as editor of the new journal, *L'Année sociologique*, he devoted much space to religious subjects (see ch. 2.2). In the preface to the second volume published in 1899 he explains this and how he had come to see religion as the basis of nearly all human institutions.

> This year, as well as last, our analyses are headed by those concerning the sociology of religion. The according of the first rank to this sort of phenomenon has produced some astonishment, but it is these phenomena which are the germ from which all others – or at least almost all others – are derived. *Religion contains in itself from the very beginning, even if in an indistinct state, all the elements which in dissociating themselves from it, articulating themselves, and combining with one another in a thousand ways, have given rise to the various manifestations of collective life.* From myths and legends have issued forth science and poetry; from religious ornamentations and cult ceremonials have come the plastic arts; from ritual practice were born law and morals. One cannot understand our perception of the world, our philosophical conceptions of the soul, of immortality, of life, if one does not know the religious beliefs which are their

primordial forms. Kinship started out as an essentially religious tie; punishment, contract, gift, and homage are transformations of expiatory, contractual, communal, honorary sacrifices, and so on. At most one may ask whether economic organization is an exception and derives from another source; although we do not think so, we grant that the question must be kept in abeyance. At any rate, a great number of problems change their aspects completely as soon as their connections with the sociology of religion are recognized. Our efforts must therefore be aimed at tracing these connections. Besides, there is no social science that is more capable of rapid progress, for the materials that have already been gathered are quite considerable and are ready to be elaborated sociologically. (1899a(i): ii/t.1960c:350–1; our italics)

His general attitude to religion as the 'open-sesame' of all institutions is seen also in a letter from Paul Lapie to Célestin Bouglé, written about this time in 1897. Both were to become members of the inner corps of the Année Sociologique group.

Basically he [Durkheim] is explaining everything *at this moment* by religion, the prevention of marriages between relatives is a religious matter, punishment is a religious phenomenon in its origins; everything is religious. I could only offer a weak protest. (Lapie 1976:8–9)

Is it being too bold to suggest that Durkheim's unbounding enthusiasm for religion as a key to understanding society is reflected in what he saw as the essence of society itself? In his famous essay written at this time, 'Représentations individuelles et représentations collectives', he states that mental life consists of a complexity of strata, too specialized for the conscious mind to pierce. This can be described as 'spiritual' and as such was at this time becoming subject to positive science (shades of Comte!). And further, if individual representational life can be labelled spiritual, social life is hyperspiritual (1898b/1924a:47–8/t.1953b:33–4).

Of the many ideas that Durkheim dealt with in the second period, some were little more than refinements of concepts and notions that he had established in the earlier period: others were quite new. He had yet to consolidate and develop the advances he had made in the second period, to add one or two more, so that all his ideas were of a piece. This was the genius of Durkheim – to weave diverse material into an all-embracing pattern. The task was taken up in the last phase of the development of his thought on religion.

5 The development of Durkheim's thought on religion

III The final formulation

1 The work continues with lectures, articles and *the* book

The third and final period can be said to start with a course of lectures on religion Durkheim gave in the Sorbonne in 1906–7 (1907f) and reaches its peak with the publication of *Les Formes élémentaires de la vie religieuse: le système totémique en Australie* in 1912. It ends with Durkheim's death in 1917. It is essentially a period of consolidation and final formulation of ideas, many of which were clear in his mind much earlier (Richard 1928:298 n.1). The feverish and creative activity of the middle period continues as Durkheim substantiated his ideas with empirical evidence. All through his academic life he was a prodigiously hard worker. While he was in Bordeaux the rector of the university said he was the hardest working of all the teachers: it is hardly likely that such endeavours were relaxed once he reached Paris. His relentless work pattern probably engendered what might have been something approaching a mental breakdown (see Lukes 1972:100 n.7; Lacroix 1981:147; Besnard 1981:3). Nothing, however, of a serious nature happened.

Durkheim continued to give a number of lecture courses at the Sorbonne and other academic institutions, including the École Normale Supérieure where he went on with his lectures on the Formation et développement de l'enseignement secondaire en France (1938a; see ch. 4). With the advent of war, however, the amount of lecturing declined (Lukes 1972:620). As in former periods, most of the lecture courses he gave were on the subject of education of one kind or another. (From the records of courses given by Durkheim throughout his academic career, 15 out of 26 were on this subject; see Pickering 1979a:101–2.)

In the middle period, Durkheim published no books at all: in the final period there was only one, to which we have just referred, which is beyond doubt his greatest work. One book which appeared posthumously touched on religious issues and was based on lectures given in this period. It was entitled *Pragmatisme et sociologie* (1955a).

The lectures on pragmatism were given in the Sorbonne in the academic year, 1913–14, with Durkheim's son, André, particularly in mind. They were largely an attack on the work of the American psychologist and philosopher, William James. One lecture was devoted to *The Varieties of Religious Experience* in which Durkheim held that James neglected the social institutions of religion, such as churches, and emphasized the interior life. He saw another weakness to the indifference of James to theological ideas, particularly whether God exists. He was more concerned with seeing whether or not beliefs about God could be reconciled with religion.

Durkheim's work on the *Année sociologique* proceeded unabated, with the publication of four volumes. The war curtailed publication and the last issue appeared in 1913. The place given to religion remained much the same in the number of reviews by Durkheim. He wrote no articles on the subject, apart from 'notes' on religious systems in primitive societies, which were mainly concerned with the problem of classification (1910a(ii)(2) and 1913a(i)(2)). Nevertheless articles and contributions which referred to religion continued to flow from his pen, and these included reviews. We estimate that they numbered 25, including those published posthumously (see Table 3.1). His interest in totemism, so much in evidence in *The Elementary Forms*, went from strength to strength, if the number of reviews (23) is a guide.

In two items Durkheim emphasizes some facets of his thought which are latent elsewhere, but never before clearly enunciated. The first appeared in the proceedings of the Société Française de Philosophie for 1913 in which Durkheim was asked to introduce a discussion of his recently published book on religion (1913b). In a lengthy and complex debate, many themes were raised: animism, naturism, reductionism, the nature of the sacred, religion as an illusion, and so on. Durkheim, however, seemed keen to put forward his idea that man possesses two components or beings within himself. The duality can be seen in terms of the soul and the body, an extension of the sacred and profane, the egoistic appetites and moral action, the individual and the social. These ideas were reiterated in the second item, an article published a year later, 'Le Dualisme de la nature humaine et ses conditions sociales' (1914a).

2 The 1906–7 lectures: 'La Religion: les origines'

The course of lectures 'La Religion: les origines', given in the Sorbonne between 1906 and 1907, was his second course on religion and heralds, as we have suggested, the emergence of the final period of Durkheim's religious thought. The lectures might be said to constitute the initial draft of *The Elementary Forms* and would probably not be known to us but for the reporting of them by Paul Fontana for the journal, *Revue de philosophie* (1907f). Although it was a journal which emanated from the Institut Catholique in Paris, and which claimed to be a liberal and 'open' publication, it is surprising nevertheless that it should have devoted 51 pages of volume VII to the work of a sociologist whose agnostic or atheistic outlook was so well known. Not surprisingly, the editor, Peillaube, found it necessary in the last of three sections, perhaps because of the criticism of readers, to state in an introductory footnote that the intention of publishing the report of the lectures was to offer a simple, objective account of them and that it did not imply editorial approval of the ideas (ibid.:620). Thanks to the journal's interest in secular theories of religion and the realization of the importance of the lectures, we at least possess an outline of what Durkheim said.

He starts by declaring the need to define religious phenomena externally so as to distinguish them from other phenomena. Only at the end of the study can one hope to define the essence of religion. The difficulty in defining religion is that as observers or actors, men have preconceived ideas which must be abandoned in order to establish a satisfactory definition. Any such definition must apply to all religions.

As in an earlier article (1899a(ii)) Durkheim rejects notions of religion based on the work of H. Spencer and Max Müller. He also states that religion cannot be defined in terms of the idea of the supernatural, of God (Réville) and of spiritual beings (Tylor), and to support his case he refers to Buddhism where such concepts are absent. More positively, he states that the definition of religious phenomena must have as its base the notion of the sacred and the profane. They are opposites, separated by interdicts. Magic is excluded from the definition since it is anti-religious. Religion is finally defined as a system of beliefs and practices related to sacred things – beliefs and practices common to a concrete collectivity.

In searching for the origin of the notion of the soul, why it is sacred in character and why the worship of souls or spirits is extended to nature, Durkheim criticizes both the animist theories of Spencer and Tylor and the naturist theory of Müller. He turns to totemism as the key. Totemism is the most primitive form of social organization known to man. The totem is the badge: it is society symbolized or hypostasized. Therefore the totem is not only the emblem of the clan, it is the centre of a religious system. Indeed, in totemism man himself is seen to be sacred and the world itself takes on a religious character. Collective totemism which refers to the entire group is differentiated from the profane. Durkheim introduces the concept of mana as religious force, which is basically the totemic principle. Religion is not an illusion. Its reality is seen in the fact that God is society transfigured or hypostasized. Historically, religion has been the point of advance for philosophy and science for it has been their predecessor.

Using the evidence of totemism, Durkheim explains the origin and qualities of the soul, spirits, genies, demons, gods. In his analysis of ritual, he develops a typology of negative rites (including interdicts) and positive rites (including sacrifice). He points to the reality of religion to those immersed in it, especially in common worship. Religion is not an aberration. When a group assembles, individual *représentations* are chased away and are seen, through common interests and beliefs, to be profane. Those who participate in such rituals feel a warmth which reassures them and gives them strength. Therefore the cult has something about it that is eternal. There exists an *élan d'intelligence* which in the absence of logical reasons is the faith without which there can be no religion.

This brief résumé of the outline of the lectures shows that they roughly correspond to *The Elementary Forms* published six years later. If Fontana's notes can be relied upon – and we have no reasons to doubt their accuracy, for in many cases there are careful references to books quoted by Durkheim – some important differences can be seen between the lectures and the book. Such differences demonstrate the development of Durkheim's thought during this period. We note the points of difference in summary form. Some will be treated in detail in future chapters.

1 There is some uncertainty in defining religion. The notion of the sacred is now included as well as reference made to a collectivity, but it lacks the sharpness of the 1912 definition.
2 The lectures make some but not exclusive use of Australian Aboriginal material. This is a distinctive feature of the book. In the lectures totemism is treated extensively and in a more general way.
3 There is, not surprisingly, no reference to the 'one well-conducted experiment' (593/415/144), nor do the lectures seem to have been written with this end in view.
4 The notion of effervescence as the fountain of religious vitality, which received added impetus from Durkheim's study of Australian ethnography, is absent, although he had made earlier references to it (see ch. 21).
5 The section on ritual in the book is more rigorously developed, with chapters on imitative, representative and piacular rites.
6 There is no reference to problems of epistemology which were so prominent in *The Elementary Forms*.
7 The notion of *représentation* is little in evidence.

It is legitimate to conclude that most, though not all Durkheim's ideas on religion, are to be found in the 1906–7 lectures. What Durkheim achieved in the period between the lectures and the book was to refine them, add to them, but above all, substantiate them by an almost exclusive and very detailed application of totemic ethnography of Australian Aboriginal tribes, with some reference to other totemic groups, notably those in North America. His concern for and developed ideas about totemism are very much within this third period.

3 *Les Formes élémentaires*

The publication of what in fact turned out to be Durkheim's most important book, *Les Formes élémentaires de la vie religieuse: le système totémique en Australie* in 1912 evoked a great number of reviews. It was a book that could not be disregarded and represented a detailed sociological analysis of religion amongst a primitive Australian people, the Arunta, with references to other totemic groups. Probably no book in the field of religion has combined such a wealth of ethnographic material with theoretical propositions. Needless to say, it contained a host of controversial points, but despite that, it was seen at the time to be a potential classic and indeed it has become so. It was quickly translated into English by an American, J. W. Swain, and published in London and New York in 1915: the translation shows signs of being hurried and although it is far from good it has not been superseded (see Nisbet 1976; also t.1975a:102–66).

Interestingly enough, the subtitle of the English translation was: *A Study in Religious Sociology* and this replaced *le système totémique en Australie*. The reason for the change has never been explained. Was it done with Durkheim's approval? Why the change anyway? Was it to emphasize the sociological nature of the book: that here was a basically new approach in the study of religious phenomena, as indeed it was? Or was it because of the book's reliance on totemism, which had come under particular criticism, that it was thought desirable to omit reference to it in the title? There is no evidence beyond the printed text itself to answer these questions. Some of the conclusions, and indeed part of the argument in the main body of the text, were concerned with the sociology of knowledge which Durkheim claimed had religious roots. Not without significance is the fact that in the third impression of the English translation of 1954 no subtitle was printed. (The writer has attempted to find out why the original change was made to the English translation by writing to the publishers involved, but they have kept no records or correspondence going back to that date.)

The main title is interesting. After rejecting the name he gave to the series of lectures he delivered in 1906–7, he adopted another title that was somewhat familiar. In the fifth volume of the *Année sociologique*, which was published in 1902, 'Formes élémentaires de la vie religeuse' appeared as a subsection of the second section of reviews called 'Sociologie religieuse'. In the introduction to the section, the authors, Hubert and Mauss, said of 'Formes élémentaires de la vie religieuse' (did they invent the phrase?) that the subsection would include items on totemism, rites, beliefs and the organization of primitive peoples (1902:190). This is very much in line with the importance Durkheim attached to his methodological approach (see ch. 6.2).

The arguments and propositions of *Les Formes élémentaires* are numerous and complex, some of which will be covered in detail in the pages ahead. For the person who has not read the book we offer an interesting review in the *Année sociologique*, which is in fact a résumé of the book. It is interesting because it was written by the author himself – reviewing his own book! – in conjunction with his nephew, Marcel Mauss (1913a(ii)(11) and (12):94–8/t.1975a:178–80). One would expect that the résumé was accurate, even if it was written not by Durkheim but by Mauss, since he did the ethnographic research. No one has decided who in fact was the author or whether they did it together. By contrast, Frazer's *Totemism and Exogamy*, vol. IV, was reviewed together with *Les Formes*. We offer the following quotation.

Durkheim's book differs from the preceding one in its method as much as in its general approach and conclusions. In a comprehensive survey Frazer tried to cover all the peoples among whom totemism in a more or less developed form is to be found. Durkheim, on the other hand, has concentrated all his efforts on a well-defined and limited group of societies; a group, however, among whom the features displayed by totemism are sufficiently pronounced as to enable the study of them to meet with most chances of success. Australia was chosen as the area for observation and everything pointed to its fitness to play this role. Nevertheless, references have sometimes been made to American totemism on those occasions when a comparison could serve to illuminate or to define more accurately the Australian facts.

Secondly, whilst for Frazer totemism is merely a disorganized accumulation of magical superstitions, for Durkheim it is a religion in the true sense of the word. What characterizes religion, in fact, is the distinction between the sacred and the profane. Thus the totem is sacred; it cannot be approached, it is held in respect, it is surrounded by prohibitions and at the same time positive virtues are attributed to it. However, what proves the religious character of totemism better than anything else is the actual analysis of the beliefs and practices of which it is composed. All the essential elements of a religion are to be found among them.

Finally, if Frazer refused to see a proper religious system in totemism, it is because he failed to recognize its social character. Durkheim has set himself the task of throwing this character into relief. The object at the centre of totemic religion, the object which is pre-eminently sacred, is not the totemic animal but the pictorial representation of it. It is because this symbol is the emblem or flag of the clan. If the symbol of the group is sacred, is this not because the sentiments inspired by the group relate to the sign which is an expression and a reminder of it? Indeed, Durkheim shows how each collectivity inspires in its members sentiments which are identical in nature with religious sentiments. In a similar way to the deity, it acts on individuals categorically, it demands sacrifices and privations from them and it gives them comfort. It requires that they should act contrary to their nature and it sustains them. These propositions have been established not only by analyses of general psychology, but also by studies of conditions of groups peculiar to Australian societies. The individual within a group is taken out of himself, goes into a genuine state of ecstasy, lives a life *sui generis* which is contrasted in its intensity and impersonality with the one the individual leads in the course of his ordinary existence. Besides, it is a fact that society produces sacred things at will and then stamps on them the characteristics of religion.

If the moral force which is the soul of religion is divested of its material symbols, what remains is collective power. This explains why, in so many lower religions, the power worshipped by the members of the cult is known in an anonymous and impersonal form; it is the Melanesian and Polynesian mana, the *wakan* of the Sioux, etc. The same idea is also to be found in Australia where the object worshipped in totemism is a vague force which is diffused throughout the animal (or vegetable) species, throughout the whole clan, at the same time as it is inherent in the totemic emblem.

Because this anonymous force is entirely moral, that is to say made up of ideas and sentiments, it can only live and act in and through particular *consciences*. Accordingly, it permeates them, and in so doing assumes individual characteristics. The fragment which each of us carries within him takes on a particular aspect by the very fact of being intermingled with our individual life, of bearing the imprint of our organism and of our temperament. Each of these fragments is a soul. That is how the idea of a soul came into being. It gives expression to the higher part of ourselves, it is the sum of the ideals which interpret collectivity in us, and which each of us incarnates in his own fashion. The author shows, by analysing Australian and American facts, how indeed the soul is merely a particularized form of the totemic force among these peoples.

Along with the idea of the soul, the idea of the personality was introduced into the domain of religion and, as a result, mythological formations of a new kind became possible. From souls to spirits, there is but a single step. Once the idea of spirits was accepted, it was to spirits that the great social or religious institutions were attributed. Thus were born, in the popular imagination, the civilizing heroes. Finally, there is a group of rites which play a leading role in the social life of these peoples, namely, initiation rites. Initiation is not peculiar to any clan; it is a tribal and even an intertribal cult, for representatives of different tribes are summoned to them. The mythical personality connected with these rites, then, occupied a separate place in religion; it was revered not by one clan but by the tribe and even several tribes. As the purpose of the initiation was to 'make men', this personality was also considered to be the creator of humanity. Thence came the idea of a great god, acknowledged by vast groups of human beings and visualized as the father of mankind. With this conception, we are already within reach of every religion which goes beyond totemism.

Such conclusions, drawn from the analysis of the beliefs, are subsequently confirmed by a study of the cult, which also determines the meaning and functions of the different rites. On this occasion, the author attempts a classification of the principal forms of the cult. First of all, he distinguishes between the negative cult and the positive cult. The first, which is made up of abstentions, consists in the observance of prohibitions. To the negative cult are naturally linked the ascetic rites which are nothing more than the exaggerated practice of the prohibitions. As for the positive cult, it includes all active ritual performances. Those studied in this book are sacrifice, all the essential elements being included in the *intichiuma*, mimetical rites, representative or dramatic rites, and expiatory rites. The last are in contrast to all the others, as doleful rites are contrasted to joyful ones: they express a special aspect of the cult. In relation to each of these kinds of rite, the author attempts to discover which collective states of the soul they express, maintain, or restore, and in this way to demonstrate the extent to which the details of ritual action are bound up in the most essential aspects of social life.

In the end, this interpretation of religion appears, above all, to be consistent with a system of actions aimed at making and perpetually remaking the soul of the collectivity and of the individual. Although it has a speculative part to play. its principal function is dynamogenic. It gives the individual the strength which enables him to surpass himself, to rise above his nature and to keep it under control. The only moral forces superior to those which the individual *qua* individual has at his command are those issuing from individuals in association. That is why religious forces are and can only be collective forces.

4 Its reception

Overall praise for the book was immediate and in some cases almost tumultuous. For example, Gustave Belot, who wrote as a philosopher interested in sociology and was often critical of Durkheim, wrote that Durkheim in his analysis of the religious sentiment 'has extricated from it one of its sources with a force, an ingenuity, and an original viewpoint, to which one cannot give too much praise' (1913a:356). Indeed, enthusiasm for the book, as well as for Durkheim's work on religion as a whole, was generous even from those who opposed him at several points. Of the many examples available, we mention one or two more. A. A. Goldenweiser wrote: 'Sharp is the author's wit and brilliant his argumentation' (1917:124). And earlier, Malinowski, then little heard of, and who was himself to become as famous as Goldenweiser, said that the book was such 'as could only be given by one of the acutest and most brilliant living sociologists' (1913:531). But praise has continued to be echoed from one generation to another, and for a case in point in more recent times we turn to the leading British anthropologist, Evans-Pritchard, who although sharply critical of Durkheim wrote of *The Elementary Forms*:

> Émile Durkheim's thesis is more than just neat; it is brilliant
> and imaginative, almost poetical; and he had an insight into
> a psychological fundamental of religion; the elimination of the
> self, the denial of individuality, its having no meaning, or
> even existence, save as part of something greater, and other,
> than the self. (1965:64)

The contemporary French sociologist, Raymond Aron, whose outlook is more akin to Weber than Durkheim, praised *The Elementary Forms* as 'le plus important, le plus profond, le plus original' of all his works (1967a:345). And this is precisely what it is. (Those who wish to encounter further examples of praise could turn to Bellah (1973:xliii–lii), Hartland (1913:92), LaCapra (1972:26), Lukes (1972:482), Worsley (1956:61); and this is but a selection!)

Evaluations of specific issues enshrined in *The Elementary Forms* will appear in the pages ahead. Here we point briefly to general strengths and weaknesses of the book raised by various scholars. The verdict of most was and still is that the book was theoretically brilliant. As Burridge has recently written, some sixty years after it was published:

> There can be few anthropological studies today which do not
> in some way stand upon the theoretical insights of Durkheim.
> (1973:49)

The conceptual framework Durkheim produced must always be

seen as 'relevant and significant'. It was later anthropologists who were able to give flesh and blood to Durkheim's theoretical skeleton (ibid.).

There were others who took the contrary view. From them the conceptual framework was weak, but Durkheim's attention to detail and his great use of ethnography was much praised. Often such critics felt that Durkheim had undermined the whole religious enterprise by denying the proclaimed truth of religion. Richard was one such person (see especially 1923), but so also was the more anthropologically renowned scholar Wilhelm Schmidt (1868–1954). Writing as a Roman Catholic as well as an anthropologist, he observed that possibly no book had reaped so many eulogies in detail and yet had been so generally repudiated in its main propositions (1926,I:579, quoted in Lowie 1937:198). Claude Lévi-Strauss, who on his own admission owed a great deal to Durkheim, wrote somewhat scathingly about Durkheim's theoretical contribution as contrasted to his ability in making ethnographical deductions. He said: 'As a theory of religion, his book is unacceptable, while the best Australian field workers hailed it as the forerunner of the discoveries they made only several years later' (1945:536).

Lévi-Strauss's comment draws attention to the fact that Durkheim's analysis of totemism was what brought forth most praise or most criticism. The subject of totemism and Durkheim's interpretation is raised in the next chapter (see ch. 6.3).

Other anthropological scholars were equally critical of Durkheim's use of ethnographical material – van Gennep, Goldenweiser, Schmidt, Malinowski, and so on. Schmidt made the interesting remark that Durkheim's failures in ethnology were due to the fact that he took such a time to produce the book, which was based on earlier plans and ideas. The sciences of ethnology and comparative religion had moved so fast that they had left behind ideas which Durkheim had acquired earlier and which he had not modified accordingly (1931:115).

Apart from the overall question of general praise and criticism of the book that was the culmination of Durkheim's academic work, there is the allied issue of trying to encapsulate *The Elementary Forms* by describing it or speaking of its essence in a few words or a sentence. Thus, Giddens has recently written: 'The main underlying body of theory [of the book] is functional in character' (1971:106). Scholars such as Talcott Parsons and Radcliffe-Brown in formulating sociological and anthropological theories have held that Durkheim, through his book, is the founder of what might be called a structural-functional approach not only to religion but to all social phenomena. Seger has written that Durkheim's functional approach to religion 'stands essentially unchanged' (1957:69). She goes on to say that modern scholars have merely added further connections, introduced negative corollaries and made necessary elaborations. Other writers have laid emphasis on this approach of Durkheim, such as Alpert, Bellah, Coser, Nisbet, and so on. A great deal turns on what is meant by function, functional and functionalism. In what precise way or ways Durkheim can be said to be a functionalist in the matter of religion is raised in some detail in chapter 16 below. Whereas early commentators appeared to praise Durkheim for his approach and indeed summed up *The Elementary Forms* as a functionalist classic, it should not be overlooked that functionalism is no longer seen as a satisfactory theory as it was held to be in the period between, say, 1930 and 1950.

But functionalism is not the only mould in which scholars have cast *The Elementary Forms*. Many social theorists have read into it the foundation or manifestation of a particular theory they support or claim to have founded. Hence Talcott Parsons sees it as being on the verge of a voluntaristic theory of action (1949:439); and again, as containing a general theory of action systems and a treatise on symbolic realism, the forerunner of modern French structuralism (1973:175). It is also basically a theory of social change according to Bellah (1959/r.Nisbet 1965:168ff.), and Pope (1973:411). Stanner, on the other hand, has written that 'the work substantially is a study of the sociology of totemism and of the social determination of categories' (1967:229). Tiryakian (1978:39) holds that its intention was to formulate a new religion, one of overcoming contemporary spiritual malaise or anomy.

We do not wish to cite further ways in which commentators have attempted to summarize in a sentence or phrase the message of *The Elementary Forms*. Our position is that all such 'reductionism' misses the enormous wealth of ideas and imagination which make up the book. It stands beyond all such compression as any classic does. Encapsulation produces distortion and is belittling. Further, it usually contains overtones which speak of either uncritical enthusiasm or denigration.

Another danger, however, of encapsulation is that the perpetrator claims to know the intention of the author. Nothing is more dangerous where it is not overtly stated. All too easily one can read into the book what was not intended. In the case of Durkheim, as we wish to show, no simple formula can do justice to his paradoxical thinking. Any formula merely distorts or oversimplifies. That there have been so many different encapsulations of *The Elementary Forms* points to its classical nature. All classics have to be interpreted: that they are thought worth interpreting makes them classics (see Introductory Remarks).

No one can deny that Durkheim's concern in *The Elementary Forms* is to unearth the origins of religion. This he openly admits, but goes on to say that he proposes to proceed '*under new conditions*' (10/8/109; Durkheim's italics). He planned to do this by exploring in what he called a scientific manner the social consequences of religion, consequences which are ever-present. Here is the one avowed purpose of his book and by that it must be judged (see 1–20/1–28/102–12). There is of course another end in view which relates to the realm of epistemology – in finding a sociological solution to the problem of categories of thought. Durkheim hoped that in studying totemistic groups he could, as it were, kill two birds with one stone. One, the problem of the origins of religion; the other that of the alleged innateness of ideas, we leave to one side, since it raises so many philosophical issues (see Introductory Remarks; 12–28/9–20).

5 Continued glory and demise

The publication of *Les Formes élémentaires* added to Durkheim's already established prestige. He continued on occasions to reiterate the motif of the book and to introduce one or two new themes (see section 1 of this chapter). The further step he planned was a definitive book on morals (see Pickering 1975). The carnage of the First World War meant a radical curtailment of his academic achievements, and as we have already noted, he turned his attention to the war effort and to the writing of pamphlets to strengthen as he hoped the morale of his beloved France (see ch. 1.7). In one of the pamphlets (1915c), he touched on religion in referring to its liberal-humanistic form as being a rallying point for the French in their hour of direst need.

So ended a sustained and determined effort to combine a scientific approach to religion with undergirding new forms of religion centred on man himself. How Durkheim's analysis of religion fared after his death and the wavering fortunes of the remnant of the Année Sociologique group are taken up in part VI (chs 27 and 28).

In the last few chapters an attempt has been made to divide the development of Durkheim's academic approach to religion into three main periods. This has meant showing in the broad sweep the many themes and ideas he raised in his work on the subject. From now on attention will be focused on a selection of the issues which have been mentioned.

Part II
Taking up Positions

6 Procedures and assumptions

Just before the Second World War Barnes and Becker, in their study of the founding fathers of sociology, wrote that:

> Critics have insisted . . . that Durkheim introduced quite as many methodological errors as he had rejected. (1938:750)

We intend in this chapter to examine a few of the alleged errors and false assumptions in the matter of method connected with his sociological approach to religion, which critics pointed out during his lifetime and which have been referred to ever since.

1 The religious beliefs of the sociologist

It has already been observed that Durkheim was from an early age an unrepentant and publicly self-confessed agnostic, even atheist (see ch. 1.2). It has also been noted that he set his heart on examining religion as a social phenomenon and this he did by using what he thought were scientific procedures. Such procedures he believed would be acceptable to any man who stood by the canons of science. He was charged, nevertheless, both in his day and subsequently, with duplicity for failing to approach religion with the neutrality and objectivity of a scientist studying given data. His atheistic outlook meant that at the outset he was biased in denying the reality of the phenomena which is held by the believer – the existence of some supernatural power (see especially, Richard 1911a, 1923 and 1925). The charge raises the long-debated issue of the personal beliefs and religious commitment of the scientist or observer in approaching religious behaviour with the intention of understanding or explaining it. Religious issues raise philosophical questions and are emotionally charged. Put in the sentiments of Max Weber, can the scientist be at least initially value-free in looking at what is most likely to involve him in a personal way? He is surely committed one way or the other. All we wish to do here is to ascertain Durkheim's position. To offer some kind of final solution to the problem is not within our terms of reference and in any case the issue is virtually insoluble.

When the subject for analysis is religion, the scientist, according to Durkheim, must be someone who has a certain natural sympathy with the believer and with the ideals of his religion. The scientist must stand where the religious person stands and see the situation through his eyes. Hostility, especially an initial hostility, is as it were counter-productive. In a spontaneous speech about his ideas on religion and given towards the end of his life Durkheim unequivocally declared the need for sensitivity towards religion on the part of the observer. In taking the aggressive atheist to task, he said: 'Let him feel it [the religious sentiment] as the believer feels it; what it is to the believer is really what it is' (1919b:101/t.1975a:184). As it is necessary to have a poetic ear to understand poetry, so it is necessary to have a religious ear in order to understand what religion is about. Durkheim employs the analogy of seeing colours:

> he who does not bring to the study of religion a sort of religious sentiment cannot speak about it! He is like a blind man trying to talk about colour. (ibid.)

Durkheim also speaks of the impossibility of communicating 'the sense of colours to a man blind from birth' in connection with instilling a sense of the social in someone who is an anarchist (1909a(2):230/t.1979a:137). And he went on to say:

> I recognized that it was hard for me to convey a notion of what society and morality are to a person whose mind is afflicted with social and moral blindness, so long as he remains in that state. (ibid.:231/138)

In the speech just mentioned, Durkheim repeatedly states that the scientist has to be 'religious'. Thus:

> There cannot be a rational interpretation of religion which is fundamentally irreligious; an irreligious interpretation of religion would be an interpretation which denied the phenomenon it was trying to explain. (1919b:102/t.1975a:185)

Durkheim here attacks those rationalists and atheists who see religion as being without any reality, that is, an hallucination, or a force ideologically poisonous or at best totally undesirable. For Durkheim, as we shall see, religious phenomena are real and therefore within the legitimate purview of the scientist (ch. 11).

In confronting 'religion in the same mental state as the believer' (ibid.:101/184), Durkheim adopts a position which at first sight might seem similar to that of Max Weber in his notion of *Verstehen*. He held that the sociologist should attempt to see the meaning of a social situation through the eyes of the person experiencing it. Here he was putting forward a formal procedure in the study of social situations, be they religious or otherwise. Durkheim's purpose was slightly different, in so far as he was not proposing what might be strictly called a method but, rather, a sympathetic attitude within a particular methodological approach. When Weber speaks, however, of the necessity of having a 'musical ear' for what is being studied, his sentiments are very close to those of Durkheim. In more recent times Joachim Wach, in many ways inclined towards a Weberian approach to the study of religious phenomena, held that 'the enquirer must feel an affinity for his subject, and he must be trained to interpret his material with sympathetic understanding' (1947:10). Such an approach continues to this day: there seems to be no other. Thus Fabian speaks of the necessity of finding 'a way in' and 'a way out' of field-work – engagement and disengagement (1979:167). Field-workers must have technical competence and at the same time a sympathy for the subject being studied.

The scientist, however, is in an ambiguous position. He has to be sympathetic to the outlook and behaviour of the religious practitioner, but he also has to stand outside and take a long, cool, objective view of what is going on. The point is that his sympathy has to be bounded by limits: it is not the same as identity. If the scientist aspires to be totally identified (and total identification is impossible anyway), then his particular approach, his analysis of the situation, will have nothing to offer. He must in some way be different. And Durkheim has no hesitation in pointing to one clear line of demarcation – no scientist can accept the dogmatism of the believer where such dogmatism makes metaphysical assertions about truth. In speaking to Free Believers in the 1913 conference, in the unrehearsed speech already referred to, he said:

> To be sure, if he [the believer] values a denominational formula in an exclusive and uncompromising way, if he believes that he holds the truth about religion in a definitive form, then agreement is impossible. (1919b:101/t.1975a:184)

More specifically, as we shall show, Durkheim rejects that reality central to belief, the existence of a supernatural power, of gods or God. For him no scientist could accept such a belief for it is directly opposed to the assumptions of science (see ch. 25.2).

He had a strong dislike for what might be called apologists for the faith, especially those who wrote 'apologetic sociology', that is, 'sociology' which is used to confirm a spiritual or ecclesiastical standpoint. Such a person was Toniolo, an obscure Italian sociologist (see 1906a(6)). One might mention other names, people not necessarily writing in the name of sociology, such as Deploige, Laberthonnière and Le Roy. Durkheim saw himself as a figure opposed to any kind of apologetics, be they in the name of religion or those dedicated to its abolition. Science stands in its own right and is to be judged by its own merits. Science saw religion, he claimed, as a system of *représentations* expressing imperfectly a reality (ibid.). The facts of religion, derived in part from history and given special treatment by sociology, are to be treated with respect. Science always adopts a reverential attitude towards facts: science needs no apologetic. The ambiguity of Durkheim's position arises from his use of the notion of reality. His assumption is to deny the proclaimed reality and to concentrate on that reality which might be said to transcend the transcendent. Thus, Durkheim could say:

> If, however, he [the believer] considers that formulae are only provisional expressions which last and can only last a certain time, if he thinks that they are all imperfect, that the essential thing is not the letter of these formulae but the reality they hide . . . I believe that up to a certain point there is an enterprise we can embark upon by common consent. (1919b:101–2/t.1975a:184–5)

Despite Durkheim's assertion that science has to be free from metaphysical speculation (1895a/1901c:139/t.1938b:141) – and who

98

would disagree with him? – the claim that science was able to declare what is real is something which indeed is to be challenged (see ch. 15). His scientism was criticized by a doctoral candidate, J. Segond, who wrote a thesis on prayer and presented it in 1911 in the University of Paris. We quote part of the conversation (1911e:33/t.1968e/r.1972:652):

> DURKHEIM: . . . mystics do not understand the essence of prayer. You have to look for it.
> SEGOND: Who knows this essence?
> DURKHEIM: We do, when we study phenomena.
> SEGOND: Phenomena are not minds.
> DURKHEIM: Let us leave that aside. . .

It is obvious that Durkheim is not content to let phenomena determine what is real. The scientist must go beyond phenomena to find reality and his superior knowledge enables him to do this. Apart from such extravagant claims, the issue of reality or essence remains very much with the philosopher, not the scientist. In philosophical circles today, however, it is seldom considered. In the last analysis, it is argued by most that what is real cannot be objectively determined, but is subjectively selected.

Durkheim, in enunciating principles by which sociology is to proceed as a science, stated that initially 'all preconceptions, no matter their kind, had to be eradicated' (1895a/1901c:31/t.1938b:31). Here he stands very much in the tradition of Descartes in doubting all ideas previously received in order to arrive at the truth. Political and religious beliefs which carry with them such emotional overtones are particularly hostile to any firm beliefs which may challenge or contradict them. It is repugnant to some people that ideas they hold dear should be examined objectively in 'cold, dry analysis' (ibid.). None the less such analysis is required in a scientific examination of social facts. No one today would quibble with such a position.

To drive home his case Durkheim gives an example of someone who does not in fact take this stand. He quotes some words from James Darmsteter, professor at the Collège de France, who was an authority on the history of religions and translator into French of the Zend Avesta.

Woe to the scholar who approaches divine matters without

99

having in the depth of his consciousness, in the innermost
indestructible regions of his being, where the souls of his
ancestors sleep, an unknown sanctuary from which rises now
and then the aroma of incense, a line of a psalm, a sorrowful
or triumphant cry that as a child he sent to heaven along
with his brothers, and that creates immediate communion with
the prophets of yore! (ibid.:33/33)

Durkheim has nothing to do with what he labels as the 'mysticism'
implied in the quotation, and mysticism for him is 'essentially a
disguised empiricism, a negation of all science' (ibid.). There can
be no doubt that Darmsteter allows his mind full imagination
in describing in somewhat idealist terms the nature of religious
sympathy. But conceding such imagination, does not Durkheim's
condemnation conflict with his demand, already mentioned, that
some kind of 'religious resonance' is required on the part of the
inquirer or listener? And supposing there is a contradiction here
in Durkheim's thought, one is tempted to suggest two possible
explanations. Either Durkheim changed his position from the
early 1890s or earlier to the period just before the First World
War, so abandoning a rigidly defined position which lacked religious sympathy, to one that was coupled with more understanding;
or that his thought in this matter indeed contains an inbuilt
paradox where the observer or listener has to be both sympathetic
and at the same time unsympathetic. Which of these alternatives
is correct is difficult to say. It depends a great deal on what
Durkheim meant by mysticism, which according to Richard he
strongly disliked and attacked (Richard 1923:130/t.1975:233; see
ch. 1.2). Is Darmsteter in fact appealing to mysticism and saying
that it is necessary to have some kind of mystical experience in
order to understand religion? Or, is he not rather putting forward
the notion that the religious observer can only do his work if he has
some kind of religious resonance with the people or phenomena he
is studying? One is inclined to believe that the first of the alternatives just mentioned is correct, and that there was a change in
Durkheim's attitude to a recognition that the sociologist who
studies religion must have a strong reverence for it. In the early
days of his writing, when he was trying to establish sociology, he
was forced to make out a case for ice-cold objectivity, but as he
grew more sure of himself in later years he was prepared to take

a less rigid stand and to see the necessity of the sociologist getting near to the religious person in order to understand the nature of religion itself.

Richard's judgment about Durkheim is too harsh and misses the point. Richard wrote:

Religion appears to be explained through the eyes of someone who considers it without living it and who sees it to be only a purely external phenomenon. (1923:234/t.1975:245)

Similar attacks came from the Catholic apologist, Deploige (1905, 1907 and 1911). Richard assumes the untenable position that the only person who is capable of understanding religion is someone who is a firm believer.

It is now generally agreed that a sociologist who embarks on a study of religious phenomena must adopt agnostic procedures and should hold an open mind about the existence of superhuman forces (see ch. 28.2). A strong denial or strong affirmation about such forces or beings undermines a scientific approach. As Stanner has written:

It is plainly a mistake to allow enquiry to be ruled by the philosophical notion that religion or metaphysical objects do not exist. They *do* exist for many peoples under study and the facts of study are what they are because of that. To ignore it is to manipulate the facts illegitimately. (1966:viii)

Although Durkheim's scientism is to be rejected, his attempt to look at religious phenomena dispassionately and to reject apologetic extremisms has led to the development of the sociology of religion and to the acceptance of a method which has proved to be very valuable. As Le Bras said:

In a period when religion was only the subject of blind squabbling and frequently bitter passions for the majority of Frenchmen, Durkheim appeared advocating a scientific study of social facts, and even if all his conclusions could not command the assent of Christians, they were presented with calm and tact. (1966:53)

Georges Davy, not a Catholic as was Le Bras, saw that Durkheim's zeal as a prophet never prevented him making an objective

study, and in Davy's eyes an honourable study of religious phenomena and their permanent significance (1960:6).

2 The careful experiment

In accordance with the aims of science Durkheim wished to establish generalizations about religion and its place in the structure of
society. Such generalizations would have universal applicability,
irrespective of the type of religion and the society in which it was
found.

To create these universals it was necessary to examine carefully
a particular society, or in other words, in the spirit of science, to
undertake 'one well-conducted experiment' from which laws could
be deduced (593/415/144; see also 1901a(iii)(17):341). Such an
'experiment' stood at the heart of *Les Formes élémentaires*.
Indeed, it might be said that the book is a writing-up of the
experiment. Durkheim felt that to concentrate on one society and
focus on its religious institutions as a whole was a far superior
methodological procedure than to follow the one then in vogue,
the comparative method (133/94). It may well be, as we have
suggested, that Durkheim adopted this method from reading
Robertson Smith's book on the Semites (see ch. 4.2).

There can be little doubt that focusing on a particular society
in order to advance anthropological and sociological knowledge
became well established as a result of Durkheim's work. Of course
ethnographic studies existed before the time of Durkheim and
indeed he relied on them in his book, but what he attempted to
do was to go beyond the ethnographic and to derive from it
generalizations which heretofore had been sought only by the
comparative method. Durkheim thus rejects the method of such
anthropologists as Frazer and Tylor, who attempted to compare
particular elements in different societies and make generalizations
about those elements (1913a(ii)(11) and (12):96/t.1975a:178). Lévi-
Strauss states what is now perhaps a truism, namely, the method
of the one well-tried experiment avoids the pitfalls of the comparative method in extracting common elements from disparate societies and from such relatedness making deductions (1945:516).

Having postulated the need to explore the relations between

religious phenomena and other social phenomena within one society, the question arises what kind of society should be selected for the experiment? It is tempting to suggest that any society would do, in the same way as any piece of zinc or any portion of human tissue can be used in experiments in the natural sciences. But Durkheim seems to reject this openness. For his 'experiment' he deliberately sought a particular type of society, one totemic in organization, and for this purpose he settled for the Arunta of central Australia. He also turned to totemic groups in North America when evidence was lacking in that tribe. He selected such societies because he believed that they exhibited the most simple of social structures – structures devoid of accretions which accumulate in the course of development. In Durkheim's eyes the need was to select for experimental purposes the most basic type of society known to man. The simpler the structures, the easier it would be to draw generalizations. Thus, the 'experiment', the raw data, rests solely on ethnographical material about the Arunta and associated tribes which, at the time that he was writing, was becoming widely known to anthropologists through a number of field-workers such as Spencer and Gillen, Mrs Parker and Strehlow.

All seems set to proceed, but logical and commonsensical as these methodological assumptions appear, several criticisms and queries arise at the very outset. We select three of them.

(a) Is it that only one experiment is really necessary?
(b) Can universals be drawn from primitive religion?
(c) Was it necessary to employ a totemic group?

Durkheim claims that his conclusions are derived from one careful study. His reasoning is clearly in line with methods used in certain natural sciences. But has he judged aright? Surely no scientist would claim that just one experiment 'proves a law', especially an initial experiment. Rather, scientific certainty is derived from repeating similar experiments which produce similar results and so 'demonstrate' the law. And in more sophisticated Popperian analysis, experiments may be performed in order to try to falsify the law or to show under what conditions the law is or is not applicable. The point is that experiments can often go wrong, mistakes are made, freak results occur, calculations turn out to be inaccurate. These errors have to be eliminated before

103

one is sure that the experiment 'works'. In his assertion about the 'one well-conducted experiment' Durkheim assumes that it is well conducted, that no miscalculations have been made, that all alien factors have been accounted for or eliminated. Strangely enough, he does not ask for further experiments to be carried out, say with other tribes, or the experiment to be tested in a modern industrial society.

In this Durkheim exhibits a dogmatic pride. He presents a QED: his conclusions can be no other than they are. That he performed an experiment of the kind he did is totally acceptable: what is to be challenged is the notion that further experiments have no merit since, a priori, the outcome will be the same. The humility and caution of the great natural scientists in making their claims appear to be absent in Durkheim, whose intention it was to make sociology a science.

What worried many critics at the time was that Durkheim, in deriving conclusions which applied to religions as a whole, made his starting-point a primitive religion. He happily moved from the Arunta to Christianity, and thence to modern humanistic forms of religion derived from it. Here was the rub. It was unpalatable that one could compare in a positive way facets of a primitive religion with those of a most sophisticated religion, which often for the critics contained ultimate truth. The Catholic modernist philosopher, E. Le Roy, attacked Durkheim at this point in the famous 1913 debate (see 1913:94) and Loisy, also a Catholic modernist and a theologian, made a similar point in a critical review (1913:46). Loisy went further when he accused Durkheim of defining religion in terms of inferior religions and not the most developed religions. Such critics did not object to Durkheim studying primitive religions *per se* and making generalizations about them. This is a laudable practice. What is wrong is to cross the line and to state that what applied to one applied to all. What relates to the primitive has to stay with the primitive. Such limitations were completely contrary to Durkheim's overall intention. With no strong personal religious conviction, van Gennep held that it was wrong to make generalizations about religion – a continuing institution – from forms such as totemism, which have ceased to be or never were vital to the institution in question (1920:43).

Now, it should be said that unlike Tylor, Frazer and Spencer,

Durkheim did not despise the religion of 'inferior' societies; he neither denigrated it nor wrote it off as superstition and hocus-pocus. He had a reverence for all religion, including primitive religion (see ch. 23). For him it was not barbaric or stupid, but had an important and significant place in the lives of its practitioners. What people did had social purpose and meaning and this applied as much to those participating in primitive religion as it did to those involved in Christianity (see ch. 11). All religions are 'species of one and the same genus' (6/4/106). Durkheim wrote:

> Primitive religions are no less worthy of respect than any other. They answer the same necessities, they play the same role, they are subject to the same causes. Just as much as any other religions, they are able to demonstrate the nature of religious life and consequently help to resolve the problem that we intend to study. (4/3/104)

In one sense this begs the issue. It is a case of *petitio principii* (see Lukes 1972:31). In the book he sets out to make generalizations derived from primitive religions which apply to those of a more sophisticated kind, whereas in the quotations just mentioned he reads into primitive religions facets of more developed religions. It has been pointed out by Raymond Aron that Durkheim was able to leap from totemic religions to religions of salvation, from the simplest to the most developed, because he held that fundamentally all religion is the same in that it is society worshipping itself (1967b, 1:65; but see ch. 16).

It should, however, be pointed out that what Durkheim was trying to do in the opening of *The Elementary Forms* was not to propose a formal definition of religion, which was to come later, but to try to defend the soundness of his scientific procedure in focusing on a primitive society. He only wished to do one thing and that was to convince his readers that religion amongst primitive peoples had to be taken with as much seriousness as amongst societies in Europe. In order to make his point he used arguments which gave too much away. He might have warded off attacks, if he had made an appeal for a sympathetic understanding of the place of religion in primitive societies in the way in which he did in his extemporaneous speech in 1913 (1913b; see section 1 of this chapter). In his arguments to demonstrate the importance of primitive religions, one sees the search for something essential behind the phenomena. This inevitably gives rise to considerable philosophical and theological problems.

As we have just seen, there were those who criticized Durkheim not so much for leaping from primitive to developed religions as in defining religion in a way that suited primitive religion. To define it thus inevitably skews the final outcome. This is not really a serious charge and Durkheim categorically repudiated it face to face with his accusers (1913b:94). In so far as his final definition of religion is concerned, it applied equally to all religions and this he always said was a basic premise of establishing the definition (see ch. 9). He always admitted the variability of the content of religion in different societies (see Belot 1909:6). It worried him in his early attempt to delineate and define religion when external characteristics were the sole criterion. He therefore sought common characteristics beneath the surface.

Today anthropologists and sociologists are less keen to make the leap that Durkheim never thought twice about making. Thus, Stanner, in his work amongst Australian pre-literate societies – the very societies on which Durkheim based his arguments – said, and it seems he had Durkheim very much in mind, that he thought he ought to take an Aboriginal religion 'as significant in its own right' and not to use the study 'mainly to discover the extent to which it expressed or reflected facts and preoccupations of the social order' (1966:vi). Stanner's intention was to study the religion as it is and 'not as a mirror of something else' (ibid.). Further, he resisted the temptation 'to draw from the single instance any conclusions about all religion' (ibid.). In contrast to Durkheim, here is a case of science proceeding slowly and carefully accumulating data from various 'experiments' and so eventually reaching, it is hoped, the generalizations. Conclusions of wide applicability are not sought in haste.

It is assumed that one of the reasons why Durkheim sees religions as 'all species of the one and same' genus' (6/4/106) is that he is an evolutionist in the broad sense of the word, that is, he holds that social institutions develop in the course of time. As history proceeds, it produces within them accretions and complexities. There is thus continuity and change. It is true that a phenomenon can be studied in any of its forms, early or late, but in order to understand what is happening it is best to analyse it as the point of its basic structure. With such a general evolutionist approach, and drawing on the methods of biology, Durkheim held that basic structures were to be found in what is primitive – what is historically early. Thus, to see religion most clearly and in its essential components it is necessary to study it in its most simple, that is, its most primitive form, before it has been 'denatured' or dissected by 'studied' reflections as man tries to explain his own actions (9/7/108). In the selection of a totemic society Durkheim thought he had found the simplest and most basic social structures known to man – a society therefore which fulfilled his initial theoretical considerations. Not without good reason, he decided that the title of the book should include the phrase *les formes élémentaires* (see chs 4.3 and 5.3). The core of his argument rests precisely on these elementary totemic forms – what they are and what they mean. In a letter Durkheim wrote to Richard in 1899 he said: 'There are . . . a certain number of elementary notions (I do not say of logical simplicity) which dominate all man's moral evolution' (1928b:299 n.1). Here indeed is Durkheim's confession of evolutionism! In fact, according to Schmidt 'Durkheim revelled in the most orthodox forms of Evolutionism' (1931:116). Evans-Pritchard went too far in calling Durkheim 'an evolutionary fanatic' (1981:161).

When Marc Boegner challenged Durkheim as to whether or not the most rudimentary forms of religion revealed its essential elements, Durkheim, interestingly enough, defended himself in part by admitting the advantages in studying more advanced forms and said:

> I will go so far as to add that a certain knowledge of more advanced forms helps in understanding the simpler forms. It is, however, with these latter that research must first concern itself. (1919b:143/t.1975a:188)

One wonders what precisely the knowledge of more advanced forms was. Are there not signs in the hiddenness of what he is saying of some uncertainty? Is he not in fact reading into primitive religions a priori elements derived from religions of advanced societies?

Was it in fact necessary for Durkheim to employ data deliberately and exclusively of a totemic tribe? Talcott Parsons thought not (1937:411). He suggested that the ethnographic details were incidental to the general theoretical analysis of religion. In one sense he is right, because if the experiment threw up conclusions which have universal validity, any society in which there is a religious system would do to 'prove' them. That is an obvious scientific inference. Is not the whole enterprise thrown into jeopardy, if this principle is denied? Seger, in supporting Parsons and attacking critics, held that the Australian material was of little value and that *Les Formes élémentaires* could have been written 'without more than passing reference to Australian or any other primitive peoples' (1957:20). Seger apparently makes little distinction between a theory and its proof and would seem to subscribe to the contention that Durkheim's theories are self-evident or based on common sense.

Yet the fact remains that religions are open to great variability and it would appear that what one can deduce from a particular religion must also be variable, for certain facets of religion are absent in one religion but present in another. Durkheim could hardly have drawn the conclusions he did about ritual, had he chosen a modern western society, where the overriding religious system might be said to be that of humanism, what he called the cult of the individual (see ch. 26). Indeed, it seems that he deliberately avoided carrying out detailed studies of the religion of his day, save those in connection with suicide (see 1897a). Stanner strongly supports the idea that it is impossible to separate the subject-matter of the book from the details of the society studied. 'In the matter of aboriginal religion . . . the details are the very stuff of the "crucial" experiment' (Stanner 1967/ r.1975:301). 'The experiment is crucial to the theory' (ibid.).

Stanner's position is strengthened by the fact that Durkheim set his sights specifically on a society that had not been secularized, even in Durkheim's sense of the term (see ch. 24). It would seem that his intention was to choose a group in which religion was all-pervasive, that is, where its influence was at a maximum and at the same time to avoid societies where religions or world-views coexist, as in pluralism. There is therefore truth in the contention that Durkheim sought for his experiment a society characterized by mechanical solidarity, that is, by sameness of belief and action amongst its members, rather than one marked by organic solidarity, which may be said to be held together by a high level of division of labour (see 1893b). In the first type of society, as Durkheim had declared in his 1893 thesis, religious and social life are virtually synonymous (ibid.:143/169). While it is evident that in the notion of mechanical and organic solidarity Durkheim was referring to ideal types, nevertheless his choice of a totemic society was one in which he believed that the influence of religion was as great as that in any society known to man.

In the course of events Durkheim's choice was not the best for his purposes. Totemic societies are not the earliest known to man nor are they the simplest (see the following section). Van Gennep was not slow to make the point in reviewing *Les Formes élémentaires*: for him Australian societies were 'highly complex', not simple and primitive as Durkheim held (1913:389/t.1975:206; and 1920:42). One sees that in Durkheim's theoretical position there is a conflict – the search for what is structurally simple – some simple, primitive form; and at the same time wanting to find a society where religion is all-pervasive, encompassing the whole of a society's life. These demands may be contrary to one another. Where religion embraces the whole of society, it is more than likely on logical grounds, to be more complex than in cases where it touches only limited areas of life, as in a modern society in the throes of secularization. It is difficult to see how one can have it both ways. Perhaps it was that Durkheim held that in a society where religion was all-encompassing, its belief-systems would be simple and straightforward and its rituals easy to understand. This would seem almost to deny his fundamental position of entering sympathetically into the religious beliefs and practices of those whom the anthropologist is studying. The observer admits this in his heart, but with his mind he is sceptical and assumes that primitive religious systems are somewhat naïve, that is, elementary. They are simple to their intellectual reasoning and in what they are trying to achieve. Continual ethnographic and anthropological research today points to an opposite conclusion.

3 The issue of totemism

As Durkheim's earlier book on suicide (1897a) was based to a large extent on statistical material and is often seen to be a classic in the use of that kind of data, so his *Elementary Forms* is a classic in its exclusive and extensive use of ethnographical material related in the main to one tribe, the Arunta. Three-fifths of the chapters are devoted to such material.

Of the many issues raised by the publication of *Les Formes élémentaires*, the one which caused most debate amongst specialists in anthropology was Durkheim's use of ethnograpic material, and in particular his interpretation of totemic societies.[1] At the time he was writing, totemism was a key issue on which a vast amount of intellectual effort was expended. When Durkheim's book was published the dust was beginning to settle and totemism was ceasing to be *the* anthropological issue. An increasing quantity of ethnographic material came to light in the period from the late 1880s to the time just before the First World War. This challenged, amongst other things, evolutionary theories, which saw totemism as a crucial stage through which every society was believed to have passed, and which was held to be the earliest societal form known to modern man. Since that time totemism has become one subject amongst others. Most of the outstanding issues seem to have been laid to rest, not least by Lévi-Strauss in his small book published in the 1960s, *Le Totémisme aujourd'hui* (1962a; see also Poole 1969).

It is interesting to note that when Durkheim introduced a discussion on his then recently published book at a meeting of the Société Française de Philosophie, there was not one reference to the religious beliefs and practices of the Arunta made either by Durkheim or his interlocutors (1913b). It was in anthropological reviews that specific questions about totemism were raised by such academics as Goldenweiser, Malinowski, Schmidt and Radcliffe-Brown in correspondence with Durkheim (see Peristiany 1960; also ch. 5.4).

With the controversies over totemism now a matter of history, those who are drawn to read *Les Formes élémentaires* do so for insight and inspiration within the confines of the sociology of religion (or perhaps epistemology), and for the brilliance and interrelatedness of ideas of a theoretical kind, not for an accurate analysis of totemic material. Durkheim cannot be seen to be an authority on totemism, and today the subject stands within the province of a highly specialised anthropology. For these reasons totemism will not be dealt with here in detail, either in itself, or in connection with *Les Formes élémentaires*, except to offer a few general comments that might be of interest. Steven Lukes has made careful résumés of the issues which can be easily consulted (1972:454, 477–82, 520–9).

To summarize Durkheim's own position, it could be said that he saw in totemism a primitive and even *ab origine* principle of social life. As a type of social organization through which every society has passed, totemism was therefore a social logos (van Gennep 1913/t.1975). It was a religious system intimately linked with the social. In it, therefore, was not only a social but also a religious logos. Perhaps by accident, but more likely by design, he chose a type of society – a pantotemism – which suited his purposes excellently.

Stanner's contention is that after 1895 – after his 'conversion' – Durkheim turned to a study of totemism, for until then he had not seen it 'either as part of a social arrangement leading to religion or as the source of all religions' (1967/r.1975:281). To help him achieve the enormous task of mastering the mass of material which then was emerging on totemism, he was aided by his nephew, Marcel Mauss, who undoubtedly provided Durkheim with selections of materials used in *Les Formes élémentaires* (see Karady 1968:xxvii n.40). As we have seen, Durkheim also reviewed a large number of books and articles on the subject in the *Année sociologique* (see ch. 4.3; also the bibliography in Pickering 1975:311–13). Very shortly after the 1895 incident, Durkheim published as the first article of the first issue of the *Année sociologique*, 'La Prohibition de l'inceste et ses origines' (1898a(ii)). Durkheim used Australian totemism to maintain his argument that the totem is a god; that it is related to exogamy, which itself rests on the incest taboo. Clearly the article forms a prelude to the later book. By 1908 such had been his reading on totemism that he knew, he said, more about the primitive people of Australia than he did about Frenchmen (1908a(3)).

Durkheim, as an armchair anthropologist, in the company of Frazer, Tylor, McLennan, Hartland and many others, relied on the findings of missionaries, colonial administrators and professional ethnographers. There have been both good and bad armchair anthropologists. In which category was Durkheim? Did he perform his 'one well-conducted experiment' with care? To answer these questions one can only rely on the comments of experts, of those who were contemporaries of Durkheim as well as those who have continued to study totemism.

There is always the problem of the reliability of sources, of the accuracy of the observation of field-workers. Van Gennep, who himself wrote extensively on totemism, accused Durkheim of never once doubting the quality of the findings of others (1913:389/ t.1975:205). Goldenweiser made the same point (1915:723ff.). For van Gennep the materials available through the works of Howitt, Spencer and Gillen were full of errors and were not to be relied on. Ethnographically, he held, Australia like South America was a 'dark continent'. Van Gennep was scathing, stating that Durkheim had gone headlong into the Australian labyrinth where so many others, such as Lang and Schmidt, had lost their way (1913:389/t.1975:206). In van Gennep's doctoral thesis published in 1920, his attack was more sustained and detailed. One of the reasons why Durkheim failed to analyse totemism correctly was because of his doctrine of society being *sui generis*, which led him to see the totem as a god (1920:40–1). The point quite simply was that Durkheim was not *au courant* with the thought of anthropologists on totemism (ibid.:68).

There was the question of the legitimacy of deductions. Wilhelm Schmidt attacked Durkheim for making totemism his pantotemism – the source of religion and deducing religious ideas from totemism: totemism is related to magic (1931:117). Goldenweiser held that it was wrong for Durkheim to see individual totemism, a belief in guardian spirits, as being an extension of clan totemism (1915:725). He also held that when Durkheim could not find relevant material amongst the Australian aboriginals (for example, there was an absence of totemic tattooing), he readily fell back on North American data (ibid.:724). Evans-Pritchard, at a somewhat later date, criticized Durkheim for being wrong in seeing the clan as the corporate group; rather it is the horde or tribe (1965:65). And, Stanner, speaking with the authority of one who has done extensive research into Australian Aborigines, said that Durkheim showed misunderstanding of Australian tribes by falsely distinguishing the totemic clan from the local group or clan and by relying too much on evidence from central Australia (1967:225).

These brief examples, where 'Durkheim the anthropologist' lays himself open to criticism, should be balanced by those of an opposite kind where his work in connection with the Arunta is praised. Goldenweiser spoke warmly of his originality (1915:727).

112

And R. H. Lowie, critical of Durkheim at many points, gives him high marks for *The Elementary Forms*, which he says is 'the only comprehensive effort since Tylor's day to unify religious data from a wholly novel angle' so that methodologically it reveals 'considerable acumen' (1925:154). He summed up the work as 'a noteworthy mental exercise' and would rank it as a land mark 'if dialectic ingenuity sufficed to achieve greatness in empirical sciences' (ibid.:157). Malinowski also spoke well of Durkheim's use of ethnographic material (1913).

About ten years after Durkheim's death, Lloyd Warner spent three years in North-East Arnhem, west of the Gulf of Carpenteria, studying groups called Murngin. His task, it was said, was to rework Durkheim's theses by undertaking original field-work. His endeavours were greatly praised by Elkin (1937), himself an authority on Australian aboriginal ethnography. Elkin held that Durkheim showed great ability in analysing the ceremonial and social life of the Arunta from secondary sources and his conviction was substantiated by the findings of Warner. In passing, it might be noted that in *A Black Civilization* (1937), Warner showed himself to be no slavish follower of Durkheim. Citing his own work on the ritual of the Murngin, he was critical of Durkheim's definition of magic and held, in opposition to Durkheim, that it could not be separated from religion. He pressed his point by stating that magical activity amongst the Murngin possessed an organizational element akin to that of religion – a point he made in great detail in an article which he published a year earlier than the book (1936).

More recently Evans-Pritchard, despite the fact that he was an authority on certain African tribes, not Australian, wrote: 'I am convinced that no field study of totemism has excelled Durkheim's analysis' (1960:24). And more specifically:

> In his treatment of totemism he shows the total inadequacy of those who take the view . . . that it is to be explained in terms of utility, and he shows, I think, convincingly that the regard paid to the totemic creatures is both secondary and symbolic. (ibid.:18–19)

Yet Durkheim's analysis was inadequate, according to Evans-Pritchard. He never asked the question, what is totemism? And he wrongly thought that North American totemism (where the word 'totem' is found) is the same as that of central Australian tribes (1981:157ff.).

We have briefly presented evidence to show that authorities have been equally divided about Durkheim's use of the totemic material. Great criticism is balanced by great praise. Much of the weakness of his position arises from the assumptions that he made about totemism and, although we do not wish to enter into a detailed consideration of these, below is presented, in summary form, generally agreed conclusions about totemism which contradicted Durkheim's assumptions.

Totemism is a pattern of social organization, not a religion or form of religion.

Not all societies have gone through a phase of totemism.

The Arunta are not the most primitive tribe known to man.

Australian totemism is not typical of totemism as a whole.

Totemism is not always associated with clans.

Totemism is not the same throughout all aboriginal tribes in Australia and elsewhere.

Totemism and clan organization are highly complex (a society which has the most primitive material culture does not necessarily have a primitive system of social organization).

Members of a primitive society do not have such uniformity of thought as Durkheim imagined.

Durkheim implied incorrectly that primitive man cannot distinguish between many things which are clearly differentiated by modern man.

7 The sacred and the profane: the ground of religion

I Defining the two poles

1 Introduction

For Durkheim, at the heart of every religion stands the sacred. Religion rests on the simple fact that men from time immemorial and in all societies have given certain objects, people and ideas an inviolable status. Around such objects which constitute the domain of the sacred, religion functions through related systems of belief and ritual. In this sense, Durkheim gives a prior place to the sacred even over religion itself. This primacy appears not only in his definition of religion, which will be discussed in a following chapter, but in his analysis and aetiology of religion.

One of the consequences of making the sacred, which is an irreducible entity, the reality of religion is that religion is treated in a much wider context than it might otherwise have been, if, for example, the base were a belief in supernatural beings or the notion of the spiritual. There can be no doubt that Durkheim's strong adherence to the sacred and his development of the concept opened up new horizons in the realm of anthropology and sociology, which through the influence of the Année Sociologique school have had lasting consequences. Durkheim must be credited for much of the responsibility for encouraging scholars to assume and develop such an approach to religion. Some would go so far as to say that, forgetting all else he wrote, this was his greatest contribution to the discipline (for example, Lalande 1932, 2:722). There are others, on the other hand, who would challenge its value and would maintain that Durkheim's strongly reasoned but rigid position has been instrumental in holding back anthropological studies of religion, as Stanner has argued in his detailed appraisal of certain aspects of Durkheim's work (1967/r.1975:290).

However, one thing is quite clear: it is that no one before, or perhaps subsequently, has so systematically and rigorously applied the concept of the sacred to the whole area of religious and even social life. Praise continues to be accorded to Durkheim's power of logical development, but at the same time, as has often been said and as we wish to demonstrate, the term has proved difficult to handle in the way he envisaged it.

We shall only briefly point to the way Durkheim developed the concept in the early periods of his academic life. By contrast, it was Hubert and Mauss who worked more on the idea than did Durkheim (see Isambert 1976). They extended the notion of the sacred from the ideas of Robertson Smith, as in their essay on sacrifice (1899).

2 Durkheim's development of the notion of the sacred

For many years Durkheim struggled to produce a definition of religion required by his conceptualist approach to science and at the same time one that would fit coherently into his system of social thought (see ch. 9). He wanted to discover a satisfactory base to analyse religion scientifically and at the same time a base that delineated the essential elements of religion, or what one might call the reality of religion. From early times he rejected those definitions which were related to theories of naturalism and animism. But despite the problems of definition, he seems always to have accepted the validity of the concept of the sacred. He was hardly a pioneer in employing the term, for he was considerably influenced by Fustel de Coulanges who used it in analysing social life in the Roman Empire. Reading Robertson Smith in 1895 obviously confirmed his predilection for the term, although he was to go well beyond Robertson Smith's use in developing the sacred-profane dichotomy (see ch. 4.2). In 1899 in his essay 'Concerning the definition of religious phenomena' there were the first signs of his developing the concept systematically. Although he was convinced of the centrality of the sacred in religious and social life, he defined religion in that essay not in terms of sacredness but of obligation. This paper could well be called an early essay on the sacred. He refers to the primacy and independence of the sacred over gods; he saw ritual as the action-element of religion which was concerned with sacred things; he points to the irreducibility of the sacred and the fundamental place of the sacred-profane dichotomy in religious and social life, and so on. A good many of his theses on the sacred appear in this early paper. They were never denied subsequently: they were merely amplified.

The notion of the sacred, and with it the profane, began to appear in various contexts within articles, lectures and books which flowed from Durkheim's pen. We shall have occasion to refer amongst others to *Professional Ethics and Civic Morals* (1950a/t.1957a), which were lectures crystallized between 1898 and 1900; *Moral Education* (1925a/t.1961a), lectures given in 1902–3; 'The determination of moral facts' (1906b); and *The Elementary Forms of the Religious Life* (1912a/t.1915d). After some hesitancy Durkheim finally took the leap and logically developed his position by defining religion in terms of the sacred. Thus, the concept was accorded an irrevocable and final place in his analysis. When precisely this leap occurred is difficult to determine. The assertion of the centrality of the sacred to religion was not made officially public until the publication of *The Elementary Forms*, although, in his lectures of 1906–7, according to the report which has been handed down to us, he came very close to his finally established position (1907f; chs 5.2 and 9.5). It would seem that Durkheim slowly developed the concept and eventually shows its most fruitful application to the whole area of ritual (see chs 17 and 18).

3 Not the sacred but the sacred-profane

Yet Durkheim did not see the sacred as an isolated concept. It does not stand on its own nor is it unitary in the sense that suicide is unitary, for the sacred is to be understood, and only has meaning, by reason of its opposite, the profane. The sacred stands as one element in a dichotomous or binary system. In 1898 in the preface to the first volume of the *Année sociologique* he wrote:

> The true character of the Roman *sacer* is very difficult to grasp and, above all, to understand if one does not see it in relation to the Polynesian *taboo*. (1898a(i):ii/t.1960c:342)

And about the same time, in a series of lectures he was giving in Bordeaux on certain aspects of morality entitled 'Physique générale des moeurs et du droit' and in connection with the sacredness of property, he expanded the idea of the sacred as consisting of things set apart, and its opposite, the notion of taboo (1950a:172ff./t.1957a:143ff.). Thus here and elsewhere he compares a concept which emerged in classical European society with one of primitive society, removed very far from the first by space and perhaps time. By so doing, he creates difficulty rather than, as was his intention, eliminating it. However, in general usage Durkheim employs the dichotomy sacred-profane, which has Latin roots, rather than sacred-taboo. Durkheim claims that he uses the notion of taboo in order to understand the profane and therefore the sacred. Interestingly enough, Frazer also associated *sacer* with taboo.

But why does Durkheim feel forced to place the sacred within a bipartite division? There appear to be several reasons. One is purely empirical. Man views the world in this way – the facts are plain to see.

We have the impression of being in communication with two sorts of reality, which are distinct in themselves and are clearly separated from each other by a line of demarcation. On the one hand there is the world of profane things, and on the other hand that of sacred things. (304/212/131)

What man sees with his own eyes is therefore a duality and this duality of things sacred and things profane is the basis of all religious thought and organization. This Durkheim never ceased to proclaim (for example, 1899a(ii):19/t.1975a:90; 50/36/113).

But another reason does not relate so much to things as they are observed, but more to the way man thinks about things. 'This duality,' he says, 'is only the objective expression of that which exists in our *représentations*' (1899a(ii):19/t.1975a:90; see ch. 15). Basically, therefore, the division of things into the sacred and profane comes from man himself, from the way he thinks about the world. The dualism exists 'in his head'. Man has devised it. It comes to the individual from society and is, as it were, turned back on to society in order that man may understand it. Durkheim wrote:

118

Sacred things are those whose *représentations* society itself has fashioned. . . . Profane things, conversely, are those which each of us constructs from our own sense data and experience; the ideas we have about them have as their subject matter unadulterated, individual impressions, and that is why they do not have the same prestige in our eyes as the preceding ones. (ibid.:25/95)

Dichotomies and paradoxes abound in Durkheim's thought. They stemmed no doubt from his philosophical leanings towards Kant and neo-Kantianism, a school of philosophy which was dominant in France at the time. He somewhat startled his colleagues by his article 'Le Dualisme de la nature humaine et ses conditions sociales' (1914a) and a debate with academics on the same subject which he introduced himself (1913b). In these, he adopted a markedly metaphysical position about the nature of man, which was based on the traditional Jewish–Christian notion that man has a soul and a body. The dualism in a social direction is seeing man as *homo duplex*, who has two irreducible components – the social and the individual. This idea he first seems to have put forward in the early 1890s in his doctoral thesis – there are in man two *consciences*: one, common to, and derived from the group; the other, unique to the individual (1893b/1902b:99/t.1933b:129–30). But Durkheim later extended the idea that what man absorbs from the social (corresponding to the soul) is sacred and what is individual, what the individual develops of himself, corresponding to the body, is profane.

> The duality of our nature is thus only a particular case of that division of things into the sacred and the profane that is the foundation of all religions, and it must be explained on the basis of the same principles. (1914a/t.1960c: 335)

There is thus an extension of the primal duality, sacred-profane, to the constituent elements of man himself. Further, each pole in no matter which set is *qualitatively* different from the other related pole. Each collects around itself data of a contrasting kind. This is borne out by the words of the previous quotation: 'they constitute two kinds of intellectual phenomena'. And Durkheim gives the reason for this by stating that 'one type is produced by a single brain and a single mind, the other by a plurality of brains and

minds acting and reacting on each other' (1899a(ii):25–6/
t.1975a:95). The profane is associated with all that is individual:
the sacred with all that is collective. We can break down the
contrast further:

> Sacred things are those whose *représentation* society itself has
> fashioned; it includes all sorts of collective states, common
> traditions and emotions, feelings which have a relationship to
> objects of general interest, etc.; and all those elements are
> combined according to the appropriate laws of social
> mentality. (ibid.)

Profane things 'are those which each of us constructs from our
sense data and experience; the ideas we have about them have as
their subject-matter unadulterated, individual impressions' (ibid.).

Already we have had occasion to mention several dichotomies
which Durkheim used. His love of them caused him readily to
extend them and the extensions are implicitly based on logic or
experience. We set out the dichotomies that have so far emerged
and add to them others of the same family which are apparent in
his work in various places.

$$\frac{\text{sacred}}{\text{profane}} : \frac{\text{plurality of minds}}{\text{single minds}} : \frac{\text{collective } \textit{représentations}}{\text{individual } \textit{représentations}} :$$

$$\frac{\text{social activity}}{\text{isolated or individual activity}} : \frac{\text{'society'}}{\text{'individual'}} : \frac{\text{collective religious phenomena}}{\text{individual religious phenomena}} :$$

$$\frac{\text{spiritual}}{\text{temporal}} : \frac{\text{soul}}{\text{body}} : \frac{\text{culture}}{\text{nature}} : \frac{\text{'new' man religiously initiated}}{\text{'old' man remaining in the profane}} :$$

$$\frac{\text{mysterious}}{\text{intelligible}} : \frac{\text{irrational}^1}{\text{rational}}$$

Granet (1884–1940), a later disciple of Durkheim, held that the
basic duality had its origins in contrasting states of social life
(1930:290). The inference is that these states preceded the
dichotomy in time. Such states were: (1) in social gathering,
assembly and effervescence; and (2) at periods of social dispersion
and isolation. Quite clearly Granet is pointing to the social life of
the Arunta who ethnographically formed the foundation of *The*

Elementary Forms (see ch. 21.2). Although Granet is right in maintaining that Durkheim pointed to some socially structured base for the concepts – and the two seasonal periods in question were associated with the sacred and the profane – one doubts whether Durkheim received such inspiration from studying the Australian Aboriginals. Admittedly he was writing about the sacred-profane dichotomy in the mid-1890s, and before articles were published by the Année Sociologique school which dealt with Australian aboriginal material, for example, his article with M. Mauss, 'De Quelques formes primitives de classification', published in 1903. A monograph raising similar problems was that by M. Mauss and H. Beuchat, 'Essai sur les variations saisonnières des sociétés eskimos. Études de morphologie sociale', written in 1906. It is legitimate to argue that Durkheim's faith in dualities was strengthened by his acquaintance with the study of what he held was the most primitive type of society known to man, namely, totemism, which is based on a system of moieties and clans. What is doubtful is whether such material initiated in his mind the sacred-profane dichotomy.

But Granet's observation raises another problem. What comes first? The concept of the sacred and profane, or a dichotomous social organization which gives rise to the concepts? There are references in Durkheim which lead to contradictory answers. On the one hand, Durkheim's sociology of knowledge suggests that social structures generate concepts, *représentations* (see ch. 15); in other words, how man lives in society gives rise to the way in which he thinks about it. But on the other hand, the way man views nature and establishes social structure is in some measure determined by concepts he already has. This last position is borne out by the fact that the sacred-profane dichotomy cannot be reduced to something else, say, nature itself: it is not to be seen in terms of some *prior* mental structure, a *représentation*. It is something *sui generis*. In Durkheim's terms, the sacred-profane dichotomy has no point of reference beyond itself. How, then, are these two contradictory approaches to be resolved? As always, Durkheim is not concerned with historical origins. These can never be determined, since we have no record of the events that took place. Rather, man lives in a dynamic society which is understood in part by seeing the two movements acting dialectically. Social structure generates concepts: concepts generate social structure.

Mary Douglas has argued that the rigid separation of the sacred and the profane is 'a necessary step' in Durkheim's theory of social integration: 'it expressed the opposition between the individual and society' (1966:21; see ch. 10). But why was it a necessary step? Does one have to accept the sacred-profane dichotomy in order to have a theory of integration by which the individual is incorporated into society? Hardly so. The extension is necessary for Durkheim because he sees society as having the characteristics of the sacred, and, having started on the path of dichotomies and dualities, it is logically necessary to extend them. Socialization thus means not only the incorporation of the individual into society, but the embracing of the sacred by the individual – 'for a long time the initiation into sacred things was also the operation by which the socialization of the individual was completed' – by this means the individual became 'a new man' (1899a(ii):26/ t.1975a:96). Thus the sacred and the profane express 'in symbolic language the duality of the individual and the social' (ibid.). Man as a species becomes sacred, which in the long run means that individuals in some way become sacred. We have already noted that Durkheim categorically argued that man is a *homo duplex* by extending the notion of the soul (and reason) and the body (and passions) to the collective (and social) and the individual (and personal)(1914a/t.1960c:336ff.).

Commentators from Durkheim's time onwards have drawn attention to his association of the dichotomy of the sacred and the profane with that of the social and the individual. Goldenweiser (1915/r.1975:217) was quick to emphasize this, as was Durkheim's admirer and critic, Gustave Belot, who wrote of Durkheim's doctrine that it 'joins morality and religion, and opposes the sacredness of the social being with the bundle of trivia which have as their foundation the needs of individuals' (1913a:338). The relation of the individual to society is a dominant theme in classical sociology and few have been more concerned with it than Durkheim himself. It is quite clear that, in answer to the critics, the solution that he attempts is basically a religious one by extending the problem of the individual and society to the area of the sacred and the profane. Not long ago Thomas Luckmann strongly supported Durkheim's position in his book *The*

Invisible Religion, in seeing the necessity of expressing the human problem of socialization in religious terms (1963/t.1967/r.1970:26). However, the relation of these two basic dichotomies is complex. Mary Douglas, forced to take into account Durkheim's doctrine of man, has somewhat modified her earlier position and written: 'The dichotomy profane and sacred is not isomorphic with that between the individual and society' (1975:xiii). Rightly, she is opposed to a simple extension so frequently made by commentators, for example, Steven Lukes, who boldly states that the sacred-profane dichotomy is of the same order as other dichotomies, being derived from the individual and social dichotomy (1972:26). If the individual is equated with socialized man, and within the moral context, then the individual is himself sacred, having a status not far removed from that of God. Lukes and others only seem to be re-echoing what Durkheim himself wrote in the 1899 essay, 'Concerning the definition of religious phenomena'. Exactly at this time Durkheim also wrote about the sacred status of man and the individual in his apologia 'Individualism and the intellectuals' (1898c/t.1969/r.1973). One can marginally solve the problem by saying that when Durkheim speaks of the sacred and the profane extended to the social and the individual, he has at the back of his mind the primitive society where this dichotomy fits, as, for example, in his description of societies characterized by mechanical solidarity (see 1893b/t.1933b). Whereas, when he suggests that the individual is sacred, he is referring to a society marked by organic solidarity (ibid.) in which greater place is given to the individual and where individual freedom is fully recognized and given quasi-sacred status (see ch. 26). It may appear that Durkheim's sacred-profane dichotomy constitutes a duality based on static concepts. If they were intended to be so, then clearly Durkheim is in considerable difficulty in extending them to the social and the individual within a modern context. But even within primitive man, the consensus element of society – the social – is linked with the social element in the individual. Man as an individual can never be totally profane. Perhaps one should differentiate between a symbolic extension of the duality, as in the case of the social and the individual in general, and an ontological extension, where one is talking about man himself as being both sacred and profane. Durkheim does not spell out this distinction and the dichotomous extensions, although fascinating by their imaginative, logical connection, do not bear close examination unless one is prepared to introduce certain conditions and to differentiate them in the ways we have suggested.

It must be stressed that in Durkheim's thought two different sets of phenomena are polarized around the sacred and the profane, two different sets of ideas. As Durkheim was to write: 'sacred things differ from profane things in their very nature and . . . their essence is different' (54/42/118). He claims that 'always and everywhere' man has visualized the sacred and the profane as separate classes of objects – 'separate genera, two worlds which have nothing in common. The forces operating in the one are not simply those found in the other raised a few degrees; they are of a different order' (53/38/15). He seemed to find evidence for this in every religion he knew: in primitive societies, in Judaism, in Christianity, and in the Greek world as well (see 1938a/1969f:33, 322/t.1977a:25,281).

4 Basic meanings

Having opened up some of the basic problems which surround Durkheim's use of the sacred-profane dichotomy, we must retrace our steps and examine closely the meanings of the words. The point was first made in 1909 by Marett in his book *The Threshold of Religion* that the concepts sacred and profane have different meanings in French compared with their English counterparts. Since these terms are crucial, it is necessary to look at their meanings in the different languages.

Latin roots

Both sacred and *sacré* are derived from the Latin *sacer*, which means holy or consecrated. But it can also mean accursed or horrible, as something devoted to a divinity for destruction, and hence criminal, impious, wicked, infamous. (Lewis and Short, *A Latin Dictionary*, 1969 edn)

Profanus literally means before or outside the temple (*profanum*). By derivation, it means that which is not sacred, or

The Sacred and the Profane I

consecrated, thus it implies unholy, common, profane: by transference, wicked, impious, unlearned, ignorant.

The French sacré and profane

Three meanings are to be distinguished for the word *sacré*:

1 holy, consecrated, as in a holy place, sacred art;
2 inviolable – that which cannot be broken – as in *'mon devoir sacré'* (my bounden duty);
3 damned, cursed, profane, bloody: *'Votre sacré chien'* (your damned dog); in this sense, an ambiguous one, the adjective is always placed before the noun.

Profane is more complex. The verb *profaner* means to profane or desecrate (a church), to violate (a grave) and to misuse (one's talents). The adjective can mean:

1(a) profane in the sense of secular (history, music);
1(b) unhallowed, ungodly;
1(c) impious, sacrilegious;
2(a) uninitiated person, outsider, layman;
2(b) an ecclesiastical person outside the fold;
2(c) an irreverent or ungodly person.

(*Harrap's New Standard French and English Dictionary*, 1972)

English meanings

The Oxford Dictionary (1933) offers five meanings of the word sacred:

1 consecrated to (a deity); dedicated, set apart (to some person);
2 of things, places, persons, set apart for or dedicated to some religious purpose; to various animals and plants that have been considered sacred to certain deities;
3 as an epithet to royalty;
4 secured by religious sentiment, reverence, sense of justice etc., against violation in encroachment; of a person or his office sacrosanct, inviolable;
5 accursed (from Latin *sacer*) (now rare).

The verb profane means to desecrate, violate, misuse, or (rare) to blaspheme. The adjective implies:

125

1 pertaining to the sacred or biblical, that is, secular, lay, common; as opposed to ecclesiastical; also of persons, not initiated, therefore uninitiated, lay, Philistine;
2 applied to things or people regarded as unholy, or as desecrating what is holy or sacred; unhallowed, ritually unclean or polluted, especially the rites of an alien religion;
3 characterized by disregard or contempt of sacred things, especially taking God's name in vain, irreverent, blasphemous, impious, irreligious.

Durkheim's meanings

What did Durkheim imply by the sacred? He focuses on a meaning that is common in all three languages – that which is consecrated or holy. In one place he writes of the sacred as that which is set apart (1906b/1924a:103/t.1953b:70) – that which society holds in its highest esteem which is not to be challenged or desecrated. In another place, sacred things are said to be 'invested with a particular dignity that raises them above our empirical individuality, and that confers upon them a sort of transcendent reality' (1925a:11/t.1961a/r.1975:197).

And what of the profane? Here Durkheim is far less precise. The profane is that which threatens, undermines or abolishes the sacred, 'destroys its essential attributes' (1906b/1924a:103/t.1953b:70). It is therefore negatively defined in relation to the sacred. This approach raises many problems which will be considered in the pages ahead as well as those associated with the concept of the sacred.

5 The sacred's own binary system

Durkheim begins his task of analysing religion by focusing on what he holds is a rigid, universal binary system – the sacred and the profane. But as he proceeds he is forced to modify such a clear bipartite approach for the reason that one pole contains its own binary system. The sacred is not 'one' but 'two'. Durkheim develops this idea in a complex passage (584ff./409ff.) where he refers to Robertson Smith as originally observing the ambiguity of the sacred itself. Durkheim argues that two kinds of religious forces exist:

1 beneficent powers or forces, impersonal or diffused, anthropo-morphic, protectors, gods, holy places, inspiring love and grati-tude (we would call these benevolent and 'pure' forces);
2 evil or impure powers, productive of disorder, death, sickness, for example, corpses, menstrual blood (by contrast, we would call these malevolent and impure forces).

As would be expected, each is opposed to the other – one forbids the other – each is locked in a radical antagonism – and 'thus the whole religious life gravitates about two contrary poles between which there is the same opposition as between the pure and the impure, the saintly and the sacrilegious, the divine and the diabolic' (586/410).

Durkheim reminds us, however, that these two poles are not those of the sacred and the profane. Each component of the sacred stands opposed to the profane as the following excerpt makes clear:

> But at the same time as these two aspects of the religious life are opposed to one another, there exists a strong bond between them. Firstly, both the aspects maintain the same relation with profane beings: they [profane beings] must abstain from every contact with impure beings just as from very holy things. The first [impure things] are no less forbidden than the second [very holy things]; they are equally withdrawn from circulation. This is to say that they [impure things] too are sacred. Doubtless the sentiments which the two inspire are not identical; respect is one thing; disgust and horror another. However, in order that the movements be the same in both cases, it is essential that the sentiments expressed do not differ in nature. And in effect, there is horror in religious respect, above all, when it is very intense, and the fear inspired by malign powers is not as a rule without some elements of reverence. (ibid.)

Lalande is right in observing that within the duality of the sacred, what is sacred can come from opposite kinds of forces. For example, what is sacred can be created as much by purity and pure things as by impurity and impure things (1932, 2:722). Durkheim's position about the sacred can be expressed diagrammatically:

$$
\left.
\begin{array}{l}
\begin{array}{ccccc}
\text{Pure} & & \text{beneficent} & \text{collective} & \text{reverence/} \\
\text{things} & - & \text{powers} & - \;\; \text{well-being} \;\; - & \text{fear}
\end{array} \;\; - \;\; \text{joy(?)} \\[2em]
\begin{array}{ccccc}
\text{Impure} & & \text{malevolent} & \text{collective} & \text{fear/} \\
\text{things} & - & \text{powers} & - \;\; \text{ill-being} \;\; - & \text{reverence}
\end{array} \;\; - \;\; \text{dejection (?)}
\end{array}
\right\} \text{Sacred}
$$

In passing we should note that Durkheim posits a similar duality within the sphere of morality, and indeed said that the dualities were of the same order. What man calls morality contains positive and negative elements – those which point to the good, which are to be loved and sought after, and elements which relate to the forbidden, to evil, to that which is not to be violated (1906b/ 1924a:53/t.1953b:36).

The dichotomy within the sacred itself is difficult for the Englishman to grasp, for the common usage of the word sacred does not usually imply malevolent beings, or the concept of the impure. Such ideas and phenomena lie within the sphere not of the sacred but the profane (see the basic meanings given above). At the same time we should be reminded of the meaning of the French word *sacré*, which of course does permit the dichotomy and which no doubt forced Durkheim to take the path he did. As Marett said: '*L'idée du sacré* may be appropriate enough in French, since *sacré* can stand either for "holy" or for "damned"; but it is an abuse of the English language to speak of "sacredness" of some accursed wizard' (1914:110). The best example for the Englishman of what Durkheim meant is to be found in the notion of good and bad angels: both are sacred, yet one stands in opposition to the other.

Theoretically there seems to be no problem for Durkheim. Benevolent and malevolent beings, the pure and the impure, are not separate classes (genera) but two separate and opposed subclasses (species) within the class called sacred (588/411). He offers the example of menstrual blood. It is sacred. On occasions it can be used for healing, yet it is basically impure (ibid.).

Robertson Smith never explained the ambiguity within the sacred. Durkheim was perplexed by it and raised the question of how it was that evil forces have great power. Why are evil forces religious in nature? It was a particular problem for him in the light of his analysis of religion because, first, religion (the sacred) is a force in society, perhaps the most powerful force, and second, as we shall see, religion is 'created' by society (see chs 14, and 3), the overall existence of religion is for the good of society. Why should a society create forces which threaten its destruction? Such forces are an enemy to Durkheim's logic. He observed that the threat of evil is removed by piacular rites (589/412; see ch. 18). In these rites the deity is placated. Evil beings are projected in such rites as collective states about suffering in society. When suffering and misfortune befall a society, the members interpret the events as caused by beings outside the society. Piacular rites seek to appease such beings and therefore alleviate social suffering, in some cases, through vicarious human suffering. Thus religion by such anti-social collective *représentations* is able to deal with social miseries, be they short-lived or continual. Durkheim solves his dilemma at the price of a somewhat crude theory of origins, not far removed from those of Tylor and Müller which he so readily rejected. He says that religion consists *inter alia* of collective *représentations* about the ultimate welfare of a society including *représentations* which appear to threaten it. Evil *représentations* are dealt with by religion in being able to neutralize them. Thus these *représentations* are created by society – by religion – so that religion creates evil powers and at the same time provides a system to defuse them or at least control them. In general terms, this may be acceptable. What is to be challenged is Durkheim's arguments within his own system.

1 He postulates that malevolent powers are collective *représentations* of suffering which are only incidental and are briefly treated compared with his search for theories about other aspects of religion which are dealt with at length.
2 What he in fact is suggesting is that religion is based on a conceptualization of 'natural' events which are a threat to society and the individual.

If this is so, then what is at the heart of Durkheim's system is really a theodicy and religion thus becomes a means of overcoming suffering in its various forms. He rejects one theory of naturism (Müller's), only to accept implicitly another, or at least to suggest that really the base of religion is suffering. It is an inevitable conclusion of Durkheim's concept of the duality of the sacred.

6 The origin and constitution of the sacred: the stamp of society

As we have noted, the dichotomy between the sacred and the profane has parallels with, and perhaps its origins in, the contrast between community or gathered life, on the one hand, and individual or separated life, on the other. However, this fact by itself – the social structuralist origin of the dichotomy – hardly accounts for the qualities and characteristics of what constitutes the sacred *per se*, or why certain objects, words, people, actions and so on, become set apart and receive unique and inviolable status. The sacred for Durkheim seems to appear mysteriously with the selection of certain things as being categorized as sacred. From individual objects the notion of the sacred is extended to classes of similar objects, from objects to persons, to ideas, to ideals. Finally, there emerges the domain or kingdom of the sacred which includes all that is sacred and becomes an almost abstract entity (50/36/113).

Is what is sacred due to a natural feeling of awe about the thing or person in question? At a time when so much ethnographic material was being collected both in terms of artefacts and ways of living, there was an understandable tendency to account for such strange phenomena as being endowed with awe. Durkheim was one of the first to question this as a satisfactory explanation. Earlier, Robertson Smith had suggested objects were deemed to be sacred quite simply because their 'natural' qualities were inherently mysterious or useful (1889/1894:165ff.). In other words sacredness is determined according to 'naturalism' or utilitarianism. The argument against such an explanation, Durkheim held, rests on the fact that what constitutes the sacred varies from society to society. No two societies agree on its content, even where the societies are contiguous. Van Gennep adopted a similar position: the sacred is not absolute, for it is brought into play as a result of particular circumstances (1909/t.1960:12–13). Confirmation that naturalism or utilitarianism had to be rejected as a basis for what is sacred came in particular from Durkheim's study of totemism. Certain animals which were held to be sacred were not necessarily the most magnificent or superior of creatures. It was the insignificant ones which were worshipped, for example, the ant.

Thus, there exists no alternative but to see that what constitutes the sacred is relative, and from this it may be deduced that no one item is universally held to be of this category. Each society creates what is specifically sacred without any necessary recognition or awareness of what it is in other societies, or of its own inherent qualities. Such relativism creates problems in defining religion, for religion so delineated rests on a concept not on a thing, person, or god which has concrete form. In one sense anything can stand for the sacred and therefore anything can be 'religion' or 'religious'. In this way, the sacred and religion have no boundaries. But on the other hand, the acceptance of a thoroughgoing relativism completely undermines any explanation that might be based upon naturalistic or utilitarian grounds (327/339/138; see also 1913a(ii)(11) and (12)/t.1975a:178–9).

The sacred is therefore that which is decided by society. Associated with each sacred item or class of items there is a *représentation* – an idea or ideal that is supported collectively (see ch. 15). Durkheim writes in his article on the dualism of human nature and its social conditions: 'Sacred things are simply collective ideals that have fixed themselves on material objects' (1914a/t.1960c:335). This association of the sacred with *représentations collectives* Durkheim made on a number of occasions, starting with his early essay on defining religion where an empirical *représentation* is contrasted with that associated with the sacred, which is based on tradition, for which man has a special respect (1899a(ii):19/t.1975a:90). Thus sacredness has as its basis a mental concept which is not dependent on the natural or utilitarian properties of the thing, idea or person which is held to be sacred. It means that the key lies in the ideas and values which are at the basis of society and which are collectively expressed by its *représentations*.

A *représentation* is an idea or concept: it is a way of thinking about an object (see ch. 15). In *The Elementary Forms*, Durkheim spoke of the sacred character of something being superadded or superimposed (*surajouter, superposer*) on it: quite simply one might say, stamped upon it (328/229/138; 602/421/150). But who does the stamping? There can be only one answer – society. As always society is Durkheim's *deus ex machina*. He is right in suggesting that the original cause – the historic moment of decision – can seldom if ever be discovered. All one can say is that it happened

131

within the context of a society and with its approval and acceptance. The reasons for the setting apart and stamping what is specifically sacred or holy may seem to modern western eyes as being irrational rather than rational. But the individual social object is integrated within the sacred complex and is part of the total ideology of the society. Society alone has the right of imprimatur. These sentiments Durkheim frequently repeats, as for example when he writes: 'Society alone is the originator of such apotheoses' – apotheoses where people are raised through *représentations* to the level of a saint or god (304/212–13/131). The sacred cannot have a supra-social origin. There is no higher power than the social in Durkheim's eyes. If certain items are sacred, beyond a geographical or social boundary, this is because social ideas are liable to spread. Durkheim strongly supports a diffusionist approach at this point (609/427/155).

Durkheim's position is relativist in the matter of the content of the sacred. It means that the content can also change with time and can 'be acquired and lost' (Stanner 1967/r.1975:295). This is clearly in accordance with the facts. What was sacred yesterday may be less sacred today, and tomorrow totally desacralized. In speaking about the challenge of science to religion, Durkheim said that religion constituted a reality that could not be dissolved by science because religion is based on the sacred and the sacred is never dissolved – it is continually coming into existence (1909a(1); ch. 25). But to follow Durkheim to this further step means accepting the eternality of both the *concept* of the sacred and the existence of a meaningful content. Can it be said that the sacred exists in every society, whether or not the members of the society accept the concept and irrespective of the presence of sacred things within their society?

To Durkheim the answer to these questions must be an unhesitating yes. Every society is based on collective *représentations* and the sacred is not just *a* collective *représentation*, the sacred is the symbol of the collective entity. Society itself is summarized in the sacred. The *représentation* of the sacred becomes 'personified in the form of God and of every kind of sacred being' (1950a:133/ t.1957a:112). When man worships God he is in some sense worshipping the collective entity: what he offers 'to the imaginary beings of religion' he is offering to society as a whole (ibid.). Hence the sacred is the collective *représentation par excellence*.

This problem of the close relation between religion and society is dealt with in later chapters (see chs 12–14). For the moment the point we wish to make is that the logic of Durkheim's thought is such that in every society the sacred exists of necessity and in a concrete form.

7 The profane

And so to the other pole of the dichotomy, what does Durkheim mean by the profane? On this point he is obscure. He never defines the profane in the positive way he defines the sacred. Let us take one possibility suggested by English usage, the sacrilegious – an example of the profane if ever there was one. Yet Durkheim says 'the sacrilegious person is merely someone profane who has been infected with a benevolent force' (587/410). Again, as we have already noted, the sacrilegious is really part of the holy, for the saint and the sacrilegious person are part of the sub-binary system. And to clinch it, we offer a further example.

> Satan is an essential part of the Christian system; he may be an impure being but he is not a profane being. The anti-god is a god, inferior and subordinate it is true, yet he is endowed with extensive powers. He is even the object of rites, of negative ones at least. (601/420–1/149)

In the absence of a precise definition, we list some of the observations or characteristics that Durkheim noted about the profane.

1 It is the reverse or opposite of the sacred, in quality as well as degree (1899a(ii):19/t.1975a:90). It threatens the very existence of the sacred by mixture or touch; it destroys the essential attributes of the sacred (1906b/1924a:103/t.1953b:70).
2 Work is an 'eminent form of profane activity: it has no other apparent end than to provide for the temporal necessities of life; it puts us in relations with ordinary things only' (439/307).
3 Women and children in certain circumstances are profane persons (543/380).
4 It stands apart from the serious side of life – it is outside *la*

vie sérieuse (see ch. 19.1). 'The simple merry-making, the profane corroboree, has no serious object' (548/383). Durkheim also refers to the same corroboree as '*vulgaire, simple réjouissance publique*' (an ordinary, simple public act of rejoicing) (544/380).

5 In contrast to sacred things which are associated with *représentations collectives*, profane things are 'those which each of us constructs from our own sense data and experience; the ideas we have about them have as their subject-matter unadulterated individual impression, which have a relatively low prestige compared to sacred things' (1899a(ii):25–6/t.1975a:95).

6 Durkheim often refers to *les êtres profanes* (profane beings) (586/410), but nowhere does he offer an example.

7 There are a number of occasions where Durkheim implies that it approximates to the ordinary: for example, '. . . that so sacred a food may be eaten by ordinary profane persons (*par de simples profanes*)' (483/338). By implication the ordinary is profane or within the orbit of the profane. 'A man cannot enter into intimate relations with sacred things except after ridding himself of all that is profane in him. He cannot lead a religious life of even a slight intensity unless he commences by withdrawing more or less completely from the temporal (*temporelle*) life' (441–2/309). In the same paragraph there are parallel ideas about man approaching the sacred by detaching himself from base (*basses*) and trivial (*triviales*) matters which debase his nature.

8 The human body is held to be profane, as well as everything man sees as related to the body, such as sensations and sensory appetites (1914a/t.1960c:334). Man clings to his instinctual and profane nature, for 'we hold to the profane world by all the fibres of our flesh; our senses attach us to it; our life depends on it. It is not merely the natural theatre of our activity; it penetrates from every side; it is part of ourselves' (446/312). Durkheim praises Christianity for its asceticism and refers to the necessity of such asceticism for the very existence of society (452/316; see ch. 23.3). It was an observation and message that he had already proclaimed in his much earlier book *Suicide* (for example, 1897a:275/t.1951a:248).

9 Certain foods are profane, as well as matter and material

things in general (434/303). In fact, matter is 'the profane *par excellence*' (613/429/159).

10 Similarly any discipline which deals with matter must also be profane, as indeed science is, at least, says Durkheim, in the eyes of the Christian (53 n.1/39 n.1/162 n.11). Because its profane effect was clearly grasped, science was at first prevented from studying the sacred. Formerly, of course, science itself was sacred when, for example, priests were the first mathematicians and astronomers (1922a:64/t.1956a:96).

Here are some of the characteristics and effects which Durkheim associates with the profane. The list is by no means complete, but in what has been given great diversity is apparent. It has been noted that while the profane would at first sight include the impure, Durkheim in his discussion of purity and impurity would make these two categories stand within the sacred as part of the subsystem and not within the category of the profane. It should also be observed that in dealing with the profane Durkheim is not as rigidly relativist as he is in referring to the sacred. Certain categories would appear to transcend given societies to a degree that approaches the universal, for example, matter and science are by implication widely accepted as being profane. The profane in its concrete form thus appears to have a higher degree of universality than does the sacred.

Stanner, in his article on Durkheim's analysis of religion written in 1967, holds that the profane is the weaker of the concepts within the dichotomy of the sacred and the profane (1967/ r.1975:291). Few would quarrel with this. In an attempt to bring some order within the confusion of meanings Durkheim attached to the profane, he maintained that there were four basic meanings: commonness (as in work), minor sacredness, non-sacredness and anti-sacredness (the power to destroy the sacred) (ibid.:293). Because Stanner does not consider the sacred as such, he tends to include in these four groupings the minor sacred which is hardly, in Durkheim's terms, part of the profane. Durkheim readily admitted to there being 'many degrees of sacred things' (52/38/115). Nowhere does Durkheim openly declare there are degrees of profane things or that the sacred tails off into the profane, and one wonders if it is legitimate to make the extension that Stanner does. In the end he has to admit that his attempts to redeem the situation do not work and holds that such divergent characteristics cannot form a class, since the objects and ideas have so little in common. Again, with that, there can be no disagreement.

In his early writings, as we have noted, Durkheim wedded *sacer* with taboo in order to see more thoroughly the nature of the sacred. The bastard pair did not create a fruitful relationship. In the course of events Durkheim failed to develop the concept of taboo or apply it extensively in *The Elementary Forms* (but see 428/300). He used the term in his essay on the prohibition of incest (1898a(ii)) and slightly more frequently in his study of property in primitive societies in *Professional Ethics and Civic Morals* (1950a:170–1/t.1957a:143–4). There can be no doubt that the concept is useful with regard to physical things and therefore to property, and under certain circumstances, to people. However, there are limitations and ambiguity of meaning – taboo is usually taken to imply that which is forbidden or set apart – and, as a term is only found among the Polynesians and Melanesians. It is very seldom used by anthropologists today as an analytical concept. The efforts of Marett in *The Threshold of Religion* (1914) to link taboo with other ethnographical terms such as wakanda, orenda and mana, have had no lasting results.

Durkheim preferred the term interdict or prohibition to that of taboo – terms which he held were roughly synonyms. The sacred is surrounded by its laws and interdicts and these help to define the sacred: they also prevent the penetration of the profane. They are the protectors of the sacred to ensure that it is not vitiated by that which seeks to annihilate it. All this can be accepted, but we are still left with the problem of what constitutes the profane. If the interdicts are not equal to the profane and stand as insulators, from what precisely are they insulating the sacred?

8 Trying to deal with the profane

One tempting and, at first sight, obvious way of overcoming the dilemma is to make Durkheim's concept of the profane mean the ordinary, the everyday, that which pertains to the workaday world. Giddens (1971:107) and Towler (1974:63) see no difficulty at all in taking this step. They feel justified no doubt in focusing on one of the meanings of the French word *profane*. This is an attractive way out of the dilemma, but it raises difficulties if one wishes to remain within the corpus of Durkheimian thought.

To make profane equivalent to mundane is to give to the concept the idea of what is neutral, what is indifferent, what is secular. But the English word profane generally means something stronger, not areligious but anti-religious, not indifferent but irreverent, not neutral but ritually polluted. Thus the temple of God is 'profaned' by admitting foreigners into it (Ezekiel 44.7). The profane only has meaning with regard to its opposite, the sacred. In this sense it is near the French *profane*, and if the notion of the sacred is weak, so is that of the profane, and vice versa. In modern English usage there is a tendency to contrast the religious, not with the profane, but with the secular. Here is a decided shift due to a loss of the sense of the sacred and with it a loss of the idea of pollution. The secular or mundane implies something less active, less vigorous. It stands for neutrality, for disregard of and indifference to religion, and as such is not likely to bring about a loss of what is essential in religion. The French word *séculariser* is no substitute for *profane* because of its special anti-clerical meaning, although at times it may come near to it (see ch. 24 n.1). While the notion of mundane or secular is implicit in Durkheim's concept of the profane, it unwarrantably limits it, for it cannot contain other notions which we have already listed.

Perhaps it is easier to see the profane as a residual term. Thus, all that is not sacred is profane, and as we noticed earlier, Durkheim always wishes to define the profane as the opposite of the sacred. There are severe problems, however, in such an approach. One is the theoretical issue of whether or not a residuum can be said to be part of a binary system. Since the residuum does not have any well-defined characteristic, can it in any sense be seen as an opposite force against which it stands? And further, can a residual entity have any value in terms of analysis? What is left over is so vast, if one may use quantitative terms, or so diverse qualitatively that generalizations about it are never adequate, or else may contain in itself contradictory elements. The residual category in the end is like so much slag. It is practically worthless with regard to the end product and is therefore best dispensed with or used for some other purpose. This is a perennial problem with all residual categories within the social sciences.

Stanner's position is that although the profane can be seen to be a residual category, nevertheless it does contain a number of characteristics, vague though they may be. Stanner has observed from his field-work that certain objects do not fit into Durkheim's notion of the sacred nor into that of the profane, even if the profane is vaguely but positively defined (1967/r.1975:291). He found amongst the Australian Aborigines that certain objects, manufactured objects, which had utilitarian or symbolic value could not be readily placed in one category or the other. When these objects came into contact with the sacred, 'nothing happened', that is, they were not made sacred and they did not bring about desacralization. Thus within the general category of profane as defined by Durkheim he found that there were forces or objects, some of which were active and some of which were completely neutral with regard to the sacred. Thus, to put all non-sacred objects into the profane seems quite unwarrantable.

Stanner holds that the best way out of the problems posed by Durkheim's concept of the profane is to posit a third category, the mundane, the ordinary, the everyday. He believes that this not only helps to neutralize criticism against Durkheim, but is empirically justifiable and necessary. But to argue, as he does, that Durkheim implicitly admitted a third category based on the concept of the mundane is not a justified inference of what we know of Durkheim's thought (ibid.:292). It may be that Durkheim sensed some difficulty in applying the terms *sacré* and *profane* in concrete cases and that there are several instances where Durkheim sees the profane in terms of the mundane, as we have noted. There is simply no evidence at all to suggest that he would have introduced a third category and extended the dichotomy to a trichotomy. Indeed, in the last analysis Stanner seems to find that the employment of a tripartite system is not in keeping with Durkheim's thought (ibid.:294).

Stanner is probably the first person to have drawn attention to the possibility that Durkheim may have implied an internal dichotomy within the profane, parallel to that within the sacred. Referring to an aside in *The Elementary Forms* that the ambiguity of the sacred, that is, its own dichotomy, could be applied to other areas (592/413–4), Stanner suggests that there might be within

Durkheim's system 'an ennobling and a vulgarizing profane' (1967/ r.1975:294). If this were so, there would then emerge a 2–2 system:

$$\frac{\text{(propitiously) sacred } +}{\text{(unpropitiously) sacred } -} : \frac{\text{(propitiously) profane } +}{\text{(unpropitiously) profane } -}$$

Inevitably the problem arises of distinguishing empirically, 'sacred −' from 'profane +'. And indeed there are cases in Durkheim's analysis where the two seem to be very close, as in Durkheim's designation of the 'less sacred'. Given this dilemma, it is tempting to rewrite the equation in the form of a continuum. At one end there would be the propitiously sacred and at the other the unpropitiously profane. But such a solution is impermissible because of the exclusiveness and logical chasm associated with all dualisms. Durkheim's thought does not permit such continua.

Stanner admits that any notion of a dichotomy within the profane is conjecture, but adds that 'some of the problems of the dichotomy (sacred-profane) would be easier to unravel if that had been his meaning' (1967/r.1975:295). This may be so at one level, but as in the case of the suggested trichotomy, the problem that emerges within a Durkheimian framework is to work out the inner relationships between the various poles, be they based on a system of three or a system of four. But at least Durkheim's bipartite division permits a fairly straightforward analysis of the relation between the poles.

Before we turn to that relation, we would finally note Stanner's contribution at the empirical level. One advantage in proposing a category designated by the mundane is that when sacred things lose their sacredness, they revert to the ordinary, the commonplace. It is necessary when applied to ideas, for before they become profane they have to pass through the area of the mundane (1967/r.1975:296). This is an appeal to introduce dynamic terms of human interaction within the sphere of the sacred. Stanner states that strained static terms are not acceptable in empirical research and these are precisely what are contained in Durkheim's dichotomy. Just to add a third category, the mundane, does not detract from what are basically 'static, categorical forms'.

8 The sacred and the profane: the ground of religion

II The relations between them: further analysis

1 The relation between the sacred and the profane

For Durkheim the two categories, the sacred and the profane, are in watertight compartments, rigidly contained, and absolutely separated. In 1906 he wrote:

> The sacred . . . cannot, without losing its nature, be mixed with the profane. Any mixture, or even contact, *profanes* it, that is to say, destroys its essential attributes. But this separation does not leave the two orders of being that have been separated upon the same level. We see this from the solution of continuity that exists between the sacred and the profane. There is between them no common measure, they are heterogeneous and incommensurable; the value of the sacred cannot be compared with that of the profane. (1906b/ 1924a:103/t.1953b:70)

And in *The Elementary Forms*: 'They repel and contradict one another so forcibly that the mind refuses to think of them at the same time. They mutually exclude each other from the *conscience*' (342/239/143). Can Durkheim make his position any clearer when he writes:

> This heterogeneity is enough to characterize the classification of things and to distinguish it from all others because it is very special: it is *absolute*. In the history of human thought there exists no other example of two categories of things so fundamentally differentiated and so radically contrasted to each other. (53/38/115; see also 453ff./317ff.)

140

He also used other terms to express the relation, such as antagonistic, hostile and jealous, abyss, logical chasm.

What Durkheim means by the sacred and the way in which the concept is used becomes very apparent in his analysis of ritual (1912a: Book III). Early in his writings, he defined ritual – 'the action component of religion' – as 'the totality of practices concerned with *sacred things*' (1899a(ii):16/t.1975a:88). Such practices have the sacred as their subject or object, and both action and belief within the realm of the sacred are in some measure dependent on each other (see ch. 20).

As always, sacred things are completely separated from the profane, but the separation is enforced and maintained by ritual in the form of negative rites which are interdictions, taboos, ascetical practices and so on (427ff./299ff.). The various forms which these take ensure physical and symbolic separation between the sacred and that which would profane it. 'The religious life and the profane life cannot coexist in the same space' (440/308). To ensure this, temples and churches are erected. Nor can the sacred and the profane exist within the same moment of time: hence feast days and festivals have been created to give the sacred its own special allocation of time and to differentiate it from profane time. In an earlier period, about 1898–1900, in his lectures on the relationship between property and law, Durkheim described certain rituals as casting 'a girdle of sanctity' around a given object to protect 'the domain' from any trespass by outsiders (1950a:198/ t.1957a:171).

Yet despite Durkheim's postulating an extreme rigidity of separation between the sacred and the profane, there exists a no man's land which has to be traversed for particular purposes and at particular times. Institutionally an individual may move across the barrier and such a person is a priest or shaman. To do this he must be prepared by eliminating from himself all that is profane, through libations and other negative rituals of cleansing (442/309). This method of analysing religious officials and negative rituals has behind it the basic idea that religion is a force, and that the sacred and the profane constitute a force relationship, and that force becomes effective or is nullified at points of contact, which are made between the sacred and the profane (see ch. 11.4).

Frequently Durkheim's thinking about religion is analogically expressed by reference to elementary ideas about electricity. This was common enough at the time, when taboo was often regarded as negative electricity and interdicts as insulators. The sacred–profane dichotomy can be seen to represent an electromotive force with positive and negative elements which must be kept apart by adequate insulation. If the insulation breaks down, the system collapses and disintegrates. However, it is also necessary that under certain conditions two forces should be brought together in order that work be done by the electricity. This calls for means of controlling the forces or the current that may flow from one pole to the other. In crude terms, suggested by Durkheim, the man who does the controlling is the priest who needs to be protected against imminent dangers, should the powerful forces get out of hand. The machinery that he controls – one might refer to this as an electric motor – is in religious terms positive ritual which is designed to bring the worshipper, initially in an isolated and insulated profane state, into contact with the force of the sacred. Often in such rites, sacred food is eaten by the worshippers.

This kind of action means that at the heart of every positive rite, so Durkheim argues, there is a veritable sacrilege, for in coming into contact with, by touching and eating the sacred, man crosses the barrier which is deliberately there to keep the profane from the sacred. This sacrilege is allowed only under controlled circumstances and within specific areas and is accompanied by special precautions (483–4/338). This kind of action is necessary for 'something to happen' – necessary so that the force can work. If the sacred and the profane are really kept in watertight compartments, nothing happens and Durkheim admitted this when he wrote: 'if the profane were prevented from entering into relations with the sacred, the sacred would serve no useful purpose' (55/40/117). In simple electrical language, the barrier between the two has to be made *generally absolute*, and adequate insulation has to be provided. This is necessary so that the forces can be put into action. Work is achieved when careful controls are brought into play, so that the sacred and the profane can fuse or flow. In pointing to contact between the sacred and the profane, as Durkheim admits not least in his concept of positive ritual, he is attempting to give dynamic content to what appears to be a static concept. Stanner therefore is not quite fair in maintaining that the sacred–profane dichotomy is without dynamic content. But over and above that the problem as always is to combine both the static and the dynamic in an acceptable manner. And this brings home the problem of change. Durkheim openly admits that the content of the sacred changes, and indeed he gives examples. But if the sacred and the profane are involved in a dualistic relation, one must assume that the profane also changes and that the changes in one are reflected in the changes in the other. About changes in the profane Durkheim is less clear.

2 The duality accepted and attacked

Following in the footsteps of Durkheim, there have been a few anthropologists and sociologists who have fully supported the sacred–profane dichotomy. For example, at the beginning of his essay *Magic, Science and Religion* Malinowski wrote: 'In every primitive community, studied by trustworthy and competent observers, there have been two clearly distinguished domains the Sacred and the Profane' (1925:17). Parsons uses this evidence to support a similar position (1954:205ff.). Phyllis Kaberry in her study of aboriginal women in the Kimberley division in North Western Australia readily categorized their activities into sacred and profane, although she did not consider the dichotomy theoretically or refer to Durkheim's work on the subject (1939). More recently, the anthropologist, B. Ray, studying sacred space and royal shrines in Buganda has found the dichotomy to be useful (1977). He says that some languages do not have sacred and profane categories but that such categories are evidence in the structure of their thought. He goes on to maintain, however, that it is mistaken to hold that the opposition is absolute and refers to things absolutely. Eliade, the historian of religions, readily embraces the dichotomy in his book, *The Sacred and the Profane* (1959), although he does not admit that he builds on a Durkheimian framework.

On the whole, however, Durkheim has earned far more criticism than praise, not so much with reference to his concept of the sacred as to the dichotomy of the sacred and the profane and its universality. Alfred Loisy, whose long and critical review of *The Elementary Forms* is little known, held that the foundation of

Durkheim's religious theory was 'fragile' because it was constituted on the sacred–profane dichotomy (1913:48). 'In reality religions are not aware of this rigorous dualism; neither the sacred nor the profane constitutes entire worlds independent of one another. . . . The profane and the sacred are qualities of things, variable in their manifestation and intensity; they are not substantial entities. . . . Religions envisage a single economy of the universe where the sacred and profane respectively occupy their place but they are in a constant state of coordination' (ibid.). Loisy sees the sacred as a modality of religious things, but not a condition of religion. It does not extend to the base of religion nor does it represent the idea of religion, or its essential elements. It relates more to the exterior manifestations of religion (ibid.).

Belot was strongly opposed to the idea of the absoluteness of the concepts of the sacred and the profane (1913a:337–8). The absoluteness of the relationship is only one of appearance, the idea stems from Leibnitz and Kant, especially the heterogeneity of the categorical imperative. The absolute character is only so in the abstract. In practice it is not absolute, although in early societies it was more obvious than in later societies. The idea of the sacred was originally associated with a collective soul.

One of Durkheim's pupils who later became a firm disciple, Marcel Granet, in an attempt to be loyal to the teachings of his deceased master was forced to admit that 'the distinction between the sacred and the profane is less appreciable in China than among us' (1922/t.1975:147; ibid.:176 n.137). Granet was writing just after the First World War and held that the traditional, conformist Chinese religion, with a vast number of minor magical and ceremonial practices, did not permit the sharply defined dichotomy envisaged by Durkheim and so could not be held to be universal. And the case of Hinduism, we would add, is interesting. Whereas the sacred–profane dichotomy would at first sight appear to fit admirably, the sacred is not to be identified with the social. In much Hindu thought the sacred is something totally outside society. The highest caste, that of the Brahmins, is the least concerned with society and the social. And in Vedic ritual, the man who is consecrated is, in one sense, leaving society and may perform anti-social acts, though admittedly these are accepted by society. Here to say the least is a complication not envisaged by Durkheim.

Goldenweiser also criticized the dichotomy as being 'artificial' as well as establishing a 'presumption in favour of an interpretation of the sacred through some one general principle' (1917:118). Lowie likewise claimed there was no evidence for the universality of the dichotomy (1925:208).

Evans-Pritchard was always a vigorous critic of the sacred–profane dichotomy. Despite early admiration for Durkheim, and he was responsible for the English translation of many of the works of the Année Sociologique group, his last essay on Durkheim (1981) was almost vitriolic and reminiscent of the attacks of Richard. His criticism has generally been at the empirical level (for example, 1956a:313). He held that the profane and the sacred, far from being rigidly differentiated, 'are so closely intermingled as to be inseparable' (1965:65). They thus cannot be placed in separate compartments which are exclusive, and which negate one another (ibid.). In field research two concepts are of little help in classifying observable data as they do not allow for flexibility. This criticism he found to be borne out in his study of the Azande, who do not make a firm distinction between the natural and the supernatural which are allied to the sacred and the profane (1937:80ff.). In his study of their witchcraft, he saw the two ideas closely intertwined. Durkheim, on the other hand, saw a rigid line of demarcation between the two; one which it was impossible to cross or even to approach without great precautions. In his introduction to the translation of Hertz's *Death and the Right Hand*, Evans-Pritchard objected to the dichotomy as being 'almost equally vague and ill-defined' as the collective *conscience* (1960:12). His final comment was that he never found the dichotomy 'the slightest value in my field research' (1981:160). Godfrey Lienhardt, a disciple of Evans-Pritchard, who studied the Dinka, came to a similar conclusion in rejecting the dichotomy (1961:291). Raymond Firth also had no time for it (1973:366).

Other recent evidence to contradict the universality claimed by Durkheim for the sacred-profane dichotomy emerges from the field-work of Jack Goody, who found among the Lo Dagaa of northern Ghana no recognizable distinction between the natural and the supernatural. He wrote: 'But neither do the Lo Dagaa appear to have any concepts at all equivalent to the vaguer and not unrelated dichotomy between the sacred and the profane' (1961:151). The Lo Dagaa have an undifferentiated concept *tii*, which means a vague admiration, as for example for European medicines, but it can hardly be called sacred.

We have already had occasion to mention Stanner's rejection of Durkheim's concept of the profane and the associated dichotomy. Decisive are his arguments based on his knowledge of the social life of Australian Aborigines. Stanner maintains that their conceptual universe is not in fact divided into two classes (1967/ r.1975:292). Whereas much of Durkheim's tendency to use the framework of dualities may have been derived from the moiety system of the Aborigines – that no one individual can be a member of two moieties – the classes do not exhibit the absolute heterogeneity, radical opposition and profound differentiation indicated by Durkheim. Stanner observes that groups 'intermix by system while preserving their identities'. They are quite able to approach one another. '*All* the totems have meaning for *all* the groups as a condition of joint social and religious life' (ibid.). Dualisms do exist, but they are not as Durkheim characterized them nor are they as rigid. Thus the sacred–profane dichotomy has to be rejected.

Mary Douglas, who leans more heavily on Durkheim than did Evans-Pritchard, like him admits that the sacred–profane dichotomy is 'empirically inadequate' (1975:xii). She takes the position that as a unique category, but not part of a duality, the idea of the sacred is a most helpful way of examining social phenomena. But her use of the idea of the sacred emphasizes the physical characteristics which Durkheim held did not determine sacredness. Thus, she lays stress on the notions of danger and contagion and tends to play down other qualities (ibid.:xiv–xv). She not only finds this approach useful in dealing with primitive societies, but even in the modern period she stresses such characteristics by references to purity and impurity, and to danger and pollution (1966).

We have presented a brief selection of criticisms of Durkheim's dichotomy, mostly by contemporary anthropologists. Such a selection is but an indication of the general rejection of that dichotomy – a rejection which began close on the heels of the publication of *The Elementary Forms*.

Finally, another type of criticism follows, implicit in what has been written in much of this chapter, namely, that the duality proposed by Durkheim is not in fact a true duality. For a valid duality to exist, there must be a balance between the two components and a declared or recognized relationship between them. The conditions and possibilities of a duality are as follows (for convenience, S refers to sacred; P to profane):

(a) S and P must be parts of a whole;
(b) S and P must be of comparable status, power or force, as in light/darkness;
(c) S and P can be entirely isolated and separate;
(d) S and P can be in conflict with one another;
(e) S and P can be dialectically related to each other;
(f) S and P can be in a relationship where one is in the process of absorbing the other.

a Parts of a whole

For Durkheim both the sacred and the profane are parts of the totality of human experience. Such an experience is contained within the experienced world. It is a closed world without any intervention from a god or divine force. All thought can be placed in either one or other of the categories of the dichotomy (50–1/37/ 113).

b Of comparable status

It is quite evident that Durkheim does not see the sacred and the profane as of comparable status but of contrasting status. The sacred and the profane are qualitatively and quantitatively different. The sacred is all powerful: the profane seems to have no force at all, unless its force is seen as a negative force which destroys the sacred. It is lifeless and powerless. Durkheim frequently refers to the superiority of the sacred, for example, in associating the body with the profane, he states: 'we think that sensations are inferior forms of our activity, and we attribute a higher dignity to reason and moral activity (sacred)' (1914a/ t.1960c:334). He almost comes to declaring a hierarchical relation between the sacred and the profane, but rejects it (53/38/114). However, the real weakness of trying to maintain a duality rests on the fact that the profane is very much a residual category, and if it is, it is then impossible to uphold the notion of a pair of entities of roughly equal force and status.

147

c A relationship of total isolation

We have already noted that Durkheim holds that the primary relationship between the two entities is one of complete heterogeneity: they are essentially worlds that are contained in watertight compartments.

d A relationship of conflict

The duality in Durkheim's view, as we have noted, is based not only on isolation but on conflict between the sacred and the profane. It is one of total opposition. A question that arises is whether this conflict really exists empirically and much evidence suggests that it does not. Durkheim thus reads into the situation the quality he wishes to bestow upon it.

e A dialectical relationship

What is meant here is a relationship between the two components which is one of conflict but which is resolved by the emergence of a third category or force. The parallel is with Hegel's concept of thesis, anti-thesis and synthesis. Although Durkheim sees the precise content of the sacred (and therefore the profane) changing, he does not see the relationship between the two as being in any way dialectical in the sense we have indicated. It has also been noted that Durkheim admits that, under controlled circumstances, the two components may come into contact with one another.

f One absorbed by the other

Durkheim also rejected the idea that, in the face of total opposition between the sacred and the profane, one component would finally be victorious over the other, or that one was in the process of being absorbed by the other. All the evidence shows that he held that the balance, despite internal changes within each component, would always be maintained. Neither the sacred nor the profane would become conquered or would even disappear. Also, he never referred to anomic states of the sacred and the profane as he did of the division of labour, crime and suicide.

In meeting some of the conditions for a duality as mentioned above, it is clear that Durkheim's dichotomy of the sacred and the profane is acceptable. But there are two major weaknesses. One is that the relationship between the entities is basically static and does not permit any kind of movement or resolution. We have shown that he did attempt to introduce a dynamic component, but this was not developed. Within his own terminology the dichotomy remains rigid, far more so than his dichotomy of the individual and society. What is more serious, however, is the fact that the sacred and the profane are not a true duality because of the weakness of one of the members, the profane, which is a rag-bag term. Thus the dichotomy is not comparable with other well-established dichotomies, as exemplified in the thought of Kant, such as mind–body, noumena–phenomena, and, more widely and fundamentally, male–female. These, it might be argued, are ontological dualities: the sacred and the profane is a symbolic duality. But what of such symbolic dualities as black–white, yin and yang? This kind of defence does not strengthen Durkheim's case, for the components just mentioned are very much of equal status and power. Again, Durkheim continually appeals to 'facts' to substantiate the dichotomy, and as we have shown, if we turn to empirical evidence, very few anthropologists, even those who admire Durkheim, can give the backing the dichotomy requires in order to make the concept of the profane an adequate opponent of the sacred.

3 Further characteristics of the sacred

The sacred–profane dichotomy, certainly as defined by Durkheim, is difficult to accept on either theoretical or empirical grounds. This does not, however, vitiate the concept of the sacred *per se* which still continues to receive wide support. Every religion contains that which is sacred.

Durkheim's contribution to the understanding of the sacred, apart from its dichotomous relation to the profane, has been very considerable and we must, therefore, examine characteristics of the sacred other than those which we have already mentioned, some of which have become unquestionably accepted and others which are held to be of less value.

a The universality of the sacred

That the sacred is universal is implied in Durkheim's belief that the dichotomy is universal. Nevertheless, his starting point seems to have been not the dichotomy, but the concept of the sacred and this he held was to be found in all societies where certain objects, actions, ideas, values are set apart and given inviolable status (1899a(ii):25/t.1975a:95; ch. 7.1). Durkheim held that the sacred, or concepts similar to the sacred, are as universal as man himself. Whereas the actual term 'sacred' and parallel concepts may be limited to a given number of societies, the universality of the general idea has seldom been challenged, although its presence in modern western societies outside established religious institutions is open to debate (see ch. 26.6).

b The irreducibility of the sacred

For Durkheim the sacred is irreducible. It cannot be explained or adequately viewed by reference to anything else. Sacred things form 'a group of phenomena which are irreducible to any other group of phenomena' (1899a(ii):17/t.1975a:88). This does not mean that one has to be agnostic about its characteristics or the way it operates, and it is legitimate to suppose that it works according to its own 'laws' (ibid.:25/95). Nor, as has been said, are its contents eternal and fixed: they are indeed subject to time and culture. The point is that the sacred cannot be broken down into constituent parts, or explained at another level, for example, the psychological. Owing to its irreducibility, the sacred might be thought to have associations with Kant's categorical imperative. Aware of the possibility of such a link, Durkheim openly denied it (1906b/1924a:102/t.1953b:70). But given the fact that the sacred is irreducible, how is it to be studied? Clearly in terms of sociology, it is a 'social fact' and related to collective *représentations* (see 1895a). The irreducibility of the sacred is strongly supported by Eliade in *The Sacred and Profane* (1959).

c An ultimate category and the progenitor of gods

If the sacred is irreducible, there can be no higher or 'more ultimate' category within religion, and indeed within society itself. It stands above the gods themselves. Thus, an object or idea does not become sacred because it is said to come from the gods, or because it is associated with the spirit or is said to be of divine origin. Rather, it is the reverse. Certain deities receive extremely high status because the sacred is bestowed upon them. The idea of the sacred is independent of the idea of god and is prior to it, although Durkheim admits 'the notion of divinity has played a role in the religious life of people, somewhat analogous to that of the idea of the ego in psychic life' (1899a(ii):15–16/t.1975a:87).

The primacy of the sacred over the deity Durkheim saw exemplified in the case of Buddhism. Classical Buddhism pays scant or no attention to spiritual beings (ibid.:9–12/81–3). This is also true of Jainism: and Durkheim attempted to extend it to Brahminism (ibid.). A lack of gods was also evident in totemism and agrarian cults (ibid.:13/85). In all these cases, Durkheim assumed, there was a sense of the sacred. The case of Buddhism has continued to be a source of argument amongst scholars (see, for example, Spiro 1966:91–5). Buddhism aside, most anthropologists and sociologists would be prepared to admit that the prominence of spiritual beings or a god within the religion of different societies varies a great deal from society to society.

Two consequences emerge as a result of subscribing to the primacy of the sacred. The first is the corollary that what is ultimate or of the highest value in a society is sacred. Therefore what actually constitutes the sacred within a society is boundless, although subject to time and change. Durkheim postulated a large number of items held to be sacred by given societies, but which in some people's eyes are not religious.

The individual is sacred in modern western society (1898c:8/ t.1969d/r.1975:62), which means that individualism is also sacred (1950a:202/t.1957a:172; see ch. 26). ·

Individuals can become gods in certain primitive societies (1925a:119/t.1961a:104).

Some of the basic ideas of the French Revolution became sacred: motherland, liberty, reason (1899a(ii):20/t.1975a:91; 305–6/ 214/132).

So also are duty, the moral imperative, reason (1914a/t.1960c: 335).

And democracy, equality, progress (ibid.; 1909a(1):57).

Primitive science, enfolded in religion in pre-literate societies and early civilization, was held to be sacred (1922a:46/ t.1956a:77).

Rights and privileges are sacred (1950a:178/t.1957a:150).

Ideas and moral concepts – collective *représentations* (602/421/ 151).

What is ultimate in a society can thus be viewed as its most sacred idea or object. This is its *summum bonum* – its 'religion'.

The second consequence is that the sacred, since it has primacy, 'creates' what is spiritual – the gods, God himself. In the various sacred ideas which have just been listed, Durkheim points to the creation of the gods. He describes one process, which has been known from the time of the Greek philosophers, as follows:

> Besides, as much today as in the past, we see society ceaselessly creating sacred things out of nothing. If society happens to take to some man, and if it believes that it has found in him the main aspirations which preoccupy it, together with the means of satisfying them, we may be sure that such a man will be set above his fellows and virtually deified. . . . This is what happened to so many kings in whom their contemporaries had faith: even if they were not turned into gods, people saw in them at least the direct representatives of the deity. (304/212–13/131)

This argument points to the creation of saints, of spiritual beings, and gods and is amply supported by historical examples, for instance, canonization of saints in the Roman Catholic Church. Out of the sacred come the gods. As Jane Harrison has said: 'Le sacré, c'est le père du Dieu' (1912:63). It is probably too strong to say that Durkheim held that the sacred is the progenitor of God and the gods. That implies an active agency which clearly the sacred is not – it is not a person – the agency is of course society itself which uses the sacred (see ch. 12). Thus a deity is established by first passing through the stage of being a human person and gradually being raised to the status of the sacred. The process does not challenge the primacy of the sacred as a concept.

152

A god is not more 'sacred' than the 'sacred'. The process demonstrates how gods are created within the aura of the sacred. Put the other way round, it is impossible to see how a god can become a god without going through some prior stage of being holy or sacred, whilst remaining in the human sphere. One might imagine that Durkheim came to this conclusion about the role of the sacred at a late stage in the development of his thought. This is not the case. It was there at a very early time, in fact well before he had read Robertson Smith. In the *Division of Labour* he wrote:

> In the beginning, the gods are not distinct from the universe, or rather there are no gods, but only sacred beings, without their sacred character being related to any external entity as their source [animals, plants, as clan totems are the objects of worship]. But little by little religious forces were detached from the things of which they were first attributes, and become hypostatized. Thus is formed the notion of spirits or gods. (1893b/1902b:273/t.1933b:288).

The theory that the sacred creates deities is unacceptable, if the sacred is pictured as an activity which is the agent of the operations. Gaston Richard found this difficult to accept and rejected the notion that the inviolability of the human person, which Durkheim purported, could have been derived from crude ideas of the sacred and the notion of interdict, even if these were manipulated by society (1925(ii):361).

d The location of the sacred

Any object, gesture, person, idea or ideal can become sacred through the imprimatur of society, but where is the sacred located? Since society is its progenitor, it must also be its depository. In Durkheim's terminology the sacred is a social fact and part of the collective *conscience*. It is not determined by the individual's notion of what is sacred: the sacred exists outside him. This is in contradistinction to a writer like Talcott Parsons, who, in giving great importance to the concept of the sacred, holds that it is located according to the declaration of the individual, the actor (1937:451; and 1954:209–10). W. J. Goode, also influenced by Parsons, stresses the emotional and personal content of religious behaviour, and adopts a very similar position (1951:45).

153

Jack Goody has supported the view that Durkheim conceived the sacred–profane dichotomy within the actor frame of reference – that it has meaning in some sense for all people and that the concepts are present in all cultures (1961:148). But on empirical grounds, he argues, it is misleading to take the actor's perception of his situation as determining the universality of the dichotomy (ibid.:160). The danger, it should be noted, of using the actor's frame of reference is that such a subjective approach in Durkheim's eyes makes it difficult to differentiate the sacred from the profane. As we shall have occasion to note, and as we have already indicated, Durkheim carefully differentiates between individual and social phenomena within religion, as well as outside it (1899a(ii); ch. 9). What is individual is profane: what is social is sacred.

For Durkheim and for those who follow in his path, the sacred is to be located in collective beliefs and ideals, in institutional religion itself, in its creeds, in its official statements and declarations. Similarly, it is determined by negative commands, prohibitions and interdicts and in negative ritual. Yet Durkheim was not opposed to discovering 'popular beliefs' in a society, realizing that they determine the sacred. In notes taken down by Georges Davy of a lecture given by Durkheim on morality, Durkheim was reported to have said in connection with the sacredness of the self:

> In order to realize this sacred quality of life, do not turn to the outstanding academics of the day but to popular beliefs; observe the effect on the *conscience* when the sacredness is disregarded. (1968c:256)

Here Durkheim shows a mistrust of armchair anthropologists, although he was an armchair anthropologist himself. The work of the sociologist is to discover the sacred in terms of collective *représentations* in society. This, however, raises particular difficulties in dealing with a society which is religiously pluralistic. How are the society's sacred values to be ascertained (see ch. 24)?

e The indivisibility of the sacred

Durkheim admits that the sacred and indeed much of religion itself is surrounded by mystery. But he did imply that scientific analysis and explanation would uncover the mystery step by step (1899a(ii):25/t.1975a:95). We offer one example where he felt his own work had contributed to the demystification of religion. In *The Elementary Forms* he set out what he held was a mysterious facet of the sacred. 'When a sacred being subdivides itself, it remains whole and equal to itself in each of its parts . . . as far as religion is concerned, the part is equal to the whole; it has the same powers, it is equally effective' (328/229/138). Sacredness is therefore not dependent on crude physical laws. This, argues Durkheim, is an additional reason why the sacred virtue, which a thing is said to possess, is not dependent on its intrinsic or physical properties. The virtue comes from sentiments which the object calls forth and symbolizes. The notion of the sacred is through a mental process and therefore, a 'spiritual', non-material process.

Although the sacred in the last analysis is invisible and is therefore 'spiritual', it is subject, according to Durkheim, to annihilation. This is contrary to at least one interpretation of the notion of spirit, namely, that it is eternal. Durkheim's ambivalence at this point – that the sacred though spiritual is vulnerable and can be threatened by extinction – is associated with the fact that he sees the sacred as a unique or particular type of *représentation* which is subject to the threat of destruction in a way that scientific knowledge is not. This he implies when he says that 'the religious domain is protected from the *reach* of the profane' (1925a:11/ t.1961a:10/r.1975:19). In order to counteract the insecure nature of the sacred, it has to be protected from the malicious enemy, that is, from the profane through ritual and interdict. Mary Douglas reaches a similar conclusion in an article on pollution (see 1975:49). She points out that, for Durkheim, religious ideas 'float in the mind, unattached, and are always likely to shift, or to merge into other contexts at the risk of losing their essential character' (ibid.). The reason for this unique category of the sacred is that the ideas 'are not referable to any ultimate material reality', for they are 'representations of abstract ideas' (ibid.). But we might extend this conclusion further and suggest that Durkheim had to invent the profane in order to create an opposite for the sacred. It would explain the vulnerability of the sacred and the necessity for its protection. Since the sacred is threatened, it must be threatened by something, and this can only be the

155

profane. This is virtually a case of the necessity of evil that good may abound.

We have no intention of commenting on Mary Douglas's assertion that Durkheim made his sacred–profane dichotomy the basis of his 'completely sociological theory of knowledge' (1975:xv). It leads to a realm which is outside the scope of this book.

f The sacred as contagious

Deriving his ideas from totemism in which the emblems of a clan are seen to be sacred, Durkheim holds that a 'sacred character is to a high degree contagious; it therefore spreads itself out from the totemic being to everything that is closely or remotely connected with it' (318/222). A simple example is that of an animal which is held to be sacred, where the food it eats and objects which are like it are also held to be sacred. This constitutes another mysterious element of religion which Durkheim claimed he had explained. First of all, it may be observed that 'the extraordinary contagiousness of a sacred character' demands that it be ritually protected, lest it affect indiscriminately other areas and objects (455/318). Durkheim attempts his explanation by using the notion of force (see ch. 11.4). Religious powers exert themselves in many ways including physical contact: 'they always seem ready to escape from points where they reside and to enter everything passing within their range' (ibid.). He claims no originality in drawing attention to these phenomena. They had been observed before by Robertson Smith, Frazer, van Gennep and others. Durkheim claims that his contribution is within the realm of Australian totemism and presents an explanation, not based on the association of ideas as was then prominent, but by an almost biological concept of propagation through contagion (1912a: bk 3, Ch. 1, sec. IV). His position, however, is weakened by combining this with a concept from physics, namely, force, so that he often implies the idea of 'contagious' force. While the analogy of contagious diseases might be a useful analogy in understanding the extension of the sacred to objects which are not initially sacred, the introduction of other analogies is not helpful.

There can be no doubt that the notion of the contagiousness of the sacred is based more on the concept of taboo, which has been likened to negative electricity and therefore to force, than on that of the Latin word *sacer*. This is evident not only in *The Elementary Forms* (ibid.) but in a much earlier work, *Professional Ethics and Civic Morals* (1950a:172ff./t.1957a:143ff.). Here he expands the idea of contagion by touch or nearness, especially with regard to property, which itself becomes contagious as it comes into contact with the sacred. Thus:

> Property is contagious. The thing appropriated, like the sacred thing, draws to itself all things that touch it and appropriates them. The existence of this singular capacity is confirmed by a whole collection of juridical principles which the legal experts have often found disconcerting: these are the principles that decide what is called the 'right of accession'. The idea may be expressed in this way: anything to which another of less importance is added (*accedit*) communicates to it its own status in law. (ibid.:177/148)

We might also add, as has been indicated, that Durkheim did not hesitate to use other scientific analogies, for example, those which related to electricity, by referring to radiation from object to object, or from person to person. The object or person becomes sacralized by radiation or touch and so itself becomes a transmitter. He also held that sacredness could be transmitted from things to persons with the result that the things ceased to be sacred (1950a:198/t.1957a:171).

The crudity of these analogies, borrowed from various sciences, is hardly acceptable today, but Goldenweiser as early as 1915 challenged Durkheim that he had failed to produce an acceptable theory (1915/r.1975:225). Given the fact that the sacred is super-added, it is difficult to see, argued Goldenweiser, why it is so readily communicated from object to object. The Australian Aboriginal is unaware of the *raison d'être* of the sacredness of an object and he would imagine his consciousness is its source. Again, why is contagiousness peculiar to the sacred and foreign to experience outside religion? Communicability amongst primitive peoples comes in observing like objects and qualities and communicates itself through the senses. If the sacred is infectious so is the profane, which Goldenweiser implies is equated with the mundane. Goldenweiser also rejects Durkheim's attempt to derive exclusively fundamental categories from religious concepts and experience.

g The emotional content of the sacred

Society creates and sets its seal on what is sacred. It is publicly declared and reinforced by ritual. Within the individual, it is established through a process of learning or socialization: and for Durkheim the sacred is the most important part of that process. The failure of an individual to acknowledge what is sacred in society is a failure in socialization. But once the sacred is firmly embedded in the individual, it becomes associated with respect and emotion, and therefore, argues Durkheim, with 'high mental energy' (453/317). It is this energy which helps to ensure antagonism on the part of the individual and the mutual exclusion of the sacred from the profane. 'When we think of holy (*saintes*) things, the idea of a profane object cannot enter the mind without encountering grave resistance . . . because the *représentation* of a sacred thing does not tolerate this nearness' (ibid.).

The emotion associated with the sacred is of two opposite kinds. The sacred commands respect and is also an object of love and devotion – the sacred is something that is earnestly sought after: but, on the other hand, the sacred is also something to be feared (1924a:51, 68, 103/t.1953b:36,48,70). Observations about psychological ambivalence towards the sacred have become common enough, particularly as a result of Freudian analysis. But it is important to note that just as Otto's concept of the holy was not *based* on psychological factors, neither was Durkheim's concept of the sacred.[1] For Durkheim, the emotional content is attendant upon a social base: not the other way round. The psychological does not search for a socially given superstructure. However, Lévi-Strauss in commenting on Durkheim's totemism has suggested that instinct is at the basis of his theory of the sacred. He hastens to add that impulses and drives explain nothing, but are the result of other factors, such as the power of the body or the impotence of the mind (1962a/t.1969:142).

h The sacred remains mysterious

The sacred is beyond the rational and understandable, and in this respect it is akin to Otto's concept of the holy. In referring to the sacredness of morality, Durkheim implies that the sacred has something about it that speaks of 'a transcendent reality' (1925a:10/

t.1961a:11/r.1975:197). What constitutes the sacred has conferred upon it a dignity that raises it above the ordinary or 'empirical' and, in this sense, raises it above the profane. Whereas Durkheim feels that his scientific approach can get behind *some* of the mystery that pervades the sacred, he is convinced that at the present moment the amount of scientific discovery is very limited and that the sacred will remain mysterious for a long time. Science moves very slowly (see ch. 25.2). Part of the reason is that the sacred is very much set within the realm of collective *représentations*, and that a rational analysis of the formation of the *représentations* seems to be impossible. One cannot go beyond the relation of *représentations* and society. Although admitting that there is a psychological content in the *représentations*, Durkheim naturally rejects a psychological explanation, such as that of the laws of association. He says that *représentations* have their own laws, but that he cannot discover them (see ch. 15). This self-confessed failure appears in the concluding paragraph of his monograph with Mauss, 'Primitive classification'. He writes: 'Now emotion is naturally refractory to analysis, or at least lends itself uneasily to it because it is too complex. Above all when it has a collective origin it defies critical and rational examination' (1903a(i):72/ t.1963b:88). Sociology can free a study of *représentations* from the 'tautologies' which metaphysicians and psychologists have brought to the subject, but it seems that it cannot finally produce a scientific explanation of them (see ch. 15.6).

4 Conclusion

The notion of the sacred is probably more acceptable and better understood in the Catholic or Jewish world than in that of Protestantism. Judaism, in which Durkheim was nurtured, and Catholicism, for which he had early and fleeting leanings, are, through their rituals, their prohibitions affecting everyday life, their use of physical objects in worship and devotion, the best examples which Europeans have of experiencing the sacred. Protestantism, on the other hand, with its basic aim of reforming medieval Catholicism, of spiritualizing and dematerializing every aspect of religion, and therefore of eliminating superstition and reducing ritual to a minimum, is a form of religion which does not have sympathy with the concept of the sacred. In Calvinism, in particular, the sacred is found only in the realm of the spiritual. For Protestants God, Jesus Christ, the Word as found in the Bible form what is holy. Apart from condemnations of idolatry and superstition, interdicts relate entirely to the moral and spiritual, and not to ritual. Perhaps it was because of a fear, if not hatred, of the concept of the sacred, with all its consequences, that Robertson Smith found such opposition to his thought, in which the sacred played so important a part. Certainly Durkheim's concept of the sacred as the basis of religion has been strongly criticized by Protestants such as Gaston Richard and, more recently, Roger Mehl (1965/t.1970:3). That Durkheim made the social and not the individual the source of the sacred has always compounded the opposition of Protestants, especially liberal Protestants, as well as that of certain humanists. By contrast, the concept of the sacred, which is applicable to primitive societies, has found most sympathy amongst Catholics. The concept of the sacred is least understood in modern secular industrial society.

From the time of Durkheim, and indeed before, with such a writer as Robertson Smith, anthropologists and sociologists have readily subscribed to the value of analysing religion in terms of the sacred. We might mention at random Marett, Granet, Malinowski, Radcliffe-Brown, Lévi-Strauss, Leach, Parsons, Nadel, Goode and Douglas. That these and others have been inclined to accept the importance of the concept of the sacred can to a large extent be attributed to the way in which Durkheim expounded the term.

Goblet d'Alviella, a French writer in the history of religion, went further than Durkheim when he based his studies of religion on the concept of *hiérologie* or the science of the sacred (1913). Durkheim never claimed there could be a science of the sacred and was thus less ambitious in this respect than was Goblet d'Alviella. Of the sacred d'Alviella wrote:

> The domain of the sacred is not a world which is irrational, invisible, unreal or illogical, nor is it a world of pure forms or images. It is a world of powers to which, by virtue of a well-known law, the imagination of primitive man assigns an independent, substantial existence. As soon as he is able to

distinguish them in an abstract form, he makes them into souls, spirits, even gods, which assume whatever form they can. Yet the sacred is also a sphere which one enters and leaves according to certain rites; it is, in short, the idea of a quality from which results an effective force. (1913:196)

Overtones indeed of Durkheim! And, using a less reasoned approach, one might also draw attention to the work in relatively more recent times of Roger Caillois in, for example, his *L'Homme et le sacré* (1939/t.1959) and that of Eliade (for example, 1959).

As Goody has pointed out, the relevant question is not whether the sacred–profane dichotomy is universal, but whether the dichotomy is a useful analytic concept (1961:148). The weight of the evidence, as we have shown, is that the dichotomy is fraught with difficulties at the theoretical level and empirically is of not much value. Further, it raises the question of whether religion is to be identified with the sacred, or with the sacred–profane dichotomy. This dilemma is eliminated if the dichotomy as such is dropped and one accepts a unitary approach to the sacred and at the same time much that Durkheim has to say about the sacred itself. It is in this sense that the anthropologist and sociologist see analytical merit in the concept. The identification of the sacred with the social has always caused trouble – it was condemned by Ginsberg (1956:242), and before that by Belot, who saw the identification as nothing more than the expression of the collective soul (*âme collective*) (1913a:338). Such criticism is particularly poignant in examining modern western societies, where the sacred is more an individual matter and has little social content. If it is legitimate to identify the social with the sacred, then primitive societies which have a mechanical type of solidarity are the best examples of the identification. But there then remains the task of showing how the change has come about and how it is that the sacred is no longer identified with the social. This calls for a more dynamic approach than that proposed by Durkheim. Apart from this issue and the claims he made about explaining contagiousness and the indivisibility of the sacred, nearly all he said about the concept, especially within the context of ritual, is of great value.

The concept of the sacred, as an essential category of social thought, has the virtue of transcending a narrow concept of religion, defined by a system of beliefs and practices centred on superhuman beings or the supernatural. In this respect such an approach has great merit in understanding society as a whole. It is therefore more likely to fit into a theoretical framework than would the concept of religion defined in terms of a god, gods or superhuman beings (see ch. 9.1).

The whole of Durkheim's analysis of religion rests on the dichotomous relation between the concepts of the sacred and the profane. The concepts constitute the foundation on which the entire edifice is built. *The Elementary Forms*, as the culmination of his religious thought, can in some way be seen as a treatise on the sacred (Isambert 1976:50). As we proceed, we shall examine the various ways in which Durkheim uses and develops the idea, especially with regard to ritual. The ways in which he does this go well beyond those developed by any other thinker, for Durkheim sees the sacred–profane dichotomy not just as a descriptive term, but as a causal factor in understanding social life. It is for this reason that a preliminary analysis of the concepts has been placed at the very beginning of our exposition of Durkheim's thought.

Yet, as has been noted, a question mark hangs over the pair of concepts on account of the criticism that has been levelled against them. If the basic concepts are open to doubt, or at least in the way in which Durkheim uses them, is not the whole enterprise then suspect? If his systematic analysis of religion, and indeed of society, is grounded on a primal dichotomy which has to be rejected, does not his whole structure fall to the ground like a house of cards? Only a fool would write off all that Durkheim said about religion just because of the unsatisfactory nature of the sacred–profane dichotomy. If the foundation appears to be somewhat shaky, it does not mean that no part of the house is worth preserving. Very far from it. In sociological analysis today, what house rests on perfect foundations? As we have said, Durkheim has a great deal to offer, even about the concept of the sacred itself, which does not directly depend on the dichotomy, and at every stage of his thought there are fruitful and stimulating connections which emerge out of his ideas.

9 Commitment to a definition

1 Early and late attempts

Durkheim seems to have taken the academic study of religion seriously when he was at the École Normale Supérieure between 1879 and 1882. It was not, however, until almost twenty years later that he published his first article that had religion as its subject-matter – 'De la Définition des phénomènes religieux' (1899a(ii)). Its importance has all too frequently been overlooked, not least because it contained Durkheim's first attempt to define religion. By 1899, when the article was published, *The Division of Labour* (1893b), *The Rules of Sociological Method* (1895a) and *Suicide* (1897a) had all appeared in print. In these books and various early articles there were references to religion, in some cases a whole chapter or more, but there was nothing in what he said which could in any way be regarded as systematic.

Since Durkheim always thought of himself as a conceptualist, who begins his studies by classifying phenomena, one would have thought that he would have dealt with the problem of defining religion on some earlier occasion. His defence might well have been that he was not obliged to offer a definition, as up to 1889 he had seriously avoided any attempt to study religion methodically. In his first major work, *The Division of Labour*, he declared that there existed no scientific definition of religion (1893b/1902b:142/t.1933b:168). A comparative approach was called for, such as that adopted by sociologists in studying crime. He made one strong assertion, namely, that in a scientific definition of religion the notion of a god or gods could not be central. There appears to be good reason to suggest that there were periods in his life when he was uncertain how to define religion. Evidence in part comes from the fact, as we shall see, that he changed the definition from one which he put forward in the conclusion of the 1899 article to one which finally appeared in *Les Formes*

163

élémentaires (65/47/123). The alteration to a new definition was apparently carried out relatively late in the development of the book. Chapter I of Book I, 'Définition du phénomène religieux et de la religion' (inaccurately translated by Swain as 'Definition of religious phenomena and of religion') was not published in learned journals before the book appeared in 1912, whereas the Introduction, and Chapters II and III of Book I appeared in print three years before (1909d and 1909c) and were incorporated into the book virtually without alteration (the last pages of 1909d were omitted). Hence one is forced to conclude that grappling with the problem of defining religion caused him a certain amount of difficulty and perhaps uncertainty. Since the chapter in question turned out to be of crucial importance and since many of the ideas about the sacred had already appeared, it seems most likely that if Durkheim had prepared in advance the chapter of the book, it would have been published in a journal. In the lectures of 1906–7 on La Religion: les origines, which constituted an early draft of *Les Formes élémentaires*, the same hesitancy over definition is apparent. He failed to produce the final formulation which was to appear in the book, although his ideas in the lecture were not far removed from those he expressed in the book itself (1907f:532–3; see pages ahead).

When Durkheim began to establish his *sociologie religieuse* (see ch. 27), he needed to produce a scientific definition of religion which would cut through definitions put forward by scholars in allied disciplines. These Durkheim felt were inadequate, judged by the criteria he had set for the discipline of sociology. It was necessary to be rid of ideas then prevalent, which were nothing more than preconceptions and false assumptions. In *The Elementary Forms* he wrote: 'Men have been obliged to make for themselves a notion of what religion is, long before the science of religion started its methodical comparisons' (32/23). He stated that any definition would be one that would adequately embrace all religions from the most primitive to the most recent, from the most 'materialistic' to the most 'spiritual' (see, for example, 1899a(ii):2–3/t.1975a:75). All subjective and vague ideas were also to be eliminated (ibid.:2/75). No one religion, not even Christianity, was held to be the norm by which others were to be judged (ibid.:3/76). All religious 'ethnocentricism' had to be abandoned in order to produce a definition which was objective and all-embracing. As is well known, Durkheim also strongly criticized the definitions which were associated with the theories of naturism and animism. He also rejected a definition which is based upon beliefs and practices centred on a god or gods, or some concept of the supernatural, because that would have been tantamount to defining religion in terms of non-reality. Jane Harrison has suggested that the reason why sociologists and anthropologists rejected the notion of defining religion in terms of a god or spirit was that such a definition would have allowed theologians to make a contribution. She wrote: 'So long as religion was defined by its object it was, to the detriment of science, confused with theology' (1912:29). Those who wanted to adopt a scientific approach and cut their links with theologians turned to the notions of religious instinct, a feeling for mystery, or mana. Whether Durkheim rejected defining religion in terms of the deity in order to keep out theologians is difficult to say. One thing is clear: he was convinced that the notion of the sacred was the basis of religion.

2 Phenomena: wholes, parts and facts

In many respects the article, 'De la Définition des phénomènes religieux' is a direct extension of Durkheim's thought as it is presented in his manifesto for the science of sociology, *The Rules of the Sociological Method* (1895a). In his plea for the legitimate place of sociology within the scientific world, Durkheim maintained that every science is required to mark out its own territory of working – to extract phenomena from the totality of experience which it is proposed to study, and then to apply to it suitable scientific methods. Thus, the initial task in defining is one of boundary-making, by which an area, or group of facts, can be distinguished from other areas or other groups of facts. (Durkheim actually used the expression *délimiter le cercle des faits* (1899a(ii):1/ t.1975a:74).) The line of demarcation may not be knife-edge, but some form of boundary is required for the establishment of a science. Such a definition, which encloses a group of phenomena, we might call a nominal one, since it contains no truth value or essence of the phenomena in question (Robinson 1950:7–11ff.). In order to proceed with its task, science as a rule, though not invariably, calls for an early or immediate definition which is of this descriptive kind. Durkheim thus saw it as incumbent upon the sociologist of religion to define his area of working.

At the very outset he made the important distinction between religious phenomena and religion. Religion contains a number of components: these together constitute what is called religion. In the opening paragraph of the 1899 article he categorically states: 'Religion is a totality of religious phenomena, and the whole can only be defined in terms of the parts' (1899a(ii):1/t.1975a:74). In *The Elementary Forms* Durkheim speaks of defining the whole in terms of the parts (47/36/112). What the parts are he never categorically listed. Primarily he saw them as 'myths, dogmas, rites and ceremonies' (as in 49/36/112). However, religion also involves art, literature, morality and so forth, and indeed at one time 'everything was religious' (see ch. 14.3). In another direction, religion is made up of what is local and individual, as well as what is social (1899a(ii):1/t.1975a:74ff.).

Quite apart from a failure in this early essay to be committed to the precise composition of the parts, Durkheim takes up a position at the very outset which seems to contradict one of his basic positions in the *Rules*, and one that he was to repeat constantly (for example, 1913a(ii)(15)). The principle in question was derived from his neo-Kantian teacher, Charles Renouvier, at the École Normale, which was to the effect that the whole is more than the sum of its parts. This meant that no entity could be satisfactorily explained by just examining the parts and, as it were, adding them together. In forming the whole the parts create a new substance or entity. An example of this, which Durkheim felt could not be contradicted, was offered in the preface of the second edition of *The Rules*, in which he states that knowledge of the properties of bronze cannot be derived by merely adding together the knowledge of the properties of its individual components, namely, copper, tin and lead (1895a/1901c:xvi/t.1938b:xlviii; ch. 22.7). A similar example relates to the composition of the life of a cell (ibid.:xvi/xlvii; see also 1898b/1924a:40/t.1953b:28–9). Durkheim was invoking these examples as he applied the principle of wholes and parts to society; and his argument is that society can never be said to be equal to the sum of its parts, or more precisely, it is greater or different from the sum of the individuals who compose it (cf. 1925a:119/t.1961a:104). That Durkheim, in seeing society as an entity *sui generis*, was accused of social realism by Deploige and many others, such as Gaston Richard and Gustave Belot, is beside the point (see Deploige 1911; Durkheim 1913a(ii)(15); ch. 13.3). What is apposite here is the status which Durkheim gives to the social facts of religion, which is different to that which he gives to society. He is ready to apply the axiom, 'the whole is greater than the parts' to society but not to religion. If religion is a component of society, and can be seen as a whole, then the principle of the whole and parts should be applied to religion itself. It is at least logical to infer that religion is more than the sum of its component parts. Why did Durkheim demand the application of the axiom to the one and not to the other? There are several possible explanations. He might have argued that society and religion are realities (or concepts), each of a different order and therefore the axiom is applicable to society but not to religion. If this is so, what grounds are sustained for the differentiation, especially as religion is seen to be so important for society? They are never forthcoming. Arguing in terms of intention, it might be said that Durkheim almost wanted to create an aura around society to make it more sacred than the sacred, that is, more sacred than religion, and to defend it from a rational analysis. He had no hesitation in attempting to demystify religion by encouraging a simple analysis in which the whole is discovered by understanding the parts. If this is so – and in the light of what we know about Durkheim's general attitude towards society, that he raised it to the status of the sacred, and that he believed a scientific explanation of religion was possible – it is clear that he is prepared to apply the axiom of the whole being greater or different from the sum of the parts to suit his case. The argument and the analogies gave rise to considerable criticism. In 1898 Tosti accused Durkheim of 'a startling error of logic', surprising in someone so logical as Durkheim, because he completely disregarded the fact that a compound is understood both by the nature of the elements of that compound and also by the law of their interaction (1898:474). As Tosti says, Durkheim attempts 'to explain the "product" by the "product" itself, thus overthrowing the scientific conception of cause' (ibid.). What is required is to know the way in which the elements are combined and this, of course, Durkheim finds well nigh impossible to delineate. One also has to know whether the compound is a real compound in

167

which new characteristics emerge or is in fact a mere aggregation of elements and their properties (see also Leuba 1913:335; Essertier 1927:16). But these arguments apart, no matter which way one may look at it, Durkheim places religion and society on two different levels and such differentiation is unwarrantable without at least offering some reason.

Incidentally, in partnership with Hubert, Mauss in his essay on magic (1904) used the principle that the unity of the whole is more real than each of its parts – something he was not able to do in his 'Essai sur le don'. So holds Lévi-Strauss (1950:xxxviii). We would also maintain that Durkheim sees effervescent assemblies as wholes (see ch. 22.7).

Joseph Sumpf has attempted another explanation (1965). His argument is that Durkheim saw religion as being such a highly complex phenomenon that it did not possess adequate continuity and coherence to be classified as a genus. In this respect religion in Durkheim's eyes is to be contrasted with the family (as in 1888c) and with socialism (1928a/1971d:35, 38/t.1958b:5, 8) which are seen as wholes. In these it is relatively easy to establish their characteristics so that they can be subjected to scientific analysis. By contrast, Sumpf holds that religions, especially Christianity, are movements and, as such, are superstructures in which religion is not a whole beyond its parts (1965:67) – 'each part is the superstructure, each individual is the society' and, in suggesting that this was Durkheim's position, he quotes the master: 'Since the part recalls the whole, it also evokes the sentiments recalled by the whole' (328/229/139). As we make clear, Durkheim's sociological approach to religion faced the problem of the enormous complexity of religious phenomena and that he sought part of the solution in treating religion as being no more than the sum of its parts. But it is surely wrong of Sumpf to state that Durkheim saw in religion a movement and not a social institution. It is legitimate to suggest that the parallels between socialism and Christianity are very close, especially given the multiplicity of the forms of socialism which were apparent in his day and are even more so today. But Sumpf does not echo the voice of Durkheim accurately, when he points to an approach to religion in which it is almost impossible to know the content of religion (ibid.:67). Nevertheless he rightly suggests that, if religion is marked by continuity and discontinuity (and contradiction), there was need for Durkheim to find a note of continuity and this he held Durkheim discovered in the concept of 'germinal principles' which he learned from reading Robertson Smith at the important time of his 'conversion' (see ch. 4.2). If religion has so many shapes and forms, there must be some underlying principle which gives rise to them. Again, if this is so, surely it is the task of sociology to discover these principles? The weakness of Sumpf's solution is that he reads too much into Durkheim with the aid of Lévi-Straussian concepts.

We turn to issues of a more substantive kind. The opening words of the 1899 article state that the sociology of religion is concerned with social facts. Here Durkheim applies the principle set out in *The Rules of Sociological Method*, namely, that sociology in general has as its subject-matter social facts (*faits sociaux*). In a much quoted passage he describes social facts as ways of acting, thinking and feeling, which are external to the individual, which in some way control or constrain him, and which cannot be explained in terms of psychology or the natural sciences (1895a/1901c:5/t.1938b:3). Since the sociology of religion is concerned with religious facts, it can be assumed that such facts are particular kinds of social facts, which are generally associated with what is called religion. However, at the very beginning of the paper Durkheim differentiates religious phenomena from religious facts. Religious phenomena include religious facts, but extend beyond them because they embrace more than the social, that is, they contain local, individual, isolated beliefs and practices which are not part of a recognized religion. Thus, religious phenomena are of two distinct kinds: social and individual. We can state Durkheim's position in 1899 in the following way:

Religion = Σ religious phenomena
= Σ social and individual, religious phenomena
= Σ social facts and individual phenomena, of a
religious kind

(Σ = sum total)

In the preface to the second volume of *L'Année sociologique*, in which the article of defining religion appeared, Durkheim said that religious facts had to be treated 'in conformity with their nature as social facts' and that 'whether describing or explaining them, one must relate them to a particular social milieu, to a definite type of society' (1899a(i):ii/t.1960c:348).

3 Emphasis on coercive force: the attempt to be scientific

In line with his definition of a social fact, Durkheim held in the early period of his thought that the key characteristic of religion was that of constraint – its power or ability to produce some social effect. This appeared as early as 1887, when he reviewed Guyau's *L'Irréligion de l'avenir* and criticized the author for failing to take account of the 'obligatory nature of religious prescriptions' (1887b:308/t.1975a:34; see also 1886a:69/t.1975a:22). He continues:

> The Christian who for the first time eats a normal meal on Good Friday, and the Jew who for the first time eats pork, experience a remorse which it is impossible to distinguish from moral remorse. (1887b:308/t.1975a:35)

The point that Durkheim makes is that the transgression of ritual regulations brings with it censure and feelings of guilt, such as accompany an immoral act. Religious prescriptions, and with them religious behaviour patterns, carry an inner sense of obligation, perhaps not unlike Kant's categorical imperative. For Robertson Smith, ritual rather than belief exerts the power of constraint: Durkheim goes further. He contends that all religious facts – prescriptions, rituals, dogmas, myths – have the quality of obligation. Hence beliefs exert force as well as rituals. He wrote: 'There is always an exact parallel between the religious character of the beliefs and the intensity of repression which imposes respect for them' (1899a(ii):18/t.1975a:89). The latter part of the 1899 essay is almost entirely given up to making the point that socio-religious phenomena consisting of beliefs and practices are by their nature obligatory (*obligatoire*). The issue was obviously crucial to Durkheim, quite apart from its importance within his theory of religion which he was then formulating. What he has to say about the power of coercion in religion is now widely accepted with little reference to him as the exponent of the idea. He notes that in early societies where religion is virtually identical with political life, believers are forced, often by physical means, to accept given dogmas, for example, doctrines of Yahweh among the Israelites (ibid.:17/88). The denial of a given belief may bring punishment to an individual. Punitive control mechanisms are, therefore, instrumental in making deviants conform. The 'authorities' also mete out punishment for ritual offences and people are thus forced to act ritually in the same way as they are forced to act according to moral and legal demands (ibid.:20/91). Nevertheless, where in a given society the political is differentiated from the religious, spiritual sanctions 'from excommunication to penance' may be directed against offenders (ibid.:18/89). Durkheim goes so far as to suggest that religion and constraint are two almost quantifiable variables, so that 'the more religious they [beliefs] are, the more they are obligatory' (ibid.). Common sense dictates that such an extreme position is untenable and reveals an underlying circularity of argument.

The concept of constraint, although it is valuable, contains a number of difficulties, especially when such a characteristic is held to be decisive in the task of definition and classification. One of the problems – and Durkheim clearly saw this – is in distinguishing religion from morality and law, for these also exhibit the same coercive qualities. He always places great emphasis on the close relation between religion and morality, especially in primitive societies (see, for example, 1925a:9ff./t.1961a:8ff.; Davy 1911:61). Indeed, in primitive societies they are virtually indistinguishable. For analytical reasons, however, it is necessary to differentiate them and in the recent period of man's history the two have been clearly separated. If they are both characterized by constraint, and here Durkheim implies constraint employing sanction and physical force directed against the offender, how can they be distinguished? In the 1899 essay, Durkheim in a quite unwarrantable way makes the deciding factor the presence of a myth (see ch. 20). Moral and legal prescriptions relate to action, but that action is not undergirded by obligatory creeds or myths. By contrast, religious actions are directly related to such beliefs and mythologies. He was no doubt swayed by the conviction that in primitive societies motivation and reason with regard to moral action are seldom in evidence and when he referred to law and morality he was subconsciously thinking of secular examples outside those associated with myth and dogma (Ginsberg 1956:232). The way in which Durkheim marks off religious facts from moral facts is unacceptable in the light of empirical evidence (see, for example, Webb 1916:50). He saw later that it was an untenable position and had to abandon the notion of defining religion by such means. As Gustave Belot said, Durkheim attempted to define morality, and religion as well, not by content but by form. He did it in the same way, though for other reasons, as Kant tried to define morality in terms of obligation (1909:7).

There seems good evidence to show that Durkheim's reading of Robertson Smith strengthened his notion or at least convinced him that religion is essentially obligatory. In his *Lectures on the Religion of the Semites* Robertson Smith observed that all acts of worship amongst ancient peoples are not left to the choice of the worshipper but are determined by fixed rules and are mechanical in form (1889/1894:84). Thus man does not choose his religion, but it comes with a general set of social obligations and norms derived by 'his position in the family and in the nation' (ibid.:28).

Coercion implies force and force is a reality, so Durkheim would argue (see chs 11.4 and 15.2). Such a reality can legitimately be studied by science. But if religion is a constraining force, then surely this is true of science also? For Durkheim the answer is in the negative. He holds that religion, and especially institutional religion, is a force that restricts and confines individual inclinations and propensities, and therefore limits freedom (see 1897a:430/ t.1951a:375). Dogma by its very authority exerts the power which restrains and holds in check other ideas and doctrines which might challenge what is orthodox. Man until recently has been forced to accept the creed of the religion in which he has been brought up and to accept it in a way that does not permit doubt or questioning. Of course there is truth in this. But for Durkheim, by contrast, science epitomizes freedom, for science is not a coercive force. It is always open to challenge, to self-criticism or to modification (1899a(ii):18/t.1975a:89). Admittedly, science has its beliefs, its *représentations*, as does religion (see ch. 15). Although they are not obligatory, it is sensible (*sense*) to believe in them (ibid.). So science which studies force is free and religion which is a force is studied by science. This kind of argument was common enough amongst nineteenth-century rationalists. Man is free only when he is in a position to accept what reason tells him is true or desirable, and when he can, without hindrance, identify himself with that which is held to be reasonable. Durkheim and the rationalists of his day wedded reason with science in their quest for certain kinds of knowledge (see ch. 25.2). The association was one Durkheim frequently made (as in 1906e:253). An interesting example of it emerges at a date close to that of the 1899 article in a little-known newspaper account of a talk he gave to the Fédération de la Jeunesse Laïque on 22 May 1901, on Religion and Free Thought, presumably at Bordeaux.

> The speaker claimed to treat the problem scientifically. He proclaimed – he predicted – the triumph of science, but he knew that religion could not be erased by the stroke of a pen. It was necessary to satisfy needs which it had so long answered. It would be useless to maintain that the two enemies could be made to coexist by giving to each its own domain: that of externals to science, and that of deep and mysterious things to religion. This allegedly mysterious world is the world that is misunderstood. 'What then is the essential difference between religion and science? It is that religious belief is obligatory, while scientific opinion is free. The scientist has the right and even the duty to be constantly on guard against himself and his theories: the believer is walled in by his dogma.' The only possible reconciliation between science and religion would consist in finding moral ends in science itself. 'Science also must find – and science in particular – ends which transcend the individual; it must have an ideal, in other words, to make real that which is beyond us: justice and the good of others. (1901h).

Here Durkheim comes very close to positivism, which he so much disliked in Comte. But that aside, his position can be expressed as:

$$\frac{\text{religion}}{\text{science}} : \frac{\text{constraint}}{\text{freedom}}$$

The notion of constraint, which Durkheim attaches to religion but not to science, creates an inevitable ambiguity in his thought. For example, religion continues to exist, even though there are as many heterodox believers as there are orthodox (1899a(ii):27/ t.1975a:97). If religion has thus persisted, so must have its powers of coercion. Yet observers today might very well maintain that religion no longer exerts that power of constraint it once did, although beliefs of many kinds continue to be widespread. On the other hand, science today possesses powers of constraint over the general public as great as, if not greater than, those of religion. Science is the new god whose beliefs demand assent and which metes out ostracism to the non-believer (see ch. 25)! Durkheim thus puts himself in a virtually impossible position by trying to give science an immunity from something he holds odious which is present in religion. As C. C. J. Webb (1865–1954), the Oxford philosopher, observed many years ago, on the criterion of constraint alone, there is no significant means of differentiating science from religion (1916:55). The difference lies only in contrasting methods used to try to establish knowledge and truth.

Another problem is one that was with Durkheim from first to last. He argued that what is obligatory must come from a higher power, from an authority which is *ipso facto* a power more exalted than that of the individual. Durkheim rejected the idea that authority rested within the individual *conscience*. He admitted that the authority could be a god or spirit, or a non-empirical order of reality, but his emphasis on the social prevented him from taking such a position seriously. Dogmatically in the 1899 article he wrote: 'There is no moral authority superior to the individual except that of the group to which he belongs' (1899a(ii):27/t.1975a:97). This is an assumption on Durkheim's part: he either cannot or does not see the need to justify it empirically (see ch. 13). It is a glaring case of a *petitio principii* – Webb was probably the first to use this phrase of Durkheim (1916:57). Nor does Durkheim see constraint as the notion of obligation *sui generis* within the individual, as in Kant's categorical imperative (ibid.). The sense of obligation, whether in religion or in other aspects of social life, is seen as a product of that life, and therefore emanating from outside the individual and having its ultimate source in society.

One of the reasons for Durkheim's position being so unsatisfactory was because of the various meanings implied in the concept of constraint. It seems possible that he became conscious of the flaws that surrounded the concept and so did not develop the idea systematically, although he never abandoned the notion of constraint as one of the characteristics of religious belief and practice. In the limited use that he made of the term within the area of religion, it is evident that there are two distinct meanings. First, the notion of the term where people are almost physically forced to accept ideas and practices which they may not by their

174

nature be willing to accept. Second, the power that religious beliefs have over the mind when once they have been accepted, for their acceptance would seem to preclude other possibilities. Those who are caught in the religious net are so overpowered that they cannot accept other ideas. Apart from religion, Durkheim was to use the notion of constraint in many contexts and from these Lukes has perceived five different senses in which the word was employed by Durkheim. The criticisms are to some measure based on those of Sorel (Lukes 1972:12ff.). The five meanings are: the authority of legal codes, the need to follow rules to achieve a given end, the causal influence of ecological and morphological factors, the psychological compulsion in a crowd situation, and cultural determinants and the influence of socialization.

4 Individual religious phenomena: their exclusion

In the process of defining religion, Durkheim introduced the concept of constraint for several reasons. One was that he wanted to apply the ideas put forward in *The Rules* to a particular area and to demonstrate the soundness of his theoretical approach. The other was that in no area of social life is there more need to separate social from individual phenomena than in religion. The complexity of religion is such that it contains many components which require isolation for analytical purposes. Durkheim's approach calls for a careful distinction between social facts, or what we might call social-religious phenomena, from individual or private phenomena. Such a distinction is by no means easy, but Durkheim attempted it in the 1899 article when he briefly describes individual phenomena as 'innumerable religious manifestations which do not belong to any properly recognised religion' (1899a(ii):1/t.1975a:74). He was, however, able to classify various types of such phenomena. They were:

1 'scattered beliefs and practices, be they individual or local, which are not integrated into a definite system' (ibid.);
2 gods, which apart from those which people are compelled to worship, are created by anyone for his own personal use (ibid.:26/96);

3 the unorthodox beliefs of an individual about a commonly worshipped god (ibid.);
4 sacrifices, disciplines and rituals not prescribed by religious law but employed by individuals (ibid.);
5 'a free, private, optional religion fashioned according to one's own needs and understanding' (ibid.).

Durkheim was careful to exclude from individual religious phenomena, beliefs and practices of small groups, say within a church or major religious grouping (ibid.:27 n.1/99 n.28). Such phenomena, which would include domestic religion or constitute a sect, are collective in nature.

In the 1899 article the line of demarcation between what is social and what is individual is not altogether clear because, from the examples that have been given, one wonders where precisely local cults, as in the case of attachment to a local saint in the Roman Catholic Church, are to be located. From what Durkheim says they could be placed within the area of socio-religious phenomena and also within individual religious phenomena. They stand very much in the middle of what some might wish to suggest is a continuum. For others it might be seen as a 'wobbly' position. In fact Durkheim agrees with this, for he says that there is no question of discovering exact boundaries, assuming they exist; only of registering first impressions (ibid.:1/74). Be that as it may, he has no other criterion for classification.

In terms of his definition, individual phenomena do not have the force of constraint which social phenomena have. That and probably that alone marks off one set of facts from the other. In general, the criterion seems to be whether or not the individual wishes to modify what is generally intellectually received and practised. Two years after the publication of the 1899 article in the preface to the second edition of *The Rules*, Durkheim spoke of the individualizing processes within religion and morality.

Because beliefs and social practices thus come to us from without, it does not follow that we receive them passively or without modification. . . . It is for this reason that each one of us creates, in a measure, his own morality, religion, and mode of life. (1895a/1901c:xxii n.2/t.1938b:lvi n.7)

In *The Elementary Forms*, Durkheim holds that every religion has 'an individual aspect' (223/157). He also refers to individual totems and would include private gods and saints as part of individual religious phenomena. However, his treatment of such phenomena is less detailed, less carefully analysed and more quickly rejected than in the earlier article. At the beginning of *The Elementary Forms* he gives only two types of individual religious phenomena (64/46/122). They are: first, personal cults, surrounding patron saints or guardian angels, which are part of the Church's practice and teaching and are covered by the definition; and second, interior religious states, which he refers to as 'religious individualism', which relate to potentiality and the future and which cannot a priori be included in the definition (65/47/123). Interestingly enough, he also mentions folklore, which roughly corresponds to the first of the categories in the 1899 article (49/36/113; 57/47/118). Such phenomena, he holds, are the debris of past religions or have arisen spontaneously in a given locality. It would appear that folklore is included in his definition when he writes: 'a definition which did not take the facts into account would in consequence not include everything which is religious' (49/36/113). Today such phenomena might be considered the basis of what has become known as common or folk religion, to be found even in modern secularized society (see Towler 1974:ch. 8). That elements of folklore have been absorbed into Christianity all down the ages is a position Durkheim maintains along with scholars of his time and subsequently.

Durkheim's position over individual religious phenomena is much the same in the 1899 article as it is in *The Elementary Forms*, although they are excluded or assumed included in the final definition; there is, however, another radical shift in that definition and it is to that which we now turn.

5 Change in definition and the consequences

In the 1899 article Durkheim defined religious phenomena in the following way:

> Phenomena held to be religious consist in obligatory beliefs, connected with clearly defined practices which are related to given objects of those beliefs. (1899a(ii):22/t.1975a:93)

Logically he found himself forced to include individual religious phenomena, and the following rider was added to the conclusion of the article:

> In addition, the optional beliefs and practices which concern similar objects or objects assimilated into the previous ones, will also be called religious phenomena. (ibid.:28/98)

This comprehensive definition, however, was abandoned and a change was apparent in the 1906–7 lectures on the origins of religion. It gave way to what was to become his final definition, which appeared in *The Elementary Forms* and which every student of Durkheim knows. It reads:

> A religion is a unified system of beliefs and practices relative to sacred things, that is to say things set apart and forbidden, beliefs and practices which unite into one single moral community, called a church, all those who adhere to them. (65/47/123)

The change is remarkable for a number of reasons. First and foremost, Durkheim forsakes the notion of constraint or obligation as the criterion of religious phenomena or religion. He acknowledges the weakness of his former definition in a footnote in *The Elementary Forms*, but is quick to observe that both definitions in fact involve the notion of obligation and therefore they are not so violently dissimilar (65–6 n.1/47 n.1/163 n.34; and see 32 n.1/23 n.1). The later definition, using the concept of a moral community, clearly implies the idea of obligation. Durkheim admits the notion of coercion is an inadequate way of determining religious beliefs, for 'it permits an infinite number of degrees: consequently, there are cases where it is not easily perceptible' (ibid.). We have already observed that the early definition was based on form rather than content.

The content is now clearly stated as the sacred and so assumes a unique place as *the* distinguishing feature of religion. The importance of this concept in his thought and the reasons for its eventual pre-eminence have been discussed in the previous chapter. As the primacy of the sacred came to be realized, logic dictated that it had to be in the centre of the new definition. It means that religion is defined in terms of a concept, not a thing or person. But as we have seen, to use the notion of the sacred, or even that of obligation, allows the inclusion of beliefs and practices which in Durkheim's eyes are *laïques en apparence*, such as the mother country, the French Revolution, the individual, the nation, within the orbit of religion (see, for example, 1899a(ii):20/ t.1975a:91; 606/424/153). Needless to say, to cite such 'secular' ideas and movements calls forth criticism (see, for example, Ginsberg 1956:232–3; ch. 26).

In the lectures 'La Religion: les origines', Durkheim introduced for the first time the notion of the sacred into a definition, but he also included the concept of a religious community (1907f:533). This is strengthened in *Les Formes élémentaires*, where he refers to 'one single moral community, called a church' (*communauté morale, appelée une Église*). (Why Durkheim used an upper-case É is not known. We have used lower case in translation.) Durkheim was probably a pioneer in emphasizing such a characteristic within a definition of religion. By so doing he stresses the social quality of religion, in which belief and action are held and practised in common by a group. To delineate a religion therefore requires the delineation of a group or society. But one of the reasons that Durkheim emphasizes the notion of a community is that, as he is reported to have said in the lectures and as he wrote in *Les Formes élémentaires*, he wishes to differentiate magic, which he called anti-religious, from religion. (That magic has such characteristics is now generally denied (see Goody 1961:146).) Religion is differentiated by its association with a society consisting of members holding common beliefs about the sacred and profane. This is called a church and 'there is no religion without a church' (1907f:532). His final definition in the lectures was said to be: 'A system of beliefs and practices relative to sacred things – beliefs and practices common to a stipulated collectivity' (*collectivité déterminée*) (ibid.:533).

Durkheim's change in definition and his eventual commitment to that in *The Elementary Forms* lays him open to at least three charges:

(a) the charge of being reductionist;
(b) of presenting an essentialist definition of religion instead of a nominal one;
(c) of presenting a theory within a definition.

We deal with each of these charges separately.

a Reductionist

With the prominence given to the notion of community in his 1912 definition of religion, Durkheim sees that it is indeed imperative to eliminate the concept of religious individual phenomena which he had been willing, and indeed was forced to accept logically as part of his 1899 definition. Indeed, in *Les Formes élémentaires* he virtually drops the concept of religious phenomena *per se*, apart from suggesting in various places that they form a kind of general background to religion. In the earlier article he was bold enough to state that religion was a totality of religious phenomena including individual religious phenomena. Now it is a totality of social facts and, in keeping with notations in earlier sections of this chapter, we might express the change as follows:

1899   religion = Σ religious phenomena
           = Σ social facts and individual phenomena of a
             religious kind
1912   religion = Σ socio-religious phenomena (social facts)

Although in some senses Durkheim set his heart on opposing reductionism, as in the case of reducing sociology to psychology, or society to its component parts, which was his clarion call in *The Rules of Sociological Method*, he now lays himself open to being a reductionist in the realm of religion. The challenge is quite simply that he reduces religion, in the way we have noted, to socio-religious phenomena, to the exclusion of all other phenomena of a religious kind – phenomena which he had acknowledged at an earlier stage. As Barnes and Becker noted: 'It is from the individualists that the most acute and cogent criticisms of the Durkheim school have come. In fact the best statements of the individualistic position are to be found in the large literature of Durkheim criticism in France' (1938:851). The point is that Durkheim offers a sociological definition which is at the same time an *exclusive* definition, in so far as all other types of phenomena which are beyond the realm of sociology are excluded. The critics claim that the definition is dogmatic and ideological in as much as religion is seen to be focused on the social. To many scholars, let alone religious believers of his day, it created hostility, as in the case of Gaston Richard (1923) and Pater Schmidt (1931). Schmidt even wrote of the 1899 article that it overemphasized the community and undervalued the individual (ibid.:130). The definition evoked hostility from many anthropologists because of its failure to accept individual manifestations of religion and also because it rejects supernaturalism. As well as such writers as Malinowski (1913), Lowie (1925) and Radin (1938), we refer to the following authors who have been critical of Durkheim at this point.

One of the early reviews of *The Elementary Forms* to appear in England was that of the well known folk-lorist, E. S. Hartland. He praised the book as a 'brilliant volume' and added: 'We in England have perhaps hitherto made too little of the influence of society in the genesis of religion', but he was quick to add that the French school 'may go to the opposite extreme, may attach too little weight to this influence and these experiences [of individuals] and in effect ignore the part actually played by the individual' (1913:96).

A. A. Goldenweiser, the American anthropologist of German origin, in two reviews of *The Elementary Forms* – perhaps the most searching reviews of the time – accused Durkheim, amongst other things, of holding too narrow a definition of religion (1915 and 1917). In the spirit of the times, Goldenweiser demanded that any definition should include the possibility of emotional thrill and ecstasy. 'The proposition,' he stated, 'further prejudices the investigator in favour of the social elements in religion at the expense of the individual elements' (1915:721/r.1975:212). Emphasizing that the subject under discussion is religion and that in every culture religious experiences occur which are weakly institutionalized, Goldenweiser comments: 'This vast domain of religious facts is completely eliminated through Durkheim's formal method' (1917:118).

Van Gennep's biting review, published in the *Mercure de France*, also focused a great deal of attention on Durkheim's failure to take into account the place of the individual and theories related to the individual. He wrote: 'as a result of his well-known personal tendency to emphasize the collective element (social) above all else and put it in the foreground, Durkheim has neglected action, the maker of institutions and beliefs, of various individuals' (1913:391/t.1975:207). Again: 'It is obvious that in the most primitive societies, social action is more pressing than individual action . . . Durkheim's dream is to recognize in society a natural – one might almost say cosmic – reality which would consequently be subject to laws as necessary as physico-chemical laws' (ibid.:391/207–8).

Along similar lines C. C. J. Webb, in his Wilde lectures of 1914, criticized Durkheim's theory and definition of religion in so far as, along with other French sociologists, he failed to take adequate account of private religious beliefs and practices (1916:61, 131ff., 173). He admitted, however, that such sociologists had given considerable service to the philosophy of religion by stressing the social setting of religion in offering a definition which took account of the historical development of religion. Webb also stated that the starting-point must be religions, not religion, and that it was wrong to abstract a common element of all religions and so produce a minimal definition. Among his criticisms he stated that the bankruptcy of Durkheim's definition became apparent when he introduced individual or optional phenomena into the 1899 definition (ibid.:58–9). If optional phenomena can be called religious, but do not constrain individuals, and socio-religious phenomena have as their criterion constraint, either it becomes impossible to differentiate them or the definition itself becomes quite meaningless. Further, private beliefs and practices in the eyes of individuals associated with them would seem to be obligatory. It is apparent that Webb is here raising the problem we have already mentioned, namely, that of the ambiguity of the term constraint. Nor is Webb any more satisfied with the later definition of religion. The notion of the sacred is open to the charge of circularity, since, Webb assumes, the context of the sacred is determined by what is religious (ibid.:60 n.2). He states that the second definition, despite Durkheim's protest about the earlier definition being too formal and stressing obligation, is no less formal than that of 1899. There was no reference to mystery in either definition. Webb himself did not think that religion could be defined (certainly in an essentialist sense) and criticized Durkheim for claiming to have done so (ibid.:59).

Later, Morris Ginsberg has criticized Durkheim's approach to primitive religion because it accorded exclusive emphasis to group solidarity and a minimum attention to religion as a means of securing material benefits and allaying fears about the natural environment. He writes: 'Thus the religious consciousness, even in its elementary forms, must have included something more than the feeling of group solidarity' (1956:239).

The position Durkheim adopted was one against the intellectual stream of his day. Philosophers who have considered religion were, on the whole, convinced that the individual element, seen in evolutionary and historical processes, was one which was becoming increasingly prominent and important in terms of understanding the nature of religion (Høffding 1914:839). The work of W. James, cited by Gaston Richard, with its emphasis on heightened psychological awareness to be seen in exceptional individuals, also pointed in the same direction.

Richard makes the observation, unique amongst critics of Durkheim, that, in eliminating references to individual phenomena, Durkheim was expressing an innate fear of mysticism which seized him at the beginning of his life and remained with him to the end (1925(ii):362; ch. 1.2). Further, Richard argues, perhaps somewhat unjustifiably, that Durkheim seemed to associate every type of interior and personal religion with mysticism. He wrote: 'He [Durkheim] feared mysticism as much as saintliness, and criminality was in his eyes a sort of phagocytosis against saintliness and the saints' (ibid.). He recalls the well-known reference to saints in *The Rules of Sociological Method*. 'Imagine a society of saints, a perfect cloister of exemplary individuals. Crimes, properly so called, will there be unknown; but faults which appear venial to the layman will create there the same scandal that the ordinary offence does in ordinary consciousness' (1895a/1901c:68/t.1938b:69).

H. Pinard de la Boullaye (1874–1958), the Jesuit scholar in the field of comparative religions, showed himself sympathetic to some consideration of the social elements of religion (1922, see vols I–III). However, he rejects Durkheim's disregard of individual religious phenomena, together with his concept of society as *sui generis* (1922:442ff.). He holds that, according to Durkheim, a person cannot be religious unless he is a member of a church. Thus, a man's personal religion is in fact irreligious! To make a church an *essential* element of religion has to be proved – something that Durkheim attempts in his analysis of totemism, which is not convincing. Pinard de la Boullaye accepts the valid distinction between real and nominal definitions in approaching most phenomena, but he rejects the idea of relying on positive and external characteristics in considering moral realities (1922, II:3ff.). He admits the reduction implicit in Durkheim's definitions, which emphasize interdict and association, and so favour a sociological explanation of religion. There is absolute silence on the faith of the individual or in superior beings, which is common to all religions, ancient and modern. Such a belief is the historical foundation of the distinction between the sacred and the profane, and the common base of confessional organization (ibid.:4; cf. Durkheim 1899a(ii):15/t.1975a:87). Loisy argues the other way; he found the 1912 definition was based too much on abstractions and not enough on reality (1913:46).

Most of the critics of Durkheim's definition and sociological approach to religion who have been mentioned have been Protestants or ex-Catholics, with the exception of de la Boullaye. Nevertheless, it could be argued that Catholics – at least traditional Catholics – would not object to a definition of religion involving the concepts of the sacred and the Church as much as would Protestants (Isambert 1969:451). And one might note that the earlier definition, emphasizing the obligatory nature of belief and practice is also more in keeping with Catholic thought than with that of Protestants.

Reductionism usually refers to a method of scientific investigation by which a phenomenon at one level is reduced to another level in order to understand it or explain it. Thus, man can be reduced to a system of organs and cells. This would be perfectly satisfactory for understanding the human body but not the person, for such a reduction excludes his mind, his psyche, or his soul if it is believed that he has one. Some form of reduction is thus legitimate and is necessary in certain scientific inquiry. The question that arises is what can be reduced and what cannot. For Durkheim, as we have seen, social phenomena cannot be reduced to individual phenomena, and social phenomena cannot be fully understood by reference to psychological study. The complexity of the phenomenon and the relation of its parts is of crucial importance in deciding whether or not reduction can take place. Lévi-Strauss suggests that where the phenomenon is too complex, it cannot be reduced to another level and one has to adopt a structural approach (1978:9ff.). It is not surprising therefore that the debate about religion and reductionism turns on whether it is legitimate to reduce religion in any way whatsoever. The pheno-

menological study of religion, now popular amongst some students
of religion of whom Professor Ninian Smart is perhaps the best-
known exponent in the English-speaking world, would want to
deny all reductionism which would in any way detract from the
wholeness of religion (Smart 1973:45ff.).

It was noted that Durkheim was ready enough to use a reductive
methodology when he put forward the 1912 definition of religion,
in which religion is reduced to religious institutions. On the other
hand, although religion could be so reduced, what is at the heart
of religion, that is, the sacred, could not be reduced. As early as
1899 he wrote: 'Here we have a group of phenomena (the sacred)
which are irreducible to any other group of phenomena'
(1899a(ii):17/t.1975a:88). He was always ready to preach against
reductionism in general, as when he wrote in *Les Formes
élémentaires*:

Nothing arises out of nothing. The impressions made on us by
the physical world cannot, by definition, embody anything
which transcends this world. The tangible can only be made
into the tangible; the vast cannot be made into the minute.
(322/225/134)

This rather woolly statement underlines Durkheim's position
about reductionism, namely, that what is held to be *sui generis*
cannot be reduced. This applies to society and the sacred. Both
these concepts are sacred just because they cannot be reduced.
Indeed, the one way to forestall the intrusion of reductionist
procedures is to state beforehand that something is *sui generis*.
We return to our earlier point: on what grounds are social phenomena held to be *sui generis* or irreducible in contrast to other
phenomena?

b An essential definition?

It can well be argued that Durkheim moved away from a scientific
approach to religion to a non-scientific one by the way in which
he changed the definition of religion. As we have noted, his
intention in the opening paragraph of the 1899 article was to
establish a boundary-making definition – a nominal definition.
The purpose was simply to locate the phenomena to be studied.
This constitutes a procedure satisfactory to the demands of a

scientific approach (Popper 1957:26, 29). Despite any internal weakness of the first definition, at least of a substantial kind, it complied with the canons of a nominal definition. Not so that which appeared in *The Elementary Forms*. Instead of offering one or two criteria, or a family of criteria which Wittgenstein has imaginatively suggested is the best way of proceeding, Durkheim presents various concepts which he implies are necessary for locating the existence of religion. What emerges is no simple delineating definition: it thus ceases to be formal and exterior (Belot 1913a:336). It becomes a comprehensive definition which sets out to give the requirements of a religion – what is most important in religion itself. Durkheim thus presents his readers with a real or essential definition and so abandons what he held to be scientific procedure. In other places he is always ready to offer something approaching an essential definition, as when he writes: 'Above all, it [religion] is a system of ideas by means of which individuals represent to themselves the society of which they are members, and the obscure but intimate relations that they maintain with it' (322–3/225/135). Durkheim admits in *Les Formes élémentaires* that at the end of the study he will be able to offer something which we would call an essential definition (32/23). He was convinced that the sociology of religion could discover behind all the complexities and variations throughout history the true content of religious life (1899a(ii):16/t.1975a:87; see 6/4/106). The object of the sociology of religion is to distinguish what is primary from what is secondary, and to establish fundamental *représentations* and religious attitudes which are to be found in each religion (see ch. 15).

Thus, it can legitimately be argued that Durkheim begins with positing external traits which are clear to see, but at the same time in going behind such a definition, he has as his object the discovery of fundamental structures. This is very much part of scientific procedure. It is 'to reach fundamental elements which are the true components of the phenomena' (Lévi-Strauss 1945:524). The question, of course, is whether Durkheim succeeds in discovering 'the true components'. Certainly no modified or ultimate definition of religion appears at the end of the book.

c A theory?

The new definition is more than a definition, it is a theory. Durkheim 'does not only isolate a number of criteria which, he holds, mark off religion from other social phenomena – beliefs and practices centred on the sacred related to the existence of a community – but goes on to state the way these criteria are related to one another. The relation is a functional one in which beliefs and practices about the sacred are said to unite participants into a whole. Factors are thus introduced in which a specific outcome is stipulated. This can be nothing else but a theory, which appears to be proved but which in the development of *The Elementary Forms* Durkheim attempts to substantiate. As Goldenweiser says, the notion of a church 'brings in an element of standardization and of unification, which should be a matter to be proved not assumed' (1915:721/r.1975:212). Belot has also made the point in his review of the book (1913a:336), and rightly it has been repeated by other critics. How far religion itself integrates society is something that will be raised later (see ch. 16.4).

6 Reasons for the change

In the face of the hostility levelled against his definition – and probably Durkheim realized he would meet such strong opposition – why did he assume a path that seemed so hazardous? Seger probably puts the case too strongly in saying that critics showed anger (1957:36). But, if Durkheim knew he was going to draw the fire of the enemy, why did he proceed in this way? Was there some inner logic in his reasoning that forced him to adopt the course he did? There are good grounds to suggest that this was in fact the case.

First, during the period from approximately 1900 to 1906, the concept of the sacred rose to such prominence in Durkheim's thought that it was seen to be a fundamental element in the ordering of society. It was in religion more than in any other sector of society that the sacred was located. There could therefore be no alternative but to define religion in terms of that concept. As we have seen, it was impossible for him to define religion in terms of a god or gods. If he had done so, he would in his eyes have implied the actual existence of the deity or the supernatural. Science must always use data that can be said to be real (see ch. 15.2). Durkheim openly denied that God or the gods existed. Therefore to have a science based on what is false is to have no science at all. By contrast, as he was firmly convinced, the sacred had a reality which could not be denied.

Second, Durkheim soon began to be dissatisfied with the earlier definition of religion based on constraint, and for reasons we have just seen. His dissatisfaction may well have been in direct response to an attack made on him by Belot (1900:292ff.). Durkheim, argues Belot, makes his starting-point the rejection of the approaches of Spencer and Müller because of the psychological overtones of their analysis. In keeping with his idea of a social fact, he turns instead to the external characteristics of religion, not its content. By concentrating on the power of constraint, he is unable to differentiate religion from other phenomena such as morality and science. Admittedly, Durkheim intended the 1899 definition to be a preliminary one, but that it contained such weaknesses, as Belot pointed out, Durkheim was ready to accept. On this score alone it is unsatisfactory.

Third, the change may have been due to a change in his evaluation of social facts. This observation has been recently made by Stanner (1967:226). 'Facts' became less important in Durkheim's later analysis of social control, which was seen to be achieved 'by a sense of imperative duty, arising from the axiology of life, to obey rules which are necessarily objectified in religious and quasi-religious symbols' (ibid.). This change is similar to that which has been observed by other writers in as much as Durkheim, it is argued, gave greater attention to collective *représentations* rather than to morphological factors. We consider this problem in other chapters (see chs 15.4 and 20.3). What is relevant here is that the change to a new conception of social control allowed Durkheim to withdraw from the notion of external obligation and therefore from his first definition of religion.

This particular argument raises a number of questions. For one thing, it is doubtful whether Durkheim makes his starting-point social control and then relates it to other factors, such as the definition of religion. It is just as legitimate to argue that Durkheim begins with religion and then changes his concept of social control as he analyses religion. This latter argument would seem to be more cogent. Further, as we have suggested, the change of focus in Durkheim's approach to sociological explanation by giving greater emphasis to collective *représentations* is itself full of problems and difficulties. Clearly Stanner's point is taken seriously, but it is doubtful if it is as important as he would make it out to be.

In sum, Durkheim's change in definition comes about as a result of the realization that the 1899 definition is untenable and that the notion of the sacred as a substantive component of religion must receive prominence in any acceptable definition. This does not, however, eradicate the problem of his reductionism, by which he eliminated from his definition all references to individual religious phenomena.

7 The definition: consequences for the discipline

Has Durkheim been misunderstood in his definition of religion? Can he be defended? At a literal level the failure to be understood hardly arises. As a conceptualist Durkheim aims to define his terms at the outset and what he says is clear enough and without ambiguity.

Was it that he was too rigorous? No scientist can be that. Did he overstate his case? The question at issue turns on the place of private and individual religious phenomena to be included in a definition of religion. As we have seen, he emphasized such phenomena in the 1899 article, and even in *The Elementary Forms* he was ready to draw attention to them. He wrote: 'We know that there is no religion which does not have an individual aspect' (223/157). No one can deny, however, that Durkheim sees the social aspects of religion – socio-religious phenomena or the social facts of religion – are of paramount importance in examining the place of religion in society. It is the aim of *sociologie religieuse* to delineate them, to relate them to other social phenomena and, if possible, to deduce laws about them. Sociology in its task of understanding society and social behaviour must inevitably concentrate on social phenomena rather than on individual phenomena which are in any case difficult to deal with methodologically.

We raise this issue in more detail in the following chapter. In order to ensure that sociology, and therefore the sociology of religion, proceeds rigorously on its road, Durkheim perhaps feels impelled to overstate his case by ensuring that in the definition of religion all references to individual religious phenomena are excluded.

Further, because Durkheim introduced the concept of the sacred as the substantive criterion of religion, he was logically forced to exclude individual elements. Since, in his view, the sacred is essentially something collective and the individual essentially profane, no other path is possible but to eliminate the individual. Religion can hardly be a phenomenon which consists of both the sacred *and* the profane (see ch. 7.3). Of course, this means that the idea of the sacred has a social origin and therefore the explanation of religion must be sociological (see Deploige 1911/t.1938:63). Thus, the source cannot be human nature in general: it is in the nature of societies themselves (ibid.).

Given, therefore, the axioms which Durkheim held were necessary to understand society and religious phenomena, he could define religion in no other way than to exclude individual religious phenomena. It might be argued that he tried in this respect to steer sociology along a particular channel which was far too narrow and from which he was forced to eliminate phenomena he held to be irrelevant. It also seems true that he posited an essential definition which involved a theory. Hence his definition becomes an example of a *petitio principii*, for which Alpert and Lukes have justly criticized him. And about essentialist definitions Wach has written: 'Those of us who study the sociological implications of religion will err . . . if we imagine that our work will reveal the nature and essence of religion itself' (1947:4).

It may well be argued in the light of the controversies that have arisen since Durkheim's day over defining religion, that to embark upon such a task at the present time is not worth the effort. The work of the sociologist or anthropologist or even historian of religion is not to waste time on the impossible task of defining religion, but to find it and analyse it. In this respect Geertz has made a strong plea (1968a:1). Over and against the urge to bypass the problem of definition, the fact remains that an undeclared or implicit meaning always exists in the mind of the observer when he searches for religion and attempts to analyse it or to describe and explain some aspect of it. Any explanation implies a definition.

The years which followed the publication of *The Elementary Forms* witnessed the continued efforts by scholars to define religion and the pattern became polarized as a result of Durkheim's work, so that roughly there were two groups – those who would define religion in terms of gods or superhuman beings on the one hand, and those who preferred to follow Durkheim in positing the notion of the sacred or something akin to it. The debate has recently been summarized by such writers as Goody (1961), Horton (1960), and Spiro (1966).[1] It would be ridiculous to suggest that every anthropologist falls within these two camps. But Durkheim's approach, despite its early criticisms, did encourage a group of scholars to define religion in terms of the sacred and that particular approach shows no sign of waning. Declared definitions give rise to inevitable consequences. To use an inclusive definition, based on the sacred, allows a religion to embrace a much larger area and to include such phenomena as humanism, communism, nationalism and so on, than an exclusive definition which centres itself on belief and worship associated with a god or spirit. 'As one makes one's bed so one must lie in it.' Stanner, commenting on Durkheim's approach to religion in the light of his study of Australian Aboriginals, wrote a few years ago:

> It seems to me that definitions of religions – that is, of all religions and at all times – are doubtfully a matter for anthropology at all. No doubt it will one day contribute some of the adequate predicates which philosophers of religion will generalize. But if it is to do so it will certainly have to stop treating religion as the dependent variable of study. (1966:vii)

Stanner is not alone amongst anthropologists and sociologists in saying that anything approaching a definitive definition of religion stands within the province of the philosopher. For the anthropologist and sociologist, an attempt to find a real definition is not on: all he can do, and indeed must do, is to attempt a strictly working definition of religion, a boundary-making definition, which Durkheim always said he began with. Although it may be true that wrestling with definitions is a pointless task, it is not a completely futile one or one that can be embarked on carelessly. A definition, no matter of what kind, has serious consequences for any discipline and that elementary lesson Durkheim fully understood.

Thus. having defined religion in strictly sociological terms, as Durkheim did, explanations of it must inevitably be of a sociological kind. The definition has cleared the way for what Evans-Pritchard has termed a structural theory of the genesis of religion (1965:53). Religion arises out of the very nature of society: it can do no other, since individual religious phenomena have been eliminated. Admittedly, theories of social origin can be found in Fustel de Coulanges and Robertson Smith, but neither developed a theory with such boldness or ruthless logic as did Durkheim.

Yet, a mystery always seems to hang over Durkheim's approach to the definition of religion. As we have noted, despite his declared intention to produce an essential definition at the end of his study, he does not do so. He always said that initially his definition of religion was concerned with external criteria and was intended to be what we today would call a nominal definition. In the early days at least, during the second stage of his approach to religion, he saw in religion a highly complex phenomenon which in some way could not be finally understood by science. In a letter to Richard criticizing him for his analysis of religion, Durkheim wrote:

> There is nothing more vague and diffuse than religion. It is true I have defined it, but vague and diffuse things can be defined. The most tortuously complex things can be defined. Confusion can be expressed. The fact remains that in religion everything is confused. At least, that is my view of it. It stands in the same relationship to the representative life of society as does sensation to the life of the individual. Just as we experience things through their colours, etc., so society represents its life and the life of the objects related to it as sacred objects. It colours them with religiosity. Why is this? The matter is highly debatable. (1928b:299 n.1.)

10 The problem of the social and the individual in religion

Attention has been drawn to the criticisms levelled against Durkheim's final definition of religion. One of the main points at issue was his virtual elimination of individual religious phenomena from that definition. We now examine the problem not so much in terms of the definition, but within the context of methodology.

1 Religion *is* a social phenomenon

Once convinced that religion is essentially a social phenomenon, understandable and to be explained only in terms of the social, Durkheim never wavered from such a position: repeatedly he used it in sociological explorations. Aspects of the relation of religion to the social are raised in chapters ahead (see chs 12–14, especially ch. 14). For the moment it is necessary to rehearse some of his observations or assertions about the social nature of religion and its origin in society.

It is interesting that, in an early book whose subject seems prima facie to have little to do with religion, *Le Suicide* (1897a), Durkheim argues most compellingly for the social character of religion. He sees religion as 'the system of symbols by means of which society becomes conscious of itself; it is the characteristic way of thinking about collective existence' (1897a:352/ t.1951a:312). And he continues:

> Here then is a great group of states of mind which would not
> have originated if particular *consciences* had not combined
> and which result from this union and are superadded to those
> which derive from individual natures. (ibid.)

Further, the social environment produces religious ideas. He had held some time before that the religious sentiment (religion itself is not mentioned) is created by men meeting together, by social life itself. In a review written earlier he referred to 'the intersocial tendencies which give rise to religious sentiment' (1887b:309/ t.1975a:36).

That religion is pre-eminently social means that it is essentially an institution in society. Durkheim goes on to say: 'it has served for many peoples as the foundation of collective life' (1925a:79/ t.1961a:69). Just because religion is social and concerned with the ideals of society, it is able to limit individual and selfish tendencies. Durkheim is convinced that religion is able to curb egoistic suicide (1897a:ch. 2) and, since it is losing its power in society, it is less able to have this effect on what he sees as an immoral act (ibid.:430ff./t.1951a:375ff.). If religion were something individual in nature and for the benefit of individual fulfilment, it would not exert such controls over individual behaviour. It performs many functions which only make sense if religion is seen to act for the good of society (see ch. 16).

Having rejected a 'religious' or a 'spiritual' explanation of religion, together with a serious consideration of the role of the individual as a key component in religion and as a progenitor of religion, Durkheim realized that his atheistic, and at the same time social theory might be criticized for being 'materialistic'. So he declared: 'Care must be taken not to see our theory of religion as a simple revival of historical materialism' (605/423/152). The forces at work within the institution of religion are not spiritual in the orthodox sense nor material, but are, we might say, in between the two. They are moral and social. He said at an early date:

> The powers before which the believer prostrates himself are not simply physical forces, such as are given to the senses and imagination: they are social forces. They are the direct product of collective sentiments which have clothed themselves in a material covering. (1899a(ii):24/t.1975a:94)

The inevitable conclusion is that Durkheim sees religion not only possessing a social dimension – a fact that is incontestable – but that such a dimension is of overriding importance to the extent that everything that might be called individual or personal can for practical purposes be excluded. As we shall see, all that goes by the name of religion – gods, rites, beliefs, religious objects – arises out of man's social life, from his interrelationship with

194

other people. That religion is a product of society, seems to be something beyond all doubt (see ch. 14 for further consideration of this point). The assumption rests more on logic than on empirical evidence.

2 The individual admitted, but disregarded: a point of criticism

Durkheim was writing at a time when liberal humanism was in the ascendancy. Such ideology gave prominence to the individual above all else and invested him with a great measure of free will. Not surprisingly, this thinking was reflected in theology itself, where concepts of the autonomy of the individual, held to be present in Hebraic-Christian thought, were strongly emphasized. Within such a situation the position of Durkheim was ambivalent. On the one hand, he was an ardent liberal humanist, who gave the individual an ultimate place in his thought, sometimes going beyond theologians and conceding him almost divine status (see ch. 26). In this he felt he was merely reflecting what was in fact happening in the religious attitudes of intellectuals of modern western Europe. Yet on the other hand, as we have just seen, religion was essentially a social phenomenon derived from society and for the benefit of society. A paradox thus emerges which was with him throughout his life.

As we have seen in the previous chapter, Durkheim admitted that individual religious phenomena existed. He always closely associated morality with religion and he saw the presence of individual moral phenomena as much in the one as in the other. Every individual has his own religion, his own morality. In the 1899 article on defining religion, he wrote:

> Each one of us has his personal moral code, his personal approach, which differs from the common morality and general approach of society although they spring from them [forms of collective activity]. (1899a(ii):28/t.1975a:97–8)

And again, in 1906, in a discussion following his paper 'La Détermination du fait moral', he repeated the idea:

195

Each individual moral *conscience* expresses the collective morality in its own way. Each one sees it and understands it from a different angle. No individual can be completely in tune with the morality of his time. (1906b/1924a:56/t.1953b:40)

Hence there are as many moralities as there are individuals, and there are as many moralities as there are religions!

Durkheim's assertion, however, that individual religious phenomena existed was not enough to satisfy many critics, who were convinced that although he admitted the existence of the individual he in fact played down and even played out the individual. With the prevailing outlook, how could such criticism have been otherwise? His doctrine was little short of heresy.

The major issue was more specifically that Durkheim in his analysis of religion had given little or no place to the individual leader, initiator or reformer. It might be said, using a modern analogy, that he saw religion emerging as a giant corporation determined by a broad policy that was in no way influenced by a charismatic figure – a figure so much stressed by Max Weber and which at the same time appears to be so characteristic of religious movements. Richard, in an early letter to Durkheim, writing to him as the leader of the then emerging Année Sociologique group, questioned the very meagre place that Durkheim had given to the role of the individual in the emergence of religion. Much later, in 1928, the reply of Durkheim, dated 11 May 1899, was published; he wrote as follows:

I know of no religion which has truly been the work of one man. In examining the history of the Jews, this idea has been completely abandoned. In India, Buddhism existed long before the advent of the Buddha. As for Christianity, the situation is well known. I cannot comment on Islam in view of the scant data at my disposal. But in the light of what I do know, I am exceedingly sceptical. On first contact, religious ideas appear impersonal – my paper of last year [1899a(ii)?] stated this better perhaps. There are amongst them a certain number of elementary (I do not say logically simple) ideas which dominate the entire moral development of humanity. (1928b:299 n.1)

And there are other instances where Durkheim showed that he

was fully aware of the influence of individuals in the development of religious and moral ideas. For example, in his lectures on moral education which he gave around 1902–3, Durkheim said that in considering moral reformers such as Christ and Socrates – names associated with the great moral revolutions of man – they shook off the yoke of traditional discipline and did not feel too strongly the weight of external authority (1925a:60–1/t.1961a:53). But the circumstances were abnormal. Care must be taken not to confuse two different feelings – the need to substitute new rules for old, on the one hand, and an impatience with all rules and an abhorrence of all discipline, on the other. 'Under ordinary conditions, the former is natural, healthy and fruitful' (ibid.). Thus Durkheim admits the legitimacy of religious and moral reformation, but at the same time he was totally opposed to the possibility of unrestricted liberties.

Later, Marc Boegner, Protestant pastor and scholar (see ch. 23.4), posed the question at the 1913–14 conference organized by the Union of Free Thinkers and Free Believers, after Durkheim had left:

Is it possible to find in the *conscience collective* of a given time all the elements included in the religious *conscience* of the great initiators of that time, for example, Jeremiah, Jesus, in opposition to the tendencies of the collective, religious *conscience* of the period? (1919b:142/t.1975a:189)

Durkheim's later written reply was:

The question of great religious personalities and of their role is certainly an important one. It was not involved in the study that I undertook: I did not wish to put forward a hypothesis relative to such a complex problem: a problem which has never been methodically studied. (ibid.:143/189)

Apart from the work of Max Weber in his analysis of types of authority and types of leadership, the difficulties hinted at by Durkheim do not appear to have been overcome by sociologists. The merits of studying individual religious leaders have, in the main, been realized by the historian, although some sociologists and anthropologists are now turning their attention to the question.

Goldenweiser, in reviewing Durkheim's work, pointed to his

virtual obsession with the social and said that 'the lives of saints are one great argument against Durkheim's theory' and 'the psychic cast of many a savage medicine man, magician, shaman, is another' (1915:219). The point is that Durkheim's system does not provide the means of distinguishing a group of religious people of average potentialities from one that contains exceptional individuals who show unusual proclivities for the religious life (Goldenweiser 1923:372).

In a debate on the subject of science and religion, not often referred to, Durkheim criticized his former teacher Émile Boutroux for proposing a notion of religion which was essentially spiritual and the idea that religion gave rise to aspiration and novelty and hence was outside the realm of scientific consideration (1909a(1)). Interestingly enough, Durkheim admitted the existence of creative periods in religion which are dominated by prophets and forerunners. He commented: 'This religion [of ferment] represents only a moment in the history of each religion. A time always comes when a religion passes from a dynamic state to a static state, where it is fixed, where its ideal crystallizes itself into very clearly defined formulae, in a body of dogmas and rites' (ibid.:56). Durkheim therefore readily accepts the fact of religious (and social) change initiated by some creative movement (see ch. 22.6). However, such a stage quickly gives rise to one of relatively high stability and it is such stable periods that hold Durkheim's attention and interest. The developed, static stage is historically much longer than the creative stage and is thus of great importance in understanding the social behaviour of a given society. It is the day-by-day, the unchanging religious force that continually permeates society, not the voice of the occasional prophet.

The notion of the individual within religion has another dimension which, because it was omitted by Durkheim, gave rise to criticism. It usually comes from those who hold that religion is essentially an individual or private affair, expressed in such terms as 'the flight of the alone to the alone'. It is often psychologists who may take this position and one readily calls to mind the work of William James. However, Malinowski, a Catholic by upbringing, and perhaps even influenced by James, held that religion is grounded in experience away from the crowd. He said: 'the strongest religious moments come in solitude, in turning away from the world, in concentration and mental detachment'

(1925:57). Here is a field anthropologist going in the reverse direction to Durkheim. In these days it is generally agreed that the influence of society, of the external social and religious environment, in some way mediates even the most personal of religious experiences. 'Purely' individual, innate religious awareness does not exist as Durkheim indicated.

The relation between the social (society) and the individual occupied the attention of many philosophers in Durkheim's day, including Lucien Lévy-Bruhl and Henri Bergson. The question of the influence of Bergson on Durkheim is raised below (see ch. 22.2). Suffice it to say here that Bergson never openly quarrelled with Durkheim as did Richard and Tarde. Nevertheless he raised questions in *Les Deux sources de la morale et de la religion* (1932) in which he challenged the implication of Durkheim's excessive concern with the social. He thus found little or no place for that which Bergson stressed, namely, the dynamic or personal factors in religion. Bergson was ready to accept the notion of the social and *représentations collectives*, but indicated that Durkheim did not account for the tension between the collective and the individual. Why should the personal come into conflict with the social? Sociology has no answer. Durkheim and those who follow him have only one way out of the dilemma – to posit that society has an existence of its own, it constitutes reality; and the individual is a mere abstraction (Bergson 1932/t.1935:85).

Another point of criticism is that Durkheim disregards the individual element in religion to suit his convenience. To many such an element was seen as being increasingly important in the light of their reading of history in the wide sweep. The Danish philosopher Høffding (1843–1941), writing about Durkheim in 1914, emphasized the fact that 'we see the individual element more and more accentuated in the course of evolution' (1914:839). And similarly van Gennep pointed to the fact that 'the individual has grown gradually conscious of himself' (1913:391/t.1975:208). However, the growth, especially in recent times, of what is said to be individual in religion has several distinct meanings which are not clearly stated in the criticisms of Durkheim. First, one can speak of a development of individual phenomena, occurring particularly in the West, as the dominant religious groups have lost their power of control. Durkheim himself said that unorthodox opinions were growing and multiplying and that 'there are in

199

every church almost as many heterodox as orthodox' (1899a(ii):28/ t.1975a:97). The multiplication of churches and sects, within the context of individual thought, has given rise to religious pluralism and is something that Durkheim readily admitted, but did not account for. The second possibility is that, with the decline of traditional religions, man himself has become the subject of a generally diffused religion in society. Man is now man's new god. This is also very much in accordance with Durkheim's own views, as we shall show in a later chapter (see ch. 26). Again, the individual element can refer to the role of individual leaders in establishing and maintaining a religion.

If Durkheim acknowledges these aspects of the individual in religion, where is the problem? Is it that the critics have misread him or not read the full extent of his works? The issue at stake seems to be that Durkheim only asserted the facts about the individual component. He did not incorporate them in a mean-ingful way into his analysis of religion. The particular meanings of the individual just outlined, however, create problems for him. He admits to religious pluralism and unorthodoxy, but places them outside his interests by categorizing them as being of little importance compared with the social or with orthodoxy. And the cult of the individual raises other questions of how it is that what is profane and what seems structurally profane becomes sacred (see ch. 26.5). Thus all Durkheim seems to offer is lip-service to individual elements in religion.

To disregard all that is individual in religion and to see religion as a social force enveloping the individual invites the question of whether such an analysis means that the freedom of the individual is denied. According to Durkheim's reasoning, religion may be seen to act on a man in a mechanical way and without personal mediation. Freedom of the will, to be able to accept or reject religious ideas, is viewed by many as not only what occurs in religious behaviour but as that which is essential for all ethical and religious action and belief. The same kind of criticism comes from those who see that for Durkheim religion is associated with primitive group emotion and characterized by mechanical solida-rity (for example, Adams 1916:303). Factual problems about the nature of religion aside, to try to deal in detail with the problem of the freedom of the will in Durkheim is too complex to consider here. We would merely draw attention to the fact that Durkheim in his frequent and, on the whole, positive allusions to Kant does not deny the freedom of the will. He takes, as in so many other issues, a *via media*, seeing man both free and yet heavily influenced by social factors (Lukes 1972:74, 635; Pope 1973; Parsons 1975). Man is skewed towards, but not determined by, external social forces.

3 Sociology has no option

The problem which Durkheim saw more clearly than anyone else in his time was: what does the sociologist 'do' with the individual element in religion? As we have already seen, on methodological ground there is little alternative but to disregard it, at least initially, and proceed without it. As early as 1886 Durkheim held that the subject-matter of the sociology of religion was 'that aspect of religion which we see when it is viewed purely as a social phenomenon' (1886a:68/t.1975a:21). And more recently Lévi-Strauss in a similar vein said that 'subjectivities are, by hypothesis, incomparable and incommunicable' (1950:xxx). Nowadays no one denies the influence of the social or social forces at work in religion. That such agreement can be found amongst scholars is perhaps in part due to Durkheim's influence. Nevertheless there were in his day, even amongst his critics, those who would agree with him on this point. We might mention in passing C. C. J. Webb who said that the individual is always subject to the pressure of 'the social medium' (1916:133), and went on:

> The operation of this is equally seen in the encouragement
> and checking of individual trains of thought and imagination.
> Such checking takes place both where free development of
> these things would be desirable; and where it would be the
> reverse. (ibid.)

The problem is, what does the sociologist select to study? Durkheim's contention is that in examining all other types of social phenomena, the sociologist can do no other than methodologically eliminate or totally disregard what is seen to be individual. In the 1899 article on defining religion he openly said that the sociology of religion has but one subject-matter – religious facts seen as social facts, what we might call socio-religious facts.

Simon Deploige was quick to see the logic of Durkheim's position. He showed that from Durkheim's definition and concepts in the article on definition Durkheim could do no other than hold to the social importance and origin of religion (1911/t.1938:63). Since religion consists of beliefs and practices associated with obligations and since all that is obligatory is social in origin, religion must *ergo* be of social origin. Durkheim's position precludes the possibility that religion could be derived from nature or from events seen to be natural. That which is sacred is also of social origin. All that is required, then, is to understand the sacred, that is, to understand the *représentations collectives*, with which it is so closely associated. Although Deploige based his argument on Durkheim's early definition of religion, the conclusion is much the same when applied to his final definition which makes a religious community and the concept of the sacred basic to the definition.

The problem between the individual and the social becomes very apparent in Durkheim's lectures on moral education, in which he was dealing with the same problem within the realm of morality (1925a:59ff./t.1961a:52ff.). In primitive societies, since social life is consistent, differing little from one place to another, or from one moment in time to another, custom and unreflective tradition are quite adequate to control moral behaviour. Indeed, custom and tradition have such power and prestige as to have no place for reasoning and questioning. As societies become more complex, morality does not operate according to purely automatic mechanisms. Since circumstances vary, morality requires intelligence in its application. As society changes, so morality has to be flexible. Yet, while conformity must not be demanded to the exclusion of intellectual appraisal, 'moral values must still be invested with that authority without which they would be ineffective' (ibid.). It is quite clear therefore that the task of the sociologist is primarily to study that which is at the root of the individual variation, no matter whether one is considering primitive societies or modern complex societies. Goody correctly states that Durkheim admitted private cults as truly religious phenomena, but only by relating them to some more inclusive religious system (1961:147). We might say that the individual is only an appendix to the social.

Durkheim brings the sociologist face to face with the simple practical problem which confronts everyone who aims to be scientific. Individual phenomena are highly diverse: they can be as numerous as the sand on the seashore. Durkheim himself says there are as many religions as there are individuals, and this is irrespective of the problem of religious pluralism. It is practically impossible to contain and analyse so many elements, exhibiting such various characteristics. Durkheim wrote about morality in much the same way as he wrote about religion. Moral reality is divided into two – the objective and the subjective (1906b/1924a:57/ t.1953b:40). The common morality which applies to all individuals in a collectivity is that which is studied by sociology. The subjective component contains an infinite number of moralities, for every person has his own morality, judging some aspects of life to be more moral than others. No one totally accepts the morality of his day. 'The diversity of moral *consciences* shows how possible it is to make use of them in order to arrive at an understanding of morality itself' (ibid.). This diversity stands outside what sociology can contain.

The same criterion can be applied to religion: individual religions are unmanageable. Therefore for Durkheim there can be no other focal point than the social (cf. Webb 1916:56), having categorically stated that individual religious phenomena which are legion are derived from 'external, impersonal and public religion' (1899a(ii):28/t.1975a:97). The task of sociology is thus to determine public religion and to disregard the individual until such time as the public is analysed. The work of *sociologie religieuse* as a new science is to begin at the beginning and the discipline is essentially concerned with the collective (1886a:68/t.1975a:22).

The sociology of religion as we have come to know it today has in fact very largely concentrated on examining and analysing the social and external components of religion, those which can be said to have social significance. The nature of its task is such that it can do no other. In this respect it has followed the path of its major founding father.

The problem of relating the individual to the social and of examining their relations was one that obsessed Durkheim (1906b and 1925a; Lukes 1972:19–22, etc.). But it was one that he was not able to solve other than by showing how the individual became part of the social through the process of socialization, which he most clearly expounded in *Moral Education* (1925a). The problem, as one intellectually unresolved, is most obvious in considering religious phenomena as we have just seen and it is one that we shall encounter in the pages ahead.

The disciples of Durkheim did not take up the issue of the individual and the social in religion. But let it be said that Marcel Mauss, who was responsible for so much reviewing in *L'Année sociologique* of books and articles on religion, attempted in some way to deal with the issue of the place of the individual within the social. He tried to solve it by positing the concept of 'the total social phenomenon' and in stressing the complexity of the social bonds at any given time. He wanted to show that the individual had a 'social' place within society and therefore came within the province of sociology. The trouble is that the concept of the 'total social phenomenon' has proved to be vague, difficult to handle empirically, and although intellectually attractive, was not developed in any way comparable to that in which Durkheim used the concept of the social or society (see various articles in Mauss 1950).

11 'All religions are false: all religions are true'

1 Truth is the issue

Durkheim held that the scientific spirit with which he identified himself was above all concerned with truth and reality (see ch. 15). Indeed, the two were in his eyes closely associated. Truth can only be related to what is real. Science deals with reality and attempts to disclose the truth about it. It is therefore incumbent upon the scientist to declare what is true. Truth is reached by observation, classification and experimentation: it is deductive, not inductive. Science is, above all, a cognitive exercise.

But religion also claims to be cognitive. In its doctrines, its creeds, its morals, it postulates truth and reality. It speaks of the existence and nature of God or gods, and of the nature of man, and it speaks of such things not only symbolically but often ontologically. When there is a clash between the claims of religion and those of science with regard to reality and to truth, Durkheim never hesitated in openly declaring that science should be followed and the claims of religion rejected (see ch. 25).

As we have observed on more than one occasion, however, Durkheim was not a thoroughgoing anti-religious rationalist. He did not slavishly follow in the footsteps of those thinkers of the eighteenth century who held that religion was an invention of priests – a deliberate lie – which was promulgated in order to exert power and control by political and religious leaders over the populace. He would have rejected the words of Rousseau: 'All men are born good: only priests and kings make them bad' which appear in the *Social Contract* – a book which in other matters Durkheim so greatly admired (see 1918b). Thus he attempted to correct the thought of the Encyclopedists in their condemnation of religion as being totally false (see 1909a(1)). Of course reason must reject the claims of religion (ibid.:57). But what opponents of religion failed to see, he argued, was that if religion was so

205

palpably untrue, why should it have lasted for such a long time and still persist in the face of attacks? Again, Durkheim, unlike many of the atheists of his day and of previous generations, did not use religious history and later the findings of anthropology as sticks to beat contemporary religious beliefs and practices (Hughes 1958:284). H. S. Hughes goes further and says that Durkheim, unlike Pareto, kept his own disbelief strictly out of the discussions by adopting a stand that made the whole question irrelevant (ibid.). But this somewhat over-simplifies Durkheim's thought. When the occasion arose, he had no hesitation in openly declaring that he could not accept the truth-claims of religion, and he believed that other scientists thought likewise.

His position about truth located in religion was not one painted in black or white. He was convinced there was *a* truth which was not that declared by religious believers, but was a hidden truth which could be unearthed by the scientist. He wrote paradoxically: 'there are no false religions. They are all true in their own way' (3/3/104). Although this sentence appeared in the last book he wrote, he had doggedly held to the idea all his life. We might legitimately change the words slightly and say that according to him: 'all religions are false: all religions are true'. It is these ideas which we now examine.

2 'All religions are false'

Durkheim denied the truth-claims of religion because he denied the existence of an order of reality outside that which man experiences through his observations and senses. He wrote:

> It is certain that they [religions] are mistaken in regard to the real nature of things: science has proved it. The modes of action which they counsel or prescribe to men can therefore rarely have useful effects: it is not by lustrations that the sick are cured nor by sacrifices and chants that the crops are made to grow. (117/83)

There is no scientific proof that gods, or spirits, or life beyond the grave exists. There is no meta-world. The gods exist only in the mind (492/345). Thus the religious believer possesses no truth

206

about life or experience which the non-believer does not have. Durkheim's scientism is seen again in *The Elementary Forms*, where he writes:

> There is but one point at issue between science and religion: it is not the right of religion to exist, it is its right to dogmatize about the nature of things, and the special competence religion claims for itself to know about man and the world. (614/430/ 159)

That there is no world outside the present order of everyday life is also evident in the essay 'Jugements de valeur et jugements de réalité' (1911b). The book and the essay were closely dependent on each other, as Richard remarked, and were published at much the same time (Richard 1923:242/t.1975:254).

The rejection by Durkheim of the truth-claims of religion is deliberately and logically connected with his definition of religion. Religion exists, no one can deny that. Its base therefore cannot be non-reality and it cannot be defined in terms of the existence of superhuman beings or a transcendental order of reality (see ch. 9.1). Rather, as we have seen, religion is based on what is held to be sacred, which is universal and is the work of man and of society. Hence in defining religion in terms of the sacred, not in terms of spiritual powers, one is not denying its reality or rejecting its claims to exist, one is proclaiming the truth of its existence, namely, the existence of the sacred.

3 Is religion then an illusion?

Since Durkheim held that there is no spiritual force or being beyond this world, he was forced to assume that all that is religious is created by man – by individuals, but more assuredly by social activity. Thus it is man who has made the gods and invented the creeds. But religions do not claim to be man-made. They are in their own ways founded by the gods or come into existence through 'revelation'. As religions generally deny that their origins are human, it might well be argued that they constitute falsehood and illusion. For a religion to be charged with being an illusion is a more palpable accusation than being charged with falsehood.

Of course, it is true that an illusion can mean a fabrication, but it can also relate to an experience which is not understood. The first implies an invention with the intention to deceive, whereas the second suggests an inability to grasp the reality of what is happening. Durkheim sided with the second meaning rather than the first. He rejected the notion that religion is an intended deception. He would also have rejected Freud's notion that religion is a neurosis, and that of Marx and his disciples that religion is an opiate of the people. For Durkheim religion cannot be written off so easily. It is a much more subtle, complex phenomenon than most rationalists make it out to be.

Basic to Durkheim's own rationalism is the contention that only ideas which contain truth endure and are effective. He believed that no institution could persist, if it were based on a lie or an illusion. Therefore, if an institution persists, it must be founded on something essentially true. He wrote in *The Elementary Forms*:

> It is undeniably true that errors have been able to perpetuate themselves in history; but, except under a union of very exceptional circumstances, they can never perpetuate themselves thus unless they were *true practically*, that is to say, unless, without giving us a theoretically exact idea of the things with which they deal, they express well enough the manner in which they affect us, either for good or bad. . . . But an error and especially a system of errors which leads to, and can lead to nothing but mistaken and useless practices, has no chance of living. (113/80: see also 1919b:98/t.1975a:182)

Behind this notion that institutions cannot be based on illusion, Durkheim subscribes to the rationalist assumption that false ideas die, true ideas (or ideas which contain truth) persist. He argued: 'I cannot allow that a false idea could be practically effective, thanks to some skilful artifice. I can think of nothing more distasteful to my mind' (1909a(2):230/t.1979a:137). In the matter of truth or falsity of ideas, Durkheim was no relativist! Truth is truth and is absolute.

In examining religion he inverts the premise. Persistence indicates the presence of truth. Religion cannot be false or devoid of all truth for the simple reason that it has been in existence all down history and is found in every society. Many were the occasions that Durkheim argued along these lines in declaring that religious institutions must be founded on some kernel of truth and therefore must in some sense be real.[1] And if the institutions are real, their reality validates a scientific approach. In this vein he wrote:

> If the scientist takes it as axiomatic that the sensations of heat and light experienced by men correspond to some objective cause, he does not conclude that this is what it *appears* to be to the senses. (597/417–18/147; our italics)

To refute Max Müller's explanation of religion, Durkheim used the premise that truth and reality were behind all social institutions that persist. Müller's theory of naturism, not far removed from the animism of Tylor and Spencer, made the starting-point of religion spontaneous sensations about nature, coupled with a sense of awe and terror. These feelings were held to be 'religious', and in the development of religion spirits were invented and associated with these natural phenomena. However, Müller held that in the process man became religious through a misuse of language, thus implying that religion was an illusion. In his attack on such a theory, which he launched as early as 1899, but which he expanded in *The Elementary Forms*, Durkheim wrote that the theory:

> makes religion a system of hallucinations, since it reduces it to an immense metaphor with no objective value. It is true that it gives religion a point of departure in reality, to wit, in the sensations which the phenomena of nature provoke in us; but by the bewitching action of language, this sensation is soon transformed into extravagant conceptions. Religious thought does not come into contact with reality, except to cover it at once with a thick veil which conceals its real forms: this veil is the tissue of fabulous beliefs which mythology brought forth. (114/81)

4 Force, the indicator of reality

To a rationalist such as Durkheim, illusions are without power, whereas what is real exerts power: hence reality is indicated by the presence of force or power. Force has the quality of being actually observed through its effects. Nowhere does Durkheim more confidently and repeatedly use the metaphor than in Chapters VI and VII of Book II of *The Elementary Forms*; the first of those chapters is called 'The notion of the totemic principle, or mana, and the idea of force'. Force is also a much used concept in the paper Durkheim presented in 1913, 'Le Problème religieux et la dualité de la nature humaine', which introduced a discussion on *The Elementary Forms* (1913b:63, etc.).

There can be no doubt that in employing this concept, so useful in physics, and particularly in mechanics and electricity, Durkheim felt he was speaking the language of the scientist. In this way sociology itself appeared to take on a scientific characteristic, and to be associated with the natural sciences. Similarly, like other sociologists and anthropologists of his day, he did not hesitate, as we have seen, to use the metaphor of electricity when referring to certain elements of religion (see, for example, 308/215; 599/419/148). Durkheim was ready to extend these metaphors in talking about 'mystical mechanics', in which religious energy is transferred by 'a physical contact' (599/419/148). But he always stated categorically that the operations were mental ones. He often uses, in addition to force, the notion of power and speaks of religious powers. These occasions are not as frequent as those mentioning force, but the meanings of the two are much the same (see, for example, 441/309).

Durkheim held that the idea of force originally came from religion, as in the notion of spirit, and not from philosophy or science which borrowed these ideas from religion itself (292/204; 1907f:106 n.1).

In broad terms Durkheim speaks of society as 'a system of active forces' (638/447); and he readily transposes the idea to religion in general as when he writes: 'religion is not a system of ideas, it is above all a system of forces' (1919b:98/t.1975a:182). He broadly characterizes these forces as those 'which move mountains' (ibid.). It was impossible to define religion in terms of a deity or spirit because the force at work in religion, in the eyes of Durkheim, is impersonal and 'non-spiritual' (285/200). Nor is the notion of force only used in a 'metaphorical sense', but in 'one sense', religious forces are 'even material forces which mechanically engender physical effects' (270–1/190). So he writes:

We are now in a better position to understand why it has been impossible to define religion by the idea of mythical personalities, gods or spirits; it is because this way of representing religious things is in no way inherent in their nature. What we find at the origin and the basis of religious thought are not determined and distinct objects and beings possessing a sacred character of themselves; they are indefinite powers, anonymous forces, more or less numerous in different societies, and sometimes even reduced to a unity, and whose personality is strictly comparable to that of the physical forces whose manifestation the sciences of nature study. (285–6/200)

Thus, by using the metaphor of force rather than that of reality, Durkheim believes that he can again show that both society and religion can be legitimately studied by science in the same way as science studies natural phenomena. The scientist would explain phenomena by offering a theory, as he wrote:

A theory of religion above all sets out to make clear what these forces are, of what they are made, and what are their origins. (1913b:66; and see 1899a(ii):24/t.1975a:94)

He would claim that his argument is strengthened and is indeed made valid by the fact that the forces to which he points are natural, not supernatural (see pages ahead). For a scientific approach, 'everything turns on knowing if the facts of which one speaks are natural, and consequently, explicable' (1913b:100; also ibid.:93).

Durkheim speaks of force in the plural as in 'the existence of very special forces' at work in the religious life (1919b:99/ t.1975a:182). and in other examples we have given. In fact he postulates the different types of force in religion or different indicators of forces at work in it. The difficulty here lies in the diversity of indicators and it is clear that he means a different order of force in each case. Much the same thing can be said of a similar concept he frequently used, namely constraint, which we have already observed (see ch. 9.3). Indeed, the notion of constraint, which Durkheim used in his early works as in the *Division of Labour* (1893b) and *The Rules of Sociological Method* (1895a), is closely linked to that of force.

We summarize below the various indicators of force, or types of force, that Durkheim saw in religion.

1 The concepts of the sacred and the profane exert a force on society making people behave in certain ways and believe certain things (304/212/131; 326/228/137; 584ff./409ff.; and see chs 7 and 8).

2 Religion is able to exert the force of self-sacrifice and self-negation and thus in asceticism it encourages its followers to deny personal fulfilment of the instincts of sex and feeding (450/315).

3 Force is also seen in religious laws as in taboos, prohibitions, excommunications, punishments after sacrilege, which are laid down by religion: also punishments for those who deviate from religious orthodoxy (1893b/1902b:59ff./t.1933b:92ff.).

4 To act in a religious and moral way in fulfilment of duty gives boldness of action and courage to face the future (303/211/120–30).

5 Force is evident in corporate assembly when participants are involved in collective effervescence: they are caught up in forces outside themselves, for example, in gatherings amongst the Arunta, in the Crusades and in the French Revolution (see ch. 21).

6 To be involved in religious situations in general is to be aware of collective forces in which the individual is raised above himself (1913b:65).

7 A man who believes in God has more confidence in facing the trials and difficulties of the world than somebody who has no such belief (299/209/128; 1919b:99/t.1975a:182).

8 The person who participates in religious action (ritual) feels himself to be a stronger person than if he had not taken part in such action (1912a: bk III, especially 536/375; 1913b:63).

9 Force is present in the totemic principle which operates in a clan type of society (1912a: bk II, Chs VI and VII, especially 316/221).

10 In sacrificial rites, 'real' forces are at work which reanimate society in the face of vitiating circumstances that may be associated with seasonal changes, for example, the onset of winter (498ff./349ff.; 589–90/412).

In what has just been written, we have offered examples of the different ways in which Durkheim applies the concept of force to religious phenomena. They are by no means exhaustive. The metaphor is readily applied to many facets of religious life. It is evident that such indiscriminate use leads to confusion and therefore has limited analytical value.

Despite such difficulties, of which Durkheim seems oblivious, he tends to universalize and talk about religious force as if it were a unitary concept applied to a unitary reality. Since the notion of force is so central to Durkheim's thought, we mention these characteristics briefly. First, the force is natural, not supernatural (1913b:68). Second, force is not associated with individuals, but is basically collective or social in origin (1913a(ii)(11) and (12):18/t.1975a:18; 329/230). Although religious force is generated in man and is therefore human (599/419/148), it is superior to what is individual (1913b:93). Third, religious force is impersonal, that is, the source is impersonal, although it is created by man as distinct from God (and this is a further reason for suggesting it can be studied by science) (286/200). Fourth, religious force is not physical or mechanical in nature, despite what some might deduce from an examination of ritual: it is basically mental or moral in operation (325/227/136; 513ff./359ff.; 599/419/148; 1919b:68, 109). Thus primitive peoples are not materialistic in the matter of religion, but are 'spiritual' (599/419/148). Fifth, since religious forces are created by man, they depend on man to be re-created and to be released. Man thus has the power to call them into being and this is achieved by men 'coming together, thinking together, feeling together, acting together' (1919b:103/t.1975a:185).

Although today few, if any scholars would want to use the concept of force in analysing religion, there were those of Durkheim's day who, although critical of his theories, nevertheless readily accepted the metaphor of religious force, and readily applied it to totemism. Such a scholar, for example, was van Gennep, who went so far as to say 'primitive ideas are clearly energy-giving. Furthermore, all religions do the same: the thing that differs is the name given to the sources and forms of energy, and the forms in which they are visualized' (1913:390/t.1975:207). And Goblet d'Alviella, a student of comparative religion and a contemporary of Durkheim, was of the opinion, and rightly so, that Durkheim's argument against the theory of Müller was not valid. Müller's theory, as well as that of animism, used the notion of force and thus, within Durkheim's own premises, upheld the 'incontestable character of reality' in religion (1913:206).

Although the application of the metaphor of force to religious activity seems to be of doubtful merit, as we have indicated, it should be pointed out that such a metaphor does encourage the notion of movement and dynamism in religion. Durkheim never sees religion in static terms, despite his functionalism which is so often held to be conservative in its consequences (see ch. 16). Rather, religion is always something on the move, involved in making and remaking man; and this is most apparent in his key notion of collective effervescence (see chs 21 and 22). In a review of *The Elementary Forms* by himself and Marcel Mauss, there is reference to the speculative part religion plays in society and also to the fact that the principal function of religion is dynamogenic (*dynamogénique*) (1913a(ii)(11) and (12):98/t.1975a:180; 1913b:67, 80). If religion generates power – if it produces social energy – it must be seen in the mode of activity and change. Far from dampening life, it raises its pulse rate. This of course is to talk about religion in general. But Durkheim was also an evolutionist in very general terms, in so far as he held there were distinct stages in the development of a religion (see ch. 6.2). As we have seen (ch. 10.2), when a new religion emerges it is in a highly dynamic state, as in the case of a prophet initiating a new religious movement. But after a time, ideals become fixed and crystallized and a body of dogmas and rites become established. Thus religion becomes institutionalized, and incidentally, a valid subject for scientific study (1909a(1):56). This does not mean therefore that the early stages of religion contain 'more forces' than the later stages; rather, it implies that the forces in the less organized state are more volatile than they are after the religion has become firmly established. In both cases force is at work and potentially gives rise to change. Social life would be vitiated, dull, monotonous and static if religion, even in its developed stages, were absent.

Durkheim's predilection for the concept of force in analysing religious phenomena sociologically has a decidedly apologetic tone about it. As we have already shown, part of that apologetic was to employ a concept which had the hallmark of the natural sciences on it and which would encourage the reader to accept sociology as a science. But the other arm of the apologetic is to suggest that there is a reality in religion which the agnostic or atheist rationalist would otherwise deny. So Durkheim stands up boldly for religion in the face of attack! What else is one to make of the following sentence written in connection with sacrifice?

> So men do not deceive themselves when they feel at this time that there is something outside of them which is born again, that there are forces which are reanimated and a life that reawakens. (498/349)

Or again:

> Men are more confident because they feel themselves stronger; and they really are stronger because forces which were languishing are now reawakened in their *consciences*. (494/346)

It can well be argued in the light of this evidence that *The Elementary Forms* is a 'scientific tract', an apologia, for the importance of religion in social life all down the ages, and much of Durkheim's other writings on the subject bears the same stamp (see chs 1.6, 2.4, 27 and 28).

5 'All religions are true'

The truth to be discovered about religion is a hidden truth, not consciously known to the believer or participant but recognized as such by the observer or scientist. It is the latter rather than the former who knows what is really happening.

One hidden reality which the scientist can point to, which is hidden from the eyes of the participant, is that of a personal or social need. This is a particularly slippery concept to handle, as we shall see (ch. 16), but Durkheim has no hesitation in using it. The reason is clear enough. If something fulfils a need, both the need and the way in which it is fulfilled must constitute reality. Thus, he could write: 'The most barbarous or bizarre rites and the strangest myths all express some human need, some aspect of life, be it individual or social' (3/2/104). This kind of reasoning is at the basis of a functional analysis of society, where it is often argued that religion itself supplies some general need – some *sine qua non* – without which society could not exist. For reasons which are not incontrovertible, the argument is that a people and society require religion in order to satisfy some basic requirement which would not otherwise be satisfied. What precisely that requirement is is not clearly stipulated.

Not only did Durkheim hold that religious truth was centred on the fulfilment of a basic need, he also saw that the truth to be discovered in religion is symbolic truth. Behind the externalities, religious rituals and peculiar beliefs, there is the symbolization of some aspect of reality. Indeed, religion is very much a symbolic exercise, and, given that assumption, the task of the sociologist is to discern what in fact is being symbolized. At the beginning of *The Elementary Forms*, he said: 'Underlying the symbol there is reality which it represents which we must grasp, and which gives it its true meaning' (3/2/104). It is interesting that he should proceed in this way, referring to religion as a (real) force, when it is nothing more than symbolic of some reality to be discovered. But then, as we shall see, for Durkheim symbolism and symbolic representation exert a real force (ch. 15).

To say that a religion uses symbols in its language and ritual is to state what is now the obvious. But for Durkheim a religion is essentially a system of symbols and therefore the symbols themselves are not a haphazard collection, diverse and disintegrated; rather, they are interconnected to form a whole and, furthermore, what is more contentious, they relate to a specific reality. Two questions arise: is the reality one or many? If it is one, as Durkheim held, what is it? He had no hesitation in replying that the symbols of religion relate to what is sacred in religion and what is sacred is very closely related to society seen as a totality. Religion thus contains within itself the collective *représentation* of the society in which it is situated. He wrote:

> We have, however, already seen that although religious beliefs are not based on fact, they do nevertheless express the social realities, even when they interpret them by symbol and metaphor. (1950a/1969g:199/t.1957a:172)

Religion therefore contains a cognitive element relating to the reality of society, that is, how society thinks of itself and the universe in which it is situated. In at least one place, however, Durkheim sees that the system of *représentations* within religion

216

expresses the reality of a given society, but it only does so 'imperfectly' (see ch. 15).

Proceeding beyond a general social need that he sees religion fulfils, Durkheim was more specific in stating that the truth or reality of religion is in the two particular functions that it has supplied all down history. These two functions he most clearly expounded in the latter years of his life. Very briefly, one may say here that the first function is a vital or practical one, that of helping men to live together, to adapt to their conditions of existence, and to give them a sense of vitality and inner renewal. This is similar to two of the manifestations of force in religion that we have just alluded to (nos 7 and 8). The second function enables man to think speculatively by giving him a system of *représentations* which uniquely expresses the world to him. In this way there is in religion 'a science before science' (1909a(1):58; and see ch. 15). These two functions will be considered in detail later on (see ch. 16).

6 Some consequences of Durkheim's position

Durkheim's assumptions about the truth and reality of religion give rise to a number of serious consequences and problems. We raise the following.

Relativism

In rejecting the claims to truth which nearly every religion declares, Durkheim refuses to accept the cognitive component of religions and sees it today as being virtually valueless. In this respect all religions are the same. None contains the truth held as such by believers. Every pretension to divine revelation is completely disregarded. The truth that religions possess is to be seen in terms of 'hidden' truth relating to social need or function, or of a system of *représentations*. The claim applies equally to every religion. Thus, all religions are false: yet all are true. *Mutatis mutandis*, the place that one religion holds in society is that which another religion holds in another society.

Expressed differently, Durkheim's relativism about religious truth is seen in the way he held that each society has the religion that it needs. The same is to be said about morality, which is so closely associated with religion: necessary for a society's existence is a morality which fits that society. In the matter of religion and morality therefore, as in other institutions, it can be argued that a society gets what it deserves.

Durkheim deliberately adopted a relativist position, not only because in the matter of religious truth he was atheist, but also because he wanted in the development of sociology, and more particularly in his *sociologie religieuse*, to bypass the *odium theologicum*. To get involved in theological debates about religious truth, and indeed in metaphysical arguments about the ultimate nature of reality, would, he argued, prevent the development of the science of sociology (see 1895a). Science had always been impeded by theological controls and metaphysical speculation. Indeed, the history of science is the history of its growing freedom, its complete secularization, and its severance from theology and philosophy.

Yet Durkheim was not an 'absolute relativist', because his relativism could be modified by objective criteria. He admitted that no two religions are identical in content and he goes so far as to suggest that religions can be graded in a hierarchy.

Naturally, it is not impossible to arrange them [religions] in hierarchical order. Some may be said to be superior to others in the sense that they bring into play a higher order of mental functions, that are richer in ideas and sentiments, that they include more concepts and fewer sensations and images, and that their systematization is better. (3/3/104)

Durkheim made no attempt to classify religions according to such criteria, although it was his practice to employ the broad categories of primitive (*inférieure*) and advanced (*supérieure*) according to societies so classified (see, for example, 1910a(ii)(2) and 1913a(i)(2)). But he never spells out the characteristics of these divisions. And he does note, as we have seen, that religions go through stages (see section 4 of this chapter), and that it is possible to argue that the function of religion in its early formative stage is not the same as that in its more developed or established stage. Once again, Durkheim does not specify the differences. The point is, of course, that he wishes to establish broad generalizations about the nature of religion, or religions seen as a whole, without initially trying to establish variations between one religion and another. This is a logical consequence of his assertion that all religions are man-made and equally true and false,

The eternality of religion

Durkheim's proclamation that religion is a reality led him to use a phrase that appeals as little to the modern sociologist as to a thoroughgoing rationalist. In the conclusion of *The Elementary Forms*, he declares in a way that lodges itself in the memory:

There is then something eternal in religion which is destined to survive all particular symbols which have successively veiled religious thought. (609/427/156)

Richard admits the logic of Durkheim's position, since his theory of religion and of changes in religion demand that 'there must be a permanent element in it [religion] as durable as man himself' (1923:233/t.1975:245). Nevertheless, Durkheim's notion of the eternality of religion was hardly original (see ch. 16.7, especially note 3). In part the idea can be traced back to Spencer, for in a review of the English sociologist's *Ecclesiastical Institutions*, Durkheim wrote in summary:

For all that [secularization], the ideal of religion will not disappear because it contains a germ of truth already to be found in the superstitious savages. (1886a:64/t.1975a:16)

That 'germ of truth' was of course not a metaphysical truth but a 'practical' truth – practical because it relates to the nature of societies (see ch. 9.2). One could also say that it was a utilitarian truth, although utilitarian was hardly a word that Durkheim would have taken to in the light of his opposition to the utilitarian individualism of Spencer. Religious faith is based on:

practical causes, it must continue to exist as long as they exist
. . . these reasons are of a sociological kind and we must look for the change . . . in the nature of societies. (1887b:310/t.1975a:37)

Such a position is based in the long run on the conviction that there is a concomitant variation between the existence of a society and commonly held beliefs. Durkheim wrote in his early days: 'For as long as men live together they will hold some belief in common' (1886a:69/t.1975a:22). In primitive societies and indeed in advanced societies these beliefs are basically religious.There is, however, evidence to show that Durkheim was willing to extend religious beliefs to 'great ideals' and the latter would be a valid category in examining modern 'secular' society. He said to the 1914 gathering of Free Believers and Free Thinkers:

So long as human societies exist, they will draw from themselves great ideals of which men will become the servants.(1919b:103/t.1975a:186)

It is easy enough to speak about the eternality of religion if one has already admitted its truth and reality as being related to some social need. Further, social need is implied in the lasting characteristics of society and is not something ephemeral. We have already seen that Durkheim relates truth to persistence. Hence the eternality of religion! Such a stand both solves and raises problems about the future of religion (see ch. 26). According to Durkheim's argument, religion must continue, though changed in form according to the dictates of society.

7 All sociologists of religion start where Durkheim does

The assumptions which Durkheim makes in his approach to religion obviously attract intellectuals who like him do not, on the one hand, wish to take a hard-line rationalist stand in writing off religion as valueless and who, on the other, as non-believers, are convinced that religion has contributed a great amount of good to the development of human societies. Their position is that of those who give religion high marks, but who cannot accept its claims. Here they are not far removed from those liberals who reject the claims of any one religion, but who are pleased that there are others who in the past have believed and continue to believe today.

All sociologists, whether they are believers or not, and those who see sociology as a scientific activity would adopt a position of methodological agnosticism in so far as they would treat the existence of God or the truth-claims of a particular religion as a factor not to be taken at its face value (cf. Berger 1970:125). The nature of sociology is such that one either has to openly deny the truth-claims of a religion or to suggest that they are non-admissible in the search for description, explanation and prediction about social institutions. Recently, a student of Durkheim, who was so bold as to declare openly the appeal of Durkheim's stance to those who would adopt a strictly sociological approach to the study of religion, wrote:

> However, I would submit, the same understanding is shared by the whole dialectical tradition, and most of us would have difficulty in formulating an alternative understanding which did not entail the profession of religious belief or the theory of the 'priestly' lie. (Poggi 1971:259–60)

Robert Bellah is another sociologist who sees that there is no alternative but to support Durkheim's position of *via media* in sociologically rejecting the truth-claims of religion, but at the same time trying to analyse objectively its place in society. He wrote: 'The rationalist positivist tradition was decisively broken through from within by Émile Durkheim, when he recognized that religion was a reality *sui generis*' (1970:8). Both Durkheim and Weber overcame the rationalist/non-rationalist impasse. They both placed religion in a theoretical rather than a descriptive context without denying its centrality or irreducibility. But we would note that this could only be done by either completely disregarding or denying the realities held by religious believers. The plain truth of the matter is that God or spirit as an operative principle of explanation can have no place in a sociology of religion (see Pickering 1979c; Barker 1980).

8 Conclusion

Durkheim held that religion contained truth; but the truth was not the same as that discovered by the natural sciences from physical phenomena. He wrote:

Its [religion's] chief aim is not to give man a *représentation* of the physical universe, for if that were its essential task we cannot understand how it could have survived, since in this matter it is scarcely more than a tissue of lies. (322–3/225/135)

Its cognitive knowledge therefore relates to another order of reality, namely, to society – to its values, ideals, to what is sacred and profane. The knowledge it offers is symbolic knowledge which, while within the province of science, cannot be contradicted by the natural sciences. To maintain this position Durkheim sets out to deny that religion is an illusion: yet the route that he takes inevitably leads to a position where religion is still an illusion, although he would deny it. At the outset his rationalist premise that truth and reality are related to what persists has to be rejected. Man *is* able to believe what is false over long periods of time. Persistence is no criterion of truth. The process of socialization, which Durkheim so skilfully analysed in his *Moral Education* (1925a) as the way the child comes to learn and accepts the 'truth' of his society, contains within itself no supra-cultural means of establishing truth. That which is taught is true. Social knowledge is unable to break relativism. Ideology persists as well as truth: modern propaganda warfare is based on such a premise. As Goldenweiser said:

Are not the highest religions, of undisputed significance and world-wide appeal, also based on illusions? Are not ideals, in more than one sense, illusions? Should one therefore be shocked if religion were shown to have its primal roots in an illusion? Thus, Durkheim's search for a *reality* underlying religion does not seem to rest on a firm logical basis. (1915/ r.1975:211)

Maunier holds that Durkheim sees that 'the fundamental notion of religious force is the expression of the superior power which society exercises over the individual'; therefore religion is little more than the gross illusion of all humanity (1913:276).

The great illusion which arises out of Durkheim's position is that the believer or practitioner does not know what is happening. This is true whether it is the man in the street or a great religious leader. Only the scientist or sociologist knows. Beliefs and rituals do not work at their face value and according to declared aims;

222

they cannot because no god or spirit exists. But they do work in a 'magical' way, in an unknown way, that only the magician-sociologist knows about. If this is the case, then there can be no doubt that the believer is suffering from an illusion. Indeed, in one place at least, Durkheim admits that the religious person has fantasies about how religious power is exercised (1913b:67; and see 1899a(ii):24/t.1975a:94). It could well be argued that if the believer is suffering from an illusion, it is best that he be told this in the way Freud openly proclaimed religion to be a neurosis and something, therefore, to be discarded. But Durkheim will not, cannot take this step.

A premise of Durkheim's basic thought is that the scientist has superior knowledge in areas in which there are acclaimed leaders and which are part of people's everyday experience. It is evident that towards the end of his life, Durkheim was coming to a fairly firm opinion that in fact the scientist and scientific knowledge belonged to an elite and that his knowledge was superior to that of the practitioner. The scientist therefore stood above the practitioner. He stated this in the matter of morals, but it is clear that it also applies to religion (see Pickering 1979a:26; ch. 15.1; ch. 25.2).

The point is that Durkheim's rationalism was not rigorous enough. He readily sacrificed 'truth' in trying to save 'religion' and believed he was strengthening the bonds of society. His *via media* was constantly under attack, not least from fellow rationalists. Such a person, for example, was Gustave Belot who, as a sympathetic critic of Durkheim, as early as 1900 criticized Durkheim's approach to religion for its treatment of the notion of illusion. He saw that if religion were only concerned with social content, the question of its truth would scarcely come into the picture (1900:294). He pointed to early Christians faced with the legal requirement to worship Caesar. They hardly saw it as having only political meaning without any metaphysical connotation. They were not able to reconcile the two principles of state worship and Christian worship and were prepared to face persecution rather than deny the second (ibid.). He concluded:

But if the religious dogma has an extra-social content –
sociological, for example – the question of its truth is forcibly
posed and instead of troubling oneself only with the power of

223

cohesion which religions give to a society, one is forced to judge the doctrines themselves. (ibid.)

It is interesting to note that no French scholar, even within the Année Sociologique group, came to Durkheim's defence in this matter (see chs 27 and 28).

A practical consequence of Durkheim's position arises when believers are told that what they are really doing is responding to social needs rather than, for example, propitiating the gods. Does this knowledge affect their religious behaviour? Do they become unbelievers, if not sociologists? There is no clear answer. Durkheim admitted that a religious person suddenly confronted by a scientific argument against religion would not abandon his faith, something had to occur beforehand (1909a(2):59). On the other hand, the sociological approach to religion as it has developed since Durkheim's day, not least by reason of its 'secular' premises and its attempt to explain religious phenomena, has undoubtedly weakened or dislocated certain attitudes and beliefs within the religious framework (Pickering 1979c). Such considerations are not our immediate concern (but see ch. 28.2).

Durkheim's rationalism leads him to seek the truth about society. Religion helps in the discovery of such truth in so far as religion is a vehicle for revealing what society thinks about itself. In this sense the sociology of religion is a necessary component of sociology.

Part III
Beliefs and Ideas

12   God's identity revealed

1 God's locus in society

The notion of God couched in transcendental language was a
particularly difficult obstacle to the many nineteenth-century sociologists and anthropologists who, assuming religion to be fabri-
cated by man, sought to explain it in rational terms. Durkheim
believed that he had overcome such a difficulty in an original way
and, some might add, in a brilliant and daring way, by concentrating on the concept of society and showing that in society was the
locus of God. Further, such was the logic of his system that his
association of the divinity with society constituted a linchpin of
his argument – one could say a metaphysical linchpin – to demonstrate that religion performs amongst several functions that of
strengthening social bonds. Without such an assertion there can
be no proof of the function (see ch. 16).

It would be wrong to hold that Durkheim reached this conclusion about the nature and origin of God as a result of the careful
observation of sophisticated religious data. The impression given
in reading *The Elementary Forms* is that he derived the idea from
the evidence of the ethnographical material relating to the Arunta,
especially that of totemism (see 1912a:bk II, esp. 323/226/135).
The close association between God and society began to appear,
however, in the early stages of Durkheim's thought. Nor can it
be said, as we shall show, that the idea itself was original. What
was original was the way in which he used and developed the
association. Again, it is not surprising that the hypothesis, which
leads some people to deduce that it has ontological status, brought
upon the head of its author a great deal of criticism. We wish to
demonstrate that critics and commentators have often read too
much into the formula and have over-simplified Durkheim's
thought.

It is apparent that as early as 1886, when he reviewed Spencer's

Ecclesiatical Institutions, his mind was beginning to associate the notion of God with a range of ideas basically social in nature. Whilst opposing Spencer's emphasis on the individual and psychological roots of religion, he wrote:

> Once the idea of a divinity had been formed in a number of *consciences* under the influence of completely personal sentiments, it served to symbolize all sorts of traditions, customs and collective needs. (1886a:66/t.1975a:19)

The process by which 'completely personal sentiments' became all-important social symbols is not and was never explained by Durkheim. The connection, however, between what was believed about gods and spirits and what people believed about society and social behaviour is clearly stated.

At much the same time – a period thick with theories about the origin of religion – Durkheim showed in another review, on this occasion of a book by Guyau, that he accepted the fact that the gods were created by man. He held that primitive man reasoned about his relations with other men and so 'he visualized the powers of nature as beings like himself; at the same time he set them apart from himself and attributed to these exceptional beings distinctive qualities which turned them into gods' (1887b:309/t.1975a:35). Guyau's *L'Irréligion de l'avenir* had the subtitle *Étude de sociologie* and such an approach to religion which included a consideration of its origins, Durkheim applauded. At the same time he found the book inadequate because it gave priority to the speculative or cognitive role of religion.

Fundamental to Guyau's argument was the idea that the gods were not the appointed protectors and protagonists of individuals, but of society seen as the tribe, the clan, the family, the city, etc. (ibid.:309/36). Guyau developed the notion of religious evolution by positing three stages, and in the third stage, which is essentially a moral stage, the deity is seen to be the 'prop of the social order' (ibid.:301/26). Durkheim in no way wished to contradict this idea of the close relation between religion and social control.

A little later during this early period he spelt out precisely the formula we have mentioned in the early book, *Suicide*. It has already been suggested on the evidence of Richard that the book was written some time before it was published in 1897. In referring to the origin of religion, he rejects the theory that it arises through man's awareness of mysterious or dreaded natural phenomena. These things in themselves are not sufficient to account for the emergence of religion, and for the simple reason that they do not represent unmediated experience but are related to *représentations*, to ideas and values which are derived from society and which are the means by which man evaluates the phenomena (see ch. 15). He goes on to argue that the power which man sees outside himself and which is greater than himself is society and so it becomes his object of adoration. The gods are the hypostatic form of society itself.

> Religion is in a word the system of symbols by means of which society becomes conscious of itself; it is the characteristic way of thinking of collective existence. Here then is a great group of states of mind which would not have originated if individual states of consciousness had not been combined, and which result from this union and are superadded to those which derive from individual natures. (1897a:352–3/t.1951a:312)

During the second stage of the development of Durkheim's religious thought, the theme is reiterated. In the course of lectures he gave in Bordeaux between 1896 and 1900, *Leçons de sociologie: physique des moeurs et du droit* (1950a), which amongst other things related legal contracts to ritual associated with them, he remarked:

> The contract by solemn ritual binds men doubly; it binds them to one another; it also binds them to the deity, if it is the deity that was party to the contract; or to the society if the society took part in the person of its representative. Further, we know that divinity is only the symbolic form of the society. (1950a/1969g:220/t.1957a:195)

Again, earlier in the lectures, speaking of the relation between religion and property:

> The gods are no other than collective forces personified and hypostasized in material form. Ultimately, it is society that is worshipped by the believers; the superiority of the gods over men is that of the group over its members. (ibid.:189/161)

In 1906 his important essay, 'La Détermination du fait moral', produced a slight variation in the old theme, this time approaching it from the viewpoint of morality, and introducing a sentence which has become famous in Durkheim's thought. His argument is that morality begins at some point of disinterestedness, but disinterestedness becomes meaningful only when its object has a higher moral value than the individual himself. He writes:

In the world of experience I know of only one being that possesses a richer and more complex moral reality than our own, and that is the collectivity.* I am mistaken; there is another being which could play the same part, and that is the Divinity. Between God and society lies the choice. . . . I can only add that I myself am quite indifferent to this choice, since I see in the Divinity only society transfigured and symbolically expressed. (1906b/1924a:75/t.1953b:52)

Les Formes élémentaires dominates Durkheim's third and most developed stage in his religious thought. The close relation between society and God is mentioned often, but there is no extension of the idea beyond that which has already been noted. He often resorts, however, to the word 'hypostasized' as in, 'the sacred principle is nothing more nor less than society hypostasized and transfigured' (495/347).

In the essay 'Value judgments and judgments of reality', he speaks about the ideals of any given society varying with time and he suggests that men today think that such variation should occur (1911b/1924a:129–30/t.1953b:89). This allows us, he argues, to understand that the attributes accorded to God also vary in space and time. Therefore there must be some reality behind our overall conception of God – 'The changing condition of God could only be intelligible if He had to realize an ideal beyond Himself' (ibid.). By implication that ideal comes from society itself – it is society itself. This selfsame notion was expressed in a slightly different way when he said that 'when the gods die the nations die' (1913b:69). When the ideals of a nation are rejected, it means the god of the nation is rejected. And as he said in a discussion:

The gods have always been born to incarnate great collective

* Not 'collective being' as in t.1953b.

230

ideas and they die when human groups have turned to different ideas. (ibid.:99)

2 God as society hypostasized

We have referred to the word 'hypostasized' in quotations from Durkheim just given and we offer another example here. In speaking about the totemic principle, Durkheim wrote:

> The god of the clan, the totemic principle, cannot therefore be anything other than the clan itself hypostasized [*hypostasié*] and represented to the imagination in the form of the tangible species of vegetable or animal which serves as the totem. (295/206/125)

Clearly the two words 'hypostasized' and 'represented' run parallel and would seem to mean much the same thing (see ch. 15). The first, however, is a technical philosophical word which Durkheim used at least several times in his published works. It is derived from the Greek, *hypostasis*, which literally means support, or what is underneath. Later, in philosophy it came to mean substance, essence, principle; and in Christian theology in the third and fourth centuries it implied person or subject, and was employed in christological and trinitarian controversies. In English there are two verbs, hypostasize and hypostatize, which are little different in implication and both mean to embody, impersonate, or to make into or regard as a self-existent substance or person (*Oxford English Dictionary*). In philosophical terminology, 'hypostasize' 'is used of the making actual or counting real of abstract conceptions' (Baldwin 1901).

Durkheim nearly always uses the verb form, *hypostasier*, and as such it can have two meanings. One is 'to treat as substance, to be considered as an ontological reality'. The second, in a pejorative sense, is 'to treat a fictitious entity or a false abstraction as a reality' (Lalande 1932, 1:309–10). Bergson in his *L'Évolution créative* uses it in the second sense (p. 376). In a similar vein, it may be said that hypostasization is close to the now more popular term 'reification'. Durkheim does not use *hypostasier* in the pejorative way, but in the sense that something is considered to have a reality, to be a substance in an ontological sense. Thus, in the quotation above, to members of the clan, the clan is in their eyes a reality as the embodiment of the animal or vegetable. We would emphasize that it is so seen by members; for it is they who take it as a reality. To the observer this is not necessarily so. And if the second meaning is implied by Durkheim in this case, it is hardly surprising that there have been those who have criticized him for using the word in a pejorative way, in saying something is substance or reality when in fact he knows the something does not exist (see the note by Lachelier in Lalande 1932, 1:309–10).

As a rule Durkheim did not use *hypostasier* by itself. Rather, he used pairs of words in which *hypostasier* was one of them, as in 'The gods are no other than collective forces personified [*incarnées*] and hypostasized [*hypostasiées*] in material form' (1950a/1969g:189/t.1957a:161). *Hypostasier* is also coupled with *transfigurer* (transfigured) (495/347). Other pairs of words are sometimes used, for example, 'Divinity is only society transfigured [*transfigurée*] and symbolically [*symboliquement*] expressed' (1906b/1924a:52/t.1953b:75). Indeed, Durkheim used *symboliquement* as frequently as any of the words just mentioned. It would thus seem safe to conclude that Durkheim, in employing *hypostasier*, was not using the word literally but in a way that meant little more than to symbolize, manifest or express the reality of something or somebody. Durkheim's use of parallel words confirms this. *Hypostasier* implies a symbolic relation and nothing more.

Now what Durkheim does not do is to say that divinity and society (the collectivity, the clan) are *alternative* means of expressing each other symbolically. Rather, one is a reality and the other a symbolic form of it. It is a one-way process. The reality is society and God the symbolic (figurative, transfigured, hypostasized) expression of it. People wrongly assume that Durkheim equates the two. For example, Mary Douglas writes: 'the Durkheimian premise that society and God can be equated' (1970:55). If the word 'equated' is to be used, it has to be subject to modifiers. The two concepts are not interchangeable.

Critics of Durkheim all too readily say that Durkheim states that God *is* society (see, for example, the many references to the debate by modern scholars in Clark 1979; also Poggi 1971). But only in one instance is he reported to have used the *être* in the sense of meaning identity. Always, as we have just suggested, Durkheim employed a verb which indicated a strong symbolic relationship. The one exception which comes to us is not from his own pen but from the report he gave in the winter of 1905–6 in a series of lectures in the École des Hautes Études Sociales on the non-theological teaching of morality (1906e). The report of the lecture – the manuscript was never published and has been lost – was made by André Lalande, a philosopher, and published in *The Philosophical Review* in America. In it Lalande said that Durkheim declared his wish 'to prove that both historically and practically *God is Society*, and conceived in a positive manner, furnishes morality with all the support one ordinarily expects from a revealed religion' (ibid.:255). In the lecture Durkheim referred to the positivist cult of humanity, 'imperfectly realized', which nevertheless expresses 'a most profound and truly religious thought; for it is not God that disappears in humanity, it is rather humanity which discovers God in itself, and which does not for that reason adore him with any less fervor' (ibid.:256). Since this is the only example that has been found in Durkheim's writings which employs the formula 'God is Society', one is entitled to question the accuracy of Lalande's reporting. It seems unwise to use it to condemn Durkheim for using an expression with which he might never have wished to have been associated. Yet later evidence shows that the phrase remained in Lalande's mind. In a letter he wrote to Cuvillier in 1955 he recalled the occasion of the lecture he reported, 'vers 1910, je crois'; in fact, as we have just noted, it was five years earlier (the letter is in the possession of the author of the present book). He repeats what he earlier reported in saying: 'pour lui [Durkheim], Dieu, *c'était* la Société' (Lalande's italics). The reason for the assertion rests, according to Lalande, on the fact that Durkheim took the traditional attributes of God one by one, and showed that society manifested them exactly – 'the source of reason, of language, of morality, of justice, the spiritual milieu "in quo vivimus, movemur et sumus" – the Eternal Being with whom we cooperate but who utterly transcends us' (ibid.). Lalande's deduction, and he would obviously argue that of Durkheim also, is that the empirical correlation of attributes makes for an identity of being, an ontological equation.

An important sentence in *The Elementary Forms* needs to be

233

considered, where Durkheim asks the rhetorical question which is generally translated something like this: 'If, then, it [the totem] is at once the symbol of god and society, is this not because god and society are one and the same thing?' (295/206/125). The important words in the French are: 'n'est-ce pas que le dieu et la société ne font qu'un?' The implied meaning is that the two – god and society – are inextricably intermeshed, they are parts of each other, of the same totality. But they are not one and the same thing. He continues: 'How could the emblem of the group have become the form of the quasi-deity, if the group and the deity were two distinct realities?' (ibid.). What Durkheim is stating is little more than that there exists an important interconnection between the two, that they are not separate realities so isolated from each other that they are unable to be closely related. They are in fact dovetailed. And to prove his point he goes on to state, using language that has now become familiar, that the god is the clan hypostasized.

Another sentence also ought to be mentioned. In the conclusion of *Les Formes élémentaires*, where Durkheim is arguing that the concept of society is crucial in the understanding of social life, he writes in a footnote: 'Basically the concept of totality, the concept of society, the concept of divinity, are in all likelihood only different aspects of one and the same notion' (630 n.2/442 n.1). Once again, it is to be noted that Durkheim does not make a metaphysical assertion that the concepts *are* the same or that the realities behind them are identical. He merely suggests the possibility and that it *is* a possibility is reinforced by the fact that he says so in a footnote.

Further, it should be made quite explicit that nowhere, so far as we can find, does Durkheim use the phrase 'deification of society', which is so often used in connection with his close association of God and society, and which is frequently attributed to him by his critics (see ch. 13). So far as can be ascertained, Durkheim speaks of deification in one place only, as the process by which the concept of God arose (1950a/1969g:189/t.1957a:161).

Initially the association of the notion of God with that of society seems innocent enough and to some may be a truism. As Goblet d'Alviella has suggested, at its simplest sociological level it means that society is to its members as God is to the faithful (1913:202; see also 295/206/125). But as one develops the parallel, and relates it to the notion of the sacred as Durkheim does, 'God himself' becomes much more closely related to society. The danger always is to jump the parallel and make the two concepts or realities identical, or at least to suggest that one *is* the other. Critics claim that Durkheim makes such a step, but they disregard all caution. To the contrary, as we have shown, Durkheim is much more careful, and nowhere does he take the final and irrevocable step of crossing the parallel, although he does go as near as he can without actually making the jump.

What is quite clear in Durkheim's own mind is that in drawing attention to the association of the two concepts and in developing that association, he had revealed certain truths about society and at the same time shed light on the nature and origin of the concept of God.

3 'Proofs'

From time to time Durkheim attempted to offer some justification for his position about the relation between the concept of God and the concept of society and for the fact that each revealed the nature of the other. In general, he offers two types of argument: one, general and perhaps philosophical; the other, particular and sociological.

In arguing for a 'transcendental' base for a secular morality and leaning on first principles derived from Kant, he held that God as the foundation of a religious morality was 'law maker and the guardian of moral order' (see 1925a:118–20/t.1961a:103–5). But God also represents an ideal which the individual tries to realize. '*Homoiōsis toi theoi* [becoming like God], to seek and live in God's image, to merge with him – such is the basic principle of all religious morality' (ibid.). Man believes there is some part of God in him, what is called the soul which 'comes from him and expresses him through us' (ibid.). Durkheim's view of man is strongly dualistic (see 1914a). If this basic religious idea is transformed into rational terms, all that is needed is to substitute for the concept of a supernatural being some 'directly observable being', which is society (ibid.). Society, like God, constrains us, dominates us, gives us laws: it also sets before us an ideal on

235

which we reflect and to which we aspire. We can thus be assured that 'divinity is the symbolic expression of the collectivity' (ibid.). And significantly Durkheim says: 'The parallel [between God and society] is indeed so complete that in itself it already constitutes a first demonstration of the hypothesis' (ibid.). This is akin to the moral argument for the existence of God, namely. that since all moral systems need some form of authority outside themselves and that morality without this cannot exist, God, as an authority, must exist. Durkheim merely adapts this and argues that since God does not exist and society does and since a moral authority is needed, society is precisely authority formerly supplied by God. The argument is also spelt out in the important paper 'La Détermination du fait moral' (1906b/1924a:75/t.1953b:52; and see la Fontaine 1926:40).

Another type of formal 'proof' he employed, which does not take into consideration the ethical argument, appeared in the report made by Lalande already referred to in this chapter. Durkheim selected certain attributes of God established in the Jewish-Christian tradition, such as creator, sovereign, mysterious, knowing ultimate good and evil, eternal, the one 'who survives passing generations and maintains the continuity of their spiritual life' (1906e:256). But, continued Durkheim, was it not the case that these attributes of God applied almost literally to the society in which men live? 'For a barbarous people there exists an ethnic god who fights against neighbouring gods; for civilized people there is only one god who makes all men brothers. The broadening of social life has broadened the conception of God and has so given rise to monotheism' (ibid.). Thus, the qualities which we associate with society are those we attribute to God. If the ideals of each are the same, there must exist a very close relationship between the two.

The second type of argument to justify his contention about the close relation between God and society is both more sophisticated and more simple. It rests on ethnographic data which he established in his analysis of the totemism of the Arunta and which he expounded in *Les Formes élémentaires* (see ch. 6.3). Durkheim reaches a point in his study of totemism in Book II where he poses the question of what the totem is (293ff./205ff./124ff.). A two-fold answer is offered:

(a) the totem symbolizes in visible and outward form the totemic principle, mana, that is, the god;

(b) the totem also marks off one clan from another: it is the 'flag' of the clan.

Thus the totem symbolizes the two realities and therefore one is forced to conclude that these realities are very closely associated and are strongly interconnected. In a sentence we discussed a little earlier, we suggested that Durkheim indicated by use of rhetorical questions that the two realities were part of each other and part of the same totality. Further, 'the god of the clan, the totemic principle, cannot therefore be anything other than the clan itself hypostasized and represented to the imagination in the tangible species of vegetable or animal which serves as the totem' (ibid.). Hence the close relationship is established! QED!

The core of Durkheim's proof is that of identity of symbolism: the symbols of the clan (society) and the symbols of the totemic principle (god) are both expressed in the totem (see Figure 12.1).

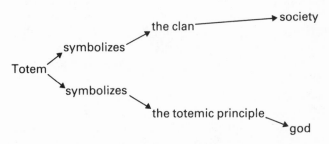

Figure 12.1   Totem and symbol

Durkheim's 'proof' seems all the more persuasive by his introduction of the word flag (*drapeau*) which he parallels with totem, so allowing the reader to infer:

$$\frac{\text{Totem}}{\text{clan}} : \frac{\text{flag}}{\text{modern society}}$$

The totem is the sacred symbol of the clan, as the flag is a sacred symbol of a modern society (see also 1913a(ii)(11) and (12):98/t.1975a:178).

The 'proof' is extraordinarily neat and it is not surprising that the very symmetry of the argument has given rise to criticism. We mention briefly some of the points.

(a) It is wrong to deduce that a clan is the same as a society, using the word society as it is generally understood (see ch. 13 below).

(b) The proof rests on the contention, say critics, that every society has passed through a period of totemism. It is now generally agreed by anthropologists that there is no evidence for such universality. Although Durkheim tended to support the notion of universality, he held that, contrary to charges made against him, his argument about what totemism revealed did not rest on such universality (134/95, including n.1). As he repeatedly said, his argument rested on 'one well-conducted experiment', not on the accumulation of experiments (ibid.) (see ch. 6.2–6.3).

(c) Durkheim holds that totemism offers the simplest form of social organization known to modern man; that was why he selected it. After all, the title of his book included the words 'elementary forms'. Such a claim for totemism is now seriously questioned, for Durkheim seems to imply that totemism leads to monotheism and not to polytheism. His 'proof' and assertions do not apply to polytheism (see pages ahead).

(d) Contrary to Durkheim's assumptions, totemism is not a religion: nor does it have a religious character (Richard 1943:156ff.; Schmidt 1931:117; etc.). It is basically a theory of human descent from a natural object, a plant or animal. Stanner, a leading authority on Australian totemism has said that the belief-systems of a totemic clan do not symbolize the clan. However, they do symbolize some aspects of reality significant to human life and experience (1967:236).

(e) It is wrong to make a parallel between a totem and a flag; one relates to a primitive society, the other to a nation. The origins of the two are different and call forth different sentiments (cf. Firth 1973:365). There are no uniform feelings towards a national flag as there are amongst primitive peoples towards their totem.

4 Criticisms

To make a *weak* association between divinity and society, that is, to assert that some dominant religious ideas are also to be found in the society in which the religion is situated, and which might be called social values, is not likely to draw forth criticism. For one thing the empirical evidence for such an assertion is overwhelmingly strong, since the ideals and structures of a society are often reflected in the attributes of the deity or deities of the society and vice-versa. For another, it leaves open the question of whether the ideas themselves, common to both the religion and to society, originate in the religion itself or in sources outside the religion but nevertheless located in society. This weak association is neither original nor provocative, and is taken for granted today amongst anthropologists and sociologists. It is the *strong* association which Durkheim pressed home, where God is held to be society symbolized or transfigured, which has given rise to much opposition and which is widely rejected by modern scholars. We have just stated that Durkheim probably never supported an even stronger association, namely, that God *is* society. For him society could never be co-extensive with and at all points the same as God. The two are not ontologically identical. Society is a much larger, more embracing concept and reality. What has to be taken more seriously is the criticism – based not on identity of God with society, but on the strong association between the two – that God is society symbolized or hypostasized (in the weak sense). To such criticism we now turn.

Durkheim's assertion that the key *représentations* of a society and its main religious ideals and beliefs are the same may be the case in some primitive societies and the fit is best in totemic societies. Hence Durkheim's 'proof', based on studies made of the Arunta. But anthropologists are by no means convinced of the fit in all primitive societies. Malinowski, for example, characterized Durkheim's position as: *vox populi, vox dei* (1925:54). He was convinced that such a position could not be accepted by anthropologists. It accords no place to individual opposition or unorthodoxy, but above all Durkheim's equation could not be upheld since society is a much larger entity than religion. More recently, Swanson has made the rather obvious point that not all

spirits and gods of a society act for the good of that society
(1960:17). Certain gods are to be ignored, ridiculed or punished.
Again, it could be argued that others behave in a hostile manner
against the well-being of society and therefore have to be
propitiated.

If some knowledge of religious systems in primitive societies
suggests that only a very few fit Durkheim's symbolic equation,
it is hardly surprising that it applies scarcely at all to modern
industrial nations. Amongst these there exists a high level of
religious differentiation, where various and opposing Christian
denominations jostle side by side and where in most countries
there is a separation of church and state. And if the state calls
itself secular, as the Third Republic in France did, what religious
bodies, all declaring their own doctrines, contain *représentations*
which correspond to those of the state? Clearly one has to look
outside the churches. But where? And how is one to derive these
general social *représentations*?

In upholding the strong association of God and society, one is
inclined to believe that Durkheim had at the back of his mind
two types of society, a primitive society based on totemism on the
one hand, and medieval Christendom, on the other. In the second,
the state is carefully differentiated from religious institutions and
therefore presents two entities whose beliefs can be compared and
where it is therefore possible to see the parallels between the
attributes of God and those of the state. But Durkheim never
seems to have worried about other examples. What of the case
of Hinduism? And in recalling Swanson's criticisms, it seems that
Durkheim's formula is difficult to apply to a polytheistic society.
To try to validate the formula, it would be necessary to establish
a group of *représentations* above the various deities, a kind of
supra-religion, some *surconscience*, as suggested by Richard,
which might be difficult in practice to establish. The example of
polytheism would seem to support the contention of Richard that
Durkheim saw totemism leading to monotheism rather than totemism giving rise to polytheism (1943:155). This would account for
Durkheim's selecting these two particular types of religion or
social organization. Of course, it could be argued that a society
which declares itself to be divine, as in the case of Hitler's
Germany, is the best example to demonstrate the association. But

to assert that is little more than to state the obvious. Society is God!

These forms of criticism merely raise in another way the problem of the tension between a religion and the society in which it is situated – tensions over, for example, the support of a war, the persecution of schismatics, the place that religious leaders should have in government, the right of education, and so forth. There is no tension where there is no differentiation between the two entities (see chs 13 and 14). But such tension can certainly be seen in early civilizations as in Israel, and perhaps in Greece and Rome. Durkheim's analysis hardly accounts for the rise of the eighth-century Jewish prophets (but see Durkheim 1919b:142–3/ t.1975a:187–9). Again, if there is such a strong association between the two concepts of divinity and society, how is it possible to account for new religious movements or religious change? As the movement is only one way, from society to God, one has to assume that all change comes from society and not from religion itself (but see ch. 14).

This inevitably brings us back to the question of reality. Reality must be society, not God (see ch. 15). This reality is known to the scientist, the sociologist, because such a person knows that 'ultimately it is society that is worshipped by the believers' (1950a/ 1969g:189/t.1957a:161). But is the worshipper convinced of this? When he has heard all Durkheim's arguments, will he then declare that he will now abandon his religion because he realizes that all along he has been worshipping not God but society? As Belot said: '[Durkheim] has seen in religion the cult of the collectivity consecrating itself to itself under the form of symbols more or less unrecognizable' (1913a:339). There is no evidence that people give up religion on such grounds or feel that when they attend mass, listen to sermons, perform *puja*, or make an animal sacrifice they are indeed worshipping society. Durkheim's assertion lacks empirical support from the experiences of those who are religious.

Are the best patriots of a society the most religious? According to Durkheim this would have to be so. What patriot would admit it, especially a modern patriot?

5 The enterprise assessed

Richard perhaps more than any other sociologist has dealt in detail with Durkheim's attempts to account for the idea of God (1943:137ff.). He seriously questioned the ability of sociology to offer a completely empirical account of the origin of the idea of God or even any kind of account of it. The only possibility, he held, was for sociology 'to assert a collective *surconscience* in which all values and judgments would be contained and through which the deification of human society would result' (ibid.). Such a possibility Richard rejects and thereby discredits the search by sociology to uncover the origin of the concept of God. John Bowker has recently raised again the question of a sociological explanation. He says that the correlation implied in the hypothesis between God and social structure must be seen to be so great that the concept of God is dependent on the latter and therefore the cause (1973:43). But he concludes that the hypothesis is 'too restricted to be even remotely probable' (ibid.). The reason is simple: social structure is not a sole and exclusive 'cause' of the concept. Social structure may be the means by which various types of concepts, such as those derived from the natural sciences, become plausible and continue in time. (In passing one ought to point to a logical fallacy in Bowker's criticism, namely, a correlation, no matter how great, can never in itself be a cause, and the way in which he posed the argument is a *non sequitur*.)

Durkheim made a daring attempt to find through rational means the locus of the concept of God. Such an attempt springs logically from his assumptions about the nature of religion, his definition of it, and particularly his concept of the sacred. It is also in line with his ventures into the sociology of knowledge in which, if one may simplify it, he holds that concepts are derived from social factors, more specifically social structure. Although no one today would support his conclusions, his strong association of the concept of God with that of society has brought home to sociologists an increased awareness of the weak form of the association. In societies dominated by one religion, its doctrines about God are reflected in the *représentations* of the society, and vice versa. The gods are not totally revealed in society: they are not completely social gods. Nevertheless they embellish different hierarchies or levels of social structure and something of the gods is buried within society (see Figure 12.2).

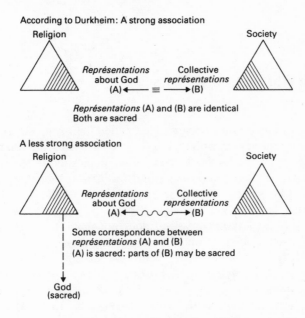

Figure 12.2   God and society

13   Society: a divine being?

1 The other side of the coin

Durkheim's assertion – what we have called the strong association of the concept of God with that of society – has led some commentators to refer to it as the doctrine of the deification of society. It cannot be stressed too strongly that the issues, though related, are not the same: they refer to different questions and are supported by different evidence. That God's nature has been revealed as society hypostasized does not mean that *ipso facto* society itself is divine, and Durkheim never said that it was. Admittedly there is evidence, which we shall discuss here and elsewhere, to show that for him society is the *ens realissimum*, that he gave it an ultimate place in his search for sociological explanation and that, as we have indicated, he also saw society as the *summum bonum* of ethical behaviour.

That God is society transfigured is, as we have indicated, prima facie a one-way process. Reality is society which becomes transfigured within religion and is epitomized as God. It is a non-reversible equation: society is not God transfigured. This particular formula therefore must be disregarded in considering the possibility that Durkheim sees society as possessing divine or quasi-divine characteristics.

There was probably no other issue which so infuriated his critics, and one believes his disciples and supporters also, as his attributing something of the divine to society (see ch. 28). Such criticisms were quickly raised and later forgotten as Durkheim's assertions in this matter were given less attention (see LaCapra in Clark 1979:130). In part, Durkheim's doctrine was a logical but not necessary development of his search for and discovery of the locus of God. He failed to convince his fellow academics, patriots, agnostics and rationalists, and he continued to antagonize the world of scholarship because the position cannot be justified by empirical data. It can be seen to apply to certain societies only, but such a proposition fails to meet the criterion of being universal and it was universal 'laws' which Durkheim set out to establish. His enthusiasm for the assertions he made about society is partially explained by his patriotism and his sense of duty which encouraged him to transfer a sense of worship evident in his young days from the God of the Jews to the god of society (see ch. 1.7). That which is worshipped must be God: society is worshipped, therefore it is God. As Stanner has noted – and he is in no way unique in such sentiments – Durkheim's 'sociocentric fixation was all-consuming' (1967:238). And Evans-Pritchard's remark is even more telling, but perhaps exaggerated: 'It was Durkheim and not the savage who made society into a god' (1956a:313).

2 Indications of divine qualities

One of the basic texts in examining Durkheim's approach to the nature of society in this respect comes from the paper La Détermination du fait moral, where he writes:

> The believer bows before his God, because it is from God that he believes that he holds his being, particularly his mental being, his soul. We have the same reasons for experiencing this feeling before the collective. (1906b/1924a:108/t.1953b:73)

Durkheim is arguing here about the moral authority of the collective and indeed the whole paper has a central theme of the need for a transcendental authority in any moral system. We have seen that he used this kind of argument in disclosing the nature of God (see ch. 12.3). To show that the functional alternative, an expression of course not used by Durkheim, is legitimate he employs the argument above, which is based on alleged individual experience. He suggests that man in coming face-to-face with society has a similar experience to that of the believer bowing before God in worship. He further suggests that the reason for the worshipper making obeisance is that he acknowledges that he is utterly dependent on God for existence. Man similarly has a reverence for society because he realizes he is utterly dependent on it for his existence. Durkheim does little to justify propositions empirically. One is tempted to deduce that it was precisely how he himself thought and that in this passage he expressed his own particular attitudes and experiences. But about other people and what they think and experience he is significantly silent, and as Richard has said, and it is true enough, such assertions cannot be proved (1943:163).

But does all this add up to the deification of society as so many critics assert? What Durkheim is offering is, as we have suggested, a functional alternative to God, where the two concepts are not identical either in Durkheim's thought or in reality, for functional alternatives never mean identity. Surely there are grounds for saying that *at certain levels*, society can be seen to be performing as 'God' in offering an authoritative base for moral behaviour. We see it in the assertion, 'it is demanded by society' or in the fact that society supplies or fulfils people's physical and emotional needs and wishes. Witness, for example, this quotation about troubled consciences arising from a failure of duty:

> This is why, in order to explain his mysterious voice that does not speak with a human accent, people imagine it to be so connected with transcendent personalities above and beyond man, which then becomes the object of a cult – the cult being, in the final analysis, only the external evidence of the authority attributed to the superhuman beings. . . . This reality in society. . . . When our conscience speaks, it is society speaking within us. (1925a:102/t.1961a:89–90)

In the association of God and society, we saw that there were two levels of association – one weak and the other strong. There are also in Durkheim's approach to the nature of society two levels of implication: first, a weak level expressed in functional terms, society acting in a way that God is said to act within the realm of moral behaviour; second, a stronger assertion, in attributing to society certain characteristics of a divine nature, for example, demanding absolute authority, giving rise to awe or adoration, the individual wish to be identified with the 'absolute'. This we shall call the divinization of society.

As we have suggested, the notion of society's 'religious' characteristics appear most clearly when Durkheim argues for a transcendental base which he sees necessary for any moral system. By a process of elimination, that is, by ruling God out, he holds that society is the only alternative left. In the debate, 'L'Efficacité des doctrines morales', which contains very important contributions by Durkheim, he sees society as 'a moral power superior to the individual, enjoying a sort of transcendence analogous to that which religions ascribe to divinity' (1909a(2):231/t.1979a:138). Bouglé's criticism during the debate seems quite right: Durkheim feels he cannot justify duty without divinizing a substratum of reality, that is, without transforming society into a divinity (ibid.:229). Durkheim's position is basically pragmatic: morality will not work unless such an authority exists. However, on other grounds, which we shall examine, he was also convinced that society possessed quasi-divine qualities.

But supposing man assumes an attitude of worship toward society, as Durkheim states, what actually is he worshipping? Society does not have a theology of itself, as many religions do, in which answers to such questions are given. The god of society – the social god – has to be deduced from observations about society. This raises severe problems. Beattie suggests two possibilities (1964:221). One is that man worships the group of people, *the collectivity*, individuals seen as a group, of which he is a member. It applies particularly in the case of totemism. The other is that he reveres *the system* of which he is part, the obligations, the duties, rights and laws by which the system operates and which is the basis of the society in which he lives. Here, we would note, Durkheim sees society as being almost identical to *la conscience collective*. Society in the first sense is 'greater' than in the second. Beattie suggests that Durkheim really implies the second rather than the first, admitting 'though sometimes he was less clear on the point' (ibid.). It is right to make this analytical differentiation, especially as Durkheim never defined society (see the following section of that chapter) and it is clear that Durkheim moves readily from one position to another without acknowledging the fact, and indeed wants it both ways. In terms of sociological explanation the second sense is usually the one implied, for it is obligations and ideals which to a very large extent control man's behaviour. On the other hand, when the notion is that of 'worshipping' society, it is likely that the first sense may be the operative one.

247

3 The nature of society: divine in what sense?

It is impossible to consider Durkheim's attributing to society characteristics which approach the divine without at the same time giving some attention to his concept of society in general. Because Durkheim never treats the subject systematically, it is therefore necessary to draw upon the whole spectrum of his written work. Further, because the concept is a key to his notion of sociological explanation, and is frequently alluded to by critics, it is impossible to treat it here other than in a brief way. We concentrate only on those aspects of the concept which bear on those characteristics of society which might be termed divine.

The most serious difficulty in dealing with Durkheim's notion of society is the fact that nowhere does he categorically define it. Despite what he sees to be the necessity in defining basic concepts, as for example, sociology (see 1895a), 'society' seems to have given rise to such enthusiasm that he overlooked the care shown in other concepts he used. This oversight is particularly poignant as society is associated with religion, and religion is defined with precision (see ch. 9). The word Durkheim generally uses is *société*, but also another word is employed, *collectivité*, as a virtual synonym (see, for example, 1906b/1924a:95). Not only does he never define these terms, he never analyses them either and, as Lukes has rightly said: '[Durkheim] uses it [society] in a deeply ambiguous way, in a multitudinous way. It covers a multitude of meanings and he never conceives it as part of his task to define it' (in Clark 1979:132). The nearest he comes to a definition, although he does not admit it as being one, is where he writes in *Moral Education* that: 'societies . . . are only permanent and organized crowds' (1925a:71/t.1961a:62). And again:

> Society is a complex of ideas and sentiments, ways of seeing and feeling, a certain intellectual and moral framework distinctive of the entire group. Society is above all a *conscience* – it is the *conscience* of the collectivity. It is this *conscience collective*. (ibid.:318/277)

Clearly in this relatively early work (1902–3), Durkheim sees society as approximating to the *conscience collective* which he expounds in *The Division of Labour* (1893b; see Lukes 1972:4).

Lukes has distinguished five ways at least in which Durkheim uses the concept of society (1972:21):

1 The social or cultural transmission or inculcation of beliefs and practices. A reality from which everything that matters to us flows.
2 The existence of an association of individuals assembled together.
3 The imposition of socially prescribed obligations. Society as a great moral power.
4 As an object of thought, sentiment and action, setting out what is good and desirable.
5 A concrete society, using the term to mean, for example, France. Reference to a particular group or institution.

See also Bellah (1973:ixff.).

In looking more closely at characteristics of society pertinent to this study, it should be noted that Durkheim repeatedly referred to society as possessing a reality which was *sui generis*, that is, in terms that can be seen to be ontological. Durkheim held that society was separate from other realities in possessing an existence or life of its own. There are those who think that society is comprised of individuals and can therefore be understood by their sum total (1895a/1901c:127/t.1938b:103; see ch. 9.2). This Durkheim strongly opposed, for to him it meant individual reductionism and would therefore make society an extension of the individual, thereby denying its *sui generis* quality. Society can never be so reduced (1925a:294/t.1961a:257). Society is more than the sum of its individuals and therefore:

$$S \neq \Sigma \ I_s$$
(S = society; I_s = individuals in the society.)

The methodological individualism of Spencer and Tarde Durkheim strongly opposed and instead embraced a form of social realism. Durkheim speaks of society as 'the *sui generis* subject formed by a plurality of individual subjects associated in such a way as to form a group; it is none other than the collective subject' (1906b/1924a:74/t.1953b:51). This 'subject', or 'collective personality' as Durkheim called it, is more than the totality of individuals who comprise it. There must be something in it beyond the sum total of the individuals, because the individuals by themselves do not have the authority and power that is in the group. Therefore society is a 'moral being [*personne morale*] qualitatively different from the individual people it comprises and from the synthesis of them which ensues' (ibid.). In *The Elementary Forms* Durkheim also refers to society as 'un être social qui représente en nous la plus haute réalité' (23/16). The group, society, collectivity has its own life, as Durkheim says, for 'human groups have a way of thinking, of feeling, and of living, differing from that of their members when they think, feel, and live as isolates' (1925a:71/t.1961a:62; see ch. 22.7). Society is therefore superior to its members, for it exerts a force over them, constrains them, but at the same time it only exists in them and through them (1950a/1969g:189/t.1957a:161). Society can only exist through individual *consciences*, and it cannot exist apart from them. It is thus a force which 'penetrates us' and 'organizes itself within us' and thus 'becomes part of our being' (299/209/128). Again, 'society is everything next to us, which envelops us and everywhere penetrates us' (1909a(2):227/t.1979a:135).

Pinard de la Boullaye held that because Durkheim saw society as a reality *sui generis*, it possessed, and alone possessed, power to mould *représentations collectives*, which in turn regulated individual thought. 'It is indeed, as one sees, the *deus ex machina* of the new positivism' (1922:446). This kind of deduction was common amongst other critics. Recently Talcott Parsons has reiterated this form of attack in assserting that Durkheim did not employ the term society 'in a common sense sociological way', which Parsons defines as being 'a concrete aggregate of human individuals' (1975:106).

In the essay 'Value judgments and judgments of reality' (1911b), Durkheim challenges those who would visualize society in static terms and, we would add, in such functional terms as are unable to admit social change. He wrote:

> To see society only as an organized body of vital functions is to diminish it, for this body has a soul [*âme*] which is the composition of collective ideals [*idéaux collectifs*]. But these ideals are not abstractions, cold intellectual *représentations*, lacking effective power. They are essentially dynamic. (1911b/ 1924a:136/t.1953b:93)

These words came in response to a question which Durkheim set

250

himself to answer, namely, whether or not society is able to create ideals. He stated that society was not only a legislator, but also the progenitor of ends and goals. In such a way society helps the individual to rise above himself. The language which he used in the above quotation, however, gave rise to alarm because of its 'theological' and 'idealist' overtones. Here is evidence enough of metaphysical speculation! And such evidence, says Gisbert, which leads to a deifying of society, has not been effaced by favourable interpreters (1959:358–9).

A logical argument can be derived from Durkheim's concept of the sacred, which demonstrates society's supra-sacred qualities. We have shown that Durkheim held that what was sacred in a given society was determined by society itself as the creator of the sacred (see ch. 7.6). The sacred is by definition that which is the most esteemed, the most holy, the most moral. But if society determines what this is, what object is sacred and what is not, society must be beyond the sacred, or at the pinnacle of what is sacred. Therefore, on rational grounds, society, when reduced to its bare essentials, must have sacred qualities. This form of reasoning was not advanced by Durkheim nor has it been put forward by commentators, but surely it must have been at the back of his mind (see ch. 26.5).

In the conclusion of *The Elementary Forms*, as we have had occasion to note (see Introductory Remarks), Durkheim deliberately enters the realm of philosophy, despite his early warnings in *The Rules of the Sociological Method* (1895a) that sociology has to keep clear of metaphysical presuppositions and thinking. In this his last book, he takes up the issue of universal categories and asserts that they have a social component in so far as they have taken from society models on which they are based (627ff./ 439ff.). One concept of particular interest is that of totality, because totality has religious manifestations, and is only the abstract form, according to Durkheim, of the concept of society. 'It is the whole which includes everything; the supreme class which encloses all other classes' (630/442/272 n.5); Kardiner and Preble (1961) maintain Durkheim gained his notion of society as a living whole from Espinas, the socio-biologist who preceded Durkheim at Bordeaux. Durkheim does not state that totality is the same as society or even divinity, but comes close to it. To associate society with totality means not only to give society supreme place in his thought, it also means that his thought comes very near to the religious.

We conclude our remarks on the semi-divine attributes of society by quoting a virtual hymn to society, a social Gloria in Excelsis:

> Society transcends the individual's *conscience*. . . . It is
> something more than a material power; it is a moral power.
> It surpasses us physically, materially and morally. Civilization
> is the result of the co-operation of men in association through
> successive generations. . . . Society made it, preserves it and
> transmits it to individuals . . . because it is at once the source
> and guardian of civilization, the channel by which it reaches
> us, society appears to be an infinitely richer and higher reality
> than our own. It is a reality from which everything that matters
> to us flows. Nevertheless it surpasses us in every way, since
> we can receive from this storehouse of intellectual and moral
> riches, at most a few fragments only. (1906b/1924a:77–8/
> t.1953b:54)

And as a doxology he writes a little later on:

> It is to society that we owe the power over matter which is
> our glory. It is society that has freed us from nature.
> (ibid.:108/73)

Indeed, there is so much in *The Elementary Forms* about society that the book is as much an 'ode' to the subject as it is a study of religion. In the closing pages of the book he wrote:

> In summing up, then, we must say that society is not at all the
> illogical or a-logical, incoherent and fantastic being which it
> has too often been considered. Quite on the contrary, the
> collective *conscience* is the highest form of psychic life, since
> it is a *conscience* of *consciences*. Being placed outside of and
> above individual and local contingencies, it sees things only
> in their permanent and essential aspects, which it crystallizes
> into communicable ideas. At the same time that it sees from
> above, it sees farther; at every moment of time, it embraces
> all known reality. (633/444)

Yet, despite this quasi-divine language that Durkheim uses in his analysis of society, he seriously denies it has metaphysical or mystical characteristics. The paradox and ambiguity of his position comes out in an earlier review on Gumplowicz.

> Undoubtedly a society is a being, a person. But this being has nothing metaphysical to it. It is not a substance more or less transcendent: it is a whole composed of parts. (1885c:632, translated in Bellah 1973:xx)

But how can one say a society is a being without reference to a metaphysical proposition and when no one is agreed about its nature or existence? Is being used symbolically? Durkheim is open to criticism because he does not say what he means by the words being or person.

One thing is clear; it is wrong to assume that when Durkheim uses the concept of society, he has in mind an ideal society – a mental image of a perfect society. He said in the debate on his paper, 'La Détermination du fait moral':

> Society has its pettiness and it has its grandeur. In order for us to love and respect it, it is not necessary to present it *other than it is*. If we were only able to love and respect that which is *ideally perfect*, supposing the word to have any definite meaning, God Himself could not be the object of such a feeling, since the world derives from Him and the world is full of imperfection and ugliness. (1906b/1924a:108/t.1953b:74; our italics only on the first group of words)

And interestingly enough, in what is most likely an allusion to Marxist thought, Durkheim adds that alongside the contemporary criticism of society as being little more than bourgeois administration, he appeals to what is neglected in such criticism, namely, society's 'most rich and moral complexity' (ibid.). Further, in the last lecture in the series on moral education, he praises the Cartesian basis of French thinking in its thirst for rationalism and for applying thought on a universal basis. On the other hand, it often exhibited the fault of being 'too simple' (1925a:321/t.1961a:279). In thinking about society there must be no abandonment of reason or falling into mysticism (ibid.:321/280). The last thing Durkheim wanted was to be accused of that (see ch. 1.2). His 'realism' comes out most strongly in *The Elementary Forms*, where he repeats the assertion that the society to which he refers is society as it 'exists and functions before our eyes' (600/420/149). As it has just been stated, according to Durkheim, society is riddled with imperfections and defects, yet such a being (*être*) inspires the sentiments of love. As the gods are both cruel and perfect so is society cruel and perfect (ibid.).

But perfect in what sense? B. R. Scharf holds that in religious activity, society presents an idealized view of itself (1970:152). This is not to be denied, for Durkheim sees all societies containing ideal elements in their *représentations collectives*. These represent amongst other things goals to which individuals and the society itself should aspire. It is evident in the moral ideals which every society possesses. But it should be noted that the realism of Durkheim's concept of society is that these ideals can be empirically ascertained. They are practical ideals. Never is society an ideal entity – a spiritual entity. When, therefore, Durkheim talks about the ideals of a society, he refers to those goals of perfection which each society maintains it should strive for. The goals are relative and not absolute, as all moral systems are in Durkheim's mind.

Once again, one sees Durkheim adopting a *via media* in rejecting materialism or a simple rationalism, but at the same time denying anything that could be called 'spiritual' or 'theological'. As Aron stated, Durkheim saw in society both the real and the ideal (1967b, 1:360).

One of the weaknesses of Durkheim is that he does not succeed in demonstrating how it is that societies and religions create ideals. Apart from collective effervescence (see chs 21 and 22), there is only one place where he offers anything approaching an explanation. He sees it in exaggeration. The emergence of ideals and divine characteristics occurs according to Durkheim by the process of society operating in and through the individual. He wrote in *Les Formes élémentaires*: 'society thus becomes an integral part of our being and *by that very fact* it is elevated and magnified' (299/209/128; our italics).

As for society being, as Durkheim called it, *sui generis*, it is evident that critics have made out of it far more than Durkheim implied. As Stanner has rightly suggested, Tarde's attack on him was beside the point because all that Durkheim was suggesting was that society is nothing more than a social system which is autonomous (1967/r.1975:283). We would add that, as such, it is not to be reduced to some other entity or to its parts, as in reductionism to individuals. In this sense it has an existence of its own, it has characteristics of its own and surely this is not in itself a staggering claim. Groups of people when acting together do not behave as individuals in themselves. The notion of *sui generis* does not of necessity imply divine-like characteristics; it is merely a way of saying that social forces are different from individual forces.

We have already considered the problem of the relation of the individual to the social, especially in the matter of religion. It is true that in many places Durkheim sees society as being superior and prior to the individual. But he also admits that society is dependent upon individuals who occupy social space and volume. There can be no society without individuals. Society therefore does not have pre-existence. It is not a timeless idea in the Platonic sense. Durkheim holds that there is a mutual interdependence between society and the individual. Each is necessary for the other and they stand in a dialectical relation (Poggi 1971:259). Society cannot exist without individuals: individuals are not 'human' unless they are part of society. Poggi holds that: 'Religion, in all its manifestation, re-enacts, reinforces, celebrates this drastic asymmetry in the – otherwise dialectical – relationship between society and the individual' (ibid.).

That Durkheim fails to define society allows his critics to do it for him and in a damaging way. For example, Goldenweiser and others believe that what he is referring to in *The Elementary Forms* is a sublimated crowd, for it is the crowd gathering together that gives strength to those who participate in it (Goldenweiser 1915:728). Thus the sublimated crowd is the source of religious rejuvenation and originality. But, as Goldenweiser continues, the crowd can consist of sages or a flock of sheep. And there is a difference! We shall attempt to show that this notion of a crowd was not what Durkheim had in mind in his theory of collective effervescence (see ch. 22). As we have noted, however, Durkheim did refer to societies as crowds, but only in the sense that they were not sublimated but permanent and organized (1925a:71/ t.1961a:62). Surely no one can take issue with that!

But not only was his concept of society seen to be little more than a sublimated crowd, it was also implied in the English-speaking world that it was associated with the notion of the group mind, as developed, for example, by McDougall in his book, *The*

255

Group Mind, published in 1920. Such a concept was strongly opposed by those liberal academics who feared it denied personal freedom and responsibility. Psychological analysis was very far from Durkheim's mind, as we shall show below (see ch. 22.1). More in keeping with Durkheim's own thought is the assertion that society in *The Elementary Forms* means not a crowd but a sib or clan. Since Durkheim does not define what he means by society, it allows him to move freely from clan to society and so make generalizations based on ethnographic material. Not surprisingly, such a step has been seriously challenged by anthropologists, for example, Lowie (1925:160). Although different clans are located in different territory, they all have much the same religion. The great god of the tribe is simply the synthesis of all the totems, just as the tribes are a synthesis of all the clans represented in them (Evans-Pritchard 1965:61). Durkheim's reasoning is that the *représentations* of the given society are those of the society at every level. Most anthropologists seem to agree that Durkheim was wrong to make these leaps in producing generalizations. Nevertheless, it should not be overlooked that such criticisms refer only to *The Elementary Forms* and, as we have shown, Durkheim's concept of society pervades the whole of his thought and is expounded in most of his writings.

So, then, what is society for Durkheim? It is clearly a manifestation of nature, an aspect of nature (cf. Mehl 1951:429). It is also a complex of the material and the mental. A society occupies social space or territory: in this sense it has an infrastructure. But it is, above all, a complexity of ideas, of ideals, of *représentations collectives*. Such a combination inevitably gives rise to difficulty and criticism. It is, as Lukes has noted (in Clark 1979:134), the cost that must be paid for using a word in a variety of ways which bring about richness and insight into the nature of social life. Ambiguity allows imagination full play. Schematically, society stands for Durkheim where God stands for the theologian. The difficulty for Durkheim is that society is, in his own words, an empirical reality, an aspect of nature, whereas God for the theologian never is this: he may be 'in this world', but ultimately he represents a reality beyond time and space. Durkheim's basically religious outlook, conscious or unconscious, encourages him, however, to attach to society a limited number of quasi-divine qualities.

4 How original was Durkheim?

Durkheim can be accused of allowing his readers to assume that he was original in attributing divine attributes to society. His implicit originality is easily contested. In France the idea that society was in some way divine was common enough and Durkheim's use of such an idea was criticized by Gustave Belot and Gaston Richard. It is inappropriate here to treat at length what has become a sterile debate about originality. We offer a few brief points.

From the times of Greek philosophers, such as Plato and Aristotle, there have been thinkers who have accorded special qualities to society, even quasi-divine qualities. One might also refer to St Augustine, Luther, Bossuet and Descartes. More appositely, in the period of the Enlightenment there were writers who, as agnostics, atheists or believers, related ideas about God to concepts in society. It is surprising that some would trace Durkheim's ideas in this matter to such forerunners. For example, Lalande thought Durkheim adopted a weak position because he was 'profoundly Kantian, for in Kantianism society takes the role generally attributed to God' (letter to Cuvillier, dated 18 May 1955; see ch. 12.2). Ginsberg pointed to Hegel's view of the history of religion in which each society manifests divine self-divination and each god manifests the spirit of the society in which it operates (1956:237). Durkheim's view, said Malinowski, was a reminder of Hegel's idea of the absolute (1913:529). And one might also point to Fichte in his *Addresses to the German Nation* in which, in tones of transcendental idealism, he refers to the glories of the German spirit enshrining all general values.

Another and much more closely related source stems from the thought of Auguste Comte. This is a particularly sensitive connection to make, because Durkheim, strong in his rejection of Comtean thought, saw that its crude positivism ended up by being the basis of a religious movement. Durkheim rightly contended that such a doctrinal outlook was harmful to his cause of establishing the science of sociology, which he claimed was based on a more profound understanding of the nature of science, although it was in the name of science that Comte developed his own brand of positivistic sociology. But the question is not so much

Durkheim's intentions and declared criticisms, but whether or not he was indeed influenced by Comte on the issue which Richard called the deification of society. Indeed, Richard had no hesitation in criticizing Durkheim for leaning heavily on Comte's positivism, and in taking over ideas such as his concept of religion of humanity (see 1943; see ch. 26). Durkheim, according to Richard, assumes uncritically that in Comte's third stage in the evolution of humanity, the Positivist, religion becomes nothing more than sociability. The process of religious evolution, according to Comte, is that religion develops from the individual to the elementary group, to the family, to the city, to humanity itself, so overcoming the distinction between nations and races (Richard 1943:144). Richard rightly believed that in an earlier period Feuerbach contributed to the notion of the deification of society, by uniting subject and object, for according to Feuerbach man is the object of man's worship. But the contemporary exponent of the deification of society, Richard held, was Durkheim himself. He was much more influenced by Comte than he was willing to admit, and despite his protest against orthodox positivism, and his poor estimation of the work of Comte, together with his esteem for Montesquieu and Saint-Simon, Richard was convinced that Durkheim's scientific rationalism was but a refinement of Comte's positivism. Nowhere was Richard's argument more firmly established than when he accuses Durkheim of deifying society. For science to claim such a metaphysical certainty that 'God is Society' is the very denial of the notion of science itself (ibid.:138). And if it was only a hypothesis to be tested, it needed a great deal of empirical evidence to substantiate it. If the task of sociology is to prove the deification of society, which Richard admits is an adventurous hypothesis, can the discipline really be called a science (ibid.)? Gustave Belot was also convinced that Durkheim had been inspired by Comte in seeing in religion 'the cult of the collectivity consecrating itself to itself under more or less unrecognizable symbols' (1913a:339).

A question which needs to be asked, but which seldom is, is whether Durkheim needed to refer specifically to the cult of the individual. If he held that society was characterized by quasi-divine qualities, or even divine qualities, and if, for example, citizens saw in it attributes formerly located in the Christian deity, why trouble about this new 'religion', this religion of man, centred, as it patently is, in society? Indeed, as we argue at the end of the book, it is unclear whether it is society or man that modern man is in fact worshipping (ch. 26.5). By underscoring the emerging religion, Durkheim was referring to an up-and-coming sect, which he hoped, one can assume, would become a church. But if this were the case, is he not denying sacred qualities to society? At least to that part of society presumably without knowledge of the cult? His position would be much more logical if he viewed society as being completely secular or neutral, which could then be gradually embraced by the new religion of humanity. Society is quasi-divine, yet is in the process of becoming quasi-divine. Does this paradox have any meaning? Hardly.

5 Criticism and evaluation

Another weakness of Durkheim's position in attributing divine qualities to society is the question of why some societies consciously divinize themselves and the vast majority do not. An example of divinization which immediately springs to mind is that of the Japanese, who in the Togugawa period venerated the Emperor as the embodiment of the genius of the Japanese people. Much the same theology occurred in the Meiji restoration (Hall 1968:28). In more recent times in the West, one could point to the divinization of society by totalitarian regimes, not least in Nazi Germany where Hitler and his supporters propagated the doctrine that the German people were a master race and, by implication, a holy people. The persecution of the Jews, another 'special' people, during the Hitler regime is significant. A further example of divinization is that of Ethiopia and Emperor Haile Selassie by the Rastafarians. Again, there are those who would extend the notion of deification to certain Communist countries where Marxist doctrine is seen to border on the infallible and where such doctrine is embodied in the society itself. The question of the Jews is interesting. For much of their history as we know it, they saw themselves as a particular people, chosen by God as vehicles of his revelation. In this sense they believed they were a sacred people in God's sight – a people set apart. Their ideal form of government was a theocracy, in which local leaders were directly answerable to God. The acceptance of a king at the time of Saul raised serious theological problems. Although they were a special people, it was anathema to them that they should be a totally divinized nation. The people of Israel sinned, rebelled against God, and for periods of their history were unworthy of their sacred trust. God, Yahweh, was always above and beyond them, never identified with them. Any such identification meant idolatry – the worst of all sins. Throughout Jewish history there is a very clear tension between the demands of Yahweh and the acts and beliefs of his people. He is always totally transcendent. For such a people to deify themselves would be unthinkable.

Now, in Durkheimian times, if one society consciously divinizes itself, it is because it is aware of a pre-determined reality, namely, the society has the quality of divinity about it and it is openly seen to be so. But if this reality is universal, why should certain societies be conscious of it and others not? Why should the sociologist reveal the hidden characteristics, which a few leaders of society have discovered throughout man's history? And what of this revelation by the sociologist in cases where societies deliberately repudiate the idea that they are in any way divine or absolute?

If, in fact, Durkheim does bestow on society divine or quasi-divine qualities which are deduced from social facts, such a conclusion is a denial of the anti-reductionism which Durkheim was so opposed to (see 1895a). Sociology could be accorded autonomy only on the principle that it explained its subject-matter at its own level, that is, the social by the social. In attacking animism and naturalism in their attempt to explain the origin of God, Durkheim upheld his anti-reductionism: 'a fact of common experience cannot give us the idea of something whose characteristic is to be outside the world of common experience' (123/87). These two attempts construct the idea of the divine out of sensations aroused in people by natural phenomena. But having affirmed his position in this way, by arguing for divine qualities about society, he denies the very principles that he wishes to uphold, although of course in reverse, in trying to raise the ordinary to the level of the divine. He can be criticized for 'reducing up' the social to the divine. Durkheim, however, attempts to save himself from such a charge, since he sees religion as a reality but only a reality of the everyday world – a reality closely related to man's experience in society. Neither man nor nature, he argues, is sacred in itself (ibid.). Sacredness must come from another source. But this will not do.

He is caught in his own ambivalence about society. If the divine is only of the order of the here-and-now, then it is hardly divine! Durkheim has either to accept this premise that the divine is nothing more than the here-and-now, which is a contradiction in terms, or deny his anti-reductionist position. Once again, he wants the best of both worlds, but he knows that the worlds are usually in conflict.

14 In the beginning: religion or society?

1 True to his own principles

The relation between religion and society posed by Durkheim must be further explored since the consequences and ramifications of his position are diverse and complex. We have already shown how, by using the concepts of society and *représentations collectives*, he attempted to demonstrate the locus of the concept of God and indeed its source. But if society is the reality behind God – and God is basically a social god – surely it is true of every facet of religion, not only the concept of God? Religion, in its totality, is derived from society. This is not to say that individuals, prophets, church leaders do not have a place. In religion as a whole – in religious institutions seen as entities of persistence – the influence of the social is of paramount significance. Therefore the locus of man's religious experience, of his religious tools, of his religious structures is in society – in socio-cultural life. What is religious is not derived from some biological or psychological source, although religion does cut into these fields, but from the social. Therefore when Durkheim attempts to use society to 'explain' religion, he is doing nothing more than being faithful to his methodological principle of avoiding reductionism, for he attempts to explain religious facts, that is social facts, by social facts.

2 All that is religious is social

Durkheim's unequivocal statement that religion is an essentially social phenomenon is to be found at the beginning of his academic life. In an early review he spoke of religion 'viewed purely as a social phenomenon' (1886a:68/t.1975a:21). And he died with

262

virtually the same theme on his lips when he wrote of his last book, in a review, that its main object was 'to demonstrate that the origins of religion are social' (1913a(ii)(6) and (7):35/ t.1975a:171). His standpoint on this matter was always misunderstood by his critics (cf. Richard 1923:247/t.1975:259). Perhaps more accurately than most commentators, van Gennep referred to Durkheim's 'well-known personal tendency to emphasize the collective element (social) above all else and to put it to the foreground' (1913:390/t.1975:207). Nor should it be overlooked that Durkheim's views were, in all probability, strengthened in reading Robertson Smith, who held that the distinction between the social and the religious was often meaningless, since every social act had reference to the gods as well as to men, and that the social body was made up of gods as well as men (1889/1894:30).

Durkheim's contention that religion is pre-eminently social and is derived from society is demonstrated or asserted in a number of different ways.[1] We have noted already that he places great emphasis on the social element in his developed definition of religion, employing the notion that a community, church or ecclesia is an integral element in the definition (65/47/123; see ch. 9.5). We have dealt in some detail with his concept of religion as something essentially social before and have no intention of going over the ground again (see ch. 10.2).

As always, Durkheim does not hesitate to contradict ideas opposed to his own. In this case he repudiates the notion that religion is essentially an individual phenomenon for the benefit of individuals, originated by individuals, individual in character. The origin and sustenance of religion is not from individuals, but from individuals working in a group.

> The only moral forces superior to those which the individual *qua* individual has at his command are those issuing from individuals in association. That is why religious forces are and can only be collective forces. (1913a(ii)(11) and (12):98/ t.1975a:180)

Religion does not further personal ends: indeed, said Durkheim, 'it exercises, at all times, a constraint upon the individual' (1893b/ 1902b:59/t.1933b:92). He had in mind here those taboos and moral directives issued in the name of religion which curb and discipline man's psychological and individual satisfactions.

It is impossible for an individual to have any religion unless he is in contact with society – unless he is part of a society. There can be no religion in a personal vacuum. As he remarked early on in his career:

Religions have only been found at the heart of established societies; among sick people who have been rigorously excluded from the rest of society by an accident (blindness allied to deafness) religious sentiment has never been found before the day it was communicated to them. (1887b:307/ t.1975a:33)

And a little later he observed that religion is unknown in the animal kingdom and that 'it is never found except where a collective organization exists' (1897a:352/t.1951a:312). Further, 'it varies with the nature of societies' and only in a group do men think religiously (ibid.).

3 The primacy of religion: all that is social is religious?

To be sure Durkheim saw religion as a social institution amongst other institutions such as law or marriage and that as such a religion is born, grows and dies. He readily admitted that all institutions, including of course religion, were subject to change (1913b:67). Religion, however, was special. It was not one of equal standing with other institutions: it was the queen of institutions. Though subject to social 'laws' and changes, it had pre-eminence. It was in fact a primal institution. Durkheim maintained such a position throughout his life. Poggi holds that for Durkheim religion is the paradigmatic institution (1971:252ff.), or the proto-institution of all other institutions. It was, as we shall see, the prototype of knowledge and of social conduct. Religion ultimately supports all other institutions. As Poggi says:

Religion directly cultivates and mobilizes attitudes of respect, devotion, submission, willingness to sacrifice oneself, etc., which all other institutions presuppose if they are to operate successfully. (ibid.:254)

One of the clearest examples of his position is to be seen in the following quotation, taken from an early work, his doctoral thesis. In it one sees what he called his broad theory of secularization (see ch. 24.3). More to the point, it discloses how he visualized religion in a primitive society – in man's earliest days. Religion, he held, embraced the entirety of life.

Originally, it [religion] pervades everything; everything social is religious; the two words are synonymous. (1893b/1902b:143/ t.1933b:169)

In this passage Durkheim seems to be arguing in terms of ideal conditions. 'Religion is equated with mechanical solidarity where an individual's thought and actions are little differentiated from those of other individuals' (Richard 1925:360). Durkheim indeed says that in societies typified by mechanical solidarity, 'we know that religion pervades the whole social life' (1893b/1902b:154/ t.1933b:8). In this sense Durkheim is arguing in terms of ideal conditions: indeed the concepts of mechanical and organic solidarity which stand at the heart of *The Division of Labour* can be interpreted as 'ideal types' not entirely dissimilar to Weber's use of the concept. A perfect example of mechanical solidarity or a perfect example of organic solidarity does not exist. Exaggerated characteristics of certain social states and conditions are made for analytical purposes. No anthropologist today would deny that in most, perhaps all primitive societies, religion as a social institution pervades great areas of life. It could be argued that when Durkheim says that in societies characterized by mechanical solidarity, the two worlds of the religious and the social are synonymous, he is exaggerating a clearly understood relationship. But Durkheim believed that he had found incontrovertible empirical evidence to show that the exaggerated connection, as we have called it, virtually existed. What he had presumed in the 1893 thesis was to be found in totemism. In the 1906–7 lectures on religion, he could triumphantly state from material he had been examining that: 'L'univers tout entier prend ainsi un caractère religieux' (1907f:98). So significant did the reporter of the lectures, Paul Fontana, see the idea to be that he had it printed in italics.

In a review in 1897 of Labriola's *Essais sur la conception matérialiste de l'histoire*, he held that according to sociologists and historians religion was the most primitive of all social phenomena, from it all other manifestations of collective activity emerged – 'Dans le principe tout est religieux' ('In the beginning all is religious') (1897e:650). Economic institutions, however, appear more rudimentary than religion but they depend on religion, which is a richer and more pervasive phenomenon, more than religion depends on them (ibid.). It is impossible to see how concepts of the deity have been influenced by economic factors to which religion cannot be reduced.

Two years later he was to modify his position slightly, when in the preface to the second volume of the *Année sociologique*, he took up the old theme once more:

> Religion contains in itself from the very beginning, even if in an indistinct state, all the elements which in dissociating themselves from it, articulating themselves, and combining with one another in a thousand ways, have given rise to the various manifestations of collective life. From myths and legends have issued forth science and poetry; from religious ornamentations and cultic ceremonies have emerged the plastic arts; from ritual practice were born both law and morals. One cannot understand our *représentation* of the world, our philosophical conceptions of the soul, of immortality, of life, unless one knows the religious beliefs which are their primordial form. (1899a(i):iv/t.1960c:350–1)

Durkheim goes on to refer also to kinship, punishment, contract, gifts and so on. But he now has doubts about one group of phenomena – economic organizations. He gives the hint that they could be derived from another source and wants to keep the question open. The general theme is that religious institutions are the source of all other institutions; and that religious ideas are the origin of other ideas. In his last book, as we have repeatedly noted, he emphasized the fact that the most fundamental ideas that man has devised – abstract categories of thought – had religious origins (see 12–15/9–11/110–12). Here are included concepts of time, space, number, cause (see also 1913a(ii)(6) and (7);35/ t.1975a:171). From the same source came all man's symbols. And further, Durkheim, together with Lévy-Bruhl, held that primitive mentality was 'essentially religious' (ibid.). It also meant that science itself had religious origins; and this allowed him to conclude:

If the main aspects of collective life began as mere aspects of
the religious life, it is obvious that the religious life must
have been the eminent form of collective life and a shorthand
expression of it viewed in its entirety. If religion has given
birth to everything that is essential in society, the reason is
that the idea of society is the soul of religion. (598–9/419/148)

Thus Poggi rightly states that religion in Durkheim's thought
'holds an unchallengeable position of supremacy' and that it stands
as the ultimate historical source of the whole institutional appar-
atus of society (1971:254). In *The Elementary Forms* Durkheim
speaks of religious forces embracing both the physical and the
moral. 'This double nature' of religion has enabled it 'to be like
the womb from which come all the leading germs of human civilization' (319/223). In these assertions it is implied that not only does
religion create other institutions, but it is the primal source of
ideas and all that is social. Hence, in the beginning was religion;
and all that was, was religious. It is possible to argue that religion
may have been the matrix of many social institutions, say on
historical grounds, but do not Durkheim's assertions mean that
religion actually creates the social, creates society? Certainly H.
S. Hughes holds that this is precisely what Durkheim meant and
that religion does give rise to society. He wrote:

The practice of religion produced a sense of solidarity, of
personal reinforcement through the group – in short, a sense
of society itself. Thus Durkheim was led to define society as
religious in origin. Religion *created* society: that was its true
function from the standpoint of positive science. (1958:285)

Statements such as these need to be treated with a certain amount
of reservation. Certainly Durkheim holds that religion gives rise
to social solidarity and cohesion. He wrote:

It is through a religion that we are able to structure a society,
the stage of unity it has reached and the degree of cohesion
of its parts. Religions are the primitive way in which societies
become conscious of themselves and their history. (1950a/
1969g:188/t.1957a:160)

Although religion produces a sense of communal unity amongst
those who adhere to it, it creates society only in this sense, as the

267

quotation just given implies. A society exists before its religion. But this implies knowledge of how things were in the beginning. Durkheim is ambivalent here. On the one hand, as we have already noted, he flatly denies the possibility of ever knowing historical origins, but, on the other, he seems to imply historical statements by pointing to elementary forms which he held existed near the beginning of man's social life. It is evident that he wishes to assert a structural relation between the two entities in holding that religion 'from the beginning' has been and always will be closely associated with the formation and persistence of society.

4 A meaningless paradox?

Two basic ideas which emerge in Durkheim's thought in relating society to religion appear to be contradictory: religion is derived from society, but in the beginning religion was the matrix of all that is social. Several questions follow. Did Durkheim understand the ambiguity of his position? Has one misread him? Is there any meaning in what he is saying?

Desroche is one who responds to the dilemma by adopting a dialectical approach (1968:61–2/t.1973:39). He argues that for Durkheim religion is a function of society only because in a different sense, society is or has been a function of religion. Without a professed religion or before the acceptance of such a religion, society is not a society. Thus, religion and society are complementary functions in a total act. Here Desroche emphasizes two types or two levels of society in asserting that according to Durkheim, society becomes itself only in a super-society (*sursociété*), the entrance to which is none other than the religious act. If religion is 'a social thing', this is not because it reflects an already established society: rather, it is social because it is an emblem of a society that is in the process of being made, which is none other than an act of self-creation. Such an interpretation, despite its plausibility, is to use a language Durkheim did not use and to read too much into his notion of society. It is more legitimate to see Durkheim's position not in dialectical terms but as a paradox which is never solved, but which contains elements of truth.

At the risk of repetition and to avoid misunderstanding, it should be observed that Durkheim was concerned with the issue of trying to establish the *fons et origo* of religion and all social institutions. For this reason he examined the most primitive group that he believed was known to man at the time, and emphasized the importance of this in *The Elementary Forms of the Religious Life* (ch. 6.2). In saying that religion was the progenitor of social institutions, Durkheim was making historical statements about the development of social life which have received general confirmation (Stanner 1967:221). For example, van Gennep has said that within semi-civilized societies religion viewed as a totality of beliefs and actions is the most social phenomenon known to man in so far as it embraces 'law, science, everything' (1913:391/ t.1975:208). Van Gennep also agrees with Durkheim in saying that most primitive societies do not differentiate social components. The social and religious are all combined. Such societies could be called religious in so far as religious ideas dominate them.

The all-pervasiveness of religion in primitive society allows some commentators to go so far as to suggest that Durkheim sees society as a religious phenomenon. This is so with Talcott Parsons (1937:427). The claim is made in conjunction with what Parsons saw as Durkheim's increasing interest in *représentations* as factors of explanation (see ch. 15.4). And H. S. Hughes follows Parsons and declares that for Durkheim, 'if religion in the end proved to be a social phenomenon, so also society turned out to be a religious phenomenon' (1958:285). Here is the paradox well and truly declared!

The reason for what appears to be a paradoxical and unresolved contradiction in Durkheim rests on the fact that he sees the social, society itself, as being sacred. Yet, on the other hand, religion is *the* locus of the sacred, it is defined in terms of the sacred, it contains the sacred ideas about society which is itself sacred. All too clearly there are the problems of identity and the danger of circular argument.

The problem comes out in another sentence in *The Division of Labour*:

It is, indeed, a constant fact that, when a slightly strong conviction is held by the same community of men, it inevitably takes on a religious character. (1893b/1902b:143/ t.1933b:169)

Thus living together (society) makes strong beliefs take on a religious character and so become part of religion. But surely the beliefs, which Durkheim admits were common to people living together and which existed before the process of intensification occurred, were religious? This he indicated in the previous sentence, when he held that people living together embraced a number of religious sentiments. Therefore, such communal living-together makes more religious what was religious before. And since religion is essentially social, society is thus an amplifier of itself. If it could be shown that society was in some way independent of its beliefs, such a position would be less ambiguous.

Let us try to re-examine the situation logically. For Durkheim it is unquestionably the case that all that is religious is essentially social and of social origin. Religion is derived from society and sustained by the social. Is it legitimate, however, to reverse the equation, as Durkheim seems to do and to say that all that is social is of religious origin – that religion gives rise to society? On grounds of logic this step cannot be taken. All X is from Y is not the same as all Y is from X, since X and Y are understood to be different. It is possible only when X and Y are identical. Now we have shown elsewhere that Durkheim could not and did not adopt this extreme position of identity (see ch. 13). He came very near to it, but did not take the ultimate step. We have just had occasion to refer to a quotation in *The Division of Labour* where Durkheim said that the two words religious and social were synonymous, but as we said then, it does not mean that the substantives, religion and society, are synonymous or identical. Durkheim was in this context referring to an idealized situation – to a primordial state of affairs of undifferentiated primitive society.

Thus Stanner seems quite right in stating that the relation between religion and society is not a symmetrical one. None the less he goes on to agree with Alpert that what Durkheim was really stating was 'the *identity* of religious thought and of social thought in general' (our italics). Identity, not being a relation, does not require either primacies or causalities to be asserted (1967/r.1975:282). In avoiding the charge of ambiguity in his own case, Stanner goes on to suggest that the key to the problem is whether one is arguing about conceptual primacy or chronological primacy, a point that will be taken up shortly.

To uphold a relationship of theses which is symmetrical would be bolstered, quite apart from the failure of logic which we have indicated, by the notion that religion creates society. This view, as we have just noted, is supported by Hughes in conjunction with Parsons. Giddens rejects the idea of Hughes, as we do, on the grounds that religion is 'the expression of the self-creation, the autonomous development of human society' (1971:110). Such an assertion is in accordance with the methods Durkheim proposed that social facts should be explained by social facts.

If one is prepared to re-phrase the theses and to take them out of their paradoxical relationship, two generalized statements emerge, which might be more generally acceptable.

1 Religion is social in origin in so far as it is derived from social interaction, of man living with fellow men in a social group. There is thus a correlation between the social and the religious, between society and religion.
2 Most social institutions as they have emerged in history were originally associated with religion and in this sense were part of religion.

Perhaps such formulations weaken Durkheim's position. They do not necessarily eliminate criticism, which could be said to apply as much to these statements as to those originally made by Durkheim. However, given the theses above, a third has to be set on its own as being inherently paradoxical, or perhaps in this case more accurately dialectical. It is that religious activity creates a sense of society or a sense of the social. In one sense this is a circular argument, since religion is itself derived from the social. On the other hand, it can be seen that when religious beliefs and practices are increased and intensified there is amongst those who adhere to them a greater sense of social coherence. And from this greater sense of society further religious ideas may emerge.

5 Further considerations

Much of the difficulty which arises out of Durkheim's two main theses about religion and society turn on whether he is making historical assertions or whether they are structural and conceptual.

Gustave Belot said of Durkheim's preface to the second volume of *L'Année sociologique* (see section 3 of this chapter) that, if his thesis about the association of religion and society is confined to strictly historical criteria and if it means that successive forms of beliefs and institutions follow one another, it is easily justified and has been upheld for a long time (1900:289). If, however, one tries to support it in more sociological terms, it is less easy to maintain. Belot held that it was difficult to determine whether certain forms and activities were born of religion, in the sense that they had come out of it, or whether they invaded it and therefore restricted it. In the matter of religion giving birth to various autonomous disciplines, the key issue is to know the principle by which the religious becomes the non-religious. What in fact brings about differentiation? And Belot said later that it is fairly clear that the family, morality, art, morals and so on have their origin in religion and that under the cover of religion and religious ideas these different functions were found, and later separated themselves from religion. This would seem to be the case historically, but if that were so the notion of origin becomes confused and is not a scientific explanation. The confusion rests on *cum hoc ergo propter hoc* (1909:30).

Much therefore turns on Durkheim's use of the ambiguous concept of origin. He was quite aware of this and he wrote: 'To be sure, if by origin we mean an absolute first beginning, the question is not a scientific one and must be dismissed out of hand' (10/8/109). It is thus impossible to find a historical moment when religion began. 'In common with every human institution, religion had no beginning' (11/10/109). Origin therefore cannot be usefully couched in historical terms. Yet in both *The Division of Labour* and *The Elementary Forms* Durkheim seems to be answering a hidden question: in the beginning what was society like? What was religion like? In the latter book, he was able to be more empirically based by using what he thought was the most primitive form of society at that time known to man. All too easily

Durkheim seems to have committed himself to a historical position and, although not primarily interested in history, gambled on historical speculation. In wanting to establish a structural or conceptual link between society and religion, he is not able to escape from historical considerations. Such considerations he might have thought would have strengthened his position, but this does not turn out to be the case.

The methodological position he most strongly proclaimed was scientific, and in searching for scientific origins – hardly a legitimate expression? – he held that the task was to find 'a way of detecting *the ever-present causes* behind the most essential forms of religious thought and practice' (11/10/109; our italics). He continues: 'these causes are most readily observed when the society under consideration is of the least complicated kind. That is why we are trying to revert to origins' (ibid.). Durkheim is therefore less worried *how* religion originated than as to *where* it originated – its locus. And where the fountain is located is where the never-ceasing supply of energy is to be found. If he cannot show the mechanisms by which it began, he claims to have found the continuing source from which it is eternally replenished. Durkheim's claim therefore is that there exists a timeless, an ahistorical relation between society and religion – a structural relation in which the two are intrinsically linked and, we would add, in an asymmetrical fashion.

Such a clarified position is not without its difficulties, however. It may be acceptable enough in general terms, but it is much more difficult to determine the nature and exactness of the correlation. The ideals of a society's religion, or of its gods, may indeed resemble the social structure of that society and its ideology at a given point of time, but is there an immediate, automatic and inevitable change in one component when the other changes? Are not both elements far more complex than Durkheim would have us imagine, far more complex than his delineation of 'the elementary forms'? It is this emphasis on elementary forms which is so deceiving. One cannot escape the problems of time and history and the question of empirical testing. Fürer-Haimendorf has noted in his study of the Apa Tanis and Daflas located in the Eastern Himalayas that their world-views challenge Durkheim's theory that religion is a reflection of social situations (1962:1). His findings suggest 'the possibility that an ideology rooted in a specific cultural background can persist with little modification in societies of very different structure and character' (ibid.). This raises the problem of a time-lag and once the factor of time is introduced, the association between religion and society as something intrinsic becomes tenuous. Fürer-Haimendorf concluded that changes in economic structure amongst the Apa Tanis were accompanied by slow changes in ideology and ritual which remain virtually unaltered despite growth in population and economy (ibid.:18). Belot, much earlier, had pointed to the question of the slowness by which functions and disciplines gained their autonomy from religion. In this respect, religion and society do not explain what is to be explained. Rather, 'each gives an account of the reverse of the problem, that is to say the slowness with which these diverse functions are differentiated, purified, and have become fully aware of the role they play' (1913a:379). Nor does Durkheim explain how the process of differentiation occurs. He hides behind such ideas as the inevitable changes in society (see ch. 22.6).

There can be no doubt that the difficulties which Durkheim faced in considering the relation between religion and society arose at a relatively early date, from say 1895 onwards (see ch. 4). The problems occurred because of the uncertainty in his own mind as to whether he saw society as the factor *par excellence* of explanation in social behaviour or whether religion was that factor. He was caught between the two and could never commit himself to the primacy of one over the other.

15 Représentations, symbols and reality

1 Introduction

In his examination of religion, Durkheim makes the assumption at the outset that what believers, religious leaders and theologians seek to achieve through practice and dogma cannot in fact be appropriated. If anything is gained, it is not related to that transcendental order of reality in which they believe. Therefore if religion achieves anything, and indeed it does achieve a great deal, it must be something quite different to what is sought by the believer. This 'something different' is known to the scientist, the objective observer standing outside the situation, who is concerned with truth. He sees a reality which is different from that claimed by the participants. The reality of the one is not that of the other. If 'reality' depended solely on sense-experience (for example, what is seen by the eyes or known from touch and hearing), it might be possible for both parties to agree about it. This is not the case. By his analysis of human experience and by the method that he uses, the scientist claims he has a greater awareness of what is real (see chs 11.8 and 25.2). The scientist stands as someone with superior knowledge, knowledge which the layman cannot understand (see, for example, 1920a:92/ t.1979a:89ff.). The scientist's claim extends to religion, which can be seen, according to Durkheim, to be a natural phenomenon in so far as it is a creation by man and by society. The problem over religion, however, which specifically interests us, is that, as has just been noted, religion is determined not according to physical characteristics relating to a thing, but is understood and communicated by way of recognized symbols and signs, not least by rituals which are overlaid with symbols. Symbols indicate a reality: they stand for something beyond themselves. The question arises as to what that reality is. Certainly the religious person is unaware of what is going on, it is argued. The assumption is therefore that all down the ages religion has been living in a perpetual darkness. 'As a matter of fact, it does not know itself. It knows neither what it is made of, nor what needs it satisfies' (614/430/159; 1909a(1)). What reality, then, does the scientist hold to lie behind the symbols? Is it that behind every religion there is a different reality? The aim of the scientist to generalize and universalize would suggest that any reality he might find would be one that would be common to all religions, irrespective of their type or form.

It is necessary to examine Durkheim's thought in a somewhat larger context in order to try to discover what he meant by reality and the relationship of reality to symbol and, more particularly, its relation to a technical word that he used extensively, *représentation*.

2 What is reality?

We have already had occasion to refer to problems associated with the concept of reelity (see ch. 6.1). Because for philosophers it relates to ontology and metaphysics, sociologists in the English and American traditions have studiously avoided it. But for Durkheim this was not so. He never seemed to hesitate to use it where he thought it appropriate. Perhaps more than anything else, his glib use of the word has caused sociologists of other traditions to steer away from him in order to maintain a purity not stained with philosophical terminology.

A very serious weakness on Durkheim's part is that he failed to define the term in an unequivocal way. It might be said that he saw reality at various levels. Physical things are real. And it is interesting to note that this idea remained with him to the end of his days when he spoke of the reality of religious 'forces' (1919b:100/t.1975a:183). Yet, on the other hand, reality is more than that which is immediately recognized on account of its physical presence or power. Indeed he himself talked of 'two sorts of reality' (304/212/131; and see 1911b/1924a:139/t.1953b:95). Reality is also infinitely complex and we can only succeed in expressing it slowly, laboriously, and by employing complex systems (1925a:321/t.1961a:279). The remarkable fact is that man can never arrive at anything but an imperfect expression of reality.

So it would appear that man both instantly recognizes what is real and yet at the same time scarcely understands it.

Thus, for Durkheim, one level of reality is related to the concrete, everyday world of experience, based on physical objects, physical necessities, human nature, psychological drives. Durkheim often seeks for explanations of social phenomena which appear to border on the physical, or are derived from physical analogies. These he put forward in the *Division of Labour* (1893b), where changes are seen in terms of population growth and moral density, all of which indicate the reality of the physical. But when Durkheim talks of force in social matters, he usually refers to moral force. Nevertheless one has at the back of one's mind that even here the physical was a fundamental reality and that, by extension, the moral exerted a force analogous to that in the physical world.

The real for Durkheim is most strongly associated with *la vie sérieuse* – the serious side of life (see ch. 19.1). He holds that art and art forms are unreal and deal with what is imaginary or what is trivial (1938a/1969f:240/t.1977a:207). The serious side of life is concerned with the necessities of existence, of what is required in order to live in a society. An obvious point of comparison is between art and ethics. The former is peripheral to existence, since certain societies have few or no art forms, whereas ethics exists in every society and controls a great deal of action (ibid.). Reality is at the heart of ethics, for, as Durkheim says, it 'either gets to grips with real objects or else loses itself in the void' (ibid.).

From this reference to the serious side of life as being what is real, it is evident that Durkheim readily went beyond what one might crudely call the common-sense or empirical notion of reality. He was prepared to apply the term to the study of social phenomena and to use it in connection with what he held to be ultimately important in this respect. Beyond all doubt society is for Durkheim a reality, not just in the sense that it might be said to exist, but because of its extreme importance in human life. In lectures on the history of the French educational system, he openly declared that the nature of reality was to be found in the 'nature of different societies' (1938a/1969f:373/t.1977a:326).

Every science studies what it considers to be a reality. For the sociologist, this reality is society or the social – the 'social is an autonomous reality' (Lévi-Strauss 1950:xxx). Yet there is always something behind the external reality which the scientist studies, there are laws and characteristics which are not immediately obvious to the ordinary observer. What is behind the reality is something which might be said to be more 'real', of greater importance than the reality itself. If this is true of physical objects, it is also true of social phenomena, of society itself. One therefore has to ask the question: what is behind society, of what does it consist? For Durkheim the answer is *représentations* of one form or another. He writes: 'Thus social life, in all its aspects and at every moment of its history, is possible only by a vast symbolism' (331/231). Hence, 'reality' at the heart of reality is a system of symbols, of *représentations* (see the following section of this chapter). But if the reality is a set of symbols, what do the symbols represent? Society? If so, Durkheim is indeed trapped in a circular argument. Apart from this problem, it is evident that ideas constitute reality (336/228/137) and that they are 'real' as a block of stone is real, although Durkheim would argue that the two sorts of reality are different. That ideas are real Durkheim demonstrates by pointing to the realm of religion, where he shows the sense of power that comes from religious belief and action. The man who participates in ritual 'feels stronger: he is stronger' (ibid.). What causes him to feel stronger? Common action but also belief. Since he has newly acquired strength, the belief must be a reality, since it acts like a physical force. All power is reality: belief is its agent. Therefore belief is real. For this reason Durkheim saw that one of the contributions that religion made to knowledge was that it provided a means showing what reality is. Thus he wrote:

> Although we see reality clearly discernible in mythologies and theologies, it is nevertheless true that we only see it magnified, transformed, and idealized. In this respect, the most primitive religions do not differ from the most recent and sophisticated. (601/421/150)

It would seem therefore that religion 'exaggerates' the case, but in so doing helps society discover reality. It could be argued that such exaggeration typifies his own thought (see ch. 28.3).

It is not suprising that Durkheim holds that reality is never completely grasped: it always remains open. While science takes over from religion and provides a more accurate kind of knowledge, which can be seen to be reality, reality in fact transcends it, as well as any other forms of knowledge. In a way that is hardly likely to appeal to those who want a definition of reality. Durkheim said that 'reality is infinite in every direction' (1938a/ 1969f:175/t.1977a:150). Thus, science cannot stipulate what is ultimately real: it can only point to reality at one level.

It is clear from what has been said, and particularly from the last reference, that Durkheim can never be accused of a naïve scientism or a simple empiricism. His thought is much too subtle for that. Suffice it to say here that he held that reality existed at various levels, or that there were various kinds of reality. Such a position leads to serious difficulties in the matter of what is social reality, and these we shall attempt to explore in the remainder of the chapter.

3 *Représentations*

Despite Durkheim's belief that reality has infinite possibilities, it is nevertheless true to say that in the way in which he used the word, the real was something that existed outside the individual. Reality is essentially objective and therefore stands 'out there'. Yet on the other hand, man is a thinking creature who is able to grasp reality only through some mental process. For Durkheim, crucial in this mental process, which of course is not a psychological process, is man's ability to create *représentations*. Indeed, man is a 'representational' creature. Man uses *représentations* in all areas of his experience and in the area of social phenomena – society itself – very little can be understood except by the use of *représentations* or symbols. They stand at the heart of social life and therefore at the heart of sociological thought.

The word *représentation* is not translated here because no English equivalent can be found for its many meanings, even if the word is confined to the context of philosophy. It can imply sentiment, volition, ideal, idea, category, symbol and myth (see ch. 20.3). Perhaps one might be so bold as to say that, in particular, *représentation* meant for Durkheim concept, category, myth. He held that man, through a *représentation*, has an idea of an external object (1925a:255ff./t.1961a:223ff.). Man cannot relate to an object without representing the thing, without having an idea of it, no matter how confused that idea might be. In this way the object is 'internalized' and 'exists' in man as a *représentation*. Sometimes the *représentation* forms a close fit to the object and is, we might say, an 'accurate' *représentation* of the object. In other cases this is not so and the *représentation* is confused or inaccurate because it is difficult to obtain such correspondence. Durkheim gives an example of this when he draws attention to the fact that we liken wind to breath, or describe light as an intangible body that goes through the air like an arrow (1920a:92/ t.1979a:89). Such a *représentation* does not correspond to reality. On the other hand, the modern scientist is able to produce a *représentation* of light or wind which is very much more accurate, although it may not be understood by people at large (ibid.). The point is that *représentations* are mental entities which may or may not correspond closely to reality or truth.

Durkheim began to consider the subject fairly systematically in an early essay 'Représentations individuelles et représentations collectives' (1898b). One of the problems that Durkheim attempted to solve was that of the emergence of new *représenta-tions*. He came to the conclusion that their birth was brought about by a process of synthesis. He drew a parallel with the growth of myths and legends. While certain aspects of religion can be understood by social morphology, for example, the way the organ-ization of the patriarchal family found its way into the Roman pantheon, or the notion of the city into that of the Greeks, such factors do not apply to the study of myths. Changes in myths can be seen only through changes in religious thought, that is, its *représentations* (see ch. 20.3). Thus, myths change through a synthesis of ideas in the same way as new *représentations* appear (1898b/1924a:43–4/t.1953b:31). Basically new *représentations* are brought into existence through laws of association in which parts combine to form a new whole. A synthesis occurs which cannot be shown to be a mere addition of the new parts. Some kind of fusion occurs which gives rise to the new totality (ibid. 43/30). Durkheim held that once a number of *représentations* had been created, they became autonomous realities 'with their own way of life' (ibid.:44/31).

Représentations constitute a wide category of entities, extending from signs to myths, from concepts to legends. Symbols come within such a category and symbol in Durkheim's thought is scarcely distinguished from other types of *représentation*. Some commentators such as Lévi-Strauss would make a distinction in Durkheim's thought between symbol and *représentation* (1945:518). It is true, as we shall see, that Durkheim does have various categories of *représentations*, such as belief, myth, idea, etc., but we would suggest that it is possible to say that when Durkheim defines society as a system of *représentations*, he comes near to stating that society is a system of symbols.

Durkheim did not hesitate to speak of various kinds or types of *représentations*. Thus, he referred to sentient (*sensibles*) *représentations* in *The Elementary Forms* (618/433). And, as indicated in the article just referred to, one of the main divisions of *représentations* that Durkheim used was to speak of individual and collective *représentations*. The first could be said to be unique to the individual as being the specific way in which the individual interprets the religion of which he is a member (see ch. 9.4 and 10). Individual *représentations* are thus numberless. The second category consists of *représentations* held by the group or society, which are external to the individual. They are therefore somewhat limited in number, but because of their collective following they hold great social significance. As we have seen, these can be said to be the subject-matter of sociology. Both in society and certainly within the religious group, the *représentations collectives* relate to sacred objects. For Durkheim they are at the heart of abstract thought, as can be seen in the paper written in conjunction with Mauss, 'De Quelques formes primitives de classification: contribution à l'étude des représentations collectives' (1903a(i)).

Durkheim holds that societies are dependent on morality for their health, if not their existence. In turn, morality rests on collective *représentations*. These *représentations* 'are as necessary for the well-being of our moral life as our food is for the maintenance of our physical life' (546/382). They are necessary therefore for social life (see Duncan 1969:158). Thus he could write:

A clan is essentially a reunion of individuals who bear the same name and rally around the same sign: take away the name and the sign which materializes it, and the clan is no longer representable. (334/233)

As early as 1898 he stated openly that the social consisted of *représentations*. He wrote: 'Whatever is social is made up of *repré-*

281

sentations, consequently it is a product of *représentations'* (1898a(ii):69). Similarly, Durkheim argued, without symbols social sentiments have a precarious existence. Without the group giving strength to them, individual temperaments easily gain control(331/231).

Not surprisingly, collective *représentations* are said to be charged with collective emotions and constitute a treasure from which individuals draw wealth. Commanding collective emotions, as they do, these *représentations* can be seen as forces acting on individuals and can thus be said to unite them (for characteristics of *représentations collectives* see 21ff./15ff.; and see ch. 16.4). Such *représentations* thus give rise to strong feelings in relation to common identification.

The earliest systems of *représentations* were religious in origin (12/9/110). And religion also constituted the first *représentation* of the relationship between things themselves, thus giving rise to the notion of causality (340/237/142). In societies where religion dominates, religious *représentations* can be seen to be part of the collective *représentations* of society. The second type of *représentations* constitute a larger category than the first (21ff./15ff.).

It is hardly surprising that the concept of *représentation* and particularly the way in which Durkheim developed it, has given rise to much controversy, particularly from sociologists and philosophers who would emphasize the need for an empirically based sociology. We shall mention some of these criticisms below, but at the moment we raise only two general lines of attack.

C. C. J. Webb was critical of the use of the term *représentation* by Durkheim, and particularly by Lévy-Bruhl, who employed it in connection with the problem of mentality amongst primitive peoples (1916:16ff.). Webb held that it was not within the province of the sociologist to question whether objects exist independently of man's consciousness of them. The problem had often presented itself to English philosophers, particularly Locke and Berkeley, that things are not 'at first perceived as they really exist' (ibid.:17). What is real or what is not real about an object is determined by the philosopher. Quite rightly, he sees that Durkheim implies that the way in which an individual views reality is determined by the influence of the group of which he is a member, that is, through the collective *représentations*. Thus society determines what is real. Gaston Richard frequently made this kind of criticism of

Durkheim, stating that the French sociologist started out by accepting the aims and methods of the scientist and ended up by being a philosopher (see, for example, 1943).

Another kind of criticism relates to Durkheim's positing the existence of some sort of 'spiritual' being behind collective *représentations*. As Lukes has pointed out, as early as 1899 in his article on defining religious phenomena, Durkheim referred to religious *représentations* emerging from the collective soul or mind and being subject to the laws of collective ideation yet to be discovered (Lukes 1972:242). The notion of a collective soul is clearly untenable to many philosophers, and to sociologists as a whole.

4 The sociological search: a change in direction?

For Durkheim the notion of *représentations* is crucial in his thought, for he sees that man is essentially a being whose life, to a very large extent, is determined by mental processes. For the sociologist, these processes are not to be seen in psychological motivation but in collective *représentations*, as ways of picturing the world, which are largely given to man or acquired by him from the society of which he is a member. The notion of *représentation* as a key to understanding man and society is present in Durkheim's thought from the very early days until his death. It is certainly prominent in *The Elementary Forms*, and also in the last thing he wrote, 'Introduction à la morale' (1920a).

For some time there have been those who held that Durkheim, in the course of his academic work, changed his position in the use of key concepts in sociological analysis and explanation. Indeed, this was noted before the time of the First World War through the observations of Gaston Richard and Georges Davy (1883–1976), a relatively late-comer to the Année Sociologique group (see ch. 2.2). Davy said that the aim of the sociologist must be to seek an explanation of the 'fundamental conditions of collective existence' (1911:43). Clearly Durkheim could well have accepted such a premise. Davy's argument about Durkheim is that in his first period of development (until about 1897), he focused on morphological factors, that is, factors which relate to the external characteristics of a social phenomenon (see, for example, 1895a/1901c:137–8/t.1938b:112–13; and see also the important article 1900c, written at the same time as the second edition of 1895a). In particular, in *The Division of Labour*, Durkheim pointed to what he called moral density which relates to the number of social units, which in turn depend upon the size of population. This type of analysis, using external characteristics, dominates *The Rules of Sociological Method* (1895a), and *Suicide* (1897a). The model of explanation follows that of the natural sciences where 'things' are held to be causal (Davy 1911:44). That Durkheim emphasizes 'things' – and he stressed that social facts were to be treated as 'things' in *The Rules of Sociological Method* – coupled with the fact that he emphasizes external characteristics has always encouraged commentators to refer to Durkheim in this respect as a positivist. What is real is therefore that which can be observed (Kardiner and Preble 1961:128).

Then, according to Davy, Richard, Parsons and others (for example, Bouglé, Benoît-Smullyan, Gurvitch), Durkheim changed his position around 1900–10, rejected morphological factors, and turned instead to ideas or *représentations* associated with social phenomena (see ch. 22.6; Pickering 1975:349). It is these – *les facteurs idéaux* – which hold the key for sociological understanding, be it of religion, of any other institution, or of society itself. That *représentations* should assume so crucial a place seems to some to be a denial of the empirical scientific method which Durkheim originally adopted. The issue has been extensively debated in the United States in recent years (see Pope 1973 and Parsons 1975) and to examine it in the light of all the available evidence is outside the scope of this book. All that can be done is to offer a few points which are derived from Durkheim's works which deal with religion.

We offer one example of the alleged volte-face in the area of religion, where the power of religion is evident. The following quotation has been cited before, but it is given here at greater length:

> The Arunta who has rubbed himself in the correct fashion
> with his churinga feels stronger; he is stronger. If he has
> eaten the flesh of an animal, which although perfectly
> wholesome is none the less forbidden, he will feel ill and die.
> (326/228/137)

It cannot be said that the man's death was initiated by some physical act which directly brought about his demise. The cause can only be a *représentation*, since it is assumed it does not contain within itself a transcendental force which has a direct physical outcome.

Davy offers an example where Durkheim argues that the cohesion of social and family groups is not founded on real, physical ties, such as neighbourhood or blood, but on the *représentation* of a mysterious consubstantiality, that is, participation in a common totem. Davy asserts that without doubt there are indeed many *things* behind these *représentations* (1911:44). The totem is simply a symbol of the collective force. But what is more important is that these *things* act on the life of societies, not by way of their intrinsic physical properties but in the manner in which they are represented to the collectivity. Thus, Davy's charge is that the operative factors are ideas not things (ibid.), and that it was Durkheim's study of religious phenomena which caused him to turn to 'spiritual' factors. But it is just as logical to argue the other way round and to suppose that a new concern with *représentations* increased his interest in religion as the cradle of sacred ideas. Parsons sees Durkheim ceasing to be a positivist in his study of religion, namely, someone who relies on what is observable. He changes to being an idealist by focusing on attributes, values, ideas (1937:441ff.). There are some grounds for arguing along these lines when one compares the 1899 article on defining religion with the 1912 book. In the first, Durkheim states that the sociology of religion deals with social facts (1899a(ii):1/ t.1975a:74), with 'only the exterior and apparent form of religion' (ibid.:16/87). In *The Elementary Forms* he notes that all religions are comparable and have certain elements in common, but these do not mean 'the external and visible characteristics' (6/4–5/106). They indicate others 'more deep rooted'. At the heart of all religious systems there exists 'a certain number of fundamental *représentations* and ritual attitudes' which 'have everywhere the same objective meaning and universally fulfil the same function' (ibid.). 'It is these permanent elements which constitute the eternal and human aspect of religion' (ibid.).

In more general terms, Davy states that reality for Durkheim ceases to be society and becomes the *représentations* of forces within society. Of course he is quite right in suggesting that

Durkheim does use the concept of *représentation* as being crucial in the search for sociological explanation, and Durkheim made the point in fact before the publication of *The Elementary Forms* and so anticipated the following sentence which comes from it:

> There is thus a part of nature where the formula of idealism applies almost literally: it is the social kingdom. There, much more than elsewhere, ideas [*idées*] constitute reality. (326/228/ 137)

But even here Durkheim is hesitant. He would only stress ideas in the social world. He does not wish to be misunderstood as being an idealist in the philosophical sense. He writes: 'Sans doute, même dans ce cas, l'idéalisme n'est pas vrai sans tempérament' ('Doubtless even in this case, idealism is only true if modified') (ibid.). The question is, what is to be tempered or modified? Idealism, to be sure. But what does this mean? It means, we hold, that reality is not solely determined by *représentations*, since certain *représentations* can be false or inadequate.

We have just shown that Durkheim held that the *représentations* of laymen about physical objects may be far removed from those of a scientist, whose *représentations* are nearer truth or reality (section 3 above). Quite clearly Durkheim rejects the monist idealism of a philosopher such as Hegel and that of the neo-Hegelians. He comes very near such thinkers, however, when he writes in a footnote: 'In a philosophical sense, the same is true of everything; for nothing exists except in *représentations*' (493/ 345). Durkheim goes on to say in the same footnote that the proposition is 'doubly true' for religious forces, since such forces correspond to the sacred which itself is not derived from 'the constitutions of things' (see ch. 7.6). It is evident that Durkheim will not be pinned down to some philosophical school. He counteracts monism by a near-dualism in which he asserts that we can never escape the duality of our nature and be completely free from physical dependence. The thing remains, as well as its *représentation*. Separating various spheres of influence, he would argue that in religious life the *représentation* is more effective than the thing itself, but the thing always remains and is understood by varying *représentations*.

There can be no doubt that there is some shift in emphasis in Durkheim's thought in turning from things (*choses*) to ideas (*représentations*). However, Durkheim's thought went through other shifts, sometimes of a more radical kind as in his definition of religion (see ch. 9). Our position is that Durkheim's change of emphasis has not been fully understood and that it has been given too much prominence by commentators. There can be no doubt that the controversy has raised important issues, but in trying to understand what he was attempting to do, these should lead us back to Durkheim to a closer examination of his work, not to wider issues. We would make the following points.

First, from the beginning of his work, Durkheim used the word *représentation* as an important, if not causal, concept in analysing social life. As we have already noted, Durkheim stressed the fact that man is a 'representational' creature. Mental processes involve *représentations* and man views society through *représentations*.

Second, the notion of coercion, seen as a force and therefore external to the individual, which was so important in his early work particularly on religion, is still contained in later concepts, including that of collective *représentations*; these, as we have observed, produce constraint over those who adhere to them.

Third, Durkheim might defend himself against the charge of shifting his ground by pointing to the fact that *représentations* are to be treated as 'things' that is, to be treated as if they were things. And this latter mode is what he meant when he talked about social facts as things in *The Rules of Sociological Method* (1895a/1901c:27/t.1938b:27). No social fact is literally a thing in the sense that a table is. The change of emphasis that Durkheim makes merely implies a change of subject-matter or a redefinition of subject-matter, and so suggests that collective *représentations* should, as social facts, be subject to the principles of *The Rules*. And let it not be forgotten that in *The Rules* Durkheim stated that ways of thinking were to be considered as social facts (ibid.:5/3). Collective *représentations* are indeed external to the individual, they exert force on others, they constitute a reality. This makes them legitimate subject-matter for scientific treatment. It has to be admitted that social facts are not identical to *représentations*, but Durkheim was still prepared to use the term social fact in the latter part of his academic life. Here, then, there is no abandonment of method. Durkheim to his dying day stated that the work of the sociologist was to be modelled on that of the scientist. There was to be no acceptance of 'philosophical explanation'.

Sociology was a discipline having its own autonomy, pursuing a scientific methodology. In this sense, therefore, there is no significant shift in Durkheim's work. After all, method very largely determines the nature of a discipline. Of course, it can be argued that in giving more prominence to *représentations* serious difficulties are encountered which make it impossible to apply a scientific method, such as that outlined in *The Rules* (see below). But that is another type of argument. *The Rules* itself is full of serious defects in many people's eyes and shows a very limited knowledge of scientific procedure. To argue that his more developed position contains serious methodological problems often gives the impression that his earlier position was much more tenable. The point is conjectural. Durkheim never actually stated that *représentations* had to be studied as things. And he never replied openly to the charges by Davy. That he did not do so may well allow us to assume that he did not believe that the charges were significant.

Fourth, as early as 1900 Durkheim stated quite clearly that it was not the task of sociology to study what might be called geographical factors, such as soil and climate, to see if they had an influence over religious and collective *représentations*, including myths and legends. Such factors were particularly useless in studying modern religions. The main argument against using them was due to the fact that such geographical factors varied in different periods of history (1900a(47)). Durkheim was thus very sceptical about the contribution that geography could make to sociology. This would seem to confirm that he never thought that 'hard things' could significantly contribute to man's understanding of social behaviour.

Fifth, those who would argue for a shift in Durkheim's thinking are hard pressed to show when precisely he changed direction in his search for sociological explanation. In the light of the points just raised, it is very difficult to indicate a particular year or period when the change might have occurred, so that if one is going to hold to this kind of interpretation of Durkheim's work, it is best to assume that it took place gradually, starting at a very early period and ending with his last works.

We would press this last point a little further and state that it is important to see that although the change does not occur around 1895 (see ch. 4), the shift to *représentations* seems most apparent when Durkheim deals with religious phenomena and their ultimate significance within the social context. Always excepting the fact that there is no 'spiritual' reality behind them, how are they to be understood as being effective, as being 'real' forces? Durkheim would seem to admit that the force of religion is generated and controlled by *représentations*. He wrote, in a quotation we have already given, that nothing exists except through its *représentation*, and he goes on to say: 'this proposition is doubly true for religious forces, for there is nothing in the constitution of things which corresponds to sacredness' (493 n.1/345 n.1). Thus the external or material properties of things have to be excluded, since they are either insignificant, or, as in some cases, the 'realities' do not have physical characteristics. It should be noted straightaway that Durkheim, in focusing on *représentations* rather than on the reality alleged by believers, brought 'religion down to earth' (in the words of Alpert) and so made a sociological approach to religion possible (1939:198).

Durkheim's position is not free from ambiguity. The use of the notion of *représentation* has the danger of allowing the reader to confuse those *représentations* which are used by the believer to represent what he sees as the reality of religion and another set of *représentations* used by the sociologist in trying to understand the way in which religious processes work. It is not difficult to see that the sociologist can have a *représentation* of a *représentation*.

Thus we return to a point that we made earlier, namely, that Durkheim readily admits to many types of *représentations* (for example, between individual and collective *représentations*), but as well he makes the distinction within the realm of collective *représentations* between those that are used by the scientist and are related to things and attempt to establish causality, and other *représentations* related to religion and values. Although his position in this respect is firmly established in *Les Formes élémentaires* (for example, 595/416/145), it is evident that he made such a distinction as early as 1899 in what we have called the second period of his development. In an ambiguous passage in the middle of his article on defining religion, he refers to empirical (*empirique*) *représentations* (1899a(ii):19/t.1975a:90). It would seem that these *représentations* are to be associated with those used by the scientist. The acceptance of such a division is therefore not late in the development of Durkheim's thought. There can be, however, for Durkheim no absolute division between religious and scientific *représentations* as there is between the sacred and the profane. Since the scientific have grown out of the religious, there can be no such water-tight compartmentalization (see ch. 14). The division between the two rests upon the superior thinking and analysis of the scientist in coming to grips with reality and in using *représentations* in a way that cannot be understood by the religious participant. The contrast between the two types of *représentation* is shown in Table 15.1.

TABLE 15.1   *Two sets of représentations*

Type	Religious	Scientific
Content	dogmas, myths, ideas, ideals	models, law, common sense (?)
Quality	distorted	precise
Related to	imagination, ideals	things
Based on	tradition	empirical observation
Gives rise to	coercion	freedom of thought
Change	very little	considerable

5 There are no unknowable symbols

It must stand to the lasting credit of Durkheim that he attempted to explain the complexity of religious symbols which abound in Arunta life. He saw the sociologist as one who could unlock the mysteries by observation and analysis and he used intricate material to demonstrate, at least to his own satisfaction, that there was little which could not be solved by the methods he advocated. He was quite clear that he could discern the reality which lay behind the *représentations*, which, as religious *représentations*, were inevitably distorted images of reality. But despite his *tour de force* in studying the totemistic system of the Arunta, the impression received in reading his work is that he appears to know what reality is before he has studied the symbols, so that he introduces a kind of dogmatism, an a priori doctrine, which starts with reality rather than symbol, and which does not predict reality from a given set of symbols.

290

The scientist claims to know reality in a way the participant does not. He claims to know that X is, for example, 'more' real than Y. Within such a framework, and in considering a sphere of religion, Durkheim states that not only do symbols convey reality, they assume reality and so become part of it. The symbol declares reality, but reality is the symbol (331/231; Duncan 1969:157). The symbol thus becomes greater than the thing. Durkheim extended his arguments from totemism by referring to the symbolic import-ance of an army's flag:

> We know what a flag is for the soldier: in itself it is but a piece of cloth. . . . The soldier who falls defending his flag certainly does not believe that he has sacrificed himself for a piece of cloth. (325–6/227–8/136–7; see earlier reference in 1911b/1924a: 127/t.1953b:87)

A more up-to-date example is where 'a used postage stamp may be worth a fortune but it is obvious that its value is in no way implicit in its natural properties' (ibid.). Durkheim's position over symbolism, to which we have already alluded, is simple enough: an external agency gives value to something which is not depen-dent on the intrinsic nature or characteristics associated with the thing itself. And, so great can be the value added that the *représen-tation* associated with the object becomes what is real. We would add that such an assertion is correct in much of the realm of religion, certainly in advanced religions. A crucifix by itself is of no value. The events associated with Christ's suffering are all-important to the believer. To desecrate a crucifix is to profane those events.

It is interesting that the examples which Durkheim gives indi-cate that the values given to an object – its symbolic worth – can be associated with economic value. The worth of anything in economic terms is derived from its rareness or scarcity. It has no 'real' worth apart from that determined by the market or, in a non-market economy, to its worth determined by society. Hence the market value or socially determined value is its real value. This kind of 'economic' thinking is strengthened by the use of the word 'superadded' which, as we have seen, Durkheim employs in referring to objects designated as sacred – value or worth is superimposed (see ch. 7.6). Durkheim sees collective *représenta-tions* attribute to things to which they refer 'properties which do not exist in any form or to any degree' (326/228/137). One might add in connection with this that he gave a high place to economic organizations certainly in terms of the emergence of social institutions (1899a(i); and see ch. 14.3). Durkheim thus cannot accept the notion of the universality of symbolic content. The same object does not symbolize the same idea the world over, nor do objects give rise to the same symbols. The properties of things, their intrinsic properties such as weight, shape, size, texture, colour, do not produce universal symbols. Hence there is no 'natural' or 'intrinsic' or 'rational' link between object and *représentation*. The link must be created through some external force and that, as we have noted, can be no other for Durkheim than society itself.

6 Things and symbols

H. D. Duncan is one who holds that Durkheim in fact treats symbols (*représentations*) as things (1969:61). With this we would concur, but we would note that by the notion of thing Durkheim implies that the entity is objective, that is, it exists outside the self and is to be analysed and understood objectively as the scientist approaches whatever phenomena he studies (625/437).

However, the aim of treating *représentations* as things can be challenged on methodological grounds. Since Durkheim never publicly contradicted what he wrote in *The Rules* (and the book went into a second and revised edition, published in 1901), one may assume that the canons of procedure that he held were always applicable. Inconsistencies and problems in applying *The Rules* to *représentations* have been noted by Claude Lévi-Strauss (1945:528; also 1950:xxvii). He says that Durkheim sought in his methodology to treat social facts as 'things', which is in keeping with Kantian ideas. But Durkheim 'oscillates between a dull empiricism and an aprioristic frenzy' (ibid.). For the one, methodical experiments are required for explanation: for the other, what is necessary is to rethink them in their logical order and this is not very fruitful. Durkheim consistently argued that *représentations collectives* are social facts and such *représentations* mean 'objectivated systems of ideas'. The solution to the dilemma according to Lévi-

Strauss is to hold that social things are psychic in nature and that 'the systems of ideas are unconscious or that unconscious psychical structures underlie them and make them possible' (ibid.). Here Lévi-Strauss offers an answer that is contrary to Durkheim's thinking, because Lévi-Strauss would make what is real and final relate to the unconscious. By contrast, sociology according to Durkheim neither knows anything of the unconscious nor wants to know it. Symbols – collective *représentations* – are the centre of sociological explanation, but their reality is always known at the level of the conscious and can therefore be always ascertained by the reasoning mind: they are in fact extensions of it.

What Lévi-Strauss was suggesting in the 1940s had to some degree been said by Talcott Parsons a few years earlier (see 1937), and was to be later repeated by other American commentators such as Bellah (1959) and Goode (1951:257). If *représentations* are seen as social facts, then these critics would argue along the lines that there has been a change in the ball game. Originally, it was one where social phenomena were to be seen to be social facts, comparable with natural facts, possessing characteristics comparable with physical facts. Parsons was amongst the first to hold that *représentations* about physical things and *représentations* about values or spiritual ideals are different and have to be treated differently (1937:431). Physical things have *représentations* which are always related to given objects so that the ideas themselves are governed by physical attributes. Distorted *représentations* are readily corrected by referring them back to the given object. Reality is the object, not the *représentation*. This is the case with scientific *représentations* and with concepts (and in this respect see 1911b/1924a:140/1953b:95). Here are *représentations* or symbols of reality (things) and they are limited to the faithful analyses of reality (things). Their object is to understand the reality. Parsons and other critics hold that Durkheim, in emphasizing collective *représentations*, is asking sociology to deal with a completely different order of reality – from 'things' to ideals, ideas, or *représentations*. That Durkheim believes that the subject-matter of sociology is *représentations* is beyond all shadow of doubt, for he categorically says so in his paper 'Jugements de valeur et jugements de réalité' (1911b:secn IV). Durkheim argues that this is so because sociology rightly deals with religion, law and morals and these for Durkheim 'are nothing more than systems of values,

293

hence ideals' (1911b/1924a:141/1953b:96). 'At the very outset sociology is concerned with the ideal' (ibid.). Sociology does not reach this position slowly by way of research, 'it sets out from there'. 'The ideal is in fact its peculiar field of study' (ibid.). Sociology has to use a scientific method in dealing with the ideal. 'The aim is to bring the ideal, in its various forms, into the sphere of nature' (ibid.). Therefore the task of sociology – of *sociologie religieuse* – is to treat *représentations* as science treats phenomena which are part of nature.

One of the reasons why Durkheim attempts to use the scientific method in dealing with ideals and values is because such ideals are related to things. Human or social *représentations* transfigure reality (ibid.:140/95). And so, 'the thing itself symbolizes the ideal and acts as the medium through which the ideal becomes capable of being understood' (ibid.:140/96). The ideal which is superadded to the object is treated as real, although not in the same way as the thing itself. There is no methodological problem, since Durkheim sees the ideal as being closely associated with the real. His idealism, such as it is, relates to the real, to things. As we have noted, he repudiates philosophical idealism and we find him saying:

> the ideal is not 'cloud cuckoo land'; it is *of* and *in* nature. It is subject to examination like the rest of the moral or physical universe. (ibid. 137/94; see also ibid. 136/93)

And again:

> Collective ideals can only be manifested and become aware of themselves by being concretely realized in material objects that can be seen by all, understood by all, and represented to all minds. (ibid.:137/94)

In the conclusion of the essay on primitive classification which Durkheim wrote with Mauss, he appears to admit, as we have noted (ch. 8.3h) the limitations of rational and critical thought (that is, science), in dealing with the ultimate problems of the subject, which includes the notion of *représentation* (1903a(i):72/ t.1963b:88). Science, as it at present stands, cannot produce a complete explanation of social phenomena.

7 Religious *représentations*. what do they represent?

As early as 1887 Durkheim was prepared to define religion as a system of *représentations* (1887b:308/t.1975a:34). Nevertheless, in a typically paradoxical way he always held that religion was more than a system of *représentations*: every religion contained an action component (see, for example, 1919b:99/t.1975a:182; see ch. 17). Religious *représentations* carry an obligatory force (1899a(ii):18/t.1975a:89). They are ready-made: and to them the individual respectfully conforms his thought (ibid.:19/90). They are not derived from individual reason, but come from the collective mind (*l'esprit collectif*) (ibid.:25/95).

Religious *représentations* are not illusions. They have to be taken seriously in so far as they symbolize reality and are necessary for the understanding of religion as well as society. But two questions emerge. First, how are they to be used for such understanding? Second, what is the reality they symbolize?

Durkheim holds that out of religious *représentations* have grown scientific *représentations*. Both of them have been used to understand the nature of the physical world. Religious *représentations* were in some ways a failure and these gave rise to more exact and acceptable ways of comprehending the universe (see ch. 25). Since one has emerged from the other, however, they cannot be totally dissimilar. But religious *représentations* have always had a wider horizon than the physical universe, for if they had been concerned only with it they would have disappeared with the emergence of modern science (322/225/135). So religious *représentations* have continued, and have continued to be at the heart of religion.

To what, then, do these *représentations* ultimately refer? Obviously to the sacred. But not all *représentations* are sacred. There can clearly be profane *représentations* which symbolize what is anti-religious, and contradict or threaten the sacred and the social. Behind a multiplicity of sacred *représentations*, is there one form of reality which is reflected in them all? To say that various symbols represent various things or different realities is to adopt a relativist position. But in this respect Durkheim is no relativist and he almost assumes an ontological or absolutist stance. He does not make such a generalization for all *représentations*. The question is only concerned with religious *représentations*. Robert Bellah is one who holds that Durkheim sees the chief aim of all religious symbolism as reproducing or representing society, not the cosmos (1973:l). Is this so? The difficulty in supporting or contradicting Bellah's position is that, as we have said before, Durkheim does not define society, but uses it as a general, universal concept, not relating it to a given territorial group. Durkheim himself admits that 'religious *représentations* are collective *représentations* which are the expression of collective realities' (13/10/111). From this it does appear that Durkheim makes the assumption that the multiplicity of collective *représentations* refer to one kind of reality. This metaphysical step is something that many commentators admit occurs, but which they cannot intellectually accept. It is not something that can be proved or substantiated empirically – that is, that religious *représentations* all refer to society, despite Durkheim's 'proof' in the case of totemism.

It is argued by Goode that Durkheim wants to see a reality behind each *représentation*, in other words that the symbols are really scientific symbols, used for making scientific statements and employed for indicating reality (1951:257). Since religious *représentations* give rise to scientific *représentations*, religious *représentations* are assumed to be like scientific *représentations*. When religious *représentations* indicate values, the question arises whether they are declaring what is real – real, that is, in the sense that scientific *représentations* declare what is real. Here there rests a contradiction between basically different attitudes towards religion. Goode assumes that 'the referents in question are ultimate, value-elements, non-scientific and non-logical in nature' (ibid.:257). This would not be acceptable to Durkheim for he sees in religion more than value-statements. For Goode, 'religion [is] the central element in the normative complex' (ibid.). One of the objections made by Goode and others to Durkheim's conclusions about religious *représentations* is that Durkheim confused scientific *représentations* with *représentations* of value, that is, religious *représentations*. In part this stems from the positivist attempt to give religion a scientific basis (ibid.:256). Such a position denies the basic fact-value dichotomy proposed by Kant, which one would imagine Durkheim would have been forced to support, given the logic of his argument about religion and science.

It should be pointed out that in an early article in 1899,

Durkheim differentiates scientific *représentations* from others, as between those which relate to thinking and those which relate to action. Science consists of *représentations*, and collective *représentations* at that, but they are not obligatory as are social *représentations collectives* (1899a(ii):20/t.1975a:91). But the dilemma really stems from Durkheim's position over religious *représentations*, which are always considered to be distorted *représentations* of an empirical reality. If they are distorted, how can they be relied upon to indicate reality, or how does one know the reality? The answer has to be that sociology, as an empirical science, is able to reveal the reality which the *représentations* inadequately express. So, once again, the science of sociology can solve the puzzle which in part sociology itself creates. The question turns on what is the reality to which religion points? Is religion a system of symbols which relate only to values of a social kind? Commentators such as Goode believe that Durkheim says this is the case.

8 Conclusion

Durkheim's use of *représentation* and the way in which he developed the concept has produced few satisfied customers and a large number of critics. For those who would see that all sociological explanation rests on symbols, his dogmatism in denying that the intrinsic qualities of a thing affect the symbol and that symbols are determined by the agency of society constitutes a serious failure. On the other hand, to speak of the necessity of symbols and ideas to those of an empirical-scientific outlook is to be accused of falling into the death-trap of idealism and the vague world of ideas. Durkheim's attempt to create a *via media* between empiricism and idealism pleases few, least of all Talcott Parsons who has argued that such a compromise is impossible to maintain, at least in the way Durkheim proposes it (1937:441ff.).

For Lévi-Strauss, Durkheim at least demonstrated one truth, namely, that society cannot exist without symbolism (1945:518). But Durkheim's failure was not so much an epistemological one, as Parsons maintained, but a failure of aim. Durkheim should have attempted, Lévi-Strauss argues, to show more clearly how symbolic thought makes social life possible. In fact he did the reverse; he tried to show that symbolism grew out of society. In this way, we would add, he made social structure prior to symbol. But is this a valid criticism of Durkheim? How far is one right in suggesting that Durkheim should have taken a different path from that which in fact he did? Surely judgment must rest only on the course of action he did in fact pursue.

A more sympathetic appraisal of Durkheim's work appears in the writing of Robert Bellah (1959/r.Nisbet 1965:169). Bellah writes: 'Thus Durkheim, in the concept of collective *représentations*, made the fundamental discovery of culture as an element analytically independent of social system, although the full significance of this insight remained somewhat obscured by his use of the word *social* to apply to both elements' (ibid.). Bellah holds that the theory makes a contribution to our understanding of social change by showing the relation of collective *représentations* to morphological factors, which have a 'reciprocal influence on social structure' (ibid.:170). This is demonstrated, according to Bellah, most clearly in *L'Évolution pédagogique* (1938a) in which Durkheim shows, for example, how morphological or social factors which aided the unification of Europe, brought about by Charlemagne, can be related to the structure of the school system, standing for representational or cultural factors. Hence Durkheim sees collective *représentations* as exerting a great influence over a period of time, when once they are institutionalized and stand in opposition to social and cultural changes. Also, when the social system is working fairly smoothly, the *représentations* will not be challenged. This only occurs when there is a great deal of social turmoil: they then contribute to the building up of a new system. This interpretation of Durkheim by Bellah, which he holds is fruitful in offering guidelines for a theory of social change, is a somewhat watered-down statement of what Durkheim was saying, attractive though it appears to be (see ch. 21). The reason is that in his comments on Durkheim, Bellah studiously avoids all Durkheim's references to reality, such as collective *représentations* constituting reality. Hence he pays no attention to what to many is a stumbling block. In a later essay, however, he does admit that 'in his social Kantianism he held that religious *représentations* are constitutive of society' (1970:8, see also 239). It would appear that Bellah supports Durkheim in admitting that *représentations* can be studied as things.

In the late 1960s H. D. Duncan made the observation that in the development of their disciplines, both of which have lent heavily on Durkheim, anthropologists have made greater use of Durkheim's analysis of symbol than have sociologists (1969:161ff.). In support of this one may point to the comment of the anthropologist R. H. Lowie, who at a much earlier date praised Durkheim for his apperceptive approach to symbol (1925:162). Lowie noted how Durkheim saw symbols intensifying the religious fervour of participants and that their fervour then subsequently was seen to flow into other channels. Duncan goes so far as to suggest that 'a social system for the anthropologist is *always* a symbolic system' (1969:161ff.). By contrast, many sociologists have adopted the crude model of the approach of natural science and have thereby excluded an approach based on symbolic interpretation. To sociologists who would follow as far as possible the approach of the natural scientist, the telling factor is that modern industrial society does not contain the degree of symbolism evident in primitive societies. Modern man attempts to live as rationally as he can and therefore to avoid all ambiguous communication. Our major concern, however, is with the sociology of religion. In traditional religions in the West there is a relatively high level of symbolism compared with other social institutions, yet Duncan's observation stands. Sociologists, in examining modern religion, have until recently eschewed symbolic analysis and preferred to see religious phenomena in terms of organization which Durkheim himself tended to disregard (see 1903a(ii)(57)). One may disagree, in some measure, with the way in which Durkheim developed his notion of *représentations* and particularly that of religious and collective *représentations*, but what he had to say remains a challenge to sociologists to reconsider their approach to the study of religious phenomena.

16 The functions of religion: a case of misunderstanding?

1 An old theoretical rock

Functionalist theory in sociology has for almost a century enjoyed an honourable and, at times, great following. In the field of religion, it has produced an acceptable method in attempting to show the important contribution that religion makes to society. During the late nineteenth century such an approach was seen to be a more promising course of procedure than the attempts made by students of religion to determine the origins of religion in a conjectured historical setting. It also had the allurement for those of a scientific inclination, in that it borrowed from biology and physiology a method which was then proving to be valuable in the study of organisms and their constituent parts. One could go further and say that in spite of the rational or atheistic outlook of many who sought the origin of religion in the dreams of primitive man or in his mistaken notion of reality, functionalism was not prima facie atheistic in its assumptions. Both believer and non-believer, both theologian and scientist, could, it was thought, happily accept a functionalist approach, since it did not start with the premise that religion was of necessity an hallucination. In functionalism metaphysical issues are not encountered at base-camp.

Many commentators, particularly when referring to *The Elementary Forms*, have tended to emphasize Durkheim's functionalism, thus playing down other elements in his approach, and indeed they have gone further and have stated that Durkheim is essentially a functionalist.[1] No one would deny Durkheim's general functionalist approach, but the danger is that in the light of the development of functionalism, what he wrote can become identifiable with the hardened or more logically extended functionalism which began to emerge in the 1920s and which proceeded to be applauded until the 1960s. It gained considerable prestige at the hands of British social anthropologists such as Malinowski and Radcliffe-Brown and in America at the hands of Talcott Parsons and Merton. The subject of functionalism is in itself extensive and no attempt is made here to treat it systematically.

Certainly the work of Durkheim gave considerable impetus to the functionalist method in sociology, especially in its application to religion. The degree to which Durkheim thought a functionalist approach was suitable to sociology can, in part, be gleaned from his manifesto for sociological procedure, *Les Règles de la méthode sociologique* (1895a), but it should be contrasted not only with the work of Spencer, who pressed biological analogies to their very limits, but also with Malinowski who held that every facet of social life could be fitted into a whole in which the parts were functionally dependent on each other (1960). Durkheim, on the contrary, proposed nothing more of the concept of function than that it be the contribution a component makes to the whole, that is, to society. It is legitimate to suggest that he saw that a more developed functionalism which makes much of such terms as equilibrium, force, stability, breaks down when such concepts are overplayed. Although he used these terms, he never reified them.

Further, *Les Formes élémentaires* is very far from being a treatise on the functional analysis of religion. Methodologically and analytically the issues are much wider. Poggi rightly says that in the book religion 'is only intermittently and to a minor extent functional, and becomes so only at a relatively late stage' (1971:248–9). And within a wider context than just religion, Hatch has observed that 'it seems inescapable that Durkheim was proposing a functionalist and utilitarian theory, yet this interpretation seems totally inconsistent with other features of his thought', for example, that one must not reduce social phenomena to their utilitarian ends (1973:200). This merely underlines the fact that Durkheim's thought is not obsessively functionalist.

2 The two major functions

In reading Guyau's *L'Irréligion de l'avenir: étude de sociologie* Durkheim seemed ready enough to support the author's contention that religion had two characteristics, performed two tasks, had two functions – one speculative and related to thought, the other practical and concerned with action (1887b:305, 308/ t.1975a:31, 34). Even the most abstract system of beliefs has practical outcomes:

> Each time any one attempts to study a collective
> *représentation*, he can rest assured that a practical and not a
> theoretical cause has been the determining reason for it. This
> is the case with that system of *représentations* we call a
> religion. (ibid.:308/34)

Durkheim maintains that Guyau's analysis is useful, if one is prepared to modify it. For Guyau religion comes from a double source: 'first the need to understand, secondly sociability' (ibid.:308/35). If, however, the order is reversed, Durkheim finds the result acceptable. These two functions very roughly correspond to the twofold division of human life – thought and action. Durkheim developed his two major functions along such a dichotomy.

He made the point strongly in 1909 in a debate on religion and science, where he said that in overcoming confessional objections to science studying religion, he did not expect that religion would disappear in the face of scientific analysis (1909a(1):58; and see ch. 25.1). The reason for his 'conservative' attitude was that, in the course of history, religion had fulfilled two very different functions. One function was vital, of a practical order. 'It helped men to live and to adapt to their conditions of existence' (ibid.). The other was a 'form of speculative thought, a system of *représentations* uniquely destined to express the world, a science before science, a science co-operating with science' (ibid.). This second function was more and more in danger of disappearing, but he implied that the first function would persist (see ch. 25.4).

It was in *The Elementary Forms* that Durkheim definitively developed the notion of these two functions. At the conclusion of the section on ritual, he writes that religious life is based on something simple and fundamental:

> It responds everywhere to one and the same need [*besoin*],
> and is everywhere derived from one and the same mental
> state. In all its forms, its object is to raise man above himself

and to make him lead a life superior to that which he would lead, if he followed only his own individual whims: beliefs express this life in *représentations*; rites organize it and regulate its working. (592/414)

And in the conclusion of the book, he extended the idea beyond religion to society itself:

There can be no society which does not feel the need at regular intervals to maintain and strengthen collective sentiments and ideas which constitute its unity and personality. This moral tonic can only be obtained by means of reunions, assemblies, and meetings, where individuals who are brought into contact with one another, mutually reaffirm their common sentiments. (601/427/156)

The function, which is associated with ritual, we call the active function. As Pécaut said in commenting on Durkheim, 'The function of religion is not to instruct believers but to help them to live; *it saves them from evil*' (1918:12; see ch. 11.4; and pages below).

The other function to which reference has already been made we call the cognitive function. This function is directly related to the other aspect of man's religious sentiment – its mental aspect. It involves faith, doctrine, dogma, theology, ideas, reason, *représentations* and so on (ch. 15.1). The issues involved often relate to the origins of the universe, of man, of suffering, of causation, of right conduct, and so on. Hence there is speculation on the nature of death, on nature itself and on the ideal (1913b:66). The cognitive function means that a religion renders society, social relationships – indeed the totality of existence – intelligible (1950a/1969g:189/t.1957a:160). In giving man the ability to think about the world, and above all an understanding of the society in which he lives, the cognitive function of religion has provided, in Durkheim's eyes, the greatest of all services to mankind. In this it has 'constructed a first *représentation*' of what the relation between things might be, that is, the notion of causality (340/237/142). He implies that 'the true function of religion is . . . to make us think, to enrich our knowledge, to add to the *représentations* that we owe to science others of a different origin and character' (595/416/145).

Durkheim always held that these two functions are in a balanced relation. Man is a thinking and an acting creature. These two facets are projected in religion. Religion helps us to think: it helps us to live (ibid.). It is little wonder therefore that critics felt that *Les Formes élémentaires* was an apologetic for religion. This is apparent in the 1913–14 conference when Durkheim accused Free Thinkers of being unaware of the depth of religion in man's being and of interpreting it only in its cognitive or intellectual role as a system of *représentations*, and perhaps in their eyes, false *représentations* (1919b:98/t.1975a:182). The point is, the man who practises religion feels a stronger, better, healthier person:

> When a man lives a religious life he believes he is participating in a force which dominates him, and which at the same time, upholds him and raises him above himself. Thus strengthened it seems to him that he is better equipped to face the trials and difficulties of existence, that he can even bend nature to his own designs. (ibid.:99/182)

In the quotations that have been presented, Durkheim holds that religion has the effect (function) through action (ritual) and belief (*représentations*) of producing in individual participants a sense of security, happiness, belonging, some inner strength. This comes from the conviction that these elements have a real effect on the experience of men and women so that they feel they are at one with the power of their god. In this way man without religion, man left to himself, would lead an inferior life. Religion is thus an ennobling institution, the most ennobling of all institutions.[2] Religion within the context of these two functions clearly supplies energy to participants. This energy cannot be derived from religion itself, since religion is not a force external to man or the world. The force or energy comes from man himself and what religion does is to release and channel that energy which man has and which comes from his being within society (595–6/417/146).

Durkheim seeks evidence for these functions of religion from the inner feelings or self-knowledge of participants. As we shall see, he was not aloof to this kind of approach, which, contrary to early proclamations, appears to cross psychological and sociological boundaries (see ch. 22.2). Apart from that, the weakness of his position rests on the extent or universality of such feelings.

The anthropologist's 'Occam's razor' – the 'If I were a horse' argument – can be applied to suggest that it is all too easy to read one's own mental or psychological reactions into a given situation. Another difficulty in examining what might be loosely called Durkheim's functionalism is that he refers to many functions, although he does not always use the word function. As in the traditional Catholic sacramental system there are two major sacraments, baptism and the mass, so for Durkheim there are two major functions, the active and the cognitive. To these are added a number of others – minor sacraments, minor functions. There is one significant difference which we shall encounter. In the Catholic system, the minor sacraments are clearly differentiated: with Durkheim the lesser functions are not clearly marked off from each other. Indeed, one function seems to give rise to another; or, one function is only slightly removed from another. To these secondary functions we shortly turn, but before we do so it should be noted that the position is made more complex because Durkheim deals with ritual in detail in Book III of *The Elementary Forms* and delineates a number of functions which seem specific only to ritual. We deal with these separately and they are only incidentally referred to in this chapter (see ch. 18.6).

3 The bases of the two functions

It has been frequently said of functionalism, and with considerable persuasion, that it is a theory that cannot be empirically substantiated. It is little more than a proposition, and a not very exciting proposition at that. At least one can speak of Durkheim as someone who attempted to prove his functional position by pointing to the bases on which the two functions worked. Hardly surprisingly, he is never satisfied with merely describing the effects of religion on society. He wants to know from where they spring and in this he points to the fact that the effects or functions are fairly constant throughout history. They must therefore come from some hidden source, some source that never varies. In speaking of the two major functions, he writes: 'It [religious life] responds everywhere to one and the same need, and is everywhere derived from one and the same mental state' (592/414). So he argues in

The Elementary Forms, but the same kind of reasoning is to be found in the early period of his approach to religion, before *The Division of Labour*. In an article of 1890, 'The principles of 1789 and sociology', he stated that although religious doctrines were not harmful or evil, 'it is quite possible and even infinitely probable that, as inadequate as they may be in their cosmological or sociological explanations, they correspond to real and legitimate needs which otherwise would not have been satisfied' (1890a/t.1973a:37). Durkheim thus sees religion growing out of a basic need (*besoin*), but it is also derived from a mental state, from a given mental disposition, which gives rise to *représentations collectives* (see ch. 15). The functions therefore do not rest on one 'cause' but two. The problem arises as to whether these two bases are connected, and if so, in what way? To such questions there are no answers, but we do know the effects – religion gives rise to action and thought, and these are mutually reinforcing (see ch. 20). We represent the situation as shown in Figure 16.1.

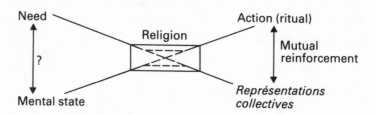

Figure 16.1   Religion, action and thought

Durkheim's argument does not convince the empirically-minded sociologist. It rests on the assumption that effects are the outcome of needs or mental states. Can these be shown to exist? It is here that the weakness emerges. It would seem that one need is that man requires help to live, but this is a very vague idea and is open to many interpretations. The mental state is that by which man comes to terms with his experience, and the need rests on the fact that man has to use *représentations* (symbols, ideas). Such needs are beyond empirical proof. They may be seen only as logical assumptions. The danger of the argument based on need is always that the advocate points to what he believes to be a need in response to an observed effect, rather than in predicting a response from a known need. In this way functionalism is said to be self-fulfilling. Whilst, therefore, Durkheim's argument is very far from being a proof, at least it is more searching than naïve propositions put forward by functionalists, who believe they follow in the Durkheimian tradition and who focus on the basic need of social coherence in society. In Durkheim's thought, this would appear to be a further or secondary function, or might it be a primary one?

4 Religion functions so as to stabilize and integrate society

It has already been observed that Durkheim's final definition of religion contained within it a theory of religion (ch. 9.5c). The definition pointed to a religiously integrated society created by common beliefs and rituals centred on the sacred. When a church or religious collectivity is considered such a thesis may appear obvious. What, however, if the theory is extended and one contrasts religion and society and suggests that religion is an agent for integrating society?

As early as 1886 in the review of Spencer's *Ecclesiastical Institutions* – we have already said that Spencer's sociology leaned heavily on functionalist ideas – Durkheim saw that law and morality had the effect of maintaining the equilibrium of society and of adapting it to the environment (1886a:67/t.1975a:20). This is also the 'role [*rôle*] of religion'. It exerts 'a regulating influence on society' (ibid.; see also, ibid.:69/23). And again, 'when it [religion] no longer fulfils its function, that is to say when it no longer ensures that adaptation of individuals or the group to external circumstances, because they have changed, confusion and uneasiness result' (ibid.:67/20). Not only here, but throughout the full extent of his academic life, Durkheim always held that society had three main regulating forces – religion, morality, law.

To speak of control as giving rise to stability implies the exercise of force or coercion, and indeed as we have seen, Durkheim held in his early days that the characteristic of religious belief and action, the most important characteristic in fact, was coercion (see ch. 9.3). The logic of the human situation is that such constraint, derived from one undifferentiated source, must have the effect of producing uniformity and social integration amongst those so moulded by the external source. To be under the influence of a religion is not only to be integrated into that 'religion', but to be integrated with those who have the same beliefs and adopt the same rituals. Admittedly, as we have seen, Durkheim abandoned the criterion of coercion as being decisive in defining religion, but he never forsook the idea of the coercive power of belief and ritual. In the 1898 essay on *représentations*, he holds it to be incontestable that religious beliefs and practices are also moral precepts, and are 'the most characteristic manifestations of collective life' (1898b/1924a:35/t.1953b:35). The mere notion of *représentations collectives*, which are essentially religious, contains in itself the possibility of social integration. Again, in his lectures on Rousseau he said:

> Since social cohesion results chiefly from a spontaneous agreement of wills, it is not possible without a certain intellectual communion. In the past, such communion resulted quite naturally from the fact that each society had its religion which was the basis of its social order. The ideas and sentiments necessary to the society's functioning were thus placed under the protection of the gods. The political system was also theological. That is why each state had its religion and one could not be a member of a state without practising its religion. (1918b/1953a:192/t.1960b:132–3)

The power of ideas held in common to make people think alike is also evident in the following passage from *The Elementary Forms*:

> We say of an individual or collective object that it inspires respect when the *représentation* which expresses it in people's *consciences* is endowed with such force that automatically it compels or inhibits actions, *regardless of every consideration relating to the useful or harmful effects of any of them.* (296/ 207/126)

Représentations collectives possess an intensity private states of *conscience* never attain (ibid.).

In a review of *The Elementary Forms* by Durkheim and Mauss these words are part of the conclusion:

> In the end, this interpretation of religion appears, above all, to be consistent with a system of actions aimed at making and perpetually remaking the soul of the collectivity and of the individual. (1913a(ii)(12):98/t.1975a:180)

What does 'the soul of the collectivity' mean? Is it a poetic term for society itself? If this is so, religion is the means by which society is made and remade: religion is instrumental in creating society. In the face of this, P. E. Hammond, in a recent article, is quite inaccurate when he says that Durkheim sees that 'religion is more the *expression* of an integrated society than it is the *source* of a society's integration' (1974:116). Yet one feels that the word soul has some force. Religion can never make society *ex nihilo*. It can only add an important ingredient to that which has already been assembled. The ingredient, or one of the chief ingredients, is *représentations collectives*. It is these which are instrumental in bringing about integration. Integration can be said to be derived from them.

At the heart of the notion of the integrative function of religion as seen in Durkheim's thought is the premise that the individual is coerced or forced into accepting beliefs and carrying out actions which are common with those of other people, but which are external to himself. For some, such as Goode (1951:257–8), the premise is to be rejected because of its mechanical implications and because it denies the freedom of the will. Be that as it may, such a premise is also basic to the concept of socialization.

It is remarkable how commentators such as Radcliffe-Brown, Parsons and Goode have concentrated on the integrative function of religion, which they see as the most important of the various functions of religion that Durkheim delineated. We would suggest that the component of integration is derived from the two major functions which Durkheim postulated and, further, that Durkheim seldom, if ever, uses the word integration, but rather refers to a number of concepts loosely associated with integration, such as coercion, equilibrium, regulating influence. The word integration is much stronger than any of these terms. As Lukes rightly says, a simplistic view that religion integrates society is an inadequate interpretation of Durkheim's notion of the function of religion (1975:297).

5 Religion as an agent for control in a negative or ascetical mode

There remains another facet of the notion of control and cohesion which must now be considered. In *The Elementary Forms* Durkheim refers to the ascetical function of ritual in which man has to perform acts which are of an unpleasant or painful kind and which have the intention of purgation or purification (see ch. 18.2). Other than this reference, there is little in the book about religion acting as a controlling force and limiting man's ambitions, desires and personal fulfilment. This effect of religion on participants, as is well known, is most clearly and almost exclusively expounded in *Le Suicide*, written during the early part of his life (but see 1893b/1902b:59/t.1933b:92). That Durkheim applauds such a task performed by religion stems from his doctrine of man. Man in himself has unlimited desires, which he attempts to satisfy but cannot (1897a:273–4/t.1951a:247). For man to pursue such goals can only produce a state of incessant unhappiness, which at the same time makes social life impossible. Much in keeping with classical Christian doctrine, Durkheim sees that the passions must be limited and harmonized. This therefore calls for the intervention of an external moral force. Physical checks would not be effective. Religion therefore acts as an agent for such control in presenting before man moral constraints which are to be accepted. Through its rituals and commands it acts as an agent in society to limit man's otherwise uncontrollable search for egoistic fulfilment (see 452/316; 446/312). Interestingly, in his lectures on socialism he wrote:

> So, today, as formerly, there are social forces, moral authorities, which must exercise this regulating influence, and without which appetites become deranged and economic order disorganized. (1928a/1971d:287/t.1958b:201)

In taking up Saint-Simon's view, Durkheim stressed with approval that religion, and particularly Christianity, through its controlling power instructed the humble to accept their lot and taught that God controlled each individual's share of the goods of their society (see ch. 23.2). A life beyond the grave contained hopes of retribution and final justice (ibid.). This kind of interpretation of Christianity, it might be added, was common enough in the intellectual armoury of agnostic and atheistic thinkers of the day. But Durkheim mentions it with approval confirming his own belief in the necessity of control in society – a system of controls mediated by religion. The controlling function of religion in limiting the desires of individuals is not only used to keep the poor and oppressed in a relatively satisfied condition; it can also act in the opposite way in curbing the power of despots through its moral prohibitions. This is to be seen when Christian nations are compared with eastern empires. Montesquieu put forward the idea with which Durkheim readily agrees (1892a/1953a:72/ t.1966a:34; see ch. 26.1).

6 How many functions?

One of the most difficult problems of coming to terms with Durkheim's functional approach to religion is the multiplicity of functions that religion is said to perform. The same goes for ritual (see ch. 18.6). As well as referring to two major functions, Durkheim also delineates one overarching function – the effect that religion has on the life of the man who participates in it. Religion elevates a man, makes him human. Durkheim wrote:

> It [religious life] responds everywhere to one and the same
> need, and is everywhere derived from one and the same
> mental state. In all its forms, its object is to raise man above
> himself and to make him lead a life superior to that which
> he would lead, if he followed only his own individual whims:
> beliefs express this life in *représentations*; rites organize it
> and regulate its working. (592/414)

With the postulation of so many functions, the problem is to discover an order of priority or whether one function is dominant. Further issues can be listed as follows:

First, some functions have subtypes or are determined by

particular analogies. Take, for example, the controlling function; it may refer to:

(a) moral prohibitions with regard to sex or liquor;
(b) keeping oppressed people satisfied;
(c) limiting the power of despots;
(d) curbing tendencies to suicide.

Even the two major functions, the active and the cognitive, are sometimes difficult to separate. The active function, which emphasizes religious actions, raises the sense of well-being in the individual when these acts are carried out. But then the cognitive function, in offering an acceptable and secure belief-system, also gives to individuals an inner satisfaction. If, therefore, one starts with a result, namely, a feeling of well-being, it is probably difficult to know whether this is derived from action or belief.

Second, most scholars, either those who have developed the work of Durkheim and approved some functional approach (and to the list of names previously given we would add J. Wach, E. O. James) or those who have criticized him, such as Gustave Belot, have tended to focus on the integrative function of religion. Such an exclusive selection, in the light of the many functions that Durkheim outlined, is a very narrow view to adopt. This function is basically derived from other functions, as we have just noted.

Third, it is trite, but nevertheless true, to say that a great deal of praise and criticism about Durkheim's functional approach turns on what is meant by 'function' and 'a functional system'. If one regards function quite simply as an effect that an institution has on society, it is perfectly admissible to speak of the various effects that religion has on society, or the various contributions that it makes to society. When, in fact, functionalism is placed within a theory of society as a number of forces which are in balance and where that balance is maintained by religion, then clearly problems arise about social change and the conservative effect religion has on society. It could well be argued that Durkheim had foreseen these problems emerging from a thoroughgoing functionalism, which for these and other reasons he assiduously avoided.

Finally, one of the difficulties in trying to produce a definitive list of functions is whether one concentrates on belief or ritual. Clearly the functions of one component are not the same as those of the other (see ch. 18.6). Alpert pointed to four functions in ritual – disciplinary, cohesive, revitalizing, and euphoric functions (1938; 1939:199ff.). He does not do justice to the two major functions of religion which Durkheim emphasized throughout his life, and which he related to belief and ritual.

If one wishes to try to piece together various functions, one might do it according to Figure 16.2 which demonstrates the complexity of their inter-relations.

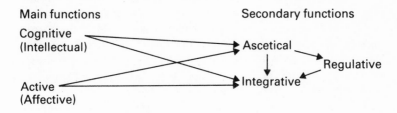

Figure 16.2   Functions of religion

7 Therefore religion is eternal

One of the consequences of holding that the two major functions are based on social need, which in turn itself is located in the very nature of man, is that religion is seen to be eternal (see ch. 11.6). Since man's nature will never change, since what is characteristic of man is intrinsic to him, religion will always persist.[3] It has been with man throughout his history and hence will continue into the future. Durkheim's position is in keeping with what he said at the outset of *The Elementary Forms*, namely, that he was searching 'for ever-present causes' (11/8/109). We offer some other examples below (see also 1898c:10/t.1969d/r.1975:66; 1909a(1):58):

> Sooner or later, custom and habit will claim their rights and that is what authorizes us to presume that religion will survive the attacks of which it is the object. For so long as men live together they will hold some belief in common. (1886a:69/ t.1975a:22)

> It is most improbable that the causes which have supported religions in the past have suddenly ceased to be effective. (1907c:51)

> There is then something eternal in religion which is destined to survive all the particular symbols which have successfully veiled religious thought. (609/427/156)

Durkheim was well aware of changes in religion and knew that to hold religion to be eternal meant that the forms of religion change, but the reality of religion or the basis of religion remains the same. This inevitably leads to thorny issues about the nature and definition of religion. However, given the hypothesis that religion is eternal, it behoves the sociologist who accepts it to try to discover religion in societies which at first sight appear to be bereft of religion. This is a particular problem in modern secularized western democracies and in Marxist societies. Durkheim overcomes the difficulty by referring to the religion of the individual or the religion of humanity (see ch. 26). The hypothesis about eternality is impossible to prove because, as we have indicated, the needs and the mental states to which Durkheim referred are beyond empirical verification or falsification. It is that there is a religious need on which religion could be said to be founded (see Spiro 1966:123 n.4). Even the argument that every society needs common ideals, morals, rules of working – and Durkheim certainly admits this – does not necessarily mean that every society has to have a religion. This line of reasoning helps to explain society rather than religion (ibid.:118). Durkheim must be true to the definition that he put forward in the beginning of *The Elementary Forms* (see ch. 9.1). Everything turns on what is sacred. If a society does not possess any ideas or values or *représentations* that are sacred, for none of them is held to be inviolate or hedged about with taboos, then that society can have no religion.

As we have suggested, Durkheim's argument for the eternality of religion was not based directly on the integrative function of religion, but on the two major functions, themselves dependent upon 'needs' and 'mental states'. In many commentators' eyes, however, the integrative function is seen to be the one of greater importance and is used in connection with arguing for the persistence of religion. But Durkheim's approach is more sophisticated. It allows him to deal with the problem of secularization or the decline of the traditional churches, and at the same time to examine new religious forms in western Europe (see chs 24 and 26). In the latter he was forced to admit that the *représentations collectives* of modern society are not found strictly within the religious institutions of society but outside them, diffused in society at large. It is quite clear that, in modern society, the moral community does not equal the Church.

The a priori reasoning in the notion of the eternality of religion means that religion is held to exist as long as man exists. It therefore cannot come to an end. One of the consequences of such a doctrinaire position is that, no matter what the external characteristics of a society are, no matter how devoid of religion it might seem to be, religion must exist hidden behind the externalities. As Durkheim was to remark:

> Even in a society which is divided into closed castes, there is always a religion common to all, and, consequently, the principles of the religious culture, which is, then, fundamental, are the same throughout the population. (1922a:39/ t.1956a:69)

Such a proposition proved to be a stone of stumbling.

8 Function, persistence and change

Our criticism of functionalism, especially that of a developed kind which is found in Talcott Parsons, as well as a more simplified functionalism which is to be seen in Durkheim, is that the theory does not deal with change.

Durkheim may not have accounted for social change in a theoretically satisfactory way, but the fact that he denied social or religious change is blatantly false (see chs 21.1 and 22.7; 1955a; Coser 1960:224). Religion both undergoes change in itself and brings about change in society. Such a statement does not need documentation. Any kind of theory which completely denies the possibility of change would be rejected by Durkheim.

Some of the criticisms that can be levelled against later functionalists because they do not allow for social change, do not apply to Durkheim. In this respect, it should be noted that Durkheim stands opposed to the pragmatism that is deeply rooted in later functionalism. His attack on the pragmatic approach of William James was precisely because the American psychologist and philosopher completely disregarded questions of truth (1955a). Durkheim rejected any analysis of religion that reduced it to a utilitarian function (Nye and Ashworth 1971:136). Religion is essentially related to values, of declaring what is true, of ends to be pursued. For Durkheim this is of primary importance and stands above any pragmatism, or any mere integrative function. Religion is directly related to some reality which is not that reality associated with integration or function. The links must be with some superstructure. He wrote in 1909:

> I believe for my part that all rites which have been practised
> by mankind correspond to something in reality, and can be,
> I do not say simply explained, but justified. (1909a(1):59)

Here are overtones of Malinowski's grand functionalism, but with the very important difference, and one to be emphasized, namely, the obvious pragmatism of Malinowski compared with the realism of Durkheim.

Whether religion can be said to be an agent for integration and stability, or whether it gives rise to social change, is a fact which in the last analysis is determined by history. Durkheim readily admitted that in the early days of a new religion, it is highly volatile, subject to persecutions, and under the sway of charismatic leaders (a phrase not actually mentioned by Durkheim) (see 1909a(1)). During this initial period a religion is obviously breaking down a unity that confronts it in order to establish another kind of unity. In this way religion stands very much as a force for revolution and change (see ch. 22.6). During such a period of its history, a religion could be said to be disruptive, endemic of division and hostility, and, to use the current word, dysfunctional. Such a period is usually followed by one of triumphalism and the success of the religion means that prophets and charismatic leaders recede, the beliefs become codified and made uniform, and ritual action is carefully established. During this period religious and sometimes secular leaders call for uniformity and integration. Durkheim's point is that these periods of integration are much longer in time than periods of change, and that during these long epochs in which a particular religion is the established or official religion, the process of socialization in which individuals become incorporated into the group becomes the most important of social factors. Therefore it is during these long time-spans that the stabilizing functions of religion are the most socially important. Since religion helped man create *représentations* and aided him to think, it is self-evident that religion can also give rise to revolutionary and socially disturbing ideas. Hence religion is both a force for destruction and for conservation.

Part IV
Ritual and Effervescent Assembly

17 Ritual

I Prolegomena

1 Introduction: prominence and neglect

Durkheim supported and, by his very support, strengthened the long-standing tradition of dividing religion into two main components – belief and ritual (see, for example, 50/36/113). For him the two categories correspond to faith, dogma, thought, *représentations*, on the one hand; and to action, cult, rite, ceremony, practice, on the other. One can go further and say that all human or social life is made up of such modes, of thought and action. But perhaps only in religion are they so obviously interrelated and interdependent. This is due to the very nature of religion itself and to the fact that the two components are related to an order of reality believed to be beyond the mundane and directly related to the gods or to the sacred.

Durkheim stressed this twofold structure of religion because he was convinced of the importance of ritual, something clearly demonstrated in his own work. Although ritual is now very much the stock in trade of the anthropologist, and to a lesser degree the sociologist, the fact remains that his chapters on ritual have been in the past, and still are, the most neglected parts of his work on religion. Even what he had to say about totemism, where admittedly in some respects he was proved to be wrong, received more attention than did his contribution to the study of ritual.

In *The Elementary Forms* he achieved a virtual balance between the two poles of belief and action. The whole of Book III is devoted to ritual (about 165 pages in the original French text, which constitutes just about a quarter of the entire volume). Book II, entitled 'The elementary beliefs', covers just over 280 pages. Admittedly more space is given to beliefs, but Books II and III form the substantive core of *The Elementary Forms*. Book I relates to definitions and rejected theories (100 pages), and there are 40 pages of conclusions. The plan and execution of the book can lead to no other deduction than that in Durkheim's mind ritual has as important a place in the structure of religion and society as does belief.

When the book appeared, however, it was remarkable that commentators, at the time and for some period following, paid scant attention to the sections on ritual. Was it that what Durkheim said about ritual was widely accepted and therefore needed no comment? Or, was his contribution to the subject one of relative insignificance compared with what he had to say about religious belief? Or, again, was it due to the fact that in the minds of intellectuals of the day, belief was held to be more important than ritual? The last of these three lines of argument would appear to be the correct one. French commentators, for example, Belot (1913a), van Gennep (1913) and to some extent Loisy (1913), seem to have been particularly guilty in ignoring either the sections of *Les Formes élémentaires* devoted to cult and rite amongst the Arunta or the generalizations that Durkheim derived from the data. The focal point seems always to be belief and *représentations*. In some respects this tradition has persisted to the present: witness, for example, Lukes' intellectual biography of Durkheim (1972), where more space could have been devoted to ritual.

On the other hand, it must not be forgotten that there have been a minority who have gone against the stream and not only commented extensively on Durkheim's treatment of ritual, but praised it. In particular, one might cite Alpert (1938 and 1939) and Talcott Parsons (1937).

By a strange coincidence Durkheim himself seems to have played down his findings on ritual rather than having emphasized them. This is borne out in his presentation of the book for discussion at the meeting of the Société Française de Philosophie on 4 February 1913. In introducing his work, he referred both to religion and to the duality of man's nature, which is a subject that appears in the book but is not central to it. He made the starting-point of his talk one of the functions of religion – its ability to raise man above himself so giving him confidence and a feeling of power. To be sure, part of this function can be ascribed to ritual. But in the turn of events the discussion that followed

centred on the social origin of religion, religion as a force, hallucination in religion, the place of the individual in religion, and so
on (1913b). Not a word about ritual! Nor did Durkheim appear
to want·to turn the discussion in that direction. Other issues
centred on the nature of religious belief, scientific thought and
the method of studying religion sociologically.

Another fact to be borne in mind is that very few of Durkheim's
writings on religion before the publication of *The Elementary
Forms* contained detailed references to ritual (see later sections
of this chapter). Most of what he wrote related to religion as a
general concept, to beliefs, *représentations* and the functions of
religion. At no point did he write in detail about the nature of
ritual. However, what he did write about it in the book did not
come as a complete surprise, since an account of his course of
lectures in the Sorbonne entitled 'La religion: les origines' had
been published much earlier (1907f). These lectures made public
much of his thinking on ritual as it was to appear in the book.
There is no evidence to suggest that anyone took up the points
he raised. The 1920s seem to have been in particular a period of
silence on the subject.

Ritual thus constitutes a forgotten chapter in Durkheim's work,
which was in part due to the writer himself. The purpose of
what follows is an attempt to bring to light what has been often
overlooked or played down.

2 Assumptions and method

Durkheim, writing as a rationalist and in the spirit of the age,
rejected or paid scant regard to the proclaimed intention of ritual.
The same attitude was adopted with regard to what the believer
himself thought he achieved in the rite. Since no god or gods
exist, prayers, ascetic acts, sacrifices, and so on, cannot bring
about that result claimed by the worshipper or religious leader.
Thus, in dealing with the Intichiuma rite of the Witchetty Grub
clan of the Arunta, Durkheim said the action did not and could
not directly bring about the fertility of the creature associated
with the totemic group (495/346). If, therefore, the doctrine or
myth of a rite is to be rejected, because the declared consequences

cannot be proved on scientific grounds, and are no part of reality, how should the observer proceed to analyse ritual?

Given such assumptions, why not disregard ritual altogether? Since it relates to falsehood and deception, let it be completely ignored, as the more moderates might suggest, or be eliminated as some Encyclopedists in the eighteenth century wanted. Although early English anthropologists, such as Tylor and Frazer, with a firm Protestant background, gave some place to ritual, ultimately they evaluated it as so much superstitious hocus-pocus (see Hamnett 1973:1). Durkheim never displayed this cynicism. He reverently rejected what the believer held that ritual meant, but he never wrote it off. Hidden in ritual is a reality of the greatest significance. Two facts could not be denied – the power of ritual to persist and, perhaps more importantly, its universality. For these reasons, if for no other, ritual for Durkheim could never be mad irrationality. If it were that, it would have died out years ago and it would not have been found to have been universal. He is reported to have said: 'Rituals are not aberrations; there are profound reasons for them in the very nature of things' (1907f:637), and going further, as he implied on other occasions, 'there is something of the eternal in ritual' (ibid.:638).

In Durkheim's analysis of religion, as we have seen (ch. 9), the gods or the deity are not accorded a central place. A divine being is not the *sine qua non* of a religious system. Such spiritual beings are to be explained by other factors. The sacred, and in this context ritual, are seen to be more important (see Isambert 1976). The reality of ritual is beyond all doubt. In a discussion on religion and science at a meeting of the Société Française de Philosophie he said:

> I myself believe that all the rituals that have been practised
> by mankind correspond to something in reality and can be
> justified, I do not say simply explained, by means of history.
> The grosser religions of the Australians have a human
> meaning as much as the actions of the most idealistic religions.
> (1909a(1):59; cf. Belot 1913a:339)

If, with Durkheim, the claims of the doctrine, theology or myth of a rite are rejected and at the same time the virtue of the ritual is upheld, how does one proceed to justify the virtue? Or, put in another way, having denied the face value of the externalities of a ritual, what method is to be adopted in studying it? How is the reality of which the observer is convinced recognized and proved? The many who take Durkheim's position and employ an alleged scientific approach have three courses open to them.

1 A low-level functionalist analysis which attempts to answer the question: what does the ritual do for social life or social solidarity (see ch. 16)?

2 As an extension of the above, but avoiding the pitfalls of functionalist language, a structural approach, which sees how ritual fits in to the structure and shape of society.

3 A psychological approach, not espoused by Durkheim, although in fact he comes very near to it at times, which sees the effect of ritual on the participants in causing a change or awakening in their emotions.

The first two of these courses, especially the second, leans heavily on a symbolic analysis. Given the presuppositions of his discipline, no other methods so far devised are valid or possible for the anthropologist or sociologist. Indeed, *the* contribution of the discipline to ritual is precisely here – its socio-symbolic interpretation. Nearly every anthropologist or sociologist today views ritual action as symbolic action (Goody 1961:152).

Such approaches to religion can only hope to find answers from facts unobserved or held to be unimportant by the actors. They are different from proclaimed ends consciously held by the participants. How else can one hope to understand ritual and to explain the persistence of such 'irrationality'? This is how Durkheim puts the issue:

> Whence could the illusion have come that with a few grains of sand thrown to the wind, or a few drops of blood shed upon a rock or the stone of an altar, it is possible to maintain the life of an animal species or of a god? (496/347)

So the motif appears once again. Religious action (and religious belief) is reduced from the acclaimed transcendental element to the level of the social: in his own phraseology, Durkheim chooses one order of reality rather than another. In this way he 'earths' religion and proceeds along a functional-symbolic path. His claim is that 'behind these outward and apparently unreasonable movements', he has discovered 'a mental mechanism which gives them a meaning and a moral significance' (496/348). To be sure, he rescues ritual from the attacks of radical rationalists, atheists and others. The cost is a form of reductionism: but, as we have noted elsewhere, sociology can assume no other course (see ch. 9.7).

3 Early ideas about ritual

In the first period of Durkheim's approach to religion, there are only one or two references to ritual. He seems to accept Guyau's view that ritual reflects man's relationship to man, which is extended to the gods (1887b:300–1/t.1975a:26–7). As a means by which religion is made visible and tangible, cult rests on a sociological relationship 'formed by an exchange of services'. Man receives something from God; he must therefore give something back to him. The final extension is where the individual loves God to such an extent that the relationship is an interior one based on adoration and ritual becomes purely symbolic. There is much in this that was close to Durkheim's thought, namely that ritual has a dominant characteristic of obligation on the part of the worshipper – *do ut des* – and that in this respect ritual is essentially a symbolic act.

In the middle period, 1895–1906, when he had an overwhelming interest in religion, belief rather than ritual dominated his thought. He was concerned with generalizations about religion (for example, what we might call its functions), rather than making generalizations derived from the minutiae of ritual. It was his disciples, such as Hubert and Mauss in their essay on sacrifice (1899), who turned to these issues. But it would be foolish to say that Durkheim disregarded ritual. He considered it in his 1899 essay, 'De la Définition des phénomènes religieux' (see ch. 9.1). In it he uses the words *pratiques religieuses* and *rite* with little or no differentiation, and in our comments in this book no distinction is made between ritual, rite, cult or practice unless it is stipulated otherwise. Durkheim shows that initially ritual is difficult to define since 'left on its own, and unrelated to anything else, it has nothing specific about it' (1899a(ii):16/t.1975a:88). Although it is not easily differentiated from other ways of behaviour, he proceeds to suggest that, apart from being obligatory, rituals are actions related to the sacred but not necessarily to the gods (ibid.:17/88). Interestingly enough, he sees that the carrying out of a person's duty towards his neighbour is ritual in nature – 'it is the best way of honouring God' (ibid.). The obligatory nature of ritual, which Durkheim emphasized in his early attempt to come to terms with ritual, contains ideas which are all too readily overlooked. That which is obligatory has to be taken seriously. It does not permit alternatives or ways of escape, it cannot be lightly subscribed to or disregarded. In brief, ritual carries with it an internal force which demands uniformity of action (see ch. 11.4).

It seems that Durkheim's theoretical attitude towards ritual was influenced by the agent of his 'conversion', Robertson Smith. His book, *The Religion of the Semites*, gave a prominent place to ritual within religion. There can be no doubt that Durkheim leaned heavily on what Robertson Smith said, but at the same time he was not uncritical of him (see ch. 4.2). Smith shocked the academic world of his time, predominantly Protestant as it was, by giving pride of place to ritual, which he considered to be more important in the lives of the practitioners than myth or belief (Smith 1889/1894:16). For Smith, myth did not contain the obligatory characteristic that ritual did. In myth 'the worshipper was often offered a choice of several accounts of the same thing, and provided that he fulfilled the ritual with accuracy no one cared what he believed about its origin' (ibid.). What was required and seen to be valuable was 'the exact performance of certain sacred acts prescribed by religious tradition' (ibid.). Durkheim sees this as an exaggeration. It is not so much that one component is more important than another, it is that they are mutually related. He wrote in the 1899 article:

> There can be no ritual without myth for a rite necessarily assumes that things are represented as being sacred and this *représentation* can only be mythical. (1899a(ii):22 n.1/ t.1975a:99 n.22)

The mutuality of myth and ritual Durkheim describes as one where 'the practices translate the beliefs into action and the beliefs are often only an interpretation of the practices' (ibid.:21/92). He continued to maintain his position even into the third period in the development of his religious thought, as is seen in the closing paragraph of Book II of *Les Formes* on the subject of religious belief, where he writes:

> But in reality, they [*représentations*] are inseparable from rites, not only because they manifest themselves there, but also because they in turn, feel the influence of these. (424/296)

So is enunciated the relation between faith and practice, which will be taken up again later in the book (see ch. 20).

4 The third period

Durkheim's thought about ritual shows a simple and strong line of development. In the earlier periods he firmly grasps certain general theoretical propositions about the importance of ritual and its relation to belief. These he never changes, but in his study of totemism and in dealing with the intricacies of the social life of his 'chosen people', the Arunta of Australia, he was forced by the sheer weight of ethnographic data to go beyond general propositions and analyse ritual in greater detail. In this way his considerable contributions to the study of ritual emerge in the third period of his religious thought. It is therefore the relevant sections of *Les Formes élémentaires* which now engage our attention, for nowhere else does he deal with the subject of ritual in such detail. There are no articles or essays which are exclusively concerned with ritual, which is itself an interesting fact, except in the early sketch of the book, given as lectures in 1906–7, to which we have already alluded (1907f; see ch. 5.2).

18 Ritual

II Classification and function

1 Definitions and basic classification

In pursuing what he held were the canons of science, Durkheim laid stress on defining his terms (see 1895a). With regard to ritual, however, a definition does not stand out as prominently as for that of religion itself, nor was it much repeated. In his early essay on defining religious phenomena, Durkheim held that ritual not only had the characteristic of obligation but related to certain objects. He defined ritual as 'the totality of practices concerned with *sacred things*' (1899a(ii):17/t.1975a:88). A similar definition appeared in Book I of *Les Formes élémentaires*, when he speaks of rites as 'rules of conduct which prescribe how man must behave in relation to sacred things' (57/41/117). Always, and this applies to much earlier reviews, Durkheim implies that ritual is the action component of religion (see ch. 17.1). Durkheim's concept of ritual is firmly set within the context of the sacred and he would thus be forced to reject any notion of ritual, such as that frequently employed at the present time, where it is associated with stylized action or ceremonial, without reference to religion which he always sees as based on the sacred.

He does not define the word cult. Is it to be taken as synonymous with rite and ritual? Generally speaking, this seems to be so, but he wrote: 'Every cult [*culte*] presents a double aspect, one negative, the other positive. In reality, of course, the two sorts of rites [*rites*] which we denominate thus are closely associated' (428/ 299). From this it appeared that Durkheim would distinguish cult from rite by implying that a cult consists of a number or cluster of rites. Indeed, one is led to assume that a society's 'total ritual' is its cult, which consists of its rituals. Nisbet agrees with this when he says: 'the cult and its rites form the essential and distinctive elements' (1974:185). But in fact Durkheim does not always make this distinction, and he often interchanges rite for cult, making the two words synonymous (434–5/304).

From what has just been said it can be readily deduced that Durkheim conceives of every ritual system containing two elements – negative and positive rites. In many respects, this simple, fundamental division is a reflection of his own approach to the sacred (see ch. 7). As his analysis unfolds, the parallels are most striking, not least in the application of those electrical analogies which we have already seen he uses, and which readily apply to a binary system, such as the sacred and the profane. Ultimately, Durkheim believes that ritual can only be understood in these terms, although as we shall see, there are some possible exceptions, as in the case of piacular rites. None the less, the overall classification is simply one of negative and positive rites.

2 Negative rites outlined: their function or effects

Negative rites are by definition those which emphasize a separation of the sacred from the profane. These embrace ascetical rites, acts of purifying, initiation rites and the keeping of holy days (bk III, Ch. I). Such rites play an extensive part in every religion (428/300). The examples Durkheim offers in connection with his selected Aboriginal peoples tend to be random. Despite his claims about the importance of this type of ritual, he does not offer extensive examples, except in referring to initiation ceremonies (447–9/313–14). Instead, his tendency is to generalize about sections or elements of rites, very short rituals or customs, which illustrate the *raison d'être* of negative rituals. His emphasis is on techniques by which man is able to isolate the two domains of the sacred and the profane.

Since negative rites state or imply that which is forbidden, evil or sinful, they are often associated with the Polynesian concept of taboo, a word basically meaning that which is withdrawn from common use (see ch. 7.3). Despite its extensive acceptance by anthropologists at the time, Durkheim had serious reservations about the term. The reason is that it is associated with the sacred and is therefore related to positive rites (428–9/300). He prefers the words interdict or interdiction, but he admits that so widely is the term taboo used that it makes it impossible to reject it in this context.

What particular forms do interdicts take in maintaining the sacred-profane dichotomy? In pointing to the Australian Aborigines Durkheim makes mention of rules and actions directed against touching the sacred, for example, against the churinga (bull-roarer), blood (especially of the initiated), hair, a corpse, eating certain sacred animals and other foods. Apart from touch, contact is prevented by not allowing people to see sacred objects – a person is removed from public view, a woman is not allowed to even glance at the instruments used in a rite, and so on. Durkheim also refers to breath as being dangerous, as well as certain sounds. Feast days in particular, in that they stipulate what is permitted as well as what is forbidden, are good cases showing the rigid division between the sacred and the profane.

Durkheim classifies rites according to their function (see ch. 16; also Table 18.1). Negative rites are those whose function it is to separate the sacred from the profane. They guarantee that the sacred is not vitiated or contaminated by the profane and they thus operate so as to ensure the continued status of the sacred. But the operation, according to Durkheim, does not often stand within an autonomous, self-defined rite. Normally such a rite functions only as an introduction and preparation for a positive rite which follows. But it often happens that the negative rite may free itself from a position of subordination and become prominent (445/311). This is most apparent in ascetic rites, where the emphasis is on privation, abstinence or suffering. Pain is an element required in such rites (446/312). Durkheim, by way of offering examples, refers to elements in initiation rites for the Arunta, where the initiate lies on a bed of leaves under which are live coals, or, as among the Urabunna, where he is beaten on the back. Circumcision is another case in point. Durkheim, who gives so much space to asceticism, as in *Le Suicide* (1897a:430/ t.1951a:375ff.) comments:

So the suffering which they impose is not arbitrary and sterile cruelty; it is a necessary school, where men form and temper themselves, and acquire the qualities of disinterestedness and endurance without which there would be no religion. (454–5/ 316)

He goes on to add that 'society itself is possible only at this price'. A key issue in the matter of negative rites is, apart from the separation of the sacred from the profane, the separation of the collective from the individual. Such rites play down and help to denigrate individual demands and values. He is reported to have said:

> During religious ceremonies when members of the group have assembled, the content of *consciences* change; the individual *représentations* – egoistic *représentations* – which take possession of them during the hours of their social life are forcibly banished because they are profane. Collective beliefs replace them, subsequently the common interests (for example making the species fertile) are considered. (1907f:637)

3 Positive rites outlined: their function or effects

Positive rites, in contrast to negative rites, bridge the gap between the worshipper and the object of his cult (see bk III, Chs II–IV). Such rites have a well-defined end – what might be called their religious or theological intention. For the Arunta, and certain North American Indians, this means for the most part the fertility of the totem species.

On the evidence of the Australian material Durkheim proposes three subtypes of positive ritual:

> sacrificial rites;
> imitative rites;
> commemorative rites.

He outlines several rites among the Australian Aborigines which were designed to ensure the fertility of the totem species, notably the Intichiuma ceremonies of the Arunta (bk III, Ch. II). He also shows variations of the ceremonies among some of the totemic groups. Durkheim argues that in cases where blood was used there was the implication of sacrifice, often the blood was that of

TABLE 18.1 *Durkheim's classification of ritual according to Book III of The Elementary Forms of the Religious Life*

Main division	General intention	Related to	Subtypes	Chapter in book	Examples of occasions	Function
Negative	To separate sacred from profane	Fear and pain	—	I	Ascetical Initiation Holy days	Eliminate individual *représentations*
Positive	To relate worshipper to divine source	Joy	1 Sacrificial	II		
			2 Imitative	III	Fertility	Euphoria
			3 Representative (commemorative)	IV	Acting out myths Awaken sentiments	Recall
		Sadness	Piacular*	V	Death Drought Plague	Expiation

* It might be argued that this, dealt with in Chapter V, constitutes a further item in the Main division. This possibility is challenged; see text.

the worshippers themselves. Sacred rocks were also used in a symbolic fashion. Contrary to what might be thought, a sacrifice was not esteemed to be a sad affair. Usually only one person or creature suffers for the sake of others, who rejoice in anticipating the consequences of the rite. The rites are usually performed when the whole group is gathered together and it is in the assembly of the group as a whole that the importance of the rites is to be located (see sections ahead).

Imitative rites are also performed for the purposes of fecundity. In this case, the propagation of the species is sought not by sacrifice but by the actions of worshippers, where the various attitudes of the animal whose fertility is sought are imitated (501/351). As in the Witchetty Grub Intichiuma of the Arunta, men pose and act in such a way as to represent the insect as it leaves the chrysalis. Other ceremonies which involve aping also occur in rites designed for rain-making. Such actions have been related to 'laws' of magic, where like is said to produce like and where anything touching an object also touches everything which has any relation of proximity or unity whatsoever with the object (510/356).

Representative or commemorative rites may also have as their intention the fertility of the species, but they involve not oblatory or imitative practices but a recollection of the past by way of a 'veritable dramatic representation' (531/372). In some examples the ceremony is clearly for the propagation of the species; in others it is more oblique and consists in the acting out of the myth. Rites of these kinds therefore involve merry-making and games, art and general enthusiasm in the form of effervescence. The myth of Thalaualla of the Warramunga tribe (to the north of the Arunta) is an example of the first kind: the myth of the snake Wollunqua among the Warramunga is an example of the second.

As one might guess from what has just been said, positive rites tend to be complete rites and are more numerous than negative rites. Furthermore, they are subject to various subtypes. Whereas negative rites separate the spheres of the sacred and the profane, and bring home to the worshipper the nature and total undesirability of the profane, positive rites directly introduce him to the sacred. Thus these rites bring him face to face with the most important elements of his society and hold before him beliefs which are the *sine qua non* of the society. This is borne out by the centrality of fertility in totemic groups; and where no sacrifice is evident, the acting out of the myth takes its place.

Once again, Durkheim makes the observation that positive rites are in contrast to negative rites seen by the nature of their gestures carried out in 'a state of confidence, joy and even enthusiasm' (556/389). Men celebrate with hope and expectation the anticipated events. The occasion may be serious and solemn, but that does not prevent liveliness and joy.

Indicated in what has just been said are two main effects or functions of positive rites – recall and euphoria. Each of these needs to be examined in a little more detail.

Recall

In referring to representative or commemorative rites, Durkheim notes that amongst the Warramunga, the ceremony takes the specific form of a dramatic representation about the single ancestor who was held to be the father of the clans (530ff./371ff.). This creation type of myth, dramatically portrayed, is similar to the Intichiuma among the Arunta. With one exception there is nothing in the rituals of the Warramunga that is related to oblation or is imitative. It consists of nothing more than the acting out of the myth, and another example that Durkheim gives is of the portrayal of the Black Snake, the ancestor Thalaualla. When the ceremony is over, the clan feels that the black snakes must inevitably increase and multiply (534/373), but the important point to note is that no gesture or act is made which can be said to call directly for or demand an increase in the fertility of the species (536/375). Durkheim therefore concludes that the function of the rite must be the dramatic representation of the myth itself. He writes:

> So the rite serves and can serve only to sustain the vitality of these beliefs, to keep them from being effaced from memory and, in sum, to revivify the most essential elements of the collective *conscience*. Through it, the group periodically renews the sentiment which it has of itself and of its unity; at the same time, individuals are strengthened in their social natures. (536/375)

In considering other rites, where the intention of fertility is less marked, such as the ceremony of the snake Wollunqua amongst the Warramunga, there seems no other object than that of acting out the myth, which gives rise to the problem of why there are so many similar totems in the same phratry. Everything centres on the myth and its re-enaction. In terms similar to those above, Durkheim states:

So we have here a whole group of ceremonies whose sole purpose is to awaken certain ideas and sentiments, to attach the present to the past, or the individual to the group. (541/ 378)

And he speaks of other ceremonies which contain only *représentations* where there is only one object and that is to commemorate the past, nothing more (542/379).

For Durkheim, representative or commemorative rites have a function that is basically one of recall, what might be termed a didactic function. Most rituals, if not all, contain actions which are themselves associated with myths or parts of myths, or belief statements (see ch. 20). To perform the ritual means to recall the myth. The obligatory nature of rites, a point that Durkheim so strongly and rightly stressed, means that rituals become occasions for the repeating of a myth or the acting out of some symbol. Thus, rituals are stipulated occasions for remembering. A more modern example would be that of the annual masses for the repose of the dead in the Roman Catholic Church, by which people remember their ancestors. Another is the Stations of the Cross. A man's memory is short: society's memory is also short. Ritual is a response to such limitations and it is probably true to say that it was man's earliest form of mass communication.

Euphoria

In considering a number of rites which contain sacrificial forms, including the Intichiuma of the Witchetty Grub clan, Durkheim comes to the conclusion that the rites have a profound effect on the participants, not only individually but as a group, and not only intellectually but emotionally (465ff./326ff.). The same can be said for other rites, imitative rites, where the fertility of the species is their declared object (501ff./351ff.). In claiming to look objectively at these rites, Durkheim came to the conclusion that their effects are indeed real, that is, they exercise, a profound influence or force over the worshippers (513/359; see ch. 11.4). The result is that all those who participate in these positive rites 'take away with them a feeling of well-being, the causes of which they cannot clearly see, but which is well founded' (ibid.). The effect is thus psychological, for the participants 'reforge their moral nature' in the rite (ibid.). 'Men,' he says, 'are confident because they feel themselves stronger; *and they really are stronger*, because the forces which were languishing are now re-awakened in their *consciences*' (494/346; our italics).

This argument assumes two basic psychological facts. The first is that in the course of everyday life a man faces from time to time feelings of weariness and a sense of drudgery, what we might call mild forms of social depression. Durkheim assumes that this is a universal condition of mankind which is self-consciously realized. He offers no proof and assumes the condition a priori. The second assumption is that by taking part in ritual, man reinvigorates himself. The evidence for this appears to be reached from what he read about the yearly communal gathering of the Arunta, which was seen as a sacred time and an occasion when religious ceremonies took place (307ff./214ff.). The social life of the Eskimos indicated the same thing (Mauss and Beuchat 1906/ t.1979).

Thus Durkheim holds that the feeling of periodic depression which permeates a society has a remedy in cultic practice, and as such, ritual answers a need that is consciously realized by society itself. If one type of ritual fails to satisfy the need, another is created. Of the French Revolution, he wrote that people 'felt the need to substitute a new cult for an ancient one that it wished to destroy' (1907f:637–8). He went on: 'when the need of a cult is not felt, society and individuals face a grave crisis because every living being ought to experience the need of always living in a state of great intensity, of openness, and of the renewal of life' (ibid.).

One result of man feeling a new creature by reason of his participation in ritual is that he is led to believe that the theological intention of the rite is achieved. According to Durkheim this is in fact illusory (513/359). One might interpose and state that a participant should say: 'I feel better by taking part in the rite'. Durkheim argues that man's rational examination of a ritual of this kind is blinded by the euphoric feelings he experiences when he participates in it. The sensations of pleasure and strength so derived put a man in a positive frame of mind so that he readily accepts the theological interpretation of the rite and believes that the animals reproduce themselves. Durkheim says: 'it is because they [positive rites] serve to remake individuals and groups morally that they are believed to have a power over things' (529/370). Again, 'the deep moral efficacy of the rite determines belief about the physical results which are themselves unreal' (1907f:637). Further, the efficacy sustains belief in the face of a lack of reason. It was true of the past: it is true today.

> [It is] from the cult as a whole that the faithful feel a warmth is being given out which reassures them. This power of awareness which transmits it even in the absence of logical reasons, is the faith without which there is no religion. (ibid.)

Thus ritual can be said to give rise to faith.

The real effect of ritual is always on the minds of the participants, and the mechanism which produces it comes from the mere fact of common assembly and mental interaction. As Durkheim wrote:

> If the real function of the cult is to awaken within the worshippers a certain state of soul, composed of moral force and confidence, and if the various effects imputed to the rites are due only to a secondary and variable determination of this fundamental state, it is not surprising if a single rite, while keeping the same composition and structure, seems to produce various effects. For the mental dispositions, the excitation of which is its permanent function, remain the same in every case; they depend upon the fact that the group is assembled, and not upon the special reasons for which it is assembled. (551/386)

Around the turn of the century he expressed similar notions about the power generated by social gathering, but in this case without reference to ritual. He said: 'When we live with people who think and feel as we do, all our ideas and emotions are reinforced by what our friends feel' (1960a). This is to be seen in festivals and public ceremonies and on every occasion when men come together, for their movements, the sound of their voices and the warmth of their words are all the more fervent. The truth is that 'the man who lives in a group has more moral energy than a man living in isolation, for he perpetually draws on this common reservoir of life' (ibid.).

4 Piacular rites

Durkheim admitted that even amongst the Arunta not all rites could be classified as either positive or negative. There existed a third category – piacular rites – whose nature might be said to be ambiguous (bk III, Ch. V; see Table 18.1). Such rites relate to occasions of sadness and misery, such as funerals, loss of the churinga, a poor harvest, drought or plague. A sense of anger may also be involved, as at times of death, as well as a general feeling of misery (562/393).

Perhaps as a result of his study of Roman religion with Fustel de Coulanges, he introduced the term piacular to deal with the problem. The Latin word *piaculum*:

> has the advantage that while it suggests the idea of expiation, it also has a much more extended signification. Every misfortune, everything of ill omen, everything that inspires sentiments of sorrow or fear necessitates a *piaculum*. (557/ 389)

This word, which implies sacrifice, is well suited for describing rites which are celebrated by those who are sad or mentally upset. In a footnote, Durkheim stated that in Pliny *piaculum* is a synonym for misfortune.

Durkheim, who is so insistent on the virtues of classification, never clearly states whether piacular rites are to be considered as a completely separate category which displays characteristics of both negative and positive rites, or whether piacular rites are to be taken as a subtype of positive rites. Clearly, they cannot be included with negative rites. Durkheim admits their ambiguous nature and goes so far as to describe the chapter on which this section is based as 'Piacular rites and the ambiguity of the notion of sacredness'.

The argument for not making piacular rites a subtype of positive rites might rest on the following facts:

(a) Durkheim makes no reference to *Le culte positif* in the heading of the chapter on *Les rites piaculaures*, as contrasted with headings for other chapters in Book III.
(b) Nowhere in the chapter on piacular rites does Durkheim categorically state that such rites are to be classified as positive.
(c) He makes much of the *occasions* of celebrating a piacular rite as if the occasion and not the function were the criterion for classification. Piacular and positive rites thus stand opposite one another according to this hallmark.

On the other hand, it could be argued that, within Durkheim's terms of definition, admittedly not so precise as one would like at times, and in contrast to negative rites, piacular rites can be placed within the general category of positive rites. We advance the following reasons:

1 Both positive and piacular rites relate the worshipper in a constructive way to the divine source acknowledged in the rite.
2 Durkheim infers, although he does not categorically state, that certain piacular rites are types of positive rite. He states: 'If mourning differs from *the other forms of the positive cult*, there is one feature in which it resembles them: it, too, is made up of collective ceremonies which produce a state of effervescence among those who take part in them' (570–1/399; our italics). The subject of effervescence is dealt with separately (see chs 21 and 22).

For what it is worth, it seems best to consider piacular rites as positive rites. The subject is debatable and certainly what is evident, on Durkheim's admission as well, is that not all rites can be easily fitted into the two-fold classification. According to Durkheim the problem is largely due to the ambivalent nature of the sacred, containing both pure and impure forces, which we considered earlier on (ch. 7.5).

5 An evaluation of Durkheim's primary classification of ritual

The basic division of ritual into positive and negative rites, as has already been stated, emerged only in the third period of the development of Durkheim's religious thought. It first appeared in the 1906–7 lectures (1907f) and was then used within the complicated sectioning of that part of *L'Année sociologique* entitled 'Sociologie religieuse'. But here it was only used in the last volume, published in 1913. Marcel Mauss, Durkheim's nephew, who was largely responsible for the reviews in this section of *L'Année sociologique* throughout its existence, used the term positive and negative rites in 1910 in a review of van Gennep's *Rites de passage* (vol. XI, p. 202). The point is that apart from the extensive use of this classification in *Les Formes élémentaires*, it was not subsequently taken up by anthropologists and sociologists. One wonders therefore whether such a classification of ritual has any merit at all. But, then, is any kind of overall classification helpful, or indeed possible in so complex a phenomenon? Often in the social sciences, classification boils down to arguments over definition. Certain classificatory systems turn out to be little more than ends in themselves, for they lead to no further analysis and high expectations turn out to be illusory. Systems of classification are thus handed down as historical monuments. Some might argue that Durkheim's classification of ritual is very much in this category – its interest is only archaic. Today, it is taken for granted that the classification of rituals – even religious rituals – is either a virtual impossibility or of doubtful consequence. Admittedly, certain kinds of rituals do hang together, such as *rites de passage*, which were originally grouped together and analysed by van Gennep, and in rituals of reversal.

It seems likely that the way Durkheim classified ritual was original. To be sure, the terms positive and negative were borrowed from mathematics or electrical theory, and they have the merit of simplicity. The classification, however, suffers from a number of serious defects, which are briefly mentioned. The most serious is that the attempt to create a universal classification is based solely on rituals practised by the Arunta and associated tribes. True, Durkheim does not set out to offer an overall classification; none the less, he supposes that his classification will have application in the widest context. Consequently he readily leaps from the Arunta, to Judaism, to Christianity, to modern forms of humanism. As with belief, so with ritual, the conclusions derived from a particular ethnographic group are immediately and without question applied to ritual in general.

Durkheim's concepts worked better with regard to negative rites, which in the main are ascetical and purgative. Such rites have a simple enough purpose – to eliminate everything that profanes or vitiates or that threatens the sacred (482/299). All religions have components of this kind, which imply that the sacred should never come into contact with the profane or some such damaging force. Nevertheless the introduction of interdicts or negative commands, although they imply the intent of negative ritual, confuses the issue. If interdicts are nothing more than commands which do not involve ritual ways of dealing with offenders, then they stand within the category of belief rather than practice.

To establish the classification, Durkheim used a simple criterion of effect centred on the sacred–profane dichotomy. Today it is generally recognized that it is impossible to create a classification on such a simple line of demarcation, and Durkheim himself admitted that certain rites may have several functions or ends (552/386). If this is so, how can a rite or family of rites be classified according to one factor and one factor alone? In a specific case, Durkheim admitted that the Intichiuma of the Arunta contained ritual elements that were both sacrificial and imitative (501/351). The classification of complex ceremonies is such that it is wellnigh impossible to establish them according to a single criterion. For these and other reasons, Leach has rightly described Durkheim's classificatory system as seeming to be 'excessively rigid' (1968:522). Further, in anthropological investigation, the way objects are used ritually prevents them being labelled sacred or profane in accordance with Durkheimian categories (Stanner 1967/r.1975:291; ch. 7.7). Particular objects can be used in various ways – at one moment sacred, at the next profane or secular.

6 Appraisal and the issue of one and many functions

Whereas Durkheim's system of the classification of ritual might appear rigid and even simplistic, it had the merit of forcing him to analyse each ritual of the Arunta separately. By so doing, he was prevented from developing a vulgar functionalism in which ritual is said to perform one and only one function (see ch. 16). Different rituals perform different functions and classification is based on such functions.

A particular ritual may perform several functions or may serve a number of different ends. Durkheim gave as a modern example the Christian liturgy or the mass, which can be used on widely different occasions, for example at a wedding as well as at a burial (551/386). He offers other examples, as in the Intichiuma ceremonies, and also in Hindu sacrifice analysed by Hubert and Mauss, where the sacrificial ritual has elements of communion, expiation, vow, and contract (Hubert and Mauss 1899). Again, negative rites can be seen as being preparatory for positive rites: penance opens the way to communion. Therefore both are necessary for each other. It can be deduced, further, that rites have considerable plasticity and 'many rites may produce the same effect and mutually replace one another' (522/386).

As we have had occasion to see, there have been those who have eagerly focused on Durkheim's functional approach to religion and in so doing have distorted his analysis (see ch. 16). Although religion is not identical to ritual, it is not surprising that some scholars have also emphasized the functions, and function, that Durkheim held ritual possessed. One such writer was Alpert, who distinguished four functions – disciplinary (or preparatory), cohesive, revitalizing and euphoric (1938:137ff.). Such functions are contained within a wide range of rituals, and clearly not all functions are contained in each rite. It is possible to argue in general terms that rituals in other societies might throw up other functions. That can be determined only by the accumulation of empirical evidence. A serious problem of Alpert's delineation of the four functions is that they are not easy to differentiate, for example, the revitalizing and euphoric functions. Where an individual gets involved in a highly excitable (euphoric) ritual, it can also be argued that he and society are thereby revitalized. The

343

external characteristics related to such functions are not clearly marked out. Our analysis of positive and negative rites has indicated a different set of functions (see the previous sections in this chapter).

Certainly, in the matter of both religion and ritual Durkheim seems to be a multi-functionalist. For thoroughgoing functionalists, such a position is unsatisfactory. They would prefer to see Durkheim as a uni-functionalist. There are some who would assert that in fact he was (for example, Radcliffe-Brown and Talcott Parsons). The question arises, was Durkheim in fact a uni-functionalist in the matter of ritual?

That Durkheim does move towards some overriding function of ritual can be seen in the development of Book III of *Les Formes élémentaires*. As he proceeds to expound positive and negative rites, he leads to the theme that rites control religious life. At the end of the section on ritual he says: 'Beliefs express this life [the religious life] in *représentation*; rites organize it and regulate its working' (*organisent . . . réglent*) (592/414). But more can be said about this rather trite observation. It will be recalled from an earlier chapter on functionalism that Durkheim in *Les Formes élémentaires* referred to the two main functions that religion performs – the speculative or cognitive function and the reinforcing or strengthening function (ch. 16.2). The first relates to belief; the second to action, to ritual. By participation in ritual a person feels stronger, and since the individual gains inner strength so society itself is strengthened. This corresponds to Alpert's revitalizing function. Durkheim wrote:

> It is society which raises him [man] above himself: we might
> even say that he is made by society, for the thing which
> makes man is that totality of intellectual assets which constitute
> civilization, and civilization is the work of society. This
> explains the *leading* role of the cult in every kind of religion.
> It is because society can only make its influence felt if it is
> active, and it is only active if the individuals of which it is
> composed are assembled together and act in common. (597–8/
> 418/147; our italics)

And again:

> The essential thing is that men are assembled together, that

sentiments are felt in common and expressed in common acts; but the particular nature of these sentiments and acts is something relatively secondary and contingent. To become conscious of itself, the group does not need to perform certain acts in preference to all others. What is necessary is that it participates in the same thought and the same action; of little importance are the visible forms under which this communion takes place. Unquestionably the external forms do not occur haphazardly; there are reasons for them: but these reasons do not depend on the central component of the cult. Hence everything leads us back to the same idea: above all, rites are the means by which the social group periodically reaffirms itself. (553/386–7)

Durkheim sees at the heart of what he designates as the chief function of ritual, and indeed every ritual, the coming together of people to take part in a common activity. Everything turns on this being together and acting together.[1] Assembly *per se* holds the key not only for ritual, but effervescent assembly as we shall see (chs 21 and 22). So the mere fact of coming together does the trick. People are transformed by it. In stirring language, Durkheim writes:

The only way of renewing the collective *représentations* which relate to sacred things is to retemper them in the very source of the religious life, that is to say, in assembled groups. Now the emotions aroused by these periodical crises through which external things pass induce the men who witness them to assemble, to see what should be done about it. But by the very fact of uniting, they are mutually comforted; they find a remedy because they seek it together. The common faith becomes reanimated quite naturally in the heart of this reconstituted group; it is born again because it again finds those very conditions in which it was born in the first place. After it has been restored, it easily triumphs over all the private doubts which may have arisen in individual minds. The image of the sacred things regains power enough to resist the internal or external causes which tended to weaken it. (494/ 346)

A person who participates in rites is forced to act in empathy with the joys and sorrows of a group (571ff./399ff.). Even when a death is involved, the participants of the ensuing ritual have nothing but sad emotions in common with each other, 'but to be in communion with one another in sadness is still to be in communion and every communion of *conscience* under whatever forms it may be raises the social pulse' (574/401).

The notion that the mere fact of assembling together explains the effectiveness of ritual contains truth and naïvety. Personal experience would seem to suggest that common participation, common encounter, very frequently increases the emotional pulse of the individuals and the social vitality of the group. But, on the other hand, a gathering can lead to social division and hostility. Durkheim seems to imply that the reasons for assembly are not important. As we shall see in a later chapter, the operative group is an ordered assembly not an *ad hoc* crowd (ch. 22.1). Nevertheless, Durkheim's argument transcends the purpose of the gathering: its intention in no way determines the outcome on the individuals and on the society.

The weakness of the principle emerges in cases where rituals are seen to be boring or where participants enter them as a matter of duty, to please a relative, for the sake of 'society', but at the same time the participant is totally removed from them mentally. In this way not only is indifference the outcome, but individual hostility or resentment may ensue. What is required as a precondition for common assembly to be effective is that the individual must come to such an assembly with certain predispositions overt or latent, for example, with a modicum of religious beliefs or a psychological attitude, conscious or unconscious, which makes him warm to the ritual.

There is, of course, in Durkheim's treatment of common assembly a methodological skating on thin ice. He gets very near to psychological explanations – certainly it is in the realm of social psychology – and such a closeness to this reductionist approach is contrary to his early principles (see 1895a). The issue will be raised in connection with effervescent assembly (ch. 22.2).

One thing apparent in his study of ritual is that enthusiasm for his analysis causes him to throw all caution to the wind. This carelessness – this exaggeration – in part stems from his great admiration for society (see chs 13; 28.3). He failed to understand – he seemed to have a fear of – individuals in isolation (a Jewish outlook?). The individual by himself is impoverished, weak, scarcely a person. With others in a society, this is not the case. It is society which gives strength, vitality, civilization, indeed makes man human. His discovery was that ritual is an agent for doing this. It brings people together, brings them out of isolation, and so makes them part of society and therefore human. But this so-called chief function is as much a technique of how rituals function within themselves as how they function in society.

Three issues emerge from Durkheim's writings on the question of one function. The first is that Durkheim never speaks about an exclusive function of ritual. Rituals perform different functions. However, as we have observed, Durkheim does emphasize a chief or main function as is witnessed in the quotation above (see ch. 16.6). But here the situation is not altogether clear. Ritual performs the chief function of controlling and organizing religious life, but also of influencing and making active individuals and society – the function of revitalization. He makes the function depend upon common assembly, as if all rituals did in fact have this characteristic. Some negative rites do not. Some rituals only involve a very few people. Durkheim seems to move all too readily from particular rites of the Arunta to the notion of common worship and praise, of large religious gatherings for that purpose which are very much part of the Judaeo-Christian tradition, and his generalization is based upon that rather than upon careful generalizations derived from the Australian rites. Delighted by his discovery (or his logic?) Durkheim sees ritual as a *sine qua non* of the maintenance of society. He is reported to have said in the 1906–7 lectures:

> It is not necessary for man's existence that he views society as the gods hypostasized, nor that he believes in the material efficacity of their rites in their physical results. But the moral and social services which the cult renders are indispensable and permanent so long as man exists, so long as there are societies. (1907f:637)

It is these 'moral and social services' which Durkheim saw as the eternal quality of religion – what made ritual eternal. He said: 'Voilà ce que le culte a d'éternel' (ibid.). What is also important to notice is that Durkheim does not state that ritual performs only one service in the maintenance of society but several. One cannot

347

pin him down to saying that ritual does this and only this. The multiplicity of rituals means a multiplicity of functions. In various ways they all contribute to the building up and strengthening of society.

The second issue is proof. We have already raised the difficulties in empirically substantiating a functional argument, especially where the intention of the rite does not correspond with the alleged social function (ch. 16.8). The danger is to argue as an armchair anthropologist, or even a field anthropologist, and to be guilty of the error of reasoning summed up in the phrase 'if I were a horse'.

The problem of proof would be considerably eased if the theological intention of the rite corresponded to its alleged social function, but there are very few cases indeed where the theologian or even the participant would agree with the sociologist or anthropologist. In the case where rituals are said to have the social function of remaking or reforging individuals and groups, Durkheim turned to the argument of Strehlow against Spencer and Gillen (529/370). Spencer and Gillen emphasized the physical function (intention) of rites. Strehlow, in questioning Australian Aboriginals, maintained that when they were asked why they celebrated the Intichiuma, replied: ' "It is because our ancestors arranged things thus. That is why we do thus and not differently" ' (530/371). Durkheim holds that such a statement is evidence for the social function of the rite and he goes on to say: 'Men celebrate it to remain faithful to the past, to keep for the group its normal physiognomy, and not because of the physical effects which it may produce. Thus, the way in which the believers themselves explain them show the profound reasons upon which the rites proceed' (ibid.). Far from being a proof of Durkheim's position, his argument shows that he has mistaken intention for authority. What in fact the rite does for the Australian in his own eyes and that which Durkheim imagines it does are completely different. Outcome is not the same as authority.

It is not that ritual, where it is found to be in operation, does not help to keep society together and contributes to its life. The issue is now seen to be that this kind of functional approach 'is so broadly applicable that it tells one virtually nothing' (Ortner 1978:4). No matter what component of society is selected, it can be shown to 'build up' the society, to strengthen it and to maintain its equilibrium. Even what appears to be a dysfunction can be said to have merit. Both the positive and the negative turn out to be positive in maintaining the solidarity of society. A functionalist approach is not wrong, it is inadequate and hence there is need to find a new way of looking at ritual; for example, as a means of controlling experience and in letting a ritual tell its own story (ibid.:5).

The third point is that if ritual is functionally essential to the life of a society, what happens if it is absent? Does the society break up? Is it necessary for social existence? Can social life and social existence be differentiated? The issue is crucial in terms of modern western society, which is virtually ritual-less. By Durkheim's reasoning, either modern society should collapse or the sociologist has to make great efforts to find ritual in a hidden form, which is a contradiction in terms.

It is not a profound observation, but nevertheless true, that Durkheim's analysis of ritual applies to pre-literate societies rather than modern societies (Giddens 1971:112). It fits best those societies characterized by mechanical solidarity. Regular moral reconsolidation of the group is necessary, because 'in the activities of day-to-day life in the profane world individuals pursue their own egoistic interests and are consequently liable to become detached from moral values upon which societal solidarity depends' (ibid.). Small-scale societies depend for their unity and existence on a strong collective *conscience* in which religion and therefore ritual are paramount. In societies marked by organic solidarity the collective *conscience* is, if not entirely absent, then minimal. In no way can it be said that modern western society is dependent for its existence on religious ritual to strengthen it regularly and reiterate its values. The unity that a nation possesses today does not depend on ritual. And even the alleged replacement of the Christian religion by the cult of the individual, so much supported by Durkheim, is virtually without ritual – something which casts doubt on its being a religion at all (see ch. 26.6).

Some, however, would disagree with this and maintain that Durkheim failed, not because he confined his attention to ritual in pre-literate societies, but because he disregarded modern secular rituals, associated, for example, in this country with Parliament, with the trooping of the colour, with domestic rituals (LaCapra 1972:233). There is some truth in this criticism. Durkheim was ready enough to point to Bastille Day as an example of what we might call secular ritual, but he did not analyse it in terms of his grandiose scheme of positive and negative rites. And one wonders whether it would be possible to do. Sacrificial rites, which are by no means universal in primitive societies, have no application in modern western life, except symbolically within the Christian tradition. Would it be too much to suggest that Durkheim, if pressed, would argue that the presence of ritual in modern society is best understood in terms of what might be called a vestigial form? And to understand that, the pre-existing full form has to be examined and from it principles derived. This is precisely what Durkheim did. Bastille Day is best understood as a time of ordered gathering on a national scale to celebrate and reaffirm an event which is held to be central to the life of the nation. It thus performs a strengthening and rejuvenating function. There is nothing in modern secular ritual which in any way corresponds to the negative rites of primitive and Catholic Christianity. In order to talk about ritual which has national significance, a great deal of effort is required to find any convincing examples. The fact of the matter is that a society based on rationalist principles has no place for ritual.

Other critics point to the weakness of Durkheim's analysis in that he readily leaps across religious traditions and vast periods of time, moving from the Arunta, taking in his stride Judaism and medieval Catholicism, and then referring briefly to modern secular ritual. Richard was particularly critical of this kind of approach. Yet, with safeguards, with care as to what in fact can be deduced, such an approach is an acceptable procedure for the anthropologist and sociologist, and has shown itself to be helpful. It is implied in the comparative method and in the approach of the structuralist and functionalist.

Durkheim's analysis of ritual is fascinating and fruitful. It has influenced a number of scholars, for example R. Will in his massive work, *Le Culte*. Goldenweiser was one of the first and in those days one of the few who praised Durkheim for his analysis of ritual. He wrote: 'Durkheim's psychological interpretation of ritual, must, on the whole, be regarded as the most satisfactory part of his analysis' (1915/r.1975:221). He applauded Durkheim for carefully pointing out the effect that ritual had on those who participated in it.

No matter how vulnerable certain of Durkheim's arguments might seem to be, his contribution to the study of ritual in bringing home its complexity and in pointing to the relation it has with other components of social life is very considerable. He saw that men have common bonds in kinship and social interests, and these are expressed in common ritual which is not only a vehicle of expression but is also a means of strengthening those ties which exist between actors. Moral life is thus openly demonstrated and intensified by ritual, and in this respect it is indeed an effective force.

19 Ritual

III Its relation to *la vie sérieuse*

1 *La vie sérieuse: la vie légère*

Durkheim in his analysis of ritual emphasized the various forms and functions that ritual can take or perform. He pointed to the complexity of structure of many rites and attempted to uncover patterns within them. To be sure, some of the characteristics of ritual which he noted hardly constituted discoveries, for they are to be found in other writers, particularly Robertson Smith, but Durkheim has the distinction of emphasizing characteristics which relate to other social components and of being systematic in his approach to ritual. We now wish to examine a characteristic of ritual which he stressed, which was unique and which has been frequently overlooked by commentators.

Durkheim contrasted positive and negative rites, as well as other rites such as piacular rituals, with secular gatherings which externally have common characteristics, and also with joyful, free outbursts within the rituals themselves. Durkheim holds that such occasions of freedom and celebration are without 'a serious object' (*objet sérieux*) (548/383). Thus he sees that 'a ritual ceremony always has an important end' (ibid.). For Durkheim, ritual is related to life in all its earnestness and therefore not to life in either its lighter side or even to life in its totality. In pursuing this idea, Durkheim introduced the expression, *la vie sérieuse* (the serious side of life) (see ch. 15.2). The essential end of ritual is thus located within *la vie sérieuse*. By contrast, those elements which are either irrelevant to or detract from *la vie sérieuse* – those anti-serious, jocular components – belong to what we would call *la vie légère* (the carefree side of life). For Durkheim this includes not only sudden outbursts of celebration, but games, drama, poetry, art, and so on (see 546/382; 548/383). The phrase, *la vie légère*, was never used by him, but we have employed it to bring out the dichotomy which perhaps existed in his own mind. Such a dichotomy amplifies the notion of *la vie sérieuse*, and in passing it will be recalled that Durkheim was someone of a serious disposition with a strong Puritan streak in him (see ch. 1.5).

2 Aspects of *la vie légère*

It is obvious that *la vie sérieuse* is associated with the social and in some way with the sacred: and by contrast, *la vie légère* is associated with the individual and in some manner with the profane (see ch. 7.2). What is meant by the term we have used, *la vie légère*, however, needs to be expanded.

As we have suggested, Durkheim argues that not every gesture and movement in ritual has meaning or a determinable reason for existence (545/381). There are some elements 'which serve nothing; they merely answer the need felt by worshippers for action, motion, gesticulation' (ibid.). This position is to be contrasted with that of Malinowski who saw in each element of ritual, and indeed the entirety of culture itself, some function which, if it was not immediately seen, was at least capable of being discovered (see Lévi-Strauss 1950:xxxvi).

Durkheim unfolds his argument in *The Elementary Forms* when he examines the occasion of the acting out of the myth of the primordial ancestor Thalaualla. He notes that the officiants perform movements such as jerking and twisting which are intended to imitate the movements of the snake-like creature (532ff./372ff.). The whole cycle of its life on earth is in this way enacted. The movements are said to please the snake, and as such, Durkheim calls them strictly religious. But in addition, there are other episodes which he says are 'epical or comical', which do not carry the same importance. One example is that of actors hiding from one another. He admits that all actions are dramas and that those of a strictly religious nature (*la vie sérieuse*) have the implications of fertility for black snakes. Such a ritual is the Intichiuma, which is a strictly totemic rite, where the *direct* object is the fertility of the species.

Dramatic gestures and movements which take place within religious rituals indicate the same processes are at work, whether or not it is the dramatic or strictly ritual which is emphasized (543/380). Furthermore, their intentions are the same, that is, argues Durkheim, to take the audience away from the real world and to transport them into another which is readily open to the imagination. What is dramatic gives the impression of entertainment, for the actors openly laugh and enjoy themselves (ibid.).

So, participants and actors readily move from one type of activity to another within the same ritual, from actions associated with *la vie sérieuse* to those connected with *la vie légère*. Durkheim notes that such a change is made without any sense of break or discontinuity (ibid.). Religious rituals as such require two criteria in order to be carried out: (a) they are to be performed on sacred ground and (b) profane people (women and children) are excluded. Consecrated ground is not insisted on for other rituals which are less 'religious' (more laicized). The subjects of some of the myths are legendary figures who have no established place in the totemic cult. These myths may have been ancient rites which have been changed, and Durkheim admits that 'the distinction between these two sorts of ceremonies is so variable that it is impossible to state with precision to which of the two kinds they belong' – that is, to simple public merry-making, or to ritual proper (544/380). He is thus prepared to accept blurred lines of demarcation.

Durkheim gives other examples in Arunta ritual. He refers to a secular corroboree as being an occasion of merry-making (548/383). Hence ritual is akin to a feast (*fête*), and by inverting the idea, Durkheim suggests that a secular occasion of rejoicing also contains within itself certain characteristics of a religious ceremony. The common factor lies in people being brought together and entering into a state of excitement or effervescence (see chs 21 and 22). 'In each case,' he says, 'cries, songs, music, violent movements, dances, the search for excitements [which] raise the ritual level' (548/383). Popular feasts often lead to excesses and 'cause men to lose sight of the distinction separating the licit from the illicit'. This observation, that many rituals are accompanied by a relaxation of moral and social sanctions and as such are seen to be joyful occasions, is commonly accepted.

It is clear to Durkheim that the dramatic element in liturgy is also associated with activities such as games and play (543–4/ 380–1). They are in his eyes but an extension of drama: he maintains that games and all the principal forms of art have been born of religion and that for a long time they retained a religious character (see ch. 14.3). The connection between ritual and games has been expanded by R. Caillois in the 1950s. Durkheim defined play as free, separate, uncertain, unproductive yet regulated make-believe, and subsumed four categories: competition, chance, simulation, vertigo. Play is in some measure separated from ordinary life but delimited within a sacred area. Again, poetry is linked to mythology: 'The truth is that there is poetry in all religion' and every rite expresses it in some degree (546/382).

The contention that art, games, story-telling, acting, are not at the centre of life is to be found in many of Durkheim's works. His argument is that no society can live on the arts. Games never hold a country together. A society has to be concerned with reality and that its members abide by and intellectually support those moral ideals which are at its very foundation. The dominance of Paris in the world of art and music in his day apart, Durkheim's major concern was for a stable and integrated nation. He therefore tended to be both personally and intellectually removed from the dominant *haute culture*.

Certainly from the days of his Latin thesis in 1892, if not before, Durkheim seems to have delighted in making the contrast between science and art. Art is action which is impelled by urgency, whereas true science is without haste (1892a/1966a:32ff./ t.1960b:5ff.). Science must be completely independent of art, it must show no regard for utility but pursue only one object, that is, knowledge. For both to perform their tasks, it is necessary that they be as sharply divided as possible and each be allowed to develop as they will. As science is still very undeveloped, it is necessary for everyday life that action be taken and that in this action art has a place (ibid.). But it is fairly clear in Durkheim's mind that in any muddling of art and science, science will eventually dominate (see ch. 25). Durkheim made a similar point in the very last thing that he wrote, where he holds that the methods employed by science and art differ and in fact there is 'a fundamental antithesis between them' (1920a:85/t.1979a:81). Science is concerned with the past and the present: art looks towards the future which it attempts to anticipate and construct (ibid.). In a lecture on the nature of sociology given in 1900, Durkheim made the point that art is basically concerned with action and practice: science with theory and knowledge (1900b:609/t.1973a:4). He also dealt extensively with the subject of art and science in the last lecture of the series entitled L'Éducation morale. He notes that every work of art is an expression of the ideal (1925a:306ff./ t.1961a:267ff.). While the difference is only a matter of degree, the ideal for realists (scientists?) is provoked in reality: for others, it is the product of internal elaboration (*un travail intérieur*). 'The idea is by definition, something that cannot be contained within reality, something that overflows from it, that goes beyond it and consequently beyond ourselves' (ibid.). The poet, the painter, the artist, is so engrossed in what he is trying to do that he becomes engulfed in it, which means that he must make sacrifices for his art. Here there is a common root with morality, for morality also commands sacrifice. But as always, everything turns on what is meant by reality. 'The domain of art is not that of the real' (ibid.). The artist must not be implausible, but he goes beyond reality. He does not subject his work to the laws of nature or of history, and therefore he encourages his public to accept notions which are scientifically absurd, that is, they have no basis in reality. Every man who sees a work of art knows this, but he does not object to what he sees or experiences, because he does not want to spoil his aesthetic pleasure. The artist's world is thus a world of images, dreams, unchecked imagination. Here Durkheim stands close to Plato. But he also holds that art is comparable to a game and that there exists a definite relationship between the two. Man looks at a work of art and his imagination is aroused. The same thing happens when he plays games, cards or dice. The competition in this case has much the same effect. When the stakes are high, argues Durkheim, the pleasure goes, for the game now becomes extremely serious. Games as well as art make man forget life and therefore take him away from reality. They stimulate the emotions, which are often unchecked by moral controls. In short, art is related to the world of leisure: *la vie sérieuse* is concerned with work, religion and morality. Yet he admitted that man cannot work all the time (ibid.:313/273). Relaxation must follow effort and 'activity must sometimes take the form of play'. But here man must be selective and assume only moral forms of leisure. In this respect, art is to be commended 'as a noble form of play'. Hence there is the need for aesthetic education. But always there is the word of warning – 'In itself, leisure is always dangerous.' 'In *la vie sérieuse* man is sustained against temptation by the obligation of work' (ibid.:314/274). A Christian idea indeed: some might say a strongly Puritan one!

Durkheim was never more forthright in his negative approach to art than when he wrote, at much the same time: 'All art is luxury; aesthetic activity is not subordinated to any useful end; it is released for the sole pleasure of the release' (1911b/1924a:125/t.1953b:85). There can be no doubt that behind Durkheim's alleged scientific objectivity, there lurks a moral disapprobation of art and the arts; their position is peripheral to society. If, however, they become prominent in society, nothing but social and moral degradation will ensue. In the course of lectures in Paris, which were to become *L'Évolution pédagogique*, Durkheim said: 'Any culture which is exclusively or essentially aesthetic contains within itself a germ of immorality, or at least an inferior morality. Indeed, art by definition moves in the realm of the unreal and the imaginary' (1938a/1969f:239–40/t.1977a:207). Durkheim once again wishes to contrast the aesthetic with the real, and would emphasize that morality (*la vie sérieuse par excellence*) which also operates in the realm of action, must come to grips with real objects or else it will cease to exert any influence. In the selfsame lectures, Durkheim attacked educational systems when they encouraged dilettantism, when they bordered on nihilism or were little worried about society. Education is utilitarian in that it is concerned with the welfare of society (ibid.:259–60/225).

The category of actions which are not related to *la vie sérieuse*, Durkheim holds, rest on the need or deep desire on the part of man for recreation (544/381). A cult does not only achieve some social end, it also provides for this secondary requirement. An accident of history? Hardly so. 'Religion has not played this role haphazardly or by some happy chance but as an inevitable consequence of its nature' (ibid.). The argument rests on a logical extension of certain given facts. The realities, argues Durkheim, in which the faithful believe, are indeed fictitious, but they 'express themselves religiously only when the imagination transfigures them' (ibid.). Intellectual forces thus make the partially imaginary religious world 'intense and tumultuous'. But the result produces

357

an excess of energy and the forces are more than required, because the symbols do not absorb them *in toto*. An excess is built up, 'which seeks to employ itself in supplementary superfluous and luxury works, that is, works of art' (ibid.). Participants 'act for the pleasure of so doing and take pleasure in all kinds of games. In so far as the beings to whom the cult is addressed are imaginary, they are not able to contain and regulate this exuberance' (ibid.). In this manner, Durkheim argues that rituals are kinds of machines whose mechanisms are unknown to their participants, but which generate surplus energy and which is then absorbed in the activities of pleasure and recreation within the mechanism itself.

3 The dichotomy evaluated

La vie sérieuse and *la vie légère* form a dichotomy which allows Durkheim to mark off ritual proper from peripheral and secondary elements within it. This offered Durkheim two advantages. First, it was a means whereby that which is socially significant is differentiated from that which is not, and is very roughly an extension of the dichotomy, the social and the individual (see ch. 10). Second, it allowed Durkheim to bring home the seriousness of life – the seriousness of *social* life – the reality of life itself. Speaking of religion in such a vein, he wrote:

> The moral forces expressed by religious symbols are real forces with which we must reckon and with which we cannot do what we will. (546/382)

Again:

> The *représentations* which it [religion] seeks to awaken and maintain in our minds are not vain images which correspond to nothing in reality, and which we call up aimlessly for the mere satisfaction of seeing them appear and combine before our eyes. (ibid.)

In Durkheim's eyes a rite loses its *raison d'être* if it 'serves only to distract'. As food is necessary for physical life, so religion and ritual are necessary for social life. The dichotomy, *la vie sérieuse* and *la vie légère*, is an attempt not only to present a scientific line of demarcation, but it also carries with it moral overtones, ethical imperatives, which are absent in the words of the dichotomy, the social and the individual. Durkheim would maintain that *la vie sérieuse* and *la vie légère* are from a common root, but have become differentiated through the course of time. Games, art, poetry, all leisure-time pursuits emerged from religion. Since religion is the *actum primum* and all society was in the beginning religious, it stands to reason that these activities had a religious foundation. Historians of early civilizations would confirm Durkheim's position, for in some cases it is clear that myths, plays, poetry, games and art have all had a religious connection visible in the civilizations of the Near East, of Greece and Rome (see, for example, Harrison 1913). The activities of *la vie légère* have become secularized in the course of time and such a movement is but a part of a continuing process of secularization, which we describe in detail in a later chapter (see ch. 24).

Durkheim's social puritanism is open to many charges and the dichotomy is not without problems of application. The most obvious charge is his denigration of works of art, of great pieces of music which are more than recreational, more than just items of fantasy or a mere provocation of the senses. Artists are not only serious in what they are doing, but their works express what is serious in man and society. Through their thought and work, many of the realities of society become manifested. For Durkheim, the achievements of artists are relegated to the carefree side of life. According to him, only the scientist and the philosopher take seriously what is real. But an extension of this turns on Durkheim's concept of science, the end of which is to produce theories about reality. This can never be the case for the artist, who, whilst he might have some kind of theory, has as his ultimate end action, not the production of theory (1900b:610/ t.1973a:4). That Durkheim has very little understanding of the nature of art form seems quite extraordinary when he was living in the centre of the art and musical world of his time (but see Tiryakian 1979a). It also means, as Bellah has noted, that in denigrating art Durkheim cuts himself off from one possible source of giving to society that which he felt it lacked, namely, a positive, lively morality (1973:xliii). Another weakness is that of conceptualization. Everywhere that Durkheim wishes to contrast *la vie sérieuse* with what we have called *la vie légère*, and particularly in *L'Éducation morale* and *Les Formes élémentaires*, he fails to make a clear distinction between the various components of that which is not serious. So it is that art, games, music, poetry, vertigo, spontaneous celebration are all spoken of as a piece and are generally described as recreational activities. Can one really accept this? Is Bach to be lumped together with whist, or Stanley Spencer with bingo! As in the notion of the profane, the weakness of the dichotomy, which we have projected, is that one of the contrasting components is really a residual term. All the weaknesses of the term profane are to be found within *la vie légère*, and even more. Durkheim was honest enough to admit that the line of demarcation between the two components was not always very clear and, as we have already noted, one activity moves into the other, often with scarce recognition on the part of participants that a change of activity has taken place. Nevertheless, it is morally necessary to differentiate these types of activities, for, as Durkheim said, a society that is based solely on recreational activities is a very weak society. On the other hand, he clearly stated that the activities of *la vie légère* are 'by no means negligible', for 'recreation is one of the forms of the moral remaking which is the principal object of the positive rite' (547/382). At least Durkheim admits the necessity for periods of recreation, which obviously strengthen *la vie sérieuse*. The abiding question is whether or not he makes an artificial line of demarcation – one which supports his moral outlook.

Durkheim's seriousness encourages him to overlook the fact that in a ritual, the priest or officiant, together with the assistants if any, are taking part in a drama or a performance. Indeed, to perform a ritual is to act, that is, to make symbolic movements – movements intended, for example, to represent a god or a religious event which, it is claimed, occurred in the past. The priest, therefore, even in his most serious moments stands before the people as an actor as well as an officiant concerned with reality.

The notion of *la vie sérieuse* as a kind of litmus paper which is able to detect what is central, religious or sacred has at first sight considerable advantage for Durkheim. It enables him to untie the complexity of rituals, to help bind together the various components of his theory and at the same time to point to those elements of society and of religion which have to be taken very seriously.

Apart from the problem of evaluating art and leisure within a total situation, the dichotomy is not as easy to apply as it first appears. There are always grey areas which fit both the serious and the less serious sides of life. There is also a circularity of argument. What is serious is decided by what is sacred: what is sacred must be serious. However, if the concepts are seen as constructs or ideal types, they have potential merit in analysing ritual, religious and other social phenomena, and need to be further explored.

20 Ritual and myth: primacy or parity?

1 The two components

As we have often stated, Durkheim divided religion into two main components: belief and ritual (see ch. 17.1). The belief component can be further divided into moral directives, interdicts, instructions, creedal statements, and myths. Myths contain religious 'truths' enshrined in stories, repeatedly recited, which are sometimes held to be historically true, sometimes not. In this chapter we consider the relation between religious belief and action, and more specifically, the interrelations between myth and ritual, especially in preliterate societies.

To say the two components are directly linked with one another is a truism. Before the middle of the nineteenth century, however, the connection was scarcely recognized when, because of the dominance of Protestant thinking in academic circles, scant attention was given to ritual in either Christian or non-Christian contexts. There, exclusive emphasis was based on belief. As we have already noted, ritual was seen as little more than pagan or Romish superstition (see ch. 17.3). Robertson Smith was amongst the first to demonstrate the importance of ritual in relation to myth or dogma. The classical scholar and admirer of Durkheim, Jane Harrison, also did much to try to establish the relation between myth and ritual in her book *Themis* (1912). It was she, along with Gilbert Murray, who showed that Greek tragedy had ritual form, often by way of a sacred dance, or ending with a formal theophany. She attempted to prove that ritual gave rise to drama and art (1913; Duncan 1960:103). In the 1930s there emerged in Britain the Myth and Ritual school led by the Old Testament scholar who had turned to anthropology, S. H. Hooke (see Hooke 1933, 1935 and 1958). The interest of the school was centred on the early civilizations of the ancient Near East, with special reference to the ritual and myths of the Jews. The school emphasized the fact that myth and ritual were very closely associated in such peoples as the Egyptians, Babylonians and Canaanites who all possessed rituals intended to secure the well-being of society, and related to the dramatic ritual of the death and resurrection of a king. In this respect the school was strongly influenced by the work of Frazer. With the ritual there was always found a myth, whose repetition had equal power with that of the action. Much of the debate surrounded the question of how common the myths and rituals were amongst the peoples with whom the Jews came into contact. The work of Hooke and his associates strengthened the notion that ritual and myth were inseparably associated with one another. From the archaeological evidence of these civilizations it was conjectured that ritual was always accompanied by myth or dogma. Through unknown factors the two elements became separated so that either the ritual or the myth has been lost to man's knowledge. Hence one may find a ritual unaccompanied by a myth or a myth seen only as a story without a ritual.

The problem of the relation between myth (and belief) and ritual has consequences as much for the sociologist as for the historian or student of religion. For example, it raises the question of whether a religion can exist or be said to be effective if, on the one hand, it has no cult or, on the other, no belief-system. If it be argued that both elements are required, what is the 'mixture' of the two? Further, within a larger context, the relation of the two, seen in either historical or structural terms, raises issues concerning the nature of society itself, a subject we have considered before (ch. 13). Does a society need common religious beliefs and some form of common action related to those beliefs, for it to exist or to be 'healthy'?

These are large questions which cannot be answered here – nor is there any attempt to deal definitively with the relation between myth and ritual – but since they are in some sense often being debated, it is profitable to examine Durkheim's approach. It was he who sharpened the debate, even if he did not originally raise the points at issue.

2 The primacy of ritual

We have already had occasion to notice the influence of the work of Robertson Smith on Durkheim, not least in stressing the importance of ritual (see ch. 4.2; ch. 17.3; Jones 1977). Robertson Smith not only counterbalanced the dominant part that myth and belief had in the study of religion by giving prominence to ritual, he went so far as to hold that rite was prior to belief (1889/1894:17ff.). This means, almost in keeping with Pareto's thinking, man acts first and reasons about his actions afterwards. Man is thus seen as essentially an acting creature who is unconditionally controlled by internal or external stimulae, and may be said to be 'irrational'. More recently the anthropologist Edmund Leach has openly declared his acceptance of Robertson Smith's position in making ritual action prior to explanatory belief (1968:524). Rituals, he holds, exert power and can therefore 'alter the state of the world because they invoke power' (ibid.). Both Smith and Durkheim saw in ritual, as we have seen, the characteristic of obligation from which there is no escape. Ritual is a force external to man which makes him behave in particular ways.

In referring to the leading role that cult plays in every religion, and to the necessity of common action in social life, Durkheim wrote at the end of *The Elementary Forms*:

> It is because society can only make its influence felt if it is active, and it is only active if the individuals of which it is composed are assembled together and act in common. In common action it becomes aware of itself and establishes itself: it is above all an active co-operation . . . thus action dominates religious life simply because it is society which is its source. (598/418/147)

Social action is thus necessary for society and religion to be effective. But the question that Durkheim does not answer categorically is whether such action is mediated by *représentations collectives*.

In reviewing the sociological study of religion by Guyau, Durkheim criticizes him for emphasizing the intellectual or speculative source of religion rather than the practical or social source. Durkheim would reverse the order and give priority to the social, which admittedly is not quite the same as ritual, but is practical and is in fact related to action. More important, Durkheim holds that faith is the 'result of practical causes' (1887b:309–10/ t.1975a:35–7).

Those who would maintain that Durkheim gives priority to action might well point to his important concept of collective effervescence, which is considered in the chapters ahead. Gathering together in religious fervour and participating in common rituals gives rise to new ideas, argues Durkheim, and strengthens those already held. Clearly action dominates such occasions which reach the height of frenzy. Man allows himself to act with a great deal of freedom.

There is also a strong hint in Durkheim, in his early article on defining religion, that he sees ritual as being prior in time to myth. He writes: 'in less advanced religions, rites are already developed and definite when myths are still very rudimentary' (1899a(ii):23 n.1/t.1975a:99 n.25). And he further suggests that all myths are 'dependent on some rite or other' (ibid.).

One thing cannot be doubted and that is that Durkheim sees in the historical development of religions – and for him Christianity stands at the pinnacle – that there has been a decline in the level of ritual and a greater emphasis on ideals (belief). In *L'Évolution pédagogique en France*, he contrasts religions of antiquity, especially the religion of Greece, with Christianity. The former were first and foremost systems of rites (1938a/1969f:323/ t.1977a:282). The rituals were intended to ensure the regular progress of the universe. By contrast, the Christian religion was more concerned with man and his soul than with nature. It was essentially an 'idealist' religion, where mind and spirit were of greater concern than the needs of the body. (See ch. 23.2.) Further, the God of the Christians was one who was to be worshipped 'in spirit and in truth'. This means of course that Christianity tended to give ritual a much smaller place than did other earlier religions. With historical development in mind, one might thus argue that Durkheim gives primacy to ritual when man's earliest religions are being considered.

Not surprisingly, there have been commentators who have held precisely this – that in Durkheim ritual is accorded primacy. Thus Goldenweiser in his analysis of Durkheim's treatment of ritual, especially of mourning rites, suggests that Durkheim views ritual as 'a spontaneous response of the group to an emotional situation' (1915/r.1975:221). It is to be contrasted with beliefs which are more reflective and speculative and are intended to be an exposition of the rites.

Talcott Parsons is one of the few commentators who in the 1930s attempted to analyse Durkheim's theory of ritual in detail (see 1937:429–41). He concluded that in the last analysis, not least due to his theory of collective effervescence, Durkheim gave priority to action rather than to thought. Social process must be 'as a *component of a system of action*' (ibid.:440). One consequence is that sociology should be a science of action – 'of the ultimate common value element *in its relations* to other elements of action' (ibid.). And Parsons goes so far as to suggest that in his theory of religion Durkheim came very near to the position that 'the central importance of religion lies in its relation to action, not to thought. But it never quite broke through' (ibid.). Similarly, Ruth Benedict concludes from her reading of Durkheim that action comes first. She is much more critical of Durkheim than is Talcott Parsons and writes:

> The contention of Durkheim and many others that religion arises from ritualism as such must be challenged, for the most extreme ritualistic formalism does not convert a council of elders or affinal exchange into an aspect even of the already existing religious complexes. Durkheim's theoretical position is untenable once it is recognized that ritual may surround any field of behavior and of itself does not give birth to religion any more than it gives birth to art or to social organization. (1934:396)

Before trying to assess the notion that ritual has primacy over belief in Durkheim's work, it is necessary to consider first other possibilities.

3 Primacy of myth and belief

Durkheim did not treat myths in the systematic way that he analysed ritual. There was no attempt to classify them as he had classified rites. Nor did he attempt to portray the functions of myth as he had attempted to portray the functions of the rites of the Arunta. Admittedly, he carefully examined their myths, but did not reach that order of generalization which he did with ritual. The beginnings of some systematic approach might be seen in his work where he collaborated with his nephew, Marcel Mauss, in the relatively early article, 'De Quelques formes primitives de classification' (1903a(i)/t.1963b), where in dealing with issues in the sociology of knowledge the two authors maintain that myths are closely related to classificatory systems (see especially ibid.:63ff./77ff.). He studiously avoided the work of Frazer on myths in the *Golden Bough*, doubtless because of its methodological pitfalls, although he originally followed him in the matter of totemism. The systematic treatment of myths is by no means easy and was to come after his time, with the structural analysis put forward by Claude Lévi-Strauss and his English admirer, Edmund Leach. Mircea Eliade has also made serious contributions to the study of the symbolism of myths from a phenomenological perspective.

On the whole Durkheim concentrated not so much on myth as on religious belief; not on stories or legends, but on rational or dogmatic statements about what was held to be religiously true. His theory centred on belief-systems or religious concepts such as the idea of God, of spirit, of the soul, and so on. How he should tackle imaginative, flamboyant stories and legends appears to be outside his methodological grasp. As Burridge has said, although Durkheim grasped myth as social fact and *représentation*, he was 'unable to realize the unparalleled opportunity presented in Australian material: myth as an integral part of culture and the social situation' (1973:193).

In the 1899 article on definition, he notes the complexity of religious *représentations* and points to the following characteristics (1899a(ii):18/t.1975a:89):

1 The object of faith can be a purely ideal being, created by the imagination.
2 It can be a directly observable, concrete reality.
3 It can be an erudite and systematized creed.
4 It can also be a few simple articles.
5 It can be a moral directive, a doctrine for living as in Christianity and Buddhism.

6 Purely cosmogonic or historical dogmas.
7 Myths and religious legends.

Perhaps part of the problem is that Durkheim finds it difficult to deal with myths because they are open to wide interpretations compared with other *représentations* which are in all probability less ambiguous. In one of the few places where he talks about myth in relation to other forms of religious thought, he writes:

Nevertheless the luxuriant growth of myths and legends, theogonic and cosmological systems, etc., which grow out of religious thought, is not directly related to the particular features of the social morphology. Thus it is that the social nature of religion has been so often misunderstood. (1898b/ 1924a:43–4/t.1953b:31)

The 'luxuriant growth' of myths mean that they cannot be related to social structure, unlike *représentations collectives*. Durkheim's conclusion here stands very much opposed to that of his later, half-disciple Lévi-Strauss, whose structural analysis can be seen as a kind of breakthrough in treating myth as an autonomous realm of thought.

Durkheim never attempted a formal definition of myth. The nearest he comes to it is in a footnote in his early essay on defining religious phenomena. In speaking about the relation of myth and ritual, he says: 'the word myth is reserved for more highly developed and more or less systematized religious *représentations*' (1899a(ii):23 n.1/t.1975a:99 n. 25). Durkheim wanted to make the distinction between myth and religious belief and he goes on: 'This restriction may be legitimate; but another word is needed to designate simpler religious *représentations*, distinguishable from myths proper by reason of their greater simplicity' (ibid.). Durkheim never found the word, and although he did not attempt to define myth with the same rigour that he defined religion, he did delineate several characteristics about myths which are generally acceptable today. Every myth contains a *représentation*, 'even very elaborated, of man and the universe' (1922a:46/t.1956a:77). He said myths and dogmas 'teach us about existence', 'describe nature to us', they have 'something majestic about them' and are 'set apart' (1899a(ii):19/t.1975a:90). Myths are thus related to the sacred (50/36/113). The 'strangest of myths . . . express some need'

(3/2/104), although Durkheim never says what that need is. They contain reality (601/421/150), but at root all mythologies demonstrate 'mental confusion' (337/235/140).

In a passage seldom referred to in *L'Évolution pédagogique*, Durkheim developed this last point. He affirmed that today different systems of logic have followed on after one another and continue to coexist (1938a/1969f:373/t.1977a:326). He writes:

> Now, there are in existence symbolic systems which in the course of history have played a role as great as, if not greater than, that of science but in which this [scientific] principle is violated at every turn: I refer to the symbolic systems of religion. Myths constantly treat of beings which at the same moment are both themselves and not themselves, which are at once single and double, spiritual and material. (ibid.)

Such mythical thinking was needed, he continues to argue, in order for societies to give expression to themselves through religious thought systems. These, though often mythical in form, had a certain logic which was not that of science, and were necessary for the survival of society. One conclusion is incontrovertible: religious *représentations*, including both myth and dogma, have their own logic, and that of myth is not identical to that of dogma.

We briefly consider occasions where Durkheim gives primacy to religious thought (myth and belief, particularly the latter). In an early review of *Ecclesiastical Institutions* by Herbert Spencer, himself a rationalist, Durkheim wrote:

> Religion, therefore, is merely a form of custom, like law and morality. What, perhaps, best distinguishes this from all others is that it asserts itself not only over conduct, but over the *conscience*. It not only dictates actions but ideas and sentiments. In short *religion starts with faith*, that is to say, with any belief accepted or experienced without argument. (1886a:68/t.1975a:21; our italics)

In *Suicide* Durkheim defined religion as a 'system of symbols by means of which society becomes conscious of itself; it is the characteristic way of thinking of collective existence' (1897a:352/ t.1951a:312). Of course, it is true that both action and ritual can be or are symbolic, but it is clear from this reference that Durkheim is thinking of beliefs, of religious *représentations*.

369

There is one place where Durkheim states quite categorically that the *raison d'être* of cults is not in their intended actions, but their effect on the mind. In referring to sacrifice in the middle of Book III of *The Elementary Forms*, he writes:

> The real reason for the existence of the cults, even those which are the most materialistic in appearance, is not to be sought in the acts which they prescribe, but in the internal and moral regeneration which these acts aid in bringing about. The things which the worshipper really gives his gods are not the goods which he places upon the altars, nor the blood which he lets flow from his veins: it is his thought. (495/346)

Durkheim's emphasis on cognition (*pensée*) is most significant. In the previous sentences he refers to the mental states (*états mentaux*) aroused by ritual. The ultimate object of the action therefore must be intellectual and here Durkheim shows not least his abiding Cartesianism.

Other evidence for the primacy of thought comes in his references to the decline of traditional western religion and the emerging new religion of humanism or individualism (see chs 24 and 26). The reason why the old rituals have ceased to be practised is because man no longer subscribes to the associated beliefs and myths. Thus, when theology is rejected, so is the ritual. 'But men cannot take part in ceremonies which seem to have no point, nor accept a faith which is totally incomprehensible to them' (615/430/ 160; but see ch. 25.3). Of course, it is true, as Durkheim sees, that one form of ritual replaces another, but it would seem that it is always belief which takes the initiative and cult follows on afterwards. This point was made quite early on in the review of Herbert Spencer and seems to contradict what he said at much the same time in examining a book by Guyau (see secn 2 of this chapter):

> Religion, therefore, is merely a form of custom, like law and morality. What, perhaps, best distinguishes this from all others is that it asserts itself not only over conduct but over *consciences*. It not only dictates actions but ideas and sentiments. In short, religion starts with faith, that is to say, with any belief accepted or experienced without argument. (1886a:68/t.1975a:21)

In modern society, which has rejected in large measure the detailed orthodox beliefs of Christianity and Judaism, vaguer beliefs rise over their ashes. But the simplicity in belief is accompanied by virtually no cult at all. Durkheim was fully conscious of this. Writing in an earlier period, he said:

> Doubtless, one cannot believe firmly in progress without it having some effect on one's way of life; however, there are no precise practices attached to such an idea. It is a faith without a corresponding ritual (1899a(ii):22/t.1975a:92)

What was applicable to a belief in the idea of progress also pertained to the cult of man, which is singularly shorn of ritual. Indeed, humanism by appeal to the reason is a ritual-less 'religion', concentrating entirely on belief (see ch. 26.6). Durkheim implied that ritual was something of the past. In writing about individualism in 1898, he said:

> For we know today that a religion does not necessarily imply symbols and rites in the full sense, or temples and priests. All this external apparatus is merely its superficial aspect. Essentially, it is nothing other than a system of collective beliefs and practices that have a special authority. (1898c:25/t.1969d/r.1975:66)

Durkheim is referring, of course, to religion in his day, and 'practices' at the end of the quotation mean moral practices. This indicates his basic attitude towards ritual, and his preference – within the context of religion – for belief, because the 'rational' is expressed better in morality than in ritual. More important, however, would be the indication that *représentations collectives* are at the base of religion and that rite is an appendix. Clearly, this is a rejection of the thought of Robertson Smith, whom he had read a few years before the publication of the article on individualism. The tendency towards a more 'rational' type of religion is seen in the decline of myth as the cognitive element and in a greater emphasis on reasoned belief. This striving after rationalism, which Durkheim felt was actually happening but which needed stressing, was mentioned in his lectures on education, where he said:

> We must disengage them [children] from their symbols,

371

present them in their rational nakedness, so to speak, and find a way to make the children feel their reality without recourse to any mythological intermediary. This is the first order of business: we want moral education to become rational and at the same time to produce all the results that should be expected from it. (1925a:13/t.1961a:11)

Here is a further example of the way in which Durkheim saw the difference between morality and traditional religion. The former did not have associated with it myth and ritual.

Another reason why it might be concluded that Durkheim gave primacy to belief (and myth) rests on the argument put forward by such scholars as Georges Davy, Gaston Richard and, in more recent times, Talcott Parsons, that in the course of Durkheim's approach to sociology he abandoned morphological factors as social determinants and turned more to *représentations*. thus supporting an 'idealist' position (ch. 15.3). Parsons went so far as to suggest that Durkheim 'in escaping from the toils of positivism has over shot the mark and gone clean over to idealism' (1937:445). Quite irrespective of whether this was the case, it should be noted that Davy held that it occurred after Durkheim became increasingly interested in religion. Religion in primitive societies is the locus of the sacred and of the collective thought of society. That Durkheim should have become increasingly interested in religion after reading Robertson Smith might seem to suggest that, since Durkheim gave prominence to mental or cognitive factors, he saw in religion the primacy of the mental over action. Those scholars who see such a change in Durkheim's thought also lay emphasis on the fact that he sees a cluster of *représentations collectives* as being necessary for a society to exist. Arguing from the evidence of totemism amongst the Arunta Durkheim holds, states Davy, that reality for the tribe is located in their beliefs (*croyances*) (1920:106). All turns on belief. What we are suggesting is that, if it is true that Durkheim places such emphasis on *représentations* as factors of explanation in the most developed stage of his thought, it is an indication of the primacy of *représentations* over ritual and action.

The question may be raised as to whether or not there is in Parsons's position some contradiction, as he had already suggested that Durkheim's thought gave primacy to action. If there is a contradiction, Parsons does not seem to be aware of it. One might defend him, however, by saying that the change which Durkheim underwent was essentially a change which caused him to seek explanatory factors, not a change in statements about the composition of religion or society. *Représentations* are only vehicles of expression. In the last analysis what is represented is society or aspects of society. Interestingly enough, Parsons in a more recent consideration of *The Elementary Forms* makes no mention of the issue of his earlier thesis that Durkheim changed to a more idealist position, and stresses instead an evolutionary approach (Parsons 1973).

That Durkheim gives primacy to myth, belief, thought, as against action is understandable in the light of his rationalist position. He and other rationalists took the view that man's prime ability is to think and to reflect. Man is indeed *homo sapiens*. This fact perhaps accounts for the scant attention Durkheim pays to myths themselves. On his own admission, he considers that they contain irrational elements in the form of stories and are based on some kind of mental confusion. His position also accounts for the reason why there are far more examples of his assertion that belief has priority over ritual rather than the reverse. And one cannot overlook the fact that for Durkheim there are commonly held beliefs at the heart of society without which it could not exist. This position he always held. Even in a society characterized by organic solidarity, it was necessary to have such a base (1893b: bk II, ch. 3). As he said: 'It is clear a society cannot hold together unless there exists among its members a certain intellectual and moral community' (1898c:10/t.1969d/r.1975:66).

4 Myth and ritual: parity of status

We have shown that there is some evidence to indicate that Durkheim held that rite takes precedence over myth and belief. In this, he followed Robertson Smith. The greater part of the evidence points in the reverse direction. But before such a conclusion is unequivocally assumed it is necessary to examine a third possibility: that ritual and myth are of equal importance and status and that it is impossible to say which has priority or primacy.

Amongst many students of religion, not least phenomenologists, this is the current 'orthodox' position – to make them equal but different. And there are many references in Durkheim which would support it.

Nowhere else does Durkheim so carefully place myth and ritual side by side as in his early paper on defining religious phenomena. For example:

> Ritual is an element of all religion, which is no less essential than faith. (1899a(ii):20/t.1975a:91)

> Since religious practices and beliefs are so interdependent, they cannot be separated by science and must belong to a single study. (ibid.:21/92)

> The practices translate the beliefs into action and the beliefs are often only an interpretation of the practices. (ibid.)

> Thought and action are closely linked to the point of being inseparable. Religion corresponds to a stage of development where these two functions are not yet dissociated. (ibid.)

Also written at much the same time was a letter to Gaston Richard (dated 11 May 1899 and published in 1928), which again shows that Durkheim sees a mutual interdependence of rite and myth, and it also indicates Durkheim's notion of the function of myth:

> The idea [of Lang] of placing myths outside religion appears to me to be monstrous. Very often – some people say it is always the case – a myth only outlines the rite on which it then proceeds. The two elements cannot be separated. The myth under its rudimentary and basic form is the *représentation* of some thing almost sacred. If this *représentation* is eliminated, what remains of religion? Myths are (1) the origin of what is practised (2) the way in which the people explain the actions of the cult. (1928b:299 n.1)

Later, and in considering moral facts, Durkheim maintained a similar position:

> There is no rite, however material it might be, that does not form a part of a more or less organized system of *représentations* that will explain and justify it. Man needs to understand what he does, though often he is easily satisfied:

this is often the reason lying behind a myth. (1906b/1924a:113/
t.1953b:76)

And this position of mutuality was reaffirmed at the end of his
life in *The Elementary Forms*, in concluding Book II on beliefs:

> Of course the cult depends upon beliefs, but it also reacts
> upon them. So in order to understand them better, it is
> important to understand it better. (424/296)

And further on in the same book, writing of the many functions
that rituals perform and how at the same time they represent a
unity, Durkheim remarks that 'in all its forms, its object [of cult]
is to raise man above himself and to make him lead a life superior
to that' he would live if left to his own devices (592/414). And
Durkheim concludes that 'beliefs express this life in terms of
représentations; rites organize it and regulate its functioning'
(ibid.). Ritual therefore dramatizes *représentations* and human
relations. In considering the ritual system of the Australian Aboriginals, he comes nearest to relating ritual and myth when he
considers the ceremony of the Black Snake amongst the Warramunga (59ff./370ff.). In it the mythical history of the ancestor
Thalaualla is ritually portrayed. The story is dramatically acted
out and to the manual actions are added hymns. The object of
the rite is not directly to increase the totemic species. Durkheim
concludes that the rite can only give vitality to the beliefs and
prevent them from being effaced from memory. The rites thus
'revivify the most essential elements of the *conscience collective*'
(536/375). In this way they form a means whereby the group
renews the sentiment it has of itself and of its notion of unity. In
addition, individuals are strengthened in their social sentiments.
A similar connection and conclusion is made in the myth of the
snake Wollunqua. Again, the object is commemorative, but at
the same time it strengthens common *représentations*.

Here, then, are a number of examples which would correct any
dogmatic assertion that Durkheim comes down heavily on one
side or the other. Cult and belief, although different in form, are
very much a whole.

5 Parity of status: difficulties and problems

In attempting to resolve the question about the priority of ritual and myth – and a relation between the two is beyond question – two procedures are open to the inquirer. The first is to answer the question historically in an attempt to ascertain the priority of the one to the other. The second is to reach a conclusion by analysing the structure or function of myth and ritual, and this inevitably opens the door to philosophical issues as well as a theory of society. These alternative approaches have already been met in connection with the relation of religion to society (see ch. 14).

One hardly needs to be reminded that it is impossible to know with any historical certainty 'what happened in the beginning'; whether belief emerged before action or vice versa, or whether the two grew together. For Durkheim, primacy in this context is not primacy in time. It is true that Durkheim was always ready to use historical data, if it shed light on the problem. Such data, however, comes relatively late in the development of mankind. Instead, Durkheim relies on 'elementary forms' which are themselves 'historical' in order to deduce his generalizations about the two components of religion. Reliance thus has to be placed upon a structural or functional approach, and here the method seems somewhat shaky because one uses evidence culled from different periods of history and from a number of different sources. One appeals to the logic of the case; to what one *sees* as the structure of various elements. Whatever conclusion is reached, it can only be little more than a hypothesis.

We have just shown that the notion of mutuality between myth and ritual was strongly supported by Durkheim, and this, in turn, may well have influenced others (for example, Hooke in the Myth and Ritual school and certainly Jane Harrison). A general knowledge of early and primitive religions would indicate, on all grounds of common sense, the close link between the two components. Rituals are the techniques for creating close relations with spirits or deities acknowledged by the believer. What the person does religiously is confirmed mentally by what he believes. What he believes reflects what he practises. In order to understand the ritual itself, man has to interpret it and understand its actual and symbolic meaning (cf. Benedict 1933:180). As Ruth Benedict has said, 'religious practices are unintelligible except by way of their mythology', and one of the clearest examples of this is the study of the dairy rituals of the Todas (ibid.). Thus it might be said that myth and ritual are two sides of the same coin. The imprint on one side helps one to understand the imprint on the other. In the case of myth and ritual, they both refer to some ultimate or defined end, consciously or unconsciously held. The mutuality is most clearly seen in the Christian eucharist.

The symmetry of the pattern is attractive: after all, structure implies some symmetry. The danger is that one imposes a symmetrical relation where in fact it does not exist. Frazer found it so attractive and was so convinced of the interdependency of ritual and myth that he tended, it is said, to invent one or other of the components where it was missing (Leach 1968:522). If one replaces belief with myth, it might be argued that every ritual has an accompanying belief. Most would want to support this hypothesis. But what of those endless beliefs which have no ritual? Or creedal statements which are not directly accompanied by rite? Again, what is one to say of those minor rituals, such as bowing to the altar in churches, which have grown up by tradition and which are not accompanied by any myth or theology? Further, one might well suggest in the matter of Judaeo-Christian myth that there was once a ritual that accompanied the creation stories of the book of Genesis. But what of other parts of the Bible? What rituals would accompany the book of Ecclesiastes? Symmetry is attractive when a *myth* is involved or where dogmas are directly associated with rites, but it is clearly the case that many theologies and dogmas exist which are not accompanied by ritual or even by moral action. It is now widely agreed amongst those who study primitive societies, let alone those dealing with more advanced ones, that there is no general rule about a myth having its associated ritual and vice versa (Ginsberg 1956:223). One can only say that it is a fruitful hypothesis which can be applied in certain cases where a mutual interdependence between myth and ritual can be established (see Kluckhohn 1942:65).

To support the concept of parity, and at the same time to avoid some of the difficulties in upholding it in the methods that have just been proposed, other types of arguments have been put forward. One, which is firmly upheld by the Myth and Ritual school of Hooke, is that the spoken word is as efficacious as the act in the eyes of participants. Therefore both myth and ritual have equal force. Another stems from Leach's attempt to interpret myth and ritual in the context of communication theory and to hold that actions 'say' things as much as 'do' things (1968:522). 'All speech is a form of customary behaviour', and 'all customary behaviour is a form of speech' (ibid.). In part what Leach is saying is true enough. But what is said in action is different from what is said by word of mouth or in the written word. One might indicate something of the other, but the medium, action or belief, determines the amount that can be communicated and the quality of what is communicated.

The difficulty about parity lies in the issue of what constitutes ritual. If ritual is said to be action in which there, amongst other qualities, is a known or conscious end, then thought, belief, myth, custom must precede the action. Further, if it is held that ritual is never spontaneous action, never based solely on impulse or psychological drive, then the question of ends becomes paramount. And this is precisely Durkheim's position. For him ritual is never uncontrolled, impulsive without thought, without in some way being directed by a mental process. This is not to say that every participant of ritual is conscious of the end. Individuals may appear to act in a way that is purely intuitive, but a closer examination would show that such actions flow out of a given belief-system. They are controlled by the parameters set by the social group. In *The Elementary Forms*, rites are to be distinguished from other actions by their *objects*, and the object of the rite is expressed in the belief (50/36/113). There is a problem here because the word object (*objet*) means either a thing, that is, the god who is to be worshipped or the animal to be sacrificed; or it can refer to the intention of the act, what the worshipper hopes to achieve in the ritual, that is, its purpose. Durkheim is often not clear about the sense in which he is using the word. No matter, however, which is intended, he states that the answer comes from the accompanying myth or dogma. In elucidation and explanation, Durkheim seeks to establish two levels of meaning. The first is that meaning which comes from dogma or myth, and we might say, by extension, to the beliefs of individual participants and another level of meaning is that which is established by the observer or the scientist who believes that he can take explanation from the level of the particular to that of the general.

So what deductions can be made about the mixture of myth and ritual in religion, defined at least in Durkheim's terms?

Whereas, as we have noted, Durkheim for a number of reasons wants to assert parity of status between ritual and belief, he secretly awards first prize to belief. This gesture ties in with his concept of collective *représentations* being essential for a society to exist. Belief of some kind, there has to be: ritual not so. In some modern forms of religion ritual scarcely exists (ch. 26.6). In *The Elementary Forms*, in the very structure of the book, Durkheim treats the belief and totemistic systems of the Arunta before their ritual, as Parsons has recently noted (1973:172). In this way Durkheim stands by the great rationalist tradition with which he was identified. He thus remains thoroughly Cartesian, but extends the scope of Cartesian analysis by taking seriously the 'irrational' myths and belief-systems of a primitive tribe. Here, Durkheim deals directly with basic sociological and philosophical problems concerning the rational and irrational, and so contributed to the continuing debate on the subject in sociology and philosophy. But for Durkheim, thought is not necessarily rational or logical or reasonable, it is basically 'representational'. It consists amongst other things of religious *représentations*, of man's view of himself, of the world, and of worlds outside this world. Durkheim admits the existence of scientific thought, but does not characterize all other thought as being irrational – a classification which is to be made by the philosopher or scientific thinker. The so-called irrational has to be understood in order that social processes may be understood. Durkheim, however, is a rationalist in so far as he maintains that human actions spring from desires and beliefs, although always with the rider that those desires and beliefs are derived from or modified by social norms – society itself. Actions, therefore, can in some sense be predicted from a known set of beliefs. Man, essentially a 'representational' creature, creates concepts and ideals by which he relates his actions. So, if the first prize is given to *représentations*, ritual comes a close second.

Whilst a simple relation between the two components of religion, myth (belief) and ritual (action), is not tenable, a study of them clarifies deeper issues in Durkheim's thought, not least about the nature of society. At the same time his analysis underlines the 'ideal' pattern of maximum religious control in cases where the two components are mutually supporting.

21 Effervescent assembly: the source of religious change and strength

I The process

1 Religious and social change

When Durkheim indicated that he was not searching for the origin of religion, he had in mind that order of origin postulated by such writers as Spencer, Tylor, Müller (see, for example, 1912a: bk I, Chs I–III). For him, and for many others subsequently, it was impossible to discover a moment in history when man created religion as the result of a reflection on dreams, or an inspirational flash in beholding the wonders of the universe, or in some similar single event or series of events. Nevertheless, Durkheim was bent on unearthing the roots of religion and he attempted to locate them, as we have noted, at the very heart of society – its social structure. A close relation exists between the components of society and religion which is itself a component of society. In this way religion is to be explained and understood in social terms, although religion is more than just the social. The demonstration of this proposition lay in logical connection rather than in empirically substantiated hypotheses. Durkheim's great achievement was in imaginatively pointing to relations between concepts, not in stating propositions which could be rigorously proved.

But to point to the social structure of society and even to speak of the functional nature of religion as being its root, still leaves a lot unsaid. If religion undergirds and strengthens society, how does one account for changes? For new doctrines? For modification of ritual? If it is suggested that as society changes so does religion, it is legitimate to argue the other way round and to say that society changes as does religion. This position is also to be found in Durkheim. One is thus faced with the threat of a circular argument. To account for change it is necessary to introduce a third force which is not identified with social structure or religion. Durkheim indeed saw, as simplistic functionalists in later generations failed to realize, that a non-functional factor has to be introduced in order to explain social change and therefore social behaviour.

Although he realized the need to posit such a factor, he did not, it seems, successfully unearth it. Critics have not been slow to point to the fact that, unlike Herbert Spencer and Karl Marx, both of whom he criticized, he did not present anything approaching a theory of change. It is true that in his early days, he employed the concept of social density in an attempt to account for the movement of societies from a state characterized by mechanical solidarity to that marked by organic solidarity (1893b: bk II, ch. V). This concept, based on biological factors and involving the increase of population in a given area, implies a growth of social interaction. An increase of social density forces a segmental form of society, such as a pre-literate society, to establish larger groups and to build towns and cities. Social density thus gives rise to modern western society. Durkheim never again extensively used the term. It is crude for purposes of explanation and treads too near biological and psychological paths to be comfortably situated in the independent domain of sociology. But to write off Durkheim at this point and to suggest that he was not aware of change, or concerned with it, or that he offered no explanation for it at all is simply not true. He was living in a rapidly changing France which had experienced the 1789 Revolution and the 1870 Franco-Prussian war and the ensuing Paris Commune. He could hardly have been oblivious to social change! Social change was central to the series of lectures that he gave on the evolution of pedagogic thought in France (1938a). Of the existence of change, he was deeply aware. None the less he seemed quite content to go no further than to refer to change in terms of historical events or to the findings of historians. For him historical evidence gives unequivocal answers. Thus, in *The Division of Labour* he writes: 'there is one truth that history teaches us' (1893b/1902b:143/ t.1933b:169; and see Bellah 1959). As part of his sociological analysis he did not produce a systematic theory which accounted for gradual changes or for what one might call, in the broadest sense, social evolution. Instead, he pointed to periods of radical or revolutionary change and concentrated on these. Nor is it surprising that such crucial changes were derived from a model of religious change and they were both basically changes in thought – in *représentations collectives*. Religious thought for Durkheim is but one category of thought in general. His approach to change is associated with his concept of effervescence, which, as Goldenweiser has rightly noted, he alone amongst sociologists of his day attempted to explore (Goldenweiser 1915/r.1975:218).

2 Collective effervescence described

A limited acquaintance with Durkheim's works would suggest that the notion of effervescence is to be found in the third period of the development of his analysis of religion, for the idea is treated in considerable detail in *The Elementary Forms* (1912a:bk II, Ch. VII). Durkheim's study of the ethnographic material on the Arunta would appear to be the source of his notion of effervescence. Such was Goldenweiser's view (1915/r.1975:218). To be sure, at first sight it receives little reference in books, essays and articles outside *The Elementary Forms*. But the assertion is not true, in that the concept is not found exclusively within that book. Two years before its publication, he wrote in his famous paper presented at the International Congress of Philosophy in Bologna, that the concept of the ideal and its contents were created and re-created by a 'new kind of psychic life' – by effervescence (1911b/ 1924a:133/t.1953b:91). But there are earlier references. Durkheim always associated the French Revolution with collective effervescence and did so not only in *The Elementary Forms*, but in a review in 1905 (1905a(ii)(2)). There are indications that he was thinking along these lines as early as 1897 in his book *Suicide* (1897a:352/t.1951a:312). Indeed, as we shall see in the pages ahead, there are many references to effervescence in his writings and lectures around 1900.

It seems most unlikely therefore that the idea came to Durkheim from the ethnographic accounts of the Australian Aborigines. One likely source is that of an outstanding essay written by his nephew, Marcel Mauss. In the classic monograph of 1906, 'Essai sur les variations saisonnières des sociétés eskimos. Étude de morphologie sociale', Mauss, working in collaboration with Beuchat, derives similar conclusions to those which Durkheim was to publish six years later in his study on the Arunta, but which in a general sense he had held for a long time. Since Mauss's findings foreshadow those of Durkheim, it is worthwhile offering details. Each year the Eskimo experience alternate phases in their social life. The two phases are centred on the seasons of summer and winter, which for the Eskimo are associated with markedly different social characteristics. In the summer, the Eskimo hunt caribou, live in tents and are all dispersed over a wide geographical area. By contrast, in the winter, when the main source of live food is fish, they come together, live in greater social density, and dwell in houses or in some cases in igloos. The effect of these seasons has a great bearing on their religious activities, for religion is subject to a similar rhythm (ibid.:96–103). During the summer there is very little religious activity, except for private and domestic cults which are nearly all associated with birth and death, although certain taboos are maintained. In winter, when people gather together, there is a radical change; myths are recited or enacted, the shaman is active especially in combating famine in the critical period from March to May. There is a great deal of dancing, often in masks, and public confession, which are used to counteract the effects of the evil spirits. Feasts of the dead are celebrated, as well as the feast of the winter solstice. On occasions, sexual licence is allowed and such sexual freedom, argues Mauss, can be seen as a very crude form of communism (ibid.:100). The summer/winter dichotomy also affects collective *représentations*, for example, the Oqomiut of Baffin Island perform a special rite which consists of two groups, children of summer and children of winter. Similarly, animals symbolize summer and winter. Thus, Mauss concludes that winter is a season in which society is in an extreme state of effervescence and activity (ibid.:125). Social activity is intense. But it is pre-eminently a religious season – winter is the time to be religious. Nevertheless, the long months passed in this way give rise to the need for a profane existence most clearly realized in summer. The point is that religion is associated with and springs from intense collective activity.

So to the Arunta (see 307–16/214–19; and 492–3/345). Australian Aborigines also experience two phases of social life. In one phase they live in small groups, in families, scattered over a wide territory, living as best they may by hunting and fishing. The second phase occurs when a clan or part of a tribe is summoned and a religious ceremony, a corroboree, is celebrated. When it is concluded, groups disperse and return to their isolated existence. In this way the cycle is repeated. The two phases are associated with contrasting levels of life – the first is uniform, dull and of a 'very mediocre intensity', making no demands on the 'lively passions'. But the second sees a dramatic change. When groups gather for the corroboree great excitement is engendered, together with exaltation and rejoicing. Restraints are relaxed: men behave like madmen, crying and shrieking and throwing themselves to the ground. When they assemble once more, 'a sort of electricity is formed by their coming together which quickly transforms them to an extraordinary degree of exaltation' (308/215). But the tempo increases, and in time individual exuberance becomes channelled into co-operative and rhythmic gestures, dances and songs. This regulated tumult is accompanied by bull-roarers. Sexual restrictions disappear and the effervescence is often so intense that 'unheard of actions' emerge. What occurs is all the more effective as it takes place at night in front of fires. Not surprisingly, the participants eventually fall to the gound exhausted.

Similar behaviour is also to be observed on the fourth day of the ceremony of the snake Wollunqua amongst the Warramunga (310–11/217). Here representatives of the two phratries – one the officiants and the other the preparers and assistants – take part. In the evening men of the two phratries – Uluuru and Kingilli – gather around a specially created mound and embark on songs. Sexual intercourse between the Uluuru wives and Kingilli men takes place which breaks the rules of exogamy. Fires are lighted. Scenes of excitement follow, with singing, dancing and processions. Finally the mound is hacked to pieces by the Uluuru. Durkheim also observes that the fire ceremonies amongst the Warramunga are even more violent (311–12/218). Thus, the Aborigines experience periods of social life, seen to be deeply religious, which are accompanied by super-excitation, freedom, openness.

3 Effervescence examined: two types or functions

The term, effervescent assembly, is used here as an alternative to collective effervescence, even as a preferred alternative. Objection might be raised that the notion of effervescent assembly stresses concreteness and social structure, absent in that of collective effervescence, which indicates diffusiveness. This is, in part, true. To imply the notion of effervescent assembly, however, is to bring out clearly a characteristic that Durkheim held was associated with collective effervescence. In the following chapter this issue is considered in detail, and it will be shown that Durkheim places emphasis on gathering in which the notion of intentionality is contrasted with accidental gathering, such as a crowd. Collective effervescence is effervescence that occurs amongst people in contact with, or in the presence of, other people. Thus, effervescent assembly refers to a purposeful gathering at which collective effervescence occurs (as in 308/215; and in 313/218 where Durkheim refers to *ces milieux sociaux effervescents*).

Durkheim's reflection on collective effervescence led him to view it in two *apparently* distinct ways.

(a) As an assembly of participants where the level of feeling is of a most intense kind, where the final outcome *may* under certain circumstances be uncertain and where it is possible that new ideas emerge. This could be called the creative function of an effervescent assembly.

(b) As an assembly of participants where the level of excitement is intense, but where those gathered together feel a bond of community and unity (as in the function mentioned above), and where as a result the members feel at the end morally strengthened. As such this might be termed the re-creative function.

Durkheim did not explicitly make this distinction and such a failure to differentiate what are in fact two types or functions gives rise to confusion. As we shall show, the two aspects are both very much present in his thought, but for analytical purposes need to be initially separated.

Creative function

In the first type of collective effervescence, Durkheim emphasizes the presence of excitement or delirium. As in the corroboree, the individual participating in the assembly fails to understand what is happening to himself – so intense are his feelings that he believes he is carried away by some external, divine force (312/218). He becomes a new being, realizing that his fellow men are also in this state of exaltation and interior transformation. He and they experience something quite different from everyday life. Involved in such activities, perhaps for days at a time, the individual is led to see the presence of two incompatible worlds – the sacred and the profane. The experience is also accompanied by the fact that many moral norms – taboos, interdicts – are totally disregarded. To a large extent, man may do whatsoever pleases him.

It is during such a period of delirium or intense communal exaltation that new sentiments, norms and ideals emerge. Out of the openness and awareness of infinite possibility comes venture and originality. Occasions of effervescence are thus periods of creativity. 'So it is in the midst of these socially effervescent milieux – out of this effervescence itself that the religious idea appears to be born' (313/218–19).

By *l'idée religieuse*, does Durkheim mean the idea of religion – the concept of religion – religion *per se*? Or does he mean new religious ideas? The short answer is that he implies both. There can be no doubt that he believed that for primitive man the reality of religion is not in individual experience, as in the personal worship of natural phenomena, but in group activity, in common ecstasy or in common ritual. But as well, and indeed for the same reason, he sees that the effervescent assembly is the source of new ideas and ideals about the most important aspects of life which are summed up in religious belief (see 604/422/151). He could not prove this second point from the data that he examined about the Arunta, since he had no historical material to work on, but he did not hesitate to point to such creative outbursts in events which were nearer home – the French Revolution. He wrote:

This tendency of society to set itself up as a god or to create gods was never more in evidence than during the early years of the French Revolution. At that particular time, under the influence of general enthusiasm, things that were purely secular in nature were transformed into sacred things by public opinion: for example, the Motherland, Liberty, Reason. (305–6/214/132)

Durkheim is more precise about the French Revolution when he speaks of the Night of the Dupes, when noblemen denounced their feudal rights and so took a totally unpredictable course of action (300 n.1/210 n.1/(especially) 164 n.42).

He made much the same point writing in a philosophical vein and not a specifically religious one, and at the same time as he was finishing, if he had not already finished, *The Elementary Forms*. In his 'Value judgments and judgments of reality', he attempted to establish the origin of the ideal, of values which transcend human experience (1911b/1924a:133ff./t.1953b:91ff.). He said: 'When individual minds are not isolated but enter into close relations with and work upon each other, from their synthesis comes a new kind of psychic life' (ibid.). Durkheim again mentions the process in connection with the emergence of new ideas in morality (1914b:35). In these moments of collective ferment or effervescence, the great ideals on which civilization rests are born.

But it is not only new ideas and ideals which emerge from collective effervescence; men also feel that in such times the ideal can indeed be realized – it is as one with the real. A man so placed thinks he is in a world quite different from his private existence and is dominated by a superhuman force. Speaking extemporaneously about contemporary religion he said:

> To explain religion, to make it rationally intelligible – and this is what the free thinker sets out to do – we must find in the world which we can comprehend by observation, by our human faculties, a source of energy superior to that which is at the disposal of the individual and which, nevertheless, can be communicated to him. I ask myself if this source can be found anywhere other than in the very special life which emanates from an assembly of men. We indeed know from experience that when men are all gathered together, when they live a communal life, the very fact of their coming together causes exceptionally intense forces to arise which dominate them, exalt them, give them a quality of life to a degree unknown to them as individuals. *Under the influence*

387

*of collective enthusiasm they are sometimes seized by a positive
delirium which compels them to actions in which even they do
not recognize themselves.* (1919b:100/t.1975a:183; our italics)

Here, and with reference to the French Revolution and Arunta,
Durkheim holds that effervescent assembly gives rise as much to
new action as to fresh ideas, for example, new rituals and festivals
(308/215; see also 1905a(ii)(2)).

The evidence from Durkheim is such that we are justified in
speaking about a creative function within collective effervescence,
and he indeed uses the phrase *effervescence créatrice* in one place
at least (611/428/157).

The re-creative function

As a rule, one imagines, effervescent assembly is not instrumental
in producing new ideas and ideals. Something much more ordinary
is the order of the day. The old remains accepted and is
unchanged. As is seen from the quotations just given, the effect
of the assembly on individuals is marked. When a gathering gives
rise to strong communal experience, it is itself a source of religious, moral and political vitality. Here is to be found the spring
of an eternally fresh realization of common, dearly-held beliefs
and actions. Man, if only momentarily, participates in an experience in which he feels himself transcended. Durkheim wrote:
'When we find ourselves at the heart of an assembly animated by
a common passion, we become capable of sentiments and actions
of which we are not capable when we are reduced to our own
efforts' (299–300/209–1/128; see also 1968c:250). This psychical
exaltation, which bestows vigour and vitality, is not only close to
individual delirium, it is in external effects close to the pathological
states witnessed in some prophets and which can be induced by
intoxicating liquors (324/226/136).

Thus, if effervescence is a vehicle for the creation of new ideas
and activities, it is also the vehicle for the re-creation and reaffirm-
ation of moral and spiritual life. The re-creative function is a
necessity for religion. Without the effervescent assembly performing such a task, religion either dies or becomes listless: with it,
it is buoyant and dynamic. He writes: 'It is for this reason that all
parties, political, economic and confessional, periodically take the
trouble to instigate meetings at which their followers can refurbish
their common faith by manifesting it in common' (300/210/128).

And in terms of beliefs , we repeat part of an earlier quotation: 'the only way of renewing collective *représentations* which relate to sacred things is to retemper them in the very source of religious life, that is to say, in the assembled groups. . . . The common faith becomes reanimated quite naturally in the heart of this reconstituted group' (494/346).

But was not all this said before in connection with ritual (see ch. 18.3)? Ritual is very often accompanied by a high level of emotional involvement and generally involves communal meeting. Both ritual and effervescent assembly reassert and fortify sentiments, beliefs, ideals. One aspect of the relation between ritual and effervescent assembly now needs to be considered.

The conquest of the anti-climax

What happens when the effervescent assembly is concluded? Durkheim sees this question to be as important as any question about the assembly itself. Effervescence, he argues, cannot last for ever: indeed it cannot last for long periods. To remain in an effervescent state is wearying. Human energies are limited, and after a point of climax, man has to return to everyday life. This is the level at which life is lived: never at that of perpetual excitement (300/209–10/128). It can be said therefore that what transpires at an effervescent assembly is an illusion in as much as it cannot persist and cannot be a continuing experience: everyday life is the reality man has to face (1911b/1924a:134/t.1953b:92).

But to return to the ordinary and face the possibility of a reaction against religious exaltation is not the end of the process. The period of exaltation remains in the memory and is part of a newly realized reality. To prevent an anti-climax it is necessary that the experience is not forgotten. Man stands in need of recalling what he has experienced. Such an anamnesis or symbolic re-enactment is achieved through sacred rituals. By this means men are drawn together and, with the help of various techniques, act out the great events of the past. In so doing, they become aware of their common bonds. Durkheim wrote: 'This revivification is the function of religious or secular feasts and ceremonies, all public addresses in churches or schools, plays and exhibitions – in a word, whatever draws men together into an intellectual and moral communion' (ibid.). It must be understood, of course, that liturgical recalling does not have as much force as the original effervescent assembly, especially when that assembly was a highly creative occasion.

Durkheim holds that the great moments of development and breakthrough, social or intellectual, have to be continually recalled in order to be effective in society and not to be forgotten. Persistence is as important as creativity for the simple reason that without such effort occasions of discovery would soon be lost. Ideas do not propagate themselves automatically or by some magic, be it in terms of rationality or an all-pervading *Geist*. Social sentiments and *représentations* have a feeble existence: they need to be ritually re-enacted (331/231; see ch. 15). Bad memory and non-rationality are part of the givenness of man.

> In fact, it is in the communal life that they [*représentations*] are formed, and this communal life is essentially intermittent. So they necessarily partake of this same intermittency. They attain their greatest intensity at the moment when the men are assembled together and are in immediate relations with one another, when they all partake of the same idea and the same sentiment. But when the assembly has broken up and each man has returned to his own peculiar life, they progressively lose their original energy. Being covered over little by little by the rising flood of daily experiences, they would soon fall into unconsciousness, if we did not find some means of calling them back into consciousness and revivifying them. (493/345)

In this way Durkheim employs the concept of collective effervescence, which is coupled with ensuing ritual, and so analyses not one event but a process. Initially, there is the effervescent assembly giving rise to what is new. This is carried forward into the continual present by regular ritual re-enactment, which keeps alive amongst worshippers those great events and gatherings that have built up their society and that proceed to invigorate it.

4 Further examples

A close inspection of Durkheim's work shows that he often resorted to the notion of collective effervescence, and applied it to various periods of history, as well as to processes in primitive societies. He held that in certain cultures and in certain eras, effervescent assemblies were common. 'There are periods in history when, under the influence of great collective upheaval, social interaction becomes much more frequent and more active. Individuals seek each other out and assemble more often. As a result there is a general effervescence characteristic of revolutionary or creative periods' (301/210–11/129). He pointed by way of example to the Carolingian period, when there were great changes in intellectual thought (1938a:78/t.1977a:65). 'This was a period in which all historians see a veritable intellectual effervescence among all peoples of Europe' (ibid.). The moral energy which had been aroused in the eleventh century to deal with problems that faced the establishment of Christendom was then channelled into the Crusades, for with them the whole of Europe entered into a state of agitation and over-excitation (ibid.:81/67). This extension from the Carolingian period 'is the only way we can explain these great religious uprisings' (ibid.:79/66). The Crusades were an endless pilgrimage. The nobles and the masses responded 'unanimously and ecstatically' to the call of Urban III. As well, this vitality gave rise to intellectual impetus in art, science and literature, culminating in scholasticism; all of which in our terms is an example of the creative type of effervescence (ibid.:88/73). Further, the effervescence associated with the Crusades was focused on Christendom itself, not on particular nations. It thus strengthened the notion of a universal Christian society.

Inevitably, Durkheim refers to the revolutions of eighteenth and nineteenth-century Europe, and the French Revolution in particular (as we have seen) as occasions of creative effervescence (see, for example, ibid.:349/305). So also was the time of the 1870 Franco-Prussian war (1911b/1924a:124/t.1953b:250). By extension, Durkheim could also speak of intellectual effervescence, where common assembly is probably less, but where, amongst intellectuals, there is something approaching feverish activity involving mutual interaction. Thus he could write:

A veritable thrust of rationalist enthusiasm occurred during the first years of the Restoration. It was from reason alone, that is to say from science, that the means of remaking the moral organization of the country were expected. It was from this intellectual effervescence that Saint-Simonism, Fourierism, Comtism, and sociology simultaneously resulted. But from the beginning of the July Monarchy this whole restlessness began to calm down. . . . The revolution of 1848 was probably only a last and necessarily feeble echo of the intellectual movement which had rendered illustrious the first part of the century. This explains why it was so quickly and easily vanquished. (1900b:613/t.1973a:11)

Such periods of vitality and breakthrough are to be contrasted with those of dullness and moral stagnation. This can apply as much to the past as to the present. Durkheim believed that at the time just prior to the First World War there was a moral coldness and indifference which indicated an impending moral bankruptcy – a period that might be designated anomic – and he hoped that the near future would once more see 'hours of creative effervescence, in the course of which new ideals will be born and new formulae emerge which will for a time serve as a guide to humanity' (611/428/157; see also 1919b:104/t.1975a:187). Durkheim said he preferred the intensity of life during the years that followed the Dreyfus affair to those that went before them (1904e:70; and see 1968c:250). That unhappy event had succeeded in giving a steady stream of collective activity of considerable intensity. 'May we not fall back again into the state of moral stagnation in which we have too long lingered' (ibid.). Durkheim is also reported to have offered another example in the *parti-socialiste* (1968c:250). (Lukes rightly suggests that in the notes compiled by Davy of what Durkheim said in a lecture, which relate to this reference, the further examples of *L'Union Sacré* and *La Morale de Guerre* were added by Davy himself and did not come from the lips of the master.)

We have briefly described the way Durkheim used the term collective effervescence, or as we prefer to call it, effervescent assembly, to refer to revolutionary departures in religious thought and action and also to the very source of religious and social energy. It is necessary to analyse the concept in more detail in the next chapter, and in examining certain criticisms levelled against it we shall be able to see some of the more fundamental issues which it raises. Before we proceed, however, a few further points might be noted. They relate to examples of effervescent assembly to which Durkheim's concept is readily applicable.

The first is the Christian eucharist, which is briefly referred to by Durkheim (609/427/156). The Last Supper celebrated by Christ with his disciples was, according to the New Testament, an event of extreme importance, of high emotional content, giving rise to new religious ideas – a great religious leader saying over bread and wine 'This is my body', 'This is my blood'. Here is a clear example of the creative type of effervescent assembly and it has always had a central place in Christian theology. It has subsequently been re-enacted, annually, weekly or daily, in response to the express command of Christ, 'Do this in remembrance of me'. Probably no religious event has been so consistently ritualized. One of the intentions of the liturgy is expressly declared to be that of anamnesis, recalling, or re-enacting the Lord's supper as it took place. The combination of creative effervescent assembly and subsequent ritual re-enactment fits admirably Durkheim's concept, and one wonders if in fact he did not derive his ideas from this source.

Another example, also within the Christian tradition, is that of glossolalia. Glossolalia or speaking with tongues is a characteristic of modern Pentecostalist sects, and as such has been known since the late nineteenth century, especially in the English-speaking world. Recently it has spread and is now to be found in most of the traditional churches. The original glossolalia occurred amongst the apostles at Pentecost (Acts 2:1–13) and has always been seen by Christians to be part of the unique event which heralded the beginning of the Church. Speaking with tongues was practised in the primitive church and modern Pentecostalists maintain that speaking with tongues is a continuing process and not just an original event. A modern glossolalia session has all the features of effervescent assembly, such as those outlined by Durkheim. It is probably the best example in the western world of collective effervescence of the re-creative type that there is at the present time. Those who speak with tongues and who practise it on a regular basis would doubt whether it could be seen as a ritual re-enacting of an original event. An anthropologist or sociologist looking at the practice of glossolalia today would doubtless feel justified in describing it as a ritual re-enacting, in which the activity is controlled by the congregational setting, where the movements seem stylized and where there would seem to be the attempt to project the first Pentecost. (For a detailed study of glossolalia, see J. Hollenweger, *The Pentecostals*, SCM Press, London 1977.)

It can also be well argued, as Mary Douglas has recently, that most revivalist sects go through a period of effervescence (1970:73–4). During this period, emotions run high, formalism is denounced, worship often involves trance states, and doctrinal differentiation is deplored. The sect then becomes sustained by the development of stable roles, formalities and the ritual re-enactment of the stage of effervescence.

Not in a strictly religious setting are the events of May 1968 in France. In the Sorbonne, where Durkheim taught, there was indeed an effervescent assembly of burning social and political importance at the time, but it does not appear to have undergone ritual re-enactment, which might be attributed, not least, to its essentially secular setting and the fact that it did not bring about a revolutionary change in political structures. But in Russia in 1917 there was revolution and the event is annually ritualized (see Lane 1981:ch. 10). How near to Durkheim's own words are those written by Boris Pasternak in *Doctor Zhivago* describing the Revolution:

> Last night I was watching the meeting in the square. It was an astonishing sight. Mother Russia is on the move, she can't stand still, she's restless and she can't find rest, she's talking and she can't stop. And it isn't as if only people were talking. Stars and trees meet and converse, flowers talk philosophy at night, stone houses hold meetings. It's like something out of the Gospels, don't you think? Like the days of the apostles. Like in St Paul – do you remember? 'You will speak with tongues and prophesy. Pray for the gift of understanding. . . .' Everyone was revived, reborn, changed, transformed. You might say everyone has been through two revolutions – his own personal revolution as well as the general one. (Boris Pasternak, *Doctor Zhivago*, Collins, Fontana, 1958, pp. 163–4)

22 Effervescent assembly: the source of religious change and strength

II Questions, criticisms and evaluation

Durkheim's theory of effervescent assembly has always had its opponents. Criticism has often been sharp, and because of this one feels that the concept was not developed after Durkheim's death. The intention of this chapter is to outline some of the points of attack and to see how far they are justified.

1 A psychological theory?

One observation that has been commonly levelled against Durkheim's theory of collective effervescence is that he adopted what is basically a psychological theory. His contention is that arising out of effervescent assembly new ideas and ideals, be they religious, moral or political, emerge because of the excitement of the moment. People gather together and their emotions are allowed and indeed encouraged to run free. For a short period anything goes and out of its springs novelty. Again, on other occasions participants emerge, feeling themselves stronger, more invigorated, more sure of their religion and moral rectitude. It is argued that such a mechanism, so central to Durkheim's thought, is hardly sociological, since it is not one that arises out of a socially controlled situation but out of uncontrolled emotion. Thus, it stands contrary to Durkheim's own attack on psychological reductionism. In staking out a unique area in which the new discipline of sociology could work, Durkheim, although admitting the validity of psychology, vigorously opposed psychological explanation within the area of sociology. The arguments that he so vigorously put forward in *The Rules of Sociological Method* are too well known to be rehearsed here (see 1895a:ch. 2; Lukes

1972:16–19, ch. 3; La Fontaine 1926). One of the more recent critics has been Evans-Pritchard, who felt that it was impossible to defend Durkheim in his analysis of effervescent assembly. He wrote:

> No amount of juggling with words like 'intensity' and 'effervescence' can hide the fact that he derives the totemic religion of the Black Fellows from the emotional excitement of individuals brought together in a small crowd, from what is a sort of crowd hysteria. (1965:68)

And Mary Douglas, writing at much the same time, takes a similar stand (1966:20). But much earlier, Delacroix in discussions with Durkheim himself (Durkheim 1913b:78), Goldenweiser in his two articles on Durkheim (1915 and 1917) and Essertier in his *Psychologie et sociologie* (1927:17–18) were amongst many who from the time of the publication of *The Elementary Forms* until the present have all suggested that the theory rests on crowd psychology. The criticism is hardly surprising, since from the 1890s onwards, particularly in France, the idea of crowd psychology was well developed. It nevertheless carried with it ideological overtones in emphasizing the irrational. Amongst the most prominent exponents of crowd psychology was Le Bon (1841–1931). whose book *Psychologie des foules* (1895) was known in this country on account of its English translation (*Crowd Psychology*, 1896). In it he developed various categories of crowds.[1] Mention must be made of the work of Gabriel Tarde (1843–1904), Durkheim's redoubtable adversary, in his *L'Opinion et la foule* (1901). The Italian sociologist and criminologist Scipio Sighele (1868–1913) in his *Psychologie des sectes* (translated from Italian into French in 1898), gave prominence, like many books on the subject at the time, to the criminal crowd and what was called sectarian criminality, and incidentally maintaining that Le Bon had freely borrowed his ideas. Delacroix himself, of whom mention has just been made, was a psychologist of religion whose book *La Religion et la foi* came out five years after the death of Durkheim. In it Delacroix held that *l'excitation collective* could be functionally explained in so far as it satisfied the gregarious instinct of individuals (1922:66). In the period when Durkheim was writing, these and other thinkers were instrumental in creating widespread interest in the spontaneous and, in what was often and still is termed, irrational collective behaviour. The charge is that Durkheim borrowed ideas from these sources without even troubling to acknowledge them.

That Durkheim catches fish from the psychological pond and fries them for his own purposes is a charge that has to be taken seriously and, we believe, to be challenged. The following points should be considered.

First, the nature of the terms used has nearly always been overlooked. Nowhere in *Les Formes élémentaires*, and seldom elsewhere, so far as we have been able to discover, does Durkheim use the word *foule*, meaning a crowd or throng. In speaking about collective effervescence, he always uses the words *rassemblement*, an assembling or gathering, and *assemblée*, gathering (and elsewhere, for example, *effervescence des assemblées* in 1968c:250). (But see use of *foule* in 1925a:71 (where *foule* is differentiated from *assemblée*), 172 and in 1897a:111.) The root meaning of *foule* is to press or to crush, and implies a large number or multitude of people who happen to be together. The emphasis is on the persons themselves, without reference to purpose or order. *Rassemblement*, however, refers to the assembling or reassembling of separate people or things. Thus in *rassemblement* the emphasis is on the *act* of coming together and refers to those involved as being of one group. A *rassemblement* can be accidental or for some purpose, and there is the implication of order, if not of intention. In military use *rassemblement* means 'fall in!' Le Bon's book was called *Psychologie des foules* not *Psychologie des rassemblements* (see pp. 529–30). Durkheim, it would seem, deliberately chooses *rassemblement* or *assemblée* and so focuses on the act of gathering, involving those of a common class or group. Such a concept is basic to his theory of ritual (see ch. 18.6). A *rassemblement* has a much stronger sense of 'we' than has a crowd. Admittedly the *rassemblement*, as we have indicated, can gather accidentally, but it quickly acquires a sense of identity and purpose and so establishes the sentiment of unity.

Although *foule* and *rassemblement* are not carefully distinguished by Sighele in his *La Foule criminelle*, he does think it necessary to distinguish a crowd from other types of gathering. He writes:

The crowd [*foule*] is a spontaneous organism, which has a

simple process of formation, and is consequently animal-like: the public [*public*] is a more complex aggregate of people, slower in taking shape and hence more human. (1901:227)

Thus Sighele and also Le Bon (1895) hold that the crowd is to be contrasted with a group that has some degree of coherence, homogeneity and purpose. Delacroix also sees the need for a similar kind of differentiation in terms of organization – an unorganized aspect and an organized one (1922:66). Our point is that Durkheim's concern was not with crowds *per se*, still less with mobs, but with gatherings which involved a group of people with some notion of purpose and identity. (This contrasts sharply with Smelser's concept of collective behaviour where action is uninstitutionalized and modifies a condition of strain (1962:73).)

Jean-Paul Sartre also underlines the element of 'we' in effervescent assembly, which is dealt with in his great book, *Critique de la raison dialectique* (1960). In referring to the events of the Bastille he sees, in some respects like Durkheim, the crucial element to be the gathering of people seeking the same goal and vibrating with the same emotions (ibid.:529ff.). Men throw down the tools and meanings which constitute their enslavement. Such action unifies them in their search for freedom. The test is a sense of unity. Action and action alone makes a 'we' out of an 'I'. But Sartre admits that such occasions are rare in the history of society.

Second, critics such as Essertier, for example, suggest that Durkheim's theory corresponds to the findings of crowd psychology, not least because Durkheim sees society *merely* as a crowd. Philippe de Félice, a later member of the Année Sociologique group, assumed in writing about mysticism and religion that Durkheim made the identification of crowd with psychology – an identification which de Félice rejects (1947:15). Bouglé, maintaining that Durkheim's treatment of crowds was the least acceptable part of his theory, held that a crowd (*foule*) was the crudest form of society to be found in which relationships are heterogeneous and without definition (1935:9). But in fairness it must be pointed out that, although Durkheim held little brief for crowds, he saw societies as 'only permanent organized crowds' (1925a:71/ t.1961a:62; see ch. 13). From this we can deduce that for Durkheim society, in any definition to be put forward, would contain these two elements – stability and organization – both of which require discipline. Such elements, absent in a crowd, Durkheim held were essential for social life (see 1925a:172/ t.1961a:150).

Seger rightly challenges the assertion that Durkheim identified crowd with society (1957:24). There is no evidence for such a connection. In one sense, we would argue, those who criticized Durkheim in this way might be excused, since Durkheim nowhere defines what he means by society, and therefore identification of the two terms might appear warrantable. But a more sympathetic general reading of Durkheim would have prevented critics such as Goldenweiser (1915 and 1917) taking this position. It may be true that Durkheim glorified society, that he glorified *assemblées*, but he hardly glorified crowds! One might hazard a guess and suggest that he had an innate fear of crowds, and we know that he was certainly no lover of revolution, certainly in his own day (see 1916c:18/t.1979a:161).

Third, according to early psychologists, the key mechanism by which crowds 'worked', by which effervescence was so effective, was located in the individuals who formed the crowds and who lost control of themselves. In a crowd, people cease to be themselves and they dissolve into the totality of other people who surround them. In this way they become 'emotionally drunk' with the collective power which engulfs them. Their own limitations are transcended, they feel they are part of a greater world, in touch with a superhuman force (see, for example, de Félice 1947:10–11). Thus, the psychological explanation turns on the individual losing his control over certain psychological drives. As an explanation of what happens in the individual Durkheim would not deny this, indeed he uses the ideas himself. But the issue at stake is not the reaction of the individual: it is the social outcome (see below).

Fourth, it was not surprising that the psychologists to whom we have referred were convinced that the crucial element in crowd psychology was the loss of rational control in individuals, and held that such behaviour was pathological (for example, Le Bon 1895). But Durkheim, despite his early references to normal and pathological social states (1893b:bk III; 1895a:ch. 3), hardly sees collective effervescence as abnormal or pathological. The truth is that it is neither: it is, in our own words, supra-normal, for it is the very opposite of pathological. It awakens and gives rise to the sacred, which is of ultimate importance to the group. The *assemblée* is therefore a 'sacred' meeting. Admittedly, Durkheim sees parallels between effervescent assembly and individual excesses, such as those seen in some prophets or in the taking of drugs, but the *rassemblement* is not to be condemned because of that. It is not pathological in the sense that a certain form of suicide could be called pathological (1897a:bk III:ch. 5). And if, today, society can be said to be in a state labelled anomic, it is because it *lacks* effervescent assemblies, rather than because it is inundated with them. Delacroix saw all crowds to be in some sense religious in so far as they transcended the rational, but for him this implied condemnation, since he was very far from enthusiastic about religious enthusiasm (1922:66).

The controversy over Durkheim's notion of collective effervescence rests on issues of causation and outcome. The effervescent assembly creates and re-creates beliefs and sentiments, that is, it *causes* beliefs to come into existence and others to be strengthened. Evans-Pritchard assumes a relationship of that order in supposing that Durkheim held that the emotional states of individuals within collective effervescence caused particular outcomes (1965:68). He therefore challenges Durkheim's alleged assumption that the participants in effervescent assemblies are in fact 'in any particular emotional state during the performance of the ceremonies' (ibid.). If they are, then the rites produce these emotional states, and hence the rites cannot be a 'product of the emotions' (ibid.). Individuals taking part in the ritual have their emotions heightened because of the effects of the rites upon them, but, adds Evans-Pritchard, 'it can hardly be an adequate causal explanation of them as a social phenomenon'. He goes on: 'The rites create the effervescence, which creates the beliefs, which cause the rites to be performed; or does the mere coming together generate them? Fundamentally Durkheim elicits a social fact from crowd psychology' (ibid.). What Durkheim indeed suggests is that the rite itself, and the people assembled together, along with an evaluation of the social circumstances (*représentation* or *sentiment*) all give rise to the effervescent exaltation (see ch. 18.6). No *one* component simply 'causes' it. Indeed Durkheim never speaks of a simple cause in this connection. He sees emerging out of a complex happening certain social consequences. It is probably not too much to say that Durkheim saw effervescent assembly as an event mysterious in nature, and not yet fully accountable scientifically. The actual mechanisms by which new ideas emerge remain unknown. One thing is quite clear, that the outcome cannot be explained by the psychological state of the individuals who compose the *assemblée*. In recent years, Horton has rightly said that an elemental individual causation is totally inadequate (1973:259). As always, for Durkheim the starting-point has to be the collective and not the individual. In his lectures on moral education, which are indeed as early as 1902, he emphasized this kind of approach:

> Thus it is that human groups have a way of thinking, of feeling, and of living differing from that of their members when they think, feel, and live as isolates. Now what we have said of crowds [*foules*], of ephemeral gatherings [*assemblées passagères*], applies *a fortiori* to societies, which are only permanent and organised crowds. (1925a:71/t.1961a:62)

Later he developed the point and said that in a group, individual minds react on each other so that they are able to achieve what is impossible or most unlikely when they are in isolation. Such a synthesis, he added, produces a *sui generis* psychic life (1911b/ 1924a:133/t.1953b:91). 'This activity is qualitatively different from the everyday life of the individual, as the superior from the inferior, the ideal from the real' (ibid.). Once again, Durkheim suggests that what emerges in effervescent assembly is not just the calculus of individual experiences, but a particular collective and corporate reality which is produced by a particular combination of individual minds. Therefore the outcome is not subject to psychological investigation, seen as the analysis of the feelings and sentiments of individuals.

Although effervescent assembly contains a social element, and therefore is subject to a sociological investigation, Durkheim openly admitted, as we have seen, that it was associated with a heightening of the emotions. 'Everyone knows how emotions and passions may break out in a crowd [*foule*] or a meeting [*assemblée*]' (1925a:71/t.1961a:62). But to accept the fact of the heightening of the emotions is not the same thing as to search for a psychological cause. Sexual emotions and feelings, prominent in marriage, do not explain the various forms of marriage or its social consequences, and the same can be said about patterns of sexual intercourse (see also Mauss 1935). Incidentally, Sorokin hints at another kind of reductionism which would be opposed by Durkheim. He argues that since a corroboree is related to seasonal variations, the causation of effervescent assembly 'at least indirectly' is geographical, and this weakens Durkheim's search for sociological explanation (1928:476). Sorokin goes on to state that geographical factors are also important in the emergence of totemism and its associated ideas – names of plants and animals connected with it. But Durkheim's arguments against the importance of geographical factors with regard to collective effervescence would likely be just as strong as those he used against the social phenomenon of suicide (see 1897a:ch. 3). And one may legitimately ask, what of the French Revolution, a frequently cited example of effervescent assembly? What geographical factors determined that? Durkheim readily pointed to the inadequacy of geographical factors in explaining religious phenomena (see 1900a(47)).

It should be noted moreover that Durkheim sees collective effervescence within the context of a social process. It is this process which is the focal point, for it is something that is socially controlled. Collective effervescence, as has been noted, has something about it that is akin to ritual. On this count it has a limited connection with the gathering of a crowd. Parsons is right in noting that crowd psychology relates to *unorganized* gatherings of people, whereas ritual has as its very essence that which is closely organized (1937:437), although, as we have noted, *rassemblement* and *assemblée* do not necessarily mean gatherings with intention. Parsons goes on to suggest that the reason critics have attacked Durkheim at this point has been due to his emphasis on the term effervescence, which is associated with emotional excitement. The same critics can make a similar attack on ritual, which 'does not fit into the intrinsic means-end schema' (ibid.). What is so often forgotten, we would argue, is that, in Durkheim's thought, over and above effervescent assembly stands society itself, a reality that is capable of being modified and strengthened by assembly. The assembly itself is never the ultimate, although it is capable of transforming society.

Thus, Durkheim does not see collective effervescence primarily, indeed if at all, in terms of crowd psychology – a point Lukes makes (1972:462). Are critics serious in asserting that Durkheim deliberately went against fundamental principles of methodology relating to psychology and sociology in his book *The Rules of Sociological Method* (1895a)? The sociologist sees collective assemblies as crucial events in social life. He asks: what are the effects of these on society? What are the social conditions which give rise to them? The issue that Durkheim was wrestling with, and it is one of considerable sociological import, is the nature of social creativity. To that we shall be turning our attention later.

2 The influence of other thinkers

When referring to collective effervescence, Durkheim makes virtually no reference to other authors. True, he mentions Stöll's *Suggestion und Hypnotismus in der Völkerpsychologie* (1894) in a footnote (300/210/164). But apart from that reference in *The Elementary Forms*, there is no reference to Le Bon or Tarde, or to other books and articles on the subject of crowd psychology. One assumes he had read the authors of the day on the subject and may have been consciously or unconsciously influenced by them, but our opinion is that the extent of such influence is by no means that suggested by certain critics. It is obvious that Durkheim did not want to be associated with such writers.

In looking for other writers on crowd psychology, who might have influenced Durkheim's thought on effervescent assembly, one might take as a likely candidate Wilhelm Wundt. Durkheim, as is well known, had a great admiration for him, partly through his visit to Germany in 1885–6 (see 1887a and 1887c). His continued interest in the work of the great German psychologist and his school is apparent in the reviews of his books by Durkheim. Wundt published his *Völkerpsychologie* in 1904 and then his *Elemente der Völkerpsychologie* in 1912 which Durkheim reviewed (1913a(ii)(8)). Gisbert has argued recently that Durkheim was much influenced by Wundt in holding that the mind is process not substance and that there exists a principle of creative synthesis. These ideas had a bearing on Durkheim's concept of social facts and what might be called group mind. The point of creativity is important as we shall see, but in Wundt's *Völkerpsychologie*, which Durkheim saw as a kind of general history of humanity (ibid.), there is little which deals with effervescence as such, despite the fact that Wundt's psychology takes into account the co-operative group and the collectivity. Indeed, Durkheim criticized Wundt for his simplistic approach, which can be seen also in Comte and Spencer. Lukes admits the parallel between Durkheim's thought on these matters and that of Wundt but doubts whether Durkheim took over relevant ideas directly from him (1972:90 n.16).

However, if one is looking for hidden influence, a stronger candidate is Bergson with his notion of *élan vital* (see LaCapra 1972:271; Lukes 1972:505–6; Durkheim 1914b; ch. 10.3). This is no occasion to explore the intellectual relations between the two great contemporary French thinkers, who had been fairly close fellow students at the École Normale Supérieure, but who later stood opposed to one another (see Peyre 1960a:28–31). Both were humanists and patriots, although of the two, Bergson was the more optimistic in believing in the unlimited progress of humanity. Further, they both denied the proclaimed truths of religion but saw their value for society. Indirectly tying morals to education, Bergson outlined the moral reforms he felt were necessary for France after the 1870–1 miseries. Above all, they had a concern for the phenomenon of vitality and enthusiasm in society, which was not a universal characteristic of philosophers of the time. Bergson's alleged anti-intellectualism was not to Durkheim's liking, in so far as Bergson held that there existed a metaphysical entity over and above, and at the same time superior to, the intellect (see ch. 10.2). This was not to be identified with the collective, which Bergson admitted, but which he held should not be in conflict with the individual, as Durkheim implied (Bergson 1932/t.1935:85). The phrase *élan vital* sums up Bergson's doctrine that there is an original life-force which passes from one generation of living beings to another by way of developed individual organisms. Perhaps inspired by these ideas and stressing the need for social vitality Durkheim at one point actually uses the term *élan collectif* (1968c:250). Gehlke maintains that Bergson influenced Durkheim on only minor points (1915:88) and Sorokin goes so far as to say that the theories of the two men are quite opposed (1928:443; and Sumpf 1965:70).

Rationalist though Durkheim was, he was also interested in what might be called the counter-Cartesian movement which was concerned with spontaneity and which may be said to stem from Victor Cousin (1792–1867) who lectured at the Sorbonne (Clark 1969:9ff.). In the latter half of the nineteenth century there were many ideas circulating amongst academics which could be seen to have some bearing on Durkheim's theory of effervescent assembly. Clearly, general influences were at work, but it is impossible to be more specific and to say that he was overwhelmingly influenced or 'seems to have freely drawn upon' one author more than another (cf. Douglas 1966:20). One thing is undeniable: Durkheim was deeply interested in spontaneity and social vitality, which he saw had a legitimate place in sociology, and these phenomena he attempted to incorporate into his work.

3 Universality and limitations

Durkheim's claim to generalize his findings, based primarily on material from the Australian Aboriginals, has been challenged from at least two directions. One challenge has been the attempt to undermine his position by pointing to later anthropological discoveries. The 'well-conducted experiment' was carried out on totemic ethnographic data and Durkheim was convinced that totemism was a universal phenomenon in as much as it was a form of social organization through which every society had passed (see ch. 6.3). On these grounds, if for no other, it seemed legitimate to him to extend his findings from the Arunta to societies at large. Totemism, however, as a general stage in evolutionary development was in fact questioned in his day and then finally rejected. Therefore, it is possible to argue that Durkheim's deductions must *ipso facto* be limited to societies which are totemic or which have passed through a stage of totemism. This form of attack is as unconvincing as is Durkheim's own attempt to extend his conclusions to society at large, based upon the extension of specific ethnographic data. To argue for or against generalizations on such premises must be rejected. If generalizations can be made at all, they are to be made only on the assumption of certain universal characteristics to be found in all societies and not just based on limited evolutionary stages. Durkheim's attempts to generalize are still valid without reference to the particular logical steps he put forward for supporting his argument. A similar argument and counter-argument rests on the existence in society of a bi-phasal type of life. Amongst the Arunta and the Eskimo, as we have observed, there are two distinct phases, in only one of which is effervescent assembly to be found. Therefore, it is maintained, it is not legitimate to extend Durkheim's theory beyond those societies which experience this type of social life. The counter-argument is that while such a bi-phasal type of social organization offers a very clear example of effervescent assembly, the same kinds of events are clearly at work in societies which do not have this form of social organization and therefore it is legitimate to extend the conclusions based on these particular types of societies. Durkheim suggests (and who would deny it?) that effervescent assemblies are to be found in other societies, whose structure is very far removed from that of the Arunta or the Eskimo. Such a methodological leap is made in the work of nearly every anthropologist and sociologist, but it weakens the notion that certain social structures give rise to particular social phenomena.

Another problem raised by Durkheim's position is that of extension and therefore identification. What is a legitimate effervescent assembly? Durkheim saw such gatherings as not only religous but also political, for both types performed a similar function. He writes:

> What essential difference is there between an assembly of Christians celebrating the main events of the life of Christ, or Jews keeping either the Exodus from Egypt or the promulgation of the Decalogue, or a gathering of citizens commemorating the institution of a new moral charter or some great event in the life of the nation? (610/427/156)

But why draw the line at political meetings? What if people are gathered together solely for recreation? Writing in 1925, Malinowski took up this point. He noted that feelings of heightened emotion do not only occur at times of collective effervescence in a primitive society, but when a person is in love, when someone conquers fear in the face of anger, or a death (1925:57–8). Disregarding individual states in which Durkheim was not specifically interested, Gaston Richard attacked his former co-worker for failing to mark off effervescent assemblies from other assemblies and failing to define occasions of true collective effervescence. Richard wrote that, according to Durkheim's thought, what was true of a religious effervescent assembly 'is no less true of a group of drinkers, gastronomes, race-goers, sportsmen, enthusiasts, and gamblers than of an association of patriots or a community of believers' (1923:236/t.1975:247). And centres of assembly could be 'cinemas, department stores, music halls, skating rinks, lecture halls, and labour exchanges!' (ibid.:236/248). And so we could go on to say that, according to Durkheim's analysis, there is little or no difference between the Ecumenical Council of Vatican II and an *ad hoc* group of students revelling in a drunken orgy in an English provincial university!

These assertions push Durkheim into a position we would suspect he would have been the first to have objected to, on the grounds of a misunderstanding of what he was asserting. To be sure, he laid himself open to such a prima-facie charge because he did not define precisely what he meant by collective effervescence. He clearly implied, however, that occasions of collective effervescence *per se* were to be marked off from other assemblies. He affirmed this in replying to a discussion about the publication of his *Elementary Forms*:

> The collective which gives rise to religion is the communion of *consciences*. It is their coalescence in the resulting *conscience* which momentarily absorbs them. But this communion is not and cannot but be intermittent by nature. It is one of the forms of social life, but there are others. There are some social relations which do not possess this character to any degree and which are not consequently religious in themselves. An example is the relations of exchange. . . . Every communion of *conscience* does not produce what is religious. It must moreover fulfil certain specific conditions. Notably it must possess a degree of unity, of intimacy, and the forces which it releases must be sufficiently intense to take the individual outside himself and to raise him to a superior life. Also, the sentiments so roused must be fixed on an object or concrete objects which symbolize them. (1913b:84)

This very important quotation, which shows clearly what Durkheim meant by effervescent assembly, demonstrates that for

407

him such an assembly stands within the area of the religious, moral and political, although this is not to deny the possibility of other limited occasions. Further, Durkheim's words here are but another example of his denial that an effervescent assembly is the same as the gathering of a crowd.

Other criteria used by Durkheim, can also help to make the distinction between what might be called a true occasion of effervescent assembly and an apparent one. First, an effervescent *rassemblement* stands within the category of the serious side of social life – *la vie sérieuse* – and would exclude gatherings relating solely to recreation, and therefore, within the modern context, football matches and student carousals (see ch. 19). The overall purpose of a recreational meeting and one which concerns society at its deepest levels is totally different. The other determining factor is that effervescent assemblies, marked by *la vie sérieuse*, are associated with actions which are ritualized. The great event itself is periodically re-enacted by ritual or myth. This is in strong contrast to recreational assemblies, or non-religious, non-political assemblies, for example, a gathering of poets or artists. When the gathering is over, the participants return to everyday life, perhaps inspired in their work, and even aware of new ideas, but they would not ritualize the event. A conference of academics would go no further than organizing another conference, and never try to repeat the conference they had just concluded! What Durkheim therefore had in mind was that effervescent assemblies are those associated with the very heart of a society and as such are recognized by the members of that society.

4 Problems of differentiation from ritual

Up to now we have challenged a number of criticisms levelled against Durkheim's concept of effervescent assembly, but it has to be admitted that the concept is not without some difficulties and confusions.

Earlier, we pointed out that Durkheim implies in effervescent assembly two functions, the creative and the re-creative. The first is dependent on a high level of effervescence, which, in a mysterious way, gives rise to novelty, for novelty is never to be had on demand. The second function is associated with common assembly and delirium which so transports the participants to a level of activity above the ordinary that they are reassured of the sacred and of the truth of their beliefs. The determining factor in both is common assembly, charged with emotional freedom and openness. Hypothetically these two functions can be differentiated, and it is theoretically possible to separate occasions when one function rather than another is seen to be at work. If a *rassemblement* produces new ideas and values which are socially acceptable, as in the case of the French Revolution and other revolutions, those new ideas can be readily identified, if of course the *rassemblement* has been subjected to historical record. But what of the assembly that has re-creation as its outcome? How can it be identified, even *ex post facto*? Clearly, one cannot demonstrate empirically that ideas are actually reinforced in individuals by collective effervescence. It is a presupposition and no testifiable means exists to demonstrate it. Therefore, the only way of identity is a negative one: where no new ideas emerge, the function must be *ipso facto* re-creative. This is a feeble method of identity. Perhaps Durkheim could have avoided it by arguing – and there would appear to be evidence for this – that the re-creative function is always present in effervescent assembly. Sometimes, however, the creative function emerges and it is thus added to the re-creative. The argument is crude and we cannot attribute to Durkheim what he did not say. When he put forward his ideas, there were no criticisms along the lines we have indicated. The point is that identity and description are dependent on outcome, and only one possible function can be empirically established. Further, although Durkheim indicates that emotional intensity accompanies an occasion of effervescence when the creative function is dominant, it cannot be easily differentiated from other occasions, still emotionally charged, when re-creation is the result.

We have also repeatedly said that the great turning-points of a society's history are periodically and dramatically portrayed in ritual – something that is necessary for social recall and therefore social assurance. Such ritual enactment is very close to effervescent assembly in which the function is re-creative. Both have two important components – they are gatherings of people with common bonds and sentiments, and both bestow some inner strength on the individual. But how, then, can one be differentiated from the other? Effervescent assembly of a re-creative kind from ritual? The answer is difficult to discover, because Durkheim did not carefully differentiate these two types of social behaviour. He saw in ritual something of effervescence and in effervescent assembly something of ritual. He wrote: 'The state of effervescence in which the assembled worshippers find themselves. . .' (525/381). He assumed that any company of worshippers would create a certain amount of delirium. It was true of the Arunta; but it is universally true whenever people meet for a religious, moral or some other serious purpose. It is found, he held, that the moral temperature of the individuals rises and something *sui generis* is created. Be that as it may, the problem is that, seen externally, it is very difficult to differentiate the two phenomena which depend on a common principle and whose functions and external effects are so similar. The notion of some kind of continuum – at one pole creative effervescence, at the other ritual – might save the day, although this is foreign to Durkheim's thought. But something of a continuum, by way of degrees of intensity, is indicated when he wrote:

> When it attains a certain degree of intensity, the collective life excites religious thought because it gives rise to a state of effervescence, which changes the conditions of psychic activity. (603/422/151)

Mary Douglas in *Natural Symbols* attempts to differentiate the conditions which give rise to collective effervescence from those which favour ritual (1970:73–4). Effervescence, she argues, is likely to occur where there exists in society a lack of opportunity of articulation within the social structure; where there is weak control over individuals by the group; where there is little distinction recognized between interpersonal and public patterns of relationships; and where society is not differentiated from the self. And in the symbolic order, effervescence will arise where symbols are diverse, where expression is spontaneous, where there is no interest in ritual differentiation, no marginality or interest in inside-outside group relations, where control of consciousness is not exalted. By contrast, ritualism occurs where these conditions for effervescence are of an opposite kind. In delineating such social conditions, Mary Douglas has usefully extended Durkheim's ideas and tried to show under what conditions effervescent activity is to the fore, and periods of history when ritual dominates. However useful such a contribution is, it does not help us solve the problem we have raised, namely, that of differentiating re-creative effervescence from ritual. Further, Mary Douglas seems to disregard Durkheim's contention that actual, if not latent, effer-vescence is present in all ritual.

5 The source of religion?

The collective assembly charged with effervescence was held by Durkheim to be the locus of religious vitality and force, and therefore to be the source of religion itself. In the assembly, man feels transformed and is therefore able to transform his environ-ment (603/422/151). The ecstasy which man so experiences takes him out of himself and he feels that he is indeed a new being (324/227/136). Religious energy – what keeps religion going – is thus to be found in effervescent assembly.

When Durkheim put this idea forward, it caused a great deal of contention. That religion was kept alive by social forces fired by common assembly was near anathema to orthodox Christians and many liberal-minded academics. For example, Gaston Richard (1923), stood firmly opposed to the notion of a collective, non-rational locus of religion; and this was reiterated by his best-known student, Roger Bastide (1930:435). The dominant thinking of the day, be it that of the humanist or believer, was that the source and origin of religion was in the individual, in his spiritual or psychic powers, in his awareness of nature, especially in coming face to face with unusual natural events. As we have stated before, Durkheim freely admitted that the individual had a place in the development of religion, but he found it difficult to accommodate the individual within his scientific framework (see ch. 10). The role of the religious virtuoso began to be analysed by his disciples, S. Czarnowski in his *Le Culte des héros et ses conditions sociales* (1915) and also by H. Hubert who wrote the preface. It might also be noted that certain early anthropologists such as Marett, Goldenweiser and Lowie placed emphasis on the individual by

411

making religious thrill, or something like it, the centre of religion itself, and that implied the centrality of the individual.

Today these issues are of little consequence. The interminable arguments as to whether or not religion is to be located in the social or the individual now seem pointless. Religion is no longer viewed as a force or a substance to be derived from one source – one fountain – as if the source can be found as the source of a river is found. Religion is seen to be too complex a phenomenon for Man to be able to say that its source or power is to be found in one specific area within the totality of human experience (see Macbeath 1952:300–1). Durkheim may well have exaggerated common assembly as the source of religion because of his great concern with the social, but he never denied the influence of individual inspiration and leadership. The social, and the religious as part of the social, were in his eyes complex entities and were certainly not thought to be synonymous. He answered an attack on his position with these words:

> M. Delacroix appears to have lost sight of the real and significant diversity of social life. This diversity allows us to understand how the religious can be social but that *not everything social is religious*. (1913b:84; our italics)

To speak of the source of religion as being something to be found in either the individual or the social is to make an assertion that is of little worth.

6 Effervescence and *représentations*

Durkheim's theory of collective effervescence is closely associated with his theory of *représentations* (see ch. 15). He saw that *représentations* had characteristics which were similar to those of social life in as much as such life is given to psychic variation and to intermittency. *Représentations* are most intense when men assemble together and when they all have a common mind and a common sentiment (493/345). Religious beliefs are but a particular case subject to the general law relating to collective *représentations* (325/227/136). The law is that collective *représentations* emerge within the context of collective delirium. Occasions of group effervescence thus constitute the mysterious spring from which collective *représentations* emerge. One argument against Durkheim is that his concept of effervescent assembly is intrinsically bound up with his concept of *représentations*. If the latter are rejected as being untenable, the former is also to be discarded. But this is not necessarily so. Durkheim's notion of effervescent assembly can be accepted irrespective of his theory of *représentations*. It is true that collective *représentations* stand at the heart of his concept of society and that therefore they are of the utmost importance for his sociology. It is also true that a common religious belief is a particular case of collective *représentations*. But over and above these observations, Durkheim's theory of effervescent assembly can stand in its own right and can be both an instrument for understanding certain religious phenomena and, in wider terms, can also be seen as the locus of social change.

So, does Durkheim's concept of effervescent assembly constitute a *theory* of religious and social change? Even viewed in terms of its creative function, it cannot be held to be a theory comparable with other theories of social change put forward by such nineteenth-century sociologists as Herbert Spencer and Karl Marx. Durkheim's theory of effervescence fails to account for gradual social transformations which take place in society. In the generally accepted sense, therefore, we cannot call his analysis a theory. His prime task was to locate one point of origin of change heretofore overlooked by historians, anthropologists and philosophers. Durkheim never suggested that effervescent assembly was the only place where ideas or religious energy originate. Nevertheless, most changes in moral, religious and political ideas emerge from communal ebullience and in this sense are social, nonrational and, for the moment, mysterious. Out of the *je ne sais quoi* excitement of the times, out of social upheaval, as in the case of the French Revolution, new ideas and hopes arise and, under such circumstances, people are so moved towards the ideal that they imagine it can be realized. The point of emergence is common excitement amongst people holding similar beliefs and values. Here is no theory of social change, but rather the locus of revolutionary, non-rational change – the emergence of ideas that have sudden and shattering consequences and produce change.

Représentations in the last analysis arise out of mental activity,

413

intellectual activity. Durkheim attempts to show in his references to effervescence, in connection with, say, the Crusades, in his lectures on higher education that the delirium that arose in the Carolingian establishment of Christendom was then channelled into the intellectual fervour of the Middle Ages, reaching a high watermark in scholasticism (1938a/1969f:79–80/t.1977a:66). The point that Durkheim stresses is that before there is intellectual change, there must be some moral or social ebullience – it is this which triggers off new ideas. He wrote:

> In order to be able to devote oneself to the work of prime, objective thought, it is necessary to have a reserve of energy available, which is in surplus to that demanded by the difficulties of day-to-day existence. When such a reserve exists, because it is not compelled to put itself to use outside, it naturally turns to the inner life, to thought and to reflection. (ibid.)

Thus effervescent activity is a necessary precursor of intellectual thought.

There is the continuing process and here Durkheim's contribution is considerable. It is not just that ideas originate, but that irrespective of their logical content they persist, not through rational reflection and argument but through ritual re-enactment – the re-enactment of the occasion of their origin. Mircia Eliade has written that the 'popular success' of Durkheim's chief work has been 'due primarily to his identification of religious experience with religious enthusiasm' and thus it is more important for an understanding of western mental outlook than for its analysis of primitive religion (1973:21).

7 The problem of creativity

Immediately preceding a reference to emotional excitement that can break out in crowds (*foules*) and assemblies (*assemblées*) Durkheim, in his lectures, *L'Éducation morale*, speaks of the nature of the collective and once again brings up his key notion that society is an entity *sui generis* (1925a:70/t.1961a:61). Not surprisingly, he uses the old analogy of bronze, whose characteristics cannot be determined from the elements which constitute it, just as the life of a cell cannot be established from a knowledge of the 'inanimate, mineral molecules, which compose it' (ibid.). We have already considered the use of this analogy and the problems it raises, amongst them the relation of wholes and parts (see chs 9.2 and 13.3). The import of the analogy in connection with collective effervescence is the imaginative yet logical link Durkheim makes between effervescent assembly and the nature of society. The point is that what emerges from an assembly cannot be analysed as merely the outcome of the activity of the individuals who take part in it. Hence creativity – the emergence of the unique – springs from a whole, the total assembly. Durkheim, deeply concerned with the problem of change, sees that new ideas and practices come into being in the course of history, in much the same way as new substances are formed out of the combination of more basic elements – substances which have qualities and characteristics which are not the calculus of those of the combining elements. This is what he implied in 'Value judgments and judgments of reality'. 'The great ideals upon which civilization rests,' Durkheim says, come from 'periods of creation and renewal' when men come close to one another and frequently gather (1911b/1924a:134/t.1953b:91). Individuals by themselves explain nothing: what is important is their interaction and their assembling. Bouglé, in an article which was to become the preface to Durkheim's *Sociology and Philosophy*, states that 'chemical synthesis' is a central point in Durkheim's thought (1924:x/ t.1953b:xxxviii), and whether or not Durkheim took this general idea from Wundt who used the phrase 'mental chemistry' is not particularly relevant at this point (Gisbert 1959:361; ch. 9.2). Durkheim, in fact, never uses the phrase mental chemistry or even chemical synthesis. What is more significant is that, in using the concept of combination, he saw that it 'produces effects that the properties of the constituent elements would not lead one to expect' (Bouglé 1924). (See also his interest in combination and creativity in 1897a:110/t.1951a:126.) Durkheim's attempt to deal with creativity and what is new in social life is a commendable sociological step. He proceeds to locate new phenomena and seek their explanation in terms of effervescent assembly. (In the more general sense, in considering the emergence of the new, Durkheim's work here parallels that of Simmel, Weber and Popper, and more recently that of Norbert Elias, who sees that unintentioned and unplanned processes emerge in social interaction.)

Goldenwesier. who incorrectly holds that Durkheim sees society as a sublimated crowd and therefore readily uses the concept of group delirium, maintains that Durkheim's theory does not account for creativity in so far as 'a crowd psychology situation may intensify or even transform a religious thrill, but it cannot create one' (1917/r.1933:371). 'Thus a series of corroborees does not make an intichiuma, nor do secular dances of the North American Indians become identified with religious dances' (ibid.). Such criticism seems to miss the point, not least because of Goldenweiser's misreading of Durkheim's analysis. Aspects of the ordinary, of the mundane, have in the course of history been sacralized. How else has the sacred been created? Despite Durkheim's own 'effervescence' about communal effervescence blinding him to certain problems, the fact remains that the value of effervescent assembly is in locating and analysing sociologically new social movements, revolutions and new religious trends characterized by revivalism. Today sociologists and anthropologists are turning their attention more and more to the unstructured elements of society rather than to the structured, concerning themselves with the jagged rather than the smooth. It is precisely here that Durkheim offers insights and a tool of analysis which can be of great value. In this matter we should mention the work of Victor Turner in his concepts of liminality and communitas, where he has attempted to explore systematically areas of social life which Durkheim was bold enough to include within his sociological perspective. In *The Ritual Process* Turner sees social life not in static terms, but as a 'dialectical process that involves successive experience of high and low, communitas and structure' (1969:83). It is a process of opposites, of contrasting experiences indispensably interlocked. Liminality and communitas stand in stark contrast to structure and status. Turner applies these concepts to a large number of situations and individuals, to many pre-literate societies, to hippies, to types of Franciscans, millenarianists, and certain eastern religious movements (for example, the Vaisnavas). He refers to such religious leaders as the Buddha, St Francis, Tolstoy, Gandhi, St John of the Cross and so on. His concepts are much wider than Durkheim's effervescent assembly, but there are parallels in so far as they are transient conditions in which there is freedom from general norms (1974:274). Turner associates Bergson's *élan vital* with liminality and communitas and thus acknowledges the influence of Bergson on his work. We have already hinted that Durkheim may have received some inspiration from that source.

Part V
Contemporary Religion

23　Durkheim's attitude to traditional religions

1 Introduction

Durkheim's analysis of religion was in the main based on ethnographic data relating to beliefs and practices of primitive peoples. But as he repeatedly showed and so often implied, he intended that his findings could be generalized and seen to be universal, and therefore it was legitimate to extend them to modern society. Indeed, the test comes in applying his theories to modern religion. He did not, however, directly examine the religious scene in Europe in his day – a scene marked by social differentiations and a plurality of denominations, nor is there any evidence to indicate that he ever intended to embark on such a task. It might well be argued that his conclusions, contrary to his own position, cannot be generalized and that his findings do not in fact apply to contemporary western society with its religious pluralism (but see Hammond 1974:116ff.).

Although Durkheim wrote no systematic treatise on contemporary religion, he did frequently consider it (for example, Protestantism and its relation to suicide), and he made a large number of references to Christianity and Catholicism. Nor was he loath to talk about contemporary religion in more general terms (see especially 1919b). To Judaism, strangely enough, his allusions were rare and brief (see ch. 1.2). But what must not be forgotten is that, in connection with the present day, Durkheim saw emerging in Europe a new religion based on humanism, which would transcend old, dying forms, namely, that of traditional western religion. Many were his references to this.

The intention of the chapters which follow is to outline Durkheim's attitudes towards the traditional religions of Europe, with the exception of Judaism; to examine his writings on what might loosely be called secularization; and finally to look at his analysis of what he believed was the religion of the future.

2 Christianity praised

Despite Durkheim's rejection of the creedal assertions of Christianity, he nevertheless displayed a high regard for it as a religion. In this respect, as we have already noted, he is markedly different from some atheistic rationalists, who saw little good in religion of any kind, let alone Christianity (see ch. 1).

Durkheim's (on the whole) generous appraisal is seen throughout his entire life, but never more so than in the early period. In the *Division of Labour*, he defends Christianity against those extremists who would attack it on grounds of its intolerance of other religions and alien thought. In contrasting Christianity with the religion of the Romans, he held that, in the matter of freedom and tolerance, the then emerging religion far exceeded those religions which had gone before it, or which might be seen to be its rivals (1893b/1902b:137/t.1933b:163). Durkheim was attempting to show that societies characterized by organic solidarity, such as those in our modern western world, paid less attention to penal law than societies marked by mechanical solidarity, such as primitive societies. In Christianity, ritual crimes which can be classified as penal crimes are given a smaller place than in other religions. And 'sacrilege, of which blasphemy is only one variety, [and] heresy under various forms, are hereafter considered the only religious forms' (ibid.). Indeed, Church leaders only resorted to penal sanctions when the fabric of Christian society was threatened by some infamous action or when it was openly attacked. They did not demand repressive action for offences of a minor kind, but only those which threatened its fundamental principles. Hence, with the passing of time, the list of crimes committed in the name of religion becomes less numerous. In a footnote Durkheim observed that the death penalty for heretics was introduced for the first time as late as 1226 and he held that this was part of the 'normal development of Christianity' (ibid). He concludes that as 'everybody knows . . . the Christian religion is the most idealistic [*idéaliste*] that has ever existed' (ibid.). Its central beliefs were broad generalizations and not rigid or narrow doctrines and practices.

In a later observation, Durkheim noted that what Christianity was able to do politically was to separate 'the temporal and spiritual, the theological and political' (1918b/1966a:192/t.1960b:133). With other religions there had been no such split – religious crime was a political crime and vice versa; and to be a member of a state meant to be a practitioner of its religion. That Christianity was responsible for the creation of two spheres gave rise to the possibility of flexibility of thought in political and moral matters, and so there emerged freedom of thought itself, which is thus directly descended from Christianity. More specifically, this freedom gained its impetus in the Middle Ages as scholasticism appeared. Here was the first deliberate attempt to create open argument in which the rights of discussants were freely admitted. In passing, one would add that the councils of the Church were doing this long before.

Durkheim developed the notion that Christianity was an 'idealistic' religion in his lectures on French higher education (1938a). *L'Évolution pédagogique en France* is a book of considerable importance in attempting to understand Durkheim's thought, not least on religion. Using a wide historical canvas, he covers the development of educational ideals and theory in the western world. The lectures demonstrate his ability as a historian who at the same time derives sociological insights from his material. Not surprisingly, he shows how certain aspects of western culture have developed in accordance with Christian ideals. His references to Christianity are extensive and detailed, and we can only hope to mention some of his more pertinent observations in conjunction with his other writings. Once again, as in his doctoral thesis, he contrasts Christianity with classical religions and notes its idealistic qualities, by which he means both a concern with personal moral values and also an emphasis on belief. For Christians, God is believed to reign over the soul of man and not over his body (1938a/1969f:323/t.1977a:282). God is not to be worshipped with material things (for example, in offerings of food), but rather he is to be the subject of the soul or mind and to be loved. Hence the Christian turns his thought inwards, to within himself as the source of life, and hence there arises the most common practice of prayer which is basically something interior. The soul – the principle of the inner life – is a direct manifestation of the divine. Christianity broke with the notion that the centre of religious activity is the material world, and so prominence was given to the spiritual, personal, the intellectual. Durkheim wrote elsewhere:

Gradually human duties are multiplied, become more precise, and pass to the first rank of importance, while others on the contrary, tend to become attenuated. One might say that Christianity itself has contributed most to the acceleration of this result. (1925a:7/t.1961a/r.1975:194)

This theme was also stated in *Professional Ethics and Civic Morals* (1950a/1969g:94/t.1957a:58).

The emphasis on the interior life, basic as Durkheim saw it to be to Christian theology, had many consequences. First, it meant that the human personality, which can be identified with the soul, became of the utmost importance and hence received ultimate status. In *Suicide* he wrote that it 'has become sacred, even most sacred in their [the Christians'] eyes, something which no one is to offend' (1897a:378/t.1951a:333). It had one practical result which was of concern to Durkheim at the time. Because what was essential in man, his psyche, was sacred, it was therefore sinful to damage it wilfully as by an act of suicide. And the Christian Church, from its early days through to Catholicism and Protestantism, has always held that suicide constituted a sinful act. It is thus nothing less than sacrilege. Durkheim's own judgment against suicide as being an immoral act is based on very similar arguments. He believed that the religion of his day – a religion of humanity – was based on such doctrines, so that suicide 'must be classed among immoral acts; for in its main principle', suicide denies the ideals of such a religion (ibid.:383/337). In brief, suicide is the violation of the personality. The person is and must be considered to be sacred, neither the individual nor the group is free to dispose of it at will. Hence an act of suicide causes society to be injured 'because the sentiment is offended on which its most respected moral maxims today rest' (ibid.).

Another consequence of the Christian doctrine of the supremacy of the individual soul was that it gave rise to modern humanism, to the cult of the individual (see ch. 26). Durkheim noted that no matter how remarkable was the place given to the individual in Roman times, it was insignificant compared with what was developed in Christianity (1950a/1969g:94/t.1957a:58). In Durkheim's moving article on individualism, written under the shadow and alarm of the Dreyfus affair, he said that 'the originality of Christianity has consisted precisely in a remarkable development of the individualist spirit' (1898c:11/t.1969d/r.1975:68). As a result of Christian doctrine, the individual was given integrity, personal rights, and allowed to express himself, within limits, as he wanted to. Durkheim held that such restricted individualism constituted in part the teaching of Christianity (ibid.). He could not identify himself with Christian morality in its entirety, nor, on the other hand, with that form of individualism which bordered on egoism.

Also, Christians were commanded to love one another and indeed mankind. Because of the sacredness of all individuals, and because their God was a god of the spirit and of love, they were encouraged to be concerned for their neighbours and, as a consequence, Durkheim held that there was a decline in the number of duties addressed specifically to the deity. On one of the rare occasions that Durkheim referred to the atonement, he wrote:

> An essentially human religion since its God dies for the
> salvation of humanity, Christianity teaches that the principal
> duty of man toward God is to love his neighbour. (1925a:
> 7/t.1961a:6–7/r.1975:194)

Durkheim saw that the history of western society could not be understood apart from a Christian doctrine which lay at its root. Christianity was the main force in forging that culture which was to become dominant in Europe and which is the foundation of modern society. It was the Church alone that was able to influence, educate and civilize the barbarians and invading Germanic peoples in the ninth century. No other comparable force was able to exert itself and to give Europe moral unity. It was without a rival, especially in the absence of any national civilization which might have opposed it. Christianity at this period was essentially international, transcending locality and region. And the monk had a definite part to play, since he was mobile, and carried the pervading culture from one country to another. He was a truly universal figure in so far as he was in one sense of no particular country, being in the service of a universal religion (1938a/1969f:49/t.1977a:39). On such a foundation arose the Carolingian renaissance and the concept of Christendom itself.

For Durkheim, what Christianity had to offer was in sharp contrast to that of rival religions around the Mediterranean, for at its heart was a contempt for the joys and pleasures of the world, a rejection of material luxury and the refinement of pleasure. In their place it substituted the joys of renunciation (ibid.:27/20). It did not praise asceticism for its own sake or embark on extreme renunciation. It extolled the virtues of humility and unpretentiousness in material and intellectual spheres, and thus it upheld the ideal of a simple way of life. This had an obvious attraction for the poor. As Durkheim said: 'Christianity was supremely the religion of those who were not great' economically or culturally (ibid.:28/21 also 1897a:282/t.1951a:254). The Church thus found itself attracting peoples who were poor, who were of non-Roman origins, and it was able to weld them together by a common faith and culture.

Quite logically the Church took the initiative in the matter of education. One reason for this was the success of the Church in its mission of converting the barbarians, notably the Germanic peoples. But at the same time, it was rooted in Roman civilization and culture, and the Latin language was at the very centre of its life. This language had therefore to be taught to the converts. Another reason, as has been noted, was that a Christian doctrine laid emphasis on faith, and therefore on thought. Hence the contents of its doctrine had to be rationally imparted to others and understood by them, and this called for educational institutions. The Church, as no other body could, entered the field of education and thoroughly developed it. Realizing this, Durkheim gave a considerable place to the role of the Church in his lectures on higher education (1938a; see especially chs 2–4, 26–7, and the following section of this chapter on the work of the Jesuits).

Within Christian education itself, Durkheim noted that it was not just concerned with facts but with basic values and indeed the whole of life. He wrote:

> Christianity was aware that the forming of a man was not a question of decorating his mind with certain ideas, nor of getting him to contract certain specific habits; it is a question of creating within him a general disposition of the mind and the will which will make him see things in general in a particular light. (1938a/1969f:37/t.1977a:29)

And the agents of education – indeed its leaders – were for the most part members of religious communities and orders. As so

many others have had occasion to observe, Durkheim emphasized
the fact that the religious life in Christianity was never one that
was totally contemplative in outlook. It was essentially communal
and had been greatly influenced by the rule of St Benedict, who
placed emphasis on work as well as on prayer and worship
(ibid.:31, 46/24, 35). In the medieval period the monasteries were
not only centres of 'research' in letters and philosophy, but were
also institutions in which aspiring intellectuals were taught (1950a/
1969g:95/t.1957a:59).

We have described in a somewhat cursory fashion Durkheim's
attitude towards Christianity in general, and by that we mean the
development of the religion up to the time of the Reformation.
The subsequent history of Catholicism and the Protestant churches
interested Durkheim in various ways, and it is to this later period
of Christian history that we now turn and consider the ways the
leaders of these religious groupings had occasion to refer to his
sociology.

3 Roman Catholicism: Durkheim's admiration and disgust

Durkheim's attitude towards modern Roman Catholicism, from
say the time of the Counter-Reformation, was very mixed. His
fleeting attraction in his teens towards this form of Christianity
has already been mentioned (ch. 1). Although he withdrew from
the possibility of conversion, there were aspects of Catholicism
he greatly respected and continued to do so to the end of his life.

In an early essay – his first to appear in the *Année sociologique*
– on the subject of incest and its origins, he noted with apparent
approval that the Roman Catholic Church saw sexual relations as
having an immediate end in the creation of a family and he went
on to observe that the same church prohibited sexual intercourse
on holy days. Strongly implanted in Durkheim's mind was the
conviction that uncontrolled sexual drives stand opposed to family
morality. This was most apparent in a discussion of the Société
Française de Philosophie on sexual education, in which he openly
stated his opposition to extra-marital sexual relations on the
grounds, amongst others, that it had a disruptive effect on family

solidarity (1911a:46/t.1979a:146). Durkheim, academically and personally such a strong supporter of the family, believed that the home in the past and the present had a religious character, which of necessity was based on collective discipline (1898a(ii):67/ t.1963a:111; and see Lukes 1972:263 n.45, etc.).

But discipline is required not only within the family, but in every area of social life. This concern with discipline is based, in turn, on Durkheim's doctrine of man. From his early writings and extending to those which appeared just before he died, there is a repeated demand for the need of discipline which is based on the firm assumption that man's instincts need to be controlled (see relevant sections in 1897a, 1925a; etc.). Man is not a creature to be liberated from social or economic oppression, from the shackles of fear and guilt, from the crippling effects of institutions, or from the degradations of capitalism. To the contrary, man's freedom comes from ensuring that his instincts are controlled by moral limits which are set by society. What makes a man a human being, and not a quasi-animal, is his acceptance of, and incorporation into what his fellow creatures have made – the culture or the civilization in which he is born. Socialization, which begins at the time of birth, is the process by which man comes to a position of acceptance and compliance; and therefore of humanness. When, however, the process is inadequate, when man openly rejects the norms and limitations set by society, when the sky is the limit, a state of anomy emerges, for man now runs wild without the boundaries within which he can operate. A position of limitless freedom and ambition gives rise to social chaos. The guarantee of social order and prevention of the anomy, which society so deeply fears, are thus dissolved when the moral limits and disciplines of society are rejected for one reason or another.

Such a doctrine of man has affinities with that of certain classical writers, for example, Plato and Aristotle. However, Durkheim chose not to mention these parallels, but to go straight to Christian sources, speaking in general terms and, surprisingly, making no reference to St Paul's writings. It is beyond doubt that Durkheim's own doctrine of man is derived from orthodox Christianity as Felix Pécaut noted (1918:4). (Pécaut (1828–98) had once been a Protestant minister, was chosen in 1880 by Ferry to organize an important teacher training college for women, and as a liberal Protestant tried to base moral education on religious feeling.)

Another aspect of the Christian doctrine of man that Durkheim adopted with modification was the notion of man's duality (see 1913b and 1914a). Man, he upheld, was possessed of two components or elements within himself, body/soul, sacred/profane, egoistic appetites/moral action, and so on. Needless to say, such a position, metaphysical in its assertions, has been widely criticized both in his day (see 1913b) and again more recently (Sumpf 1965:66ff.). The point here is not to expound Durkheim's doctrine or to criticize him, but to demonstrate his borrowing of certain Christian ideas.

Whereas the orthodox Christian doctrine of man is common to both Catholics and the majority of Protestants, we have mentioned it within the context of modern Catholicism because Durkheim was of the opinion, evident in his *Suicide*, that the spirit of discipline and moral constraint which are a necessary element of his doctrine of man, were in modern times better upheld by Catholics than by Protestants. At various periods Protestants had been subject to influences which granted considerable authority and autonomy to the individual (see the next section of this chapter), whereas the Catholic Church, in rejecting such doctrine and later setting its face against liberalism, was able to exert over its followers a clear-cut morality and to administer it through the confessional. Never let it be forgotten that Durkheim's attachment to liberalism in morals and politics was one that maintained the necessity of self-discipline and the imposition of social discipline. Any notion that liberalism should veer towards egoism or libertinism was strongly repudiated (see ch. 26.4).

The thought and practice of the Jesuits occupied a considerable place in Durkheim's lectures on higher education (1938a; pt II, chs 5–7). In their response to the impetus and success of the Protestant Reformation, the Jesuits, who helped to restore the morale and domain of the Catholic Church, broke the monopoly of higher education which had been centred solely in the universities. The Catholic Church needed to enter into close and influential relations with the growing intellectual classes. This demanded educational and social ability on the part of the Church and for the emergence of a system which would be designed to train people for specific tasks and occupations in society. The Jesuits, realizing the need, saw that it could be met only by mingling with the world and being open to its dominant ideas, even assimilating them, but at the same time using them for the ultimate good of the Church. This meant a new type of religious order which would be prepared to enter every important social area of life, to break out of the rigidity of the old communities and orders, and at the same time to be maintained and strengthened by firm self-discipline. In seeking to influence the young and operate a new type of education, the Jesuits held that it was necessary to harness Renaissance thought, which could lead so easily to Protestantism; this meant making full use of classical learning, to the point of trying to control it and demonstrate its theoretical importance for the Church. One outcome was that their students had to speak Latin in everyday conversation. So successful were the colleges founded by the Jesuits that for a time the very existence of the universities was threatened. In overlooking some of the common accusations made against the Jesuits – for example, their rigidity of goal coupled with flexibility of means, bordering on the immoral – Durkheim stated that 'Jesuit education played the major part in the formation of our national genius, and gave it the distinctive features which it exhibits in the period of its full maturity' (1938a/1969f:274/t.1977a:239). The Jesuits emphasized written exercises amongst their students, something unknown in the age of scholasticism; and eloquence or rhetoric was looked on as a superior art. On the other hand, little or no place was given to understanding classical civilization set in a historical context. Further, the classics were so taught that profane or pagan though they were, they were used as eulogies for the faith, and in so doing the Jesuits deliberately 'denatured the ancient world' (ibid.:287/250; see also ibid.:293/255). They turned classical literature, which was so popular at the time and which was basically non-Christian, into a form which was held to be inspired by Christianity. With the Jesuits the love of learning for its own sake was lost. But here Durkheim seemed to praise the Jesuits for giving to education a specific purpose, that of making pupils faithful Catholics (ibid.:291/254), for Durkheim himself saw education in utilitarian terms because all knowledge and learning were for men's avocations in life (ibid.:265/230). Jesuit education, however, was crammed, intensive and highly competitive to the point of endangering the mind in the demand for written work and a lack of thoughtfulness on the part of students. On the other hand, Jesuits laid it down as axiomatic that there must be a close and personal link between the teacher and the pupil – something absent in medieval universities. The pupil was never left to his own ingenuity or by himself. The aim was as much to help the student as to prevent misconduct.

Durkheim concluded that the Jesuit system was well grounded in the conditions of the sixteenth century, but that the Jesuits applied their principles too rigidly. In coming too close to the student, they inhibited all freedom of movement, so that in the end their method became what we should today call counterproductive (ibid.:302–3/264).

But, by and large, compared with Protestantism, Durkheim saw in Catholicism in the nineteenth century a more rigorous, robust church capable of resisting profaning influences such as the intrusion of science and freedom of thought (1907c:51; see the following chapter).

Durkheim's attitude towards the Catholic Church was, however, ambivalent and he tempered words of praise with those of condemnation. He had a strong dislike of large, powerful bodies exercising control that can border on the despotic. This clearly emerges in his lectures on higher education in France where he writes:

When a body in authority, any body in authority, is fired by
a love of regimentation, when it has a tendency to make
everything conform to a single unique norm, it experiences an
instinctive horror for everything which is the result of whim
and imagination. Anything which might disturb the established
order takes on the appearance of a scandal which must be
avoided; and since elective affinities are necessarily
incompatible with programmes which have been decreed . . .
every effort is made to suppress them by restricting freedom.
(1938a/1969f:141/t.1977a:121)

Such sentiments are associated with a similar dislike of a rigid hierarchy. Richter has said:

As for his refusal to recognize bureaucracy as part of a normal
society, he identified bureaucracy with hierarchy, and
hierarchy with the Roman Catholic Church. As a 'survival'
from an earlier stage, this type of organization was obsolete.
(1960:203)

431

Thus, it was the nature of the structure of the Roman Catholic Church that Durkheim found quite unacceptable.

It was at an academic colloquium held in Paris in 1905 on the Separation of Church and State that Durkheim, speaking as a leading sociologist, caused uneasiness among his fellow discussants by referring to the Catholic Church as a 'sociological monstrosity'. The relevant part of the discussion reads:

> DURKHEIM: I shall only give you an impression: I believe the mistrust of the bishops [towards lay associations] is not without foundation. The law [of Separation], in the measure to which it will give more autonomy to lay people, will remove the Catholic Church from the abnormal position it is in now. The Church, from a sociological point of view, is a monstrosity.

> [Desjardins said that the Roman Catholic Church was not so much a monstrosity as miraculous.]

> DURKHEIM: It is the same thing. . . . It is abnormal that an association so vast and diffuse, which itself links up complex moral groups – where, as a consequence, so many causes of differentiation are bound to be at work – should be subject to such an absolute intellectual and moral homogeneity. (1905e:370)

Durkheim's very sinister word '*un monstre*' was such a forceful one that not only did it electrify the colloquium, it caused one of its members, Abbé Hemmer, to refer to it in a subsequent article in which he inverted the implication of the phrase:

> Durkheim has well said that the ancient institution of Christ is a sociological monstrosity. On this acceptable verification is founded in apologetics one of the proofs of the divinity of the Church ('Reflexions sur la situation de l'Église en France au début du XXe siècle', *La Quinzaine*, 1(3),1905, p. 4).

So Durkheim, in Hemmer's eyes, did stalwart service for the Catholic Church!

Were there other sources that made Durkheim openly hostile to Roman Catholicism? Lukes has made the point, and it is a common enough one, that Durkheim was 'a good anti-clerical' (1972:534). Such an accusation has to be concretely related to the specific historical situation of the day in which the clergy were able to control the political attitudes of their flocks. This was particularly obnoxious to Durkheim, as the prevailing clerical outlook was frequently royalist or right wing. The Dreyfus affair witnessed an upsurge in French Catholicism in the direction of hierarchical authoritarianism. As an ardent Dreyfusard, Durkheim saw that large sections of the Catholic Church, sustained by the local clergy, rallied to the cause of nationalistic triumphalism. It is little wonder therefore that Durkheim's anti-clericalism was all the more confirmed by the events of the affair (see ch. 1.4).

As Durkheim was ambivalent towards modern Catholicism, so there were some sections of the Catholic population similarly disposed towards him. Durkheim's contention that from available statistics suicide rates were lower in Catholic areas than in Protestant ones (see the following section of this chapter) carried ideological consequences and clearly pleased some Catholic apologists, particularly, as Richard noted, German Catholic clergy (1923:136/t.1975:240). It can also be argued in another direction that there exists common ground between Durkheim and Catholic theologians in so far as they both give a prominent place to institutional forms, and see that truth is located in rationality rather than in human consciousness or religious experience, as was common with many Protestants at the time.

These considerations apart, there was considerable objection from Catholic intellectuals to Durkheim's thought.[1] No Catholic apologist finding comfort in what Durkheim said about suicide would be equally pleased when he uncritically stated what Guyau had written: 'It is often the most Catholic countries which provide most criminals' (1887b:303/t.1975a:29). But other points of contention were much more serious: they related to Durkheim's assumptions about the nature of religion studied sociologically, his denial of the truth-claims of all religion, not least those of Christianity, that all religion is man-made, that the most important element of religion is its social component. These points we have already considered in detail in previous chapters. Nevertheless, Catholic opposition to Durkheim in the main was weak because the Church possessed no sociological thinker of his stature, comparable, let us say, with the Protestant sociologist, Gaston Richard (see the following section). Opposition tended to be more vociferous after Durkheim died, for it was aroused by the attempt of the Durkheimian, Paul Lapie, the French government's director of primary education, to introduce Durkheimian sociology into teacher training colleges (see ch. 27.3). While Durkheim was alive, the only serious academic opposition came from the French-speaking Belgian Simon Deploige (1905–7 and 1911; see ch. 4.1). But as Durkheim noted, not only had Deploige misunderstood elements of his thought, but he had very little to offer sociology save a return to Thomism (1907b and 1913a(ii)(15)). In the period after Durkheim's death, no comparable attack was launched by Catholics, and it has been said that they were not unhappy to support the arguments of Gaston Richard, not least because of his standing as a professor of sociology at the University of Bordeaux. This 'accidental' ecumenical venture was later streng-thened when Richard was asked to contribute to a series 'Actual-ités scientifiques et industruelles' edited by Jacques Chevalier in the 1930s. Chevalier was a right-wing Catholic, an 'integrist' who later served in the Petain government. He was a firm admirer of Richard and had been influenced by Le Play and Bergson.

After the Second World War one sees a remarkable change amongst certain liberally inclined Catholics. No longer is sociology seen to be an enemy of the Church, but now it is a handmaid. By its examination of the facts it can show the Church the inner workings of its institutions and is therefore to be welcomed. In the vanguard of the movement was the revered Catholic medieval historian and sociologist, Gabriel Le Bras, who became the patron of Catholic 'religious sociology' (see ch. 27.1 n.1). Influenced by Durkheim and his nephew, Marcel Mauss, Le Bras was convinced of the academic value of sociology in the study of religious phenomena and supported the contention of certain clerics that the application of sociology to the Church at the present time would equip the clergy with a means of combating the decline of religious institutions in France, which had occurred for over a century.

4 Protestantism: did Durkheim understand it?

Durkheim's attitude towards Protestantism was tepid, if not cold. He showed little of the ambivalence he had for Catholicism.

References to Protestantism are thinly scattered and, as readers might guess, it is in *Suicide* that most of his writings on the subject are to be found. As is well known, in searching for causal factors contributing to suicide, he attempted to discover whether various forms of religion had any bearing on rates of suicide and he found that, particularly in Switzerland, suicide tended to be higher amongst Protestants than amongst Catholics (1897a:bk III, ch. II). In his search to explain such a social fact – his methodological procedure need not detain us – he compared what he held were the social characteristics of Protestantism with those of Catholicism, which had significance in relation to suicide. Protestants, he noted, have fewer common beliefs and practices than have Catholics, the believer relies on his own conscience about his faith, and therefore his approach to religion is individualistic. The result is that the Protestant churches tend to be loosely integrated, for they exert very little control, nor do they inculcate a sense of religious loyalty and devotion as does the Catholic Church. Protestantism admits to a great deal of free inquiry, and for this and for other reasons there is to be found within it a strong desire for education. Amongst many variable factors, which are themselves interrelated, he holds that one provides the clue for tendencies towards suicide. It is the tendency to free inquiry. Yet it was something about which Durkheim was ambivalent. On the one hand, he strongly favoured it, but, on the other, he was aware that it weakens moral life. Towards the end of *Suicide*, he concludes that 'religion, therefore, modifies the inclination to suicide only to the extent it prevents men from thinking freely' (1897a:430/t.1951a:375). Catholics in the past have been able to do this, and Protestants to a less extent, but no religion today is able to exert sufficient control over individuals to prevent free inquiry, not even Catholicism. He adds, perhaps hinting at liberal Protestantism:

> When religion is merely a symbolic idealism, a traditional philosophy, subject to discussion and more or less a stranger

to our daily occupation, it can hardly have much influence on us. (ibid.:431/376)

Durkheim always saw ritual as a key element of religion (see part IV of this book). Protestantism was particularly vulnerable here, for Durkheim said in his lectures on moral education that the autonomy of morality in Protestantism is further accentuated by the fact that ritual is minimized. The moral function of divinity thus becomes its sole *raison d'être* (1925a:8/t.1961a:7/r.1975:195). As its specifically religious characteristics become eroded, spiritualistic philosophy, argued Durkheim, takes over from Protestantism, and in this sense Protestantism itself stands close to the long-standing evolution of history towards secularization (see the following chapter).

This is no occasion to challenge point by point Durkheim's assessment of Protestantism in relation to suicide. Some Protestant thinkers, for example, Gaston Richard, were fully aware of its implications and were therefore hostile towards him. However, it could be well argued that Durkheim wrote very much as an outsider and that his generalizations about Protestantism were far from accurate. Certainly some of the things he said hardly applied to the Calvinists in France, amongst whom there existed at the time he wrote, and still exists, a great sense of community and integration, in part engendered by years of persecution. L'Église Réformée as a minority group has striven to maintain its own identity and has thus created relatively close ties between its members. Durkheim admits such characteristics of small religious groups (1897a:155/t.1951a:156/t.1975:44). All the arguments to explain high suicide rates amongst Protestants could be applied to Jews, but, as Durkheim noted, their rates were particularly low. Durkheim was thus forced to find reasons which applied to Jews, but which did not apply to Protestants. This shifting of ground greatly weakens Durkheim's attempt to find a scientific explanation of the phenomenon he had unearthed.

The generalizations he tried to make about Protestantism raise the question of the value of such a term as Protestantism within sociological explanation. Protestantism exists within so many forms – from small sects like the Mennonites, to established churches such as the Lutheran Church – that it becomes very difficult to make universal statements about Protestantism which have a general significance. This difficulty is compounded by the fact that with the inroads of liberal thought into many Protestant churches there is to be found, on the one hand, dogma as rigidly held as that in the Roman Catholic Church, and, on the other, sets of beliefs which are little differentiated from humanism. The attempt to speak in broad terms is a failure that is to be seen also in Max Weber. Generalizations usually flounder when the Church of England is taken into consideration. Durkheim noted this to be the case in examining rates of suicide and found that amongst Protestant countries England had the lowest rates (ibid.:160ff./ 160ff./48ff.). Yet England is the country most famous for its individualism and for freedom of speech! Durkheim is thus forced to offer various lame reasons for the exception to his 'rule' – the Anglican Church is more integrated than Protestant churches; there are more clergy per capita in England than in any other Protestant country; there exists a hierarchical form of church government; and there are national laws relating to the observance of Sunday. Perhaps Anglicanism was to him something of a theological and a sociological mystery, as it is to many continental thinkers.

In his lectures, *L'Évolution pédagogique en France*, Durkheim did not give the Protestant churches much credit for the development of education in his country. But he noted that at the time of the Reformation amongst the Anglo-Saxon and Germanic peoples, humanism was very rapidly curbed (1938a:314/ t.1977a:274). In fact Lutheranism was basically indifferent towards humanism and the advocacy by Luther for a study of the classics had the sole object of equipping preachers adequately for their task (ibid.:326/285). In this respect Luther, together with Melanchthon, were far removed from the outlook of Erasmus and the leaders of the Renaissance in Latin countries. Durkheim wrote: 'The fact is that Protestantism had a feeling for secular society and its temporal interests which Catholicism neither possessed nor could possess' (ibid.:327/285). The result was that humanism never made the headway in Germany that it did in France in the sixteenth century.

To be fair, Durkheim did point to some qualities in Protestantism with which he was sympathetic – the notion of free inquiry, an emphasis on morality, and perhaps a minimizing of ritual. And he also admitted that in the change in educational theory towards a concern for nature and science that came at the time of the French Revolution, Protestant countries were of service in fostering the new pedagogy, because the religion 'was already sensitive to the non-clerical [*laïque*] side of society' (1938a/1969f:334–5/t.1977a:292).

Initially, it seemed that much in Durkheim's *Suicide* attracted some Protestant ministers, as well as German Catholic priests, although obviously for different reasons. Gaston Richard commented that they were 'too ingenuous' (1923:136/t.1975:240).

Gaston Richard (1860–1945), to whom many references have been made, was an early collaborator with Durkheim and worked with him on the *Année sociologique* (see ch. 2.4; Pickering 1975:343–59; 1979b). Having been brought up as a Catholic and having rejected the faith and spent a short time as a non-believer while he was at the École Normale Supérieure, he became a Protestant and remained a strong supporter of the Église Réformée to his dying day. Until his withdrawal, Richard was the sole Protestant in the Année Sociologique group, and perhaps the only member committed to any traditional religion (see ch. 27.2). Whilst at the École he became a friend of Durkheim and although he was never a member of the closest circle around Durkheim, he was, because of his early writings and doctorat d'état, a senior member of the *équipe* (see various articles in *RFS*, XX, 1979). In 1907, after ten years of co-operation with Durkheim, he withdrew from the group. Earlier, when Durkheim left the University of Bordeaux in 1902, Richard followed him as lecturer in sociology, and became a professor in 1906. There he remained until he died. Cut off from Durkheim's group, he became for a while an isolated figure. He was known to be the most outspoken critic of Durkheim and was frequently referred to as 'le vieil adversaire de Durkheim'. One of the causes for the rift and then hostility to Durkheim and his followers was over the question of religion. As we have seen, he held that in many respects Durkheim failed in his work to live up to the goal he had set himself, namely, a scientific approach to social phenomena. He in fact made metaphysical statements about religion and therefore ceased to be scientific. Durkheim also, he argued, denied the freedom of the individual and his contribution to the development of religion. It is evident that behind much of Richard's criticism there is implied

Durkheim's failure to understand Protestantism and indeed Christianity as well (see chs 27 and 28).

Another outspoken critic from the Protestant ranks was Marc Boegner (b.1881), who became an outstanding leader of the Église Réformée and a member of the Académie Française. At the conference of the Union of Free Thinkers and Free Believers held in 1914, it was his questions which Durkheim chose to answer in writing (see 1919b/t.1975a; also Poulat 1970). His questions on the whole tended to be critical and raised such issues as studying religion in its most primitive forms, the place of Australian Aboriginals amongst primitive peoples, the role of individual leaders in the evolution of religion and the relation between higher religions and those of a more primitive form (1919b:142–3/t.1975a:187–9; ch. 10.2).

5 A liberal or a medievalist?

In this chapter we have tried to demonstrate that Durkheim had considerable respect for Christianity. He pointed to its doctrines as being crucial in understanding the emergence of modern western society, for the Europe of his day had grown out of a Christendom based on strong religious beliefs. It is also clear that Durkheim held dear some of the values embedded in Christianity, notably its doctrine of man and its demand for discipline and self-control. He seemed to reject much of Protestantism, because he saw that it was far too individualistic and tended to encourage egoism. What clearly appealed to Durkheim most were the humanistic qualities that he saw in Christianity – a willingness to suffer for other people which is inherent in its doctrine of God and in the story of Jesus Christ dying for mankind. Christians were commanded to love their neighbours, to be concerned for the things of the spirit which ultimately leads to a concern for the individual. In all this speaks the honest liberal humanist, who does not condemn Christianity as being an evil that has to be eliminated, or a force which has done little good for society. Its contribution to culture has been crucial and its doctrine of man, expressed in orthodox terms has elements that are to be commended and which could be said to form part of the *raison d'être* of secular humanism.

That Durkheim was a convinced liberal and an ardent supporter of the Third Republic, no one can deny. But there is lurking behind this conviction not only the need for strict discipline, but a harking back to the ideals of the high Middle Ages. Dedicated though he was to the hopes of an emerging society based on democracy and free thought, Durkheim nevertheless, in his exploration of the history of Christianity, saw in the medieval period a most desirable combination of Christian belief, academic excellence and an integration of thought and action – something like praxis. Now it has been lost. He wrote in his lectures on higher education in France:

Nothing could be further from the truth than this view of the Middle Ages [that the Middle Ages was a sort of interval], and consequently nothing is more inappropriate than the name which we give to this epoch. Far from its being a mere period of transition without any originality of its own between civilizations which were brilliantly original it is rather the period of gestation for the fertile seeds of an entirely new civilization. (1938a/1969f:39/t.1977a:31)

Again, when Durkheim points to Abelard as the most representative figure of the medieval period, does he not indicate that there are in him virtues of the highest order? He had a:

brilliant dialectic, faith grounded in reason, and that curious mixture of religious fervour and a passion for knowledge which was a distinguishing mark of this great era. (ibid.:85/70; see also 84/69)

When speaking of scholastic philosophy, he notes that its characteristic is the mutual interpenetration of 'reason and faith within a single system of ideas which renders them inseparable from one another' (ibid.:112–13/96). Here it seems we have that perfect combination of faith and reason that Durkheim the rationalist sees to be ultimately desirable. Such unity, which existed in the medieval period, projected an ideal for which he strove in the twentieth century. Whilst he was unflinching in his support for *La Nation* and for liberal democracy, and whilst he rejected traditional Christian morality, though retaining a great deal of it, there is nevertheless beneath such externalities a secret longing for the ideals and aspirations of a much earlier period than his own.

Durkheim's respect for traditional western religion was basically a respect for something in the past, for a dying social force. The claims of that religion which had helped to found Europe could no longer be accepted by thoughtful people such as himself. For centuries in fact, longer than anyone had realized, that force had been diminishing and was now virtually spent. But for what reasons? It was a question to which Durkheim frequently addressed himself.

24 Secularization: the history of mankind

1 The inevitability of religious change

Although Durkheim had something approaching an innate warmness towards all religions, and in particular, as we have shown, towards Christianity, he did not believe that traditional religions would persist in Europe, nor did he think it desirable that they should. It was patently evident to him, as to many intellectuals of his day in France and elsewhere, that Christian belief and practice had reached their last days. It was no surprise to him that it should be so. In a frequently quoted sentence, he wrote: 'Les anciens dieux vieillissent ou meurent, et d'autres ne sont pas nés' – 'The old gods are growing old or are dying and other gods have not been born' (610–11/427/156). No gospel is immortal and that of the Christians is no exception. Every religion thus faces death. But some observers would note that, if traditional Christianity was on its death bed at the turn of the century, it has proved to be a long time dying. Religions are much more resilient than is often imagined.

Religious change is very much part of Durkheim's sociology. Although he wrote nothing systematic on it, especially in relation to the modern period, there are many references to it in his earliest writings as well as in his last.

There are, of course, two distinct issues – one is religious change *per se*, and the other is religious change implying a decline or weakening of religion within society, especially in its institutional forms. It is the latter issue that is associated with the contentious term secularization. Durkheim generally has at the back of his mind such a term. In some respects he saw secularization in far more radical terms than do many modern sociologists. Nevertheless, he had a paradoxical approach to the subject: religion is dying and society is becoming secular; yet, on the other hand, religion is alive and will always be a component of social life.

442

2 Words used by Durkheim relating to religious change and secularization

To describe the diminution of religious institutions, Durkheim did not use a French word which has a root in common with the English word secularization. The term secularization in its modern context is basically Anglo-Saxon. Rather, he employed several words, *déclin, affaiblissement, régression*. For example, he spoke about a weakening (*affaiblissement*) of religion in the *Rules* (1895a:162/t.1938b:132) and God 'progressively withdrawing' (*déclin*) from his relationships with man in the *Division of Labour* (1893b/1902b:144/t.1933b:169). At first sight, these are acceptable terms. For example, no one would object to the word decline (*déclin*). But reflection on the term regression (*régression*) suggests an ideological component, for it implies a 'reversion to a less developed form' (*Oxford English Dictionary*), and the same idea is indicated in the French. Gaston Richard attacks Durkheim precisely at this point. He holds that Durkheim is not sympathetic towards the claims and social facts of religion (1923:126/ t.1975:229). This is evident, if nowhere else, in Durkheim's adoption of the word *régression*. Sarcastically, Richard writes:

> Even before it was scientifically constituted, the history of religions had its inescapable law. The law was that the evolution of religion is regression or rather dissolution. (ibid.:133/236)

It is undeniable that for Durkheim the development of social institutions in the history of mankind has been accompanied by a regression of religion. He stated this in his first and last books, *Division of Labour* (1893b/1902b:144/t.1933b:169) and *The Elementary Forms of the Religious Life* (613/429/158).

Durkheim was being merely descriptive when he said that religion had now lost most of its sovereign power (*son Empire*) (1897a:283/t.1951a:255; see also 1900a(47)). One clear indication of its weakened state was its failure to control men's minds (*consciences*). This is evident if one compares a primitive society with a modern society: a primitive society is dominated by religion and, indeed, one can go so far as to say that one of the characteristics of primitiveness is religious domination. For a society to become

443

intensely religious means going back to the starting-point, that is, to becoming primitive. As Durkheim wrote:

> Unless the great societies today helplessly crumble and we return to little social groups of long ago, that is, unless humanity returns to its starting point, religion will no longer be able to exert very deep or wide sway over consciences. (1897a:430–1/t.1951a:375).

Thus, for Durkheim, regression would seem to be an unfortunate word to describe the decline in religious institutions unless it is used in a paradoxical sense. Durkheim would make it mean a loss of religious control, implying that it stands for a state in society in which traditional religion is outside the concern of man. Yet, as Richard rightly says, it means a return to a former state, and in Durkheim's terms this means society's return to religious domination. Hence two opposite meanings are contained in the one word. However, Durkheim envisages regression not just in terms of what might be called institutional religion. There is, over a wide historical sweep, a decline in the use of penal law, which Durkheim associates with religious law, and also a decrease in the number 'of proverbs, adages, dicta, etc. as societies develop' (1893b/1902b:144/t.1933b:170; see also 1901a(i)/t.1973b). This, he holds, is another proof in showing that collective *représentations* move towards generality and indeterminism, for in 'the fundamental conditions of the development of societies . . . there is a decreasing number of collective beliefs and sentiments which are both collective enough and strong enough to take on a religious character' (1893b/1902b:144/t.1933b:170).

The ambiguity that Durkheim exhibits about the term regression persists throughout his approach to secularization (this is also noted by Gluckman 1962:19–20). The ambiguity is based on his own ambivalence towards religion itself – a denial of its truth-claims, on the one hand, and a worship of its practical effects, on the other.

Disregarding for the present the ambiguities in the use of the word regression, we shall assume that in speaking of the decline of contemporary religion we refer only to its weakened institutional condition.

For analytical purposes, *déclin*, and the associated words just mentioned, must be separated from *séculier* (secular) and *laïque* (lay), which possess distinctive French connotations.[1] Their association with anti-clericalism and the separation of church and state has had a long history. It would be wrong to assume that a church forced to become 'secularized' or 'laicized' in the French sense, and therefore shorn of clerical, episcopal or papal domination, would suffer a priori a loss in respect or in allegiance. Nevertheless to Durkheim and others, such a loss of power within society would mean a loss of control and a weakened position as an agent of socialization. To be *laïque* or *séculier* is to be shorn of social power. Hence in the last analysis, *sécularisation* may mean secularization in the English sense. Whereas Durkheim may claim to be a scientific observer of the decline of traditional religion, he is also someone who lends support to its continual weakening, as for example in welcoming the separation of church and state (1905e) and, as we shall show, by propagating his scientific theories of religion (see ch. 28.2).

3 Age-long secularization

Durkheim sees the decline of religious institutions occurring along two time-scales. First, over a wide historical spectrum, in which secularization has been in progress for millennia. Second, in more recent times, in which there has been an acceleration of the process due to particular circumstances in western society. We shall deal with each idea separately.

For Durkheim the waning of religious institutions is not something new. It did not begin in the so-called modern period. Rather, it has been a continual process from the time that man's civilization began to develop. One could almost say that it is the story of man's social evolution, or at least a large part of it. Such a position logically emerges from Durkheim's notion that in the beginning everything was religious (see, for example, 1897e; ch. 14.3). The passage of time has meant that from a position of being encased in religion, societies have been able to dislodge most, if not all, social areas from religious domination. By man's discoveries and changes in his thought and values, areas of social life have been able to discard their religious ideology and become autonomous. In the history of secularization, ethics, art, philosophy, science, and so, on have eliminated all their original religious premises. The process has been at work throughout history: man's history is the history of his secularization.

Such thinking goes back to the first of Durkheim's books. Here he took a stand from which he never moved and to which he frequently alluded. The well-known passage is in *The Division of Labour*:

If there is one truth that history teaches us beyond doubt, it is that religion tends to embrace a smaller and smaller portion of social life. Originally, it pervades everything; everything social is religious; the two words are synonymous. Then little by little, political, economic, scientific functions free themselves from the religious function, constitute themselves apart and take on a more and more acknowledged temporal character. God, who was at first present in all human relations, progressively withdraws from them; he abandons the world to men and their disputes. At least, if he continues to dominate it, it is from on high and at a distance, and the force which he exercises, becoming more general and more indeterminate, leaves more place to the free play of human forces. (1893b/1902b:143/t.1933b:169)

He reiterated the same point in lectures given a little later in 1895–6 entitled L'Histoire du socialisme:

But in fact, as one advances in history, from inferior society to the city, from city to Christian peoples, one observes consistently that religion withdraws more and more from public life. (1928a:326/t.1958b:225)

The phenomenon of decline is linked in *The Division of Labour* with the contrast Durkheim made between societies marked by mechanical solidarity and those characterized by organic solidarity. The former are segmental, in which social life is regimented: empirically such societies are associated with primitive peoples. By comparison, societies marked by organic solidarity allow greater individual freedom, in which social life is more differentiated, and such societies are identified with those in the modern western world. Durkheim sees religion as being a dominant agent for control in societies characterized by mechanical solidarity; whereas in those typified by organic solidarity it is far less influential. Thus there is a regression of religion as societies change from possessing one type of solidarity to another. The movement appears to be inevitable and means a virtual devolution of religion. Little wonder, then, that Richard, in referring to ideas in the *Division of Labour*, wrote: 'It [religion] is a form of solidarity condemned to retrogression or disintegration by the very laws of its formation and development' (1923:233/t.1975:244–5).

In extending his thesis about organic solidarity, Durkheim saw one outcome of what we call secularization was that as social life becomes free from religious control, so religious thought turns to personal life. Unable to control public affairs, religion's only hope is to gain control and influence over followers in their personal lives. Thus the history of religion is the history of the development of its privatization. Belot pointed to privatization as being a key characteristic of western religion in his day (1909:37), and it would appear that such an idea was fairly common amongst French intellectuals at the turn of the century. More recently it has been emphasized by Berger (1967:133).

4 Recent secularization

Although the secularizing process has been with man for the length of his history, it has not proceeded uniformly and there have been fluctuations and accelerations, certainly in the western world in recent epochs. Such secularization, so much the stock in trade of modern sociologists of religion, became apparent, it is said, in the late eighteenth and early nineteenth centuries. It is often associated with the rise of industrialization. But Durkheim, in company with Max Weber, does not locate recent secularization either within that epoch or with its associated social characteristics (see the section below). He would make its point of emergence earlier, around the fifteenth and sixteenth centuries at the time of the Renaissance and Reformation, arising out of the breakup of medieval religion (1907c:51). A shift in thought occurred then that was in the direction of individualism. In the revival of Greek and Roman studies, which was at the heart of the Renaissance, man, not God, became the centre of the universe (see 1938a; chs. 15 and 17). At the Reformation, there was a different movement afoot, but the result was much the same. Authority in religious matters was seen by the reformers to be located no longer in an institution exercising temporal power, but in the individual and in his interpretation of the Bible. The basis for religious truth thus shifts from public to private authority (see ch. 23.4).

So it is that Protestantism, by changing the seat of religious authority from the Church to the individual helps to bring about a loss of religious power and control in society, and with it an overall diminution of religious institutions. Also, the right of the individual to choose in matters of religious truth must inevitably give rise to a pluralist society, which itself accelerates secularization. In locating the origins of recent secularization in the Renaissance and Reformation, Durkheim's position is but a logical development of his all-embracing theory of secularization.

As Durkheim was to say many times, religion does not have the same role in society today that it had in the past. Since it is 'a primordial phenomenon, it must yield more and more to the new social forms which it has engendered' (1899a(i):iv/ t.1960c:352–3). He saw no need to substantiate such a proposition about contemporary secularization, because for him it was wellnigh self-evident. In contrast to his study on suicide, a more precise analysis of the contemporary religious scene by way of statistics, say of church membership or attendance, was quite unnecessary. Indeed, in the review of a book on the subject, he doubted the value that could be derived from such analyses, not least that for religious rites of passage (1903(ii)(57)). Although there was a decline in the baptisms and marriages solemnized in church in Paris in the late nineteenth century, Durkheim held that such evidence in itself was a poor indicator of the state of religious belief (ibid.). (There is implied here a primacy of belief over ritual (see ch. 20).) He held that other indicators, much more conclusive about the state of contemporary religion, were available and these did not at the same time require the use of statistics or surveys. That modern religion was in a state of decline or going through a process of secularization could be shown, in Durkheim's eyes, in the following ways.

1 The loss of the temporal power of the Church, especially the Roman Catholic Church, is to be seen in the separation of Church and State which has taken place in so many countries in recent

times. What the Church has to offer is not openly supported by rulers: it may even be rejected. The modern state has no desire to be aligned with the beliefs and practices of any particular brand of Christianity, indeed with Christianity at all. Witness the separation of the Church and State in France in 1905 when the anti-clerical Third Republic was strong enough to overcome such ecclesiastical opposition as was then offered. The Church is given no option of assuming or rejecting an alliance with the state. Forced by its weakened condition, it has to assume a private role in society and, as we have said, to influence individuals as best it can. The truth of the matter is that the Church has now become a voluntary society.

2 Religion today allows itself to be the subject of scientific inquiry and of objective historical research. Formerly, until perhaps the eighteenth century, such an approach, especially in the Catholic Church, would have been unthinkable. It would have constituted an anathema and be seen as the work of heretics. That religion can now do no other than allow the scientist to pass through its doors and examine it as he does other phenomena means that it has lost control over its own affairs. The sacred of which it has been guardian, whether it be the sacred of some relic, the Bible, or the sacraments, is rendered profane by the possibility of uncovering what is believed to be the *raison d'être* of the sacred (1893b/1902b:270/t.1933b:285; 1907c; 1909a(1):517–8; and see following chapter).

3 In a similar way, Durkheim measured the secularized state of society in terms of the inability of religious institutions to enforce rules relating to sacrilege. A truly religious society is one where sacrilege is severely punished. As Durkheim wrote: 'A religion which tolerates acts of sacrilege abdicates any sway over men's minds' (1898c:12/t.1969d:27/r.1975:69). In religious societies schisms are also unknown or, if known, are not tolerated. Today, these criteria no longer exist. Sacrilege against the Church is not severely dealt with – hardly even considered. Indeed, can sacrilege be said to exist at all? Those who defame the Church, flout its rules, criticize its beliefs and deride its rituals, all go about their business unpunished, unmolested, and are looked upon as acceptable citizens.

4 The institutional weakness of the Church is paralleled by its inability to control the lives of individuals, although that sphere

is the one that alone remains to it. By way of example, Durkheim pointed to suicide. As we have seen, men in the past held to religious beliefs and were subject to religious disciplines in such a way as to prevent them committing suicide: this is no longer the case (see ch. 23.3–23.4). Also, that there was not more opposition towards the separation of Church and State was evidence of the weakened state of religion at the time (1907c:51).

5 Durkheim rejected the doctrines of traditional religion, but so did the vast majority of his colleagues in the universities. This probably was an indicator to Durkheim that most of the intellectual world was composed of non-believers. If the Church thus failed to hold the most intelligent members of society, its position as an intellectually respectable force is seriously open to question. In the matter of truth, science is to be followed rather than religion (see ch. 25.2). In his lectures, published as *Moral Education*, he wrote:

> All religious ideas are social in origin; and, on the other hand, they still remain the pre-eminent form of public and private thought for the vast majority of men. To-day, it is true, among more advanced thinkers science has replaced religion. (1925a:79/t.1961a:69)

Elsewhere, with apparent approval, he quotes an idea from Guyau to the effect that all those of superior intelligence (meaning men), can do without religion, but not so the masses, women and children (1887b:303/t.1975a:29). That women as distinct from men need religion is implied in his *Suicide* (1897a:231/t.1951a:215). The woman's more 'natural' religiosity is seen to be a ready protection against the tendency to suicide.

So much for the evidence that Durkheim gives for modern secularization. But is he fooling us or is his thinking muddled? He seems to imply that religion remains very much part and parcel of many people's lives, even in the late nineteenth century. He is ready enough to admit the persistence of religion, despite his references to growing secularization. Where does he stand? The answer is that he is completely convinced about an accelerating secularization of traditional religions. This is to be seen in the loss of the social and political power of the churches, and also in the wide acceptance of science amongst intellectuals as a truth system to replace that of religion. And even in the populace at large, although the people still might be called religious and be associated with the churches, the influence of religion over their public and private lives, especially the former, is very much less marked than in previous centuries.

5 The effects of secularization on society

In considering the effects of secularization on society, Durkheim adopted what now appears a romantic position, based at least on an admiration of the medieval church. Here he follows in the path of Auguste Comte. In a discussion of his book, *Les Formes élémentaires*, at a meeting of the Société Française de Philosophie in 1913, he observed that when nations lost their religious faith they quickly fell into moral and social decay (1913b:69). He said:

> Since the gods are only personified collective ideals – a fact to which every weakening of faith bears witness – the collective ideal obviously becomes weakened itself; and it can only become weaker if the social vitality is itself damaged. In a word, if the gods are only the nations conceived symbolically, it is inevitable that the nations die when the gods die. The believer himself cannot fail to recognise this important sociological factor.

The fact that when religion decays the nation also decays was a contention that Durkheim knew was made often enough by others. For himself, however, he was firmly convinced of its truth, not through casual observation but by reason of his own theorizing, as is seen above. The onslaught of decadence, which comes as a direct result of a declining religion, was not due to the gods taking their vengeance on a disbelieving people (ibid.), but through ensuing moral poverty. This is a logical extension of Durkheim's assertion that the *représentations* of a society, which include moral directives and goals, stand at the heart of religion. The *représentations* of a society correspond to the *représentations* of its religion. If the second lose their power, so must the first.

Along similar lines Durkheim argued that a society could exist only when its members were within 'a certain intellectual and

451

moral community' (1898c:10/t.1969d:25/1975a:66; see also 1886a:69/ t.1975a:22). Human beings can only live together when there exists a set of commonly held beliefs. That, Durkheim thought, was a sociological truism (ibid.). It follows, therefore, that the more demanding and the more widely adhered to are the common beliefs, the greater will be the social cohesion amongst members of a society (see ch. 16). Durkheim wrote in *Suicide*:

> Now, a religious society cannot exist without a collective *credo* and the more extensive the *credo* the more unified and strong is the society. (1897a:158/t.1951a:159/r.1975a:47)

If this notion applies to a religious society, it applies equally to society in general. Since a secularized society implies a lack of universally held religious beliefs, and since on Durkheim's own confession, religious *représentations* are closely identified with the collective *représentations* of society, a secularized society prima facie must be less firmly integrated than one that is religious. A decline of religion in a society must have a weakening effect on the social cohesion of that society itself. In this way, secularization thus becomes an instrument for the erosion of social life. But is the matter in fact as simple as this?

6 Religious change, not secularization?

Although a diminution of religion spelt moral decay in a society, and although Europe was in a state approaching that of anomy, Durkheim did not hold that the end of religion had come. God is not dead: a new god is taking his place. This is both a social fact and is also logically necessary for a society to continue to exist. In brief, at the present time, it is not so much a question of secularization, of society reaching a state of secularity where religion is completely eliminated, but one of religious metamorphosis. He wrote:

> For if it is true that religion is, in a sense indispensable, it is no less certain that religions change, that yesterday's religion could not be that of tomorrow. (1898c:10/t.1969d:25/r.1975a:66)

What is at stake therefore is religious movement and the problem is to account for the decline of the old and the emergence of the new. This means in sociological terms that religious change is to be seen as part of social change, and Durkheim's alleged failure to produce a theory of social change is to return to a monotonous chorus.

In chapter 22 above, we had occasion to show that in place of a theory of change, Durkheim offered the concept of collective effervescence seen in its creative mode, which is derived from religious activity and which could itself be seen as a religious phenomenon. Although this 'irrational' explosive mechanism accounts for revival and the emergence of new ideas, it can hardly account for a decline or reversal. There is no 'negative' effervescence to show how the old is discarded. The old merely seems to 'fade away'. Apart therefore from the phenomenon of effervescence, Durkheim suggests that religion changes as the society in which it is set changes. He wrote in an early review: 'History teaches us that religions have evolved and changed with the very societies which gave birth to them' (1887b:307/t.1975a:33). Here Durkheim stresses the social component of religion and its close relation to society. In an important footnote in one of his early writings, he said, having stated some of the timeless functions performed by religion:

> But it must be understood that the importance we thus attribute to the sociology of religion does not in the least imply that religion must play the same role in present-day societies that it has played at other times. In a sense, the contrary conclusion would be more sound. Precisely because religion is a primordial phenomenon, it must yield more and more to the new social forms which it has engendered. (1899a(i):v n./t.1960c:352 n.6)

But what precisely these forms are is not stipulated. And when he says that religion embraces 'a smaller and smaller portion of social life', he makes an obvious assertion and one that was commonly held at the time. What is needed is explanation: not the rehearsal of facts already known. Here, Durkheim seems to be in the muddle that he was in when he tried to explain suicide in his book of 1897. There are a number of factors at work which appear to be related but which cannot be easily separated.

7 Some suggested explanations

In one place Durkheim attributes the decline of traditional religions to inevitable events. 'The communion of minds,' he says,
'can no longer form around particular rites and prejudices, since
rites and prejudices have been swept away *in the natural course of
things*' (1898c:11/t.1969d:26/r.1975:67; our italics). So the scientific
Durkheim, without any clearly enunciated reason appeals to
'nature' – the course of events – a mysterious force over which man
has no control – to explain secularization. It is hardly necessary to
be reminded that the whole of *The Rules of Sociological Method*
was a cry against such imprecision and such 'mysticism'.

In a somewhat similar vein, he wrote in lectures on moral
education that:

> But gradually things change. Gradually, human duties are
> multiplied, become more precise, and pass to the first rank
> of importance; while others on the contrary tend to become
> attenuated. (1925a:7/t.1961a:6/r.1975:194)

One of the few places where Durkheim differentiates ritual from
belief in his reference to contemporary secularization is here in
these lectures. Usually he speaks of religion in this context as a
blanket term. He went on to say:

> Although there are religious duties – rites addressed only to
> divinity – the place they occupy and the importance
> attributed to them continue to diminish. (ibid.)

Durkheim implies elsewhere that religious practice and indeed
certain religious beliefs go by the board on the grounds that there
are now more demands made by society on people's lives. This, in
turn, suggests changes in values and, somehow or other, religious
values diminish in importance compared with other values. It was
in his lectures on custom and law, given also at the turn of the
century, that Durkheim put forward these ideas about the effect
of the tempo of modern life. It is the enemy of religious practices:
they are abandoned quite simply because there are other things
to do. He said: 'The demands of a busier life tended to reduce
the importance of ritual formalities' (1950a:227/t.1957a:194).
Beyond this not very profound observation, Durkheim offers no
further explanation.

At the 1913–14 Conference of the Union de Libres Penseurs et de Libres Croyants, Durkheim suggested that contemporary religious life was languishing and that revivals were short-lived, not because people had turned away from confessional formulae but 'because our power for creating ideals has weakened . . . because our societies are undergoing a phase of profound agitation' (1919b:103–4/t.1975a:186). The enthusiasm of our forefathers for religion has therefore disappeared. Religion no longer thrills us, because many of its aspects 'have passed into common usage to such a degree that we are no longer conscious of them, or because they do not meet our current aspirations' (610/427/156). Hence changes in society, not changes in religion itself, bring about secularization. It is the general state of society which is the cause and it is here that we encounter difficulty and confusion. Durkheim spoke of several characteristics of the age in which he lived:

1 In *Suicide* (1897a) and in his comments on anti-Semitism (1899d), he said that modern man was living in 'decadent times', or in a period of agitation. This is indicated by social and political crises, such as those in 1848 with the European revolutions, in 1870–1 with the Franco-Prussian war and the Commune, and in 1894 and for a while thereafter with the Dreyfus affair (see ch. 1.4).

2 Another characteristic of the period of transition which Durkheim felt society was going through was marked by a loss of ideals and divinities 'which do not meet the requirements of the new aspirations which have come to the fore'(1919b:103–4/t.1975a:186).

3 The period is also characterized by 'moral coldness' which implies a moral mediocrity (610/427/156). Men are indifferent to constraints and virtues projected and imposed by religious and civil authorities.

4 Along with these characteristics, and indeed contained within them, there stands Durkheim's concept of anomy. It is impossible to consider this subject in detail here, other than to say that it is a state of society that Durkheim described as disaggregated (*désagrégé*), or in a state of disintegration (1897a:326/t.1951a:289). As a synonym for anomy, Durkheim also used *dérèglement* – a disordered state or dissoluteness

455

(ibid.:281/253). For the individual, it is the 'malady of infinite aspirations' as men and women reject the moral norms of society or have not been satisfactorily socialized in them.

Durkheim sees these as characteristics of modern society; they are close to characteristics which were described earlier on and can be seen to be the result of secularization. There obviously exists a correlation between them and the decline of traditional religion. Which is cause and which is effect is not established. Often Durkheim is little more than descriptive. Something much more decisive is needed to get beyond mere description and the possibility of circularity of argument. For Durkheim, it is science which both breaks the old and creates the new.

The importance Durkheim attaches to science in our understanding of modern society, and in particular of religious change, is considered in the following chapter, at the end of which Durkheim's approach to secularization will be assessed.

25 The invasion of religion by science

1 Science, the real cause of secularization

Running through all Durkheim's writings, even from the earliest, there is an unbroken strand which states simply and categorically that religion, both in the early days of man and now, has suffered a persistent decline due to one fact and one fact alone, the continual advance and acceptance of scientific thought and practice. At the turn of the century, he spoke of the 'triumph of science' over religion (1901h). Another sociologist, Herbert Spencer, held a similar view (1886a), while the philosopher, J. M. Guyau vigorously maintained that science was in the process of taking over religion (1887b). Triumph implies competition, if not hostility, between science and religion. The clash was obvious in the case of pagan religions, which in Durkheim's day were held to be shot through with superstitious practices and beliefs. These were the very antithesis of science. But Christianity, despite its sophisticated and philosophically based theology (as, for example, in the system of Aquinas), was not exempt. It, too, had to face the challenge of science with its certain knowledge about the world of physical phenomena. Science had advanced through being given its own autonomy and that autonomy meant complete freedom to use whatever methods it wished. Antagonism between science and religion was inevitable, because many religions in the past made assertions of truth in areas of experience which had now become the province of science. The conclusions which science has reached are very different from the truths proclaimed by the churches. Antagonism or the possible accommodation on the part of religion are thus the only possible outcomes.

For obvious reasons, religions, especially those of the West, have always been afraid that their claim to knowledge should be undermined by a rival authority, even though that authority might be some other religion. Reason and freedom of thought, which

Durkheim axiomatically allied with science, can also be seen as two further enemies (see ch. 9.2). Speaking about the scholastic period of the Middle Ages, Durkheim wrote:

> For the moment one introduces reason, criticism and the spirit of reflectiveness into a set of ideas which up to that time has appeared unchallengeable it is the end: the enemy has gained a foothold. (1938a/1969f:87/t.1977a:73)

Every time a new science was founded, the Christian Church rose in arms to oppose it (1893b/1902b:270/t.1933b:285). At first the clash was with the natural sciences in their study of the physical world. Then, in the late nineteenth century, the enemy came even closer to the 'City of God': the human and social sciences, psychology and sociology, went so far as to take as their subject man's behaviour in his innermost being and in the very society in which he lives. In 1893 Durkheim wrote:

> Christianity itself, although it instantly gave individual reflection a larger place than any other religion, could not escape this law. To be sure, the opposition was less acute as long as scholars limited their researches to the material world since it was originally abandoned to the disputes of men. Yet, as this surrender was never complete, as the Christian God does not entirely ignore things of this world, it necessarily happened that, on more than one point, the natural sciences themselves found an obstacle in faith. But it is especially when man became an object of science that the resistance became fierce. The believer, indeed, cannot but find repugnant the idea that man is to be studied as a natural being, analogous to others, and moral facts as facts of nature. (ibid.)

Here Durkheim appears as an early proclaimer of the notion that Christianity has become its own grave-digger – an idea that has recently become popular, not least through the writings of Peter Berger (for example, 1967). Indeed, in speaking of religious changes in the direction of secularization, Durkheim openly declares that 'Christianity itself has contributed most to the acceleration' (1925a:7/t.1961a:6/r.1975:194). The reason is that Christianity has, by some form of dialectical process, given rise to ideas and institutions, which, once they have established their independence, turn round and deal deathly blows to the source of their origin. One fact, in particular, has been responsible for the decline of Christian thought – the insistence on the part of Christians to assert the truth about God, the world and man. This has given rise to science, which now denies the truths that Christianity originally put forward. If religions assert doctrines about reality which can be studied by science, the religions cannot deny or forbid critical analysis. From a scientific point of view, the doctrines may well be heresies (1890a/t.1973a:37).

The very action of science in investigating areas of experience which are held dear by religion can be, and nearly always is, sufficient to destroy the religious interpretation of the phenomena in question (see chs 16.8 and 28.3). The alternative explanation put forward in the name of science is convincing enough for people to reject religious explanation and doctrine. Offering a scientific explanation for what was once held to be a distinctly religious phenomenon is thus in itself a destructive process. In a review of Fouillée's *Les Éléments sociologiques de la morale*, Durkheim wrote, concerning the religious character of moral phenomena – and what he said also applies to religion – that 'the very fact of treating them scientifically has the effect of profaning them' (1907a(3):355). And later in *The Elementary Forms* he stated:

> Once science came into being, it assumed a profane character, especially in the eyes of the Christian religion; consequently as it emerged it could not be applied to sacred things. (53 n.1/ 39 n.1/162 n.11)

But the opposition on the part of the Church to science entering the temple, examining holy books, analysing the psychological qualities of religious individuals, can no longer be sustained. The defensive walls have been breached. Durkheim said:

> the fact that the scientific spirit attacks it [religion] and questions it with the same freedom of thought that it applies to other natural phenomena goes to prove that it has lost its ascendancy which enabled it to be protected from profane thought. (1907c)

Thus, religion is impotent to prevent science undertaking its work and its work is such as to erode religion.

Interestingly enough, although Durkheim was thoroughly

convinced that science profaned religion, he rejected the idea that it profaned morality. In 1906 he said:

> I wish to stress the fact that this science [sociology] permits the empirical study of moral facts, while at the same time not destroying the *sui generis* religious character which is inherent in them and which distinguishes them from all other human phenomena. (1906b/1924a:89/t.1953b:62)

Durkheim felt that such a position prevented the adoption of utilitarian empiricism (ibid.), but he also wanted to protect, at least theoretically, what he saw as the religion of the future from being profaned by the intrusion of science (see ch. 26). To sustain his position he was forced to differentiate between religious phenomena and moral phenomena, and to maintain that morality is not above criticism and is therefore subject to reason and argument, whereas religion is held to be beyond modification by science. The sacred in religion is founded on dogmatism not discussion, which it does not admit (ibid.:70/49). He constantly speaks of the close relation between religion and morality. He once saw law and morality as being almost identical to religious belief, although the first two were not based on obligatory beliefs as was religion (1899a(ii):19/t.1975a:73; see ch. 9.3). The logic of his position is that there must be two kinds of the sacred. One operates in religion and is fragile: the other in morality, which admits examination but which is immune from the deleterious effects of criticism. Science in this case does not undermine the validity of morality. Such differentiation is unwarrantable.

The attack of science is on religious belief, not on religious action. Durkheim is a rationalist to the extent that he believes that once a person's faith has been undermined, he will cease to be involved in the ritual. He wrote at the conclusion of *The Elementary Forms*:

> Men cannot take part in ceremonies which seem to have no point, nor accept a faith which is totally incomprehensible to them. In order to extend religion or simply keep it alive, its justification is necessary, that is to say, there has to be a theory about it. (615/430/160)

Yet Durkheim will not go the whole hog: he will not admit that the decline of traditional religions has been brought about by science and science *alone*. Religion is resilient and an attack on its beliefs will not necessarily destroy it, especially if religious sentiments are strong. He wrote in one of his early books:

> Faith is not uprooted by dialectic proof; it must already be deeply shaken by other causes to be unable to withstand the shock of argument. (1897a:171/t.1951a:169/r.1975:55)

Infuriatingly Durkheim does not spell out what these other causes are.

2 The superiority of science as a source of knowledge

In those areas of experience or reality where science legitimately enters – and what area can it not or will it not enter? – science rather than religion, Durkheim held, discovers the truth (see chs 11.8 and 15.1). He sees the superiority of science over religion, not least in the sociological fact that amongst intellectuals of his day – 'amongst more advanced thinkers' – science has superseded religion, and even taken its place (1925a:59/t.1961a:69). His adulation of science virtually turned science into a religion. Science is in fact liberation. 'We liberate ourselves through understanding', there is no other way (ibid.:132–3/116). And what provides understanding? Science. It is 'the well spring of our autonomy' (ibid.).

He was opposed to every religion which claimed to dogmatize about objective knowledge and reality. Christianity did not proclaim truth and it had no right to pretend it did. In the conclusion of *The Elementary Forms* he wrote:

> There is but one point at issue between science and religion: it is not the right of religion to exist, it is its right to dogmatize about the nature of things, and the special competence religion claims for itself to know about man and the world. (614/430/159)

Such a claim by Durkheim means that the adherents of religion should accept the findings of science and attempt to change their own views and doctrines accordingly. He hinted at this even in an early review (1887b:311/t.1975a:38) and was just as outspoken at the 1913–14 conference, where he said that free believers should not dogmatize, and that they should overlook their denominational formulae in order to have an openness of mind in seeing religion objectively (1919b:75/t.1975a:184; see also 1909a(1):60). His position implies that any allegedly scientific statement has precedence over a religious one on the same subject. Religion in its cognitive element has no alternative but to bow before science and rational thought. Thus, when a religion proclaims that the object of worship is to adore the divinity, such an activity cannot form a legitimate objective study, since God for the scientist does not exist. Further, theology can never be a scientific study, since it does not deal with reality.

The truth science proclaims is certain, although it is always open to challenge by the scientist. And when successfully challenged, it is forced to change. In this sense there is a steadfastness in scientific knowledge which places it above all other knowledge, for example, metaphysical knowledge. No other discipline has given man knowledge to such a degree as science and, furthermore, it is a knowledge that can be applied to everyday life.

> Once the authority of science is established, it must be taken into consideration. We can go beyond science because of the pressures of necessity; however, it must be our starting point. We can affirm nothing it denies, deny nothing it affirms, and establish nothing which directly or indirectly contradicts the principles on which it depends. (616/430/160)

The threat of science to religion was amply demonstrated in Durkheim's eyes by the fact that religious leaders themselves on so many occasions tend to oppose the conclusions of science. That they should even attempt to do this proclaims how they fear the discoveries and conclusions of science, which are in direct opposition to their own proclamations of truth.

In his debate on science and religion, he observed that while science could proclaim no privileged position (surely with a note of sarcasm), religion did not have a science of itself, that is, it did not really know what it was doing (1909a(1):60). He later wrote in *Les Formes*:

> It is certain that they [religions] are mistaken in regard to the real nature of things: science has proved it. The modes of action which they counsel or prescribe to men can therefore

rarely have useful effects: it is not by lustrations that the sick are cured nor by sacrifices and chants that the crops are made to grow. (117/83)

It is the task of science, not theology, to reveal all and to discover the truth of religion. It and it alone is competent to do this. Thus, the assumption is that all down the ages religion has been living in a perpetual world of darkness (614/430/159).

For this reason, therefore, the enlightened religious person should welcome, not revile, science for its work in establishing truth. He wrote at an early date:

Let those who view anxiously and sadly the ruins of ancient beliefs, who feel all the difficulties of these critical times, not ascribe to science an evil it has not caused but rather which it tries to cure! Beware of treating it as an enemy! (1897a:170/ t.1951a:169/r.1975:56)

The evil which science, and here Durkheim means sociology, is trying to cure is the morally weakened state of society brought about by the decline of traditional beliefs, which in turn have been weakened by science!

There is no logical reason why religion should not judge science, and indeed there have been many theologians who have done this. But to Durkheim such a counter-attack will not be successful. And it will not be successful because religion has lost once and for all its ability to speak truth, truth about man, truth about the world.

From now on, faith no longer exercises over the system of *représentations*, which we can call religious, the same hegemony as before. Confronting it stands a rival power [science], its offspring which will subject it to its own criticism and control. All the signs indicate that this control will continually increase and be ever more effective, while no limit can possibly be fixed on its future influence. (616/431/ 160–1)

As we have indicated, the most recent and serious challenge to religion from the sciences is now the social sciences, and in particular sociology. His oft-repeated chorus is that sociology, as he defines and expounds it, is every whit a science and comparable with say, biology or physics (see 1895a). By extension, it is possible to argue, as Deploige does (1911/t.1938:373), that the sociology of religion as a science is now directly replacing religious faith and thus is becoming a new kind of theology offering a reasonable account of faith, and even comparable to that of the great theological systems of previous ages. In this sense, Durkheim's *sociologie religieuse* is the faith of today and tomorrow and the years to come (see chs 27 and 28). This 'new theology' would be:

bound to depend upon the different sciences as soon as they come into existence; the social sciences first, because religious faith has its origins in society; psychology, because society is a synthesis of human *consciences*; finally, the natural sciences because man and society are functions of the universe and can only be artificially separated from it. (615/431/160)

These are the words with which he ends the two sections on religion in the conclusion of his great book on the subject.

3 Science is not god!

Yet, Durkheim was no naïve rationalist who believed that ideas in isolation, or contained in a vacuum, could bring about social change. Traditional religion, in fact, is not at the point of dissolution just through the discoveries of science. In one of his early reviews, that on Guyau's *L'Irréligion de l'avenir*, he takes up this position by saying that:

If the only mistake that religions had ever made was to be in disagreement with scientific truths, they would still be in a healthy state today. (1887b:301/t.1975a:37)

He states that if society needs religion, religion would either modify its own doctrine in order to embrace new ideas or else would deny science altogether. We might add that this kind of movement, of religion absorbing some of the findings of science, was visible in the churches of his day among liberal Christians of both Catholic and Protestant persuasions. On the other hand, it is also clear that traditionalists, faced with the threat of science, hardened their dogmas and veered towards fundamentalism, either papal or biblical. Unaided science, however, does not bring about secularization, and for two reasons. The first relates to the nature of religion; the second, to the nature of science.

The force of logic, reason and argument will not 'stamp out faith': 'logic can just as easily be used to defend as to attack it, and the theologian can reason just as well in order to prove it as the free thinker to refute it' (ibid.). Durkheim openly declared that 'religion could not be erased at the stroke of a pen' (1901h). The point is that the scientific, rational refutation of a particular religious belief would not automatically cause people to give up their practice of religion. It is not so much a question of specific beliefs but the general inclination to belief. An overall attitude towards belief is at the heart of every religious person. Preachers, Durkheim said, were aware of this. He wrote:

> they devote much less attention to establishing directly and by methodical proofs the truth of any particular proposition of the utility of such and such an observance, than to awakening or reawakening the sentiment of the moral comfort attained by the regular celebration of the cult. Thus they create a predisposition to belief, which precedes proofs, which leads the mind to overlook the insufficiency of the logical reasons, and which thus prepares it for the proposition whose acceptance is desired. This favourable prejudice, this impulse towards believing, is just what constitutes faith. (514/360)

Similarly, a rational or scientific attack on a particular ritual may not have much effect:

> the true justification of religious practices does not lie in the apparent ends which they pursue, but rather in the invisible action which they exercise over the mind and in the way in which they affect our mental status. (ibid.)

But much the same thing applies to a 'belief' in science. It is not the existence of scientific ideas and truths which is necessary, but the general acceptance of science by society at large (298/208/127). For the populace to be aware of scientific achievements and thinking, there is the need to teach and preach science as well as practise it. There is nothing automatic in the propagation of scientific ideas (see ch. 2).

What has just been said confirms the fact that Durkheim saw the growth of new ideas as issuing from some haphazard and non-rational process, as distinct from the rationality of the ideas themselves. It is well known that the general acceptance of the findings of science has often been slow. And secularization, although it has been continuous, has at the same time been far from uniform. Nor are religion and free thought to be inversely correlated according to some precise mathematical formula. The relationship between them is complex. The growth of scientific ideas in society as a whole depends very much on the *conscience collective*, on the common outlook of society itself. Although Durkheim sees religion and free thought as being closely related in an inverse fashion, he is cautious about a more precise relationship.

> Religion, the eminent form of the common conscience, originally absorbs all representative functions with practical functions. The first are not dissociated from the second until philosophy appears. But this is possible only when religion has lost something of its hold. This new way of representing things clashes with collective opinion which resists it. It has sometimes been said that free thought makes religious beliefs regress, but that supposes, in its turn, a preliminary regression of these same beliefs. It can arise only if the common faith permit. (1893b/1902b:269–70/t.1933b:285)

And Durkheim goes even as far as to suggest that religion itself has been of great value to science by holding before it the fact that it is not God! He wrote in an early review:

> The great service which it has rendered to science has been to remind it constantly of its limits and that is why it has lasted. Some day might not this sentiment about the limits of our knowledge, confirmed as it is by long experience, permeate science itself and become an integral element of scientific thought? (1887b:311/t.1975a:38)

4 Only a partial take-over?

From what has just been said, it is evident that Durkheim did not believe that science would suddenly supplant religion, or that it could act as a surrogate religion. Complete victory was not envisaged. His approach was more subtle. He wrote: 'For in asking that religion become an object of science, I do not mean at all that it should be swallowed up by science' (1909a(1):58).

It has already been observed that Durkheim, like so many others, divided religious phenomena into two distinct compartments – belief and practice (see ch. 17). Religion makes statements about the world and man's experience of it, as well as about an alleged world which is beyond the senses. At the same time religion demands that man makes a response in terms of action, be that action ritualistic or ethical.

Durkheim's analysis of contemporary secularization and the future of religion is based on the contention that science has virtually taken over the cognitive or speculative function of religion (see ch. 16). As Durkheim was to write towards the end of his life: 'Born of religion, science is tending to substitute itself for religion in everything that concerns the cognitive and intellectual functions' (613/429/159; see also 1909a(1):58). This is what in fact is happening and the cosmological component of theology, for example, is now little in evidence (1909a(1):58).

Yet science is not in a position to engineer a complete take-over. The affective function – the ritual component – cannot be controlled by the new empire-builder. This remains in the hands of religion. Although science is responsible for changing man's beliefs by changing the content of one function, it can never be a substitute for religion and can never be a religion in itself. That there is no *complete* demise of religion even within the speculative sphere is not due so much to the nature of religion as to the nature of science. Science is never fully realized in so far as its work is never finished. 'It is fragmentary, incomplete' (615/431/160). It advances slowly, deliberately, but is sure of every step it takes. Its knowledge to date, therefore, is only partial. This fact has certain practical consequences and one is that religion is thus entitled to claim some area in which it can speculate, but not be certain about. He wrote:

Even the most rational and laicized religions cannot and never will be able to do without some special form of speculation which, although it has the same object as science itself, nevertheless is not really scientific. In these religions the obscure intuitions of sensations and sentiment often take the place of logical reasoning. (615–16/431/160)

Religion, in terms of its claim to knowledge, is allowed a certain autonomy, but it is much smaller than it used to be and must continue to diminish as science progresses. If 'God' is allowed any place at all, he is of necessity a 'god of the gaps'.

That science moves slowly and that man cannot wait for it to complete its knowledge has a practical outcome of another kind (1904a(5):383/t.1979a:32). In everyday living man has to act. For this he needs knowledge, but if there is no scientific knowledge available, he must act with what 'knowledge' he possesses in hope and faith. This is true in the realm of morality as well as in other areas of life. In directing action, religion has a full part to play. It is still required to perform some controlling function over man's instinctual and social behaviour, although its power in this respect is considerably weaker than once it was (1886a:68/t.1975a:21). It is therefore legitimate for religion to proceed as a social necessity, provided of course that it realizes its limited sphere of influence.

5 Resultant confusion

To point to religion in the future as a necessary element in society forced Durkheim into an extremely difficult position. As we have just seen, religion today ceases to be for the most part, although not entirely, a vehicle for explaining human experience. But since its claims to knowledge are now assumed by science, sacred knowledge becomes profane knowledge (see ch. 8). As we have had occasion to remark before, Durkheim's attempt to differentiate religion from science was full of difficulty and the position he gave in his theory to religion in the future does not solve the problem: rather, it compounds it. That the two components of religion can be readily dealt with in such a way that one component almost disappears and the remaining one can proceed virtually unharmed and so continue to maintain its identity is an extraordinary piece of surgery. Even the most extreme functionalist today would have hesitations at this point.

But this raises an important theoretical problem. It is Durkheim's failure to explicate the cognitive component of religion. The following are some of the aspects which are involved in mental activity associated with religion:

1 explanation of events by positing a cause;
2 statements about gods, spirits – their existence, their characteristics;
3 the origins of the universe;
4 doctrine of man, 'anthropology' – his nature and place in the universe;
5 statements about moral behaviour;
6 directives about ritual action.

All these elements may be, or are, contained within the myths of a religion or in its doctrines or theology. The point to note is their diversity. When Durkheim speaks of a take-over by science, he has in mind the explanation of natural events. And he would certainly add that since truth was the object of science, that element of the cognitive function of religion relating to the existence of gods and spirits and that relating to the origins and development of the universe would also be superseded by scientific knowledge. But on this all now agree that science has to be agnostic. The other aspects are clearly outside the realm of science itself, although as we have indicated, he associates science with a certain doctrine of man and a humanistic moral system. Nevertheless, in the face of the complex nature of the cognitive element of religion, it is difficult to see how Durkheim can maintain that scientific thought is a more perfect form of religious thought (613/429/158). There is no unbridgeable gulf between the two: they differ only in the matter of degree (Lenoir 1918:588). One would like to suggest that, with a slight stretching of the point, it would be safe to conclude from Durkheim's thought that the man who is devoted to science is indeed a 'religious' man. Durkheim would hardly allow the equation to be reversed, however!

His former teacher, Boutroux, attacked Durkheim for claiming too much for science. According to Boutroux, science has no right to determine reality or to 'weaken' it by references to the normative, and its sole task is that of ordering and systematizing reality (Durkheim 1909a(1):60). But Durkheim used science in a different way. 'Science for him [Durkheim] explains things rationally, that is, it causes them to emerge from a given principle in accordance with a logical necessity' (ibid.). In practice, with reference to religion, it meant looking at religion in exclusively objective terms. Thus, for Durkheim, science when applied to religion meant more than an open, empirical analysis, and despite protests to the contrary, Durkheim's approach contains rationalist overtones.

The most serious weakness of Durkheim's position, then, stems from the fact that he means so many different things by science – observation, experimentation, logical reasoning, freedom of thought, individualism. Further, religion itself, having given birth to science, is not adequately differentiated from science. In an important article on *Suicide*, Nye and Ashworth observed that Durkheim found it problematic in separating, by way of definition, science from religion. They observed that he did not make the usual nominalistic separation by stating that science treated as 'useful' what religion considered was 'real' (Nye and Ashworth 1971:137).

The position is further muddled by Durkheim's equation that totemism is primitive science (see ch. 6.3). The assertion is also strengthened by the contention that science has been born out of religion and is hence basically of the same nature (see 342/239/143–4). Religion is thus the mother: science the daughter. There must therefore be mother-daughter similarities. Confusion reigns, as Belot says, because the process of parturition is not clearly defined (1913a:374). Durkheim fails to separate social knowledge from knowledge about the physical universe. Since he cannot differentiate religious knowledge from that derived from science, his epistemology is dominated by confusion.

It was always a point of surprise to Richard that Durkheim, in nailing his flag to the mast of science, could so blatantly disregard the basic assumptions of science. Richard follows the colossus of Enlightenment philosophy, Kant, whose system of thought enabled scientific analysis to proceed unchecked by metaphysical speculation, although such speculation found a place elsewhere within his system. Durkheim himself, as Richard knew, was a neo-Kantian who, one assumes perhaps falsely, accepted many of the basic ideas of Kant in the matter of science and philosophical speculation. Richard wrote in 1911 that it was remarkable:

how he [Durkheim] has been able to believe that with the wings of a sociologist he has flown over the abyss created by Kant, the abyss between science and morality, between knowledge and religion, between the world of facts and the world of values, how he has been able to confuse the applicability of a technical knowledge with a prescription of *conscience* and finally to draw from a precarious ethnographical induction on the forms of savage or primitive cults, a judgment on the value of the deepest religious experiences. (1911a(i):332)

Richard could not understand how Durkheim had confused two very different sets of ideas. First, sociology as a science in the very limited sense of the word, as a study concerned with social phenomena and social relationships; and second, metaphysical speculation, 'which appeals to this science . . . and tries to resolve general problems of morality, religious philosophy, and theory of knowledge' (ibid.:331). Richard concluded: 'the two endeavours seem to me not only different but contradictory' (ibid.).

Another aspect of the epistemological confusion relates to religious belief in the future. It will be very severely restricted since man has very little area in which to speculate. But what will be the content? Perhaps more than Durkheim realized, if Richard's logical development of Durkheim's position is accepted –

If the most clearly defined religion which has the most social form, totemism, is the very science of primitive peoples, the intellectual equivalent of our religion is not faith in God, it is our science, on condition that it is widened to include not only the group – mathematics, physics, biology – but the sociology of religion, including the theory of collective understanding. (Richard 1923:240/t.1975:251)

Again, if, as Durkheim maintains, the speculative and rational elements of religion are fast disappearing, though a small remnant will always remain, what is left to religion? Little more than the activist function. But on what is this based? Nothing more than a collective emotion, nothing more than an irrational way of life (Richard hints at this, ibid.:233/245). It is like suggesting that a man with his head cut off or with vital organs missing can function almost as well as he did before such losses. By depriving religion of its intellectual dimension it becomes emasculated and such a vestigial and irrational form must quickly give way to the complete demise of religion itself. But this is contrary to what Durkheim wants!

6 Appraisal of Durkheim's analysis of secularization

Before some attempt is made to assess Durkheim's approach to secularization, two issues raised earlier have to be briefly reviewed – that the process of secularization has been afoot throughout man's history and that modern industrialization in western Europe is not a significant factor in that process.

The thesis that the whole of history is the history of secularization can be accepted only within such a wide framework that its value as a proposition becomes extremely questionable. Durkheim's position rests on two assumptions: first, that in the beginning 'all was religious'; and second, since then, there has been a continual and gradual, but none the less apparent, diminution of the control of religion over social life. The first seems very much like Auguste Comte's notion of a theological stage. Indeed, openly critical though Durkheim was of Comte, there is much in his treatment of religion that is reminiscent of Comtean thought, more especially in the matter of religious change (see Richard 1943). The first of the propositions is extremely difficult to prove, not least because we know nothing about the history of preliterate societies. What kinds of lives people lived in such societies before they were discovered by western man is lost to knowledge for ever, or at least, is difficult to reconstruct with certainty. Also, our anthropological understanding of preliterate societies shows no certainty that the totality of life within such societies has been dominated by religion to the extent Durkheim would have us believe. Mary Douglas has forcibly argued that different levels of religious commitment are to be found between tribe and tribe, and that virtually secular primitive societies are now known to exist (1970:chs 1 and 7).

The second proposition which needs to be supported by precise historical knowledge is a far from easy task, as sociologists and historians have discovered. Only rough indicators can be found to measure levels of religious dominance or commitment, but even if broad indicators are used, religion, when it often seems to be on the decline, suddenly receives strength through revival. This is most apparent in western society over the past two hundred years, where the levels of religion and secularization present a highly complex picture. 'Little by little' is Durkheim's phrase about the growth of secularization, but the uniformity suggested by it can hardly be substantiated. Durkheim's statements about religion in general do not allow for revivals or changes through external pressure, as in the cases of armed conquest or aggressive evangelization. Marc Boegner was quick to criticize Durkheim for this in response to Belot's exposition of *Les Formes* in 1914 (Boegner 1919:139). The notion of general secularization as a historical process which has occurred from the beginning of man's social existence cannot be supported, or, if it is accepted in very broad terms, adds up to little.

Another problem is that of explaining the process of autonomy – a point on which Durkheim remains silent. If all social institutions have been born in the womb of religion, how have they become separated? How have they cut themselves off from their mother? Apart from referring to the growth of science, the nearest Durkheim comes to offering even a clue is to be seen in the changes that societies undergo when they move from those characterized by mechanical solidarity to those marked by organic solidarity. In the second type, beliefs and sentiments of a collective kind are relatively weak: hence in a society of organic qualities, individualism based on private ideals and beliefs is more prominent than in societies labelled mechanical. But, once again, whence comes the change? Durkheim is strong on indicators, for example, changes in types of law and religion itself could be an indicator, but weak on causal factors. As is commonly known, the nearest he comes to positing reasons for change in this particular context is in the increase in population, bringing with it an increase in moral density which causes the former type of society – segmentary society – to break up. The inadequacy of this theory of change has been criticized enough to make further comment unnecessary (see ch. 22.7). But it hardly accounts for the emergence of the autonomy of institutions, freed from religious control. How does science that is religious become non-religious? What makes it proceed in such a direction?

It is at first surprising that in seeking for causes which might be said to contribute to recent secularization, Durkheim, unlike many sociologists before and after him, pays scant attention to factors under the general heading of industrialization. He makes but a passing reference to Spencer's theory that secularization is the result of the popularization of scientific knowledge, which has been brought about by industrial progress (1886a:64/t.1975a:16). According to Spencer, what has been eroded in religion is the fundamental belief in supernatural causation. The agent has been science, propagated by the handmaid of industry. Further, Spencer believed that religion had acquired a more moral and spiritual content by the growth of free inquiry and the 'sentiment of independence', with which Durkheim agrees (1909a(1):5), but disagrees with him in that such qualities have been precipitated, 'awoken and fostered' by the development of industrial societies (1886a:67/t.1975a:20). In this connection, the nearest that Durkheim comes to mentioning industrialization – and this is but the vaguest hint – is in his *Professional Ethics*, when he refers to a weakening of religious formalities occurring as life becomes busier (1950a:227/t.1957a:193; see ch. 24.7).

The reason why Durkheim almost completely disregards industrialization as a key factor in the recent decline of religious institutions is simply that he rejects morphological factors and embraces those relating to ideas. It is not the effects of industrialization, of work habits, of repetitive labour, of the growth of areas of poverty and distress which adversely affect traditional religion. Rather, it is changes in ideas and values about the world, the supernatural, man's relationships with man, that determine changes in the direction of secularization. The key is in collective *représentations* and changes here are not to be attributed to the industrial revolution but to earlier revolutions, the Renaissance and the Reformation. Durkheim does not consider the possibility that the industrial revolution has itself brought about changes in collective *représentations*.

So how, then, is Durkheim's approach to secularization to be assessed? We can readily accept the fact that in very general terms secularization has been in process for a long time; that today western man lives in a society that is highly secularized in so far as religious institutions have lost their power; that man lives in a pluralist society; that there are certain elements in Christian theology that appear to have given rise to the recent secularization; and that on the whole the process or processes are continuing in the direction they originally took, with no sign of reversal. All this, actually or latently found in Durkheim, is frequently commented on today and generally accepted. The indicators he used for the growth of secularization are particularly convincing, in some ways more so than detailed statistics.

At the level of explanation and interpretation, Durkheim's analysis is extraordinarily neat. Using as a base the two prime functions of religion, he shows how the growth of science so operates as to explain secularizing tendencies but at the same time to allow the continued existence of some form of religion in the future. By logical ingenuity he is able to derive conclusions and explanations which suit his purposes admirably. It is brilliant but not convincing. Everything turns on the acceptance of the two functions and his theory of society. On both points, as we have seen, he is open to criticism. He is befogged by his adulation of science. No one would deny the growth of scientific thought as a factor of overwhelming importance in the process of secularization. And Durkheim is to be praised in that he does not take a crudely rationalist position in the matter of the propagation of scientific knowledge. But in his hands science is seen both as a tool for destroying religion and also as an instrument for pointing to the conservation of religion. Religion, therefore, must continue! Durkheim's explanation fails because it is not radical enough.

26 The new religion: the cult of man or society?

1 Prognostication and the characteristics of a future religion

That religion will persist in some form, Durkheim, as we have seen, was in no doubt. As religions are social phenomena, none is immortal; but 'neither is there any reason to believe that humanity will be incapable of inventing new ones in the future' (611/428/157). The process of such creativity is perpetual, for it is deep in man and society.

But what form will religion now take, as the traditional religions are dissolving? Durkheim was ambivalent about the sociological temptation to predict the outcome. On the one hand, he felt it was unwise to foretell the future:

> one would like to try to imagine the composition of a future religion, that is to say, a religion more conscious of its social origins. Of course, one must be very cautious in doing this. It is quite pointless to try to guess in what precise form such a religion would be able to express itself. What one can foresee are the social forces which will give birth to it. (1919b:103/ t.1975a:186)

This is very much the cautious Durkheim, trying not to damage the science he has been spawning by hazardous guesses which might easily prove to be wrong (see also 1907c). And again, in one of the first things he wrote (a review of Spencer's *Ecclesiastical Institutions*), he says:

> For so long as men live together, they will hold some belief in common. What one cannot foresee and what only the future will be able to decide, is the particular form in which this faith will be symbolized. (1886a:69/t.1975a:22–3; see also 1887c:311/t.1975a:38)

There are, nevertheless, plenty of instances where scientific

476

caution is thrown to the winds and where he is prepared to chance his arm about the new forms of religion. Marc Boegner did not hesitate to point out his inconsistencies (Boegner 1919:141) – his reluctance to prophesy as a scientist and yet a readiness to talk freely about the emergence of a new religion. Indeed, one might add, to state that there will be religion at all in the future is to play the role of prophet.

Obviously stemming from his conception of the relationship between science and religion (see the previous chapter), he stated that future religions would be basically rational.

> All that can be surmised is that they will continue to be further penetrated by rationality than even the most rational religions today, and that the social sense, which has always been the soul of religion, will be asserted more directly and more decisively than in the past, without being shrouded in myths and symbols. (1907c:51)

In *Suicide*, published some ten years before, Durkheim noted that any new religion would have to admit freedom of thought, the right of criticism and of individual initiative to a greater extent than that displayed amongst the liberal Protestants of his day (1897a:431/t.1951a:375). But he was also quick to comment that such a movement would mean that religion in the future would be able to limit suicide even less than traditional religions, since for him, freedom of thought and suicide were positively correlated.

In addition to freedom from prevailing myths and a greater place given to free thought, Durkheim seemed to imply that every man would carry out his religious inclinations as he wanted to. He wrote that the day would come 'when the only form of worship will be that which each of us will freely perform in his own heart' (63/46/122). Does this imply that all social characteristics of religion would disappear and individual manifestations be triumphant? If so, the sociology of religion would be out of business! Despite this somewhat obscure remark, Durkheim implied that the new religion would indeed have social characteristics, which like all else of the Third Republic would be 'laïque en apparence'. They were as follows.

1 It would express the unity of society and its most sacred values.

2 It would hold periodic meetings when individuals would be given the opportunity of affirming the values of society by some ritualistic expression. Such meetings would also provide inspiration and new insight into social life (610/427/156).

3 The new form of religion would contain some references to 'objective knowledge' about the social and personal worlds in which people live. The degree of knowledge would be determined by science, which would increasingly control this aspect of religion. In the meantime, religion would continue to speculate in areas of experience so far not penetrated by science. As just stated, the new religion would have a faith or theory based on reason (612/428/157; 615/430/160).

4 The new religion would have justice as one of its basic themes. Durkheim said at the 1913–14 conference: 'We aspire to a higher justice than any of the existing formulae can express in a way that will satisfy us' (1919b:104/t.1975a:186–7)

Durkheim received encouragement about the possibility of a new form of religion emerging in western society from the fact that the French Revolution had produced, within recent memory, new religions and new collective *représentations*. He wrote:

At that particular time, under the influence of general enthusiasm, things purely secular in nature were transformed into sacred things by public opinion, for example, the Motherland, Liberty, Reason. A religion was established which had its dogmas, its symbols, its altars, and its holy days. It was to these spontaneous aspirations that the cult of Reason and the Supreme Being attempted to give some form of official recognition. It is true that this religious revival lasted only a very short time because the patriotic enthusiasm which at first caught the imagination of the masses gradually waned. (305–6/214/132)

What had happened in the French Revolution was not only sociologically interesting, but it seemed to give him hope that the future religion, although not the same as that generated by the Revolution, would be of a similar kind. He saw that if men had created gods in response to those traumatic events, they could continue to make them in other similar situations. Thus, the means of creation, as always, would be in the effervescent gathering in which deities are born out of blind psycho-social forces (see ch. 22).

He realized, of course, that it was not sufficient that gods were thought to exist. They had to be present in people's minds 'with sufficient force so that the *représentations* which they express are effective' (1913b:69). The gods must be believed in with a collective faith, 'for the faith of each can only be strong if it is shared by everyone' (ibid.). Interestingly enough, Durkheim's thought here bears strong resemblances to some kinds of Protestantism in so far as he stresses the importance of faith – faith which is held by the individual and with little reference to practice or cult.

2 The source of religious revival: the working classes

Religion is a product of man, it is derived from humanity, from society. Durkheim said: 'There is an idea that we absolutely have to get used to; it is that humanity is left on this earth to its own devices and can only count on itself to direct its own destiny' (1919b:105/t.1975a:187). Humanity is a blanket-like term lacking sociological precision. Where in society or in what section of society will the new religious forms emerge?

As we have seen, Durkheim believed that at the time in which he lived, there existed a social languishing, a lack of nerve, moral mediocrity, a virtual state of anomy (see ch. 24.5) – a judgment doubted by Richard and others (1923:237/t.1975:248). For Durkheim, this 'state of uncertainty and confused agitation cannot last forever' (611/427/157). Therefore, the day will come when societies will experience 'creative effervescence' and from this, 'new ideals will be born and new formulations emerge which will for a time serve as a guide to humanity' (ibid.). So the religion of the future will come into existence.

Quite out of the blue, Durkheim locates the emergence of revival in the near future as arising within the working classes. This unheralded commitment to such a group was made at the 1913–14 Conference of Free Thinkers and Free Believers. He proclaimed:

One can go further and say with some precision that it is

among the working classes [*les classes populaires*] in particular that these new forces are in the course of formation. (1919b:104/t.1975a:187)

The reason why Durkheim committed himself to this position was probably because he felt that *les classes populaires* had a collective warmth, an openness and enthusiasm, which by contrast were absent in the middle classes.

The reference to the working classes is surprising, for they are so seldom referred to in Durkheim's sociology. Indeed, the oft-repeated criticism against his sociology is that there is virtually no reference to social conflict, and it nowhere deals with class division or class antagonism. Here Durkheim appears to follow Auguste Comte in paying scant regard to the problem, although Comte tried to promulgate his church of humanity amongst the working classes. Durkheim saw that religion had a controlling and consoling function within the various classes of society (see ch. 16.5). When religion was an effective force, it warned masters and the rich that worldly interests were not the highest goals of life and had to be subordinated. To the workers, religion offered consolidation and contentment by holding before them compensatory justice in a world to come. This world was also seen to be created, sustained and controlled by God himself, complete with its class divisions (1897a:283/t.1951a:254–5).

One is tempted to conclude that in pointing to the working classes as the source of religious revival, Durkheim, like Comte again (who included the female sex), was indulging in bourgeois romanticism. And romantic ideas about the proletariat can also be found in Marx. Now that history has moved on, Durkheim's prophecies are seen to be false. The working classes in the West have not been the heralds or devotees of a new religion. The form of religion found amongst them at the present time is diffused, containing elements of superstition and simple beliefs. This is not to say that such folk religion is unimportant, but it is very far removed from that kind of religion Durkheim thought would emerge in the period in which we live (see Towler 1974:ch. 8). Religion in the West today, in either its traditional or humanistic forms, is located, if anywhere, mainly in the middle classes.

3 The emergence of an old French religion?

Throughout his academic career Durkheim never ceased to indicate that his own beliefs corresponded to those of the religion of the future (see ch. 1.6). Referring to his position in what we would call the early period in the development of Durkheim's religious thought, Richard has written:

> In his correspondence and in open conversation which I had with him, Durkheim took delight in saying that we have no other religion than that [the inviolability of the person] and that was all he would retain of the religion of humanity, dear to Auguste Comte. The inviolability of the human person was for him only the transformation of the Roman concept of the Sacred and the Jewish notion of interdict. (1925(ii):361)

Thus here and throughout his writings, Durkheim is seen to join the ranks of others of his time in declaring that the religion-to-be will be a species which has been variously called the religion of humanity, individualism, the cult of man, the cult of personality, and so on. In this form of religion, man dethrones God and puts himself on it.

That man has become a god to himself is in recent times an idea of the Enlightenment, stemming philosophically from Kant and his *Critique of Pure Reason* (1781) – it will be recalled that Durkheim himself was a neo-Kantian. Nowhere was the notion of the man-god so practically worked out as in France, which became the seed-bed of humanized, lay religions, in part helped by the thought of J.-J. Rousseau. The Revolution itself can be seen to be in some way a religious movement. As de Toqueville is reported to have said, it was 'a political revolution which had the effect of a religious revolution and in a way assumed the aspect of one'. An outcome of the failure of the 'religion' of the Revolution was Saint-Simon's *Nouveau Christianisme* (1823), the teaching of which was propagated by his disciples such as Bazard, Enfantin and others. In another direction his ideas were taken up and developed by Auguste Comte, in his highly theological and ritualized religion of humanity. The Third Republic gained the reputation for spawning governments which were overtly committed to humanism and its political counterpart, liberalism.

In this it was supported by many middle-class intellectuals and academics. Needless to say, lay religion in France has been subject to a great deal of analysis (see Charlton 1963; Weill 1925). Durkheim's 'religious' outlook was in general very much that of the *idéologues* of the Third Republic, for he reflects in perhaps a more sophisticated way an idealism dominant in his day – that of a worship of science coupled with a self-assured belief in the progressive independence of men from the religious institutional oppression of previous generations. But he did not only reflect it, he proclaimed it and, as we have seen, he was one of the most outspoken upholders of the Republic (see chs 1 and 2).

However, for Durkheim, the point of origin of such a religion was not the French Revolution, the Reformation, the Renaissance, scholasticism, the decline of Greek and Roman polytheism, or the demise of oriental theocracies (1893b/1902b:146/ t.1933b:171). The development of the cult of man corresponds to the growth of secularization (see ch. 24). Indeed the two are closely related: they are almost identical. Individualism has thus been in progess without cessation all through history (ibid.). In the beginning, 'society is everything, the individual nothing' (1897a:382/t.1951a:336). But the path has been in the direction of the individual and, like that of secularization, has not been 'straightforward' but nevertheless has proceeded 'without a break in continuity'. Granet (1930:291) observed that this important relationship is seen in a key passage in *The Division of Labour*:

> As all the other beliefs and the other practices take on a character which is less and less religious, the individual becomes the object of some kind of religion. We have a cult of the dignity of the person, which like every strong cult already has its superstitions. (1893b/1902b:147/t.1933b:172)

Here is 'an inevitable law against which it would be idle to inveigh' (ibid.). Durkheim thus puts forward one of those laws which he thought sociology should attempt to produce in accordance with the guidelines he set out in the *Rules* (1895a). But he is silent about the inner workings of the law. Even if there is a correlation between the growth of secularization and the growth of individualism, how is it that one is related to the other? What is the causal connection? There is no answer. All that Durkheim can do is to point to certain historical periods and religions and show how they have accelerated the process. In this, Christianity is singled out as giving greater impetus to the movement than any other religion. Even to the Greeks and Romans, the cult of humanity as described by Durkheim was 'quite unknown' (1938a/1969f:372/t.1977a:325). As Christianity most assuredly cut the path of secularization, so it opened the door for science and freedom of thought, and hence the cult of man (1898c:11/t.1969d:26/r.1975:68). The Renaissance constituted another surge in the same direction (1938a/1969f: chs 15 and 16). One is tempted to deduce that, according to Durkheim, the heritage *par excellence* of simple or primitive societies, and indeed that of Christianity itself, is human sacredness, the sentiment of personal dignity.

Thus, through historical processes, society has now reached a position where man has ascribed to human personality something of the transcendental. Durkheim wrote at the turn of the century:

> There remains nothing that man may love and honour in common, apart from himself. This is why man has become a god for men, and it is why he can no longer turn to other gods without being untrue to himself. (1898c:11/t.1969d:26/ r.1975:67)

In transforming himself into god, man does not worship an individual man, but disregards the multitude of individual differences and posits universal qualities and characteristics. It is man in general whom he worships:

> The cult of which he is at once both object and follower does not address itself to the particular being that constitutes himself and carries his name, but to the human person, wherever it is to be found, and in whatever form it is incarnated. Impersonal and anonymous, such an end soars far above all particular consciences and can thus serve as a rallying-point for them. (ibid.:9/23/64)

Expressed in terms in keeping with Durkheim's definition of religion, man has made himself sacred. In his lectures on moral education, Durkheim stated: 'Don't we say, casually, that the human person is sacred, that we must venerate him?' (1925a:8/ t.1961a:10/r.1975:197).

We have outlined the main tenets of Durkheim's version of religion centred on man. The immediate likeness to Comte's religion of humanity has already been suggested and was raised in an earlier chapter (ch. 13.4). To this issue we briefly return.

Scholars, including Richard, would agree that Comte's concept of the religion of humanity was by no means the same as that which Durkheim used. Comte's notion was much more general in seeing humanity as a universal, unitary concept covering the whole of mankind, past, present and future. Durkheim feared that such a concept bordered on the metaphysical. His own notion was more sociological. Man received his exalted place in certain societies: only in them is it legitimate to talk about the cult of the individual. Each society has different values just as each religion is different in the content of its beliefs. If the deification of man occurs in a society, it is because that society has brought about such sacralization. Should Durkheim claim any originality in connection with the cult of man, it would be in this kind of analysis, for there is no universal 'god' of man in Durkheim as there is in Comte. To be sure, Durkheim saw that the religion of the future in modern western society would be what we might loosely call humanism. He seemed to imply that such a religion would grow as western civilization expanded. But this is not what Comte meant by the religion of humanity, which involved a Catholic type of cult and theology and was missionary in outlook. Such characteristics and aims were anathema to Durkheim. For him, the new religion would arise from below, from the thought of academic liberals, who would allow each society to create its own 'gods' which would be closely tied to the *représentations* each society developed. Richard overlooked these differences between Comte's religion of humanity and Durkheim's close assocation of society and divinity. He made a more sweeping condemnation of Comte's positivism and Durkheim's rationalism in so far as claims were made by both in the name of science but which were beyond scientific proof. Comte and Durkheim entered the realm of metaphysics in what they were asserting and they degraded the discipline, by committing a fundamental error about the nature of religion, stating that it is basically a collective phenomenon or a collective emotion (Richard 1943:136–7). Incidentally, Belot criticized Durkheim on historical grounds claiming that the idea of a god of humanity or simply a god of society was relatively late in the development of the notion of God. Divinities of nature, which were earlier, had little interest in the welfare of society (1909:17).

Saint-Simon was probably a greater influence on Durkheim than Comte and some of this is to be seen in those sections devoted to Saint-Simon in the course of lectures he gave on socialism (1928a). Durkheim indeed admitted that Saint-Simon – Comte was his secretary – was the more important of the two in the development of sociology. Certainly, in the realm of the analysis and theory of religion, Gurvitch is convinced that Durkheim was more influenced by Saint-Simon than by Comte (1965:24). But even here questions are to be raised. Durkheim held that Saint-Simon's *Nouveau Christianisme*, based on the unity of humanity, love and god, and extending from time to eternity, led very easily to pantheism which was clearly something Durkheim strongly rejected. Further, as in the case of the religion of humanity, its protagonists had a strong sense of mission (cf.1928a:276/ t.1958b:190). And this, from a slightly different point of view, confirms what we have suggested already, namely, that both polytheism and pantheism ill fit Durkheim's association of the concepts of God and society.

4 The heresy of egoism

Durkheim never exclusively fixed on one term to describe the religion he was convinced was going to become dominant in the western world and which had been developing for centuries. He sometimes referred to it as individualism, or moral individualism, as the cult of man, or the cult of the individual, or, again, as the cult of the human personality. One term he certainly avoided was that of the religion of humanity because of its association with Auguste Comte. And the notion of personality, although sometimes used by Durkheim, was not extensively employed, perhaps not least because it could be associated with psychology, and Durkheim would keep that discipline at a safe distance from sociology. He realized the term individualism contained ambiguities which he wanted to avoid. Although the phrase the cult of man has strong religious connotations, and some might think contains irrational overtones, Durkheim had no qualms in using it. It seems on the whole to be a useful term to employ, especially when one considers what Durkheim was referring to.

All the traditional religions have had their heretics, who in the eyes of the orthodox are more dangerous than members of other religions. Durkheim believed that the cult of the individual was no exception and was capable of heretical exposition. His article 'Individualism and the intellectuals' (1898c) contains a clarification of what is meant by moral individualism or the cult of man and at the same time is a refutation of a similar but dangerous belief. But such calls to orthodoxy had already appeared in *Suicide* (1897a) and subsequently in an important article, 'Two laws of penal evolution' (1901a:(i)). The heresy that can spring from individualism is that of egoism, seen as the fulfilment, even saturation, of individual needs and sensory appetites. The egoistic man, as distinct from him who follows the cult of man, thinks only of himself and places himself as an individual at the pinnacle of his values. Egoism is thus anti-social; indeed, it is the enemy of society and, as such, has to be curbed by the practice of self-discipline and social controls. These are undermined, if egoism becomes dominant. English utilitarian egoism, such as that of Herbert Spencer, is an obvious example of the heresy, for it emphasizes 'the tangible, empirical individual as realized in each particular *conscience*' (1901a(i):89/t.1973b:302). Durkheim employs Kant's arguments to reject such individualism and sees the value of extending the concept of human personality, in general, to humanity as a whole, to man as universal being, and thus abstracting him from concrete and particular forms (ibid.). If one's faith rests in this generalized form, the shortcomings and evils of egoism are nullified, for in this case the individual man is now seen to be part of man in general, and this means a concern for the state of others, as well as for the individual. In practical terms, it implies commitment to the liberty of others, to their rights, and to the notion of social and economic justice. It implies, as Durkheim says, the old adage: ' "do not unto others that which you would not wish done to you" ' (ibid.). Again, writing in 1906, he said:

The human personality is a sacred thing; one dare not violate it nor infringe its bounds, while at the same time *the greatest good is in communion with others*. (1906b/1924a:51/t.1953b:37; our italics)

Durkheim's 'Individualism and the intellectuals' was a defence against the heresy that he and other Dreyfusards were charged with; an individualism which undermined the well-being of society by the following of selfish, individual ends. Durkheim showed that the cult of man, which he followed, was indeed the very opposite of the heresy with which he was charged and that the form of individualism to which he subscribed was associated with that of Kant, in particular, as well as that of Rousseau. Like their doctrines, his own transcended the individual and showed that 'duty consists in averting our attention from what concerns us personally' (1898c:8/t.1969d:24/r.1975:61). Put into more 'religious' and at the same time functionalist terms, Durkheim held that the person who admits his belief in individualism, as he defines it, performs the same useful action as the ancient Roman when he observed his traditional rites which upheld collective and national sentiments (ibid.:12/27–8/69; see also 1950a/t.1969g:94ff./ t.1957a:58ff.).

5 But who is god? Man or society?

In rejecting the heresy of egoism, Durkheim unwittingly raised the fundamental question about the nature of the cult of man and its theological or philosophical substantiation. To posit grounds for rejecting egoism but at the same time to accept the cult of man tempts one to ask whether, in the eyes of Durkheim, man in fact represents the highest order of existence, or whether there is not something which transcends man himself. Is man, universal man, in fact the ultimate of Durkheim's system?

The issue at stake is but another facet of the problem which confronted Durkheim, namely, the relation of the individual to society. It is centred on such issues as the problem of socialization, of the individual adopting social norms and culture, of the problem of freedom and social absorption, of the relation of individual *représentations* to collective *représentations*, and now, once again, it turns up in the issue of the sacredness of the individual and the ultimate authority of society.

Although Durkheim refused to define religion in terms of divine being or beings, and went so far as to deny categorically their existence, he was willing enough to refer to man's nature as being in some sense divine, for he 'has something of that transcendental majesty which the churches have at all times given to their Gods' (1898c:8/t.1969d:21/r.1975:62). Again, 'man has become a god for men' and therefore 'we belong to no temporal being because we are kin to God' (1897a:379/t.1951a:334; see also 1906e:256). So if the gods do not exist, man does, and here we have an empirical reality they do not possess. But man has not always been sacred; how does he become so? Sacredness is not inherent in man. 'Society has consecrated the individual and made him pre-eminently worthy of respect' (ibid.:106/72). Again, 'It is society that instituted it [cult of the individual] and made of man the god whose servant it is' (ibid.:84–5/59).

In another context, as we have seen, Durkheim virtually deified society, as is witnessed in the distorted statement 'God is society'. No matter how ambiguous such a statement is, it does imply that society has associated with it *représentations* that are held to be divine. It is the mysterious transcendental 'other' before which men must bow. As Durkheim admitted, there is in reality only one force greater than man himself and that is society. In speaking of the emergence of a rational morality, he wrote:

All that we needed was to substitute for the conception of a supernatural being the empirical idea of a directly observable being, which is society – provided we do not view society as an arithmetic sum of individuals, but as a new personality distinct from individual personalities. We have shown how society so conceived constrains us since it dominates us. (1925a:199/t.1961a:104)

Durkheim saw that a rational morality was one that was 'demanded by society' (ibid.:103/90). Under these circumstances the collectivity takes unto itself the role of divinity. If society declares what and who God is, it must itself be God. He was caught in a paradox. Nationalist though he was, Durkheim also saw that nationalism had to be subject to the highest control of universal humanistic values (Schoffeleers and Meijers 1978:49). In this respect there exists a supra-national creed emanating from western society which will and should engulf the whole of humanity. Durkheim is never free from such ideology. The conclusion is inevitable: the subject is equated with the object.

Yet there is contrary evidence in Durkheim's writings, not only from passages that have already been given but also in a sentence he wrote in *Suicide*. 'But today he [man] has acquired a kind of personality which places him above himself as well as above society' (1897a:378/t.1951a:333). But how is it that man can be above society, when society makes him god?

Durkheim wants it both ways. He suggests that there now exists a cult of man in which man is god, but although god is without a limit, man is far from being so and must be subject to limitations because his instincts have to be controlled, and society as an entity *sui generis* exerts those controls. Since society is ultimate power, it must be god. And of course, as we have indicated (see ch. 13), in the last analysis society is made equivalent to *La Nation*, the country, a whole society (see, for example, 1925a:123/t.1961a:107). *La Patrie* is very much the incarnation of humanity (Mitchell 1931:104; and see ch. 1.6). But if it is a case of 'my country right or wrong', is this not likely to conflict with universal concepts of humanity? Durkheim's position assumes that *La Patrie* is a manifestation of humanistic ideals as he envisaged them. What if a society does not possess them? Further, in the West, consensus values are minimal (see Lane 1981:225ff.). Where in such diversity stands 'God'? Can Durkheim really maintain that his god – humanity – is found in society – in *La Patrie*? Would he acknowledge it in the so-called civil religion of the United States (see Warner 1962; Cole and Hammond 1974; Schoffeleers and Meijers 1978; Gehrig 1981)? The old problem emerges – how does one differentiate national values, which may be seen to be sacred, from the cult of man; again, from the state itself, and also from churches? Durkheim's enthusiasm for the concept of humanity blinds him to these issues.

Durkheim was never able to explain satisfactorily the relation between the individual and society. The introduction of the cult of man in no way helps the problem; indeed, it aggravates it. Nor does a dialectical juggling with the terms provide a way out, for example, in the merging of the two entities. Despite the canonization of man proposed by Durkheim, it remains a historical fact that the individual is often in conflict with society. Indeed, it could well be argued that he has gained his rights, achieved justice and freedom of thought, not by co-operation with society but by fighting against it. Man has triumphed, not through the agency of

489

society but in spite of it. If therefore there exists conflict between the individual and society, which of them can be labelled god or the ultimate?

It is a matter of debate whether or not the cult of man is a point of difference in Marxist and Durkheimian thought. Marx would abolish religion in order to make man man: Durkheim would make man god. Here Durkheim's ideas more nearly resemble Feuerbach's; for example, when Durkheim writes 'Man has become a god for men' (1897a:378/t.1951a:334). In his speech in 1914 to the Conference of Free Thinkers and Free Believers, Durkheim makes the following point which may refer to a Marxist, whose name is unknown:

> A short time ago, an orator, gesticulating prophetically
> towards the heavens, told us they were emptying and urged
> us to turn our eyes towards the earth, that is to say, to occupy
> ourselves above all with pursuing our economic interests to
> the best of our ability. This formula has been called impious.
> From my position one can say it is false. No, there is no need
> to fear that the heavens will ever become finally depopulated,
> for we ourselves populate them. (1919b:103/t.1975a:186).

6 Can the cult be justified? Its theology and ritual

Durkheim's conviction that a new religion was emerging brought upon him a great deal of criticism both during his life and afterwards. Needless to say, attacks came from many quarters, from committed Christians, be they Catholic or Protestant (see chs 23, 27 and 28). Obviously there were those who, as agnostics or atheists, openly rejected the possibility or desirability of some future religion. For them, the whole movement of humanism was one of liberation from religion in any form. Also, there were those who felt that Durkheim's theoretical position was wrong, in so far as it demanded the persistence of religion. Amongst these van Gennep. He wrote in his review of *The Elementary Forms*:

> the progress of humanity has consisted in the growing
> secularization of all mental and practical activities, and in the
> proportional disintegration and destruction of religion. As for

replacing religion with another sociological imperative, I do not see the point of it, nor do I consider even its possibility. (1913:91/t.1975:208)

A few years earlier Belot disagreed with Durkheim and seriously doubted the value of trying to create or uphold any form of religion in the present day (1909). He advocated that religion should be allowed to die and morality alone take its place. For him, unlike Durkheim, morality is of a different and an independent source from that of religion. Not surprisingly, such criticism still persists. In a recent book dealing with Durkheim's concept of morality and the religion of the individual, Wallwork wrote:

> But Durkheim is less than convincing when he predicts, on evolutionary grounds, that traditional religions are destined to be replaced by the new cult of man because they conflict with the modern scientific *weltanschauung*. (1972:149)

There is limited value in quoting similar words of criticism from other sociologists, philosophers and theologians. We need to turn to a more detailed examination of his concept of the religion of individualism.

Durkheim wrote: 'This cult of man has for its first dogma the autonomy of reason and for its first rite freedom of thought' (1898c:10/t.1969d:24/1975:65). On what grounds does Durkheim assert these and similar doctrinal utterances? Unlike Comte's religion of humanity, Durkheim's cult of the individual, and indeed the creed of humanism in general, has never been officially or authoritatively formulated. To suggest as Durkheim does that reason is its prime doctrine is hardly a reason for justifying it! Since Durkheim rejects revelation, he feels he must find some equivalent. The foundation of the religion, as we have seen, is the ideological enthronement of man. Durkheim attempts to show this as a movement which has been evolving over a long period of time. There is also a theological reason for accepting the religion. As he writes;

> We know indeed that the sacred character which still marks the individual today is founded in reality; it is no more than the expression of the very high value that has accrued to individual personality through the conscience and dignity it is invested with. (1950a/1969g:199/t.1957a:172)

491

Durkheim holds that his doctrine of man, having some affinity with that of Christianity (see ch. 23.3–23.4) is at the basis of the new religion. 'The most significant part of our being,' he said, 'which we call the soul, comes from Him [God] and expresses Him through us' (1925a:119/t.1961a:104). Using Christian language Durkheim, as it has been repeatedly said, closely associates God with society. What is divine in man is the social (1913b; 1914a; ch. 8). 'We all carry the imprint of divinity' (1925a:119/t.1961a:104).

Because the cult of man does not exist in a form that is instantly recognized, Durkheim was forced to argue for its existence. And as well as pointing to what he held were historical facts, many of his arguments are reminiscent of the theologian trying to prove the existence of God, and sometimes one sees in him the scholastic philosopher arguing ontologically. For example, in 'Individualism and the intellectuals', after he has presented with approval Kant's concept of morality based on man *in abstracto*, he goes on to assume that from this, as we have noted, the human person is sacred and has something about him of the transcendental which churches have always bestowed upon their gods (1898c:8/t.1969d:21/r.1975:62). So man is a divine being by deduction! And, with his customary logic, Durkheim sees that as man treated his gods in the past, so he treats man now, offering him respect and worship. Since man must never profane his gods, so man today must never profane man. He wrote:

> Whoever makes an attempt on a man's life, on a man's liberty, on a man's honour inspires us with a feeling of horror, in every way analogous to that which the believer experiences when he sees his idol profaned. Such morality is therefore not simply a hygienic discipline or a wise principle of economy. It is a religion of which man is, at the same time, both believer and god. (ibid.:8/21–2/62)

On these grounds alone man should not commit suicide (as he argued in his book on the subject, see 1897a:383/t.1951a:337), and we might add that such a reason should prevent him going to war or committing murder or other violent crimes! However, the question of crime in Durkheim is problematic and ambivalent – something that has been carefully pointed out by Richard (see Richard 1925(ii):361). Durkheim's argument for the existence of his religion is very much like the moral argument for the existence of God. Man is a moral creature, but a moral system does not have authority unless there is a moral being superior to man: since a moral system exists, a moral being exists. Similarly, for Durkheim, man is a moral creature, whose moral system needs to be undergirded by some authority superior to himself, that is, a religion: therefore the religion exists. And he goes so far as to admit this in his *Suicide*, when he wrote that the cult of human personality is that on which all our morality rests (1897a:379/ t.1951a.334). Time and time again, Durkheim admitted that an ethical system needs an authority above itself and therefore a humanistic ethic requires a humanistic religion (see 1908a(2); 1909a(2)/t.1979a). One may well ask the question whether any person is persuaded not to commit suicide or murder because he worships man? Empirical evidence is certainly required if Durkheim's position is to be substantiated. There can be no doubt that at the time Durkheim wrote there were a large number of middle-class intellectuals, especially French liberals, who held views which were in some way in keeping with those of Durkheim. Within the working classes, from whom Durkheim hoped a religious revival would spring, little that would pass for the cult of man has ever existed or exists today. This we have already noted. Durkheim made no attempt to try to prove his case, undertook no empirical research to strengthen his position, other than pointing to changes of thought in the intellectual climate of society. Yet those who are highly committed to humanism today are most reluctant to use the kind of terminology that Durkheim felt to be so important in delineating the religion of the future.

One of the most severe problems that faces all liberal humanists is that of suffering. Humanism contains an essentially optimistic ethic. How does such an ethic or religion cope with violence, national disasters, war or concentration camps? Durkheim may say that man worships man, but man does not hesitate to slaughter his fellow beings. Humanistic appeals do not assuage evil, only force does that. Durkheim himself was shattered by the holocaust of the First World War, which decimated his own select body of students. One wonders if, as a result of the war, he did not abandon his faith in the religion of the future which, just before the declaration of war, he had so much praised (see 1919b). The loss of his son André hastened his death: but had not his own faith in the future also died (see ch. 1.8)?

In his essay 'The dualism of human nature', Durkheim comes to the brink of considering questions of theodicy, where he attempts to show how idealism and monism cannot incorporate notions of sin and suffering (1914a; see also 1913b). He admits that these are accommodated in various kinds of dualistic systems. However, the notions of sin and suffering have no place in the creed of the religion of the future. He openly rejects those traditional religions which have placed suffering at the centre of their beliefs. He wrote:

> The great religions of modern man are those which insist the most on the existence of the contradictions in the midst of which we struggle. These continue to depict us as tormented and suffering. (1914a:213/t.1960c:331–2)

And then, in approving primitive religions, he adds, 'the crude cults of inferior societies breathe forth and inspire a joyful confidence' (ibid.). It is evident that Durkheim – on the eve of the outbreak of war, let it be noted once again – would solve the problems of suffering and evil by repressing them and throwing up a smoke-screen of self-generated happiness. (The relation of theodicy to sociology was considered by Richard towards the end of his life (1943).)

Can man, can society make man sacred? In one sense, of course, it is possible. As we saw earlier, anything can be designated sacred by society (see ch. 7.6). But to make man sacred is not to achieve something of the same order as saying that gods exist who are sacred. The first is visible to the naked eye; the second is not: the first is not surrounded by mystery; the second is. Man is never hidden, existing beyond human sight. He does not have to be revealed in some non-rational way. He can never be sacred in the same way as the gods are (1906b/1924a:93/t.1953b:71).

To say that the cult of man has 'as its first rite freedom of thought' is to make one doubt whether Durkheim in stating this was totally oblivious to his analysis of ritual, for it bears little relation to his early ideas on the subject and certainly to what he was to write on it in *The Elementary Forms*. Was he unaware that the cult of man is a cult without a cultus?

As it is generally understood, humanism is essentially anti-ritualistic. To humanists religious ritual – ritual in any form – speaks of either superstition or irrationality. And Durkheim's own ambivalence is apparent, on the one hand, in an intellectual realization of the need of ritual within a religion and, on the other, a personal distaste for it. Of ritual in the modern context, Durkheim wrote in a way that almost contradicts what he said in *The Elementary Forms* (see ch. 20.3):

> For we know today that a religion does not necessarily imply symbols and rites in the full sense, or temples and priests. All this external apparatus is merely its superficial aspect. Essentially it is nothing more than a system of collective beliefs and practices which have special authority. (1898c:10/ t.1969d:25/r.1975:66)

However, what are these practices, which are supported by a special authority, and which are associated with the cult of man? From other contexts we may deduce that they are great national observances such as Bastille Day. But such occasions are social, they do not relate to the sacredness of the person, and there are no rites which openly declare such a faith. Once again, on this evidence alone, one may ask whether the god at the back of Durkheim's mind is society rather than man. Gluckman, referring to the *Division of Labour*, observed that Durkheim emphasized that as religious formalism began to decline the god of humanity began to emerge (1962:19ff.). Gluckman also noted that in primitive societies social relations are ritualized, but not so in modern societies. Ritual becomes more general as it turns itself into congregational worship, and then vanishes almost entirely. Thus, ritual in western industrial society seems destined to extinction despite any ascendancy in human values.

Comte's religion of humanity had more logic in it than Durkheim's cult of man. Comte fully understood the necessity of ritual for a religion; and with that firmly in his mind took it as his task to introduce in great detail a sophisticated ritual, in part borrowed from rites of the Roman Catholic Church, but which had humanity as its object of worship. (Soviet leaders seem to follow Comte rather than Durkheim in recent attempts to strengthen civic ritual in the USSR (see Lane 1981).)

In many respects Durkheim felt that what historical religions had done in the past for society, the cult of man could achieve in the future. For Durkheim the most important characteristic was the force that a religion exerted over the individual *conscience*; by this means a religion was able to influence people in their moral behaviour and to call forth acts of self-denial and asceticism. The major issue turns on whether a self-consciously generated and internalized ideal can gain not only respect and following but can be raised to a transcendental status which is necessary for a religion to exist. Here it would appear that there is at least one internal inconsistency. In his lectures which covered Bazard's development of Saint-Simon's *Nouveau Christianisme*, he attacked both Bazard and Saint-Simon for proposing a religious system which in opposite ways led to pantheism, where all that exists, be it material or non-material, is divine (1928a/1971d:260/ t.1958b:234–5). Such a system, in addition to other weaknesses, was not able, argued Durkheim, to restrain egoism and psychological drives and demands. It makes no call for self-sacrifice. Unchecked liberty would give rise to social chaos, not harmony. There must be an appeal from outside the system for man to be loyal and obedient to the system's demands. It must have an authority greater than that of the individual. Christianity had been successful in this respect, because its god was over and above the world and called for men to be obedient to the demands of control (ibid.:258/232). Apart from the issue of pantheism, the criticism which Durkheim levels against *Nouveau Christianisme* is equally applicable to what he saw as the religion of the future. The new religion, however, is no different from Saint-Simon's. Witness his platitudinous attitude to the cult of the individual, written at the time of the Dreyfus affair:

> This religion of humanity has all that is required to speak to its believers in a tone that is no less imperative than the religions it replaces. Far from confining itself to indulging our instincts, it offers us an ideal which infinitely surpasses nature. (1898c:9/t.1969d:23/r.1975:63–4)

But above all, in contrast to Comte once again, Durkheim can point to no church, no organization by which men assemble and jointly express their faith and practice. Its controlling force over society is minimal. Evans-Pritchard was wrong in stating that Durkheim envisaged a secularist church of the kind that arose out of the French Revolution (1962:32). One response in defence of

Durkheim is to suggest that membership of the religion is identical to that of society, since the society's beliefs would correspond to those of its members. But such a condition would mean that the society was characterized by mechanical solidarity and this flatly contradicts Durkheim's own thinking about the emergence of the cult of man. Again, it is difficult to say that society equals the Church in a pluralistic world, for such a proposition is clearly a failure to be realistic.

In the light of what has been said, the question arises as to whether what Durkheim was proclaiming constituted a religion, as he claimed it was. The answer is clearly in the negative. The cult of man, as we have observed, is without a ritual and without a church. As such, and in accordance with Durkheim's own definition of what constitutes a religion, it cannot in any way be so designated (see ch. 9.5). The basic elements are missing and therefore the proclamation that the cult of the individual is a religion is unconvincing (see, for example, 1898c:8/t.1969d:21/ r.1975:62; see also 1950a/1969g:104/t.1957a:69).

Another reason for saying this was that Durkheim never claimed to be, nor was he in fact, a founder of a secular religion. If Durkheim had a strictly religious task, it was as a theologian of a religion that he claimed was already in existence. Richard calls Durkheim's cult of man the daughter of Comte's religion of humanity which he saw as a systematic combination of positivism and humanism, but this was not really the case (1935:19; 1943; see ch. 13.4). It may be true, as Richard also stated, that Durkheim's concept of the religion of the future was one facet of his *sociologie religieuse* (see chs 27 and 28). However, Durkheim did not want to turn his sociology into a religion as Comte had done (611/427/ 156). He claimed that in the first place his task was merely to point to what in fact was happening in the course of history, and unlike Comte, he did not seek to propagate the faith or encourage the practice in terms of ritual, or again to create a church. He did not see himself as a preacher, evangelist or missionary for a *religion*. But at the same time it can be justifiably said that he attempted to give some scientific basis to the religion which stemmed from his theory of society, where divinity is society symbolically transformed (Goblet d'Alviella 1913:220).

7 Basically a system of morality

Durkheim was firmly convinced that his analysis of what he thought was the religion of the future was both academically and politically acceptable. He seemed sure that in emphasizing a reverence for science and a reverence for man and bringing them together he had breached the gap between religion and science, which many intellectuals, both believers and non-believers, had for a long time seen as being a great, if not unbridgeable gulf (see Aron 1967b, 2:41). From now on, thanks to him, the scientist and the fair-minded (that is, the liberal) theologian can meet on common ground. Since Durkheim's time, the relation between religion and science has gone through many phases of rapprochement and hostility. Certainly the dream he had has never materialized. The 'best' of science and the 'best' of religion cannot in fact dwell happily in the same bed. Contrary to what Durkheim hoped, one cannot have it both ways.

In the broad sweep, however, Durkheim was right on two counts. First, there has been a continual decline of traditional western religions. Second, and more in keeping with this chapter, there has been a growth in the acceptance of the ideals of humanism, defined in the widest terms, and to be found particularly amongst intellectuals. The notion of Kantian man remains triumphant and, in the absence of God, man continues to think of himself as a self-legitimating being. This needs to be carefully documented for present-day society, but one can immediately point to the Charter of the United Nations, to Charter 77 and to the speeches of leading politicians in the West. The most 'sacrilegious' attitude a person may take today is to be anti-humanistic, to be racialist, or an opponent of Charter 77. Further, this humanistic outlook has in recent years become dominant in the churches themselves, both Protestant and Catholic, where the classical themes of salvation and redemption based on the work of Christ and the theology of St Paul have fallen into the background in the face of the dominant concern with personal relations, the ethic of love, and social justice.

We have stated that Durkheim was no founder of the cult of man and that, despite his proclamation to the contrary, he was dealing with hardly a religion at all. More precisely, he was advocating what we might call a functional alternative to a traditional religion, as when he wrote:

> This cult, moreover, has all that is required to take the place of the religious cults of former times. (1950a/1969g:104/ t.1957a:69)

But the alternative is not another religion; it is in fact a moral system. Such is the conclusion of many scholars (for example, Giddens 1978:99). This striving for a secular morality – some form of Christian ethic, shorn of theological dogma, ritual and a church – was clearly evident not only in Durkheim but also in such thinkers and political leaders of his time as Renouvier, Guyau, Desjardins, Barrès, Buisson and Péguy before his conversion to Catholicism.

Durkheim was optimistic about this morality, which was at the foundation of the Third Republic. Apart from the question of its 'truth', he was convinced that such a morality would stand firm in the face of scientific inquiry and rational criticism, for they both had given rise to it. Such a morality would be free from the undermining forces of scientific investigation. One wonders whether the events of history and subsequent changes in society which occurred after his death would have shaken his optimism – we might point to the final stages of the First World War (see ch. 1.7), the rise of Hitler, the growth of communism, and the development of a permissive morality. Durkheim's unshakeable hope was based very largely on the legacy of Christianity, as he himself admitted. He was living in an immediate post-Christian age, which was still relying on the capital and goodwill of Christian ideology and structures. These have continued to be eaten away and the capital expended. What price his optimism today?

Part VI
Postscript

27 *Sociologie religieuse*: a hope that quickly fades

1 Durkheim's vulnerability

This book has been about Durkheim's *sociologie religieuse*. What has been attempted is a commentary on some of the key aspects of his sociological analysis of religion rather than a systematic account of it. Nevertheless it is hoped that what has been written forms an adequate presentation of the aims and achievements of what was, for Durkheim, one of the most important, if not *the* most important, aspects of his sociology.

There is no doubt that Durkheim's influence on the sociology of religion has been enormous. It could well be argued that in terms of theory the discipline has not developed beyond the pioneering work undertaken by Durkheim, on the one hand, and Max Weber, on the other. This may appear strange in the light of some of the critical points that have been raised here, but the fact of the matter is that Durkheim's imaginative and fertile mind pointed to social interconnections and concepts which have shown themselves to be fruitful in empirical work long after they were first advanced.

Much of the criticism that has been levelled against Durkheim has arisen on account of what we have constantly referred to as his *via media* position. It is very easy to attack anyone who takes to the middle of the road. The internal logic of extremism may provide the enemy with plenty of ammunition and the man in the middle gets double fire. Such vulnerability was particularly apparent in Durkheim's day in the very country where he hoped his ideas would be acceptable. He rejected not only militant, atheistic rationalism, but also a commitment to a religious position; not only a crude materialistic empiricism, but also any adherence to idealism. In the bitter controversies between believer and non-believer in France around the turn of the century, he introduced a note of sanity and mutual recognition by being objective and in trying to appeal to both sides (Le Bras 1966:53). The critics, as we have seen and as we shall emphasize in the pages ahead, saw a great deal that was wrong in his *sociologie religieuse*, but to the liberal minded he stood as someone who calmed troubled waters. That today in the sociology of religion one can find Catholics, Protestants, non-Christians and non-believers working side by side without entering into perpetual conflict is in part due to the vision that Durkheim had for the discipline.

As we began with an historical note, so we end with one. In this postscript attention is drawn, amongst other things, to the fortune of Durkheim's *sociologie religieuse*, especially in the period between the wars.

2 The eclipse of Durkheim's *sociologie religieuse*

The term *sociologie religieuse*, frequently used by Durkheim, approximately corresponds to what today is meant by the sociology of religion.[1] Richard claimed that Durkheim had coined the word (1923:126/t.1975:230). Be that as it may, one thing is certain, the term appeared in the first issue of the *Année sociologique*, published in 1898, and was thereafter repeatedly employed to refer to a section of reviews. It immediately followed the first section, *sociologie générale*, and it was often the longest section. This, of course, may be explained by the large number of books being written in the field of religion at the time.[2] Of great significance is the fact that Durkheim saw religion as the key to understanding society (see ch. 28.1). After his death, *sociologie religieuse* in the way he had formulated it, entered into a period of limbo for a number of years. To try to account for such a demise, it is necessary to examine briefly the fortunes of Durkheimianism after the First World War and also to look at the place *sociologie religieuse* held amongst devoted disciples dedicated to the task of extending and propagating their master's work.

Both the Année Sociologique group and the journal went into a state of decline after the death of Durkheim in 1917. Part of the reason was that no immediate or obvious successor could be found to follow him. There was no one of his stature in the *équipe* – no one with his ability and vitality, no one with the charismatic qualities he possessed – who could take over where he had left off. Perhaps the reason for this, and it was certainly the cause of the weakened state of the group, was the carnage of the war in which many of the most promising disciples were killed, such as David, Hertz, Bianconi, and not least his own son, André. Weakened, and with no obvious leader, those who tried to carry on the work of their founder were unable to achieve the pre-eminence of the school which it had had in earlier decades (see Craig 1979; Geiger 1979; Weisz 1979).

The journal, *L'Année sociologique*. which in its early days had been so successful in the academic world of France and elsewhere, was re-started under the editorship of Marcel Mauss, on whose shoulders almost by default the mantle of Durkheim had fallen. Publication was painfully slow and the first volume of the new series did not appear until 1925. It turned out to be of enormous length, something like 1,000 pages: but the second and last volume, published two years later, was a tenth of the size. The new series, as a second child, died in early infancy.

Somewhat more successful was the *Collection de l'Année sociologique, Annales sociologiques*. The editorial committee contained such Durkheimians as Bouglé, Fauconnet, Mauss, Simiand and Halbwachs. In part, the articles came from meetings of the Institut Française de Sociologie and consisted of five series, each dealing separately with general sociology, *sociologie religieuse*, legal and moral sociology, economic sociology, and social morphology. The series was produced between 1934 and 1942.

The intellectual world of France seemed less enthusiastic about sociology after the war than it had been when Durkheim was alive. The encouraging impetus which was formerly centred on him waned. The university authorities were not keen to develop the subject and student interest was correspondingly weakened. Durkheim's chair was annulled in 1919, although the subject did not disappear from the Sorbonne. It was also taught in the universities of Bordeaux and Strasbourg (see *RFS*, XX(1), 1979). Some of Durkheim's disciples, however, were able to obtain university chairs in the late 1920s and in the 1930s, and Célestin Bouglé occupied the influential post of director of the École Normale Supérieure. An antipathy to Durkheimians was nevertheless apparent in the Académie, who found themselves very much on the defensive (Craig 1979:279). Although certain individuals were thus moderately successful, Durkheimians as a whole were precariously placed. The impact on academic life once achieved by *le grand maître* and his team had gone. Nevertheless the group continued to hold together until the Second World War and Bouglé could still talk of 'notre école sociologique' in 1938 (Bouglé 1938:41).

How did *sociologie religieuse* fare within Durkheimian sociology itself during the days of diminution? One scholar at least has declared that a weakness soon began to appear in the place *sociologie religieuse* held within the wider discipline. With the publication of *Les Formes*, which was meant to be the pinnacle of achievement for its author and his colleagues, Durkheim went too far according to Wilhelm Schmidt, who said, admittedly a number of years later, that the book 'in fact marked the beginning of a decline' (1931:123). One thing seems quite clear: *sociologie religieuse* between the wars no longer held pride of place as it formerly did when Durkheim held the reins.

To account for this one might point to the fact that it was Durkheim himself who had shown such interest in religion and had so brilliantly applied sociological techniques to its study. He was now dead and no one trained by him, no one amongst those who joined the Année Sociologique group after the war, had anything approaching his conviction of the centrality of religion in a scientific explanation of social phenomena. This is not to say that no one of the *équipe* turned to the study of religious phenomena. But there is a notable decline and a lack of interest amongst members, not least in Marcel Mauss himself, who had written so much on the subject in the *Année sociologique* when his uncle was editor. Not without interest is the fact that Mauss ceased to concern himself with religion in the way he had up to the time of the First World War, perhaps due to the pressure of his mentor. Further, those later disciples who wrote on religion did not become well known, for example, Philippe de Félice (1880–1964), who wrote several books (see de Félice 1947) and who contributed reviews to the original series of the *Année sociologique*, as well as to the second. He originally studied theology and was probably the only person who had been trained in that discipline. He had differences with Durkheimian thought, and although he had been taught by Hubert, he left the group in 1927 and lectured in the Protestant Faculty of Theology in Paris. Another name that might be mentioned is that of Stefan Czarnowski (1897–1937), a Celtic scholar of Polish descent who had studied under Durkheim, Mauss and Hubert. He made some contributions to the second series of the *Année sociologique* and his thesis, *Le Culte des héros et ses conditions sociales* (1915), became well known. He died prematurely at the age of 40. It is possible to speculate, as Evans-Pritchard did, that the young Robert Hertz (1881–1915), who had written extensively on religious subjects, would have assumed leadership in this area had he lived (Evans-Pritchard 1960:16 n.1, 24). He had planned to write on the subject of sin, pardon and auricular confession. Marcel Granet also showed much interest in religion as in *La Religion des Chinois* (1922) but he wrote very much as a Sinologist and ethnographer rather than as someone primarily concerned with theoretical issues in the sociology of religion.

Admittedly, *sociologie religieuse* continued to occupy an honoured place, as it had done formerly, in the reviews of the new series of the *Année sociologique*, and not surprisingly since Mauss declared that he wanted to continue the policy of the first series. The section, *sociologie religieuse*, still followed *sociologie générale*, and in the first volume, 164 pages, or about 15 per cent of all pages, were devoted to the subject. In the *Annales*, to which reference has just been made, that which dealt with *sociologie religieuse*, edited by Mauss, with the help of Granet, was extraordinarily thin, with only two original articles, one by Granet and the other by Czarnowski, to which were added very few reviews (1939). In Series E on social morphology, Halbwachs wrote an article on 'La Morphologie religieuse' (Fascicule 2, 1937).

If one examines books written on Durkheim's sociology during the 1920s, it is to be noted that time and time again very little place is given to his analysis of religion. Sometimes it is completely omitted. Much is written about his quest for the scientific method, his work on the division of labour and on suicide, and a great deal on the philosophical problems of the concept of *représentations collectives*. But apart from references to the notion of the sacred, which meant so much to Durkheim, and also to the relation between deity and society, the French scholars refer to little else. The cult of the individual and Durkheim's analysis of ritual are completely forgotten.

Why was it that amongst those of his most fervent disciples and those who joined the faithful band after the First World War, a general interest in the study of religion waned? Evans-Pritchard rightly notes that Durkheim and his disciples had, despite their agnosticism, accorded an enormous importance to the ideals of the collective and had sympathy, even admiration of religious idealism (1960:16 n.1). But he reads too much into the alleged common ideas of the group. It was Durkheim rather than his disciples who gave so prominent a place to religion and who was willing to be committed to writing about it in such positive terms, not least in considering religio-humanistic ideals in modern society. The question is this: if religion was so crucial to the understanding of society, as Durkheim clearly held it was, why was it that his colleagues did not seize on the fact and after his death develop such theoretically important ideas?

Two reasons suggest themselves. One, that within the *équipe* Durkheim was unique in his enthusiasm for things religious. In this sense he was without parallel and none of his colleagues possessed the enthusiasm for religion which we have suggested he had. After all, as has been repeatedly said, the Année Sociologique group was agnostic and rationalist virtually to a man. It is therefore not surprising that no one worked in the field of religion out of the conviction of its importance in society. None seemed willing to bear testimony in the academic world to this crucial position upheld by Durkheim. Durkheim seemed specially placed with little chance of a successor. To be sure, his aim was that members of the *équipe*, using the tools of sociology, should specialize in specific areas such as law, economics, crime, the family, and so on. A team of religious specialists was not required but the fact that no one developed *sociologie religieuse* is of great significance.

Apart from the predilections of those who were members of the group, one has to face the possibility that one of the reasons why so few were prepared to work in the realm of religion was that they secretly disagreed with some of Durkheim's assertions on the subject. For example, Cuvillier said that 'above all, the thesis which claims to derive logical values from religion and make it the mother of science seems to have scandalized his contemporaries' (1953:51). Other issues of this kind are taken up in the next chapter. But one point might be raised now. It relates to the cult of man. As we have seen, van Gennep, rationalist and anthropologist, but not a member of the group, openly attacked

Durkheim at this point. To the thorough-going rationalist, religion is a thing of the past: it is associated with ideals and a way of life which cannot be accepted by modern man. For Durkheim, a completely religionless society was intellectually impossible and emotionally frightening. In the eyes of his colleagues, such a concern for religion was best forgotten – it was a streak they wished was not present. Nothing is more telling than the fact that, so far as we know, no one disciple spoke or ever wrote about the religion of the future, or indeed of the present, as being that of man himself.

3 The storming of teachers' training colleges

Whereas Durkheimian sociology suffered a general decline within the academic world after the First World War, its followers did not hesitate to promulgate it when and wherever they could. Their enthusiasm, determination and effectiveness, as we have just said, nowhere nearly matched that of the original team and its master. But where opportunities arose they took them and were not loth to make use of political openings for the dissemination of their brand of sociology. One way in which they were able to achieve this was in the appointment of their members to chairs in various French universities. Another kind of opportunity, which brought the discipline into national prominence if not disrepute, opened up shortly after the end of the war.

In 1920, Paul Lapie (1869–1927), who had been director of primary education in the French government since 1914, decided to introduce into teachers' training colleges, les Écoles Normales Primaires, a course in sociology, especially covering those aspects of sociology which applied to education and morality (see Richard 1923:125ff.; Marjolin 1937:702; Bouglé 1938:35ff.; Geiger 1979). Lapie had joined Durkheim's *équipe* at its inception, spent some time in Tunis, and then became a colleague of Gaston Richard, teaching philosophy at the University of Bordeaux. He was convinced of the need to imbue future teachers with general culture, with an adequate knowledge for personal reflection, as over against specialized learning. This, he held, was necessary for a democratic society in which citizens should be free, open people.

Although he was critical of Durkheim for being politically too conservative – Lapie had strong socialist leanings – he nevertheless wished to ensure that the sociology of Durkheim was used in preparing teachers for their work. His intention was to raise the standard of instruction in colleges and also to insist that sociology be a compulsory subject, even have a place of honour (Bouglé 1938:36). Bouglé maintained that in courses given under the title, Notions de Sociologie appliquées à la Morale et à l'Education, there were references at the end to religion, art and science (ibid.; and see pages ahead). It was these that caused an uproar, with shouts of socialism and irreligion! Needless to say, the hostility that was aroused came from scholars and intellectuals who were opposed to the sociology of Durkheim on account of its philosophical presuppositions, and one academic referred to this 'ersatz humanism' which was called sociology (ibid.:36–7). Prominent in the attack were both Catholics and Protestants. Gaston Richard wrote the powerful article entitled 'L'Athéisme dogmatique en sociologie religieuse' which was published in 1923 and to which we have often referred. He stated that the followers of Durkheim along with their sympathizers, were trying to monopolize the teaching of sociology in France to the exclusion of all other types of sociology, and in particular a type of sociology of religion which Richard held was incompatible with the Christian faith (1923:126/ t.1975:229). The issue flared up again in 1927 involving Herriot, Minister of Public Instruction, and such academic figures as E. Le Roy, J. Chevalier, professor of philosophy at Grenoble, and Duguit, dean of the Faculty of Law at Bordeaux. The elimination of *la sociologie religieuse* from syllabuses in teachers' training colleges was demanded. Once again Richard attacked the government and Durkheimians as well (Richard 1928). The question for him was not so much that sociology should not be taught but that it was exclusively that of Durkheim and did not allow other approaches. In short, what was being presented was not a liberal understanding of sociology but a dogmatic one. Jean Izoulet, an eccentric professor of sociology at the Collège de France, wrote in an indictment which has become well-known: 'the obligation of teaching the sociology of M. Durkheim in 200 Normal Schools in France is the gravest peril our country has known for some time' (1928:247). At one stage, Bouglé was invited to appear before the Académie des Sciences Morales et

Politiques to offer an explanation of the situation. Earlier in the troubles, Lapie was almost forced to resign over the affair.

The fact remains, however, that wherever sociology was to be found in state institutions it was nearly always based on that of Durkheim. As late as 1939 it seemed necessary to Achille Ouy, writing in the *Revue internationale de sociologie*, to attack Durkheimians vehemently for their abiding and powerful influence in the educational and academic worlds. He went so far as to say that many independent sociologists were united only in their opposition to 'Durkheimian imperialism' (1939:343). Van Gennep, a casualty of the exclusivism of Durkheim's policy, was never given a professorship in France or asked to join the Année Sociologique group, either while Durkheim was alive or during the inter-war period (see Zumwalt 1982:307). This can be rightly seen as an academic scandal. Those who opposed what van Gennep called the renewal of Comtean sociology had to take refuge in the Collège de France and the Institut. Somewhat bitterly he observed:

> In the tight group the Durkheimians mounted the assault from these positions and in approximately twenty years made themselves masters. Whoever was not part of the group was 'marked' (quoted in Zumwalt 1982:302; see also Leclercq 1948:56).

The influence of Durkheimian sociology between the wars in colleges and lycées is to be gleaned from an examination of the *manuels* used in teaching students (see Cuvillier 1953:48). The Third Republic insisted on the teaching of philosophy in the lycées as a compulsory subject. In the Écoles Normales Primaires, at the time we are considering, students in their first year studied psychology and pedagogy; in their second, sociology; and in their third, the philosophy of science and morality. For all these courses the syllabuses were closely tied to the *manuels* which were similar to the so-called readers used commonly in American universities today. The *manuel* consisted of a number of short extracts from the works of selected authors, which were often preceded by a paragraph or two of introduction. Students were examined in their knowledge of these texts. After the First World War Durkheimians were asked to edit *manuels* on sociology and this of course meant placing emphasis on Durkheimian sociology. Take, for example, a *manuel* for second-year students in the colleges of education that appeared in the early 1920s. It was entitled *Notions de sociologie* and was edited by Hesse and Gleyze with a preface by Paul Fauconnet, a prominent member of the Année Sociologique group (the 7th edition was published in 1935. See Geiger 1979:258 n.3). Another *manuel* appeared in 1930, *Éléments de sociologie*, edited by Bouglé and Raffault, both Durkheimians.[3] In the section on religion and society, most of the extracts were from works by Durkheim, though there were some by Lévy-Bruhl, Fustel de Coulanges and Loisy. And there was another section, From Religion to Science, in which, once again, there were several extracts from the Durkheimian school. Seldom were anti-Durkheimians given much space, although Gaston Richard is referred to in one instance where a part of his study of women in society is printed (1909). As the years passed, so the emphasis on Durkheimian sociology waned and temporarily fell out of favour.

The documentation of the renewed interest in Durkheim, which began in France in the 1970s and was partly due to earlier studies of his work made in the United States and England, is beyond the scope of this book. What arises from the brief observations made here about the decline of Durkheimian sociology between the wars in the country of its birth is that its influence was relatively more widespread in colleges and lycées than in the academic world at large, in which the earlier impetus was lost. Further, there appeared to be the realization that within Durkheim's theory as a whole, one apparent weakness was in its *sociologie religieuse*. To be sure, there were no great defenders of the faith, but perhaps one of the reasons for this was the realization of some of its theoretical weaknesses. It is these which must now be summarily considered.

28 *Sociologie religieuse*: a case of exaggerated claims?

The enfeeblement of the Année Sociologique group in the 1920s and 1930s, together with the weakening of the ideals which it represented, certainly stands as a historical judgment on Durkheim's aim that his sociology should be part of the theoretical and ideological foundation of *La Nation* – the new revitalized France. But it was not only the failure of a dream that was at stake. His *sociologie religieuse*, on which the dream was in part based, turned out to be the most vulnerable element of his scientific advances, at least during that period. There are doubtless many ways of trying to account for the weakness (see Faublée 1977:37). Much of what has been written in this book has indicated both the riches and the poverty of his thought on religion. In trying to understand what was in any case a partial eclipse, we would point in summary form to two issues which repelled would-be supporters at that time (and probably have done so subsequently) – the claim that religion is the proto-institution, and the alleged effect that *sociologie religieuse* has on religion itself. Both issues have been dealt with before, but they are now briefly reconsidered in the light of the historical situation.

1 Religion as demiurge

That Durkheim gave religion pre-eminence in his sociological imagination is beyond all doubt. It has been the theme of this book. That he did so is based on the conviction that perhaps historically and certainly structurally religion is the fountain-head of civilization. As Duncan says: 'Durkheim selected religion because he believed it to be the primal act (just as Freud selected sex, Marx economics, etc.)' (1969:159). Durkheim made the point as early as 1899 when he wrote in the preface to the second volume of the *Année sociologique* that sociology is a primordial

513

phenomenon – the germ from which all other phenomena are derived (1899a(i):iv/t.1960c:350; Belot 1913a:334; ch. 14.3). Parodi (1919:136) also noted that what economic factors were for Karl Marx religion was for Durkheim, but whereas such factors remained paramount for all historical materialists following in the footsteps of Marx, the dominance of religion, as we have just seen, was not so for Durkheim's followers.

There can be no doubt that his near fixation on religion, as some would call it, was manifested in the close association of religion with the social. It was an attempt on his part to explain social facts by reference to the social facts of religion (ch. 14.3). This began to emerge in what has been called the second period in the development of his thought, and shortly after the turning-point which occurred with his reading of Robertson Smith (see ch. 4.2). Apart from the evidence of his own writings, the letter from Paul Lapie to Célestin Bouglé written during this period stated that Durkheim saw religion not only as a requirement for society but as the linch-pin for understanding it (see ch. 4.4). The letter was written at much the same time as Durkheim was composing the preface to the second volume of the *Année sociologique*. And in an article of the same period, 'Représentations individuelles et représentations collectives', there is another example of his belief that religion is crucial to an adequate comprehension of society.

> It is perhaps impossible to understand how the Greek or
> Roman pantheon came into existence unless we go into the
> constitution of the city, the way in which primitive clans slowly
> merged, the organization of the patriarchal family.
> Nevertheless the luxuriant growth of myths and legends, the
> organic and cosmological systems, etc., which grow out of
> religious thought, is not directly related to the particular
> features of social morphology. (1898b/1924a:43–4/t.1953b:31)

Admittedly Durkheim shows ambivalence here. Is it that religion explains the social, or the social explains religion? (See Lukes 1972:233; Jones 1974.) It seems undeniable, however, that in the quotation Durkheim points to the prime place religion has in explaining other social phenomena.

But as we have also seen Durkheim, from his early days until his last, gave religion a prime place on what must be seen to be utilitarian grounds. Religion provides man with so much – with so much that cannot be obtained from any other source. Thus, just before the First World War he could say:

> The man who lives according to religion is not only one who visualizes the world in a certain way, who knows what others do not know, he is above all a man who feels within himself a power of which he is not normally conscious, a power which is absent when he is not in the religious state. The religious life implies the existence of very special forces. (1919b:99/ t.1975a:182)

If such forces are at work in society, what greater social forces can exist? None. For none can achieve what religion achieves. As he and Mauss together wrote about *The Elementary Forms*, these forces are 'aimed at making and perpetually remaking the soul of the collectivity and of the individual' (1913a(12):98/t.1975a:180).

In religion Durkheim saw the apex of reality, one might almost say the incarnation of reality. As any incarnation allows the human being to see in concrete form the meaning of an otherwise hidden deity, so religion, in the concreteness of its beliefs and rituals, allows society to see its hidden reality. It thus provides the key to the understanding of society itself. It is *le clef de voûte* (the keystone) of society; it explains society. Thus, Durkheim's sociology is really a *sociologie religieuse* in the sense that sociology is in the last analysis about religion and is therefore 'religious'. *Sociologie religieuse* is thus a term justified in two senses.

The place that religion can have in examining and explaining social phenomena as a whole is an issue open to debate amongst sociologists today as well as in the past. Not surprisingly many sociologists of religion give it a position of considerable importance, if not of centrality, and in so doing certainly follow in the tradition of Durkheim, and perhaps Max Weber. Thus, the American sociologist, Robert Bellah, could write quite recently that with a correct comprehension of the nature of religion, religion can be seen to be more and more important in the understanding of human experience and is central to the cultural preoccupation of contemporary man (1970:241). He states what is now generally accepted, that religion is a traditional mode by which man interprets the world. In more recent times, however, man has increasingly turned to the social sciences for a fresh interpret-

515

ation of his existence. Side by side with this, the social sciences themselves have increasingly recognized the importance of religion in such an understanding (ibid.:246).

As we have seen, Durkheim always stressed the cognitive element in religion, namely, its use by man in his thinking about the universe in which he lives. If this is in fact the case that religion plays so central a part in man's mental make-up, then the sociologist standing outside religion and outside the society which he is studying, must be prepared to admit the prime place that religious phenomena have in man's total experience. We have just seen that in the mid-1890s, when Durkheim held that religion was the fountain of all social institutions, several of his disciples were highly sceptical of his 'religiosity', though they did not openly contradict him. In trying to make religion explain everything social, in maintaining that religion is *le clef de voûte*, Durkheim went too far and made claims that could not be substantiated. It might be argued, and many anthropologists have done so subsequently, that in preliterate society religious phenomena, broadly defined, are central to the lives of primitive peoples. But in attempting to make generalizations that are not qualified by time, Durkheim fell into serious error, for he would have to maintain that the centrality of religion in early societies also pertains in modern societies. No matter how religion is defined, no matter its hallmarks of identity, providing such hallmarks clearly differentiate it from other phenomena, the fact remains that modern industrial society is not determined by religious values and practices. To understand life as a whole in the contemporary world of the West is to search for keys which are certainly not to be found within religion. Durkheim's infatuation with religion blinded him to the nature of modern society. It might be suggested that any weakness at this point could be overcome by the stress that Durkheim gave to what he saw as the pervading religion of the society of his day, the cult of the individual (see ch. 26). This, however, is to move from one position of weakness to another. The carnage of the First World War, the years of depression which followed it, and the rise of European dictatorships crushed any hopes of a triumphant humanism, which was implied in Durkheim's notion of the emerging religion of the individual.

Why should religion have assumed so central a place in Durkheim's thought? The question has seldom been asked, and more to the point, never satisfactorily answered. Perhaps it is an impossible question since the inner workings of Durkheim's mind will never be known. But the issue is not without importance, because by taking the stand he did, Durkheim seemed to be swimming against the stream in proclaiming the centrality of religion to a world that intellectually and politically would reject such a proposition.

There are three ways in responding to the question: one, by pointing to Durkheim's conviction which was sustained by empirical data derived from primitive and advanced societies; two, arising from the centrality of religion based on his theoretical system; three, from a personal quest, religious in nature.

It is clear from empirical evidence alone, from ethnographic studies which Durkheim had read, for he had never lived in a primitive society, that religion is central to the life of a society. This fact is proclaimed in numberless articles, reviews and books, from *The Division of Labour* to *The Elementary Forms*. In this respect a piece of evidence has recently come to light which bears out this point which was raised earlier (see ch. 27 n. 2). In a letter to the German, H. Uzener, Durkheim wrote about the policy of the *Année sociologique*:

> Everything that relates to the history of religions has a very important place in our collection. (6.5.1898, in *Études durkheimiennes. Bulletin d'information*, 7, p. 4)

But it was not just the importance of religion *per se*, say as an extensive force within society that struck Durkheim, it was because it helped to explain society – religion made sense of society. By it alone society could be understood. Based on his assertion that Durkheim moved away from morphological factors to *représentations collectives* to explain social phenomena, Richard argued that Durkheim turned to religious beliefs and ideas because *représentations collectives* are to be found in the heart of religion, and certainly so in a primitive society. *Ergo* to study religion is in fact to study society itself. We have rejected the notion of a radical change in Durkheim's thought (ch. 15.4), but Richard's assertion about the importance of *représentations collectives* for Durkheim's theory and their location within religion is readily accepted. The point is that logic rather than evidence dictated Durkheim's position.

517

Often there have been the hints that Durkheim's great interest in religion may have sprung from a religious quest, nestled deep in his psyche. As Evans-Pritchard has written, Durkheim had 'an almost obsessive interest in religion' (1960:16). He could not get religion out of his system – to the thoroughgoing rationalist that seems obvious. How far the religious quest dominated his academic appraisal of religion is extremely difficult to reckon. How is one ever going to assess the depth of an alleged spiritual search, since he never openly spoke about it? All that can be demonstrated, and has been done in this book, is to show the parallel between Durkheim's great interest in religion and such facts of his private life as are available and which might be said to be religious. One cannot go beyond that association. A causal connection is out of the question until further evidence has been obtained and that seems most unlikely.

The conclusion must be that no simple reason lies behind Durkheim's academic fascination with religion. He projected what he considered were scientific criteria which pointed to the crucial role that religion plays in society and how far that sprang from a religious quest must remain a mystery for ever shrouding the affair.

2 The alleged destructiveness of Durkheim's *sociologie religieuse*

In Platonic thought the demiurge is creator, but in Gnosticism he is sometimes the author of evil and destruction. For Durkheim, as we have suggested, religion was the creative demiurge, co-operating with society to produce society. But there might also be seen to be a Gnostic side. Durkheim's analysis of religion can be held to be destructive. Creation becomes associated with death through the mediation of science. It has been seen already that when science enters and examines the domain of religion, it usually secularizes and destroys it (see chs 16.8 and 25.1). The queen of all social institutions suffers in this way, whether it be physics, or biology, or historical criticism, or psychology which worms its way into her. And if these sciences secularize, so does sociology, so does *sociologie religieuse*. It is a science which perhaps more than any other undermines the very subject it is studying (see Berger 1970:ch. 2; Martin, Mills and Pickering 1980). The queen must lose her crown by the very agency which pointed to it. It is not surprising, therefore, that some have gone so far as to declare Durkheim's *sociologie religieuse* intrinsically anti-religious, despite protests on the part of Durkheim to the contrary (Richard 1923:126/t.1975:228). Far from being an apologist for religion, as some critics of Durkheim have alleged, he unconsciously, even deliberately, sets out to undermine that to which he was so closely attached. Unworried about the professional consequences it might have to himself, Richard constantly attacked Durkheim for the deleterious effect that his sociology had on religious faith. Durkheim's sociology, *dite religieuse*, as Richard scathingly referred to it, had, according to '*le vieil adversaire de Durkheim*' one clear object, the destruction of religion itself (see ch. 23.4). Through the work of Durkheim, Richard held, 'religion is on the dissecting table awaiting vivisection, standing alongside is the surgeon, scalpel in hand' (1923:239/ t.1975:251). Indeed, Durkheim's sociology is not worthy of the name (Richard 1935:23).

So, if religion, seen as the creator-demiurge of society, was the agent through which members of Durkheim's *équipe* and many rationalist intellectuals during the 1920s and 1930s became disillusioned with Durkheim's approach to religion, the destructive-demiurge, *sociologie religieuse*, was a point of departure for intellectuals who were believers. Today, the fears of destruction voiced by Richard, Deploige and others, go unheeded and seem inappropriate. The sociology of religion, with less pretentious hopes than those voiced by Durkheim but still using many of his propositions and assumptions, proceeds and has now achieved an accepted and respected place within the discipline of sociology. Even more is this approach contained within the discipline of anthropology. Nevertheless, the main argument put forward by Durkheim, that the intrusion of science into the field of religion desacralizes it, has never been challenged. Religion cannot prevent scientific investigation but such investigation tends to erode theological beliefs and practices, be they of a primitive religion or a more modern one. In most people's minds, such an investigation weakens what is at heart the mysterious and the transcendental. Durkheim's theory of the sacred, namely, that society alone determines what is sacred, casts doubts on the validity of holding anything to be sacred, even man himself. Why should anyone accept for himself the sacredness of a belief or action on such grounds? Once one knows that society is the agent, the game is up. Every type of sociology of religion, which claims to understand the workings of what might be held to be a divine institution in human terms, inevitably weakens the basic concepts of that institution. Richard might fire his salvoes against Durkheim but the fact of the matter is that he never wrote systematically on the sociology of religion. Indeed he never taught it, and so never showed how it might be carried out in such a way as to avoid the dangers he saw in Durkheim's approach. (Richard's last book (1943), written at the end of his life, does not meet this point.)

Yet there is no alternative. No one wants to return to the days of Galileo and the Inquisition. Science must have its say. Freedom of investigation must be allowed. Methodological agnosticism or atheism is the basis of all modern science, and natural 'causation', once it is established, is a preferred explanation of an event or phenomenon that was originally called mysterious or mystical. If there is a scientific explanation standing over against a religious explanation, then what is established by science will win the day. Of course the attack stemming from scientific analysis may not mean the extermination of religion. What often happens is that the believer, under such pressure, moves his base from one level to another, if possible out of the range of scientific fire. In the face of secularizing challenges, religious doctrines have to be modified. But such modifications carry the possibility of demolishing the entire structure. Out with the bath-water may go the baby. Durkheim is right: man's search for knowledge takes him away from the empire once claimed by religion towards a smaller empire cut back by the development of science, admittedly not immediately, not suddenly, but gradually. Thus, when sociology, which adopts the scientific standpoint, enters the realm of the religious, the believer has to be careful of the ground on which he is standing. He may no longer follow the paths he used to, for sociology may have made them precarious. The dilemma is insurmountable. It is the believer who faces the challenge of the sociologist, not the believer who challenges the sociologist. And to redefine the situation may in the end bring about no situation at all.

3 A final look

Durkheim has been called the Moses of sociology (*RFS*, XX:304). The title is only partially apt. Durkheim was indeed able to lead sociology out of a country of 'oppression', where associated with the work of Comte and Le Play, it was derided. Further, it was not the case of one man journeying by himself to a new country but rather leading others – his *équipe* – who would take over from him when he was gone and attempt to develop the subject. The analogy is wrong, however, because it was Joshua who finally led the Jews into the Promised Land, not Moses. Durkheim, by contrast, successfully brought religion to an academic country of milk and honey. The title thus has merit, not only because of its religious and Jewish associations, but because both 'Moses' found themselves triumphantly leading people who were aspiring to find a new territory.

A leader of great stature, which undoubtedly he was, Durkheim was as well a child of his period, a product of his country. Isambert has made the observation that in the emergence of sociology in France, religious questions were constantly mixed up with the attempt to establish social science (1969:439). One has but to recall Saint-Simon's *Nouveau Christianisme*, Comte's religion of humanity, and Le Play's strong support for the Catholic religion, especially the Ten Commandments as a 'cement' of society. The vacuum, which the French Revolution created by the blows it dealt to the Roman Catholic Church, sociologists, along with others, have seemed keen to fill. Durkheim was no exception when he readily pointed to that religion which he thought was already in existence in modern society, the worship that man accords to man. The fact that Durkheim criticized the efforts of his predecessors for their failure to establish a sound method and their inability to analyse the religious situation aright, in no way deflected him from taking what in the last analysis is a very similar position.

We have attempted to show that some of the criticisms levelled against Durkheim were unjustified. Certain commentators have read too much into his analysis and forced it into positions, we are convinced, he would not have permitted. Nevertheless, it is true that he attempted to explain society by religion and religion

521

by society, and the validity of the cries of some critics has to be accepted. The paradox contains truths but they do not run the distance Durkheim wished them to. His imagination and the vitality of his logic encouraged him to go 'for the big one', to throw caution to the wind, and to try to 'explain' religion. Sympathetic commentators would say that Durkheim was guilty of exaggeration, not only with regard to religion but to other sociological issues. Lukes has gone so far as to say that probably every major proposition Durkheim advanced was false (in Clark 1979:147ff.). This is probably an exaggeration in itself but despite it, the same writer testifies to the greatness of Durkheim's thought. Perhaps the hiatus can be accounted for by the fact that often whole theories cannot be accepted, but when a particular society is examined parts of the theory offer flashes of insight and understanding to the field-worker. They need modification but they are seen as being of enormous value and give rise to new hypotheses (see Turner 1974:23). The danger of unsympathetic or negative criticism often means that in chopping off extremities and exaggerations the ideas themselves become completely rejected or negated. Durkheim breaks his own rules, to be sure, but in so doing opens up vistas which had heretofore remained hidden. He overworked the concept of the sacred and the profane, but no one has contributed more to our understanding of the place of the sacred in social experience than Durkheim. He rigidly classified ritual but in so doing opened up new ways of analysis. He saw the importance of effervescent assembly, which seems initially to be such an unpromising sociological concept, but which turns out to be valuable in analysing sudden changes in society. Above all, he brought home the social component of religion – that religion is mediated socially and permeates society – as no other sociologist had done before. He may have been thought to have presented an apologia for religion expressed in social terms, but behind this remains truths no one can now deny (Webster 1913:845; see ch. 11.5). If Durkheim had been content to confine himself solely to facts, to description, not only would the results have been tedious, he would never have advanced the science with which he is so closely identified. It is only by being daring that new positions are taken, new fields opened up, and science makes strides into the future. He adopted strong views and held them strongly. There is something in Durkheim, in an oblique way, which points to Kuhn's notion of the progress of science in leaping forward by the discovery of a new paradigm.

Durkheim's eventual triumph, after the partial eclipse between the wars, is that his work is now regarded as fundamental to the development of sociology. In the sociology of religion the advances that have been made have frequently been an extension of his theoretical ideas. Theory within the subdiscipline, however, has not moved much farther on: no one opened up or developed more issues than he did.

Notes

1 Durkheim's religious quest I Adolescent changes, family life and personal beliefs

1 The Jews who lived in the region of Alsace-Lorraine were Ashkenazic Jews, who had migrated to the area from Germany since the sixteenth century. They possessed their own courts of law and controlled their affairs with as little help as possible from Gentile authorities. They tended therefore to be somewhat isolated from French society. They spoke Yiddish and Hebrew and had little knowledge of French even at the time of the Revolution. It gave Jews French citizenship and so put an end to the self-government of the Ashkenazic Jews. Sephardic Jews, who settled in Spain, Portugal and western France, were assimilated more easily into the countries to which they had migrated. Differences between Sephardic and Ashkenazic Jews persisted into the nineteenth century.

3 The development of Durkheim's thought on religion I The early period

1 There are some parallels in the personal religious attitudes of Fustel de Coulanges and Durkheim. Fustel was a staunch Free Thinker who had a deep attachment to the Catholic Church (see ch. 23.3). His hope, unlike that of Durkheim, was that he would be buried according to the rites of the Church, in order to give substance to his esteem for the tradition of his ancestors (Lalande 1906:252–3). Interestingly enough, Durkheim dedicated his Latin thesis on Montesquieu (1892a) to Fustel.

6 Procedures and assumptions

1 The nature of Australian totemism can be described as follows. The basic unit of the social life of the Aborigines is the clan. At the centre

of totemism is the belief that the descent groups are associated with animal species. These species are said to protect the members of the group. On the other hand, the members of the group do not eat or kill the given species or animal. On the contrary they encourage the species to multiply through the agents of periodic rituals, but the rule is relaxed at these rituals and the species are religiously consumed. This procedure marks off Australian totemism from other forms of totemism. Further characteristics are the belief in the presence of some all-pervading power which Durkheim associated with mana and the fact that the Arunta have no cult of the dead. The key to Durkheim's explanation was the Intichiuma ceremonies (see ch. 18).

7 The sacred and the profane: the ground of religion I Defining the two poles

1 See 53 n.1/39 n.1/162 n. 11. Here Durkheim mentions the dichotomy rational–irrational but does not develop it extensively anywhere (see Pickering 1979a:14–18).

8 The sacred and the profane: the ground of religion II The relations between them: further analysis

1 The two words sacred and holy are often used synonymously. Robertson Smith used the dichotomy holy and common (1889/ 1894:140ff.). He referred to the Hebrew root of holy (kodesh) and was content to let holy and sacred be substituted for each other. About the time of the First World War the notion of the holy received prominence through the work of Rudolph Otto (1869–1937), the Protestant theologian and professor at Marburg University. His book *Das Heilige*, published in 1917 and translated as *The Idea of the Holy* six years later, was a reaction against psychological and rational theories of religion. Using the approach of comparative religion, he held that religion was essentially the confrontation of the human mind with a Something, which is immediately felt as a transcendent presence, but whose character is only gradually understood. Otto associated the presence with the numinous, from the Latin *numen*, a supernatural divine power. At the heart of religion is the awe and majesty of things, peoples, places and events. The awareness of the 'totally other' is felt through awe and is also intellectually recognized. It is a *mysterium tremendum et fascinans*, which is not reducible to a psychological state. Otto's definition of the

525

holy is thus an essentialist one. But his notion of the numinous has marked differences from Durkheim's concept of the sacred, despite the fact that for both of them the terms were irreducible and absolute and were not determined by psychological drives or realities. For Otto, the numinous implied the presence of a transcendent reality, which could be known by its intrinsic qualities. Basically it is a distinctive *sui generis* mode of human experience and knowledge, but it is mediated through the individual. For Durkheim, on the other hand, the sacred has no reality other than the social designation of certain acts, things and persons, set apart for reverence and worship. Questions of feeling and emotion on the part of the practitioners are of secondary consequence. The nature of the sacred is not determined by inherent qualities, which is so in the case of the numinous.

Durkheim kept fairly strictly to the use of the term sacred and for him it was not an alternative for holy, although the notion of the holy in a general sense is implied in the sacred. He does, however, from time to time employ the word holy as in holy (*saintes*) things (for example, 1899a(ii):16/t.1975a:87).

9 Commitment to a definition

1 Briefly, it might be mentioned that those who would define religion in terms of the sacred are Marett (1914), Granet (1922), Malinowski (1925), Parsons (1951), Goode (1951), Radcliffe-Brown (1952). Those who tend to use the Spencer–Tylor base in religion as being in terms of a god, spirit or superhuman being are Evans-Pritchard (1956a), Firth (1959), Goody (1961), Spiro (1966).

11 'All religions are false: all religions are true'

1 For example, 1899a(ii):25/t.1975a:94; 1909a(1):57; 3/2/103–4; 100/83; 322/225/134; 1913b:63, 67; 1919b:99; 1950a/1969g:188/t.1957a:160; see also Goldenweiser 1915/r.1975:217.

14 In the beginning: religion or society?

1 We offer the following references where religion is said to be social in essence or origin: 1887b:307 and 309/t.1975a:33 and 36; 1893b/1902b:59/

t.1933b:92;1925a:79/t.1961a:69;1913a(ii)(6)and(7):35/t.1975a:175;605/
433/152.

16 The functions of religion: a case of misunderstanding?

1 We might mention the following: Alpert (1939:198ff.); Lévi-Strauss (1945:516ff.); Lowie (1925:153); Parodi (1913:520); Pécaut (1918:112); Seger (1957:59).

2 See also similar references: (122/86; 326/228/137; 595/416/145; 1913b:63; 1919b:99–100/t.1975a:182–3; see ch. 11.4).

3 The notion that religion binds society together and so performs a cohesive function, and that at the same time it is eternal, is probably the least original part of Durkheim's work. In proposing these ideas he stands towards the end of a long line of predecessors who held similar views. For example, Critias, a disciple of Socrates, taught that the gods had been invented to maintain social order. Much later, the powerful French historian and patriot, Michelet (1798–1874), although a religious man, held that Catholicism would die and likewise Christianity itself. But that was not to be the fate of religion which would in the years ahead, he argued, centre on patriotism, liberty, the Fatherland (see Chadwick 1975:200). This was similar to the attitude of Durkheim to the religion of the future (see ch. 26). Hippolyte Taine (1828–93), a critic and philosopher of no religious persuasion, who was much moved by the Franco-Prussian war, held that it was necessary to maintain religion in order to conserve society. His position in part emerged from his Positivism, especially in applying to moral sciences the method of biology. One can quote other writers such as de Bonald (1753–1840), the political theorist, expelled by the French Revolution. He wrote the influential book, *Théorie du pouvoir politique et religieux*, where he held that religion was necessary in all societies. Similarly, de Maistre (1753–1821), lawyer and politician, an anti-revolutionary, supported a virtual theocratic outlook, but at the same time showed tolerance in the matter of religion. Like all the others he saw religion as a requirement for society to exist.

18 Ritual II Classification and function

1 Durkheim attempts to convince himself and his readers that the clearest example of his position about the social key in understanding ritual is to be seen in the most primitive of all rituals known to man, totemic

527

ritual. His argument rests on two hypotheses (553/387). (1) Ties of blood unite men as do traditions and common interests. When men assemble they become aware of their moral unity. (2) By actions and thoughts, primitive men affirm that they are like the animals of the species in which they find consubstantiality. Thus, imitative rites are the first rites to appear, since they emerge as the totemic cult by which man attempts to identify himself with the species from which he believes he is descended and which dominates his social life. In this way he thinks he participates in the nature of an animal. Men affirm their collective existence and they do this in their minds and through the material acts in which they imitate the animal. These processes of *représentation* translate and maintain a sentiment of pride, self-confidence and veneration. Hence, conscious unity amongst the Aboriginals, engendered and heightened by the religious assembly, causes them to perform imitative acts expressive of the totem. Having convinced himself that this is a true analysis of totemic ritual, Durkheim goes on to declare that the sentiments and processes are wholly comparable to those found amongst worshippers in more advanced and idealistic religions, and here Durkheim obviously is referring to Jews and Christians (554/387). Therefore, for both primitive and modern man, security, respect and social solidarity are awakened by the sheer influence of ritual involvement, which always emerges in the regular assembly of people and which in this respect is said to exert a real force – a collective force.

Durkheim stated his position on what he saw to be the essential role of ritual at the end of the chapter on commemorative or representative rites, which constituted a category of positive rites. He had yet to deal with piacular rites. The question therefore arises whether the generalization he made about ritual relates solely to positive rites, or whether it includes all ritual, including negative and piacular rites.

Durkheim commits himself to universality on the grounds that 'the other rites we have been studying are probably only variations of this essential rite', i.e. totemic ritual (553/387). In the difficult paragraph which this sentence introduces and which concludes the chapter, Durkheim states that other rites – non-imitative, non-commemorative rites – stem from the totemic cult which itself was once imitative and then became utilitarian in attempting to seek a declared religious end, when the totemic animal gave way to the more personal hero (god), and the imitative rites became commemorative rites, which later gave rise to sacrifice, to communion and to oblation. Durkheim's claim for universality with regard to a basic ritual function would thus rest upon an evolutionary argument rather than a structural one. In fact of course he wants to claim both. The ritual principle can be derived from history as well as through immediate observation. 'But, at bottom, all these different practices are only variations of one and the same theme: everywhere their basis is the same state of mind, interpreted differently according to the situations, the moments of history and the disposition of worshippers' (555/388).

At the beginning of the ensuing chapter (Ch. V), Durkheim applies his generalizations to state that positive rites give rise to a condition of confidence, joy, enthusiasm, among the participants; and similarly, other rites relate to sad occasions. His thinking about ritual in general terms is clear. The basic function of ritual is to reproduce in men's minds common sentiments in accordance with the tenor of the rites themselves. He says: 'Oft repeated experiences have shown that the rites generally do produce effects which we expected of them and which are the reason for their existence' (556/389). Positive rites produce joy and enthusiasm: negative rites penitence and sorrow. So then, ritual is basically a technique for controlling the minds, feelings and sentiments of those people who participate in such religious activity. The end is not a theological goal but one which gives rise to a particular mental state, determined by the characteristics of the ritual itself. The particularity of the end varies. Ritual actions are therefore means of achieving ends. Such a position gives rise to basic problems of the relationship between action and *représentation*, between ritual and myth (see ch. 20).

22 Effervescent assembly: the source of religious change and strength II Questions, criticisms and evaluation

1 *A comparison in summary form of the work of Le Bon and Durkheim in the matter of crowd psychology and collective effervescence*

	Le Bon	Durkheim
Concentrated on	*foule*	*assemblée, rassemblement*[a]
	was more than individuals: a collective mind law of mental unity	more than individuals, a corporate identity, *sui generis*
	individual minds weakened (become autonomous), gives rise to new properties/ ideas	individual minds strengthened gives rise to new properties/ ideas
	religious in nature, but seen personally as 'evil'	source of religion, 'sacred' gatherings, and personally(?) admired
	categorized as irrational	categorized as supra-normal(?)

	Le Bon	Durkheim
Stressed	classification of crowds, unconscious motives, role of leaders, law of mental unity	emergence of new ideas and ideals, strengthening of present ideas and ideals

Le Bon admired Spencer, because the latter stood for reason against emotion; for men against women; for governing elites against democracy; for rationalism against religion. The influence of Spencer on Le Bon is clearly evident. Le Bon, unlike Durkheim, emphasized the terrifying effect crowds had on those who were opposed to them and their goals.
ª *Rassemblement* for Le Bon was a heterogeneous, non-anonymous crowd.

23 Durkheim's attitude to traditional religions

1 Marjolin, in his article of the 1930s, refers to the opposition of Catholics to Durkheimians, but the evidence he offers does not appear convincing (1937:696–7). Those who wrote against Durkheimian thought were not, by our reckoning, of high sociological or theological standing, and their attempts were confined to pamphlets and Catholic-biased *manuels* used in higher education. One source of opposition, the followers of Le Play, was not prominent in the academic world in this period. For the attacks by liberal Catholics during Durkheim's lifetime, see the contributions of E. Le Roy and Père Laberthonnière at a meeting of the Société Française de Philosophie on 4 February 1913 (see Durkheim 1913b).

24 Secularization: the history of mankind

1 The words *séculier* and *laïque*, which were much used in France in Durkheim's day and indeed before, were associated with the notion of lay control and anti-clericalism, as for example, in the secularization or laicization of education. Against the background of Roman Catholicism, the wish of many was to curb the power of the hierarchy and that of the local priest because of their alleged interference in matters of state and their control over people's lives. Anti-clericalism, which has a long history in France, did not necessarily imply a disregard of religion, although many anti-clericals were agnostics or atheists. Anti-clericalism was not levelled against Protestants and Jews, who often on religious and political grounds found themselves allied to anti-

clericals. The question centred on power, the power wielded by the Catholic Church. However, there were some French Catholics, usually middle-class intellectual laymen, who genuinely desired to increase the power of the laity within the church and to limit that of the hierarchy. This was apparent in the debates which led to the separation of church and state in 1906. The separation was a triumph for the anti-clericalism of the Third Republic. One reaction amongst certain liberal-minded Catholics at the time was that they supported the *associations culturelles* proposed by the government which would be responsible for organizing and maintaining local churches, presbyteries and seminaries. These *associations* were condemned by the 1906 papal encyclical *Gravissimo* (see McManners 1972:147ff.). In a debate on the separation of church and state, Durkheim rightly observed that the proposed lay groups would never succeed, for it was very difficult for any institution organized monarchically to become quickly democratic in structure (1905e; and see ch. 23.3).

27 *Sociologie religieuse*: a hope that quickly fades

1 Durkheim never defined the term, *sociologie religieuse*, and assumes that its meaning is obvious. The words appear in his early writings and at the inception of the *Année sociologique*. Not surprisingly it occurs in *Les Formes élémentaires* and is in the heading of the opening chapter. After all, *sociologie religieuse* is the subject of the book! J. W. Swain translated the term as 'religious sociology' and to *The Elementary Forms of the Religious Life* he added the subtitle, *A Study in Religious Sociology*, although in later editions the addition was dropped (see ch. 5.3).

In French usage today there are three closely allied phrases, *sociologie religieuse*, *sociologie de la religion*, *sociologie des religions* (Isambert 1969:436). The first is usually associated with 'religious sociology' in which the parameters of the discipline are set by theological considerations. *Sociologie de la religion* is approximately equivalent to what Durkheim meant by *sociologie religieuse* and is an attempt to apply sociological assumptions and methods to the phenomenon of religion. In deference to the challenge of phenomenologists, there are those who would speak of the *sociologie des religions*, the sociology of religions. Preference for this phrase rests on the contention that either there is no such thing as religion, or that religions cannot be lumped together for the purposes of making sociological generalizations derived from the amalgam. Both theoretically and indeed practically, all that can be achieved scientifically is to make generalizations about each religion, or even, within the Christian context, each denomination. Such an approach to religions rather than to religion has also been strongly emphasized by certain scholars outside France (see Smart 1973).

531

It seemed legitimate to J. Cazeneuve to refer recently to the *sociologie religieuse* of Lucien Lévy-Bruhl (1857–1939), a contemporary of Durkheim, and on the edge of the Année Sociologique group (*ASRel,* 20, 1965:75–7). Lévy-Bruhl's notions of 'pre-religion' and 'prelogical mentality' are far-reaching concepts which in this respect are parallel with those of Durkheim's *sociologie religieuse.* Desroche, in introducing the special issue of the journal in which Cazeneuve's article appears, studiously avoids the term *sociologie religieuse* (ibid.:3–6).

Perhaps because of the ambiguity of its meaning, the term religious sociology was not much employed in the English-speaking world until after World War II. It then became used for that sociology which applied itself to ecclesiastical institutions, with the direct or indirect intention of increasing the effectiveness of local churches or denominations. Often the research was financed by them. Amongst Catholics on the Continent where studies were initiated in the 1940s and 1950s, considerable encouragement came from the Catholic medieval scholar, Gabriel Le Bras who pressed for strictly empirical sociological studies. In those days the hierarchy of the Church laid down clearly the legitimate parameters within which religious sociology could work. A typical study suggested by a prominent Catholic sociologist and theologian was that religious sociology should undertake research on whether the powers exercised by the Pope, priests and bishops corresponded to those set by canon law (Leclercq: 1948:143).

The term sociology of religion, rather than religious sociology, has the air of 'scientific' respectability that would allow it to be placed happily alongside the sociology of the family, the sociology of law, and other similar sociologies. This is what Durkheim wanted *la sociologie religieuse* to be. It is quite clear that the term *sociologie religieuse* raised no problems in Durkheim's own mind, nor were there such problems publically raised in the minds of his disciples. The sub-discipline itself including the name given to it was perfectly acceptable.

From the time of Durkheim until the Second World War, and indeed after it, when the sociology of religion and religious sociology began to develop, Durkheim's *sociologie religieuse* was the one type of the sociology of religion which dominated the scene but which at the same time was not itself developed. For the French and for others, *sociologie religieuse* meant that form of the sociology of religion set by Durkheimian assumptions and conclusions. Sociology of religion was, apart from the studies of Max Weber, Durkheim's *sociologie religieuse.*

After the Second World War, as sociology itself developed in Britain and North America, the sociology of religion began to be more widely established. With such development, however, there was a shift away from Durkheim's specific approach to a more eclectic one in which the methodology and assumptions of Durkheim were challenged and modified, in some way due to the growing influence of the work of Max Weber especially in the United States. But one fundamental principle remained. It was the contention that there exists a phenomenon called religion which embraces all individual religions. Such an assumption stems directly from the nineteenth-century claim amongst liberal thinkers that there does indeed exist a phenomenon called religion and that it is possible to create a science or several sciences devoted to the subject. (For the history of the sociology of religion see, for example, Wach 1945; Bellah 1970; and Desroche 1969.)

2 The section entitled *sociologie religieuse* was under the direction of Durkheim's immediate assistant, Marcel Mauss. Some of the ablest thinkers, including Durkheim himself, undertook reviews on the subject. A parallel term was *anthropologie religieuse*, which was used less frequently but also appeared in the first number of the *Année sociologique* (I:208). In the second issue Durkheim openly declared that *sociologie religieuse* would hold a central place in the journal (II:iv). In both these volumes about a quarter of the entire number of pages was given to the section on *sociologie religieuse* and it was often the longest section of all (see Alpert 1939:47–53). The policy continued throughout the entire series and it has been calculated that out of 2,073 reviews in the twelve volumes of the *Année sociologique* 581, or 28 per cent, dealt with religious subjects (Nandan 1975:121). There were of course articles (*mémoires originaux*) on religion. Richard called *la sociologie religieuse 'la branche maîtresse'* of the *Année sociologique* (Essertier 1930:245).

3 Other *manuels* were edited by Déat, René Hubert, Souriau, and Davy.

Bibliographies

The intention of the bibliographies presented below is twofold. First, to offer a comprehensive selection of references to religion in the writings of Durkheim, along with references by other authors to his study of religion or some aspect of his life and work related to religion. This was the object of the bibliographies given in the author's *Durkheim on Religion* (1975). Those bibliographies have now been brought up-to-date. Second, to list the references in the text of this book so that the reader may find the necessary details of each reference. In both bibliographies there are items which do not specifically mention Durkheim's analysis of religion, but which are referred to in the text. They are marked with an asterisk*. The placing of items in these various categories, in the last analysis, rests on subjective factors and no completely objective division is possible.

The use of abbreviations and symbols is to be found in Abbreviations, and References, Notation, Translations, at the beginning of the book.

1 Durkheim and religion

This bibliography consists primarily of a selection of books, articles and reviews written by Durkheim in which reference is made to religion. The dating enumeration is that of Lukes (1972) which has been extended by the present author (1978; and see References, Notation, Translations). References to reviews, the subject-matter of which is marriage but which also mention religion, have been excluded, for example, 1899a(iv)(19),(21).

*1885c   Review. 'Gumplowicz, Ludwig, *Grundriss der Soziologie*', *RP*, XX, pp. 627–34.
1886a   Review. 'Herbert Spencer – *Ecclesiastical Institutions:*
(part of) *being part VI of the Principles of Sociology*. London, 1885' *RP*, XXII, pp. 61–9.

t.1974a   by R. A. Jones, 'Durkheim's Critique of Spencer's *Ecclesiastical Institutions'*, *Sociological Enquiry*, 44(3), pp. 205–14.

t.1975a   by J. Redding and W. S. F. Pickering, in W. S. F. Pickering (ed.), *Durkheim on Religion. A selection of readings with bibliographies and introductory remarks*, Routledge & Kegan Paul, London and Boston.

*1887a   'La Philosophie dans les universités allemandes', *Revue internationale de l'enseignement*, XIII, pp. 313–18, 423–40.

1887b   Review, 'Guyau – *L'Irréligion de l'avenir, étude de sociologie*. Alcan, 1887', *RP*, XXIII, pp. 299–311.

t.1975a   by J. Redding and W. S. F. Pickering (see 1886a).

1887c   'La Science positive de la morale en Allemagne', *RP*, XXIV, pp. 33–58, 113–42, 275–84 (Wundt on religion, pp. 116–18).

*1888c   'Introduction à la sociologie de la famille', *Annales de la Faculté des Lettres de Bordeaux*, pp. 257–81.

t.1978a   by M. Traugott, in M. Traugott (ed.), *Émile Durkheim on Institutional Analysis*, University of Chicago Press, Chicago and London.

1890a   'Les Principes de 1789 et la sociologie', *Revue internationale de l'enseignement*, XIX, pp. 450–6.

t.1973a   by M. Traugott, in R. N. Bellah (ed.), *Émile Durkheim on Morality and Society*, University of Chicago Press, Chicago and London.

*1892a   *Quid Secundatus Politicae Scientiae Instituendae Contulerit*, Gounouilhou, Bordeaux.

t.1937b   (French) by F. Alengry, 'Montesquieu: sa part dans la fondation des sciences politiques et de la science des sociétés', *Revue d'histoire politique et constitutionelle*, 1, pp. 405–63 (r.1953a).

t.1960b   See 1953a.

1893b   *De la Division du travail social: Étude sur l'organisation des sociétés supérieures*, Alcan, Paris.

1902b   2nd edition by Durkheim.

t.1933b   by G. Simpson, with Preface, *The Division of Labor in Society*, Macmillan, New York.

1895a   *Les Règles de la méthode sociologique*, Alcan, Paris.

1901c   2nd edition by Durkheim.

t.1938b   by S. A. Solovay and J. H. Mueller, *The Rules of Sociological Method*, edited, with an introduction by G. E. G. Catlin, University of Chicago Press, Chicago, and (1950) Free Press, Chicago.

1897a	*Le Suicide: étude de sociologie*, Alcan, Paris.
t.1951a	by J. A. Spaulding and G. Simpson, *Suicide: A Study in Sociology*, edited, with an introduction by G. Simpson. Free Press, Chicago, and (1952) Routledge & Kegan Paul, London (r. bk II, ch. 2 in Pickering 1975, see 1886a).
1897e	Review, 'Antonio Labriola – *Essais sur la conception matérialiste de l'histoire*', *RP*, XLIV, pp. 645–51.
*1898a(i)	'Préface', *AS*, I, pp. i–vii.
t.1960c	by K. H. Wolff, in K. H. Wolff (ed.), *Emile Durkheim 1858–1917. A Collection of Essays; with Translations and a bibliography*. Ohio State University Press, Columbus, Ohio. (Republished as *Essays in Sociology and Philosophy*, Harper & Row, New York, 1964.)
1898a(ii)	'La Prohibition de l'inceste et ses origines', *AS*, I, pp. 1–70.
t.1963a	with an introduction, by E. Sagarin, *Incest. The Nature and Origin of the Taboo by Émile Durkheim*, Lyle Stuart, New York.
1898a(iii)(13)	Review. 'Marcel Mauss – "La Religion et les origines du droit penal", deux articles parus dans la *Revue de l'historie des religions*, 1897', *AS*, I, pp. 353–8.
1898b	'Représentations individuelles et représentations collectives', *RMM*, VI, pp. 273–303 (r.1924a).
t.1953b	see 1924a.
1898c	'L'Individualisme et les intellectuels', *RB*, 4th series, X, pp. 7–13.
t.1969d	by S. and J. Lukes, 'Individualism and the intellectuals', *Political Studies*, XVII, pp. 19–30 (r.Pickering 1975, see 1886a).
t.1973	by M. Traugott (see 1890a).
1899a(i)	'Préface', *AS*, II, pp. i–iv.
t.1960c	by K. H. Wolff (see 1898a(i)).
1899a(ii)	'De la Définition des phénomènes religieux', *AS*, II, pp. 1–28.
t.1975a	by J. Redding and W. S. F. Pickering (see 1886a).
*1899b	Contribution to 'Enquête sur la guerre et le militarisme', *L'Humanité nouvelle*, May 1899, pp. 50–2.
1899d	Contribution to H. Dagan, *Enquête sur l'antisémitisme*, Stock, Paris, pp. 59–63.

1900a(45)	Review. 'Lasch, Richard, *Religiöser Selbstmord und seine Beziehung zum Menschenopfer*', *AS*, III, pp. 480–1.
1900a(47)	Review. 'Ratzel (Friedrich) – *Anthropogeographie, Erster Teil: Grundzüge der Anwendung der Erdkunde auf die Geschichte*, 2ᶜ éd., Engelhorn, Stuttgart, 1899', *AS*, III, pp. 550–8.
*1900b	'La Sociologie en France au XIXe siècle', *RB*, 4e série, XII, pp. 609–13, 647–52.
t.1973a	by M. Traugott (see 1890a).
1900c	'La Sociologia ed il suo dominio scientifico', *Rivista Italiana di Sociologia*, IV, pp. 127–48.
t.1960c	by K. H. Wolff (see 1898a(i)).
1901a(i)	'Deux Lois de l'évolution pénale', *AS*, IV, pp. 65–95.
t.1973b	by T. A. Jones and A. T. Scull, 'Two laws of penal evolution', with an introduction, *Economy and Society*, 2, pp. 278–308.
t.1978a	by M. Traugott (see 1888c).
*1901a(iii)(17)	Review. 'Steinmetz, S. R., *Die neueren Forschungen zur Geschichte der menschlichen Familie*', *AS*, IV, pp. 340–2.
1901h	'Compte-rendu d'une conférence sur "Religion et libre pensée" devant les membres de la Fédération de la Jeunesse laïque, donnée 22 Mai 1901', *La Petite Gironde*, 24 May 1901. (A report of Durkheim's speech.)
*1902a(i)	'Sur le totémisme', *AS*, V, pp. 82–121.
1903a(i)	(with M. Mauss) 'De Quelques formes primitives de classification. Contribution à l'étude des représentations collectives', *AS*, VI, pp. 1–72.
t.1963b	by R. Needham, *Primitive Classification*, with an introduction by R. Needham, Cohen & West, London.
1903a(ii)(57)	Review. 'E. Fournier de Flaix – "Statistique et consistance des religions à la fin du XIXe siècle" ', *AS*, VI, pp. 550–1.
1903c	(with P. Fauconnet) 'Sociologie et sciences sociales', *RP*, LV, pp. 465–97.
t.1905d	'Sociology and the social sciences', *Sociological Papers*, 1, pp. 258–80 (pp. 473–84 omitted).
*1904a(5)	Review. 'Lévy-Bruhl, L., *La Morale et la science des moeurs*', *AS*, VII, pp. 380–4.

t.1979a   by H. L. Sutcliffe, in W. S. F. Pickering (ed.), *Durkheim: Essays on Morals and Education*, with introductions, Routledge & Kegan Paul, London and Boston.

*1904e   Contribution to: 'L'Élite intellectuelle et la démocratie', *RB*, 5e série, I, pp. 705–6.

t.1973a   by M. Traugott (see 1890a).

1905a(ii)(2)   Review. 'Pellison (Maurice) – "La Sécularisation de la morale au XVIIᵉ siècle", *La Révolution française*, No. 1903, pp. 385–408', *AS*, VIII, pp. 381–2.

1905e   Contribution to discussion: 'Sur la Séparation des églises et de l'état', *Libres entretiens*, 1ère série, pp. 369–71, 496–500.

1906a(6)   Review. 'Toniolo (Giuseppe) – *L'Odierno problema sociologico*. Firenze, 1905', *AS*, IX, pp. 142–3;

1906b   'La Détermination du fait moral', *BSFP*, VI, pp. 169–212 (r.1924a).

t.1953b   See 1924a.

1906e   Lecture on Religion and Morality delivered in the École des Hautes Études in the winter of 1905–6. Summary by A. Lalande in 'Philosophy in France (1905)', *PR*, XV, pp. 255–7.

*1907a(3)   Review. 'Fouillée, Alfred, *Les Éléments sociologiques de la morale*', *AS* X, pp. 354–61.

1907a(17)   Review. 'Frazer (J. G.) – *Lectures on the Early History of the Kingship*. Macmillan, London, 1905', *AS*, X, pp. 411–15.

1907b   'Lettres au Directeur de *La Revue néo-scolastique*', *RNS*, 14, pp. 606–7, 612–14 (first letter dated 20 October 1907, second letter, 8 November 1907).

1907c   Contribution to: '*La Question religieuse: enquête internationale*', *MF*, LXVII, p. 51. (r. in a volume of the same title edited by F. Charpin, Paris, *Société du Mercure de France*, 1907, pp. 95–7).

1907f   'Cours de M. Émile Durkheim à la Sorbonne', *Revue de philosophie*, 7(5), pp. 528–39; 7(7), pp. 92–114; 7(12), pp. 620–38. (A summary by P. Fontana of the 1906–7 course of lectures on 'La Religion: les origines'.)

*1908a   Contribution to discussion: (1) 'Pacifisme et patriotisme', *BSFP*, VIII, pp. 44–9, 51–2, 66–7, 69. (2) 'La Morale positive: examen de quelques difficultés', *BSFP*, VIII, pp. 189–200. (3) L'Inconnu et l'inconscient en histoire', *BSFP*, VIII, pp. 229–45.

539

t.1979a   (2) by H. L. Sutcliffe (see 1904a(5)).

1909a   Contribution to discussion: (1) 'Science et religion', *BSFP*, IX, pp. 56–60. (2) 'L'Efficacité des doctrines morales', *BSFP*, IX, pp. 219–31.

t.1979a   (2) by H. L. Sutcliffe (see 1904a(5)).

1909c   'Examen critique des systèmes classiques sur les origines de la pensée religieuse', *RP*, LXVII, pp. 1–28, 142–62. (This corresponds to Chs II and III of 1912a.)

1909d   'Sociologie religieuse et théorie de la connaissance', *RMM*, XVII, pp. 733–58. (This corresponds to the Introduction of 1912a, pp. 754–8 have been omitted.)

1910a(ii)(2)   Note. 'Systèmes religieux des sociétés inférieures', *AS*, XI, pp. 75–6. (Unsigned: probably by Durkheim.)

t.1975a   by J. Redding and W. S. F. Pickering (see 1886a).

*1911a   Contribution to discussion: 'L'Éducation sexuelle', *BSFP*, XI, pp. 33–8; 44–7.

t.1979a   by H. L. Sutcliffe (see 1904a(5)).

1911b   'Jugements de valeur et jugements de réalité', in *Atti del IV Congresso Internazionale di Filosofia*, Bologna, 1911, vol. I, pp. 99–114 (r. in *RMM*, 1911, XIX, pp. 437–53, and in 1924a).

t.1953b   See 1924a.

1911c   Articles : (1) 'Éducation', pp. 529–36, (2) 'Enfance', pp. 552–3 (with F. Buisson), (3) 'Pédagogie', pp. 1538–43, in *Nouveau Dictionnaire de pédagogie et d'instruction primaire*, publié sur la direction de F. Buisson, Hatchette, Paris ((1) and (3) r. 1922a).

t.1979a   by H. L. Sutcliffe (see 1904a(5)).

1911e   Examination of thesis. J. Segond, *La Prière. Étude de psychologie religieuse*, *RMM*, supplément janvier, pp. 32–3. (r. 1975 in V. Karady (ed.), *Durkheim, E. Textes*, 3 vols., Les Éditions de Minuit, Paris, 2, pp. 137–40).

t.1968e   by S. Lukes (r. Lukes 1972:649–53).

1912a   *Les Formes élémentaires de la vie religieuse. Le système totémique en Australie*, Alcan, Paris.

t.1915d   by J. W. Swain, *The Elementary Forms of the Religious Life: A Study in Religious Sociology*. Allen & Unwin, London; Macmillan, New York.

t.1975a   certain sections by J. Redding and W. S. F. Pickering (see 1886a).

1913a(i)(2)   Note. 'Systèmes religieux des sociétés inférieures', *AS*, XII, pp. 90–1 (Unsigned: probably by Durkheim.)

t.1975a   by J. Redding and W. S. F. Pickering (see 1886a).

1913a(ii)(6)   Review. 'Lévy-Bruhl – *Les Fonctions mentales dans les*
& (7)   *sociétés inférieures*, Paris, 1910'. 'Durkheim (Émile) –
            Les Formes élémentaires de la vie religieuse. *Le Système
            totémique en Australie*, Paris, 1912', *AS*, XII, pp. 33–7.
t.1972   by A. Giddens, *Émile Durkheim: Selected Writings*,
            Cambridge University Press, Cambridge, pp. 246–9.
            (First paragraph and references omitted.)
t.1975a   by J. Redding and W. S. F. Pickering (see 1886a).

*1913a(ii)(8)   Review. 'Wundt, Wilhelm, *Elemente der
            Völkerpsychologie*', *AS*, XII, pp. 50–61.

1913a(ii)(9)   Review. 'Patten – *The Social Basis of Religion*, New
            York, 1911', *AS*, XII, pp. 79–80.

1913a(ii)(10)   Review. 'Visscher (H.) – *Religion und soziales Leben
            bei den Naturvölkern*. 2 vols Schergens, Bonn, 1911',
            AS, XII, pp. 83–8.

1913a(ii)(11)   Review with M. Mauss. 'Frazer – *Totemism and
& (12)   *Exogamy*. vol. IV', and 'Durkheim – *Les Formes
            élémentaires de la vie religieuse*. *Le système totémique
            en Australie*', *AS*, XII, pp. 91–8.
t.1975a   by J. Redding and W. S. F. Pickering (see 1886a).

1913a(ii)(15)   Review. 'Deploige, Simon – *Le Conflit de la morale et
            de la sociologie*. Louvain, 1911', *AS*, XII, pp. 326–8.

1913b   Contribution to discussion: 'Le Problème religieux et
            la dualité de la nature humaine', *BSFP*, XIII, pp.
            63–75, 80–7, 90–100, 108–11.

1914a   'Le Dualisme de la nature humaine et ses conditions
            sociales', *Scientia* XV, pp. 206–21.
t.1960c   by C. Blend, in Wolff 1960 (see 1898a(i)).

*1914b   Contribution to discussion: 'Une nouvelle position du
            problème moral', *BSFP*, XIV, pp. 26–9, 34–6.

*1915b   with E. Denis, *Qui a voulu la guerre? Les origines de
            la guerre d'après les documents diplomatiques*, Colin,
            Paris.
t.1915e   *Who Wanted War? Origins of the War according to
            Diplomatic Documents*, Colin, Paris.

1915c   *L'Allemagne au-dessus de tout: la mentalité allemande
            et la guerre*, Colin, Paris.
t.1915f   *Germany Above All: German Mentality and the War*,
            Colin, Paris.

*1916a   *Lettres à tous les Français*, Comité de publication, Paris
            (see letters 1, 5, 10, 11).

*1916c Contribution to: 'La Grandeur morale de la France: L'école de demain', *Manuel général de l'institution primaire, Journal hebdomadaire des instituteurs et des institutrices*, 83 (17), pp. 217–18.

t.1979a by H. L. Sutcliffe (see 1904a(5)).

1917b Contribution to discussion: 'Vocabulaire technique et critique de la philosophie', *BSFP*, XV, pp. 1–2 (see *Sacré*).

Published posthumously

1918b 'Le "Contrat social" de Rousseau', *RMM*, XXV, pp. 1–23, 129–161 (r.1953a).

t.1960b See 1953a.

1919b Contribution to discussion in F. Abauzit *et al.*, *Le Sentiment religieux à l'heure actuelle*, Vrin, Paris, pp. 97–105, 142–3; (r.*ASRel*, 1969, 27, pp. 73–7; 1971, 30, pp. 89–90.)

t.1975a by J. Redding and W. S. F. Pickering (see 1886a).

*1920a 'Introduction à la morale', with an Introductory note by M. Mauss, *RP*, LXXXIX, pp. 79–97.

t.1979a by H. L. Sutcliffe (see 1904a(5)).

1922a *Éducation et sociologie*, introduction by Paul Fauconnet, Alcan, Paris.

1968f new edition.

t.1956a by S. D. Fox, *Education and Sociology*, introduction by S. D. Fox and foreword by T. Parsons, Free Press, Chicago.

1924a *Sociologie et philosophie*, preface by C. Bouglé, Alcan, Paris. (Reproduces 1898b, 1906b and 1911b.)

1951b new edition.

t.1953b by D. F. Pocock, *Sociology and Philosophy*, with an introduction by J. G. Peristiany, Cohen & West, London.

1925a *L'Éducation morale*, introduction by Paul Fauconnet, Alcan, Paris.

1963c new edition.

t.1961a by E. K. Wilson and H. Schnurer, *Moral Education: A Study in the Theory and Application of the Sociology of Education*, edited, with an introduction, by E. K. Wilson, Free Press, New York (r. ch. 1, in Pickering 1975, see 1886a).

1928a *Le Socialisme. Sa définition, ses débuts, la doctrine Saint-Simonienne*, edited by M. Mauss, Alcan, Paris.

1971d	new edition.
t.1958b	by C. Sattler, *Socialism and Saint-Simon*, edited, with an introduction by A. W. Gouldner, Antioch Press, Yellow Springs, Ohio; and (1959) Routledge & Kegan Paul, London.
1928b	Part of a letter from Durkheim to G. Richard, dated 11 May 1899. Published in Richard 1928, pp. 298–9 n.1.
1938a	*L'Évolution pédagogique en France*, 2 vols, Alcan, Paris. I 'Des origines à la Renaissance' with an introduction by Maurice Halbwachs; II. 'De la Renaissance à nos jours'.
1969f	new edition.
t.1977a	by P. Collins, *The Evolution of Educational Thought. Lectures on the Formation and Development of Secondary Education in France*, introduction by M. Halbwachs and a translator's introduction, Routledge & Kegan Paul, London and Boston.
1950a	*Leçons de sociologie: physique des moeurs et du droit*, foreword by H. N. Kubali, introduction by G. Davy, L'Université d'Istanbul, Istanbul, Presses Universitaires de France, Paris.
1969g	new edition.
t.1957a	by C. Brookfield, *Professional Ethics and Civic Morals*, Routledge & Kegan Paul, London.
*1953a	*Montesquieu et Rousseau, précurseurs de la sociologie*, foreword by A. Cuvillier, introductory notes by G. Davy, Rivière, Paris. (Reproduces 1918b, together with a translation of 1892a into French by A. Cuvillier.)
1966a	new edition.
t.1960b	by R. Manheim, *Montesquieu and Rousseau. Forerunners of Sociology*, foreword by H. Peyre, University of Michigan Press, Ann Arbor.
1955a	*Pragmatisme et sociologie. Cours inédit prononcé à la Sorbonne en 1913–14 et restitué par Armand Cuvillier d'après des notes d'étudiants*, Vrin, Paris.
t.1960c	lectures 1–5, 13 and 14 by C. Blend, in Wolff 1960 (see 1898a(i)).
*1960a	'Les Raisons d'être. Morale de la société en général', *Annales de l'Université de Paris*, 1, pp. 54–6.
1968c	' "La Morale". Notes de cours prises par G. Davy'. In Lukes 1968, 2, pp. 248–60.

2 On Durkheim and religion

ABAUZIT, F. *et al.* 1919 *Le Sentiment religieux à l'heure actuelle*, Vrin, Paris.

ADAMS, G. P. 1916 'The interpretation of religion in Royce and Durkheim,' *PR*, 25, pp. 297–304.

ALEXANDER J. C. 1982 *Theoretical Logic in Sociology*, vol. 2. *The Antinomies of Classical Thought: Marx and Durkheim*, Routledge & Kegan Paul, London, Melbourne and Henley.

ALPERT, H. (1938), 'Durkheim's functional theory of ritual', *Sociology and Social Research*, 23, pp. 103–8. (r. in R. A. Nisbet, 1965, *Émile Durkheim*, Prentice-Hall, Englewood Cliffs, New Jersey, pp. 137–41.)

ALPERT, H. 1939 *Émile Durkheim and his Sociology*, Columbia University Press, New York.

ALPERT, H. 1959 'Emile Durkheim, a perspective and appreciation', *ASR*, 24, pp. 462–5.

D'ALVIELLA, GOBLET see Goblet d'Alviella.

ANONYMOUS 1913 Review. '*Les Formes élémentaires de la vie religieuse. Le système totémique en Australie*', *RMM*, 21 (supplément), pp. 1–3.

ANONYMOUS 1917 Obituary notice on Durkheim, *RMM*, 24, pp. 749–51.

*ANONYMOUS 1918 'Nécrologie – Émile Durkheim', *RP*, 85, pp. 95–96.

ARON, R. 1967a *Les Étapes de la pensée sociologique*, Gallimard, Paris.

ARON, R. 1967b *Main Currents of Sociological Thought*, 2 vols, Basic Books, New York. (1968 Weidenfeld & Nicolson, London) (English translation by R. Howard and H. Weaver of lecture course, Les Grandes Doctrines de sociologie historique. Approximates to 1967a.)

*AUBERY, P. 1962 *Milieux juifs de la France contemporaine*, Plon, Paris.

*BALDWIN, J.M. 1901 *Dictionary of Philosophy and Psychology*, Macmillan, New York and London.

BARKER, E. 1980 'The limits of displacement: two disciplines face each other', in D. Martin, J. O. Mills, W. S. F. Pickering (eds), *Sociology and Theology: Alliance and Conflict*, Harvester, Brighton.

BARNES, H. E. and BECKER, H. 1938 *Social Thought from Lore to Science*, 2 vols, Heath, Boston.

BASTIDE, R. 1930 'Un grand Sociologue français. M. Gaston Richard, Directeur de l'Institut Internationale de Sociologie', *Revue du christianisme social*, II, pp. 428–37.

BASTIDE, R. 1935 *Éléments de sociologie religieuse*, Colin, Paris.

BAUM, G. 1975 *Religion and Alienation. A Theological Reading of Sociology*, Paulist Press, New York.

BEATTIE, J. 1964 *Other Cultures. Aims, Methods and Achievements in Social Anthropology*, Cohen & West, London.

BEATTIE, J. 1966 'Ritual and social change', *Man*, n.s., 1, pp. 60–74.

BELLAH, R.N. 1959 'Durkheim and history', *ASR*, 24, pp. 447–61.

BELLAH, R. N. 1968 'Religion – II The sociology of religion', *International*

Encyclopedia of the Social Sciences, Macmillan and the Free Press, New York, vol. 13, pp. 406–14.

BELLAH, R. N. 1970 *Beyond Belief. Essays on Religion in a Post Traditional World*, Harper & Row, New York.

BELLAH, R. N. (ed.) 1973 *Emile Durkheim on Morality and Society*, introduction by R. N. Bellah, University of Chicago Press, Chicago and London.

BELOT, G. 1900 'La Religion comme principe sociologique', *RP*, 49, pp. 288–99.

BELOT, G. 1909 'Morale et religion', in R. Allier, G. Belot, *et al.*, *Morales et religions*, Alcan, Paris, pp. 1–38.

BELOT, G. 1913a 'Une Théorie nouvelle de la religion', *RP*, 75, pp. 329–79.

BELOT, G. 1913b 'L'Idée de Dieu et l'athéisme', *RMM*, 21, pp. 151–76.

BELOT, G. 1919 'La conception sociale de la religion' in F. Abauzit *et al.*, *Le Sentiment religieux à l'heure actuelle*, Vrin, Paris, pp. 105–34.

BENDIX, R. and ROTH, G. 1971 *Scholarship and Partisanship. Essays on Max Weber*, University of California Press, Berkeley, Los Angeles and London.

*BENEDICT, R. 1933 'Myth', *Encyclopedia of the Social Sciences*, Macmillan, London, vol 11, pp. 178–81.

BENEDICT, R. 1934 'Ritual', *Encyclopedia of the Social Sciences*, Macmillan, London, vol. 13, p. 396–7.

BENEDICT, R. 1938 'Religion', in F. Boas (ed.), *General Anthropology*, Heath, New York, pp. 627–65.

BENOIT-SMULLYAN, E. 1948 'The sociologism of Émile Durkheim and his school', in H. E. Barnes (ed.), *An Introduction to the History of Sociology*, University of Chicago Press, Chicago, pp. 499–537.

BERGENSEN, A. J. 1978 'A Durkheimian theory of "witch hunts" with the Chinese cultural revolution of 1966–1969 as an example', *JSSR*, 17, pp. 19–29.

BERGER, P. L. 1967 *The Sacred Canopy*, Doubleday, New York.

*BERGER, P. L. 1970 *A Rumour of Angels*, Allen Lane, London.

*BERGSON, H. 1932 *Les Deux Sources de la morale et de la religion*, Alcan, Paris (English translation by R. A. Audia and C. Brereton, *The Two Sources of Morality and Religion*, Macmillan, London, 1935).

*BESNARD, P. 1979 'La Formation de l'équipe de *l'Année Sociologique*', *RFS*, XX(1), pp. 7–31.

BESNARD, P. 1981 'Une Étude sur Durkheim et la politique', *Études durkheimiennes. Bulletin d'information*, 6, pp. 1–5.

BESSE, DOM 1913 *Les Religions laïques. Un romantisme religieux*, Nouvelle Librairie Nationale, Paris.

BIERSTEDT, R. 1966 *Émile Durkheim*, Weidenfeld & Nicolson, London.

BIRNBAUM, N. and LENZER, G. 1969 Introduction to *Sociology and Religion: A Book of Readings*, Prentice-Hall, Englewood Cliffs, New Jersey.

BIBLIOGRAPHIES

BIROU, A. 1959a 'Religion e ideal en el pensamiento de Durkheim', *Revista mexicana de sociologia*, 21, (3), pp. 1001–40.

BIROU, A. 1959b *Sociologie et religion*, Les Éditions Ouvrières, Paris.

BOCOCK, R. J. 1970 'Ritual: civic and religious', *BJS*, 21, pp. 285–98;

BOCOCK, R. J. 1974 *Ritual in Industrial Society*, Allen & Unwin, London.

BOCOCK, R. J. 1979 'The symbolism of the father – a Freudian sociological analysis', *BJS*, 30(2), pp. 206–17.

BOEGNER, M. 1919 Contribution to discussion in F. Abauzit *et al.*, *Le Sentiment religieux à l'heure actuelle*, Vrin, Paris, pp. 134–42.

*BOUGLÉ, C. 1924 'Le Spiritualisme d'Émile Durkheim', *RB*, 62, pp. 550–3, r.1924a as preface to Durkheim's *Sociologie et philosophie*.

BOUGLÉ, C. 1930 'Quelques souvenirs', in 'L'Oeuvre sociologique d'Émile Durkheim', *Europe*, 22, pp. 281–4.

BOUGLÉ, C. 1935 *Bilan de la sociologie française contemporaine*, Alcan, Paris.

BOUGLÉ, C. 1938 *Humanisme, sociologie, philosophie; remarques sur la conception française de la culture générale*, Hermann, Paris.

*BOURDEL, P. 1974 *Histoire des Juifs de France*, Albin Michel, Paris.

BOURGIN, H. 1938 *De Jaurès à Léon Blum. L'École Normale et la politique*, Fayard, Paris.

BOWKER, J. 1973 *The Sense of God*, Clarendon Press, Oxford.

*BRANFORD, V. 1918 'Durkheim, a brief memoir', *SR*, 10, pp. 77–82.

BRUNO, A. 1914 'L'origine della religione e il totemismo', *Revista Italiana di Sociologia*, Sept.–Dec. 1914, pp. 749–54.

BRYANT, C. G. A. 1976 *Sociology in Action. A Critique of Selected Conceptions of the Social Role of the Sociologist*, Allen & Unwin, London.

BUDD, S. 1973 *Sociologists and Religion*, Collier-Macmillan, London.

*BUISSON, F. 1916 'Le vrai sens de l'Union Sacrée', *RMM*, 23, pp. 633–56.

BURRELL, S. 1981 'Sport as ritual: interpretation from Durkheim to Goffman', *Social Forces*, 60(2), pp. 354–76.

BURRIDGE, K. O. L. 1973 *Encountering Aborigines: A Case Study: Anthropology and the Australian Aboriginal*, Pergamon, New York.

CAILLOIS, R. 1939 *L'Homme et le sacré*, Gallimard, Paris (English translation by M. Barash, *Man and the Sacred*, Free Press, Chicago, 1959).

CANTONI, R. 1963 'La Sociologia religiosa di Durkheim', *Quaderni sociologici*, 12(3), pp. 239–71.

CAZENEUVE, J. 1971 *Sociologie du rite*, Presses Universitaires de France, Paris.

*CHADWICK, O. 1975 *The Secularization of the Nineteenth Century*, Cambridge University Press, Cambridge.

CHARIN, F. 1907 *La Question religieuse. Enquête internationale*, Société du Mercure de France, Paris.

*CHARLTON, D. G. 1963 *Secular Religions in France, 1815–1870*, Oxford University Press, London.

546

CHATTERTON-HILL, G. 1912a 'L'Étude sociologique des religions', *Revue d'histoire et de littérature religieuses*, 3, pp. 1–42.

CHATTERTON-HILL, G. 1912b *The Sociological Value of Christianity*, A. & C. Black, London.

CIPRIANI, R. 1977–8 'Per una definizione dell ambito della sociologia della religione: da Durkheim e Yinger', *Sociologia*, 11(2/3), pp. 141–50; 12(1/2), pp. 49–66.

*CLARK, T. N. 1968 'Émile Durkheim and the institutionalization of sociology in the French university system', *EJS*, 9, pp. 37–71.

*CLARK, T. N. 1969 Introduction to *Gabriel Tarde: On Communication and Social Influence: Selected Papers*, University of Chicago Press, Chicago and London.

CLARK, T. N. 1973 *Prophets and Patrons*, Harvard University Press, Cambridge, Mass.

CLARK, T. N. (ed.) 1979 'Emile Durkheim today', *Research in the Sociology of Knowledge, Sciences and Art*, 2, pp. 123–53.

COLE, W. A. and HAMMOND, P. E. 1974 'Religious pluralism, legal development, and societal complexity: rudimentary forms of civil religion', *JSSR*, 13(2), pp. 177–89.

COSER, L. A. 1960 'Durkheim's conservatism and its implications for his sociological theory', in K. Wolff (ed.), *Emile Durkheim, 1858–1917*, Ohio State University Press, Columbus, Ohio, pp. 211–32. (Republished as *Essays on Sociology and Philosophy*, Harper & Row, New York, 1964.)

COSER, L. A. 1971 *Masters of Sociological Thought. Ideas in Historical and Social Context*, Harcourt, New York.

*CRAIG, J. E. 1979 'Maurice Halbachs à Strasbourg', *RFS*, XX, pp. 273–92.

CUVILLIER, A. 1953 *Où va la Sociologie française?* Librairie Marcel Rivière, Paris.

*CZARNOWSKI, S. 1915 *Le Culte des héros et ses conditions sociales*, Alcan, Paris.

DANSETTE, A. 1948 *Histoire religieuse de la France contemporaine*, vol. 1, Flammarion, Paris; 1951, vol. 2 (English translation published by Herder & Herder, New York, 1961).

DAVY, G. 1911 *Émile Durkheim. Choix de textes*, Louis-Michaud, Paris.

DAVY, G. 1919 'Émile Durkheim: I. L'Homme', *RMM*, 26, pp. 181–98.

DAVY, G. 1920 'Durkheim: II. L'Oeuvre', *RMM*, 27, pp. 71–112.

DAVY, G. 1960 'Émile Durkheim', *RFS*, I, pp. 3–24.

DELACROIX, H. 1913 'Le Problème religieux et la dualité de la nature humaine', *BSFP*, XIII, pp. 75–80.

DELACROIX, H. 1922 *Le Religion et la foi*, Alcan, Paris.

DEMERATH, N. J. and HAMMOND, P. E. 1968 *Religion in Social Context*, Random House, New York.

DE PLAEN, G. 1972 'L'Anthropologie religieuse chez Freud et Durkheim. Position du problème', *Cahiers philosophiques africains*, 2, pp. 25–37.

DEPLOIGE, S. 1905–7 'Le Conflit de la morale et de la sociologie', *RNS*,

12, pp. 405–17; 13, pp. 49–79, 135–63, 281–313; 14, pp. 329–54, 355–92.

DEPLOIGE, S. 1907 'Réponses aux lettres de M. Durkheim', *RNS*, 14, pp. 607–11, 614–21.

DEPLOIGE, S. 1911 *Le Conflit de la morale et de la sociologie*, Dewit, Bruxelles. (Reproduction of articles 1905–7.) (English translation by C. C. Miltner, *The Conflict between Ethics and Sociology*, Herder, St Louis and London, 1938.)

DESROCHE, H. 1968 *Sociologies religieuses*, Presses Universitaires de France, Paris (English translation by J. K. Savacool, *Jacob and the Angels: an Essay in Sociology of Religion*, with a foreword by N. Birnbaum, University of Massachusetts Press. Amherst, Mass., 1973.)

DESROCHE, H. 1969 'Retour à Durkheim? D'un texte peu connu à quelques thèses méconnues', *ASRel*, 27, pp. 79–88.

DOUGLAS, J. D. 1967 *The Social Meanings of Suicide*, Princeton University Press, Princeton, New Jersey.

DOUGLAS, M. 1966 *Purity and Danger. An Analysis of Concepts of Pollution and Taboo*. Routledge & Kegan Paul, London.

DOUGLAS, M. 1968 'Pollution', *International Encyclopedia of the Social Sciences*, Macmillan and Free Press, New York, vol. 12, pp. 336–42.

DOUGLAS, M. 1970 *Natural Symbols. Explorations in Cosmology*, Barrie & Rockliff, London.

DOUGLAS, M. 1975 *Implicit Meanings*, Routledge & Kegan Paul, London, Boston and Henley.

DUNCAN, H. D. 1960 'The development of Durkheim's concept of ritual and the problem of social disrelationships', in K. H. Wolff (ed.), *Émile Durkheim 1858–1917*. Ohio State University Press, Columbus, Ohio, pp. 97–117.

DUNCAN, H. D. 1969 *Symbols and Social Theory*, Oxford University Press, New York.

*DUVEAU, G. 1957 *Les Instituteurs*, Éditions du Seuil, Paris.

DUVIGNAUD, J. 1965 *Durkheim; sa vie, son oeuvre*, Presses Universitaires de France, Paris.

EDWARDS, A. 1977 'Life as fashion parade: the anthropology of Mary Douglas', *New Blackfriars*, 58, pp. 131–9.

*ELIADE, M. 1959 *The Sacred and the Profane*, Harcourt, Brace, New York.

ELIADE, M. 1973 *Australian Religions: An Introduction*, Cornell University Press, New York.

ELKIN, A. P. 1937 Review. '*A Black Civilization* by W. Lloyd Warner, Harper, New York.' *Oceania*, 8(1), pp. 119–20.

*ESSERTIER, D. 1927 *Psychologie et sociologie*, Alcan, Paris.

ESSERTIER, D. 1930 *Philosophes et savants français du XXᵉ siècle. V Sociologie*, Alcan, Paris.

*EVANS-PRITCHARD, E. E. 1937 *Witchcraft, Oracles and Magic among the Azande*, Clarendon Press, Oxford.

EVANS-PRITCHARD, E. E. 1956a *Nuer Religion*, Clarendon Press, Oxford.

EVANS-PRITCHARD, E. E. 1956b 'Religion', in E. E. Evans-Pritchard (ed.), *The Institutions of Primitive Society*, Blackwell, Oxford, pp. 1–11.

EVANS-PRITCHARD, E. E. 1960 Introduction to the translation by R. and C. Needham of R. Hertz's *Death and The Right Hand*, Cohen & West, London, pp. 9–24.

EVANS-PRITCHARD, E. E. 1962 *Essays in Social Anthropology*, Faber, London.

EVANS-PRITCHARD, E. E. 1965 *Theories of Primitive Religion*, Clarendon Press, Oxford.

EVANS-PRITCHARD, E. E. 1981 *A History of Anthropological Thought*, edited by André Singer, with an introduction by E. Gellner, Faber, London.

*FABIAN, J. 1979 'Text as terror: second thoughts about charisma', *Social Research* (Fall/Autumn), pp. 166–203.

FAUBLÉE, J. 1977 'L'École sociologique française et l'étude des religions dites "primitives" ', *AS*, 3e série, 28, pp. 19–39.

*FAUCONNET, P. 1927 'The Durkheim school in France', *SR*, 19, pp. 15–20.

*DE FÉLICE, P. 1947 *Foule en délire. Extases collectives*, Albin Michel, Paris.

FILLOUX, J.-C. 1970 Introduction and notes. Émile Durkheim, *La Science sociale et l'action*, Presses Universitaires de France, Paris. (A selection of previously published articles by Durkheim.)

FILLOUX, J.-C. 1975 'La Société selon Durkheim', *Recherche sociale*, 53, pp. 41–53.

FILLOUX, J.-C. 1976 'Il ne faut pas oublier que je suis fils de rabbin', *RFS*, XVII(2), pp. 259–66.

FILLOUX, J.-C. 1977 *Durkheim et le socialisme*, Librarie Droz, Geneva and Paris.

*FIRTH, R. 1959 'Problem and assumption in an anthropological study of religion', *Journal of the Royal Anthropological Institute*, 89(2), pp. 129–48.

FIRTH, R. 1973 *Symbols, Public and Private*, Allen & Unwin, London.

FORDE, D. 1958 *The Context of Belief: a Consideration of Fetishism among the Yakö*, Liverpool University Press, Liverpool.

FOUILLÉE, A. 1911 *La Pensée et les nouvelles écoles anti-intellectualistes*, Alcan, Paris.

FÜRER-HAIMENDORF, C. 1962 *The Apa Tanis and their Neighbours: A Primitive Civilization of the Eastern Himalayas*, Routledge & Kegan Paul, London.

*FUSTEL DE COULANGES, N. D. 1864 *La Cité antique*, Paris (English translation by W. Small, *The Ancient City*, New York, 1873).

*GEERTZ, C. 1968a *Islam Observed*, Yale University Press, New Haven and London.

GEERTZ, C. 1968 'Religion – I. Anthropological study', *International Encyclopedia of the Social Sciences*, Macmillan and Free Press, New York, vol. 13, pp. 398–406.

*GEHLKE, C. E. 1915 'Émile Durkheim's contributions to sociological theory', *Studies in History, Economics and Public Law*, 63, pp. 7–188.

*GEHRIG, R. 1981 'The American civil religion debate: a source of theory construction', *JSSR*, 20(1), pp. 51–63.

*GEIGER, R. 1979 'La Sociologie dans les écoles normales primaires. Histoire d'une controverse', *RFS*, XX, pp. 257–67.

GELLNER, E. 1962 'Concepts and society', *Transactions of the Fifth World Congress of Sociology (Washington).* (r.I.C. Jarvie and J. Agassi (eds), 1973, *Cause and Meaning in the Social Sciences*, Routledge & Kegan Paul, London and Boston.)

GENNEP, A. VAN *See* van Gennep A.

*GIDDENS, A. 1970 'Durkheim as a review critic', *SR*, n.s., 18, pp. 171–96.

GIDDENS, A. 1971 *Capitalism and Modern Social Theory: An Analysis of the Writings of Marx, Durkheim and Weber*, Cambridge University Press, Cambridge.

GIDDENS, A. 1972 *Émile Durkheim: Selected Writings*, Cambridge University Press, Cambridge.

GIDDENS, A. 1978 *Durkheim*, Collins, London.

GILBERT, M. 1978 'Neo-Durkheimian analyses of economic life and strife: from Durkheim to the social contract', *SR*, n.s., 26, pp. 729–54.

GINSBERG, M. 1956 *On the Diversity of Morals*, vol. I, Heinemann, London, pp. 230–42.

GISBERT, P. 1959 'Social facts and Durkheim's system', *Anthropos*, 54, pp. 353–69.

GLUCKMAN, M. 1962 'Les Rites de Passage', in M. Gluckman (ed.), *Essays on the Ritual of Social Relations*, Manchester University Press, Manchester.

GOBLET D'ALVIELLA, COMTE 1913 'La Sociologie de M. Durkheim et l'histoire des religions', *Revue de l'histoire des religions*, 67, pp. 192–221.

GOLDENWEISER, A. A. 1915 Review. '*Les Formes élémentaires de la vie religieuse*', *American Anthropologist*, 17, pp. 719–35 (r.Pickering 1975).

GOLDENWEISER, A. A. 1916 'The views of Andrew Lang and J. G. Frazer and Émile Durkheim on totemism', *Anthropos*, X–XI, pp. 948–70.

GOLDENWEISER, A. A. 1917 'Religion and society: a critique of Émile Durkheim's theory of the origin and nature of religion', *Journal of Philosophy, Psychology and Scientific Methods*, 14, pp. 113–24. (Reproduced in *History, Psychology and Culture*, Kegan Paul, London and Norwood, Mass., 1933, pp. 361–73.)

GOLDENWEISER, A. A. 1923 *Early Civilization: an Introduction to Anthropology*, Harrap, London.

GOODE, W. J. 1951 *Religion among the Primitives*, Free Press, Chicago.

GOODY, J. 1961 'Religion and ritual: the definitional problem', *BJS*, 12, pp. 142–64.

GRAFTON, H. G. 1945 'Religious origins and sociological theory', *ASR*, 10, pp. 726–39.

GRANET, M. 1922 *La Religion des Chinois*, Presses Universitaires de France, Paris (English translation with an introduction by M. Freedman, *The Religion of the Chinese People*, Blackwell, Oxford, 1975).

GRANET, M. 1930 'La Sociologie religieuse de Durkheim', in 'L'Oeuvre sociologique d'Émile Durkheim', *Europe*, 22, pp. 287–92.

GREENBERG, L. M. 1976 'Bergson and Durkheim as sons and assimilators: the early years', *French Historical Studies*, IX(4), pp. 619–34.

GURVITCH, G. 1937 'La Science des faits moraux et la morale théorique chez E. Durkheim', *Archives de philosophie du droit et de sociologie juridique*, 7, pp. 18–44.

GURVITCH, G. 1938 *Essais de sociologie*, Recueil Sirey, Paris.

GURVITCH, G. 1950 *La Vocation actuelle de la sociologie vers une sociologie différentielle*, Presses Universitaires de France, Paris (3rd edn, 2 vols, 1957 and 1963).

GURVITCH, G. 1965 Introduction and Notes to C. H. de Saint-Simon, *La Physiologie sociale, oeuvres choisies*, Presses Universitaires de France, Paris.

GUSTAFSSON, B. 1972 'Durkheim on power and holiness', in T. H. Biezais (ed.), *The Myth of the State*, Almquist & Wiksell, Stockholm, pp. 20–30.

HABERT, O. 1913 'La Religion primitive d'après l'école sociologique', *Revue du clergé français*, 75, pp. 513–43.

HALBWACHS, M. 1918 'La Doctrine d'Émile Durkheim', *RP*, 43, pp. 353–411.

HALBWACHS, M. 1925 *Les Origines du sentiment religieux*, Delamain, Boutelleau et Cie, Paris (English translation by J. A. Spaulding, *Sources of Religious Sentiment*, Free Press, New York, 1962).

*HALL, J. W. 1968 'A monarch for modern Japan', in R. E. Ward (ed.), *Political Development in Modern Japan*, Princeton University Press, Princeton, New Jersey.

HAMÈS, C. 1969 'Le Sentiment religieux à l'heure actuelle. Un texte peu connu de Durkheim. À propos de la parution des *Formes élémentaires de la vie religieuse*', *ASRel*, 27, pp. 71–2.

HAMMOND, P. E. 1974 'Religious pluralism and Durkheim's integration thesis', in A. W. Eister (ed.), *Changing Perspectives in the Scientific Study of Religion*, Wiley, New York, pp. 115–42.

HAMNETT, I. 1973 'Sociology of religion and sociology of error', *Religion*, 3, pp. 1–12.

HARRISON, J. E. 1912 *Themis*, Cambridge University Press, Cambridge.

*HARRISON, J. E. 1913 *Ancient Art and Ritual*, Oxford University Press, London.

HARTLAND, E. S. 1913 Review. 'Australia: totemism. *Les Formes élémentaires de la vie religieuse*', *Man*, 13(6), pp. 91–6.

HARTLAND, E. S. 1914 *Ritual and Belief. Studies in the History of Religion*. Williams & Norgate, London.

HATCH, E. 1973 *Theories of Man and Culture*, Columbia University Press, New York and London.

HAWKINS, M. J. 1979 'Comte, Durkheim and the sociology of primitive religion', *SR* 27(3), n.s., pp. 429–46.

HÉBERT, M. 1912 'Note sur l'article de M. Chatterton-Hill', *Revue d'histoire et de littérature religieuses*, 3, pp. 43–52.

HØFFDING, H. 1914 '*Les Formes élémentaires de la vie religieuse*', *RMM*, 22, pp. 828–48.

HONIGSHEIM, P. 1960 'The influence of Durkheim and his school on the study of religion', in K. H. Wolff (ed.), *Émile Durkheim 1858–1917*, Ohio State University Press, Columbus, Ohio, pp. 233–46.

*HOOKE, S. H. (ed.) 1933 *Myth and Ritual. Essays on the Myth and Ritual of the Hebrews in relation to the Culture Patterns of the Ancient East*, Oxford University Press, London.

*HOOKE, S. H. (ed.) 1935 *The Labyrinth. Further Studies in the relation between Myth and Ritual in the Ancient World*, SPCK, London.

*HOOKE, S. H. (ed.) 1958 *Myth, Ritual and Kingship*, Clarendon Press, Oxford.

HORTON, R. 1960 'A definition of religion and its uses', *Journal of the Royal Anthropological Institute*, 90, pp. 201–25.

HORTON, R. 1973 'Lévy-Bruhl, Durkheim and the scientific revolution', in R. Horton and R. Finnegan (eds), *Modes of Thought*, Faber, London, pp. 249–300.

*HUBERT, H. 1915 Preface to S. Czarnowski, *Le Culte des héros et des conditions sociales*, Alcan, Paris.

*HUBERT, H. and MAUSS, M. 1899 'Essai sur la nature et la fonction du sacrifice', *AS*, II, pp. 29–138 (English translation by W. D. Halls, with a foreword by E. E. Evans-Pritchard, *Sacrifice: Its Nature and Function*, Cohen & West, London 1964).

*HUBERT, H. and MAUSS, M. 1902 'Introduction. Deuxième section. Sociologie religieuse', *AS*, V, pp. 189–91.

*HUBERT, H. and MAUSS, M. 1904 'Esquisse d'une théorie générale de la magie', *AS*, VII, pp. 1–146. (English translation by R. Brian with a foreword by D. F. Peacock, *A General Theory of Magic*, Routledge & Kegan Paul, London and Boston, 1972.)

HUGHES, H. S. 1958, *Consciousness and Society*, Vintage, New York.

ISAMBERT, F.-A. 1969 'The early days of French sociology of religion', *Social Compass*. XVI(4), pp. 435–52.

ISAMBERT, F.-A. 1976 'L'Élaboration de la notion de sacré dans l'"École" durkheimienne', *ASRel*, 42, pp. 35–56.

IZOULET, J. 1928 *La Métamorphose de l'église; ou la sociologie, fille du décalogue, au Collège de France*, Albin Michel, Paris.

JONES, R. A. 1974 'Durkheim's critique of Spencer's *Ecclesiastical Institutions*', *Sociological Inquiry*, 44(3), pp. 205–14.

JONES, R. A. 1977 'On understanding a sociological classic', *AJS*, 83(2), pp. 279–319.

JONES, R. A. 1981 'Robertson Smith, Durkheim and sacrifice: an historical context for *The Elementary Forms of the Religious Life*', *Journal of the History of the Behavioral Sciences*, 17(2), pp. 184–205.

*KABERRY, P. 1939 *Aboriginal Women, Sacred and Profane*, Routledge, London.

KARADY, V. 1968 'Présentation de l'édition', in M. Mauss, *Oeuvres*, 3 vols, Les Éditions de Minuit, Paris, pp. i–liii.

KARADY, V. (ed.) 1975 *Durkheim, É. Textes*, 3 vols, Les Éditions de Minuit, Paris.

KARDINER, A. and PREBLE, E. 1961 *They Studied Man*, Secker & Warburg, London.

*KLUCKHOHN, C. 1942 'Myths and rituals: a general theory', *Harvard Theological Review*, 35, pp. 45–79.

KÖNIG, R. 1962 'Über die Religionssoziologie bei Émile Durkheim', in D. Goldschmidt and J. Matthes (eds), *Probleme der Religionssoziologie*, Kölner Zeitschrift für Soziologie und Sozialpsychologie, Köln und Opladen, West Deutscher Verlag, Sonderheft 6, pp. 36–49.

LACAPRA, D. 1972 *Émile Durkheim: Sociologist and Philosopher*, Cornell University Press, Ithaca and London.

LACROIX, B. 1976 'La Vocation originelle d'Émile Durkheim', *RFS*, XVII, pp. 213–45.

LACROIX, B. 1981, *Durkheim et le politique*, Presses de la Fondation Nationale des Sciences Politiques, Paris, and Presses de L'Université de Montréal, Montréal.

LACROZE, R. 1966 *Éléments d'anthropologie*, Vrin, Paris.

LA FONTAINE, A. P. 1926 *La Philosophie d'É. Durkheim*, Vrin, Paris.

LALANDE, A. 1906 'Philosophy in France (1905)', *PR*, 15, pp. 252–62.

LALANDE, A. 1932 *Vocabulaire technique et critique de la philosophie*, 3 vols, Alcan Paris.

LALANDE, A. 1955 Letter to A. Cuvillier (owned by W. S. F Pickering).

LANE, C. 1981 *The Rites of Rulers. Ritual in Industrial Society – The Soviet Case*, Cambridge University Press, Cambridge.

LAPIE, P. 1976 'Extrait d'une lettre de Paul Lapie à Célestin Bouglé, datée du 7 Mai 1897', *Études durkheimiennes. Bulletin d'information*, 3, pp. 8–9.

LEACH, E. R. 1954 *Political Systems of Highland Burma*, Bell, London.

LEACH, E. R. 1968 'Ritual' in *International Encyclopedia of the Social Sciences*, Macmillan and Free Press, New York, vol. 13, pp. 520–6.

*LE BON, G. 1895 *Psychologie des foules*, Alcan, Paris.

LE BRAS, G. 1960a 'Emile Durkheim et la sociologie des religions', *Annales de l'Université de Paris*, I, pp. 45–6.

LE BRAS, G. 1960b 'Problèmes de la sociologie des religions', in G. Gurvitch (ed.), *Traité de sociologie*, vol. , PUF, Paris, pp. 79–102 (English translation by G. S. Jones and A. Duncan, 'Some problems of the sociology of religion', in N. Birnbaum and G. Lenzer, (eds), *Sociology and Religion. A Book of Readings*, Prentice-Hall, Englewood Cliffs, New Jersey, 1969, pp. 430–45.)

LE BRAS, G. 1966 'Note sur la sociologie religieuse dans *l'Année Sociologique*', *ASRel*, 21, pp. 47–53.

BIBLIOGRAPHIES

LECLERCQ, J. 1948 *Introduction à la sociologie*, Institut de recherches économiques et sociales de l'Université de Louvain.

LEMONNYER, A. 1913 Review. '*Les Formes élémentaires de la vie religieuse*', *Revue de sciences philosophiques et théologiques*, pp. 535–7.

LENOIR, R. 1918 'Emile Durkheim et la conscience moderne', *MF*, 127, pp. 577–95.

LENOIR, R. 1930 'Lettre à R. M.' in 'L'oeuvre sociologique d'Émile Durkheim', *Europe*, 22, pp. 292–6.

LE ROY, E. 1913 Contribution to discussion: 'Le Problème religieux et la dualité de la nature humaine', séance du 4 février 1913, *BSFP*, 13, pp. 63–113.

LEUBA, J. H. 1913 'Sociology and psychology: the conception of religion and magic and the place of psychology in sociological studies', *AJS*, 19, pp. 323–42.

LÉVI-STRAUSS, C. 1945 'French sociology', in G. Gurvitch and W. E. Moore (eds), *Twentieth Century Sociology*, Philosophical Library, New York, pp. 503–37.

LÉVI-STRAUSS, C. 1950 'Introduction à l'oeuvre de Marcel Mauss', in G. Gurvitch (ed.), *Marcel Mauss: Sociologie et anthropologie*, Presses Universitaires de France, Paris.

LÉVI-STRAUSS, C. 1960 'Ce que l'ethnologie doit à Durkheim', *Annales de l'Université de Paris*, I, pp. 47–52.

LÉVI-STRAUSS, C. 1962a *Le Totémisme aujourd'hui*, Presses Universitaires de France, Paris (English translation by R. Needham, *Totemism*, Beacon Press, Boston, Mass., 1963; 1969 Penguin, London.)

LÉVI-STRAUSS, C. 1962 *La Pensée sauvage*, Librarie Plon, Paris (English translation by R. Needham, *The Savage Mind*, Weidenfeld & Nicolson, London, 1966).

*LÉVI-STRAUSS, C. 1978 *Myth and Meaning*, Routledge & Kegan Paul, London, Boston and Henley.

LIENHARDT, R. G. 1956 'Religion', in H. L. Shapiro (ed.), *Man, Culture and Society*, Oxford University Press, New York, ch. XIV.

*LIENHARDT, R. G. 1961 *Divinity and Experience: the Religion of the Dinka*, Clarendon Press, Oxford.

LOISY, A. 1913 'Sociologie et religion' (a review of *Les Formes élémentaires de la vie religieuse*), *Revue d'histoire et de littérature religieuses*, 4, pp. 45–76.

LOWIE, R. H. 1925 *Primitive Religion*, Routledge, London.

LOWIE, R. H. 1937 *The History of Ethnological Theory*, Harrap, London.

LUCKMANN, T. 1963 *Das Problem der Religion in der modernen Gesellschaft*, Verlag Rombach, Freiburg (English translation, *The Invisible Religion. The Problem of Religion in Modern Society*, Macmillan, New York, 1967).

LUKES, S. 1968 'Émile Durkheim: an Intellectual Biography', D.Phil. thesis, Oxford University, 2 vols.

LUKES, S. 1972 *Émile Durkheim. His Life and Work. A Historical and*

Critical Study, Harper & Row, New York (1973, Allen Lane, London).

LUKES, S. 1975 'Political ritual and social integration', *Sociology*, 9(2), pp. 289–308.

LUPU, I. 1931 *Die Grundlagen der Gesellschaft, das Recht und die Religion in der Durkheimschule: Ihr besonderer Widerhall in der Jenenser Jerusalemschen Soziologie*, Viata Romacascâ, Iasi.

MACBEATH, A. 1952 *Experiments in Living*, Macmillan, London.

MCFARLAND, H. N. 1954 'Theories of the social origin of religion in the tradition of Émile Durkheim', Ph.D. thesis, Columbia University.

*MCMANNERS, J. 1972 *Church and State in France, 1870–1914*, SPCK, London.

MAÎTRE, J. 1966 'La Sociologie du catholicisme chez Czarnowski, Halbwachs, Hertz et van Gennep', *ASRel*, 21, pp. 55–68.

MALINOWSKI, B. 1913 Review. '*Les Formes élémentaires de la vie religieuse*', *Folklore*, 24, pp. 525–31. (r.in Malinowski, 1963, *Sex, Culture and Myth*, Rupert Hart-Davis, London).

MALINOWSKI, B. 1925 'Magic, science and religion', in J. D. Needham (ed.), *Science, Religion and Reality*, Sheldon Press, London. (r.in B. Malinowski, 1948, *Magic, Science and Religion and other essays*, Free Press, Chicago).

*MALINOWSKI, B. 1926 *Myth in Primitive Psychology*, Norton, New York. (r.in Malinowski, 1948, *Magic, Science and Religion and other essays*, Free Press, Chicago).

*MALINOWSKI, B. 1960 *A Scientific Theory of Culture and other essays*, Oxford University Press, New York.

MALINOWSKI, B. 1963 *Sex, Culture and Myth*, Rupert Hart-Davis, London.

MARETT, R. R. 1914 *The Threshold of Religion*, Methuen, London.

MARJOLIN, R. 1937 'French sociology – Comte and Durkheim', *AJS*, 42, pp. 693–704.

MARTIN, D., MILLS, J. O., and PICKERING, W. S. F. (eds.) 1980 *Sociology and Theology: Alliance and Conflict*, Harvester, Brighton.

MAUBLANC, R. 1930 'Durkheim professeur de philosophie', *Europe*, 22, pp. 296–303.

MAUNIER, R. 1913 Review. '*Les Formes élémentaires de la vie religieuse*', *RIS*, 1913, p. 276.

MAUSS, M. 1925 'In memoriam, l'oeuvre inédite de Durkheim et de ses collaborateurs', *AS*, n.s., 1, pp. 7–29.

*MAUSS, M. 1927 'Lucien Herr', *AS*, n.s., 2, p. 9.

*MAUSS, M. 1935 'Les Techniques du corps', *Journal de psychologie normal et pathologique*, 32, pp. 271–93 (English translation by B. Brewster, 'Techniques of the body', *Economy and Society*, 1973, 2(1), pp. 70–88).

*MAUSS, M. 1950 *Sociologie et anthropologie*, introduction à l'oeuvre de Marcel Mauss par Claude Lévi-Strauss, Presses Universitaires de France, Paris.

555

MAUSS, M. 1968 *Oeuvres.*, 3 vols, edited by Victor Karady, Les Éditions de Minuit, Paris.

MAUSS, M. 1979 'L'Oeuvre de Mauss par lui-même', *RFS*, XX, pp. 209–20.

*MAUSS, M. with BEUCHAT, M. H. 1906 'Essai sur les variations saisonnières des sociétés eskimos. Étude de morphologie sociale', *AS*, IX, pp. 39–132 (English translation by J. J. Fox, with an introduction by J. J. Fox, *Seasonal Variations of the Eskimo. A Study in Social Morphology*, Routledge & Kegan Paul, London, Boston and Henley 1979).

MEHL, R. 1951 'Dans quelle mesure la sociologie peut-elle saisir la réalité de l'Église'. *Revue d'histoire et de philosophie religieuses*, 31, pp. 429–38.

MEHL, R. 1965 *Traité.de sociologie du protestantisme*, Delachaux et Niestlé, Neuchâtel (English translation by J. H. Farley, *The Sociology of Protestantism*, SCM, London, 1970).

*MERCIER, P. 1966 *Histoire de l'anthropologie*, Presses Universitaires de France, Paris.

MITCHELL, M. M. 1931 'Émile Durkheim and the philosophy of nationalism', *Political Science Quarterly*, 46, pp. 87–106.

MOL, H. 1979 'The origin and function of religion: a critique of, and alternatives to, Durkheim's interpretation of the religion of Australian Aborigines', *JSSR*, 18(4), pp. 379–89.

MOORE, S. F. and MYERHOFF, B. G. (eds) 1977 *Secular Ritual*, Van Gorcum, Amsterdam.

*NANDAN, Y. 1975 *L'École durkheimienne et son opus*, Édition du Centre National de la Recherche Scientifique, Paris.

NISBET, R. A. 1965 *Emile Durkheim* (with selected essays), Prentice-Hall, Englewood Cliffs, New Jersey.

NISBET, R. A. 1974 *The Sociology of Émile Durkheim*, Oxford University Press, New York.

NISBET, R. A. 1976 Introduction to Émile Durkheim's *The Elementary Forms of the Religious Life*, new edition, Allen & Unwin, London.

NYE, D. A. and ASHWORTH, C. E. 1971 'Émile Durkheim: was he a nominalist or a realist?' *BJS*, 22, pp. 133–48.

O'DEA, T. 1966 *Sociology of Religion*, Prentice-Hall, Englewood Cliffs, New Jersey.

OLIVER, I. 1976 'The limits of the sociology of religion. A critique of the Durkheimian approach', *BJS*, 27(4), pp. 461–73.

*ORTNER, S. B. 1978 *The Sherpas through their Rituals*, Cambridge University Press, London.

OUY, A. 1939 'Les Sociologies et la sociologie,' *RIS*, 47, pp. 245–75, 463–91.

PARODI, D. 1913 'Le Problème religieux dans la pensée contemporaine', *RMM*, 21, pp. 511–25.

PARODI, D. 1919 *La Philosophie contemporaine en France. Essai de classification des doctrines*, Alcan, Paris.

PARSONS, T. 1937 *The Structure of Social Action*, Free Press, Chicago.

PARSONS, T. 1949 'The theoretical development of the sociology of religion', in *Essays in Sociological Theory, Pure and Applied*, Free Press, Chicago, pp. 52–66.

PARSONS, T. 1951 *The Social System*, Free Press, Chicago.

PARSONS, T. 1954 *Essays in Sociological Theory* (revised edition), Free Press, Chicago.

PARSONS, T. 1968 'Durkheim, Émile', *International Encyclopedia of the Social Sciences*, Macmillan and Free Press, New York, vol. 4, pp. 311–20.

PARSONS, T. 1973 'Durkheim on religion revisited: another look at *The Elementary Forms of the Religious Life*', in C. Y. Glock and P. E. Hammond (eds), *Beyond the Classics? Essays in the Scientific Study of Religion*, Harper & Row, New York, pp. 156–80.

PARSONS, T. 1975, 'Comment on "Parsons' interpretation of Durkheim" and on "Moral Freedom through Understanding in Durkheim" ', *ASR*, 40(1), pp. 106–11.

PEACOCK, J. S. 1975 *Consciousness and Change*, Blackwell, Oxford.

PÉCAUT, F. 1918 'Émile Durkheim', *Revue pédagogique* 72, pp. 1–20.

PERISTIANY, J. G. 1960 'Durkheim's letter to Radcliffe-Brown', in K. H. Wolff (ed.), *Émile Durkheim 1858–1917*, Ohio State University Press, Columbus, Ohio, pp. 317–24.

PEYRE, H. 1960a 'Durkheim: the man, his time and his intellectual background', in K. H. Wolff (ed.), *Émile Durkheim 1858–1917*, Ohio State University Press, Columbus, Ohio, pp. 3–31.

*PEYRE, H. 1960b Foreword to Durkheim's *Montesquieu and Rousseau* (see Durkheim 1953a).

PICKERING, W. S. F. (ed.) 1975 *Durkheim on Religion*, Routledge & Kegan Paul, London, Boston and Henley.

PICKERING, W. S. F. 1978 'Complément à la bibliographie de Durkheim', *Études·durkheimiennes: Bulletin d'information*, 2, pp. 9–14.

PICKERING, W. S. F. 1979a Introductions to Morals and Education in W. S. F. Pickering (ed.), *Durkheim: Essays on Morals and Education*, Routledge & Kegan Paul, London, Boston and Henley.

PICKERING, W. S. F. 1979b 'Gaston Richard: collaborateur et adversaire', *RFS*, XX pp. 163–82.

PICKERING, W. S. F. 1979c 'The sociology of religion: a discipline that undermines religion?' *King's Theological Review*, 2(1), pp. 1–7.

PINARD DE LA BOULLAYE, H. 1922 *L'Étude comparée des religions*, vol. I, Beauchesne, Paris; 1925, Vol. II; 1931, Vol. III.

POGGI, G. 1971 'The place of religion in Durkheim's theory of institutions', *EJS*, 12, pp. 229–66.

POGGI, G. 1972 *Images of Society: Essays on the Sociological Theories of Tocqueville, Marx and Durkheim*, Standford University Press, Standford, and Oxford University Press, London.

POOLE, R. C. 1969 Introduction, 'C. Lévi-Strauss, *Totemism*', Penguin, London.

POPE, W. 1973 'Classic on classic: Parsons' interpretation of Durkheim', *ASR*, 38, pp. 349–415.

BIBLIOGRAPHIES

*POPPER, K. 1957 *The Poverty of Historicism*, Routledge & Kegan Paul, London, Boston and Henley.

POULAT, E. 1966 'Le Développement institutionnel des sciences religieuses en France', *ASRel*, 21, pp. 23–36.

POULAT, E. 1970 'La Conception sociale de la religion. Retour à un texte peu connu de Durkheim', *ASRel*, 30, pp. 87–90.

RADCLIFFE-BROWN, A. R. 1952 *Structure and Function in Primitive Society*, Cohen & West, London.

RADIN, P. 1938 *Primitive Religion: its Nature and Order*, Hamish Hamilton, London.

RAY, B. 1977 'Sacred space and royal shrines in Buganda', *History of Religions*, 16(4), pp. 363–73.

*RICHARD, G. 1909 *La Femme dans l'histoire. Étude sur l'évolution de la condition sociale de la femme*, Doin, Paris.

RICHARD, G. 1911a 'Sociologie et métaphysique', four articles, *Foi et vie*, June–July, 1911.

    (i) 'A propos de M. Durkheim' (1 June 1911).

    (ii) 'Brève Histoire des variations de M. Durkheim' (16 June 1911).

    (iii) 'La Distinction sociologique du bien et du mal chez M. Durkheim' (1 July 1911).

    (iv) 'La Sociologie religieuse de M. Durkheim et le problème des valeurs' (16 July 1911).

RICHARD, G. 1923 'L'Athéisme dogmatique en sociologie religieuse', *RHPR*, 1923, pp. 125–37, 229–61 (English translation by J. Redding and W. S. F. Pickering, in Pickering 1975).

RICHARD, G. 1925 (i) Sociologie religieuse et morale sociologique. La théorie solidariste de l'obligation', *RHPR*, 1925, pp. 244–61.

    (ii) 'La Morale sociologique et la pathologie de la société', *RHPR*, 1925, pp. 346–68.

RICHARD, G. 1928 'L'Enseignement de la sociologie à l'école normale primaire', *L'Éducateur protestant*, 7, pp. 198–208, 233–43, 295–307 (includes a letter from Durkheim to Richard, dated 11 May 1899, pp. 298–9 n.1).

RICHARD, G. 1935 'Avant-propos inédit', *RIS*, 43 (supplément), pp. 9–33.

RICHARD, G. 1943 *Sociologie et théodicée. Leur conflit et leur accord*, Les Presses Continentales, Paris.

RICHTER, M. 1960 'Durkheim's politics and political theory', in K. H. Wolff (ed.), *Émile Durkheim 1858–1917*, Ohio State University Press, Columbus, Ohio, pp. 170–210.

ROBERTSON, R. 1970 *The Sociological Interpretation of Religion*, Blackwell, Oxford.

*ROBINSON, R. 1950 *Definition*, Clarendon Press, Oxford.

RUNCIMAN, W. G. 1969 'The sociological explanation of religious beliefs', *EJS*, 10, pp. 149–91.

SAHAY, A. 1976 'The concept of morality and religion. A critique of the Durkheimian world view', *Sociological Analysis and Theory*, 6(2), pp. 167–85.

*SARTRE, J.-P. 1960 *Critique de la raison dialectique*, vol. 1, Gallimard, Paris.

SCHARF, B. R. 1970 'Durkheimian and Freudian theories of religion: the case of Judaism', *BJS*, 21, pp. 151–63.

SCHMIDT, W. 1926 *Der Ursprung der Gottesidee; Eine Historisch-Kritische und Positive Studie*, vol. 1, Aschendorffsche Verlag, Munich.

SCHMIDT, W. 1931 *The Origin and Growth of Religion: Facts and Theories* (translated by H. J. Rose), Methuen, London.

SCHOFFELEERS, M. and MEIJERS, D. 1978 *Religion, Nationalism and Economic Action*, van Gorcum, Assen.

SEGER, I. 1957 *Durkheim and his Critics on the Sociology of Religion*, Bureau of Applied Social Research, Columbia University, New York.

SHAW, D. W. D. 1978 *The Dissuaders. Three Explanations of Religion*, SCM Press, London.

*SIGHELE, S. 1898 *Psychologie des sectes*, Giard, Paris.

*SIGHELE, S. 1901 *La Foule criminelle. Essai de psychologie collective*, Alcan, Paris.

SIMPSON, G. 1963 *Émile Durkheim: Selections from his Work with an Introduction and Commentaries*, Crowell, New York.

SKORUPSKI, J. 1976 *Symbol and Theory. A Philosophical Study of Theories of Religion in Social Anthropology*, Cambridge University Press, Cambridge.

*SMART, N. 1973 *The Phenomenon of Religion*, Macmillan, London.

*SMELSER, N. J. 1962 *Theory of Collective Behaviour*, Routledge & Kegan Paul, London.

*SMITH, W. R. 1889, *Lectures on the Religion of the Semites*, Edinburgh (2nd edn, A. & C. Black, London, 1894).

SOROKIN, P. 1928 *Contemporary Sociological Theories through the first quarter of the twentieth century*, Harper & Row, New York.

SPIRO, M. E. 1966 'Religion: problems of definition and explanation', in M. Banton (ed.), *Anthropological Approaches to the Study of Religion*, Tavistock, London, pp. 85–126.

STANNER, W. E. H. 1966 *On Aboriginal Religion*, Oceania Monograph 11, University of Sydney, Sydney.

STANNER, W. E. H. 1967 'Reflections on Durkheim and aboriginal religion', in M. Freedman (ed.), *Social Organization: Essays Presented to Raymond Firth*, Frank Cass, London, pp. 217–40 (r.Pickering 1975).

STEINER, F. 1956 *Taboo*, Cohen & West, London.

*STÖLL, O. 1894 *Suggestion und Hypnotismus in der Völkerpsychologie*, Koehler, Leipzig.

SUMPF, J. 1965 'Durkheim et le problème de l'étude sociologique de la religion', *ASRel*, 20, pp. 63–73.

SWANSON, G. E. 1960 *The Birth of the Gods: the Origin of Primitive Beliefs*, University of Michigan Press, Ann Arbor.

*TARDE, G. 1901 *L'Opinion et la foule*, Alcan, Paris.

TAYLOR, S. 1963 'Some implications of the contribution of É. Durkheim to religious thought', *Philosophical and Phenomenological Research*, 24, pp. 125–34.

TIMASHEFF, N. S. 1955 *Sociological Theory. Its Nature and Growth*, Random House, New York.

TIRYAKIAN, E. A. 1962 *Sociologism and Existentialism: Two Perspectives on the Individual and Society*, Prentice-Hall, Englewood Cliffs, New Jersey.

TIRYAKIAN, E. A. 1964 'Introduction to a bibliographical focus on Émile Durkheim', *JSSR*, III(2), pp. 247–54.

TIRYAKIAN, E. A. 1978 'Durkheim and Husserl: A comparison of the spirit of positivism and the spirit of phenomenology', in J. Bien (ed.), *Phenomenology and the Social Sciences: A Dialogue*, Martinus Nijhoff, The Hague, Boston and London.

TIRYAKIAN, E. A. 1979a 'L'École durkheimienne à la recherche de la société perdue: le début de la sociologie et son milieu culturel', *Cahiers internationaux de sociologie*, LXVI, pp. 97–114.

TIRYAKIAN, E. A. 1979b 'Durkheim's *Elementary Forms* as *Revelation*', in B. Rhea (ed.), *The Future of the Sociological Classics*, Allen & Unwin, London.

*TOSTI, G. 1898 'Suicide in the light of recent studies', *AJS*, 3, pp. 464–78.

TOWLER, R. 1974 *Homo Religiosus: Sociological problems in the study of religion*, Constable, London.

TRAUGOTT, M. (ed.) 1978 *Émile Durkheim on Institutional Analysis*, University of Chicago Press, Chicago and London.

TURNER, B. S. 1971 'Sociological founders and precursors: the theories of religion of Émile Durkheim, Fustel de Coulanges and Ibn Khaldun', *Religion*, I, pp. 32–48.

TURNER, V. W. 1968 *The Drums of Affliction*, Clarendon Press, Oxford.

*TURNER, V. W. 1969 *The Ritual Process. Structure and Anti-Structure*, Aldine, Chicago.

TURNER, V. W. 1974 *Dramas, Fields, and Metaphors. Symbolic Action in Human Society*, Cornell University Press, Ithaca and London.

*VAN GENNEP, A. 1909 *Les Rites de passage*, Emile Nourry, Paris (English translation by M. B. Vizedom and G. L. Caffee, *The Rites of Passage*, introduction by S. T. Kimball, Routledge & Kegan Paul, London, 1960).

VAN GENNEP, A. 1913 Review. 'Les Formes élémentaires de la vie religieuse', *MF*, 101, pp. 389–91 (English translation by J. Redding and W. S. F. Pickering in Pickering 1975).

VAN GENNEP, A. 1920 *L'État actuel du problème totémique*, Leroux, Paris.

WACH, J. 1945 'Sociology of religion', in G. Gurvitch and W. E. Moore (eds), *Twentieth Century Sociology*, Philosophical Library, New York.

WACH, J. 1947 *Sociology of Religion*, Routledge & Kegan Paul, London.

*WACH, J. 1951 *Types of Religious Experience Christian and non-Christian*, Routledge & Kegan Paul, London.

WALLACE, R. A. 1977 'Émile Durkheim and the civil religion concept', *Review of Religious Research*, 18(3), pp. 287–90.

WALLIS, W. D. 1914 'Durkheim's view of religion', *Journal of Religious Psychology*, 7, pp. 252–67.

WALLWORK, E. 1972 *Durkheim: Morality and Milieu*, Harvard University Press, Cambridge, Mass.

WARNER, W. L. 1936 'The social configuration of magical behaviour: a study in the nature of magic', in R. H. Lowie (ed.), *Essays in Anthropology Presented to A. L. Kroeber in Celebration of his Sixtieth Birthday*, University of California Press, Berkeley, pp. 405–15.

WARNER, W. L. 1937 *A Black Civilization*, Harper, New York and London.

WARNER, W. L. 1959 *The Living and the Dead: A Study in the Symbolic Life of Americans*, Yale University Press, New Haven.

WARNER, W. L. 1962 *American Life: Dream and Reality*, University of Chicago Press, Chicago.

WEATHERLY, U. G. 1917 Review. '*The Elementary Forms of the Religious Life*', *AJS*, 22, pp. 561–3.

WEBB, C. C. J. 1916 *Group Theories of Religion and the Individual*, Allen & Unwin, London.

WEBSTER, H. 1913 Review. '*Les Formes élémentaires de la vie religieuse*', *AJS*, 18, pp. 843–6.

*WEILL, J. G. 1925 *Histoire de l'idée laïque en France au XIXᵉ siècle*, Alcan, Paris.

*WEISZ, G. 1979 'L'Idéologie républicaine', *RFS*, XX, pp. 83–112.

WESTLEY, F. R. 1978a 'The complex form of the religious life: A Durkheimian view of new religious movements', Ph.D. thesis, McGill University, Montreal.

WESTLEY, F. R. 1978b ' "The Cult of Man": Durkheim's predictions and new religious movements', *Sociological Analysis*, 39(2), pp. 135–45.

WHITE, H. W. 1977 'Reductive explanations of religion with special reference to Durkheim', Ph.D. thesis, McGill University, Montreal.

WILL, R. 1925 *Le Culte*, vol. 1, Librairie Istra, Strasbourg; 1929, vol. 2, Alcan, Paris; 1935, vol. 3, Alcan, Paris.

WILSON, E. K. 1973 Introduction to English translation of *L'Éducation morale*, (see Durkheim 1925a).

WOLFF, K. H. (ed.) 1960 *Émile Durkheim, 1858–1917: A Collection of Essays, with Translations and a Bibliography*, Ohio State University Press, Columbus, Ohio. (Republished as *Essays on Sociology and Philosophy*, Harper & Row, New York, 1964.)

WORMS, R. 1917 'Émile Durkheim', *RIS*, 25, pp. 561–8.

WORSLEY, P. M. 1956 'Émile Durkheim's Theory of Knowledge', *SR*, n.s., 4, pp. 47–62.

*WUNDT, W. 1904 *Völkerpsychologie*, Theil, Leipzig.

*WUNDT, W. 1912 *Elemente der Völkerpsychologie*, Leipzig (English translation by E. L. Schaub, *Elements of Folk Psychology*, Macmillan, New York, 1916).

BIBLIOGRAPHIES

ZEITLIN, I. M. 1968 *Ideology and the Development of Sociological Theory*, Prentice-Hall, Englewood Cliffs, New Jersey.

ZUMWALT, R. 1982 'Arnold van Gennep: The Hermit of Bourg-la-Reine', *American Anthropologist*, 84, (2), pp. 299–313.

Name Index

(excluding names in the bibliographies)

Subject Index

(Where recognized translations have been made, Durkheim's books, articles and reviews are given according to the English title. Only the more important items relating to religion have been indexed.)

571